APPLIED ETHICS

Arctic Ocean
Greenland Sea
Greenland
Baffin Bay
Beaufort Sea
Alaska
Iceland
Norway
Sweden
Hudson Bay
Canada
Gulf of Alaska
United Kingdom
Denmark
Netherlands
Germany
Poland
Belgium
France
Italy
Spain
Portugal
North Pacific Ocean
North Atlantic
United States of America
Mediterranean Sea
Morocco
Western Sahara
Algeria
Lybia
Mexico
The Bahamas
Cuba
Haiti
Dominican Republic
Puerto Rico (US)
Hawiian Islands (U.S.)
Belize
Honduras
Guatamala
El Salvador
Nicaragua
Costa rica
Panama
Mauritania
Mali
Niger
Chad
Senegal
Gambia
Guinea Bissau
Guinea
Sierra Leone
Liberia
Ivory Coast
Ghana
Togo
Benin
Burkina
Nigeria
Cameroon
Venezuala
Guyana
Suriname
French Guiana (France)
Colombia
Ecuador
Congo
Gabon
Brazil
Peru
Bolivia
Angola
Namibia
Paraguay
Chile
Argentina
Uruguay
South Pacific Ocean
South Atlantic Ocean
Falkland Islands
S.Georgia Islands
Antarctica
U. K.
NETHERLANDS
GERMANY
POLAND
English Channel
BELGIUM
LUXEMBOURG
CZECH REPUBLIC
SLOVAKIA
FRANCE
SWITZERLAND
AUSTRIA
HUNGARY
ROMANIA
Bay of Biscay
SLOVENIA
CROATIA
BOSNIA
SERBIA
YUGO -SLAVIA
MONTENEGRO
ANDORRA
PORTUGAL
SPAIN
ITALY
MACEDONIA
Adriatic
ALBANIA
Tyrrhenian Sea
GREECE
Ionian Sea
Mediterranean Sea

Arctic Ocean
Bering Sea
Finland
Russian Federated Republic
Estonia
Latvia
Lithuania
Byelarus
Ukraine
Kazakhstan
Mongolia
Sea of Okhotsk
Black Sea
Caspian Sea
Aral Sea
Georgia
Uzbekistan
Kyrgyzstan
Bulgaria
Turkey
Azerbaijan
Armenia
Turkmenistan
Tajikistan
Syria
Lebanon
Israel
Iraq
Iran
Afghanistan
Jordan
Sea of Japan
N. Korea
S. Korea
Japan
China
East China Sea
Nepal
Bhutan
Egypt
Kuwait
Pakistan
Saudi Arabia
U.A.E.
India
Oman
Myanmar
Vietnam
Taiwan
Pacific Ocean
Hong Kong
Philippine Sea
Laos
Sudan
Yemen
Bangladesh
Thailand
South China Sea
Philippines
Kampuchea
Ethiopia
Somalia
Sri Lanka
Brunei
Malaysia
Malaysia
Uganda
Kenya
Rwanda
Burundi
Tanzania
Lake Tanganyika
Singapore
Indonesia
Papua New Guinea
Indian Ocean
Solomon Islands
Arafura Sea
Malawi
Zambia
Mozambique
Zimbabwe
Madagascar
Botswana
Coral Sea
Australia
Swaziland
Lesotho
New Zealand
Estonia
Latvia
Lithuania
Russian Federated Republic
Byelarus
Ukraine
Moldova
Kazakhstan
Romania
Caspian Sea
Aral Sea
Black Sea
Georgia
Bulgaria
Macedonia
Uzbekistan
Kyrgyzstan
Azerbaijan
Greece
Turkey
Turkmenistan
China
Armenia
Syria
Lebanon
Israel
Iran
Afghanistan
Iraq
Egypt
Jordan
Kuwait
Pakistan

APPLIED ETHICS
A Multicultural Approach

edited by

LARRY MAY

SHARI COLLINS SHARRATT

both at Washington University, St. Louis

PRENTICE HALL, Englewood Cliffs, New Jersey 07632

Library of Congress Cataloging-in-Publication Data

Applied ethics: a multicultural approach/edited by Larry May and Shari Collins Sharratt.
p. cm.
Includes bibliographical references.
ISBN 0-13-068842-8
1. Ethical problems. I. May, Larry. II. Sharratt, Shari Collins.
BJ1031.A66 1994
170—dc20 93-5395
CIP

Acquisitions editor: Ted Bolen
Copy editor: Virginia Rubens
Production coordinator: Peter Havens
Editorial assistant: Nicole Gray
Cover design: Bruce Kenselaar
Editorial/production supervision
and interior design: Rob DeGeorge
Cover photo: Paul Gauguin, *Ta Matete,* 1892.
Bale, Musee. Giraudon/Art Resource, N.Y.

A Paramount Communications Company
Englewood Cliffs, NJ 07632

Printed in the United States of America

10 9 8 7 6 5

ISBN 0-13-068842-8

PRENTICE-HALL INTERNATIONAL (UK) LIMITED, *London*
PRENTICE-HALL OF AUSTRALIA PTY. LIMITED, *Sydney*
PRENTICE-HALL CANADA INC., *Toronto*
PRENTICE-HALL HISPANOAMERICANA, S.A., *Mexico*
PRENTICE-HALL OF INDIA PRIVATE LIMITED, *New Delhi*
PRENTICE-HALL OF JAPAN, INC., *Tokyo*
SIMON & SCHUSTER ASIA PTE. LTD., *Singapore*
EDITORA PRENTICE-HALL DO BRASIL, LTDA., *Rio de Janeiro*

Contents

Preface

This book will fill an existing gap in the literature used in applied ethics courses. The major anthologies in applied ethics contain essays written almost exclusively by American social and moral philosophers. These anthologies leave the student with the impression that there are no viewpoints other than those expressed by Americans, and that ethical and social philosophy has little to do with perspectives of other nations and cultures. More and more courses that include the perspectives of diverse cultures are being added to the curriculum. There is no applied ethics volume comparable to ours—indeed philosophy has been very slow to respond to the call for multiculturalism in our curricula.

Our volume addresses various topics in applied ethics from Western and nonwestern perspectives. As a result, the typical instructor will have an easier time approaching the material than if the material were segregated, or if the issues were not already well known in the West. Nonetheless, since our book devotes significant attention to the moral perspectives of many different cultures and ethnicities, students will come away from our text having a deeper appreciation for other cultures. We believe that the increasing emphasis on multiculturalism and internationalism across disciplines has set the stage for a very positive reception for a book like ours.

Let us briefly address some of the terminology in the book. We have chosen to use the term "American Indian" rather than "Native American" because of the increasing use of the former instead of the latter in such titles as "American Indian Studies" and because many American Indian people believe that the term "Native American" does not adequately capture their identity since many non-Indians may also claim to be Native Americans. We have used the term "African American" when referring to Blacks living in America and have retained the term "Blacks" when the designated group was not restricted to Americans.

Many people provided us with valuable suggestions and assistance throughout the year that we worked on this project. We would like to thank Margaret Battin, Karen Warren, Iris Young, Mary Mahowald, and Marilyn Friedman for valuable suggestions about the book's format and selections. We are especially grateful to Dana Klar from Washington University's Center for American Indian Studies for help with some of the multicultural material. In addition, Kenneth Sharratt, Marilyn Broughton, and Debi Katz have helped in the more technical phases of the book's production. The following reviewers provided helpful suggestions and useful insights: Richard Farr, University of Hawaii at Manoa; James A. Gould, University of South Florida; Karen Hanson, Indiana University; Howard McGary, Rutgers University; Elane O'Rourke, Moorpark College; Donald Porter, College of San Mateo; Robert W. Smith, Mesa Community College; and Maurine Stein, Prairie State College. And finally we would like to thank Ted Bolen, Wayne Spohr, Rob DeGeorge, Nicole Gray, and the rest of the Prentice Hall staff for their invaluable help and support during the last year.

APPLIED ETHICS

Introduction

Our first resource is human compassion, gained through the clear use of our minds, which will allow us to make the best use of the human family. And another of our best resources emerges when we think clearly about the peoples who have alternative answers to the questions that are not being answered by our society. For the first time . . . it is possible . . . to make the world our library.

—John Mohawk[1]

This anthology presents a new approach to the study of applied ethics. Its premise is that the issues in applied ethics are addressed too often from narrow North American perspectives, with little attention paid to viewpoints from other cultures. The 55 essays collected here attempt to present a wide view of the standard issues in contemporary applied ethics such as abortion, euthanasia, world hunger, discrimination, war, and the environment. To these standard issues we have added discussions of gender roles, violence, human rights, and AIDS. We have attempted to find the very best recent literature—indeed, over half the essays in our book have been written in the last five years. In addition, more than half the essays either take a non-Western perspective or address themselves to the international context of an applied ethics issue, and many of the essays are written by people who are indigenous to the cultures about which they are writing.

Each section of our anthology begins with a well-known essay on a major issue such as hunger, war, or abortion. This is followed by a very recent essay, usually responding to the "classical" essay. In addition, each section includes several essays that approach the topic from Third World perspectives, and many sections have pieces that relate the topic of the section to relevant international issues. It is our intention to broaden the range of perspectives, in addition to making the issues come alive in ways they often do not when a more limited range of perspectives is considered.

THE CASE FOR A MULTICULTURAL APPROACH TO ETHICS

Lawrence Blum offers the following definition of multiculturalism:

> Multiculturalism involves an understanding, appreciation and valuing of one's own culture, and an informed respect and curiosity about the ethnic cultures of others. It involves a valuing of other cultures, not in the sense of approving of all aspects of those cultures, but of attempting to see how a given culture can express value to its own members.[2]

In this view—a view we largely share—a multicultural approach to ethics, or any subject, does not require that we be uncritical of the practices and beliefs of other cultures. Indeed, just as a consideration of the many distinctly North American perspectives on abortion does not require that we agree with all of these views, so a consideration of the many diverse cultural perspectives on applied ethics issues does not require that we agree with all of these views either.

Our approach to multiculturalism begins with a sincere belief in the words written 100 years ago by John Stuart Mill:

> Only through diversity of opinion is there, in the existing state of human intellect, a chance of fair play to all sides of the truth.[3]

The key component in the case for multiculturalism is diversity of opinion. To give just one example: In the contemporary American debate on abortion, virtually no one defends late-term abortions. But we have included an essay by several Chinese physicians who defend this practice in countries such as theirs which are struggling to curb a population explosion. We have included this essay not because we necessarily agree with it, but because we think that it is important that this opinion be heard and reflected upon to see whether there is any part of the truth that is revealed by such a consideration.

Another important part of the case for multicultural approaches to ethics, and to other subjects, is to combat the ethnocentrism and racism that often result from ignorance of other peoples and cultures. There is little doubt that our ignorance of people who are different from ourselves has, historically, contributed to much hatred and violence. By remaining uninformed about people of other cultures, we miss the opportunity to see how much alike they are to us, and avoid having to try to understand the basis for our differences.

Yet another argument in favor of a multicultural approach to ethics, or to any other subject, has to do with the importance of understanding those who are our competitors, and those who we hope will eventually be our partners in the development of the global village. In the past, the restricted vision of traditional approaches in the West worked to a limited extent only because the world was cut into many self-contained units. In a fragmented world, one group could survive simply by closing its doors and regarding everyone else as the enemy. With increasing global interdependence this narrow approach is becoming counterproductive. John Mohawk makes the case well when he says:

> We are living in a world in which difference is just a simple fact of life, but our collective thinking has yet to truly come to grips with this reality. This *has* to change. A workable world mentality means that we are going to have to make peace with those who are different from us.[4]

The reach of many issues today—environmental degradation, racial and sexual oppression, the AIDS epidemic—is global. Intellectual disciplines such as applied ethics cannot afford to be myopic, since the survival of the West will surely depend in the near future on its ability to understand the much more populous areas of the Third World, as well as disparate cultures that exist side by side with, and sometimes within, Western cultures.

Finally, there is a strong moral case for discussions of cultures different from one's own. Such discussions foster respect for others. Respect is generally recognized as a moral value by most cultures. And the most important component of respect is an appreciation for another person as different from oneself. An appreciation for different cultures will make us better able to appreciate differences among individuals, especially between ourselves and those who in many minor, and some major, ways are different from us. If it is true that understanding breeds respect, then a consideration of a diverse set of cultural perspectives, such as those contained in this anthology, will advance the moral goal of increasing respect among peoples and individuals in the world.

WHAT DOES ETHICS CONCERN?

According to many Western and non-Western perspectives, ethics generally is understood to address the question: How ought we to lead our lives? Ethics, as a branch of philosophy, raises a number of questions that can be addressed conceptually or theoretically, namely:

- Is ethical knowledge possible?
- What are the sources of such knowledge?
- What are the theoretical strategies for resolving conflicts among these sources?
- Which are the most important values and how are they related to each other?

Applied ethics pursues these various conceptual or theoretical questions within the framework of particular contemporary issues.

In Western thought, it is common to distinguish between two large subgroups of questions in ethics. *Personal ethics* deals with the questions

- What determines the rightness or wrongness of particular actions?
- What determines how social responsibility will divide into the individual shares of responsibility for the members of a community?

Then there are large-scale, collective issues in ethics, which we will call *social ethics*, such as

- What determines the rightness or wrongness of various social policies?
- What are communities collectively responsible for?

There is a long-standing controversy in Western thought about the relationship between personal and social ethics. Some thinkers have believed that ethics mainly concerns what one's individual conscience tells one to do, and that one should not be concerned about what the society at large could do. Others, such as the utilitarians, have thought that ethics primarily concerns deciding what is best for the society at large, with each person's own happiness counting for no more than any other person's happiness. Some non-Western approaches deny that there is a significant difference between these two approaches.

Neither of these approaches, personal or social, excludes the other. Indeed, environmental ethics is a clear case of a blend between the two: It involves a set of issues that ultimately require collective action, yet it also involves issues that individuals in North America, for instance, face every day in the way they decide about such personal matters as whether to use a recycling bin. All issues in ethics have a personal dimension in that they have an effect on individual lives and call for some kind of judgment on the individual's part. In addition, most ethical issues have a social dimension in that, for their resolution, they require some sort of group action by the community at large. In this text, we will stress social ethics first, in order to push ourselves to think about the effects of our actions on distant parts of the world, thereby extending the horizon of our ethical gaze.

WHERE DO WE BEGIN?

In any study of ethics, the first and most difficult question we face concerns the subject matter itself: What do we study in an ethics course? What data, if any, are we concerned with? There are three types of "data" most commonly mentioned in ethics:

- Intuitions
- Rules and codes
- Social roles

Some philosophers would also include *reason* as a major source of ethical knowledge. But it seems to us that reason alone cannot tell us very much in ethics, unless it has something to operate on. Although rationality is terribly important in ethics, since it sets the ground rules for discussion and deliberation, an appeal to reason alone is unlikely to lead very far in ethics.

The most commonly cited "data," especially in Western approaches to ethics, are people's *intuitions*. Intuitions concern what people actually think, especially after they have engaged in reflection about what is right and wrong. Most discussions of ethics begin with what people think is wrong about such issues as starvation or murder. Of course, there is significant disagreement about such things, and so an appeal to intuitions alone will not resolve many ethical questions. What one can hope for, indeed what our book aims at, is an increasingly reflective approach toward one's intuitions, informed by an understanding of the intuitions and reasoning of a wide spectrum of the population. As we will see, there is an emerging consensus concerning issues raised in certain ethical questions. On some other issues, we are far away from anything remotely resembling a consensus.

Rules and *codes* are another important starting point in ethics. Most communities have explicit or implicit sets of moral rules and taboos, and many societies have codes of conduct that are enforced against their members in much the same way that civil laws are enforced. These rules and codes often reflect the considered judgments of many people over many generations. In this sense, rules and codes often represent an intergenerational consensus about what is right or wrong. But codes and rules can conflict with an individual person's intuitions when applied to a particular case. In such cases of conflict it is not clear that the rules or codes should be given priority over one's intuitions. One such example is

Huck Finn's dilemma: He was drawn toward his friend, Jim, and was inclined not to turn him in as a runaway slave; but Huck was also strongly motivated by the rules of his society, which dictated that slaves were property, and when they escaped they were in effect stealing from their masters. It is extremely important that we not treat any code or set of rules (or intuition) as unchallengeable, for like the slavery rules, even the consensus of a community may be ethically flawed.

Social roles are another interesting starting point for ethics discussions. Taking on, or having been thrust into, a particular role such as "father" or "mother," "teacher" or "friend," "employer" or "employee," is often thought to involve a change in one's moral status. Social roles create obligations or expand our responsibilities. Understanding what is the status of these roles may be an important first step toward understanding what is right or wrong to do in a given situation. But like rules and codes, social roles may conflict with intuitions, and worse yet, the different roles each person assumes may offer conflicting guidance about what is right or wrong in particular cases. So again, we should not, indeed we cannot, regard social roles as unimpeachable sources of ethics. Rather, we need to consider intuitions, rules, codes, and social roles as each providing input into a process of ethical deliberation. What is crucial in such a process is the ability to resolve conflicts that exist among these sources of ethical knowledge.

HOW ARE MORAL JUDGMENTS MADE?

In Western thought there are three standard ways of making moral judgments, especially in cases in which there are conflicts among our sources of ethical knowledge:

- Consequentialism—of which utilitarianism is the most prominent variation.
- Deontological theory—of which Kantianism and rights theory are the most prominent variations.
- Virtue theory—of which Aristotelianism and Thomistic theory are the most prominent variations.

Each of these theoretical perspectives has achieved prominence, and for each perspective there are significant groups of defenders among contemporary moral philosophers.

Consequentialism is the view that judgments about whether an action is morally right should be made based on an assessment of the probable effects, or consequences, of alternative acts that are open to the person in question. Consequentialists contend that an act is morally right insofar as it maximizes the best results for everyone. But there is considerable disagreement about how to assess what is the best consequence. Is pleasure or happiness the main basis for deciding what is best? Or is there some other criterion, such as goodness, that should be the basis for deciding what is best for everyone? Another question that arises is this: Should greater emphasis be placed on short-term or long-term effects? And also, should we take account of the effects that application of a particular rule would have on the society at large?

Some consequentialists, such as classical utilitarians, believe that a person can measure the quantity of happiness likely to be produced by an act, and the quantity of happiness likely to be produced by all alternative acts, and then by comparing these quantities decide which act is morally best. Duties and rights are reconceived as merely rules of thumb for guiding us toward what is best for everyone. We begin our readings with an excerpt from John Stuart Mill's book *Utilitarianism*, at the end of which he argues that rights are merely highly likely to advance the greatest happiness for the greatest number. Rights, on this view, have no intrinsic value.

Other consequentialists, such as rule utilitarians, take a more subtle view of moral duties and rights. Rather than weighing the likely consequences of alternative acts, these consequentialists weigh the likely consequences of alternative rules. If a rule, such as "honesty is the best policy," has been proven to be productive of very good consequences, and no other more useful rule is applicable, then the right thing to do is to conform to the rule of honesty. Both duties and rights are understood as forms of rule. On this view it would be right to act according to a weighty rule, such as the honesty rule, even though it appears that better consequences could be had in this one case by acting dishonestly. Duties and rights have weight here, but the weight is still a function of their ability to produce the best consequences in the society as a whole.

Deontological theory is the view that we should perform those acts that conform to duties and rights, quite independently of the consequences. In general, deontological views characterize morally right acts as those that display the most intrinsic value. The value of an act is determined by examining the act in light of moral principles. Here are two common deontological principles:

- Always treat a person as an end, never as a means only.
- Treat people the way you would want to be treated.

Deontological theorists are generally concerned about what a person intends to do, rather than about the actual results of what that person does. Some deontological theorists believe that the principles used to assess acts must be universal in scope, and others believe that it is sufficient that the principles reflect a consensus in a particular society.

Our second reading is by Ronald Dworkin, one the the best-known contemporary defenders of a deontological approach to rights. Dworkin argues that rights should be treated as trump cards. Whenever they are applicable, they should not be overridden by considerations of social well-being. If a government is willing to disregard a person's fundamental rights for some useful social purpose, that government fails to respect the dignity of the person, and thereby undermines the idea of equality and justice within its domain. For example, when a government denies fundamental rights of free speech to one of its citizens, Dworkin argues, that government insults the citizen, and the government thereby undermines respect for law. Deontological theory is attractive because of its firm stand against the denial of rights to any citizen. Many of the essays in our book embrace such a perspective.

Virtue theory is the view that judgments about what is morally right should be made in terms of promoting good character or other natural ends. The key to making good judgments is to have developed good habits to which one can merely refer now that one is uncertain about what to do. Morality is very much a matter of context as well as habit; the virtuous person is supposed to have developed a fine sense of appropriateness that is sensitive to differences in context. In this respect, virtue theory shares much in common with various non-Western perspectives, such as Buddhism. Unlike consequentialism and deontological theory, virtue theory focuses on the person's character rather than the person's behavior.

One way of understanding the virtuous life is in terms of conforming to what is "natural." In deciding what to do, one should pursue the path that is most in keeping with what is most natural in a given context. In this sense, virtue theory and *natural law* theory share much in common. Natural law theory is the view that morality is grounded in something larger than our human circumstances, namely in a natural (in many cases God-given) order. Natural law theory is most prominently espoused by Catholic theorists and by other theorists who support a strong connection between religion and ethics. Natural law has been understood, at least since Thomas Aquinas, as God's eternal law applied to natural entities, most especially to humans. In its more recent manifestations, there has been much controversy in natural law theory as to what precisely is the relationship between God's law and human laws.

Each of these theories may give a different answer to the question of how to resolve a particular conflict between sources of ethical knowledge. There is no consensus about which of these theories is best. Our view is that each of these theories contains a grain of truth, and that some combination of these theoretical perspectives may turn out to be the best overall theory. Until such a combination is devised, it is worthwhile to consider each perspective seriously whenever one is faced with a conflict of sources of ethical knowledge. This may seem unsatisfactory to those who were hoping that ethics would always provide a single solution to any ethical question. On our view, ethics is not a science that provides such solutions; rather, the study of ethics enriches one's deliberations but leaves the conclusion of those deliberations often unresolved.

WHAT ARE SOME OF THE CHIEF VALUES?

In most Western discussions of ethics, from a philosophical perspective, various values are subjected to the most intense conceptual scrutiny. Each of these values can be understood from the standpoint of personal or social ethics. Among the chief values are

- autonomy
- justice
- responsibility
- care

Autonomy is often thought to be a paradigmatic value in personal ethics. Being autonomous means being true to our own principles and acting in a way which we have chosen or which we endorse. Autonomy is closely connected to self-respect, for the person who is true to his or her own principles generally esteems himself or herself. Autonomy also has a social ethics dimension. For autonomy to be maintained and maximized in a population it is crucial that social institutions be designed to minimize interference with the life choices of individuals. Highly intrusive institutions will make it much more difficult for individuals to attain autonomy. In the field of medicine, the more fully patients are informed about treatment options, the more likely they are to make autonomous decisions.

Justice is also sometimes characterized as a value of personal ethics. In this view, justice is best understood as giving to each person his or her due, based on what that individual has a legitimate right to. When rights are understood as a contract between two equal parties, they undergird a personal ethics conception of justice. But justice also is concerned with the fair distribution of goods and services within a society. The fairness of distributions is not solely determined by contractual rights. This is especially true, as we will see in several of our essays, when we approach distributive justice from a global perspective. It may be true that no one is owed our help to be saved from starvation, but it seems to many philosophers that it would be unjust to spend one's resources on luxuries while others die highly painful deaths from starvation because they have no resources with which to purchase food.

Responsibility, like justice, has a personal and social orientation. Responsibility can be understood as accountability for the consequences that one has explicitly and directly caused. According to this understanding, one can limit one's responsibility simply by not doing very much that has effects in the world. But if we think of the consequences of what people have failed to do, as well as what they have explicitly done, then responsibility can be seen as a social category that is related to our membership in various communities. This latter sense of responsibility implies that in order to avoid acting irresponsibly, people will have to worry about their contribution, or lack of contribution, to group action as well as about their own individual personal actions. For example, racist violence on one's campus may not seem to be a particular student's responsibility if that student did not engage in the violence. But if the student could have helped in preventing the violence, but chose not to, there is a sense in which the student may share responsibility for that violence.

Care has recently been discussed as a decidedly different value from justice. Justice, even in its social, distributive form, calls for us to be impartial in assigning to people what is considered their due. But care calls for partiality, especially toward those who cannot protect themselves and to whom we are in special relationships. Our own children may not be owed any more than children in distant parts of the world; indeed our own children are probably owed less, given their already privileged position. But there is a value in preferring one's own child and striving to aid him or her. In our section on gender roles, we will encounter a recent dispute on whether and to what extent justice and care are different.

This concludes a brief overview of some of the main currents in contemporary Western philosophical approaches to ethics. In the next section we will explain how an emphasis on multiculturalism will further enrich our deliberations about both personal and social ethics.

A BRIEF ACCOUNT OF SOME NON-WESTERN PERSPECTIVES

The main non-Western perspectives represented in this anthology are these:

- African
- Buddhist
- Indian Hindu
- Islamic
- American Indian

We have also included a significant number of both Western and non-Western feminist pieces. As will become clear, there is considerable overlap among many of these non-Western perspectives. It is for this reason that it is sometimes appropriate to talk of a Third World perspective, even though each of these non-Western perspectives is unique. In the remainder of this introduction we will give a very brief overview of these perspectives.

The question of whether there is a single, distinct African perspective is hotly debated. What most of our authors mean by an African perspective is one that is centered on several traditional key ideas. Ifeanyi Menkiti provides a good summary of some of these ideas. Africans deny that the concept of a person

> can be defined by focusing on this or that physical or psychological characteristic of the lone individual. Rather man is defined by reference to the environing community . . . the reality of the community takes precedence over the reality of individual life histories, whatever these may be . . . persons become persons only after a process of incorporation. Without incorporation into this or that community, individuals are considered to be mere danglers, to whom the description "person" does not fully apply.[5]

In addition, as we will see, the experiences of poverty and hunger, so prevalent in many parts of Africa, have meant that Africans put much more emphasis on economic considerations than on political rights such as the right to free speech. Furthermore, the well-being of the community is paramount, and the well-being of the individual is inextricably linked to that of the community. Claude Ake's essay on African conceptions of human rights is a good place to begin to understand the ethical perspective that is connected to the view of personhood central to traditional African thought.

The Buddhist ethical perspective, unlike the African, is thoroughly individualistic in orientation: "The ultimate responsibility for any act rests with the individual."[6] But this individualistic orientation does not lead to selfishness or self-centered regard for maximizing the pleasures of one's life. Rather, the Buddhist ethical perspective values patience, compassion, self-sacrifice, kindness, and love. These virtues are to be pursued for the betterment of the person, if not in this life then in the next, as each person attempts to move closer to an ideal state of harmony with self and nature. The Buddhist perspective so strongly stresses compassion that it sometimes is understood as supporting an injunction against harm to any living thing. As we will see, Buddhism has many insights for discussions of human rights and environmental ethics. The essay by Kenneth Inada in the first section is a good place to start.

Indian Hindu perspectives on ethics share many features in common with Buddhist perspectives, but there are also important differences. I. C. Sharma has provided a good summary of some of the key Indian ethical ideas. Indian philosophies all start with the idea of a person who is suffering, and "who is to be rescued from endless torture, misery, disease, destruction, old age, even death."[7] For most Indian philosophers, the path to take in ending suffering is as important as the ending of suffering itself. Mohandas Gandhi epitomizes one of the great differences between Hindu and Buddhist ethical perspectives. Gandhi stressed an active intervention into the world to make it better, whereas Buddhists often prefer a more patient and passive approach. Gandhi's nonviolence and pacifism, as we will see, are inspired by a drive toward mitigating as much suffering as one can in the present. This orientation can also be seen in the essay by Guha in the section on environmental ethics, in which he criticizes those who place wilderness preservation ahead of relieving human suffering.

Traditional Islamic perspectives on ethics are deeply intertwined with religious conceptions. Like some Hindu perspectives, Islamic ethics is highly activist and interventionist. Most interestingly for our purposes, Islamic ethics are highly partialist. The Koran specifies that there will be strict rules for the ethical conduct of males, and quite different, some would say even stricter, rules for women. In addition, non-Muslims are to be treated quite differently from Muslims. This ethical perspective shares some features in common with those Western philosophers in the virtue ethics tradition who have argued for different sets of norms for how one behaves toward one's family members and toward those who are outside of one's family. But the Islamic perspective is especially difficult to reconcile with any claims of universal human rights, or of women's equal rights, as we will see in the essays about Islam in the sections on human rights and on gender roles.

American Indian perspectives, although often quite different from tribe to tribe, are deeply infused with a respect for the group, as is true for African perspectives. Added to this is a respect for

> the integrity and inherent importance of the natural world. . . . This is a very central belief which seems consistent across many Native American cultures—that the Earth is a living, conscious being that must be treated with respect and loving care.[8]

American Indians are also deeply affected by the extreme forms of suffering and discrimination their people have been forced to withstand while living in a dominant white society. Their insights are particularly important, as we will see, both in discussions of environmental ethics and in those on racial and gender discrimination.

Finally, let us say just a few words about feminism, a perspective that falls in between Western and non-Western philosophies. Many recent feminist writings have stressed the importance of relationships and interdependence rather than autonomy and individual rights. In this respect some feminist perspectives share many views in common with African and American Indian perspectives.[9] Most feminists have offered often cogent critiques of Western ethical views, especially concerning the nature and importance of justice, the commitment to universal principles, the rigidity of gender roles, as well as the status of pregnant women and the distribution of health care. Essays addressing these subjects can be found in the following sections of our anthology.

Let us end this introduction with a comment about method. While we have tried to provide a representative sample of Western and non-Western perspectives on applied ethics, we have not provided a sample of differences in method that exist in non-Western philosophical writing about ethics. Rather we have tried to find pieces that all have an argument that can be analyzed in terms of Western philosophical methods. In this sense, the essays all speak to one another, in terms of arguments and counterarguments, even though this method may not be common in the cultures in question. Nonetheless, even though most of our essays are Western in form, we feel that they are not so "Westernized" as to misrepresent their cultural perspectives.

It is our hope that this anthology will spawn future works in applied ethics by those who take non-Western perspectives. In constructing our book we found a large literature—larger than most Western-trained philosophers would expect to find. Hopefully, our success will cause other Western philosophers to explore Third World perspectives on applied ethics in greater depth. We would be grateful to hear from anyone who is working in this area or who knows of good essays that we have not included here. We have provided a brief bibliography at the end of each chapter to point the reader toward some of the essays that we were not able to include in this book.

NOTES

1. John Mohawk, "Epilogue: Looking for Columbus," *The State of Native America,* edited by M. Annette Jaimes. (Boston: South End Press, 1992), p. 443.
2. Lawrence Blum, "Antiracism, Multiculturalism, and Interracial Community: Three Educational Values for a Multicultural Society," a monograph published by the University of Massachusetts, Boston, 1991.
3. John Stuart Mill, *On Liberty* [1859] (Indianapolis: Hackett Publishing, 1978), p. 46.
4. John Mohawk, "Epilogue," p. 442.
5. Ifeanyi Menkiti, "Person and Community in African Traditional Thought," in *African Philosophy,* 3rd ed. edited by Richard Wright (Lanham, MD: University Press of America, 1984), pp. 171–72.
6. Stephan Beyer, *The Buddhist Experience* (Belmont, CA: Wadsworth, 1974), p. 10.
7. I. C. Sharma, *Ethical Philosophies of India* (New York: Harper & Row, 1965), p. 55.
8. Annie Booth and Harvey Jacobs, "Ties that Bind: Native American Beliefs as a Foundation for Environmental Consciousness," *Environmental Ethics,* vol. 12 (Spring 1990), pp. 30, 32.
9. See Sandra Harding's fascinating essay, "The Curious Coincidence of Feminine and African Moralities," in Eva Kittay and Diana Meyers, eds., *Women and Moral Theory* (Totowa, NJ: Rowman and Littlefield, 1987).

I

Human Rights

In each of our chapters, rights play a prominent role, so it is important to begin by understanding what rights are. Human rights are rights that people have by virtue of simply being human. Such rights are thought to exist universally. This universality is attested to by the fact that the United Nations' Universal Declaration of Human Rights was ratified with no dissenting votes. But in spite of this fact, there is quite a lively debate about the nature, extent, justification, and enumeration of human rights. We begin our anthology with this topic because it is central to all of the subsequent discussions—environmental rights; the right to be fed; the rights of those fighting in, or the right not to have to fight in, wars; the rights of sexual and racial equality; the right to health care; the right to free choice; as well as the right to life and the right to die.

In general, rights are considered to be extremely important moral considerations. Rights form the basis upon which individuals can make claims against other individuals or against whole societies or governments. If Jones has a right of free speech, then she has a strong basis for complaint if someone tries to prevent her from speaking, regardless of whether anyone wants to hear what she says. Indeed, according to the deontological tradition, the existence of a right provides an individual with a nearly unchallengeable basis for exercising that right, even when the vast majority of fellow citizens would be better off if the individual were not allowed to exercise her right. From a deontological point of view, rights are anti-majoritarian, or as Ronald Dworkin puts it, trump cards, which outweigh considerations of collective happiness or well-being.

Hardly anyone, at least in Western societies, denies that there are human rights; but there is a long-standing debate about what is the basis of these rights and about which are the most fundamental human rights. The latter debate has centered around the distinction between civil and economic rights. Civil rights concern the basic political status of members of a society, and include such things as the rights to vote, speak, assemble, and participate equally in political affairs. Economic rights concern the livelihood and survival of a person in terms of food, shelter, clothing, and medical supplies. Many socialists, feminists and members of certain non-Western societies have challenged the Western-oriented dominance of civil over economic rights.

In some non-Western societies, as we will see, there is also a serious question raised about whether there are human rights that are universal in scope, or whether rights vary according to gender or race. Another challenge often brought against conceptions of human rights is that they are too focused on the individual rather than on the group. Ancient and medieval discussions of ethics in the West, especially discussions of natural rights, did not have this emphasis. The universalistic and individualistic dimensions of a Western conception of rights are products of the modern age. In a sense, some of the non-Western approaches we will examine resemble ancient and medieval Western conceptions much more than they do modern ones, and there are interesting parallels between premodern and non-Western approaches that would be interesting to explore.

Our first reading is one of the best-known discussions of consequentialist ethics in general. John Stuart Mill, a defender of utilitarianism, presents one of the most plausible interpretations of utilitarianism, that is, the theory of ethics that equates moral rightness with the maximization of pleasure and the minimization of pain. Mill explains the importance of distinguishing between pleasures qualitatively. He argues that the test for deciding which of two pleasures is the best is simply which is preferred by those who have experienced both. Mill's general defense of the principle of utility proceeds from the idea that only when people prefer or desire something do we have any basis for regarding that thing as good. He then proceeds to show that happiness is the only thing that is desired for its own sake. Virtue and rights are valued in terms of their promotion of happiness or utility. At the end, Mill recognizes that justice is a term for various moral requirements that protect rights, and that while justice is merely a form of social utility, it is an especially important and weighty kind of utility.

Our second reading is taken from one of the most prominent defenders of rights, Ronald Dworkin. Dworkin is a defender of a deontological approach to ethics. In his essay he explains why rights need to be conceived as things that are not just very weighty forms of utility and hence as not being subject to legislative negotiation. The members of any society need to know that their government will respect them, and not exploit them for the betterment of the society against their will. On his account, rights operate as protectors of individual dignity, and as guarantors of equal respect within societies. To this end, Dworkin, like most Western theorists, focuses on civil or political rights as the most fundamental of human rights.

Claude Ake takes a socialist perspective on rights. Like consequentialists, Ake argues that rights are only justifiable if they promote the best kind of society. In his view the best society is not the one that maximizes aggregate happiness or well-being, but the one that leads to the greatest amount of economic development and liberation for the members of society. Ake contends that, especially in Africa, economic considerations outweigh civil or political considerations. The two greatest problems for Africans are starvation and fascism. Combatting these problems would lead to quite a different way of ordering human rights than is typical among liberal Western theorists, he argues.

A similar point is made by Charlotte Bunch. She points out that the greatest problem facing women around the globe is the oppression and violence directed by men who are, by and large, in positions of power over women. Protecting women's civil or political rights will not necessarily end such practices as sexual slavery, nor diminish the extent to which men are able to exercise arbitrary power over the lives and livelihoods of women. As was true for Ake, Bunch does not claim that human rights are unimportant. Rather, she criticizes the way in which human rights have traditionally been conceptualized. Until the actual problems faced by women are treated as of equal concern with the problems faced by men, human rights discussions will not have much to offer women.

Abdullahi Ahmed An-Na'im discusses a society in which the very legitimacy of human rights is called into question by the practices of the religious leadership. An-Na'im points out that some societies, such as those in the Islamic world, do not clearly endorse the view that all people should be accorded the same fundamental protections. Islamic society is partialist, in the sense that non-Muslims are treated quite differently from Muslims. The equal respect which Dworkin holds to be the hallmark of human rights theory is lacking in practice, although arguably it is something that can be justified by reference to some main Islamic texts. In those societies that do not accept the principle of equal respect, talk of human rights will not have much meaning, he concludes.

We end this section with a discussion of Buddhist conceptions of ethics and the application of Buddhism to the human rights debate. Kenneth Inada spends most of his essay discussing Buddhist conceptions of human nature. It is unusual in the West for discussions of human rights to focus on human nature in this way. Indeed, rights theorists tend to ignore such things and to focus instead, in a legalistic way, on theories and strategies for confronting offending institutions and governments that have abused the human rights of their members. Such an aggressive adversarial approach is quite inconsistent with the patient, compassionate, cooperative approach that characterizes the Buddhist perspective. A Buddhist conception of human rights would focus on the creation and maintenance of harmony in society rather than on the claims that individuals would bring against one another.

The discussions of Buddhist and Islamic perspectives could lead to a broader discussion of approaches to the field of ethics. In the West, ethics is often seen as similar to law. The pursuit of human rights is thus seen as quite similar to the pursuit of legal rights through the adversarial court system. But perhaps ethics should not be conceived in such a legalistic fashion. Perhaps ethics is, and should be, more concerned with cooperation and compassion than with the positing of claims by one person against another person. This is a subtext of our anthology and will recur in several other contexts.

Utilitarianism

John Stuart Mill

John Stuart Mill was one of the leading intellectuals of the nineteenth century. He was a member of Parliament as well as a popular philosopher. He was the author of A System of Logic *(1843),* On Liberty *(1859),* Utilitarianism *(1861),* Considerations on Representative Government *(1861),* The Subjection of Women *(1869), and* Principles of Political Economy *(1871).*

Mill's defense of the principle of utility is the most influential modern account of a consequentialist moral theory. In this excerpt from his book Utilitarianism, *Mill clearly sets out the principle of the greatest happiness for the greatest number and defends it against several of the most obvious objections. He then offers a limited defense of the principle. He ends by explaining the intimate relationship between utility and rights.*

WHAT UTILITARIANISM IS

The creed which accepts as the foundation of morals "utility" or the "greatest happiness principle" holds that actions are right in proportion as they tend to promote happiness; wrong as they tend to produce the reverse of happiness. By happiness is intended pleasure and the absence of pain; by unhappiness, pain and the privation of pleasure. To give a clear view of the moral standard set up by the theory, much more requires to be said; in particular, what things it includes in the ideas of pain and pleasure, and to what extent this is left an open question. But these supplementary explanations do not affect the theory of life on which this theory of morality is grounded—namely, that pleasure and freedom from pain are the only things desirable as ends; and that all desirable things (which are as numerous in the utilitarian as in any other scheme) are desirable either for pleasure inherent in themselves or as means to the promotion of pleasure and the prevention of pain.

Now such a theory of life excites in many minds, and among them in some of the most estimable in feeling and purpose, inveterate dislike. To suppose that life has (as they express it) no higher end than pleasure—no better and nobler object of desire and pursuit—they designate as utterly mean and groveling, as a doctrine worthy only of swine, to whom the followers of Epicurus were, at a very early period, contemptuously likened; and modern holders of the doctrine are occasionally made the subject of equally polite comparisons by its German, French, and English assailants.

When thus attacked, the Epicureans have always answered that it is not they, but their accusers, who represent human nature in a degrading light, since the accusation supposes human beings to be capable of no pleasures except those of which swine are

Reprinted with permission of Hackett Publishing Co., from *Utilitarianism*, by John Stuart Mill, edited by George Sher, 1979. [Edited]

capable. If this supposition were true, the charge could not be gainsaid, but would then be no longer an imputation; for if the sources of pleasure were precisely the same to human beings and to swine, the rule of life which is good enough for the one would be good enough for the other. The comparison of the Epicurean life to that of beasts is felt as degrading, precisely because a beast's pleasures do not satisfy a human being's conceptions of happiness. Human beings have faculties more elevated than the animal appetites and, when once made conscious of them, do not regard anything as happiness which does not include their gratification. I do not indeed, consider the Epicureans to have been by any means faultless in drawing out their scheme of consequences from the utilitarian principle. To do this in any sufficient manner, many Stoic, as well as Christian, elements require to be included. But there is no known Epicurean theory of life which does not assign to the pleasures of the intellect, of the feelings and imagination, and of the moral sentiments a much higher value as pleasures than to those of mere sensation. It must be admitted, however, that utilitarian writers in general have placed the superiority of mental over bodily pleasures chiefly in the greater permanency, safety, uncostliness, etc., of the former—that is, in their circumstantial advantages rather than in their intrinsic nature. And on all these points utilitarians have fully proved their case; but they might have taken the other and, as it may be called, higher ground with entire consistency. It is quite compatible with the principle of utility to recognize the fact that some kinds of pleasure are more desirable and more valuable than others. It would be absurd that, while in estimating all other things quality is considered as well as quantity, the estimation of pleasure should be supposed to depend on quantity alone.

If I am asked what I mean by difference of quality in pleasures, or what makes one pleasure more valuable than another, merely as a pleasure, except its being greater in amount, there is but one possible answer. Of two pleasures, if there be one to which all or almost all who have experience of both give a decided preference, irrespective of any feeling of moral obligation to prefer it, that is the more desirable pleasure. If one of the two is, by those who are competently acquainted with both, placed so far above the other that they prefer it, even though knowing it to be attended with a greater amount of discontent, and would not resign it for any quantity of the other pleasure which their nature is capable of, we are justified in ascribing to the preferred enjoyment a superiority in quality so far outweighing quantity as to render it, in comparison, of small account.

Now it is an unquestionable fact that those who are equally acquainted with and equally capable of appreciating and enjoying both do give a most marked preference to the manner of existence which employs their higher faculties. Few human creatures would consent to be changed into any of the lower animals for a promise of the fullest allowance of a beast's pleasures; no intelligent human being would consent to be a fool, no instructed person would be an ignoramus, no person of feeling and conscience would be selfish and base, even though they should be persuaded that the fool, the dunce, or the rascal is better satisfied with his lot than they are with theirs. They would not resign what they possess more than he for the most complete satisfaction of all the desires which they have in common with him. If they ever fancy they would, it is only in cases of unhappiness so extreme that to escape from it they would exchange their lot for almost any other, however undesirable in their own eyes. A being of higher faculties requires more to make him happy, is capable probably of more acute suffering, and certainly accessible to it at more points, than one of an inferior type; but in spite of these liabilities, he can never really wish to sink into what he feels to be a lower grade of existence. We may give what explanation we please of this unwillingness; we may attribute it to pride, a name which is given indiscriminately to some of the most and to some of the least estimable feelings of which mankind are capable; we may refer it to the love of liberty and personal independence, an appeal to which was with the Stoics one of the most effective means for the inculcation of it; to the love of power or to the love of excitement, both of which do really enter into and contribute to it; but its most appropriate appellation is a sense of dignity, which all human beings possess in one form or other, and in some, though by no means in exact, proportion to their higher faculties, and which is so essential a part of the happiness of those in whom it is strong that nothing which conflicts with it could be otherwise than momentarily an object of desire to them. Whoever supposes that this preference takes place at a sacrifice of happiness—that the superior being, in anything like equal circumstances, is not happier than the inferior—confounds the two very different ideas of happiness and content. It is indisputable that the being whose capacities of enjoyment are low has the greatest chance of having them fully satisifed; and a highly endowed being will always feel that any happiness which he can look for, as the world is constituted, is imperfect. But he can learn to bear its imperfections, if they are at all bearable; and they will not make him envy the being who is indeed unconscious of the imperfections, but only because he feels not at all the good which those imperfections qualify. It is better to be a human being dissatisfied than a pig satisfied; better to be Socrates dissatisfied than a fool satisfied. And if the fool, or the pig, are of a different opinion, it is because they only know their own side of the question. The other party to the comparison knows both sides.

It may be objected that many who are capable of the higher pleasures occasionally, under the influence of temptation, postpone them to the lower. But this is quite compatible with a full appreciation of the intrinsic superiority of the higher. Men often, from infirmity of character, make their election for the nearer good, though they know it to be the less valuable; and this no less when the choice is between two bodily pleasures than when it is between bodily and mental. They pursue sensual indulgences to the injury of health, though perfectly aware that health is the greater good. It may be further objected that many who begin with youthful enthusiasm for everything noble, as they advance in years, sink into indolence and selfishness. But I do not believe that those who undergo this very common change voluntarily choose the lower description of pleasures in preference to the higher. I believe that, before they devote themselves exclusively to the one, they have already become incapable of the other. Capacity for the nobler feelings is in most natures a very tender plant, easily killed, not only by hostile influences, but by mere want of sustenance; and in the majority of young persons it speedily dies away if the occupations to which their position in life has devoted them, and the society into which it has thrown them, are not favorable to keeping that higher capacity in exercise. Men lose their high aspirations as they lose their intellectual tastes, because they have not time or opportunity for indulging them; and they addict themselves to inferior pleasures, not because they deliberately prefer them, but because they are either the only ones to which they have access or the only ones which they are any longer capable of enjoying. It may be questioned whether anyone who has remained equally susceptible to both classes of pleasures ever knowingly and calmly preferred the lower, though many, in all ages, have broken down in an ineffectual attempt to combine both.

From this verdict of the only competent judges, I apprehend there can be no appeal. On a question which is the best worth having of two pleasures, or which of two modes of existence is the most grateful to the feelings, apart from its moral attributes and from its consequences, the judgment of these who are qualifed by knowledge of both, or, if they differ, that of the majority among them, must be admitted as final. And there needs be the less hesitation to accept this judgment respecting the quality of pleasures, since there is no other tribunal to be referred to even on the question of quantity. What means are there of determining which is the acutest of two pains, or the intensest of two pleasurable sensations, except the general suffrage of those who are familiar with both? Neither pains nor pleasures are homogeneous, and pain is always heterogeneous with pleasure. What is there to decide whether a particular pleasure is worth purchasing at the cost of a particular pain, except the feelings and judgment of the experienced? When, therefore, those feelings and judgment declare the pleasures derived from the higher faculties to be preferable *in kind*, apart from the question of intensity, to those of which the animal nature, disjoined from the higher faculties, is susceptible, they are entitled on this subject to the same regard.

I have dwelt on this point as being part of a perfectly just conception of utility or happiness considered as the directive rule of human conduct. But it is by no means an indispensable condition to the acceptance of the utilitarian standard; for that standard is not the agent's own greatest happiness, but the greatest amount of happiness altogether; and if it may possibly be doubted whether a noble character is always the happier for its nobleness, there can be no doubt that it makes other people happier, and that the world in general is immensely a gainer by it. Utilitarianism, therefore, could only attain its end by the general cultivation of nobleness of character, even if each individual were only benefited by the nobleness of others, and his own, so far as happiness is concerned, were a sheer deduction from the benefit. But the bare enunciation of such an absurdity as this last renders refutation superfluous.

According to the greatest happiness principle, as above explained, the ultimate end, with reference to and for the sake of which all other things are desirable—whether we are considering our own good or that of other people—is an existence exempt as far as possible from pain, and as rich as possible in enjoyments, both in point of quantity and quality; the test of quality and the rule for measuring it against quantity being the preference felt by those who, in their opportunities of experience, to which must be added their habits of self-consciousness and self-observation, are best furnished with the means of comparison. This, being according to the utlitarian opinon the end of human action, is necessarily also the standard of morality, which may accordingly be defined "the rules and precepts for human conduct," by the observance of which an existence such as has been described might be, to the greatest extent possible, secured to all mankind; and not to them only, but, so far as the nature of things admits, to the whole sentient creation. . . .

OF WHAT SORT OF PROOF THE PRINCIPLE OF UTILITY IS SUSCEPTIBLE

It has already been remarked that questions of ultimate ends do not admit of proof, in the ordinary acceptation of the term. To be incapable of proof by reasoning is common to all first principles, to the first premises of our knowledge, as well as to those of our conduct. But the former, being matters of fact, may be the subject of a direct appeal to the faculties which judge of fact—namely, our senses and our internal consciousness. Can an appeal be made to the same faculties on questions of practical ends? Or by what other faculty is cognizance taken of them?

Questions about ends are, in other words, questions what things are desirable. The utilitarian doctrine is that happiness is desirable, and the only thing desirable, as an end; all other things being only desirable as means to that end. What ought to be required of this doctrine, what conditions is it requisite that the doctrine should fulfill—to make good its claim to be believed?

The only proof capable of being given that an object is visible is that people actually see it. The only proof that a sound is audible is that people hear it; and so of the other sources of our experience. In like manner, I apprehend, the sole evidence it is possible to produce that anything is desirable is that people do actually desire it. If the end which the utilitarian doctrine proposes to itself were not, in theory and in practice, acknowledged to be an end, nothing could ever convince any person that it was so. No reason can be given why the general happiness is desirable, except that each person, so far as he believes it to be attainable, desires his own happiness. This, however, being a fact, we have not only all the proof which the case admits of, but all which it is possible to require, that happiness is a good, that each person's happiness is a good to that person, and the general happiness, therefore, a good to the aggregate of all persons. Happiness has made out its title as *one* of the ends of conduct and, consequently, one of the criteria of morality.

But it has not, by this alone, proved itself to be the sole criterion. To do that, it would seem, by the same rule, necessary to show, not only that people desire happiness, but that they never desire anything else. Now it is palpable that they do desire things which, in common language, are decidedly distinguished from happiness. They desire, for example, virtue and the absence of vice no less really than pleasure and the absence of pain. The desire of virtue is not as universal, but it is as authentic a fact as the desire of happiness. And hence the opponents of the utilitarian standard deem that they have a right to infer that there are other ends of human action besides happiness, and that happiness is not the standard of approbation and disapprobation.

But does the utilitarian doctrine deny that people desire virtue, or maintain that virtue is not a thing to be desired? The very reverse. It maintains not only that virtue is to be desired, but that it is to be desired disinterestedly, for itself. Whatever may be the opinion of utilitarian moralists as to the original conditions by which virtue is made virtue, however they may believe (as they do) that actions and dispositions are only virtuous because they promote another end than virtue, yet this being granted, and it having been decided, from considerations of this description, what *is* virtuous, they not only place virtue at the very head of the things which are good as means to the ultimate end, but they also recognize as a psychological fact the possibility of its being, to the individual, a good in itself, without looking to any end beyond it; and hold that the mind is not in a right state, not in a state conformable to utility, not in the state most conducive to the general happiness, unless it does love virtue in this manner—as a thing desirable in itself, even although, in the individual instance, it should not produce those other desirable consequences which it tends to produce, and on account of which it is held to be virtue. This opinion is not, in the smallest degree, a departure from the happiness principle. The ingredients of happiness are very various, and each of them is desirable in itself, and not merely when considered as swelling an aggregate. The principle of utility does not mean that any given pleasure, as music, for instance, or any given exemption from pain, as for example health, is to be looked upon as means to a collective something termed happiness, and to be desired on that account. They are desired and desirable in and for themselves; besides being means, they are a part of the end. Virtue, according to the utilitarian doctrine, is not naturally and originally a part of the end, but it is capable of becoming so; and in those who live it disinterestedly it has become so, and is desired and cherished, not as a means to happiness, but as a part of their happiness.

To illustrate this further, we may remember that virtue is not the only thing originally a means, and which if it were not a means to anything else would be and remain indifferent, but which by association with what it is a means to comes to be desired for itself, and that too with the utmost intensity. What, for example, shall we say of the love of money? There is nothing originally more desirable about money than about any heap of glittering pebbles. Its worth is solely that of the things which it will buy; the desires for other things than itself, which it is a means of gratifying. Yet the love of money is not only one of the strongest moving forces of human life, but money is, in many cases, desired in and for itself; the desire to possess it is often stronger than the desire to use it, and goes on increasing when all the desires which point to ends beyond it, to be compassed by it, are falling off. It may, then, be said truly that money is desired not for the sake of an end, but as part of the end. From being a means to happiness, it has come to be itself a principal ingredient of the individual's conception of happiness. The same may be said of the majority of the great objects of human life: power, for example, or fame, except that to each of these there is a certain amount of immediate pleasure annexed, which has at least the semblance of being naturally inherent in them—a thing which cannot be said of money. Still, however, the strongest natural attraction, both of power and of fame, is the immense aid they give to the attainment of our other wishes; and it is the strong association thus generated between them and all our objects of desire which gives to the direct desire of them the intensity it often assumes, so as in some characters to surpass in strength all other desires. In these cases the means have become a part of the end, and a more important part of it than any of the things which they are means to. What was once desired as an instrument for the attainment of happiness has come to be desired for its own sake. In being desired for its own sake it is, however, desired as *part* of happiness. The person is made, or thinks he would be made, happy by its mere possession; and is made unhappy by failure to obtain it. The desire of it is not a different thing from the desire of happiness any more than the love of music or the desire of health. They are included in happiness. They are some of the elements of which the desire of happiness is made up. Happiness is not an abstract idea but a concrete whole; and these are some of its parts. And the utilitarian standard sanctions and approves their being so. Life would be a poor thing, very ill provided with sources of happiness, if there were not this provision of nature by which things originally indifferent, but conducive to, or otherwise associated with, the satisfaction of our primitive desires, become in themselves sources of pleasure more valuable than the primitive pleasures, both in permanency, in the space of human existence that they are capable of covering, and even in intensity.

Virtue, according to the utilitarian conception, is a good of this description. There was no original desire of it, or motive to it, save its conduciveness to pleasure, and especially to protection from pain. But through the association thus formed it may be felt a good in itself, and desired as such with as great intensity as any other good; and with this difference between it and the love of money, of power, or of fame—that all of these may, and often do, render the individual noxious to the other members of the society to which he belongs, whereas there is nothing which makes him so much a blessing to them as the cultivation of the disinterested love of virtue. And consequently, the utilitarian standard, while it tolerates and approves those other acquired desires, up to the point beyond which they would be more injurious to the general happiness than promotive of it, enjoins and requires the cultivation of the love of virtue up to the greatest strength possible, as being above all things important to the general happiness.

It results from the preceding considerations that there is in reality nothing desired except happiness. Whatever is desired otherwise than as a means to some end beyond itself, and ultimately to happiness, is desired as itself a part of happiness, and is not desired for itself until it has become so. . . .

ON THE CONNECTION BETWEEN JUSTICE AND UTILITY

In all ages of speculation one of the strongest obstacles to the reception of the doctrine that utility or happiness is the criterion of right and wrong has been drawn from the idea of justice. The powerful sentiment and apparently clear perception which that word recalls with a rapidity and certainty resembling an instinct have seemed to the majority of thinkers to point to an inherent quality in things; to show that the just must have an existence in nature as something absolute, generically distinct from every variety of the expedient and, in idea, opposed to it, though (as is commonly acknowledged) never, in the long run, disjoined from it in fact. . . .

The idea of justice supposes two things—a rule of conduct and a sentiment which sanctions the rule. The first must be supposed common to all mankind and intended for their good. The other (the sentiment) is a desire that punishement may be suffered by those who infringe the rule. There is involved, in addition, the conception of some definite person who suffers by the infringement, whose rights (to use the expression appropriated to the case) are violated by it. And the sentiment of justice appears to me to be the animal desire to repel or retaliate a hurt or damage to oneself or to those with whom one sympathizes, widened so as to include all persons, by the human capacity of enlarged sympathy and the human conception of intelligent self-interest. From the latter elements the feeling derives its morality; from the former, its peculiar impressiveness and energy of self-assertion.

I have, throughout, treated the idea of a *right* residing in the injured person and violated by the injury, not as a separate element in the composition of the idea and sentiment, but as one of the forms in which the other two elements clothe themselves. These elements are a hurt to some assignable person or persons, on the one hand, and a demand for punishment, on the other. An examination of our own minds, I think, will show that these two things include all that we mean when we speak of violation of a right. When we call anything a person's right, we mean that he has a valid claim on society to protect him in the possession of it, either by the force of law or by that of education and opinion. If he has what we consider a sufficient claim, on whatever account, to have something guaranteed to him by society, we say that he has a right to it. If we desire to prove that anything does not belong to him by right, we think this done as soon as it is admitted that society ought not to take measure for securing it to him, but should leave him to chance or to his own exertions. Thus a person is said to have a right to what he can earn in fair professional competition, because society ought not to allow any other person to hinder him from endeavoring to earn in that manner as much as he can. But he has not a right to three hundred a year, though he may happen to be earning it; because society is not called on to provide that he shall earn that sum. On the contrary, if he owns ten thousand pounds three-per-cent stock, he *has* a right to three hundred a year because society has come under an obligation to provide him with an income of that amount.

To have a right, then, is, I conceive, to have something which society ought to defend me in the possession of. If the objector goes on to ask why it ought, I can give him no other reason than general utility. If that expression does not seem to convey a sufficient feeling of the strength of the obligation, nor to account for the peculiar energy of the feeling, it is because there goes to the composition of the sentiment, not a rational only but also an animal element—the thirst for retaliation; and this thirst derives its intensity, as well as its moral justification, from the extraordinarily important and impressive kind of utility which is concerned. The interest involved is that of security, to everyone's feelings the most vital of all interests. All other earthly benefits are needed by one person, not needed by another; and many of them can, if necessary, be cheerfully forgone or replaced by something else; but security no human being can possibly do without; on it we depend for all our immunity from evil and for the whole value of all and every good, beyond the passing moment, since nothing but the gratification of the instant could be of any worth to us if we could be deprived of everything the next instant by whoever was momentarily stronger than ourselves. Now this most indispensable of all necessaries, after physical nutriment, cannot be had unless the machinery for providing it is kept unintermittedly in active play. Our notion, therefore, of the claim we have on our fellow creatures to join in making safe for us the very groundwork of our existence gathers feelings around it so much more intense than those concerned in any of the more common cases of utility that the difference in degree (as is often the case in psychology) becomes a real difference in kind. The claim assumes that character of absoluteness, that apparent infinity and incommensurability with all other considerations which constitute the distinction between the feeling of right and wrong and that of ordinary expediency and inexpediency. The feelings concerned are so powerful, and we count so positively on finding a responsive feeling in others (all being alike interested) that *ought* and *should* grow into *must*, and recognized indispensablity becomes a moral necessity, analogous to physical, and often not inferior to it in binding force.

If the preceding analysis, or something resembling it, be not the correct account of the notion of justice—if justice be totally independent of utility, and be a standard *per se*, which the mind can recognize by simple introspection of itself—it is hard to understand why that internal oracle is so ambiguous, and why so many things appear either just or unjust, according to the light in which they are regarded. . . .

It appears from what has been said that justice is a name for certain moral requirements which, regarded collectively, stand higher in the scale of social utility, and are therefore of more paramount obligation, than any others, though particular cases may occur in which some other social duty is so important as to overrule any one of the general maxims of justice. Thus, to save a life, it may not only be allowable, but a duty, to steal or take by force the necessary food or medicine, or to kidnap and compel to officiate the only qualified medical practitioner. In such cases, as we do not call anything justice which is not a virtue, we usually say, not that justice must give way to some other moral principle, but that what is just in ordinary cases is, by reason of that other principle, not just in the particular case. By this useful accommodation of language, the character of indefeasibility attributed to justice is kept up, and we are saved from the necessity of maintaining that there can be laudable injustice.

The considerations which have not been adduced resolve, I conceive, the only real difficulty in the utilitarian theory of morals. It has always been evident that all cases of justice are also cases of expediency; the difference is in the peculiar sentiment which attaches to the former, as contradistinguished from the latter. If this characteristic sentiment has been sufficiently accounted for; if there is no necessity to assume for it any peculiarity of origin; if it is simply the natural feeling of resentment, moralized by being made coextensive with the demands of social good; and if this feeling not only does but ought to exist in all the classes of cases to which the idea of justice corresponds—that idea no longer presents itself as a stumbling block to the utilitarian ethics. Justice remains the appropriate name for certain social utilities which are vastly more important, and therefore more absolute and imperative, than any others are as a class (though not more so than others may be in particular cases); and which, therefore, ought to be, as well as naturally are, guarded by a sentiment, not only different in degree, but also in kind; distinguished from the milder feeling which attaches to the mere idea of promoting human pleasure or convenience at once by the more definite nature of its commands and by the sterner character of its sanctions.

Taking Rights Seriously

Ronald Dworkin

Ronald Dworkin is professor of jurisprudence at Oxford and professor of law at New York University. His books include Taking Rights Seriously *(1977),* A Matter of Principle *(1985),* Law's Empire *(1986), and* A Bill of Rights for Britain *(1990)..*

This is one of the best-known recent statements of the deontological approach to rights. Dworkin argues that rights must be understood as extremely important moral concerns, and cannot be outweighed merely because a majority would be better off by violating the rights of an individual. Rights need extremely strong protection because they are necessary for the dignity and equal respect of individuals, especially when those individuals form a minority within a society. Dworkin believes that the right to free speech is a paradigm example of a right that should be given extremely strong weight—what he elsewhere has called treating rights as trump cards. Dworkin concludes that only when governments respect rights will respect for the law be generally reestablished.

THE RIGHTS OF CITIZENS

The language of rights now dominates political debate in the United States. Does the Government respect the moral and political rights of its citizens? Or does the Government's foreign policy, or its race policy, fly in the face of these rights? Do the minorities whose rights have been violated have the right to violate the law in return? Or does the silent majority itself have rights, including the right that those who break the law be punished? It is not surprising that these questions are now prominent. The concept of rights, and particularly the concept of rights against the Government, has its most natural use when a political society is divided, and appeals to cooperation or a common goal are pointless.

Reprinted with permission of Ronald Dworkin, from *Taking Rights Seriously,* by Ronald Dworkin, Harvard University Press, 1977. [Edited]

The debate does not include the issue of whether citizens have *some* moral rights against their Government. It seems accepted on all sides that they do. Conventional lawyers and politicians take it as a point of pride that our legal system recognizes, for example, individual rights of free speech, equality, and due process. They base their claim that our law deserves respect, at least in part, on that fact, for they would not claim that totalitarian systems deserve the same loyalty.

Some philosophers, of course, reject the idea that citizens have rights apart from what the law happens to give them. Bentham thought that the idea of moral rights was "nonsense on stilts." But that view has never been part of our orthodox political theory, and politicians of both parties appeal to the rights of the people to justify a great part of what they want to do. I shall not be concerned, in this essay, to defend the thesis that citizens have moral rights against their governments; I want instead to explore the implications of that thesis for those, including the present United States Government, who profess to accept it.

It is much in dispute, of course, what *particular* rights citizens have. Does the acknowledged right to free speech, for example, include the right to participate in nuisance demonstrations? In practice the Government will have the last word on what an individual's rights are, because its police will do what its officials and courts say. But that does not mean that the Government's view is necessarily the correct view; anyone who thinks it does must believe that men and women have only such moral rights as Government chooses to grant, which means that they have no moral rights at all.

All this is sometimes obscured in the United States by the constitutional system. The American Constitution provides a set of individual *legal* rights in the First Amendment, and in the due process, equal protection, and similar clauses. Under present legal practice the Supreme Court has the power to declare an act of Congress or of a state legislature void if the Court finds that the act offends these provisions. This practice has led some commentators to suppose that individual moral rights are fully protected by this system, but that is hardly so, nor could it be so.

The Constitution fuses legal and moral issues, by making the validity of a law depend on the answer to complex moral problems, like the problem of whether a particular statute respects the inherent equality of all men. This fusion has important consequences for the debates about civil disobedience; I have described these elsewhere[1] and I shall refer to them later. But it leaves open two prominent questions. It does not tell us whether the Constitution, even properly interpreted, recognizes all the moral rights that citizens have, and it does not tell us whether, as many suppose, citizens would have a duty to obey the law even if it did invade their moral rights.

Both questions become crucial when some minority claims moral rights which the law denies, like the right to run its local school system, and which lawyers agree are not protected by the Constitution. The second question becomes crucial when, as now, the majority is sufficiently aroused so that Constitutional amendments to eliminate rights, like the right against self-incrimination, are seriously proposed. It is also crucial in nations, like the United Kingdom, that have no constitution of a comparable nature.

Even if the Constitution were perfect, of course, and the majority left it alone, it would not follow that the Supreme Court could guarantee the individual rights of citizens. A Supreme Court decision is still a legal decision, and it must take into account precedent and institutional considerations like relations between the Court and Congress, as well as morality. And no judicial decision is necessarily the right decision. Judges stand for different positions on controversial issues of law and morals and, as the fights over Nixon's Supreme Court nominations showed, a President is entitled to appoint judges of his own persuasion, provided that they are honest and capable.

So, though the constitutional system adds something to the protection of moral rights against the Government, it falls far short of guaranteeing these rights, or even establishing what they are. It means that, on some occasions, a department other than the legislature has the last word on these issues, which can hardly satisfy someone who thinks such a department profoundly wrong.

It is of course inevitable that some department of government will have the final say on what law will be enforced. When men disagree about moral rights, there will be no way for either side to prove its case, and some decision must stand if there is not to be anarchy. But that piece of orthodox wisdom must be the beginning and not the end of a philosophy of legislation and enforcement. If we cannot insist that the Government reach the right answers about the rights of its citizens, we can insist at least that it try. We can insist that it take rights seriously, follow a coherent theory of what these rights are, and act consistently with its own professions. I shall try to show what that means, and how it bears on the present political debates. . . .

CONTROVERSIAL RIGHTS

The argument so far has been hypothetical: if a man has a particular moral right against the Government, that right survives contrary legislation or adjudication. But this does not tell us what rights he has, and it is notorious that reasonable men disagree about that. There is wide agreement on certain clearcut cases; almost everyone who believes in rights at all would admit, for example, that a man has a moral right to speak his mind in a nonprovocative way on matters of political concern, and that this is an important right that the State must go to great pains to protect. But there is great controversy as to the limits of such paradigm rights, and the so-called "anti-riot" law involved in the famous Chicago Seven trial of the last decade is a case in point.

The defendants were accused of conspiring to cross state lines with the intention of causing a riot. This charge is vague—perhaps unconstitutionally vague—but the law apparently defines as criminal emotional speeches which argue that violence is justified in order to secure political equality. Does the right of free speech protect this sort of speech? That, of course, is a legal issue, because it invokes the free-speech clause of the First Amendment of the Constitution. But it is also a moral issue, because, as I said, we must treat the First Amendment as an attempt to protect a moral right. It is part of the job of governing to "define" moral rights through statutes and judicial decisions, that is, to declare officially the extent that moral rights will be taken to have in law. Congress faced this task in voting on the anti-riot bill, and the Supreme Court has faced it in countless cases. How should the different departments of government go about defining moral rights?

They should begin with a sense that whatever they decide might be wrong. History and their descendants may judge that they acted unjustly when they thought they were right. If they take their duty seriously, they must try to limit their mistakes, and they must therefore try to discover where the dangers of mistake lie.

They might choose one of two very different models for this purpose. The first model recommends striking a balance between the rights of the individual and the demands of society at large. If the Government *infringes* on a moral right (for example, by defining the right of free speech more narrowly than justice requires), then it has done the individual a wrong. On the other hand, if the Government *inflates* a right (by defining it more broadly than justice requires) then it cheats society of some general benefit, like safe streets, that there is no reason it should not have. So a mistake on one side is as serious as a mistake on the other. The course of government is to steer to the middle, to balance the general good and personal rights, giving to each its due.

When the Government, or any of its branches, defines a right, it must bear in mind, according to the first model, the social cost of different proposals and make the necessary adjustments. It must not grant the same freedom to noisy demonstrations as it grants to calm political discussion, for example, because the former causes much more trouble than the latter. Once it decides how much of a right to recognize, it must enforce its decision to the full. That means permitting an individual to act within his rights, as the Government has defined them, but not beyond, so that if anyone breaks the law, even on grounds of conscience, he must be punished. No doubt any government will make mistakes, and will regret decisions once taken. That is inevitable. But this middle policy will ensure that errors on one side will balance out errors on the other over the long run.

The first model, described in this way, has great plausibility, and most laymen and lawyers, I think, would respond to it warmly. The metaphor of balancing the public interest against personal claims is established in our political and judicial rhetoric, and this metaphor gives the model both familiarity and appeal. Nevertheless, the first model is a false one, certainly in the case of rights generally regarded as important, and the metaphor is the heart of its error.

The institution of rights against the Government is not a gift of God, or an ancient ritual, or a national sport. It is a complex and troublesome practice that makes the Government's job of securing the general benefit more difficult and more expensive, and it would be a frivolous and wrongful practice unless it served some point. Anyone who professes to take rights seriously, and who praises our Government for respecting them, must have some sense of what that point is. He must accept, at the minimum, one or both of two important ideas. The first is the vague but powerful idea of human dignity. This idea, associated with Kant, but defended by philosophers of different schools, supposes that there are ways of treating a man that are inconsistent with recognizing him as a full member of the human community, and holds that such treatment is profoundly unjust.

The second is the more familiar idea of political equality. This supposes that the weaker members of a political community are entitled to the same concern and respect of their government as the more powerful members have secured for themselves, so that if some men have freedom of decision whatever the effect on the general good, then all men must have the same freedom. I do not want to defend or elaborate these ideas here, but only to insist that anyone who claims that citizens have rights must accept ideas very close to these.[2]

It makes sense to say that a man has a fundamental right against the Government, in the strong sense, like free speech, if that right is necessary to protect his dignity, or his standing as equally entitled to concern and respect, or some other personal value of like consequence. It does not make sense otherwise.

So if rights make sense at all, then the invasion of a relatively important right must be a very serious matter. It means treating a man as less than a man, or as less worthy of concern than other men. The institution of rights rests on the conviction that this is a grave injustice, and that it is worth paying the incremental cost in social policy or efficiency that is necessary to prevent it. But then it must be wrong to say that inflating rights is as serious as invading them. If the Government errs on the side of the individual, then it simply pays a little more in social efficiency than it has to pay; it pays a little more, that is, of the same coin that it has already decided must be spent. But if it errs against the individual it inflicts an insult upon him that, on its own reckoning, it is worth a great deal of that coin to avoid.

So the first model is indefensible. It rests, in fact, on a mistake I discussed earlier, namely the confusion of society's rights with the rights of members of society. "Balancing" is appropriate when the Government must choose between competing claims of right—between the Southerner's claim to freedom of association, for example, and the black man's claim to an equal education. Then the Government can do nothing but estimate the merits of the competing claims, and act on its estimate. The first model assumes that the "right" of the majority is a competing right that must be balanced in this way; but that, as I argued before, is a confusion that threatens to destroy the concept of individual rights. It is worth noticing that the community rejects the first model in that area where the stakes for the individual are highest, the criminal process. We say that it is better that a great many guilty men go free than that one innocent man be punished, and that homily rests on the choice of the second model for government.

The second model treats abridging a right as much more serious than inflating one, and its recommendations follow from that judgment. It stipulates that once a right is recognized in clear-cut cases, then the Government should act to cut off that right only when some compelling reason is presented, some reason that is consistent with the suppositions on which the original right must be based. It cannot be an argument for curtailing a right, once granted, simply that society would pay a further price for extending it. There must be something special about that further cost, or there must be some other feature of the case, that makes it sensible to say that although great social cost is warranted to protect the original right, this particular cost is not necessary. Otherwise, the Government's failure to extend the right will show that its recognition of the right in the original case is a sham, a promise that it intends to keep only until that becomes inconvenient.

How can we show that a particular cost is not worth paying without taking back the initial recognition of a right? I can think of only three sorts of grounds that can consistently be used to limit the definition of a particular right. First, the Government might show that the values protected by the original right are not really at stake in the marginal case, or are at stake only in some attenuated form. Second, it might show that if the right is defined to include the marginal case, then some competing right, in the strong sense I described earlier, would be abridged. Third, it might show that if the right were so defined, then the cost to society would not be simply incremental, but would be of a degree far beyond the cost paid to grant the original right, a degree great enough to justify whatever assault on dignity or equality might be involved.

It is fairly easy to apply these grounds to one group of problems the Supreme Court faced, imbedded in constitutional issues. The draft law provided an exemption for conscientious objectors, but this exemption, as interpreted by the draft boards, has been limited to those who object to *all* wars on *religious* grounds. If we suppose that the exemption is justified on the ground that an individual has a moral right not to kill in violation of his own principles, then the question is raised whether it is proper to exclude those whose morality is not based on religion, or whose morality is sufficiently complex to distinguish among wars. The Supreme Court held, as a matter of Constitutional law, that the draft boards were wrong to exclude the former, but competent to exclude the latter.

None of the three grounds I listed can justify either of these exclusions as a matter of political morality. The invasion of personality in forcing men to kill when they believe killing immoral is just as great when these beliefs are based on secular grounds, or take account of the fact that wars differ in morally relevant ways, and there is no pertinent difference in competing rights or in national emergency. There are differences among the cases, of course, but they are insufficient to justify the distinction. A government that is secular on principle cannot prefer a religious to a nonreligious morality as such. There are utilitarian arguments in favor of limiting the exception to religious or universal grounds—an exemption so limited may be less expensive to administer, and may allow easier discrimination between sincere and insincere applicants. But these utilitarian reasons are irrelevant, because they cannot count as grounds for limiting a right.

What about the anti-riot law, as applied in the Chicago trial? Does the law represent an improper limitation of the right to free speech, supposedly protected by the First Amendment? If we were to apply the first model for government to this issue, the argument for the anti-riot law would look strong. But if we set aside talk of balancing as inappropriate, and turn to the proper grounds for limiting a right, then the argument becomes a great deal weaker. The original right of free speech must suppose that it is an assault on human personality to stop a man from expressing what he honestly believes, particularly on issues affecting how he is governed. Surely the assault is greater, and not less, when he is stopped from expressing those principles of political morality that he holds most passionately, in the face of what he takes to be outrageous violations of these principles.

It may be said that the anti-riot law leaves him free to express these principles in a non-provocative way. But that misses the point of the connection between expression and dignity. A man cannot express himself freely when he cannot match his rhetoric to his outrage, or when he must trim his sails to protect values he counts as nothing next to those he is trying to vindicate. It is true that some political dissenters speak in ways that shock the majority, but it is arrogant for the majority to suppose that the orthodox methods of expression are the proper ways to speak, for this is a denial of equal concern and respect. If the point of the right is to protect the dignity of dissenters, then we must make judgments about appropriate speech with the personalities of the dissenters in mind, not the personality of the "silent" majority for whom the anti-riot law is no restraint at all.

So the argument fails, that the personal values protected by the original right are less at stake in this marginal case. We must consider whether competing rights, or some grave threat to society, nevertheless justify the anti-riot law. We can consider these two grounds together, because the only plausible competing rights are rights to be free from violence, and violence is the only plausible threat to society that the context provides.

I have no right to burn your house, or stone you or your car, or swing a bicycle chain against your skull, even if I find these to be natural means of expression. But the defendants in the Chicago trial were not accused of direct violence; the argument runs that the acts of speech they planned made it likely that others would do acts of violence, either in support of or out of hostility to what they said. Does this provide a justification?

The question would be different if we could say with any confidence how much and what sort of violence the anti-riot law might be expected to prevent. Will it save two lives a year, or two hundred, or two thousand? Two thousand dollars of property, or two hundred thousand, or two million? No one can say, not simply because prediction is next to impossible, but because we have no firm understanding of the process by which demonstration disintegrates into riot, and in particular of the part played by inflammatory speech, as distinct from poverty, police brutality, blood lust, and all the rest of human and economic failure. The Government must try, of course, to reduce the violent waste of lives and property, but it must recognize that any attempt to locate and remove a cause of riot, short of a reorganization of society, must be an exercise in speculation, trial, and error. It must make its decisions under conditions of high uncertainty, and the institution of rights, taken seriously, limits its freedom to experiment under such conditions.

It forces the Government to bear in mind that preventing a man from speaking or demonstrating offers him a certain and profound insult, in return for a speculative benefit that may in any event be achieved in other if more expensive ways. When lawyers say that rights may be limited to protect other rights, or to prevent catastrophe, they have in mind cases in which cause and effect are relatively clear, like the familiar example of a man falsely crying "Fire!" in a crowded theater.

But the Chicago story shows how obscure the causal connections can become. Were the speeches of Hoffman or Rubin necessary conditions of the riot? Or had thousands of people come to Chicago for the purposes of rioting anyway, as the Government also argues? Were they in any case sufficient conditions? Or could the police have contained the violence if they had not been so busy contributing to it, as the staff of the President's Commission on Violence said they were?

These are not easy questions, but if rights mean anything, then the Government cannot simply assume answers that justify its conduct. If a man has a right to speak, if the reasons that support that right extend to provocative political speech, and if the effects of such speech on violence are unclear, then the Government is not entitled to make its first attack on that problem by denying that right. It may be that abridging the right to speak is the least expensive course, or the least damaging to police morale, or the most popular politically. But these are utilitarian arguments in favor of starting one place rather than another, and such arguments are ruled out by the concept of rights.

This point may be obscured by the popular belief that political activists look forward to violence and "ask for trouble" in what they say. They can hardly complain, in the general view, if they are taken to be the authors of the violence they expect, and treated accordingly. But this repeats the confusion I tried to explain earlier between having a right and doing the right thing. The speaker's motives may be relevant in deciding whether he does the right thing in speaking passionately about issues that may inflame or enrage the audience. But if he has a right to speak, because the danger in allowing him to speak is speculative, his motives cannot count as independent evidence in the argument that justifies stopping him.

But what of the individual rights of those who will be destroyed by a riot, of the passer-by who will be killed by a sniper's bullet or the shopkeeper who will be ruined by looting? To put the issue in this way, as a question of competing rights, suggests a principle that would undercut the effect of uncertainty. Shall we say that some rights to protection are so important that the Government is justified in doing all it can to maintain them? Shall we therefore say that the Government may abridge the rights of others to act when their acts might simply increase the risk, by however slight or speculative a margin, that some person's right to life or property will be violated?

Some such principle is relied on by those who oppose the Supreme Court's recent liberal rulings on police procedure. These rulings increase the chance that a guilty man will go free, and therefore marginally increase the risk that any particular member of the community will be murdered, raped, or robbed. Some critics believe that the Court's decisions must therefore be wrong.

But no society that purports to recognize a variety of rights, on the ground that a man's dignity or equality may be invaded in a variety of ways, can accept such a principle. If forcing a man to testify against himself, or forbidding him to speak, does the damage that the rights against self-incrimination and the right of free speech assume, then it would be contemptuous for the State to tell a man that he must suffer this damage against the possibility that other men's risk of loss may be marginally reduced. If rights make sense, then the degrees of their importance cannot be so different that some count not at all when others are mentioned.

Of course the Government may discriminate and may stop a man from exercising his right to speak when there is a clear and substantial risk that his speech will do great damage to the person or property of others, and no other means of preventing this are at hand, as in the case of the man shouting "Fire!" in a theater. But we must reject the suggested principle that the Government can simply ignore rights to speak when life and property are in question. So long as the impact of speech on these other rights remains speculative and marginal, it must look elsewhere for levers to pull.

WHY TAKE RIGHTS SERIOUSLY?

I said at the beginning of this essay that I wanted to show what a government must do that professes to recognize individual rights. It must dispense with the claim that citizens never have a right to break its law, and it must not define citizens' rights so that these are cut off for supposed reasons of the general good. Any Government's harsh treatment of civil disobedience, or campaign against vocal protest, may therefore be thought to count against its sincerity.

One might well ask, however, whether it is wise to take rights all that seriously after all. America's genius, at least in her own legend, lies in not taking any abstract doctrine to its logical extreme. It may be time to ignore abstractions, and concentrate instead on giving the majority of our citizens a new sense of their Government's concern for their welfare, and of their title to rule.

That, in any event, is what former Vice-President Agnew seemed to believe. In a policy statement on the issue of "weirdos" and social misfits, he said that the liberals' concern for individual rights was a headwind blowing in the face of the ship of state. That is a poor metaphor, but the philosophical point it expresses is very well taken. He recognized, as many liberals do not, that the majority cannot travel as fast or as far as it would like if it recognizes the rights of individuals to do what, in the majority's terms, is the wrong thing to do.

Spiro Agnew supposed that rights are divisive, and that national unity and a new respect for law may be developed by taking them more skeptically. But he is wrong. America will continue to be divided by its social and foreign policy, and if the economy grows weaker again the divisions will become more bitter. If we want our laws and our legal institutions to provide the ground rules within which these issues will be contested then these ground rules must not be the conqueror's law that the dominant class imposes on the weaker, as Marx supposed the law of a capitalist society must be. The bulk of the law—that part which defines and implements social, economic, and foreign policy—cannot be neutral. It must state, in its greatest part, the majority's view of the common good. The institution of rights is therefore crucial, because it represents the majority's promise to the minorities that their dignity and equality will be respected. When the divisions among the groups are most violent, then this gesture, if law is to work, must be most sincere.

The institution requires an act of faith on the part of the minorities, because the scope of their rights will be controversial whenever they are important, and because the officers of the majority will act on their own notions of what these rights really are. Of course these officials will disagree with many of the claims that a minority makes. That makes it all the more important that they take their decisions gravely. They must show that they understand what rights are, and they must not cheat on the full implications of the doctrine. The Government will not re-establish respect for law without giving the law some claim to respect. It cannot do that if it neglects the one feature that distinguishes law from ordered brutality. If the Government does not take rights seriously, then it does not take law seriously either.

NOTES

1. See Chapter 8.
2. He need not consider these ideas to be axiomatic. He may, that is, have reasons for insisting that dignity or equality are important values, and these reasons may be utilitarian. He may believe, for example, that the general good will be advanced, *in the long run*, only if we treat indignity or inequality as very great injustices, and never allow our *opinions* about the general good to justify them. I do not know of any good arguments for or against this sort of "institutional" utilitarianism, but it is consistent with my point, because it argues that we must treat violations of dignity and equality as special moral crimes, beyond the reach of ordinary utilitarian justification.

The African Context of Human Rights

Claude Ake

Claude Ake is professor of political science at the University of Port Harcourt in Nigeria. He is the author of A Theory of Political Integration *(1967),* Revolutionary Pressures in Africa *(1978), and* A Political Economy of Africa *(1981).*

Ake points out that Western conceptions of human rights are not very interesting or useful for African societies. He contends that if a person is starving to death, the right to free speech does not do him or her much good. Ake also argues that a strong emphasis on rights will block various development policies. He believes that socialism rather than what he calls procedural liberalism provides the best grounding for a conception of human rights that will effectively address the current problems of hunger and fascism in African countries. In this context, collective rights, especially those of disadvantaged groups, will be of greater concern than individual rights.

Nobody can accuse Africa of taking human rights seriously. In a world which sees concern for human rights as a mark of civilized sensitivity, this indifference has given Africa a bad name. It is not unlikely that many consider it symptomatic of the rawness of life which has always been associated with Africa. I am in no position to say with any confidence why Africa has not taken much interest in human rights but I see good reasons why she should not have done so.

Before going into these reasons let us be clear what we are talking about. The idea of human rights is quite simple. It is that human beings have certain rights simply by virtue of being human. These rights are a necessary condition for the good life. Because of their singular importance, individuals are entitled to, indeed, required to claim them and society is enjoined to allow them. Otherwise, the quality of life is seriously compromised.

The idea of human rights, or legal rights in general, presupposes a society which is atomized and individualistic, a society of endemic conflict. It presupposes a society of people conscious of their separateness and their particular interests and anxious to realize them. The legal right is a claim which the individual may make against other members of society, and simultaneously an obligation on the part of society to uphold this claim.

The values implicit in all this are clearly alien to those of our traditional societies. We put less emphasis on the individual and more on the collectivity, we do not allow that the individual has any claims which may

Reprinted by permission of *Africa Today*, *Vol. 34*, No. 142, pp. 5–13, ©1987.

override that of the society. We assume harmony, not divergence of interests, competition and conflict; we are more inclined to think of our obligations to other members of our society rather than our claims against them.

The Western notion of human rights stresses rights which are not very interesting in the context of African realities. There is much concern with the right to peaceful assembly, free speech and thought, fair trial, etc. The appeal of these rights is sociologically specific. They appeal to people with a full stomach who can now afford to pursue the more esoteric aspects of self-fulfillment. The vast majority of our people are not in this position. They are facing the struggle for existence in its brutal immediacy. Theirs is a totally consuming struggle. They have little or no time for reflection and hardly any use for free speech. They have little interest in choice for there is no choice in ignorance. There is no freedom for hungry people, or those eternally oppressed by disease. It is no wonder that the idea of human rights has tended to sound hollow in the African context.

The Western notion of human rights lacks concreteness. It ascribes abstract rights to abstract beings. There is not enough concern for the historical conditions in which human rights can actually be realized. As it turns out, only a few people are in a position to exercise the rights which society allows. The few who have the resources to exercise these rights do not need a bill of rights. Their power secures them. The many who do not have the resources to exercise their rights are not helped any by the existence of these rights. Their powerlessness dooms them.

The idea of human rights really came into its own as a tool for opposing democracy. The French Revolution had brought home forcefully to everyone the paradox of democracy, namely that its two central values, liberty and equality, come into conflict at critical points. There is no democracy where there is no liberty for self-expression or choice. At the same time there is no democracy where there is no equality, for inequality reduces human relations to subordination and domination. The French Revolution and Jean Jacques Rousseau revealed rather dramatically the paradoxical relation between these two central values of democracy by leaning heavily towards equality. They gave Europe a taste of what it would be like to take the idea of equality and the correlative idea of popular sovereignty seriously.

Bourgeois Europe was horrified. The idea of a popular sovereign insisting on equality and having unlimited power over every aspect of social life was unacceptable. For such power was a threat to the institution of private property as well as the conditions of accumulation. So they began to emphasize liberty rather than the collectivity. This emphasis was also a way of rejecting democracy in its pure form as popular sovereignty. That was the point of stressing the individual and his rights and holding that certain rights are inalienable. That was the point of holding that the individual could successfully sustain certain claims and certain immunities against the wishes of the sovereign or even the rest of society. It is ironical that all this is conveniently forgotten today and liberal democrats can pass as the veritable defenders of democracy.

CHANGING STATUS OF HUMAN RIGHTS IN AFRICA

Africa is at last beginning to take interest in human rights. For one thing, the Western conception of human rights has evolved in ways which have made it more relevant to the African experience, although its relevance still remains ambiguous. Because human rights is such an important part of the political ideology of the West, it was bound to register in Africa eventually. Human rights record is beginning to feature in Western decisions of how to relate to the countries and leaders of Africa. Western decisions on this score have been made with such cynical inconsistency that one wonders whether human rights record really matters to them at all. However, our leaders ever so eager to please are obliged to assume that it matters and to adjust their behavior accordingly. Also the authoritarian capitalism of Africa is under some pressure to be more liberal and thereby create political conditions more conducive to capitalist efficiency.

If these are the reasons why Africa is beginning to take more interest in human rights, they are by no means the reason why she ought to do so. The way I see it is that we ought to be interested in human rights because it will help us to combat social forces which threaten to send us back to barbarism. Because it will aid our struggle for the social transformation which we need to survive and to flourish. To appreciate this let us look at the historical conditions of contemporary Africa.

I hope we can all agree that for now, the most salient aspect of these conditions is the crisis. It has been with us for so long we might well talk of the permanent crisis. No one seems to know for sure what its character is but we know its devastating effects only too well. We Africans have never had it so bad. The tragic consequences of our development strategies have finally come home to us. Always oppressed by poverty and deprivation, our lives become harsher still with each passing day as real incomes continue to decline. We watch helplessly while millions of our people are threatened by famine and look pitifully to the rest of the world to feed us. Our social and political institutions are disintegrating under pressure from our flagging morale, our dwindling resources and the intense struggle to control them. What is the problem? I am not sure. But I am convinced that we are not dealing simply or even primarily with an economic phenomenon. There is a political dimension to it which is so critical, it may well be the most decisive factor.

This is the problem of democracy or the problem of political repression. A long time ago our leaders opted for political repression. Having abandoned democracy for repression, our leaders are delinked from our people. Operating in a vacuum, they proclaim their incarnation of the popular will, hear echoes of their own voices, and reassured, pursue with zeal, policies which have nothing to do with the aspirations of our people and which cannot, therefore, mobilize them. As their alienation from the people increases, they rely more and more on force and become even more alienated.

CONSEQUENCES OF THE PROBLEM OF DEMOCRACY

The consequences of this are disastrous. In the first place it means that there is no development. Political repression ensures that the ordinary people of Africa who are the object of development remain silent, so that in the end nobody really speaks for development and it never comes alive in practice. Development cannot be achieved by proxy. A people develops itself or not at all. And it can develop itself only through its commitment and its energy. That is where democracy comes in. Self-reliance is not possible unless the society is thoroughly democratic, unless the people are the end and not just the means of development. Development occurs, in so far as it amounts to the pursuit of objectives set by the people themselves in their own interest and pursued by means of their own resources.

Another consequence of repression is the brutalization of our people. Look around you. The willful brutalization of people occurring among us is appalling. Human life is taken lightly, especially if it is that of the underprivileged. All manner of inhuman treatment is meted out for minor offenses and sometimes for no offenses at all. Ordinary people are terrorized daily by wanton display of state power and its instruments of violence. Our prison conditions are guaranteed to traumatize. The only consensus we can mobilize is passive conformity arising from fear and resignation. As we continue to stagnate this gets worse.

Yet another disaster threatens us. I am referring to fascism. In all probability this is something which nobody wants. But we might get it anyway because circumstances are moving steadily in that direction. All the ingredients of fascism are present now in most parts of Africa: a political class which has failed even by its own standards, and which is now acutely conscious of its humiliation and baffled by a world it cannot control; a people who have little if any hope or sense of self-worth yearning for redeemers; a milieu of anomie; a conservative leadership pitted against a rising popular radicalism and poised to take cover in defensive radicalism. That is what it takes and it is there in plenty. If Africa succumbs it will be terrible—fascism has always been in all its historical manifestations.

It seems to me that for many African countries the specter of fascism is the most urgent and the most serious danger today. Unless we contain it effectively and within a very short time, then we are in a great deal of trouble.

If this analysis is correct, then our present agenda must be the task of preventing the rise of fascism. To have a chance of succeeding this task requires a broad coalition of radicals, populists, liberals and even humane conservatives. That is, a coalition of all those who value democracy not in the procedural liberal sense but in the concrete socialist sense. This is where the idea of human rights comes in. It is easily the best ideological framework for such a coalition.

AN AFRICAN CONCEPTION OF HUMAN RIGHTS

We have now seen the relevance of human rights in the African context. But on a level of generality which does not tell us very much and so does not really settle the question of the applicability of the Western concept of human rights. I do not see how we can mobilize the African masses or the intelligentsia against fascism or whatever by accepting uncritically the Western notion of human rights. We have to domesticate it, recreate it in the light of African conditions. Let me indicate very briefly how these conditions redefine the idea of human rights.

First, we have to understand that the idea of legal rights presupposes social atomization and individualism, and a conflict model of society for which legal rights are the necessary mediation. However, in most of Africa, the extent of social atomization is very limited mainly because of the limited penetration of capitalism and commodity relations. Many people are still locked into natural economies and have a sense of belonging to an organic whole, be it a family, a clan, a lineage or an ethnic group. The phenomenon of the legal subject, the largely autonomous individual conceived as a bundle of rights which are asserted against all comers has not really developed much especially outside the urban areas.

These are the conditions which explain the forms of consciousness which we insist on misunderstanding. For instance, ethnic consciousness and ethnic identity. It is the necessary consciousness associated with non-atomized social structures and mechanical solidarity. Ethnic consciousness will be with us as long as these structural features remain, no matter how we condemn it or try to engineer it out of existence.

All this means that abstract legal rights attributed to individuals will not make much sense for most of our people; neither will they be relevant to their consciousness and living conditions. It is necessary to extend the idea of human rights to include collective human rights for corporate social groups such as the family, the lineage, the ethnic group. Our people still think largely in terms of collective rights and express their commitment to it constantly in their behavior. This disposition underlies the zeal for community development and the enormous sacrifices which poor people readily make for it. It underlies the so-called tribalist voting pattern of our people, the willingness of the poor villager to believe that the minister from his village somehow represents his share of the national cake, our traditional land tenure systems, the high incidence of cooperative labor and relations of production in the rural areas. These forms of consciousness remain very important features of our lives. If the idea of human rights is to make any sense at all in the African context, it has to incorporate them in a concept of communal human rights.

For reasons which need not detain us here some of the rights important in the West are of no interest and no value to most Africans. For instance, freedom of speech and freedom of the press do not mean much for a largely illiterate rural community completely absorbed in the daily rigors of the struggle for survival.

African conditions shift the emphasis to a different kind of rights. Rights which can mean something for poor people fighting to survive and burdened by ignorance, poverty and disease, rights which can mean something for women who are cruelly used. Rights which can mean something for the youth whose future we render more improbable every day. If a bill of rights is to make any sense, it must include among others, a right to work and to a living wage, a right to shelter, to health, to education. That is the least we can strive for if we are ever going to have a society which realizes basic human needs.

Finally, in the African context, human rights have to be much more than the political correlate of commodity fetishism which is what they are in the Western tradition. In that tradition the rights are not only abstract, they are also ascribed to abstract persons. The rights are ascribed to the human being from whom all specific determinations have been abstracted: the rights have no content just as individuals who enjoy them have no determination and so do not really exist.

All these problems which usually lurk beneath the surface appear in clear relief when we confront them with empirical reality. Granted, I have the freedom of speech. But where is this freedom, this right? I cannot read, I cannot write. I am too busy trying to survive I have no time to reflect. I am so poor I am constantly at the mercy of others. So where is this right and what is it really? Granted, I have the right to seek public office. That is all very well. But how do I realize this right? I am a full-time public servant who cannot find the time or the necessary resources to put up the organization required to win office. If I take leave from my work, I cannot hold out for more than one month without a salary. I have no money to travel about and meet the voters, even to pay the registration fees for my candidature. If I am not in a position to realize this right, then what is the point of saying that I have it? Do I really have it?

In Africa liberal rights make less sense even as ideological representations. If rights are to be meaningful in the context of a people struggling to stay afloat under very adverse economic and political conditions, they have to be concrete. Concrete in the sense that their practical import is visible and relevant to the conditions of existence of the people to whom they apply. And most importantly, concrete in the sense that they can be realized by their beneficiaries.

To be sure, there are rights which are realizable and there are people in Africa who effectively realize their rights. However, the people who are in a position to realize their rights are very few. They are able to realize their rights by virtue of their wealth and power. The litmus test for rights is those who need protection. Unfortunately these are precisely the people who are in no position to enjoy rights. Clearly, that will not do in African conditions. People are not going to struggle for formalities and esoteric ideas which will not change their lives.

Therefore, a real need arises, namely, to put more emphasis on the realization of human rights. How is this to be? Not in the way we usually approach such matters: by giving more unrealizable rights to the powerless and by begging the powerful to make concessions to them in the name of enlightened self-interest, justice and humanity. That approach will fail us always. Rights, especially those that have any real significance for our lives are usually taken, not given—with the cooperation of those in power if possible, but without it if necessary. That is the way it was for other peoples and that is the way it is going to be in Africa.

The realization of rights is best guaranteed by the power of those who enjoy the rights. Following this, what is needed is the empowerment by whatever means, of the common people. This is not a matter of legislation, although legislation could help a little. It is rather a matter of redistributing economic and political power across the board. That means that it is in the final analysis a matter of political mobilization and struggle. And it will be a protracted and bitter struggle because those who are favored by the existing distribution of power will resist heartily.

CONCLUSION: HUMAN RIGHTS AND SOCIAL TRANSFORMATION

It is at this point that the ideal of human rights is fully articulated for it is now that we see its critical dialectical moment. Initially part of the ideological prop of liberal capitalism, the idea of human rights was a conservative force. It was meant to safeguard the interests of the men of property especially against the threatening egalitarianism of popular sovereignty. It was not of course presented as a tool of special interests but a universal value good for humanity. That went down well and it has been able to serve those who propagated it behind this mystification.

But ideas have their own dynamics which cannot easily be controlled by the people who brought them into being. In case of human rights, its dynamics soon trapped it in a contradiction somewhat to the dismay of its protagonists. Fashioned as a tool against democracy, the idea became an important source of legitimation for those seeking the expansion of democracy. But in Europe, this contradiction never fully matured. An agile and accommodating political class and unprecedented affluence saw to that.

In Africa, prevailing objective conditions will press matters much further particularly the question of empowerment. In all probability, the empowerment of people will become the primary issue. Once this happens, the social contradictions will be immensely sharpened and the idea of human rights will become an asset of great value to radical social transformation. I cannot help thinking that Africa is where the critical issues in human rights will be fought out and where the idea will finally be consummated or betrayed.

Women's Rights as Human Rights: Toward A Re-Vision of Human Rights

Charlotte Bunch

Charlotte Bunch is the director of the Center for Global Issues and Women's Leadership at Rutgers University. She is the author of Passionate Politics: Feminist Theory in Action *(1987). She is the editor of seven books, including* Class and Feminism *(1974) and* Learning Our Way: Essays in Feminist Education *(1983).*

Bunch criticizes the Western conception of human rights as leaving women's rights largely out of the picture. Many women's rights are socioeconomic—that is, centered on food, shelter, and work. In addition, political oppression and systematic forms of violence against women are not taken as seriously as rights to free speech and press—rights that are only marginally important to many women, especially those in the Third World. Bunch concludes with some practical guidelines for transforming Western conceptions of human rights to ensure that women's rights are also counted as human rights.

Significant numbers of the world's population are routinely subject to torture, starvation, terrorism, humiliation, mutilation, and even murder simply because they are female. Crimes such as these against any group other than women would be recognized as a civil and political emergency as well as a gross violation of the victims' humanity. Yet, despite a clear record of deaths and demonstrable abuse, women's rights are not commonly classified as human rights. This is problematic both theoretically and practically, because it has grave consequences for the way society views and treats the fundamental issues of women's lives.

Reprinted by permission of *Human Rights Quarterly, Volume 12,* Number 4, November 1990.

This paper questions why women's rights and human rights are viewed as distinct, looks at the policy implications of this schism, and discusses different approaches to changing it.

Women's human rights are violated in a variety of ways. Of course, women sometimes suffer abuses such as political repression that are similar to abuses suffered by men. In these situations, female victims are often invisible, because the dominant image of the political actor in our world is male. However, many violations of women's human rights are distinctly connected to being female—that is, women are discriminated against and abused on the basis of gender. Women also experience sexual abuse in situations where their other human rights are being violated, as political prisoners or members of persecuted ethnic groups, for example. In this paper I address those abuses in which gender is a primary or related factor because gender-related abuse has been most neglected and offers the greatest challenge to the field of human rights today.

The concept of human rights is one of the few moral visions ascribed to internationally. Although its scope is not universally agreed upon, it strikes deep chords of response among many. Promotion of human rights is a widely accepted goal and thus provides a useful framework for seeking redress of gender abuse. Further it is one of the few concepts that speaks to the need for transnational activism and concern about the lives of people globally. The Universal Declaration of Human Rights,[1] adopted in 1948, symbolizes this world vision and defines human rights broadly. While not much is said about women, Article 2 entitles all to "the rights and freedoms set forth in this Declaration, without distinction of any kind, such as race, colour, sex, language, religion, political or other opinion, national or social origin, property, birth or other status." Eleanor Roosevelt and the Latin American women who fought for the inclusion of sex in the Declaration and for its passage clearly intended that it would address the problem of women's subordination.[2]

Since 1948 the world community has continuously debated varying interpretations of human rights in response to global developments. Little of this discussion, however, has addressed questions of gender, and only recently have significant challenges been made to a vision of human rights which excludes much of women's experiences. The concept of human rights, like all vibrant visions, is not static or the property of any one group; rather, its meaning expands as people reconceive of their needs and hopes in relation to it. In this spirit, feminists redefine human rights abuses to include the degradation and violation of women. The specific experiences of women must be added to traditional approaches to human rights in order to make women more visible and to transform the concept and practice of human rights in our culture so that it takes better account of women's lives.

In the next part of this article, I will explore both the importance and the difficulty of connecting women's rights to human rights, and then I will outline four basic approaches that have been used in the effort to make this connection.

BEYOND RHETORIC: POLITICAL IMPLICATIONS

Few governments exhibit more than token commitment to women's equality as a basic human right in domestic or foreign policy. No government determines its policies toward other countries on the basis of their treatment of women, even when some aid and trade decisions are said to be based on a country's human rights record. Among nongovernmental organizations, women are rarely a priority, and Human Rights Day programs on 10 December seldom include discussion of issues like violence against women or reproductive rights. When it is suggested that governments and human rights organizations should respond to women's rights as concerns that deserve such attention, a number of excuses are offered for why this cannot be done. The responses tend to follow one or more of these lines: (1) sex discrimination is too trivial, or not as important, or will come after larger issues of survival that require more serious attention; (2) abuse of women, while regrettable, is a cultural, private, or individual issue and not a political matter requiring state action; (3) while appropriate for other action, women's rights are not human rights per se; or (4) when the abuse of women is recognized, it is considered inevitable or so pervasive that any consideration of it is futile or will overwhelm other human rights questions. It is important to challenge these responses.

The narrow definition of human rights, recognized by many in the West as solely a matter of state violation of civil and political liberties, impedes consideration of women's rights. In the United States the concept has been further limited by some who have used it as a weapon in the cold war almost exclusively to challenge human rights abuses perpetrated in communist countries. Even then, many abuses that affected women, such as forced pregnancy in Romania, were ignored.

Some important aspects of women's rights do fit into a civil liberties framework, but much of the abuse against women is part of a larger socioeconomic web that entraps women, making them vulnerable to abuses which cannot be delineated as exclusively political or solely caused by states. The inclusion of "second generation" or socioeconomic human rights to food, shelter, and work—which are clearly delineated as part of the Universal Declaration of Human Rights—is vital to addressing women's concerns fully. Further, the assumption that states are not responsible for most violations of women's rights ignores the fact that such abuses, although committed perhaps by private citizens, are often condoned or even sanctioned by states. I will return to the question of state responsibility after responding to other instances of resistance to women's rights as human rights.

The most insidious myth about women's rights is that they are trivial or secondary to the concerns of life and death. Nothing could be farther from the truth: sexism kills. There is increasing documentation of the many ways in which being female is life-threatening. The following are a few examples:

- Before birth: Amniocentesis is used for sex selection leading to the abortion of more female fetuses at rates as high as 99 percent in Bombay, India; in China and India, the two most populous nations, more males than females are born even though natural birth ratios would produce more females.[3]
- During childhood: The World Health Organization reports that in many countries, girls are fed less, breast fed for shorter periods of time, taken to doctors less frequently, and die or are physically and mentally maimed by malnutrition at higher rates than boys.[4]
- In adulthood: the denial of women's rights to control their bodies in reproduction threatens women's lives, especially where this is combined with poverty and poor health services. In Latin America, complications from illegal abortions are the leading cause of death for women between the ages of fifteen and thirty-nine.[5]

Sex discrimination kills women daily. When combined with race, class, and other forms of oppression, it constitutes a deadly denial of women's right to life and liberty on a large scale throughout the world. The most pervasive violation of females is violence against women in all its manifestations, from wife battery, incest, and rape, to dowry deaths,[6] genital mutilation,[7] and female sexual slavery. These abuses occur in every country and are found in the home and in the workplace, on streets, on campuses, and in prisons and refugee camps. They cross class, race, age, and national lines; and at the same time, the forms this violence takes often reinforce other oppressions such as racism, "able-bodyism," and imperialism. Case in point: in order to feed their families, poor women in brothels around U.S. military bases in places like the Philippines bear the burden of sexual, racial, and national imperialism in repeated and often brutal violation of their bodies.

Even a short review of random statistics reveals that the extent of violence against women globally is staggering:

- In the United States, battery is the leading cause of injury to adult women, and a rape is committed every six minutes.[8]
- In Peru, 70 percent of all crimes reported to police involve women who are beaten by their partners; and in Lima (a city of seven million people), 168,970 rapes were reported in 1987 alone.[9]
- In India, eight out of ten wives are victims of violence, either domestic battery, dowry-related abuse, or among the least fortunate, murder.[10]
- In France, 95 percent of the victims of violence are women; 51 percent at the hands of a spouse or lover. Similar statistics from places as diverse as Bangladesh, Canada, Kenya, and Thailand demonstrate that more than 50 percent of female homicides were committed by family members.[11]

Where recorded, domestic battery figures range from 40 percent to 80 percent of women beaten, usually repeatedly, indicating that the home is the most dangerous place for women and frequently the site of cruelty and torture. As the Carol Stuart murder in Boston demonstrated, sexist and racist attitudes in the United States often cover up the real threat to women; a woman is murdered in Massachusetts by a husband or lover every 22 days.[12]

Such numbers do not reflect the full extent of the problem of violence against women, much of which remains hidden. Yet rather than receiving recognition as a major world conflict, this violence is accepted as normal or even dismissed as an individual or cultural matter. Georgina Ashworth notes that:

> The greatest restriction of liberty, dignity and movement and at the same time, direct violation of the person is the threat and realization of violence. . . . However violence against the female sex, on a scale which far exceeds the list of Amnesty International victims, is tolerated publicly; indeed some acts of violation are not crimes in law, others are legitimized in custom or court opinion, and most are blamed on the victims themselves.[13]

Violence against women is a touchstone that illustrates the limited concept of human rights and highlights the political nature of the abuse of women. As Lori Heise states: "This is not random violence. . . . [T]he risk factor is being female."[14] Victims are chosen because of their gender. The message is domination: stay in your place or be afraid. Contrary to the argument that such violence is only personal or cultural, it is profoundly political. It results from the structural relationships of power, domination, and privilege between men and women in society. Violence against women is central to maintaining those political relations at home, at work, and in all public spheres.

Failure to see the oppression of women as political also results in the exclusion of sex discrimination and violence against women from the human rights agenda. Female subordination runs so deep that it is still viewed as inevitable or natural, rather than seen as a politically constructed reality maintained by patriarchal interests, ideology, and institutions. But I do not believe that male violation of women is inevitable or natural. Such a belief requires a narrow and pessimistic view of men. If violence and domination are understood as a politically constructed reality, it is possible to imagine deconstructing that system and building more just interactions between the sexes.

The physical territory of this political struggle over what constitutes women's human rights is women's bodies. The importance of control over women can be seen in the intensity of resistance to laws and social changes that put control of women's bodies in women's hands: reproductive rights, freedom of sexuality whether heterosexual or lesbian, laws that criminalize rape in marriage, etc. Denial of reproductive rights and homophobia are also political means of maintaining control over women and perpetuating sex roles and thus have human rights implications. The physical abuse of women is a reminder of this territorial domination and is sometimes accompanied by other forms of human rights abuse such as slavery (forced prostitution), sexual terrorism (rape), imprisonment (confinement to the home), and torture (systematic battery). Some cases are extreme, such as the women in Thailand who died in a brothel fire because they were chained to their beds. Most situations are more ordinary like denying women decent educations or jobs which leaves them prey to abusive marriages, exploitative work, and prostitution.

This raises once again the question of the state's responsibility for protecting women's human rights. Feminists have shown how the distinction between private and public abuse is a dichotomy often used to justify female subordination in the home. Governments regulate many matters in the family and individual spheres. For example, human rights activists pressure states to prevent slavery or racial discrimination and segregation even when these are conducted by nongovernmental forces in private or proclaimed as cultural traditions as they have been in both the southern United States and in South Africa. The real questions are: (1) who decides what are legitimate human rights; and (2) when should the state become involved and for what purposes. Riane Eisler argues that:

> the issue is what types of private acts are and are not protected by the right to privacy and/or the principle of family autonomy. Even more specifically, the issue is whether violations of human rights within the family such as genital mutilation, wife beating, and other forms of violence designed to maintain patriarchal control should be within the purview of human rights theory and action. . . . [T]he underlying problem for human rights theory, as for most other fields of theory, is that the yardstick that has been developed for defining and measuring human rights has been based on the male as the norm.[15]

The human rights community must move beyond its male defined norms in order to respond to the brutal and systematic violation of women globally. This does not mean that every human rights group must alter the focus of its work. However it does require examining patriarchal biases and acknowledging the rights of women as human rights. Governments must seek to end the politically and culturally constructed war on women rather than continue to perpetuate it. Every state has the responsibility to intervene in the abuse of women's rights within its borders and to end its collusion with the forces that perpetrate such violations in other countries.

TOWARD ACTION: PRACTICAL APPROACHES

The classification of human rights is more than just a semantics problem because it has practical policy consequences. Human rights are still considered to be more important than women's rights. The distinction perpetuates the idea that the rights of women are of a lesser order than the "rights of man," and, as Eisler describes it, "serves to justify practices that do not accord women full and equal status."[16] In the United Nations, the Human Rights Commission has more power to hear and investigate cases than the Commission on the Status of Women, more staff and budget, and better mechanisms for implementing its findings. Thus it makes a difference in what can be done if a case is deemed a violation of women's rights and not of human rights.[17]

The determination of refugee status illustrates how the definition of human rights affects people's lives. The Dutch Refugee Association, in its pioneering efforts to convince other nations to recognize sexual persecution and violence against women as justifications for granting refugee status, found that some European governments would take sexual persecution into account as an aspect of other forms of political repression, but none would make it the grounds for refugee status per se.[18] The implications of such a distinction are clear when examining a situation like that of the Bangladeshi women, who having been raped during the Pakistan–Bangladesh war, subsequently faced death at the hands of male relatives to preserve "family honor." Western powers professed outrage but did not offer asylum to these victims of human rights abuse.

I have observed four basic approaches to linking women's rights to human rights. These approaches are presented separately here in order to identify each more clearly. In practice, these approaches often overlap, and while each raises questions about the others, I see them as complementary. These approaches can be applied to many issues, but I will illustrate them primarily in terms of how they address violence against women in order to show the implications of their differences on a concrete issue.

1. Women's Rights as Political and Civil Rights. Taking women's specific needs into consideration as part of the already recognized "first generation" political and civil liberties is the first approach. This involves both raising the visibility of women who suffer general human rights violations as well as calling attention to particular abuses women encounter because they are female. Thus, issues of violence against women are raised when they connect to other forms of violation such as the sexual torture of women political prisoners in South America.[19] Groups like the Women's Task Force of Amnesty International have taken this approach in pushing for Amnesty to launch a campaign on behalf of women political prisoners which would address the sexual abuse and rape of women in custody, their lack of maternal care in detention, and the resulting human rights abuse of their children.

Documenting the problems of women refugees and developing responsive policies are other illustrations of this approach. Women and children make up more than 80 percent of those in refugee camps, yet few refugee policies are specifically shaped to meet the needs of these vulnerable populations who face considerable sexual abuse. For example, in one camp where men were allocated the community's rations, some gave food to women and their children in exchange for sex. Revealing this abuse led to new policies that allocated food directly to the women.[20]

The political and civil rights approach is a useful starting point for many human rights groups; by considering women's experiences, these groups can expand their efforts in areas where they are already working. This approach also raises contradictions that reveal the limits of a narrow civil liberties view. One contradiction is to define rape as a human rights abuse only when it occurs in state custody but not on the streets or in the home. Another is to say that a violation of the right to free speech occurs when someone is jailed for defending gay rights, but not when someone is jailed or even tortured and killed for homosexuality. Thus while this approach of adding women and stirring them into existing first generation human rights categories is useful, it is not enough by itself.

2. Women's Rights as Socioeconomic Rights. The second approach includes the particular plight of women with regard to "second generation" human rights such as the rights to food, shelter, health care, and employment. This is an approach favored by those who see the dominant Western human rights tradition and international law as too individualistic and identify women's oppression as primarily economic.

This tendency has its origins among socialists and labor activists who have long argued that political human rights are meaningless to many without economic rights as well. It focuses on the primacy of the need to end women's economic subordination as the key to other issues including women's vulnerability to violence. This particular focus has led to work on issues like women's right to organize as workers and opposition to violence in the workplace, especially in situations like the free trade zones which have targeted women as cheap, nonorganized labor. Another focus of this approach has been highlighting the feminization of poverty or what might better be called the increasing impoverishment of females. Poverty has not become strictly female, but females now comprise a higher percentage of the poor.

Looking at women's rights in the context of socioeconomic development is another example of this approach. Third world peoples have called for an understanding of socioeconomic development as a human rights issue. Within this demand, some have sought to integrate women's rights into development and have examined women's specific needs in relation to areas like land ownership or access to credit. Among those working on women in development, there is growing interest in violence against women as both a health and development issue. If violence is seen as having negative consequences for social productivity, it may get more attention. This type of narrow economic measure, however, should not determine whether such violence is seen as a human rights concern. Violence as a development issue is linked to the need to understand development not just as an economic issue but also as a question of empowerment and human growth.

One of the limitations of this second approach has been its tendency to reduce women's needs to the economic sphere which implies that women's rights will follow automatically with third world development, which may involve socialism. This has not proven to be the case. Many working from this approach are no longer trying to add women into either the Western capitalist or socialist development models, but rather seek a transformative development process that links women's political, economic, and cultural empowerment.

3. Women's Rights and the Law. The creation of new legal mechanisms to counter sex discrimination characterizes the third approach to women's rights as human rights. These efforts seek to make existing legal and political institutions work for women and to expand the state's responsibility for the violation of women's human rights. National and local laws which address sex discrimination and violence against women are examples of this approach. These measures allow women to fight for their rights within the legal system. The primary international illustration is the Convention on the Elimination of All Forms of Discrimination Against Women.[21]

The Convention has been described as "essentially an international bill of rights for women and a framework for women's participation in the development process . . . [which] spells out internationally accepted principles and standards for achieving equality between women and men."[22] Adopted by the UN General Assembly in 1979, the Convention has been ratified or acceded to by 104 countries as of January 1990. In theory these countries are obligated to pursue policies in accordance with it and to report on their compliance to the Committee on the Elimination of Discrimination Against Women (CEDAW).

While the Convention addresses many issues of sex discrimination, one of its shortcomings is failure to directly address the question of violence against women. CEDAW passed a resolution at its eighth session in Vienna in 1989 expressing concern that this issue be on its agenda and instructing states to include in their periodic reports information about statistics, legislation, and support services in this area.[23] The Commonwealth Secretariat in its manual on the reporting process for the Convention also interprets the issue of violence against women as "clearly fundamental to the spirit of the Convention," especially in Article 5 which calls for the modification of social and cultural patterns, sex roles, and stereotyping that are based on the idea of the inferiority or the superiority of either sex.[24]

The Convention outlines a clear human rights agenda for women which, if accepted by governments, would mark an enormous step forward. It also carries the limitations of all such international documents in that there is little power to demand its implementation. Within the United Nations, it is not generally regarded as a convention with teeth, as illustrated by the difficulty that CEDAW has had in getting countries to report on compliance with its provisions. Further, it is still treated by governments and most nongovernmental organizations as a document dealing with women's (read "secondary") rights, not human rights. Nevertheless, it is a useful statement of principles endorsed by the United Nations around which women can organize to achieve legal and political change in their regions.

4. Feminist Transformation of Human Rights. Transforming the human rights concept from a feminist perspective, so that it will take greater account of women's lives, is the fourth approach. This approach relates women's rights and human rights, looking first at the violations of women's lives and then asking how the human rights concept can change to be more responsive to women. For example, the GABRIELA women's coalition in the Philippines simply stated that "Women's Rights are Human Rights" in launching a campaign last year. As Ninotchka Rosca explained, coalition members saw that "human rights are not reducible to a question of legal and due process. . . . In the case of women, human rights are affected by the entire society's traditional perception of what is proper or not proper for women."[25] Similarly, a panel at the 1990 International Women's Rights Action Watch conference asserted that "Violence Against Women is a Human Rights Issue." While work in the three previous approaches is often done from a feminist perspective, this last view is the most distinctly feminist with its woman-centered stance and its refusal to wait for permission from some authority to determine what is or is not a human rights issue.

This transformative approach can be taken toward any issue, but those working from this approach have tended to focus most on abuses that arise specifically out of gender, such as reproductive rights, female sexual slavery, violence against women, and "family crimes" like forced marriage, compulsory heterosexuality, and female mutilation. These are also the issues most often dismissed as not really human rights questions. This is therefore the most hotly contested area and requires that barriers be broken down between public and private, state and nongovernmental responsibilities.

Those working to transform the human rights vision from this perspective can draw on the work of others who have expanded the understanding of human rights previously. For example, two decades ago there was no concept of "disappearances" as a human rights abuse. However, the women of the Plaza de Mayo in Argentina did not wait for an official declaration but stood up to demand state accountability for these crimes. In so doing, they helped to create a context for expanding the concept of responsibility for deaths at the hands of paramilitary or right-wing death squads which, even if not carried out by the state, were allowed by it to happen. Another example is the developing concept that civil rights violations include "hate crimes," violence that is racially motivated or directed against homosexuals, Jews or other minority groups. Many accept that states have an obligation to work to prevent such rights abuses, and getting violence against women seen as a hate crime is being pursued by some.

The practical applications of transforming the human rights concept from feminist perspectives need to be explored further. The danger in pursuing only this approach is the tendency to become isolated from and competitive with other human rights groups because they have been so reluctant to address gender violence and discrimination. Yet most women experience abuse on the grounds of sex, race, class, nation, age, sexual preference, and politics as interrelated, and little benefit comes from separating them as competing claims. The human rights community need not abandon other issues but should incorporate gender perspectives into them and see how these expand the terms of their work. By recognizing issues like violence against women as human rights concerns, human rights scholars and activists do not have to take these up as their primary tasks. However, they do have to stop gatekeeping and guarding their prerogative to determine what is considered a "legitimate" human rights issue.

As mentioned before, these four approaches are overlapping and many strategies for change involve elements of more than one. All of these approaches contain aspects of what is necessary to achieve women's rights. At a time when dualist ways of thinking and views of competing economic systems are in question, the creative task is to look for ways to connect these approaches and to see how we can go beyond exclusive views of what people need in their lives. In the words of an early feminist group, we need bread and roses, too. Women want food and liberty and the possibility of living lives of dignity free from domination and violence. In this struggle, the recognition of women's rights as human rights can play an important role.

NOTES

1. Universal Declaration of Human Rights, *adopted* 10 December 1948, G.A. Res. 217A(III), U.N. Doc. A/810 (1948).
2. Blanche Wiesen Cook, "Eleanor Roosevelt and Human Rights: The Battle for Peace and Planetary Decency," Edward P. Crapol, ed. *Women and American Foreign Policy: Lobbyists, Critics, and Insiders* (New York: Greenwood Press, 1987), 98–118; Georgina Ashworth, "Of Violence and Violation: Women and Human Rights," *Change Thinkbook II* (London, 1986).
3. Vibhuti Patel, *In Search of Our Bodies: A Feminist Look at Women, Health, and Reproduction in India* (Shakti, Bombay, 1987); Lori Heise, "International Dimensions of Violence Against Women," *Response,* vol. 12, no. 1 (1989): 3.
4. Sundari Ravindran, *Health Implications of Sex Discrimination in Childhood* (Geneva: World Health Organization, 1986). These problems and proposed social programs to counter them in India are discussed in detail in "Gender Violence: Gender Discrimination Between Boy and Girl in Parental Family," paper published by CHETNA (Child Health Education Training and Nutrition Awareness), Ahmedabad, 1989.
5. Debbie Taylor, ed., *Women: A World Report, A New Internationalist Book* (Oxford: Oxford University Press, 1985), 10. See Joni Seager and Ann Olson, eds., *Women In The World: An International Atlas* (London: Pluto Press, 1986) for more statistics on the effects of sex discrimination.

6. Frequently a husband will disguise the death of a bride as suicide or an accident in order to collect the marriage settlement paid him by the bride's parents. Although dowry is now illegal in many countries, official records for 1987 showed 1,786 dowry deaths in India alone. See Heise, note 3 above, 5.
7. For an in-depth examination of the practice of female circumcision see Alison T. Slack, "Female Circumcision: A Critical Appraisal," *Human Rights Quarterly* 10 (1988): 439.
8. C. Everett Koop, M.D., "Violence Against Women: A Global Problem," presentation by the Surgeon General of the U.S., Public Health Service, Washington D.C., 1989.
9. Ana Maria Portugal, "Cronica de Una Violacion Provocada?", *Fempress* especial "Contraviolencia," Santiago, 1988; Seager and Olson, note 5 above, 37.
10. Ashworth, note 2 above, 9.
11. "Violence Against Women in the Family," Centre for Social Development and Humanitarian Affairs, United Nations Office at Vienna, 1989.
12. Bella English, "Stereotypes Led Us Astray," *The Boston Globe,* 5 Jan. 1990, 17, col. 3. See also the statistics in Women's International Network News, 1989; United Nations Office, note 11 above; Ashworth, note 2 above; Heise, note 3 above; and *Fempress*, note 9 above.
13. Ashworth, note 2 above, 8.
14. Heise, note 3 above, 3.
15. Riane Eisler. "Human Rights: Toward an Integrated Theory for Action," *Human Rights Quartely* 9 (1987):297. See alo Alida Brill, *Nobody's Business: The Paradoxes of Privacy* (New York: Addison-Wesley, 1990).
16. Eisler, note 15 above, 291.
17. Sandra Coliver, "United Nations Machineries on Women's Rights: How Might They Better Help Women Whose Rights Are Being Violated?" in Ellen L. Lutz, Hurst Hannum, and Kathryn J. Burke, eds., *New Directions in Human Rights* (Philadelphia: Univ. of Penn. Press, 1989).
18. Marijke Meyer, "Oppression of Women and Refugee Status," unpublished report to NGO Forum, Nairobi, Kenya, 1985 and "Sexual Violence Against Women Refugees" Ministry of Social Affairs and Labour, The Netherlands, June 1984.
19. Ximena Bunster describes this in Chile and Argentina in "The Torture of Women Political Prisoners: A Case Study in Female Sexual Slavery," in Kathleen Barry, Charlotte Bunch, and Shirley Castley, eds., *International Feminism: Networking Against Female Sexual Slavery* (New York: IWTC, 1984).
20. Report given by Margaret Groarke at Women's Panel, Amnesty International New York Regional Meeting, 24 Feb. 1990.
21. Convention on the Elimination of All Forms of Discrimination Against Women, G.A. Res. 34/180, (1980).
22. International Women's Rights Action Watch, "The Convention on the Elimination of All Forms of Discrimination Against Women" (Minneapolis: Humphrey Institute of Public Affairs, 1988), 1.
23. CEDAW Newsletter, 3rd Issue (13 Apr. 1989), 2 (summary of U.N. Report on the Eighth Session, U.N.Doc. A/44/38, 14 April 1989).
24. Commonwealth Secretariat, "The Convention on the Elimination of All Forms of Discrimination Against Women: The Reporting Process—A Manual for Commonwealth Jurisdictions," London, 1989.
25. Speech given by Ninotchka Rosca at Amnesty International New York Regional Conference, 24 Feb. 1990, 2.

Islam, Islamic Law and the Dilemma of Cultural Legitimacy for Universal Human Rights[1]

Abdullahi Ahmed An-Na'im

Abdullahi Ahmed An-Na'im is currently professor of law at the University of Khartoum. He is the author of Toward an Islamic Reformation: Civil Liberties, Human Rights and International Law *(1990). He has edited* Human Rights in Africa: Cross Cultural Perspectives *(1990), and* Human Rights in Cross Cultural Perspectives *(1992).*

Islamic societies, like African ones, generally do not place a high value on the protection of human rights. An-Na'im argues that human rights need to be perceived as culturally legitimate in order for them to be given more than lip service. Since countries are largely left unsupervised in terms of the protection of the human rights of their own citizens, the leaders must be persuaded that the human rights of all their citizens are deserving of equal respect. But in Islamic cultures a deep division exists between those who are Muslim and those who are not, as well as between men and women. As long as these divisions exist, appeals to universal human rights will continue to clash with deeply held cultural and religious views.

Although Islam is often discussed in the contexts of North Africa and the Middle East, in fact the majority of Muslims live outside this region. The clear majority of the Muslims of the world live in the Indian sub-continent.[2] The Muslim population of Indonesia alone is equal to the combined Muslim population of Egypt and Iran, the largest countries of the so-called Muslim heartland of North Africa and the Middle East. In terms of percentage to the total population, Muslims constitute 97% of the total population of Pakistan, 82.9% of that of Bangladesh and 80% of that of Indonesia. While Muslims constitute slightly less than half the population of Malaysia, Islam is perceived as an important element of Malay ethnicity which receives special protection under the constitution.[3] As we shall see, Pakistan has been struggling with the meaning and implications of its purported Islamic identity since independence. Bangladesh also appears to be heading in the same direction. It is therefore important to consider the Islamic dimension of human rights policy and practice in South and Southeast Asia.

It is important to note that Islamic norms may be more influential at an informal, almost subconscious psychological level than they are at the official legal or policy level. One should not therefore underestimate the Islamic factor simply because the particular

Reprinted from *Asian Perspectives on Human Rights,* Claude E. Welch and Virginia Leary (editors), 1990, by permission of Westview Press, Boulder, Colorado. [Edited]

state is not constituted as an Islamic state, or because its legal system does not purport to comply with historical Islamic law, commonly known as Shari'a.[4] Conversely, one should not overestimate the Islamic factor simply because the state and the legal system are publicly identified as such. This is particularly important from a human rights point of view where underlying social and political attitudes and values may defeat or frustrate the declared policy and formal legal principles.

This chapter is concerned with both the sociological as well as the legal and official impact of Islam on human rights. The chapter begins by explaining the paradox of declared commitment to human rights, on the one hand, and the low level of compliance with these standards in daily practice, on the other. It is my submission that this paradox can be understood in light of the competing claims of the universalism and relativism of human rights standards. It is my thesis that certain standards of human rights are frequently violated because they are not perceived to be culturally legitimate in the context of the particular country. To the extent that political regimes and other dominant social forces can explicitly or implicitly challenge the validity of certain human rights norms as alien or at least not specifically sanctioned by the primary values of the dominant indigenous culture, they can avoid the negative consequences of their violation.

Such analysis would seem to suggest the need for establishing cultural legitimacy for human rights standards in the context of the particular society. However, this enterprise raises another problem. If indigenous cultural values are to be asserted as a basis of human rights standards, we are likely to encounter "undesirable" aspects of the indigenous culture. In other words, while it may be useful to establish cultural legitimacy for human rights standards, certain elements of the indigenous culture may be antithetical to the human rights of some segments of the population. This chapter will illustrate the dilemma of cultural legitimacy for human rights in the Islamic tradition.

THE HUMAN RIGHTS PARADOX

1988 marked the fortieth anniversary of the Universal Declaration of Human Rights, which was adopted by the General Assembly of the United Nations on the 10th of December 1948.[5] Several U.N. and regional human rights conventions have since been ratified as binding international treaties by scores of countries from all parts of the world.[6] At the domestic level, many human rights receive strong endorsement in the constitutional and legal system of most countries of the world. Moreover, human rights issues are continuously covered by the news media as a supposedly important consideration in national and international politics.

Despite these formal commitments to human rights, and apparently strong concern with their violation, there is a mounting crisis in practical compliance with human rights standards throughout the world. Gross and consistent violations of human rights in many countries are recorded daily. Activist groups and non-governmental organizations continue to charge almost every government in the world of involvement or complicity in violating one or more human rights in its national and/or international policies.[7]

This glaring disparity between apparent commitment in theory and poor compliance in practice is what may be called the paradox of human rights. On the one hand, the idea of human rights is so powerful that no government in the world today can afford to reject it openly.[8] On the other hand, the most basic and fundamental human rights are being consistently violated in all parts of the world. It is therefore necessary to understand and resolve this paradox if human rights are to be respected and implemented in practice. As correctly stated by Jenks: "The potentially tragic implication of this paradox is the ever-present danger that the denial of human rights may, as in the past, express, permit and promote a worship of the State no less fatal to peace than to freedom; by failure to make a reality of the Universal Declaration of Human Rights and United Nations Covenants of Human Rights we may leave mankind at the mercy of new absolutism which will engulf the world."[9]

One obvious explanation of the dichotomy between the theory and practice of human rights is the cynical manipulation of a noble and enlightened concept by many governments and politicians in all countries of the world. It may therefore be said that this is merely the current manifestation of an ancient phenomenon in human affairs. However, without disputing the historical validity of this analysis, one can point to the other side of the coin as the concrete manifestation of another ancient phenomenon in human affairs, namely the capacity of people to assert and realize their rights and claims in the face of adversity and cynicism. From this perspective, what is therefore significant is not the cynical abuse of the human rights idea, but the fact that oppressive governments and ambitious politicians find expressing their support of human rights useful, if not necessary, for gaining popular support at home and legitimacy abroad. This tribute paid by vice to virtue is very significant and relevant to future efforts at bridging the gap between the theory and practice of human rights.

In order to hold governments to their declared commitment to human rights, it is essential to establish the principle that human rights violations are not matters within the exclusive domestic jurisdiction of any state in the world.[10] Under traditional international law, national sovereignty was taken to include the right of each state to treat its own subjects in whatever manner it deemed fit. Consequently, it was perceived to be un-warranted interference in the internal affairs of a sovereign state for other states to object to or protest any action or policy of that state towards its own subjects. The Charter of the United Nations (UN) apparently endorsed these notions. Article 2.7 expressly stated that the Charter does not "authorize the United Nations to intervene in matters which are essentially within the domestic jurisdiction of any state or shall require the Members to submit such matters to settlement under the present Charter." Other authoritative statements of international law continue to emphasize the traditional definition of national sovereignty. For example, these notions feature prominently in the 1970 UN Declaration on Principles of International Law Concerning Friendly Relations and Co-operation among States in Accordance with the Charter of the United Nations.[11]

However, Article 2.7 of the UN Charter stipulates that the principle of non-interference in matters essentially within the domestic jurisdiction of any state shall not apply to UN action with respect to threats to the peace, breaches of the peace and acts of aggression. It could be argued that serious and consistent violations of at least some fundamental human rights constitute a threat to international peace and security, and are therefore within this exception to the "essentially domestic jurisdiction" clause of the UN Charter. In other words, since serious and consistent violations of certain human rights constitute a threat to international peace and security, the UN can act against the offending state because the matter is beyond the "essentially domestic jurisdiction" of the state. It may also be possible to construe some of the language of the above cited

1970 UN Declaration on Friendly Relations as permitting international action in promoting and protecting at least some fundamental human rights.

Despite its problems, national sovereignty appears to be necessary for the exercise of the right of peoples to self-determination. In any case, it is too strongly entrenched to hope for its total repudiation in the foreseeable future. Nevertheless, it is imperative to overcome national sovereignty objections to international action for the protection and promotion of human rights without violating the legitimate scope of such sovereignty. "The renunciation of intervention [in the internal affairs of states] does not constitute a policy of nonintervention; it involves the development of some form of *collective intervention*."[12]

In order to support this position, it is necessary to repudiate any plausible argument which claims that action in support of human rights violates the national sovereignty of the country. It has been argued, for example, that the established international standards are not consistent with the cultural traditions or philosophical and ideological perspectives of the given country.[13] It is not enough to say that this argument may be used as a pretext for violating human rights because such manipulation would not be viable if there is no validity to the argument itself. In other words, this argument is useful as a pretext precisely because it has some validity which makes the excuse plausible. It is therefore incumbent upon human rights advocates to address the element of truth in this argument in order to prevent its cynical abuse in the future.

THE LEGITIMACY DILEMMA

If we take the UN Charter and the Universal Declaration of Human Rights as the starting point of the modern movement for the promotion and protection of human rights, we will find it true that the majority of the peoples of Africa and Asia had little opportunity for direct contribution to the formulation of these basic documents. Since the majority of the peoples of these two continents were still suffering from the denial of their collective human right to self-determination because of colonial rule and foreign domination at the time, they were unable to participate in the drafting and adoption processes.[14] It is true that some of the representatives of the older, mainly Western, nations were sensitive to the cultural traditions of the unrepresented peoples,[15] but that could have hardly been a sufficient substitute for direct representation.

Many more African and Asian countries subsequently achieved formal independence and were able to participate in the formulation of international human rights instruments. By ratifying the UN Charter and subscribing to the specialized international instruments which incorporated and elaborated upon the Universal Declaration of Human Rights, the emerging countries of Africa and Asia were deemed bound by those earlier documents in addition to the subsequent instruments in which they participated from the start. Thus, the vast majority of the countries of Africa and Asia can be seen as parties to the process by which international human rights standards are determined and formulated. Nevertheless, this official and formal participation does not seem to have achieved the desired result of legitimizing international human rights standards in the cultural traditions of these peoples. This failure is clearly illustrated, in my view, by the lack of sufficient popular awareness of and support for these standards among the majority of the population of the countries of Africa and Asia. Given this lack of awareness and support for the international standards, it is not surprising that governments and other actors are able to evade the negative consequences of their massive and gross violations of human rights throughout Africa and Asia.

It is my submission that formal participation in the formulation and implementation processes by the elites of African and Asian countries will never achieve practical respect and protection for human rights in those regions unless that participation reflects the genuine consensus of the population of those countries. I would further suggest that the peoples of these regions have not had the chance to develop such consensus by re-examining their own cultural traditions in terms of universal and international human rights. It seems that the elites of these countries have come to the international fora where human rights standards were determined and formulated without a clear mandate from their own peoples.

As an advocate of international human rights, I am not suggesting that the international community should scrap the present documents and start afresh. This would be an impracticable and dangerous course of action because we may never recover what would be lost through the repudiation of the present instruments and structures. What I am suggesting is that we should supplement the existing standards and continue to develop them through the genuine participation of the widest possible range of cultural traditions. In furtherance of this approach, it is incumbent on the advocates of human rights to work for legitimizing universal standards of human rights within their own traditions.

However, this approach presents us with the other horn of the dilemma. Almost every existing cultural tradition (including philosophical or ideological positions) in the world has some problems with respect to the full range of fundamental human rights. Generally speaking, for example, whereas the liberal tradition(s) of the West have difficulties in accepting economic, social and cultural rights and in conceiving of collective rights such as a right to development, the Marxist tradition has similar difficulties with respect to civil and political rights.[16] More specifically, prevailing notions of freedom of speech under the Constitution of the United States, for instance, may protect forms of speech and expression which advocate racial hatred in violation of the international standards set by the Covenant for the Elimination of All Forms of Racial Discrimination of 1965.

The main difficulty in working to establish universal standards across cultural boundaries is the fact that each tradition has its own internal frame of reference and derives the validity of its precepts and norms from its own sources. When a cultural tradition relates to other traditions and perspectives, it is likely to do so in a negative and perhaps even hostile and antagonistic way. In order to claim the loyalty and conformity of its own members, a tradition would normally assert its own superiority over, and tend to de-humanize the adherents of, other traditions. This tendency would clearly undermine efforts to accord members of other traditions equality in status and rights, even if they happen to live within the political boundaries of the same country.[17]

Nevertheless, I believe that all the major cultural traditions adhere to the common normative principle that one should treat other people as he or she wishes to be treated by them. This golden rule, which may be called the principle of reciprocity, is shared by all the major traditions of the world. Moreover, the moral and logical force of this simple proposition can easily be appreciated by all human beings of whatever cultural tradition or philosophical persuasion. If construed in an enlightened manner so that the "other" includes all other human beings, this principle is capable of sustaining universal standards of human rights.

In accordance with this fundamental principle of reciprocity, I would take universal human rights to be those rights which I claim for myself, and must therefore concede to others. The practical implications of this fundamental principle would have to be negotiated through the political process to develop consensus around specific policies and concrete action on what the majority or other dominant segment of the population would accept for itself and would therefore have to concede to minorities and individuals. Although theoretical safeguards and structures may be devised to ensure the constitutional and human rights of all individuals and groups, the ultimate safeguard is the goodwill and sense of enlightened political expediency of the majority or other dominant segment of the population. Unless the majority or dominant segment of the population is persuaded to respect and promote the human rights of minorities and individuals, the whole society will drift into the politics of confrontation and subjugation rather than that of reconciliation and justice.

THE LEGITIMACY DILEMMA IN THE MUSLIM CONTEXT

When I consider Shari'a as the historical formulation of my own Islamic tradition I am immediately confronted with certain inadequacies in its conception of human rights as judged by the above stated principle of reciprocity and its supporting arguments. In particular, I am confronted by Shari'a's discrimination against Muslim women and non-Muslims and its restrictions on freedom of religion and belief. Unfortunately, most contemporary Muslim writings on the subject tend to provide a misleadingly glowing view of Shari'a on human rights without any reference to the above cited problematic aspects of Shari'a.[18] Moreover, some of those Muslim authors who are willing to candidly state the various features of conflict and tension between Shari'a and current standards of human rights tend to take an intransigent position in favor of Shari'a without considering the prospects of its reconciliation with current standards of human rights.[19]

It is true that Shari'a had introduced significant improvements in the status and rights of women as compared to its historical contemporaries of between the seventh and nineteenth centuries A.D.[20] Under Shari'a, Muslim women enjoy full and independent legal personality to own and dispose of property and conclude other contracts in their own right. They are also guaranteed specific shares in inheritance, and other rights in family law. However, Shari'a did not achieve complete legal equality between Muslim men and women. Whereas a man is entitled to marry up to four wives and divorce any of them at will, a woman is restricted to one husband and can only seek judicial divorce on very limited and strict grounds. Women receive only half a share of a man in inheritance, and less monetary compensation for criminal bodily harm (*diya*). Women are generally incompetent to testify in serious criminal cases. Where their testimony is accepted in civil cases, it takes two women to make a single witness.[21] Other examples of inequality can be cited. In fact, the general rule of Shari'a is that men are the guardians of women, and as such have the license to discipline them to extent of beating them "lightly" if they fear them to become unruly.[22] Consequently, Shari'a holds that Muslim women may not hold any office involving exercising authority over Muslim men.

Similarly, Shari'a granted non-Muslim believers, mainly Christians and Jews who submit to Muslim sovereignty, the status of *dhimma*, whereby they are secured in person and property and permitted to practice their religion and regulate their private affairs in accordance with their own law and custom in exchange for payment of a special tax, known as *jiziya*.[23] Those classified by Shari'a as unbelievers are not allowed to live within an Islamic state except with a special permit of safe conduct, known as *aman*, which defines their status and rights.[24] If the residence of a *musta'min*, an unbeliever allowed to stay within an Islamic state under *aman*, extends beyond one year, some Shari'a jurists would allow him to assume the status of *dhimma*. However, neither *dhimma* nor *aman* would qualify a non-Muslim to full citizenship of an Islamic state or guarantee such a person complete equality with Muslim citizens.[25] For example, Shari'a specifically requires that non-Muslims may never exercise authority over Muslims.[26] Consequently, non-Muslims are denied any public office which would involve exercising such authority.

The third example of serious human rights problems with Shari'a indicated above is freedom of religion and belief. It is true that *dhimma* and possibly *aman*, would guarantee a non-Muslim a measure of freedom of religion in that he would be free to practice his officially sanctioned religion. However, such freedom of religious practice is inhibited by the limitations imposed on non-Muslims in public life, including payment of *jiziya*, which is intended by Shari'a to be a humiliating tax.[27]

Another serious limitation of freedom of religion and belief is the Shari'a law of apostasy, *ridda*, whereby a Muslim would be subject to the death penalty if he should repudiate his faith in Islam, whether or not in favor of another religion.[28] Some modern Muslim writers have argued that apostasy should not be punishable by death.[29] However, this progressive view has not yet been accepted by the majority of Muslims. Moreover, even if the death penalty is abolished, other serious consequences will remain, such as the possibility of other punishment, confiscation of the property of the apostate and the nullification of his or her marriage to a Muslim spouse.[30] In contrast, non-Muslims, including Christians and Jews, are encouraged to embrace Islam. Whereas Muslims are supported by the State and community in their efforts to proselytize in order to convert non-Muslims to Islam, non-Muslims are positively prohibited from undertaking such activities.

All of the above features of discrimination against Muslim women and non-Muslims and restrictions on freedom of religion and belief are part of Shari'a to the present day. Those aspects of discrimination against Muslim women which fall within the scope of family law and inheritance are currently enforced throughout the Muslim world because Shari'a constitutes the personal law of Muslims even in those countries where it is not the formal legal system of the land.[31] Discrimination against non-Muslims and the Shari'a law of apostasy are enforced in those countries where Shari'a is the formal legal system. For example, Article 13 of the Constitution of the Islamic Republic of Iran expressly classifies Iranians in terms of their religious or sectarian belief. By the terms of this Article, Baha'is are not a recognized religious minority, and as such are not entitled even to the status of second class citizens under the principle of *dhimma* explained above. Moreover, as recently as January 1985, a 76-year-old man was executed for apostasy in the Sudan.[32]

What is more significant for our present purposes, however, is the fact that all of these and other aspects of Shari'a are extremely influential in shaping Muslim attitudes and policies even where Shari'a is not the formal legal system. In other words, so long as these aspects of Shari'a are held by Muslim legislators, policy makers and executive officials to be part of their cultural tradition, we can only expect serious negative consequences for human rights in predominantly Muslim countries, regardless of whether or not Shari'a is the basis of the formal constitutional and legal system of the land. . . .

NOTES

1. A first draft of this chapter was prepared under a grant from the Woodrow Wilson International Center for Scholars, Washington, D.C. The statements and views expressed herein are those of the author and are not necessarily those of the Wilson Center. I have prepared the final draft of this chapter while holding the position of Ariel F. Sallows Professor of Human Rights at the College of Law, University of Saskatchewan, Canada in 1989–90.
2. For statistics on Muslim peoples and their percentages of the total population of all the countries of the world see, Richard V. Weeks, ed., *Muslim Peoples: A World Ethnographic Survey,* second ed. (Westport CT.: Greenwood Press, 1984), pp. 882–911.
3. F. A. Trindade and H. P. Lee, editors, *The Constitution of Malaysia: Further Perspectives and Developments* (Singapore: Oxford University Press 1986), pp. 5–12. See further the review of this book by Abdullahi A. An-Na'im in *Columbia Journal of Transnational Law* 26 (1988), pp. 1101–1107.
4. It is misleading to think of Shari'a as merely law in the strict modern sense of the term. Shari'a is the Islamic view of the whole duty of humankind, and includes moral and pastoral theology and ethics, high spiritual aspirations and detailed ritualistic and formal observance as well as legal rules in the formal sense. See S. G. Vesey-Fitzgerald, "The Nature and Sources of the Shari'a," in M. Khadduri and H. J. Liebesny, eds., *Law in the Middle East* (Washington: The Middle East Institute, 1955), pp. 85ff.; and Majid Khadduri, "Nature and Sources of Islamic Law," *George Washington Law Review* 22 (1953), pp. 6–10.
5. For the full text of the Universal Declaration of Human Rights see Ian Brownlie, ed., *Basic Documents on Human Rights,* second ed. (Oxford: Clarendon Press, 1981), pp. 21–27.
6. These include the International Convention on the Elimination of All Forms of Racial Discrimination of 1965; the International Covenant on Economic, Social and Cultural Rights and the International Covenant on Civil and Political Rights, both of 1966; and the Convention on the Elimination of All Forms of Discrimination Against Women of 1979. For the texts of these instruments, see *ibid.* pp. 150–63, pp. 118–27 and pp. 94–107, respectively. There are three regional conventions currently in force for Europe, the Americas and Africa. See *ibid.* pp. 242–57 and pp. 391–416 for the European and American Conventions respectively. The African Charter is included as Appendix I in Claude E. Welch, Jr. and Ronald I. Meltzer, eds., *Human Rights and Development in Africa* (Albany: State University of New York Press, 1984), pp. 317–29.
7. See, for example, the Annual Reports of Amnesty International, and the periodic reports of Human Rights Internet and the Minority Rights Group. Of special interest to the subject of this paper, see Lawyers Committee for Human Rights, *Zia's Law: Human Rights under Military Rule in Pakistan* (New York/Washington: The Lawyers Committee for Human Rights (1985). The Lawyers Committee has also published two other reports on human rights in Pakistan: *Violations of Human Rights in Pakistan* June 1981; and *Justice in Pakistan* July 1983.
8. Louis Henkin, Introduction, in Louis Henkin, ed., *The International Bill of Rights: The Covenant on Civil and Political Rights* (New York: Columbia University Press, 1981), p. 1.
9. C. Wilfred Jenks, *The World Beyond the Charter in Historical Perspective* (London: George Allen and Unwin, Ltd., 1969), pp. 130–31.
10. Henkin, *The International Bill of Rights,* pp 3–8. See generally, Richard Falk, *Human Rights and State Sovereignty* (New York: Holmes & Meier, 1982).
11 G.A. Res. 2625 (XXXV 1970). For the full text of this Declaration see Louis Henkin, Richard C. Pugh, Oscar Schachter and Hans Smit, eds., *Basic Documents Supplement to International Law: Cases and Materials,* second ed. (St. Paul, MN.: West Publishing Co., 1987), pp. 75–83.
12. Richard Falk, *Legal Order in a Violent World* (Princeton: Princeton University Press, 1968), p. 339. Emphasis added.
13. This argument was recently advanced by official spokesmen of the Islamic Republic of Iran. See Edward Mortimer, "Islam and Human Rights," *Index on Censorship* (1983), p. 5.
14. Only eleven African and Asian countries were founding Members of the U.N., with seven more joining over the next ten years. Jenks, *The World Beyond the Charter in Historical Perspective,* p. 92.
15. See, for example, "Human Rights, Comments and Interpretations," a symposium edited by UNESCO, London, 1949, reprinted in *Human Rights Teaching,* IV (1985), pp. 4–31.
16. These conceptual difficulties and cultural differences were the underlying cause of the development of two separate covenants, one for civil and political rights and the other for economic, social and cultural rights, rather than a single bill of human rights as originally envisaged. Henkin, *The International Bill of Rights,* pp. 5–6.
17. See, generally, Patrick Thornberry, "Is there a

Phoenix in the Ashes? International Law and Minority Rights," *Texas International Law Journal* 15 (1980), p. 421.

18. See, for example, Ali Abedl Wahid Wafi, "Human Rights in Islam," *Islamic Quarterly* 11 (1967), p. 64; and Isma'il al-Faruqi, "Islam and Human Rights," *Islamic Quarterly* 27 (1983), p. 12. One of the better and more constructive works by contemporary Muslim authors is Riffat Hassan's "On Human Rights and the Qur'anic Perspectives," *Journal of Ecumenical Studies* 19 (1982), p. 51.
19. See, for example, Tabandeh, *A Muslim Commentary on the Universal Declaration of Human Rights* (London: F. T. Goulding and Co., 1970).
20. On the relative improvements in the status of women introduced by Shari'a, see Ameer Ali, *The Spirit of Islam* (London: Christophers, 1922), pp. 222–57; and Fazlur Rahman, "Status of Women in The Qur'an," in G. Nashat, ed., *Women and Revolution in Iran* (Boulder, CO.: Westview Press, 1983), p. 37.
21. For sources and discussion of these aspects of Shari'a, see Abdullahi Ahmed An-Na'im, "The Rights of Women and International Law in the Muslim Context," *Whittier Law Review* (1987), pp. 493–97.
22. Verse 4:34 of the Qur'an. The Qur'an is cited here by number of chapter followed by number of verse in that chapter.
23. Verse 9:29 of the Qur'an. See *The Encyclopedia of Islam, New Edition,* vol. II, p. 227; and Majid Khadduri, *War and Peace in the Law of Islam* (Baltimore: The Johns Hopkins Press, 1955), p. 177 and pp. 195–99.
24. Khadduri, *War and Peace in the Law of Islam,* pp. 163–69; Muhammad Hamidullah, *The Muslim Conduct of State,* 5th edition (Lahore: Sh. M. Ashraf, 1966), pp. 201–02.
25. Majid Khadduri, "Human Rights in Islam," *The Annals of the American Academy of Political and Social Science* 243 (1946), p. 79. Cf. Majid Khadduri, *The Islamic Concept of Justice* (Baltimore and London: The Johns Hopkins University Press, 1984), p. 233.
26. This is held to be so because verses of the Qur'an, such as 3:28, 4:144, 8:72 and 73, etc. prohibit Muslims from taking non-Muslims as *awliya*, guardians and supporters.
27. This connotation is reflected in the language of verse 9:29 of the Qur'an which requires that *dhimmis* pay *jiziya* in humiliation and submission.
28. Khadduri, *War and Peace in the Law of Islam,* p. 150; Rudoph Peters and Gert J. De Vries, "Apostasy in Islam," *Die Welt des Islams* XVII (1976–77), p. 1.
29. See, for example, A. Rahman, *Punishment of Apostasy in Islam* (Lahore: Institute of Islamic Culture, 1972).
30. On these other consequences of apostasy see Abdullahi Ahmed An-Na'im, "The Islamic Law of Apostasy and its Modern Applicability: A Case from the Sudan," *Religion* 16 (1986), p. 212.
31. Coulson, *A History of Islamic Law,* p. 161; Herbert Liebesny, *The Law of the Near and Middle East* (Albany: State of New York Press, 1975), p. 56.
32. For a full explanation and discussion of this case see An-Na'im, "The Islamic Law of Apostasy and its Modern Applicability: A Case from the Sudan."

A Buddhist Response to the Nature of Human Rights

Kenneth K. Inada

Kenneth K. Inada is a professor of philosophy at the State University of New York at Buffalo. He is the author of Nagarjuna *(1970)* and Guide to Buddhist Philosophy *(1985). He edits the* Journal of Buddhist Philosophy.

Inada contends that a Buddhist perspective places much more importance on the fluidity of human relationships than does a Western perspective. This means that a Buddhist conception of human rights will be softer, more accommodating, and more flexible than a Western conception of human rights; it will be more compassionate, more forgiving, and less inclined to set up strong oppositions between parties. In contrast to the Western perspective, a Buddhist conception of human rights is less interested in legal formalities and more interested in the nurturance of feelings that will promote humanistic existence.

It is incorrect to assume that the concept of human rights is readily identifiable in all societies of the world. The concept may perhaps be clear and distinct in legal quarters, but in actual practice suffers greatly from lack of clarity and gray areas due to impositions by different cultures. This is especially true in Asia, where the two great civilizations of India and China have spawned such outstanding systems as Hinduism, Buddhism, Jainism, Yoga, Confucianism, Taoism and Chinese Buddhism. These systems, together with other indigenous folk beliefs, attest to the cultural diversity at play that characterizes Asia proper. In focusing on the concept of human rights, however, we shall concentrate on Buddhism to bring out the common grounds of discourse.

Alone among the great systems of Asia, Buddhism has successfully crossed geographical and ideological borders and spread in time throughout the whole length and breadth of known Asia. Its doctrines are so universal and profound that they captured the imagination of all the peoples they touched and thereby established a subtle bond with all. What then is this bond? It must be something common to all systems of thought which opens up and allows spiritual discourse among them.

In examining the metaphysical ground of all systems, one finds that there is a basic feeling for a larger reality in one's own experience, a kind of reaching out for a greater

Reprinted by permission of Westview Press, from *Asian Perspectives on Human Rights,* edited by Claude E. Walsh and Virginia Leary, 1990.

cosmic dimension of being, as it were. It is a deep sense for the total nature of things. All this may seem so simple and hardly merits elaborating, but it is a genuine feeling common among Asians in their quest for ultimate knowledge based on the proper relationship of one's self in the world. It is an affirmation of a reality that includes but at once goes beyond the confines of sense faculties.

A good illustration of this metaphysical grounding is seen in the Brahmanic world of Hinduism. In it, the occluded nature of the self (*atman*) constantly works to cleanse itself of defilements by yogic discipline in the hope of ultimately identifying with the larger reality which is Brahman. In the process, the grounding in the larger reality is always kept intact, regardless of whether the self is impure or not. In other words, in the quest for the purity of things a larger framework of experience is involved from the beginning such that the ordinary self (*atman*) transforms into the larger Self (*Atman*) and finally merges into the ultimate ontological Brahman.

A similar metaphysical grounding is found in Chinese thought. Confucianism, for example, with its great doctrine of humanity (*jen*), involves the ever-widening and ever-deepening human relationship that issues forth in the famous statement, "All men are brothers." In this sense, humanity is not a mere abstract concept but one that extends concretely throughout the whole of sentient existence. Confucius once said that when he searched for *jen*, it is always close at hand.[1] It means that humanity is not something external to a person but that it is constitutive of the person's experience, regardless of whether there is consciousness of it or not. It means moreover that in the relational nature of society, individual existence is always more than that which one assumes it to be. In this vein, all experiences must fit into the larger cosmological scheme normally spoken of in terms of heaven, earth and mankind. This triadic relationship is ever-present and ever-in-force, despite one's ignorance, negligence or outright intention to deny it. The concept that permeates and enlivens the triadic relationship is the *Tao*. The *Tao* is a seemingly catchall term, perhaps best translated as the natural way of life and the world. In its naturalness, it manifests all of existence; indeed, it is here, there and everywhere since it remains aloof from human contrivance and manipulation. In a paradoxical sense, it depicts action based on non-action (*wu-wei*), the deepest state of being achievable. The following story illustrates this point.

A cook named Ting is alleged to have used the same carving knife for some 19 years without sharpening it at all. When asked how that is possible, he simply replied:

> What I care about is the way (*Tao*), which goes beyond skill. When I first began cutting up oxen, all I could see was the ox itself. After three years I no longer saw the whole ox. And now—now I go at it by spirit and don't look with my eyes. Perception and understanding have come to a stop and spirit moves where it wants. I go along with the natural makeup, strike in the big hollows, guide the knife through the big openings, and follow things as they are. So I never touch the smallest ligament or tendon, much less a main joint. . . . I've had this knife of mine for nineteen years and I've cut up thousands of oxen with it, and yet the blade is as good as though it had just come from the grindstone.[2]

Such then is the master craftsman at work, a master in harmonious triadic relationship based on the capture of the spirit of *Tao* where the function is not limited to a person and his or her use of a tool. And it is clear that such a spirit of *Tao* in craftsmanship is germane to all disciplined experiences we are capable of achieving in our daily activities.

Buddhism, too, has always directed our attention to the larger reality of existence. The original enlightenment of the historical Buddha told of a pure unencumbered experience which opened up all experiential doors in such a way that they touched everything sentient as well as insentient. A Zen story graphically illustrates this point.

Once a master and a disciple were walking through a dense forest. Suddenly, they heard the clean chopping strokes of the woodcutter's axe. The disciple was elated and remarked, "What beautiful sounds in the quiet of the forest!" To which the master immediately responded, "you have got it all upside down. The sounds only make obvious the deep silence of the forest!" The response by the Zen master sets in bold relief the Buddhist perception of reality. Although existential reality refers to the perception of the world as a singular unified whole, we ordinarily perceive it in fragmented ways because of our heavy reliance on the perceptual apparatus and its consequent understanding. That is to say, we perceive by a divisive and selective method which however glosses over much of reality and indeed misses its holistic nature. Certainly, the hewing sounds of the woodcutter's axe are clearly audible and delightful to the ears, but they are so at the expense of the basic silence of the forest (i.e., total reality). Or, the forest in its silence constitutes the necessary background, indeed the basic source, from which all sounds (and all activities for that matter) originate. Put another way, sounds arising from the silence of the forest should in no way deprive nor intrude upon the very source of their own being. Only human beings make such intrusions by their crude discriminate habits of perception and, consequently, suffer a truncated form of existence, unknowingly for the most part.

Now that we have seen Asian lives in general grounded in a holistic cosmological framework, we would have to raise the following question: How does this framework appear in the presence of human rights? Or, contrarily, how does human rights function within this framework?

Admittedly, the concept of human rights is relatively new to Asians. From the very beginning, it did not sit well with their basic cosmological outlook. Indeed, the existence of such an outlook has prevented in profound ways a ready acceptance of foreign elements and has created tension and struggle between tradition and modernity. Yet, the key concept in the tension is that of human relationship. This is especially true in Buddhism, where the emphasis is not so much on the performative acts and individual rights as it is on the matter of manifestation of human nature itself. The Buddhist always takes human nature as the basic context in which all ancillary concepts, such as human rights, are understood and take on any value. Moreover, the context itself is in harmony with the extended experiential nature of things. And thus, where the Westerner is much more at home in treating legal matters detached from human nature as such and quite confident in forging ahead to establish human rights with a distinct emphasis on certain "rights," the Buddhist is much more reserved but open and seeks to understand the implications of human behavior, based on the fundamental nature of human beings, before turning his or her attention to the so-called "rights" of individuals.

An apparent sharp rift seems to exist between the Western and Buddhist views, but this is not really so. Actually, it is a matter of perspectives and calls for a more comprehensive understanding of what takes place in ordinary human relationships. For the basic premise is still one that is focused on human beings intimately living together in the selfsame world. A difference in perspectives does not mean noncommunication or a simple rejection of another's view, as there is still much more substance in the nature of conciliation, accommodation and absorption than what is initially thought of. Here we propose two contrasting but interlocking and complementary terms, namely, "hard relationship" and "soft relationship."

The Western view on human rights is generally based on a hard relationship. Persons are treated as separate and independent entities or even bodies, each having its own assumed identity or self-identity. It is a sheer "elemental" way of perceiving things due mainly to the strong influence by science and its methodology. As scientific methodology thrives on the dissective and analytic incursion into reality as such, this in turn has resulted in our perceiving and understanding things in terms of disparate realities. Although it makes way for easy understanding, the question still remains: Do we really understand what these realities are in their own respective fullness of existence? Apparently not. And to make matters worse, the methodology unfortunately has been uncritically extended over to the human realm, into human nature and human relations. Witness its ready acceptance by the various descriptive and behavioral sciences, such as sociology, psychology and anthropology. On this matter, Cartesian dualism of mind and body has undoubtedly influenced our ordinary ways of thinking in such a manner that in our casual perception of things we habitually subscribe to the clearcut subject–object dichotomy. This dualistic perspective has naturally filtered down into human relationships and has eventually crystallized into what we refer to as the nature of a hard relationship. Thus, a hard relationship is a mechanistic treatment of human beings where the emphasis is on beings as such regardless of their inner nature and function in the fullest sense; it is an atomistic analysis of beings where the premium is placed on what is relatable and manipulable without regard for their true potentials for becoming. In a way it is externalization in the extreme, since the emphasis is heavily weighted on seizing the external character of beings themselves. Very little attention, if any, is given to the total ambience, inclusive of inner contents and values, in which the beings are at full play. In this regard, it can be said that postmodern thought is now attempting to correct this seemingly lopsided dichotomous view created by our inattention to the total experiential nature of things. We believe this is a great step in the right direction. Meanwhile, we trudge along with a heavy burden on our backs, though unaware of it for the most part, by associating with people on the basis of hard relationships.

To amplify on the nature of hard relationships, let us turn to a few modern examples. First, Thomas Hobbes, in his great work, *Leviathan,*[3] showed remarkable grasp of human psychology when he asserted that people are constantly at war with each other. Left in this "state of nature," people will never be able to live in peace and security. The only way out of this conundrum is for all to establish a reciprocal relationship or mutual trust that would work, i.e., to strike up a covenant by selfish beings that guarantees mutual benefits and gains, one in which each relinquishes certain rights in order to gain or realize a personal as well as an overall state of peace and security. This was undoubtedly a brilliant scheme. But the scheme is weak in that it treats human beings by and large mechanically, albeit psychologically too, as entities in a give-and-take affair, and thus perpetuates the condition of hard relationships.

Another example can be offered by way of the British utilitarian movement which later was consummated in American pragmatism. Jeremy Bentham's hedonic calculus[4] (e.g., intensity of pleasure or pain, duration of pleasure or pain, certainty or uncertainty of pleasure or pain, purity or impurity of pleasure or pain, etc.) is a classic example of quantification of human experience. Although this is a most expedient or utilitarian way to treat and legislate behavior, we must remind ourselves that we are by no means mere quantifiable entities. John Stuart Mill introduced the element of quality in order to curb and tone down the excesses of the quantification process,[5] but, in the final analysis, human nature and relationships are still set in hard relations. American pragmatism fares no better since actions by and large take place in a pluralistic world of realities and are framed within the scientific mode and therefore it is unable to relinquish the nature of hard relationships.

In contemporary times, the great work of John Rawls, *A Theory of Justice*,[6] has given us yet another twist in pragmatic and social contract theories. His basic concept of justice as fairness is an example of the reciprocal principle in action, i.e., in terms of realizing mutual advantage and benefit for the strongest to the weakest or the most favored to the least favored in a society. Each person exercises basic liberty with offices for its implementation always open and access available. It is moreover a highly intellectual or rational theory. It thus works extremely well on the theoretical level but, in actual situations, it is not as practical and applicable as it seems since it still retains hard relationships on mutual bases. Such being the case, feelings and consciousness relative to injustice and inequality are not so readily spotted and corrected. That is to say, lacunae exist as a result of hard relationships and they keep on appearing until they are detected and finally remedied, but then the corrective process is painfully slow. Thus the theory's strongest point is its perpetually self-corrective nature which is so vital to the democratic process. Despite its shortcomings, however, Rawls' theory of justice is a singular contribution to contemporary legal and ethical thought.

By contrast, the Buddhist view of human rights is based on the assumption that human beings are primarily oriented in soft relationships; this relationship governs the understanding of the nature of human rights. Problems arise, on the other hand, when a hard relationship becomes the basis for treating human nature because it cannot delve deeply into that nature itself and functions purely on the peripheral aspects of things. It is another way of saying that a hard relationship causes rigid and stifling empirical conditions to arise and to which we become invariably attached.

A soft relationship has many facets. It is the Buddhist way to disclose a new dimension to human nature and behavior. It actually amounts to a novel perception or vision of reality. Though contrasted with a hard relationship, it is not in contention with it. If anything, it has an inclusive nature that "softens," if you will, all contacts and allows for the blending of any element that comes along, even incorporating the entities of hard relationships. This is not to say, however, that soft and hard relationships are equal or ultimately identical. For although the former could easily accommodate and absorb the latter, the reverse is not the case. Still, it must be noted that both belong to the same realm of experiential reality and in consequence ought to be conversive with each other. The non-conversive aspect arises on the part of the "hard" side and is attributable to the locked-in character of empirical elements which are considered to be hard stubborn facts worth perpetuating. But at some point, there must be a break in the lock, as it were, and this is made possible by knowledge of and intimacy with the "soft" side of human endeavors. For the "soft" side has a passive nature characterized by openness, extensiveness, depth, flexibility, absorptiveness, freshness and creativity simply because it remains unencumbered by "hardened" empirical conditions.

What has been discussed so far can be seen in modern Thailand where tradition and change are in dynamic tension. Due to the onslaught of elements of modernity, Buddhism is being questioned and challenged. Buddhist Thailand, however, has taken up the challenge in the person of a leading monk named Buddhadasa who has led the country to keep a steady course on traditional values.[7]

> The heart of Buddhadasa's teaching is that the Dhamma (Sanskrit, Dharma) or the truth of Buddhism is a universal truth. Dhamma is equated by Buddhadasa to the true nature of things. It is everything and everywhere. The most appropriate term to denote the nature of Dhamma is *sunnata* (Sanskrit, *sunyata*) or the void. The ordinary man considers the void to mean nothing when, in reality, it means everything—everything, that is, without reference to the self.

We will return to the discussion of the nature of the void or *sunnata* later, but suffice it to say here that what constitutes the heart of Buddhist truth of existence is based on soft relationships where all forms and symbols are accommodated and allows for their universal usage.

Robert N. Bellah has defined religion as a set of normative symbols institutionalized in a society or internalized in a personality.[8] It is a rather good definition but does not go far enough when it comes to describing Buddhism, or Asian religions in general for that matter. To speak of symbols being institutionalized or internalized without the proper existential or ontological context seems to be a bit artificial and has strains of meanings oriented toward hard relationships. Bellah, being a social scientist, probably could not go beyond the strains of a hard relationship, for, otherwise, he would have ended in a nondescriptive realm. The only way out is to give more substance to the nature of religious doctrines themselves, as is the case in Buddhism. The Buddhist Dharma is one such doctrine which, if symbolized, must take on a wider and deeper meaning that strikes at the very heart of existence of the individual. In this respect, Donald Swearer is on the right track when he says:

> the adaptation of symbols of Theravada Buddhism presupposes an underlying ontological structure. The symbol system of Buddhism, then, is not to be seen only in relationship to its wider empirical context, but also in relationship to its ontological structure. This structure is denoted by such terms as Dhamma or absolute Truth, emptiness and non-attachment. These terms are denotative of what Dhiravamsa calls "dynamic being." They are symbolic, but in a universalistic rather than a particularistic sense.[9]

Swearer's reference to an underlying ontological structure is in complete harmony with our use of the term soft relationship. And only when this ontological structure or soft relationship is brought into the dynamic tension between tradition and modernity can we give full accounting to the nature of human experience and the attendant creativity and change within a society.

Let us return to a fuller treatment of soft relationships. In human experience, they manifest themselves in terms of the intangible human traits that we live by, such as patience, humility, tolerance, deference, non-action, humaneness, concern, pity, sympathy, altruism, sincerity, honesty, faith, responsibility, trust, respectfulness, reverence, love and compassion. Though potentially and pervasively present in any human relationship, they remain for the most part as silent but vibrant components in all experiences. Without them, human intercourse would be sapped of the human element and reduced to perfunctory activities. Indeed, this fact seems to constitute much of the order of the day where our passions are mainly directed to physical and materialistic matters.

The actualization and sustenance of these intangible human traits are basic to the Buddhist quest for an understanding of human nature and, by extension, the so-called rights of human beings. In order to derive a closer look at the nature of soft relationships, we shall focus on three characteristics, namely, mutuality, holism, and emptiness or void.

MUTUALITY

Our understanding of mutuality is generally limited to its abstract or theoretical nature. For example, it is defined in terms of a two-way action between two parties and where the action is invariably described with reference to elements of hard relationships. Except secondarily or deviously, nothing positive is mentioned about the substance of mutuality, such as the feelings of humility, trust and tolerance that transpire between the parties concerned. Although these feelings are present, unfortunately, they hardly ever surface in the relationship and almost always are overwhelmed by the physical aspect of things.

What is to be done? One must simply break away from the merely conceptual or theoretical understanding and fully engage oneself in the discipline that will bring the feelings of both parties to become vital components in the relationship. That is, both parties must equally sense the presence and value of these feelings and thus give substance and teeth to their actions.

Pursuing the notion of mutuality further, the Buddhist understands human experience as a totally open phenomenon, that persons should always be wide open in the living process. The phrase, "an open ontology," is used to describe the unclouded state of existence. An illustration of this is the newborn child. The child is completely an open organism at birth. The senses are wide open and will absorb practically anything without prejudice. At this stage, also, the child will begin to imitate because its absorptive power is at the highest level. This open textured nature should continue on and on. In other words, if we are free and open, there should be no persistence in attaching ourselves to hard elements within the underlying context of a dynamic world of experience. The unfortunate thing, however, is that the open texture of our existence begins to blemish and fade away in time, being obstructed and overwhelmed by self-imposed fragmentation, narrowness and restriction, which gradually develop into a closed nature of existence. In this way, the hard relationship rules. But the nature of an open ontology leads us onto the next characteristic.

HOLISM

Holism of course refers to the whole, the total nature of individual existence and thus describes the unrestrictive nature of one's experience. Yet, the dualistic relationship we maintain by our crude habits of perception remains a stumbling block. This stunted form of perception is not conducive to holistic understanding and instead fosters nothing but fractured types of ontological knowledge taking. Unconscious for the most part, an individual narrows his or her vision by indulging in dualism of all kinds, both mental and physical, and in so doing isolates the objects of perception from the total process to which they belong. In consequence, the singular unified reality of each perceptual moment is fragmented and, what is more, fragmentation once settled breeds further fragmentation.

The Buddhist will appeal to the fact that one's experience must always be open to the total ambience of any momentary situation. But here we must be exposed to a unique, if not paradoxical, insight of the Buddhist. It is that the nature of totality is not a clearly defined phenomenon. In a cryptic sense, however, it means that the totality of experience has no borders to speak of. It is an open border totality, which is the very nature of the earlier mentioned "open ontology." It is a non-circumscribable totality, like a circle sensed which does not have a rounded line, a seamless circle, if you will. A strange phenomenon, indeed, but that is how the Buddhist sees the nature of individual existence as such. For the mystery of existence that haunts us is really the nature of one's own fullest momentary existence. Nothing else compares in profundity to this nature, so the Buddhist believes.

Now, the open framework in which experience takes place reveals that there is depth and substance in experience. But so long as one is caught up with the peripheral elements, so-called, of hard relationships one will be ensnared by them and will generate limitations on one's understanding accordingly. On the other hand, if openness is acknowledged as a fact of existence, then the way out of one's limitations will present itself. All sufferings (*duhkha*), from the Buddhist standpoint, are cases of limited ontological vision (*avidya*, ignorance) hindered by the attachment to all sorts of elements that obsess a person.

Holism is conversant with openness since an open experience means that all elements are fully and extensively involved. In many respects, holistic existence exhibits the fact that mutuality thrives only in unhindered openness. But there is still another vital characteristic to round out or complete momentary experience. For this we turn to the last characteristic.

EMPTINESS

Emptiness in Sanskrit is *sunyata*.[10] Strictly speaking, the Sanskrit term, depicting zero or nothing, had been around prior to Buddhism, but it took the historical Buddha's supreme enlightenment (nirvana) to reveal an incomparable qualitative nature inherent to experience. Thus emptiness is not sheer voidness or nothingness in the nihilistic sense.

We ordinarily find it difficult to comprehend emptiness, much less to live a life grounded in it. Why? Again, we return to the nature of our crude habits of perception, which is laden with unwarranted forms. That is, our whole perpetual process is caught up in attachment to certain forms or elements which foster and turn into so-called empirical and cognitive biases. All of this is taking place in such minute and unknowing ways that we hardly, if ever, take notice of it until a crisis situation arises, such as the presence of certain obviously damaging prejudice or discrimination. Then and only then do we seriously wonder and search for the forms or elements that initially gave rise to those prejudicial or discriminatory forces.

Emptiness has two aspects. The first aspect alerts our perceptions to be always open and fluid, and to desist from attaching to any form or element. In this respect, emptiness technically functions as a force of "epistemic nullity,"[11] in the sense that it nullifies any reference to a form or element as preexisting perception or even post-existing for that matter. Second and more importantly, emptiness points at a positive content of our experience. It underscores the possibility of total experience in any given moment because there is now nothing attached to or persisted in. This latter point brings us right back to the other characteristics of holism and mutuality. Now, we must note that emptiness is that dimension of experience which makes it possible for the function of mutuality and holism in each experience, since there is absolutely nothing that binds, hinders or wants in our experience. Everything is as it is (*tathata*), under the aegis of emptiness; emptiness enables one to spread out one's experience at will in all directions, so to speak, in terms of "vertical" and "horizontal" dimensions of being. As it is the key principle of enlightened existence, it makes everything both possible and impossible. Possible in the sense that all experiences function within the total empty nature, just as all writings are possible on a clean slate or, back to the zen story, where the sounds are possible in the silence (emptiness) of the forest. At the same time, impossible in the sense that all attachments to forms and elements are categorically denied in the ultimate fullness of experience. In this way, emptiness completes our experience of reality and at the same time, provides the grounds for the function of all human traits to become manifest in soft relationships.

It can now be seen that all three characteristics involve each other in the selfsame momentary existence. Granted this, it should not be too difficult to accept the fact that the leading moral concept in Buddhism is compassion (*karuna*). Compassion literally means "passion for all" in an ontologically extensive sense. It covers the realm of all sentient beings, inclusive of non-sentients, for the doors of perception to total reality are always open. From the Buddhist viewpoint, then, all human beings are open entities with open feelings expressive of the highest form of humanity. This is well expressed in the famous concept of *bodhisattva* (enlightened being) in Mahayana Buddhism who has deepest concern for all beings and sympathetically delays his entrance to nirvana as long as there is suffering (ignorant existence) among sentient creatures. It depicts the coterminous nature of all creatures and may be taken as a philosophic myth in that it underscores the ideality of existence which promotes the greatest unified form of humankind based on compassion. This ideal form of existence, needless to say, is the aim and goal of all Buddhists.

As human beings we need to keep the channels of existential dialogue open at all times. When an act of violence is in progress, for example, we need to constantly nourish the silent and passive nature of nonviolence inherent in all human relations. Though nonviolence cannot counter violence on the latter's terms, still, its nourished presence serves as a reminder of the brighter side of existence and may even open the violator's mind to common or normal human traits such as tolerance, kindness and noninjury (*ahimsa*). Paradoxically and most unfortunately, acts of violence only emphasize the fact that peace and tranquillity are the normal course of human existence.

It can now be seen that the Buddhist view on human rights is dedicated to the understanding of persons in a parameter-free ambience, so to speak, where feelings that are extremely soft and tender, but nevertheless present and translated into human traits or virtues that we uphold, make up the very fiber of human relations. These relations, though their contents are largely intangible, precede any legal rights or justification accorded to human beings. In brief, human rights for the Buddhist are not only matters for legal deliberation and understanding, but they must be complemented by and based on something deeper and written in the very feelings of all sentients. The unique coexistent nature of rights and feelings constitutes the saving truth of humanistic existence.

NOTES

1. *Lu Yu* (The Analects of Confucius): VII, 29.
2. *The Complete Works of Chuang Tzu,* translated by

Burton Watson (New York: Columbia University Press, 1960), pp. 50–51.

3. Thomas Hobbes, *Leviathan* (New York: Hafner, 1926).
4. Jeremy Bentham, *An Introduction to the Principles of Morals and Legislation* (New York: Hafner, 1948).
5. John Stuart Mill observed, "It is better to be a human being dissatisfied than a pig satisfied; better to be a Socrates dissatisfied than a fool satisfied." *Utilitarianism,* cited in Louis P. Pojman, *Philosophy: The Quest for Truth* (Belmont, CA: Wadsworth, 1989), p. 357.
6. John Rawls, *A Theory of Justice* (Cambridge: Harvard University Press, 1971). Rawls also has a chapter on civil disobedience but it too is treated under the same concept of justice as fairness and suffers accordingly from the elements of hard relationships.
7. Donald K. Swearer, "Thai Buddhism: Two Responses to Modernity," in Bardwell L. Smith, ed., *Contributions to Asian Studies,* Volume 4: Tradition and Change in Theravada Buddhism (Leiden: E.J. Brill, 1973), p. 80. "Without reference to the self" means to uphold the Buddhist doctrine of non-self (Sanskrit, *anatman*) which underlies all momentary existence and avoids any dependence on a dichotomous self-oriented subject—object relationship. For an updated and comprehensive view of Buddhadasa's reformist's philosophy, see Donald K. Swearer, ed., *Me and Mine: Selected Essays on Bhikkhu Buddhadasa* (Albany: State University of New York Press, 1989).
8. Robert N. Bellah, "Epilogue" in Bellah, ed., *Religion and Progress in Modern Asia* (New York: Free Press, 1965), p. 173.
9. Swearer, "Thai Buddhism," p. 92.
10. Etymologically *sunyata* (in Pali, *sunnata*) means the state of being swollen, as in pregnancy, or the state of fullness of being. Thus, from the outset the term depicted the pure, open and full textured nature of experiential reality.
11. Kenneth Inada, "Nagarjuna and Beyond," *Journal of Buddhist Philosophy* 2 (1984), pp. 65–76, for development of this concept.

HUMAN RIGHTS—SUPPLEMENTARY READINGS

ANIKPO, MARK. "Human Rights and Self-Reliance in Africa," in *Emerging Human Rights,* Shepherd and Anikpo, editors. New York: Greenwood Press, 1990.

BELL, DIANE. "Considering Gender: Are Human Rights for Women Too? An Australian Case," in *Human Rights in Cross Cultural Perspective,* An-Na'im, editor. Philadelphia: University of Pennsylvania Press, 1991.

COBBAH, JOSIAH. "African Values and the Human Rights Debate." *Human Rights Quarterly,* vol. 9(3), August 1987.

DONNELLEY, JACK. "Human Rights and Development: Complementary or Competing Concerns," in *Human Rights and Third World Development,* Shepherd and Nanda, editors. New York: Greenwood Press, 1985.

HARE, R.M. "Rights and Justice," in *Moral Thinking.* Oxford: Oxford University Press, 1981.

LIXIAN, CHENG. "A Tentative Discussion of Human Rights." *Chinese Studies in Philosophy,* vol. 17(1), Fall 1985.

PENNOCK, J. ROLAND. "Rights, Natural Rights, and Human Rights—A General View." *NOMOS 23: Human Rights.* New York: New York University Press, 1981.

SCANLON, THOMAS. "Rights, Goals and Fairness," in *Public and Private Morality,* Hampshire, editor. Cambridge, England: Cambridge University Press, 1978.

TIBI, BASSAM. "The European Tradition of Human Rights and the Culture of Islam," in *Human Rights in Africa,* An-Na'im and Deng, editors. Washington, DC: The Brookings Institution, 1990.

WIREDU, KWASI. "An Akan Perspective on Human Rights," in *Human Rights in Africa,* An-Na'im and Deng, editors. Washington, DC: The Brookings Institution, 1990.

ZEIDAN, SHAWKY. "A Human Rights Settlement: The West Bank and Gaza," in *Human Rights and Third World Development,* Shepherd and Nanda, editors. New York: Greenwood Press, 1985.

ZION, JAMES. "North American Indian Perspectives on Human Rights," in *Human Rights in Cross Cultural Perspectives,* An-Na'im, editor. Philadelphia: University of Pennsylvania Press, 1991.

II

Environmental Ethics

There is yet no ethic dealing with man's relation to land and to the animals and plants which grow upon it. Land . . . is still property. The land-relation is still strictly economic, entailing privileges but not obligations.

The extension of ethics to this third element in the human environment is, if I read the evidence correctly, an evolutionary possibility and an ecological necessity.

—Aldo Leopold[1]

Legally, the environment has no rights. Property rights are still the premier means of addressing the environment. Presently in the United States, the only way for natural objects or ecosystems to be protected is through the assertion of a human being's legal rights. In order to have a legal claim concerning an environmental harm, one must have "standing," which is the capacity to challenge an action in a court. The harm must be an "injury in fact;" can be in the past, present or future; and must be capable of being redressed by the court. The environment may also be legally protected through legislation. However, in order to make any progress, one needs factual and conceptual arguments to persuade those in power that consideration for the environment goes beyond traditional property value concerns.

Many people link the environmental crisis to a general shortage of ethics. The historically unparalleled levels of consumption and the consequent environmental degradation has brought into question the earth's carrying capacity. Many assert that without reevaluations of and drastic changes in our ways of life, we will not come out of this crisis.

Environmental ethics considers limitations on the freedom of exercising property rights, and concerns the further extension of our ethical duties to the environment. This reconceptualization of the environment as an object of moral concern carries with it a radical reconceptualization of key elements within the Western tradition.

Human rights, which were discussed in the previous section, and the environment are inextricably linked. Many have argued that the right to a clean, livable environment is an absolute prerequisite for all other human rights. Human rights approaches, or anthropocentric approaches, only consider the environment as it relates to human interests. Anthropocentrism asserts that we only have ethical duties to humans, thus precluding direct duties to the environment.

A broader approach is sentientist, represented in this chapter in Bernard Rollin's essay. This view asserts that all sentient beings have interests that matter to them, and they have intrinsic value. The environment has merely an instrumental value for sentient beings; that is, the environment serves as a means to the sentient beings' ends. Rollin argues that it is nonsensical to attribute intrinsic value or direct moral concern to natural (nonsentient) objects. He maintains that nonetheless, we can derive a strong argument against the destruction of natural objects. By placing the emphasis on sentience, Rollin broadens the moral domain from anthropocentrist views.

Others insist that the environment is a tool for economic development that must be used in order to guarantee basic human rights. William K. Reilly argues from this perspective. Reilly argues for sustainable economic growth that is in harmony with environmental protection. He cites examples of the developed world's higher concern with the quality of the environment and lower birth rates, and states that this results in a qualitatively healthier economic growth. In calling for "good growth," Reilly asserts that it is possible to raise the standard of living for all, without subsequent environmental degradation. Although Reilly nods in the direction of stewardship of natural systems, his focus is not on duties to the environment, but on the economic benefits for humans that can be reaped through this "good growth."

Others argue for a type of environmental rights, often to guarantee that differing property rights and competing interests will not further despoil the environment. It is asserted that we have ethical obligations to all of nature. To grant our obligations to all of nature is to recognize the interrelated nature of ecosystems, which are composed of living and nonliving entities. In direct contrast to the aforementioned views, it is claimed that both living and nonliving matter have inherent value and "standing" for ethical consideration. This view is often called "deep ecology" and is also known as the "biocentric" or "ecocentric" approach. Deep ecology broadens our ethical duties even further than a sentientist approach does. From the viewpoint of deep ecology, the entire ecosystem has intrinsic value, and may not be used (as an instrument) to merely further specific interests. We are obliged to take the entire ecosystem into account as an object of moral concern while pursuing our human interests.

J. Baird Callicott's essay brings the traditional American Indian views to the environmental ethics debate, and through his presentation we see yet another extension of the moral domain. Callicott asserts that traditional American Indian views did not draw a sharp line between living and nonliving matter, and considered rocks, rivers, and other natural entities "very much alive." He asserts that for American Indians being "alive" means that the concept of consciousness and awareness that humans experience is considered to be shared with other entities, such as rivers and rocks. One's place in the world was dependent on maintaining good relations with all natural entities in the environment.

In some ways similar to the American Indian approach is that of Taoism. Chung-ying Cheng argues for the inclusion of the Tao and its teachings in environmental ethics. Cheng points out that Western attitudes toward nature center on the external relation of humans to their surroundings, premised upon a dichotomy between the human and nonhuman worlds. In contrast, the Chinese center on the internal relation of humans to their surroundings, premised upon an integrated and interdependent harmony of humans and the world. Westerners, while viewing themselves apart from nature, have studied and then manipulated, dominated, and exploited the world for their pursuits. The conception of humans as separate lends itself to the desire for and exercise of conquest and domination. In contrast, the Chinese tradition represented in both Confucianism and Taoism maintains an internalist, integrated view of nature. Cheng states that traditional Chinese views do not place humans opposite nature, in a hostile manner. Rather, in the Chinese view, it is necessary to cultivate the internal connection to nature, for one's own well-being. Cheng presents the "ecological principle of nature," which is derived from the Tao, and can teach us not to impose ourselves on things. This imposition has often been in the form of domination and exploitation, which Karen J. Warren also addresses.

Warren draws some connections between feminism and the environment in adopting a perspective known as "ecofeminism." Ecofeminism claims that there are similarities between nature and women in that patriarchy attempts to control and dominate both. The similarities Warren has noted include the facts that women and nature are criticized for not conforming to rationality as the paragon of knowledge; that women are symbolically represented in natural terms and the description of nature in feminine terms; and that women and nature historically lack the political power necessary to raise themselves from inferiorized status to full moral consideration. Warren asserts that the maintenance of the patriarchal system of domination over both nature and women is achieved through the unequal distribution of power and privilege. As we will see, this unequal distribution of power and wealth carries over into all aspects of life, including world hunger and poverty.

Ramachandra Guha enters the debate here, and criticizes the deep ecology movement for ultimately leading to further deprivation in the Third World. Guha claims that there is no significant difference between the anthropocentrist and deep ecology approaches. He asserts that environmental problems stem from the appetites of consumers and the military, and from the sociopolitical base that sustains them. Further, Guha specifically objects to the emphasis that environmentalists have placed on wilderness preservation. He asserts that in the Third World, preserving the wilderness sometimes means depriving countries of the means necesary to develop economically. Guha argues that we need to radically reconceive our institutions in order to avoid further destruction of the environment and address the inequity that exists between the developed world and the Third World.

Guha's view may not be immediately incompatible with deep ecology, for consumer and military appetites are also a target of its charges. However, the deep ecologists extend our moral duties beyond the human domain, while Guha is more concerned with political action to address the deprivation of Third World human conditions. Bettering these conditions means that we may have to accept no-growth for those nations that have been exploiting the environment for their seemingly insatiable, and certainly unsustainable, economic and industrial growth.

While Reilly argues for sustainable growth and asserts that affluence leads to environmental protection, Guha argues that growth and environmental protection have been at the expense of most members of the Third World, thus morally mandating a radical change in the appetite for growth. The next section concerning world hunger and poverty will further illuminate the connections Guha asserts between environmental degradation and exploitation of Third World peoples.

NOTE

1. Aldo Leopold, *A Sand County Almanac* (New York: Oxford University Press, 1966), p. 217.

Environmental Ethics and International Justice

Bernard E. Rollin

Bernard E. Rollin is a professor of philosophy, professor of physiology and biophysics, and Director of Bioethical Planning at Colorado State University. He has written six books, including Animal Rights and Human Morality *(1981) and* The Unheeded Cry: Animal Consciousness, Animal Pain, and Science (1989). *At Colorado State, Professor Rollin established the first course in animal rights and veterinary ethics.*

Rollin argues that although it makes no sense to grant natural, nonsentient objects intrinsic value or moral value, these objects must become central to our ethical deliberations. He bases the value of these objects in the instrumental value they have for animals and people. Rollin asserts that the instrumental value approach will place a better check on the harmful treatment of the environment than endowing nonsentient natural objects with "quasi-mystical rhetorical status." Further, he points out the international and global dimensions of pollution, since pollution does not respect property rights or political boundaries. With great concern about the exploitation of nonhuman sentient beings (which also does not recognize political borders), Rollin extends our ethical domain to include all sentient beings, as they possess intrinsic value. However, the environment remains a concern only insofar as it has instrumental value to sentient beings.

The past two decades have witnessed a major revoltuionary thrust in social moral awareness, one virtually unknown in mainstream Western ethical thinking, although not unrecognized in other cultural traditions; for example, the Navajo, whose descriptive language for nature and animals is suffused with ethical nuances; the Australian Aboriginal people; and the ancient Persians. This thrust is the recognition that nonhuman entities enjoy some moral status as objects of moral concern and deliberation. Although the investigation of the moral status of nonhuman entities has sometimes been subsumed under the global rubric of environmental ethics, such a blanket term does not do adequate justice to the substantial conceptual differences of its components. . . .

The question of environmental ethics in relation to international justice must be analyzed into two discrete components. First are those questions that pertain to direct objects of moral concern—nonhuman animals whose sentience we have good reason to suspect—and that require the application of traditional moral notions to a hitherto ignored domain of moral objects. Second are those questions pertaining to natural objects

Reprinted by permission of Westview Press, from *Problems of International Justice*, edited by Steven Luper-Foy, 1988. [Edited]

or abstract natural objects. Although it is nonsensical to attribute intrinsic or direct moral value to these objects, they nonetheless must become (and are indeed becoming) central to our social moral deliberations. This centrality derives from our increasing recognition of the far-reaching and sometimes subtle instrumental value these objects have for humans and animals. Knowing that contamination of remote desert areas by pollutants can destroy unique panoplies of fragile beauty, or that dumping wastes into the ocean can destroy a potential source of antibiotics, or that building a pipeline can have undreamed-of harmful effects goes a long way toward making us think twice about these activities—a far longer way than endowing them with quasi-mystical rhetorical status subject to (and begging for) positivistic torpedoing.

THE ENVIRONMENT AND INTERNATIONAL JUSTICE

How do both of these newly born areas of moral concern relate to issues of international justice? In the case of issues pertaining to moral awareness of the questions involved in the preservation and despoliation of nonsentient natural objects, processes, and abstract objects, the connection becomes increasingly clear as our knowledge increases. The interconnectedness of all things occupying the biosphere, the tenuousness and violability of certain natural objects and events whose permanence and invulnerability were long taken for granted have become dramatically clearer as environmental science has developed and the results of cavalier treatment of nature have become known.

Even those lacking any moral perspective on the instrumental values in nature now ought to have some prudential ones. Thus, even if one does not care about poisoning the air that other people and animals breathe, prudential reason would dictate that one realize that one is also poisoning oneself. Thus, the question of control of the actions of those who would or could harm another or everyone for the sake of selfish interests begins to loom large as our knowledge of environmental impact of individual actions begins to grow. These effects therefore enter into the dialectic of social justice. What constraints can legitimately be placed upon my freedoms in order to protect the environment? What social or individual benefits balance what costs to the environment or to natural objects? How much ought aesthetic values weigh against economic ones? Whole bureaucracies like the Environmental Protection Agency in the United States exist to ponder and regulate such questions in almost all civilized countries, and recent legal thinking has sought ways to codify the importance of natural objects in the law—for example, by granting them legal standing.[1] (Such a granting can and should be based on a realization of their instrumental value, not on intrinsic value; we already have such a precedent in legal standing for ships, cities, and corporations.)

Nevertheless, increased environmental knowledge has driven home a major but often ignored point: Environmental effects do not respect national boundaries. I recall traveling more than twenty years ago to the northernmost regions of eastern Canada that can be reached by road—areas inhabited almost exclusively by Native Americans to whom the benefits accruing from technological progress were manifestly limited. I was appalled to discover that in this land of few roads and fewer amenities, atmospheric pollutants such as sulfur dioxide and hydrogen sulfide reigned supreme—an unwelcome gift from factories hundreds of miles away across the U.S. border. I had no doubt that the respiratory systems of those native people were paying a heavy, and totally unjustified, price for another country's prosperity in which they did not share.

Similar examples abound. When propellant gases released by people in affluent societies (possibly) succeed in tearing a hole in the ozone layer, which hole then has cataclysmic effects on global weather, penetration of noxious rays, and so on, we again see that environmental damage does not respect national boundaries.

In a slightly different vein, one can consider underdeveloped countries struggling to raise the living standards of their populace. To do so, they must exploit and perhaps despoil resources and environments that, from the point of view of a detached observer, ought to be left alone or whose exploitation will or may in some measure ultimately threaten the whole biosphere. The detached observer may well be (and probably is) where he is in virtue of similar despoliation routinely engaged in by his country generations before environmental consciousness had dawned. Is the underdeveloped country to bear a burden of poverty just because its awakening is happening a hundred years late? Or is the new environmental knowledge to count for naught in the face of the need for development?

An excellent example of this point was recently given by an environmental scientist, Michael Mares, in an article in *Science*. Echoing the point we just made, Mares asserts that "broad-scale ecological problems have little to do with national boundaries. In our complex world, where multiple links of commerce, communications, and politics join all countries to a remarkable degree, the suggestion that ecological problems of large magnitude can or should be solved only at a local level is unrealistic. We are all involved in biospheric problems."[2]

Using the case of South America, for which massive extinction of species has been predicted and where wholesale destruction of rain forests has occurred, Mares points out that one cannot look at this situation strictly as South America's problem, but as one caused by global as well as local pressures with global and local consequences. With South American countries in economic difficulties, can one really expect governments there to take a long-run ecological perspective rather than acceding to short-term gain? If other countries in an immediate position to adopt a long-run perspective wish to do so, they must help South America with the requisite expertise as well as with significant financial assistance. . . .

The ultimate example is, of course, the ecological catastrophe of the nuclear winter that is projected to follow nuclear war. Those who would suffer from the effects of such a winter far outnumber the belligerents. Thus, nuclear war becomes a pressing matter not only to those nations with a penchant for annihilating one another, but even to those simple innocents thousands of miles and cultural light years away from the principals who have no notion of the ideological and economic disputes leading to the conflagration and no allegiance to either side.

Yet another striking example of the need for international cooperation and justice in environmental matters comes from the burgeoning area of biotechnology and genetic engineering. For some time, the United States has led in genetic engineering and also in attempts to create rules and guidelines for its regulation. Interest groups have brought suit against projects that might have untoward and unpredictable environmental consequences—for example, the ice nucleation experiments in California that use genetically engineered bacteria to protect crops from frost.[3] Demands for stringent federal regulation of such work have persisted, primarily on the grounds that such activities could wreak havoc with the environment in undreamed-of ways. What is all too often forgotten is that genetic engineering is a problem for international regulation, not merely for national rules. By and large, the technology for doing pioneering work in genetic engineering is relatively inexpensive, compared, for example, to the need for enormous amounts of capital to build particle accelerators. Thus, stringent regulation or even abolition of genetic engineering in a country such as the United States would not alone solve the problem; regulation would merely move genetic engineering into countries less concerned with potential national and global catastrophe. The net effect is that probably riskier, less supervised work would be done under less stringent conditions. Thus, by its very nature, genetic engineering must be controlled internationally if national control is to be effective.

The point about genetic engineering can be made even more strongly when one contemplates its use for military purposes. If there is a real possibility of environmental disaster arising adventitiously out of benign applications of biotechnology, this is a fortiori the case regarding those uses whose avowed purpose is destructive and whose sphere of effect is unpredictable. So much is manifest in the ratification of the Biological Weapons Convention of 1975, widely cited as the world's first disarmament treaty, "since it is the only one that outlaws the production and use of an entire class of weapons of mass destruction."[4] In October 1986, steps were taken to strengthen the verificational procedures of the treaty, but these essentially boil down to merely voluntary compliance, with no system of sanctions or enforcement.

The final example of environmental problems depending for their solution on some system of international justice concerns the extinction of species. Such problems fall into two distinct categories given the argument we have developed, although this distinction has traditionally been ignored. In my view, we must distinguish between threats of extinction involving sentient and nonsentient species. In the case of sentient species, the fact that a species is threatened is trumped by the fact that its members are sentient. First and foremost, the issue involves harming individual, direct objects of moral concern, just as genocide amounts to mass murder, not the elimination of an abstract entity.

Thus, from the point of view of primary loci of moral concern, killing *any* ten Siberian tigers is no different than killing the *last* ten. Our greater horror at the latter stems from invoking the relational value dimension to humans—no human will ever again be able to witness the beauty of these creatures; our world is poorer in the same way that it would be if one destroyed the last ten Van Goghs, not just any ten; the loss of the last ten tigers may lead to other losses of which we are not aware. But we should not lose sight of the fact that the greater harm is to the animals, not to us. For this reason, I will discuss the destruction of sentient species separately, along with cases where individual animals are destroyed and hurt without endangering the species.

This still leaves us with the case of species extinction involving nonsentient species—plants or animals in whom we have no reason to suspect the presence of consciousness. Such extinction is not necessarily an evil. Few (albeit some) bemoaned the eradication of the smallpox virus, and David Baltimore recently remarked that, in his view, all viruses could be eradicated with no loss (save perhaps to intrinsic value theorists).[5] On the other hand, most cases of extinction presumably would be cases of (relational) evil because nonsentient species that do not harm us or other sentient creatures directly or indirectly are at worst neutral, and their loss is both an aesthetic loss for their uniqueness and beauty (the humblest organisms often contain great beauty—

in symmetry, adaptation, complexity, or whatever, as my friend the parasitologist discovered), or a loss of a potential tool whose value is not yet detected (as a source of medicine, dye, and so on), or as crucial to the ecosystem in some unrecognized way.

The destruction of myriad species is a major problem. The greatest threat lies in the tropics, where species diversity is both the richest and under the greatest threat. It has been estimated that only one in ten to one in twenty species in the tropics are known to science.[6] A hectare of land in the Peruvian Amazon rain forest contains 41,000 species of insect alone, according to a recent count.[7] A *single tree* contained 43 species of ant. In ten separate hectare plots in Borneo, 700 species of tree were identified, matching the count for all of North America![8] According to a report in *Science*, "The continued erosion of tropical rain forests—through small-scale slash and burn agriculture at one extreme to massive timber operations at the other—is . . . closing in on perhaps half the world's natural inventory of species. Most biologists agree that the world's rain forests will be all but obliterated at some point in the next century."[9] Furthermore, small parks and preserves could not harbor numbers and varieties of species proportional to their size. Thus, standard conservation compromises do not represent a viable solution to the problem.

Other habitats holding a large diversity of species also are threatened. These include coral reefs, coastal wetlands, such as those in California, and large African lakes. The last have been especially threatened by the attempt to cultivate within them varieties of fish not indigenous to the area. A mere documentation of species unknown to science and possibly threatened would require the life work of twenty-five thousand taxonomists; currently there are a mere fifteen hundred such individuals at work.[10] Standard techniques of conserving representative members of such species in zoos and herbaria or perserving germ plasm in essence represent the proverbial drop in the bucket, although they are of course better than nothing.

Scientists who have devoted a great deal of study to these issues again echo the point cited earlier from Mares: These concerns are not local, but international. Michael Robinson puts the point dramatically: "We are facing 'the enlightenment fallacy.' The fallacy is that if you educate the people of the Third World, the problem will disappear. It won't. The problems are not due to ignorance and stupidity. The problems . . . derive from the poverty of the poor and the greed of the rich."[11] *Science*, in concluding its analysis, asserted that "the problems are those of economics and politics. Inescapably, therefore, the solutions are to be found in those same areas."[12]

Some recognition of this politico-economic dimension of environmental problems has been slowly forthcoming politically. There are, for example, indications that policies of the World Bank, which lends development money to countries, are being restructured to take more cognizance of environmental concerns. The bank has been criticized for funding the Polonoroeste project in Brazil, which would have destroyed large forest areas in Brazil in order to allow mass migration of farmers from impoverished areas, and for funding cattle ranching projects in Africa that promote desertification.[13]

Thus, even a cursory examination of some major environmental issues affecting the nonsentient environment indicates that those problems are insoluble outside of the context of international justice. The question then becomes: What, if any, philosophical basis exists for a system of international justice in this area? History has shown, after all, that attempts to create viable machinery of international justice in any area, ranging from an end to genocide to the prevention of war, have run the gamut from laughable to ineffectual. Self-interest has always trumped justice; the situation among nations, it is often remarked, is essentially the Hobbesian "war of each against all." This historical point again blunts even the pragmatic justification for attributing intrinsic value to the nonsentient environment. After all, widespread recognition in the Western tradition of the intrinsic value of humans has not at all assisted in the development of effective mechanisms to ensure that such value is respected.

Ironically, if we begin with the Hobbesian insight, it actually may be easier to provide a rational (and pragmatically effective) basis for a system of international justice regarding environmental concerns rather than human rights. After all, there is no pragmatic reason for a nation to sacrifice its sovereignty in the international arena regarding matters of human rights. If a given country benefits significantly from oppressing all or some of its citizenry, what positive incentive is there for that nation to respond to other nations' protests, and what incentive is there for other nations to protest? In the latter case, of course, there may be moral or ideological reasons for a nation to protest another's human rights policies, but such concerns usually give way to more pragmatic pressures—for example, if the oppressive country stands in a mutually beneficial trade or defensive relationship with the concerned nation.

In the case of global environmental concerns—destruction of the ozone, pollution of air and water, nuclear winter, dangers arising out of genetic engineering, loss of species—*everyone* loses (or might lose) if these concerns are not addressed. A leitmotif of our discussion has been precisely the global nature of such concerns. We have, in the case of all of the examples cited previously, something closer to what game theorists call a game of cooperation rather than a game of competition. That is, if one nation loses its fight with an environmental problem, or simply does not address it, any other nation could, and in many cases would, be likely to suffer as well. Thus, if the United States, through excessive use of fluorocarbons, weakens the ozone barrier, the results will not be restricted to the United States, but will have global impact.

By the same token, even if a given nation X stands to gain by ignoring environmental despoliation, others may lose and, without a system of regulation, may in turn bear the brunt of Y's or Z's cavalier disregard of other aspects of the environment. Furthermore, there is good reason to believe that the short-run gains accruing to a nation by a disregard of environmental concerns may well be significantly outweighed in the long run by unforeseen or ignored consequences. Thus, the wholesale conversion of African grasslands into grazing lands for domestic animals not ecologically adapted to such an environment may yield short-term profits, but in the long run lead to desertification, which leaves the land of no use at all. By the same token, cavalier disregard of species loss in the deforestation of the tropics may certainly provide short-term windfall profits, but at the expense of far richer resources. *Time* magazine recounted a number of examples of these riches.

> These threatened ecosystems have already proved a valuable source of medicines, foods and new seed stock for crops. Nine years ago, for example, a strain of perennial, disease-resistant wild maize named *Zea diploperennis* was found in a Mexican mountain forest, growing in three small plots. Crossing domestic corn varieties with this maize produces hardy hybrids that should ultimately be worth billions of dollars to farmers. A great many of

> the prescription drugs sold in the U.S. are based on unique chemical compounds found in tropical plants. For example, vincristine, originally isolated from the Madagascar periwinkle, is used to treat some human cancers. Scientists are convinced that still undiscovered forest plants could be the source of countless new natural drugs.[14]

The fundamental argument, however, is still the Hobbesian one of rational self-interest. Any country, if utterly unbridled in its pursuit of short-term economic gains, or in its cavalier disregard for the impact of its activities on other nations, can permanently harm the interest of other nations. An irresponsibly genetically engineered microorganism does not respect national boundaries or military power, nor does oceanic or atmospheric pollution. The consequences of lack of control of environmental damage can range from loss of potential benefits—such as loss of new medication derived from plants, or loss of the delight and wonder in seeing a fragile tundra aglow in wildflowers—to positive and serious harm—the dramatic rise in cancers or other diseases produced by environmental despoliation of air, water, or the food chain, or even to a new ice age or tidal waves resulting from destruction of the ozone. Given modern technology, virtually any nation can damage any or all nations in any number of these ways; hence, a situation ripe for Hobbesian contractualism is reached.

In Hobbesian terms, of course, individuals engaged in a war of each against all are rendered equal by their ultimate vulnerability to harm and death by action on the part of others or combinations of others. Thus, we rationally relinquish our natural tendency toward rapaciousness in recognition of others' similar tendency, and our vulnerability thereto. Unrestricted greed is sacrificed for security and protection from the unrestricted greed of others, and a sovereign who, as it were, builds fences protecting each from all is constituted by each individual surrendering a portion of his or her unbridled autonomy. As we have seen, a precisely analogous situation exists regarding environmental vulnerability, and thus rationality would dictate that each nation surrender some of its autonomy to an international authority in order to protect itself, or the whole world including itself, from major disaster. This is of course especially clear, as we have seen earlier, in matters pertaining to biological warfare, where any nation can effectively annihilate any or all others.

In summary, then, the relevance of a viable mechanism of international justice to environmental ethical concerns is manifest. Indeed, many if not most environmental issues, and certainly the most vexing and important ones, entail major global consequences and thus cannot be restricted to local issues of sovereignty. An environmental ethics is inseparable from a system of international justice, not only in terms of policing global dangers and verifying and monitoring compliance with international agreements, but also in terms of implementing the distributive justice necessary to prevent poor countries from looking only at short-term gains. The rain forests are not only a problem for the countries in which they are found; if other developed nations are to benefit from the continued existence of the rain forests, we must be prepared to pay for that benefit. No country should be expected to bear the full brunt of environmental concerns. Classical economics does not work for ecological and environmental concerns; each unit pursuing its own interest will not enrich the biosphere, but deplete and devastate it. As E. O. Wilson put it in a recent conference on biodiversity, "The time has come to link ecology to economic and human development. . . . What is happening to the rain forests of Madagascar and Brazil will affect us all."[15] In other words, if a tree is felled in a primeval forest and there is no one else around, one should care about it anyway. . . .

Nonetheless, the situation is not hopeless. The case of the Canadian harp seal hunt dramatically illustrates that nations can be motivated by a moral concern that is actually inimical to self-interest. The European Economic Community recently banned the importation of seal products derived from the barbaric Newfoundland hunt. This was done despite the fact that at least some European nations derived economic benefit from the seal hunt and despite the fact that the European public was a major traditional consumer of seal products. This case dramatically illustrates that human consciousness is being increasingly sensitized to the suffering and interests of animals.

Cynics might argue that the seal case derives from the sentiment attached to the furry cuteness of baby seals and the jarring image of their slaughter by clubbing—big eyes and blood on the white snow. Although there is some truth in this claim, it is by no means all. Until recently, moral concern as embodied in the "humane ethic" was highly selective and favored the cute, cuddly, and familiar. Thus, for example, the Animal Welfare Act of 1966 and 1970, the only legal constraint on animal research in the United States, exempted from its very limited purview (it concerned itself only with food, caging, transport, and so on and disavowed concern with the actual content and conduct of research) rats, mice, and farm animals, in fact, 90 percent of the animals used in research. For purposes of the act, a dead dog was defined as an animal, a live mouse was not. Recently, however, things have changed. With the rise of an articulated moral concern for sentient beings by philosophers such as Peter Singer, Tom Regan, Steven Sapontzis,[16] and myself, that concern has captured the social imagination nationally and internationally. New guidelines and laws extend concern even to the more prosaic and unlovely animals, and a new amendment to the Animal Welfare Act in the United States, which I helped to draft, now mandates control of pain, suffering, and distress, which is a direct insult to the ideology of science that treated these as unknowable. Similar thrusts have occurred in other countries; in Germany, a new law bans animal research for military and cosmetic purposes, as does a new Dutch law. By the same token, many countries, such as Britain, Switzerland, and Denmark, have put constraints on confinement agriculture—"factory farming"—even though a price is paid in "efficiency" and cost to the consumer.

We sometimes forget that there is an international dimension even to animal research and factory farming. Unilateral and major constraints on such practices by one country for the sake of moral concern for animals, with other countries not making similar moves, can lead, for example, to an erosion of the legislating country's agricultural economy if the constraints make its products prohibitively more expensive and drastically reduce a market for them. But a universal constraint applicable to all countries would merely put all competitors back at the same starting gate. Public education also can convince consumers to "put their money where their morality is."

In the case of animals in science, a parallel problem arises. Multinational corporations, and even individual researchers, when unable to do a particular kind of experiment in one country will simply go to another. Given that experimenters then are shifting the suffering from one animal to another who is not different morally, this is not a just solution. Here we cannot even use the rationalization we do with humans—"Their culture makes things tolerable to them that are not tolerable to us"—because, as a Dutch colleague of mine said, "All dogs bark in the same language." Thus, scientific research must also be regulated by internationally accepted rules, else the burden of injustice is merely shifted from one innocent animal to another who happens to be living in a different place. For this reason, the European Economic Community member nations are drafting rules designed to govern all member nations, which is a step in the right direction because it would probably be impractical for companies smarting under such rules to move out of Europe altogether to less enlightened countries.

There are many areas of animal abuse where the network of interests and thus the need for rules are obviously international. There are other cases—for example, a horrendous blood sport practiced in a small country—where there are fewer international connections and implications. Nonetheless, the key to stopping all such evils is, in the final analysis, the same. It lies in a widespread philosophical extension of widespread moral notions. Thus, the philosophical basis for a system of international justice that can stop, for example, the slaughter of rhinoceroses for frivolous consumer goods such as ornamental knives and aphrodisiacs (which reduced the black rhino population from 65,000 in 1970 to 4,500 today),[17] or the killing of the snow leopard for fur, lies in the expanded moral vision of many people in diverse nations. Such expanded awareness is contagious and creates a new gestalt on animals that finds expression in legislation, boycotts, embargos, and the like. Such concern is likely to manifest first on a national level, with demands for regulation of research and mandated protection of research animals (including recent demands for housing that respects their telos); legal constraints on agricultural practices that yield efficiency at the expense of animals' suffering; restriction of frivolous and painful testing on animals, such as the LD 50 and Draize tests used in developing cosmetics and the like; tighter controls imposed over zoos, circuses, and rodeos; and so on.

But as I said, animal exploitation does not stop at national boundaries, nor does moral concern for animals. Thus, such abuses as traffic in rare birds where vast shipments of them arrive dead and dying; unregulated transport of all varieties of animals; the murder of porpoises in pursuit of tuna; the slaughter of migrating whales in the Faroe Islands as a sport and "cultural tradition," will—whether happening in any or all countries—be subjected to international pressures for regulation. These inevitably will result in tighter monitoring and restriction of such activities, which in turn will require international cooperation of the sort that is starting to develop in order to control the drug traffic.

It is perhaps not totally utopian to suggest that expanded concern for animals, a concern crossing geopolitical barriers, may lead to expanded concern for other human beings in countries not one's own, in a lovely dialectical reversal of the traditional wisdom preached by St. Thomas Aquinas and Immanuel Kant, suggesting that concern for animals is merely disguised concern for human beings.

NOTES

1. See the seminal discussion in Christopher Stone, *Should Trees Have Standing? Toward Legal Rights for Natural Objects* (Los Altos, Calif.: William Kaufmann, 1974).
2. Michael Mares, "Conservation in South America: Problems, Consequences, and Solutions." *Science* 233 (1986):734.
3. For a discussion of various ethical issues surrounding genetic engineering, see my "The Frankenstein Thing," in J.W. Evans and A. Hollaender (eds.), *Genetic Engineering of Agricultural Animals* (New York: Plenum, 1986).
4. *Science* 234 (1986): 143.
5. *Time,* November 3, 1986, p. 74.
6. *Science* 234 (1986):149.
7. Ibid.

8. Ibid.
9. Ibid.
10. Ibid., p. 150.
11. Ibid.
12. Ibid.
13. *Science* 234 (1986):813.
14. *Time*, October 13, 1986, p. 80.
15. Ibid.
16. Steven Sapontzis, *Morals, Reason, and Animals* (Philadelphia: Temple University Press, 1987).
17. *Science* 234 (1986):147.

The Green Thumb of Capitalism: The Environmental Benefits of Sustainable Growth

William K. Reilly

William K. Reilly was Administrator of the United States Environmental Protection Agency from 1989 to 1993.

Reilly represents the "good growth" position. He asserts that economic growth is not only essential but can benefit the environment through conservation, efficient resource use, renewables, and recycling. Reilly illustrates his position with examples from the developed world. He connects affluence, lower population growth, cleaner technology, and corporate accountability for pollution to the cleaner environment enjoyed in Western nations. He sees good economic growth as the solution to the developing nations' poverty, hunger, and pollution. Economic growth, he argues, leads to a reduction of poverty and stabilization of population growth, which when achieved, will lead to a reduction of environmental problems.

Murmurs of agreement rippled through the business world last year when the new chairman of Du Pont, Edgar S. Woolard, declared himself to be the company's "chief environmental officer." "Our continued existence as a leading manufacturer," he said, "requires that we excel in environmental performance."

Ed Woolard has plenty of company these days. The sight of CEOs wrapped in green, embracing concepts such as "pollution prevention" and "waste minimization," is becoming almost commonplace. Businessmen increasingly are acknowledging the value, to their profit margins and to the economy as a whole, of environmentally sound business practices—reducing emissions, preventing waste, conserving energy and resources. Government is trying to help by creating market incentives to curb pollution, by encouraging energy efficiency and waste reduction, and by developing flexible, cost-effective regulatory programs. The recognition by business leaders and government that a healthy environment and a healthy economy go together—that in fact, they reinforce each other—reflects a growing awareness throughout society of this profound reality of modern life.

Less has been said or written, however, about the other side of the coin—the environmental benefits of a prosperous, growing economy. Many environmentalists remain ambivalent—and some openly suspicious—about many forms of economic growth and development. Entire industries are viewed as unnecessary or downright illegitimate by a shifting subset of activist, although not mainstream, environmentalist opinion: offshore oil development, animal husbandry, plastics, nuclear energy, surface mining, agribusiness. These skeptics equate growth with pollution, the cavalier depletion of natural resources, the destruction of natural systems, and—more abstractly—the estrangement of humanity from its roots in nature. Studs Terkel's trenchant comment about corporate polluters—"They infect our environment and then make a good buck on the sale of disinfectants"—remains a common attitude among certain activists. At the grass-roots level, conflicts over industrial pollution, waste disposal, and new development tend to erupt with particular intensity and passion. One activist recently put it to me directly: In relation to waste incinerators, he said, "People think we're NIMBYs (Not-In-My-Backyard). But we're not. We're NOPEs (Not-On-Planet-Earth)."

The skepticism of some environmentalists toward growth is grounded in painful experience. Historically, economic expansion has led to the exploitation of natural resources with little or no concern for their renewal. At some levels of population and economic activity the damage from such practices was not readily apparent. But growing populations, demands for higher living standards, and widespread access to the necessities of modern life in economically advanced societies—and even in developing countries that provide raw materials to richer consumers—have created steadily increasing pressures on the environment. These include air and water pollution, urban congestion, the careless disposal of hazardous wastes, the destruction of wildlife, and the degradation of valuable ecosystems. Up to half of the wetlands in the lower 48 states that were here when the first European settlers arrived are gone; and the United States continues to lose 300,000 to 500,000 acres of this ecologically—and economically—productive resource to development every year. Furthermore, the byproducts of rapid industrialization have become so pervasive that they are altering the chemical composition of the planet's atmosphere, depleting stratospheric ozone and adding to atmospheric carbon dioxide.

Economic development based on unsustainable resource use cannot continue indefinitely without endangering the carrying capacity of the planet. Old growth patterns must change—and quickly—if we are to ensure the long-term integrity of the natural systems that sustain life on Earth.

GREAT EXPECTATIONS

To achieve *sustainable* growth—growth consistent with the needs and constraints of nature—we need to secure the link between environmental and economic policies at all levels of government and in all sectors of the economy. Harmonizing economic expansion with environmental protection requires a recognition that there are environmental benefits to growth, just as there are economic benefits flowing from healthy natural systems. Most environmentalists realize this, and a growing number are working creatively toward new policies that serve the long-term interests of both the environment and the economy.

How does economic growth benefit the environment?

First, growth raises expectations and creates demands for environmental improvement. As income levels and standards of living rise and people satisfy their basic needs for food, shelter, and clothing, they can afford to pay attention to the quality of their lives and the condition of their habitat. Once the present seems relatively secure, people can focus on the future.

Within our own country, demands for better environmental protection (for example, tighter controls on land development and the creation of new parks) tend to come from property owners, often affluent ones. Homeowners want to guarantee the quality of their surroundings. On the other hand, environmental issues have never ranked high on the agenda of the economically disadvantaged. Even though the urban poor typically experience environmental degradation most directly, the debate proceeds for the most part without their active participation.

The correlation between rising income and environmental concern holds as true among nations as it does among social groups. The industrialized countries with strong economies and high average standards of living tend to spend more time and resources on environmental issues, and thus to be better off environmentally. Between 1973 and 1984, when Japan emerged as a global economic power, it also took significant steps to clean up its historic legacy of pollution; and the energy and raw material used per unit of Japanese production decreased by an impressive 40 percent. In contrast, the developing nations, mired in poverty and struggling to stay one step ahead of mass starvation, have had little time and even less money to devote to environmental protection. Some of the world's worst and most intractable pollution problems are in the developing world and Eastern Europe.

Recent United Nations data analyzed by the World Resources Institute (WRI) show that the rivers with the highest levels of bacterial contamination, including urban sewage, are in Colombia, India, and Mexico. The WRI also reports consistently higher levels of sulfur dioxide and particulate air pollution in cities in Eastern Europe and the Third World than in most (although not all) of the cities of the developed world. And it is in Third World countries like Brazil, Indonesia, and Colombia that tropical rain forests are being lost at such alarming rates; while in Africa, India, and China, deserts are growing amid ever-worsening water shortages.

GROWTH LOWERS BIRTH RATES

Economic growth can mitigate these resource and environmental pressures in the developing nations in two closely related ways: by reducing poverty, and by helping to stabilize population growth. Many global environmental problems result from the activities of those supposed villains, the profit-hungry multinational corporations, than from the incremental, cumulative destruction of nature from the actions of many individuals—often the poor trying desperately to eke out a living. These actions range from the rural poor in Latin America clearing land for title, for cattle, or for subsistence farming; to gold miners, electroplaters, and small factories releasing toxic substances into the air and water; to farmers ruining fields and groundwater with excessive applications of pesticides.

In the developing nations especially, the population explosion of the past few decades (developing countries have more than doubled in population just since 1960) has greatly intensified the accumulating pressures on the environment. Even though the *rate* of increase is starting to fall in most of the Third World, population growth in countries such as Mexico, the Philippines, Kenya, Egypt, Indonesia, and Brazil has contributed and will continue to contribute to global degradation, to loss of natural resources, to poverty, and to hunger. Continued rapid population growth will cancel our environmental gains, and offset environmental investments.

One widely acceptable strategy that can make an important contribution to lowering fertility rates is education. The World Bank has drawn attention to the close correlation between education of children—specifically, bringing basic literacy to young girls—and reduction in the birthrate. Economic growth also offers hope for some relief. As countries grow economically, their fertility rates tend to decline; in most developed nations the birthrate has dropped below replacement levels, although it is creeping back up in some countries. Stable populations coupled with economic growth mean rising per capita standards of living. Education and economic development are the surest paths to stabilizing population growth.

A WALK ON THE SUPPLY SIDE

The benefits of economic growth just described—higher expectations for environmental quality in the industrialized countries, and reduced resource demands and environmental pressures related to poverty and swelling populations in the developing nations—show up on the demand side of the prosperity/progress equation. But economic expansion contributes on the supply side as well—by generating the financial resources that make environmental improvements possible.

In the United States, for example, economic prosperity has contributed to substantial progress in environmental quality. The gains this country has made in reducing air and water pollution since 1970 are measurable, they are significant, and they are indisputable. In most major categories of air pollution, emissions on a national basis have either leveled off or declined since 1970. And the improvements are even more impressive when compared with where we would be without the controls established in the early 1970s.

Air emissions of particulates went down by 63 percent between 1970 and 1988; the EPA estimates that without controls particulate emissions would be 70 percent higher than current levels. Sulfur dioxide emissions are down 27 percent; without controls, they would be 42 percent higher than they are now. Nitrogen oxide, which is up about 7 percent from 1970 levels, would have increased by 28 percent without controls. Volatile organic chemicals are down 26 percent; without controls, they would be 42 percent higher than today's levels. Carbon monoxide is down 40 percent; without controls, it would be 57 percent higher than current levels. And without controls on lead, particularly the phase-in of unleaded gasoline, lead emissions to the air would be fully 97 percent higher than they are today. Instead, atmospheric lead is down 96 percent from 1970 levels.

Similar, although more localized, gains can be cited with respect to water pollution. In the Great Lakes, thanks to municipal sewage treatment programs, fecal coliform is down, nutrients are down, algae are down, biological oxygen demand is down. Twenty years ago pollution in Lake Erie decimated commercial fishing; now Lake Erie is the largest commercial fishery in the Great Lakes. The Potomac River in Washington, D.C., was so polluted that people who came into contact with it were advised to get an inoculation for tetanus. Now on a warm day the Potomac belongs to the windsurfers.

It cost the American taxpayers, consumers, and businessmen a great deal of money to realize these gains. The direct cost of compliance with federal environmental regulations is now estimated at more than $90 billion a year—about 1.7 percent of gross national product (GNP), the highest level among western industrial nations for which data are available. Yet the United States achieved its remarkable environmental progress during a period when GNP increased by more than 70 percent.

We can learn two important lessons from the U.S. experience of the past two decades. First, our environmental commitments were compatible with economic advancement; the United States is now growing in a qualitatively better, healthier way because we made those commitments. And second, it was not just good luck that substantial environmental progress occurred during a period of economic prosperity. Our healthy economy paid for our environmental gains; economic expansion created the capital to finance superior environmental performance.

ECO-CATASTROPHE IN EASTERN EUROPE

The contrast between the U.S. experience and that of the Soviet Union and Eastern Europe over the past two decades is both stark and illuminating. While the United States prospered and made a start on cleaning up, Poland, Hungary, Romania, East Germany, Czechoslovakia, and the Soviet Union were undergoing an environmental catastrophe that will take many years and hundreds of billions of dollars to correct. In Eastern Europe, whole cities are blackened by thick dust. Chemicals make up a substantial percentage of river flows. Nearly two-thirds of the length of the Vistula, Poland's largest river, is unfit even for industrial use. The Oder River, which forms most of Poland's border with East Germany, is useless over 80 percent of its length. Parts of Poland, East Germany, and Romania are literally uninhabitable; zones of ecological disaster cover more than a quarter of Poland's land area. Millions of Soviets live in cities with dangerously polluted air. Military gas masks were issued in 1988 to thousands of Ukrainians to protect them from toxic emissions from a meat-processing plant.

The Soviet Union and its former satellites are plagued by premature deaths, high infant mortality rates, chronic lung disorders and other disabling illnesses, and worker absenteeism. The economic drain from these environmental burdens, in terms of disability benefits, health care, and lost productivity is enormous—15 percent or more of GNP, according to one Eastern European minister with whom I spoke.

The lifting of the Iron Curtain has revealed to the world that authoritarian, centrally planned societies pose much greater threats to the environment than capitalist democracies. Many environmental principles were undefendable in the absence of private property: Both the factory and the nearby farmland contaminated by its pollution were the property of the state. And the state, without elections, was not subject to popular restraints or reform. Equally important, decisions to forgo environmental controls altogether, in order to foster all-out, no-holds-barred economic development, now can be seen to have done nothing for the economy. The same policies that ravaged the environment also wrecked the economy. There is a good reason that no economic benefits have been identified from all the pollution controls these nations avoided: Healthy natural systems are a *sine qua non* for all human activity, including economic activity.

What has happened in the United States and Eastern Europe is convincing evidence that in the modern industrial world prosperity is essential for environmental progress. Sustainable economic growth can and must be the engine of environmental improvement; it must pay for the technologies of protection and cleanup.

CLEANER TECHNOLOGIES

The development of cleaner, more environmentally benign technologies clearly makes up a central element in the transition to sustainable patterns of growth. Technology, like growth, can be a mixed blessing. Technological progress has given many of the Earth's people longer, healthier lives, greater mobility, and higher living standards than most would have thought possible just a century ago. Technology has alerted us to environmental concerns such as stratospheric ozone depletion and the buildup of "greenhouse" gases in the atmosphere.

But the adverse consequences to the environment from new technology, while neither intended nor anticipated, have also been significant. Twentieth-century industrial and transportation technologies, heavily dependent on fossil fuels for their energy and on nonrenewable mineral and other resources for raw materials, have contributed substantially to today's environmental disruptions. So, too, has the widespread use of certain substances—asbestos, chlorofluorocarbons (CFCs), PCBs, a number of synthetic organic chemicals—which have proved to be hazardous to human health or the environment or both.

But if technological development has caused many of the environmental ills of the past and present, it also has a vital role to play in their cure. This "paradox of technology," as Massachusetts Institute of Technology President Paul Gray calls it, is increasingly accepted by environmentalists and technocrats alike. In fact, some environmentalists and legislators are more inclined to invest faith in technology even than are the captains of industry. Gus Speth, a co-founder of the Natural Resources Defense Council and now president of World Resources Institute, has called for a "new Industrial Revolution" in which "green" technologies are adopted that "facilitate economic growth while sharply reducing the pressures on the natural environment."

I share this enthusiasm for the promise of technology, especially after observing firsthand the truly encouraging results of bioremediation in cleaning up Alaska's Prince William Sound after the Exxon *Valdez* oil spill. When I first saw the full scale of that disaster, my initial thought was: Where are the exotic new technologies, the products of genetic engineering, that can help us clean this up? It was immediately clear that conventional oil spill response technology was overwhelmed.

Not long after the spill, EPA's research and development staff brought together 30 or so scientists to develop a program of bioremediation. This program does not involve any genetically engineered organisms—just applications of nutrients to feed and accelerate the creation of naturally occurring, oil-eating microbes.

Having been to Alaska several times to check on the progress of the cleanup, I've seen what bioremediation can do to minimize the effects of a massive crude oil spill—especially below the surface of the shoreline. Those areas of shoreline that were treated only by washing or scrubbing still have unacceptably high levels of subsurface oil contamination—much higher than the areas treated with nutrients. The success of bioremediation is, in fact, virtually the only good news to result from that tragic oil spill.

Biotechnology also has great potential for many other environmental applications. Last February, I urged biotechnology companies to give a high priority to locating and developing microorganisms that can safely and inexpensively neutralize harmful chemicals at hazardous waste sites, as well as other pollutants in the air and water.

Other technologies, such as space satellites and sensors, increasingly sophisticated environmental monitoring and modeling capabilities, will give us the information base we need to respond appropriately to global atmospheric changes. The recent international agreement to phase-out ozone-depleting CFCs before the end of this century was greatly facilitated by scientific studies of the Antarctic ozone hole and the rapid development of safe substitutes for CFCs. And continued advancements in medical technology and in our understanding of the role of environmental factors in human health will continue to enhance human life expectancy and freedom from disease.

COMMUTING BY COMPUTER

President Bush recently called attention to the environmental and social benefits of a technological advance known as "telecommuting": working from home or a neighborhood center close to home, sending messages and papers back and forth via fax or computer. By giving Americans an attractive alternative to driving, telecommuting helps reduce harmful auto emissions, from smog precursors to carbon dioxide. It also saves energy, relieves traffic congestion, and according to some studies, can even increase productivity by 20 percent or more.

As a fan of face-to-face communication, who believes also that creativity is often stimulated by the chance encounter, I must confess to a bit of skepticism about some of the virtues attributed to telecommuting. But environmentally and economically, it has incontestable appeal. And as congestion grows in many American cities, the appeal of telecommuting will also increase. Recognizing this, the federal government and several states have tried telecommuting in pilot projects; the EPA is among the federal agencies testing the concept at selected locations.

Many other environmentally beneficial technologies are changing for the better the way humans interact with the environment. Miniaturization, fiber optics, and new materials are easing the demand for natural resources. As older plants and equipment wear out, they are replaced by more efficient, less polluting capital stock. The evolution of energy will continue with clean coal technologies and with the commercialization of economically competitive, non-polluting, renewable energy technologies such as photovoltaic solar cells. New self-enclosed industrial processes will prevent toxic substances such as lead and cadmium, which are almost impossible to dispose of safely, from entering the ambient environment. The wise manufacturer is already asking new questions about products—not just how will the product be used, but how will it be disposed, and with what effects?

A RESOURCE SAVED IS A RESOURCE EARNED

Corporations such as Dow, 3M, Monsanto, Du Pont, Hewlett-Packard, Pratt & Whitney, Union Carbide, and others have curtailed emissions and saved resources through a wide variety of successful pollution-prevention techniques. Dow's Louisiana division, for example, recently designed and installed a vent recovery system to recapture hydrocarbon vapors that were being released as liquid hydrocarbons were loaded into barges. The new system recovers 98 percent of the vaporized hydrocarbons, abating hydrocarbon emissions to the atmosphere by more than 100,000 pounds a year.

As environmentalists have been pointing out for years, a pollutant is simply a resource out of place. By taking advantage of opportunities for pollution prevention, companies not only can protect the environment, they can save resources and thus enhance productivity and U.S. competitiveness in an increasingly demanding international market.

Accordingly, the EPA has made the encouragement of pollution prevention one of its leading priorities. At the same time, the administration is pursuing an innovative regulatory approach that builds on traditional command-and-control programs with economic incentives to harness the dynamics of the marketplace on behalf of the environment. By engaging the market in environmental protection, we can end the kind of signals to the economy that will encourage cleaner industrial processes and the wise stewardship of natural resources. The Department of Energy is involved as well; DOE is placing heavy emphasis on increasing energy efficiency and the commercialization of renewable energy technologies.

These governmental efforts are badly needed because the development of environmentally and economically beneficial new technology has been slowed by the high cost of capital in the United States—a direct consequence of the immense federal budget deficit. The deficit drives up interest rates, slows the pace of economic expansion, and discourages modernization and other environmentally friendly investments. While there are many reasons to bring the federal deficit under control, the need to free capital for environmental investments is certainly an important one.

Deficit spending is, unfortunately, not the only government policy inhibiting environmental improvements. A wide range of regulatory requirements and subsidies, in the United States and in many other countries, lead to market distortions that encourage inefficiencies while promoting the unsustainable use of timber, water, cropland, and other resources. The Foundation for Research on Economics and the Environment (FREE), a free-market think tank based in Seattle, Washington, and Bozeman, Montana, has done pioneering work in the field of "New Resource Economics"; FREE argues that hundreds of millions of dollars could be saved and much environmental damage avoided every year by discontinuing subsidized clear-cutting in national forests and by curtailing heavily subsidized water development projects. For similar reasons, the Reagan administration opposed development on coast barrier islands, which required heavy subsidies for bridges, flood insurance, and seawalls, and also exposed taxpayers to the costs of disaster relief when the inevitable hurricanes devastated the fragile handiwork of human beings.

ACCOUNTING FOR POLLUTION

One important step toward achieving greater harmony between economic and environmental policies would be for the government to consider seriously some long-overdue changes in the way the nation's economic health and prosperity are evaluated. As environmentalists and economists at think tanks like Resources for the Future have been pointing out for years, traditional economic accounting systems such as GNP and NNP (net national product) are poor measures of overall national well-being. They ignore or undervalue many nonmarket factors that add immeasurably to our quality of life: clean air and water, unspoiled natural landscapes, wilderness, wildlife in its natural setting. President Bush's Clean Air Act proposals for curtailing sulfur dioxide emissions, which are precursors of acid rain, will significantly improve visibility in the northeastern United States. People literally will be able to see farther. But we have not yet found a way to put a price tag on a scenic vista.

At the same time, GNP and NNP fail to discount from national income accounts the environmental costs of production and disposal, or the depletion of valuable natural capital such as lost cropland and degraded wetlands. The Exxon *Valdez* oil spill, a terrible environmental disaster, shows up as a *gain* in GNP because of all the goods and services expended in the clean-up. Without a realistic measure of national welfare, it is difficult to pursue policies that promote healthy, sustainable growth—growth that draws on the interest on stocks of renewable natural capital—in place of policies that contribute to the depletion of the capital itself.

The effort to develop a more comprehensive measure of national welfare should be just one part of an overall national strategy to achieve environmentally sound, sustainable economic growth. Such a strategy should be based on two fundamental premises:

First, economic growth confers many benefits, environmental and otherwise. Growth provides jobs, economic stability, and the opportunity for environmental and social progress. Only through economic growth can the people of the world, and especially the poor and hungry, realize their legitimate aspirations for security and economic betterment. And second, not all growth is "good" growth. What the world needs is healthy, sustainable, "green" growth: growth informed by the insights of ecology and wise natural resource management, growth guided by what President Bush refers to as an ethic of "global stewardship."

At the recent White House conference on global climate change, the president said, "Strong economies allow nations to fulfill the obligations of stewardship. An environmental stewardship is crucial to sustaining strong economies. . . . True global stewardship will be achieved . . . through more informed, more efficient, and cleaner growth."

A "GOOD GROWTH" STRATEGY

Good growth means greater emphasis on conservation, greater efficiency in resource use, and greater use of renewables and recycling. Good growth unifies environmental, social, and economic concerns, and stresses the responsibility of all individuals to sustain a healthy relationship with nature.

Good growth enhances productivity and international competitiveness and makes possible a rising standard of living for everyone, without damaging the environment. It encourages broader, more integrated, longer-term policy-making. It anticipates environmental problems rather than reacting to the crisis of the moment.

Good growth recognizes that increased production and consumption are not ends in themselves, but means to an end—the end being healthier, more secure, more humane, and more fulfilling lives for all humanity. Good growth is about more than simply refraining from inflicting harm on natural systems. It has an ethical, even spiritual dimension. Having more, using more, does not in the final scheme of things equate to being more.

Good growth can illuminate the path to a sustainable society—a society in which we fulfill our ethical obligations to be good stewards of the planet and responsible trustees of our legacy to future generations.

Traditional American Indian and Western European Attitudes Toward Nature: An Overview

J. Baird Callicott

J. Baird Callicott is a professor of philosophy and natural resources at the University of Wisconsin, Stevens Point. He is the author of Companion to a Sand County Almanac: Interpretive and Critical Essays *(1987), and* In Defense of the Land Ethic: Essays in Environmental Philosophy *(1989), and coauthor of* Clothed in Fur and Other Tales: An Introduction to an Ojibwa World View *(1982).*

Callicott attempts to bring out the parallel between Aldo Leopold's land ethic and the land ethic of the traditional American Indians. Callicott acknowledges that there is no one world view of all North American Indians, and that the different tribes have richly varied cultures. However, Callicott emphasizes that there is a unity among the tribes concerning the attitudes and beliefs of the people in relation to the environment. Reverence and respect for nature is the unifying thread Callicott traces through various tribal accounts, settler accounts, and ethnographic reports. Callicott argues that this provides a fairly reliable record of American Indian attitudes toward nature. Callicott further argues that those who deny the relevant wisdom of American Indian world views for contemporary environmental ethics are mistaken.

I

In this paper I sketch (in broadest outline) the picture of nature endemic to two very different intellectual traditions: the familiar, globally dominant Western European civilization, on the one hand, and the presently beleaguered tribal cultures of the American Indians, on the other. I argue that the world view typical of American Indian peoples has included and supported an environmental ethic, while that of Europeans has encouraged human alienation from the natural environment and an exploitative practical relationship with it. I thus represent a romantic point of view; I argue that the North American "savages" were indeed more noble than "civilized" Europeans, at least in their outlook toward nature.

I do not enter into this discussion unaware of the difficulties and limitations which present themselves at the very outset. In the first place, there is no *one* thing that can be called *the* American Indian belief system. The aboriginal peoples of the North American continent lived in environments quite different from one another and had culturally adapted to these environments in quite different ways. For each tribe there

Reprinted by permission of J. Baird Callicott and *Environmental Ethics* from *Environmental Ethics, Vol. 4,* No. 4, 1982. [Edited]

were a cycle of myths and a set of ceremonies, and from these materials one might abstract *for each* a particular view of nature. However, recognition of the diversity and variety of American Indian cultures would not obscure a complementary unity to be found among them. Despite great internal differences there were common characteristics which culturally united American Indian peoples. Joseph Epes Brown claims that

> this common binding thread is found in beliefs and attitudes held by the people in the quality of their relationships to the natural environment. All American Indian peoples possessed what has been called a metaphysic of nature; all manifest a reverence for the myriad forms and forces of the natural world specific to their immediate environment; and for all, their rich complexes of rites and ceremonies are expressed in terms which have reference to or utilize the forms of the natural world.[1]

Writing from a self-declared antiromantic perspective, Calvin Martin has more recently confirmed Brown's conjecture:

> What we are dealing with are two issues: the ideology of Indian land-use and the practical results of that ideology. Actually, there was a great diversity of ideologies, reflecting distinct cultural and ecological contexts. It is thus more than a little artificial to identify a single, monolithic ideology, as though all Native Americans were traditionally inspired by a universal ethos. Still, there were certain elements which many if not all these ideologies seemed to share, the most outstanding being a genuine respect for the welfare of other life forms.[2]

A second obvious difficulty bedeviling any discussion of American Indian views of nature is our limited ability accurately to reconstruct the abstract culture of New World peoples prior to their contact with (and influence from) Europeans. Documentary records of pre-contact Indian thought simply do not exist. American Indian metaphysics existed embedded in oral traditions. Left alone an oral culture may be very tenacious and persistent. If radically stressed, it may prove to be very fragile and liable to total extinction. Hence, *contemporary* accounts by contemporary American Indians of *traditional* American Indian philosophy are vulnerable to the charge of inauthenticity, since for several generations American Indian cultures, cultures preserved in the living memory of their members, have been both ubiquitously and violently disturbed by transplanted European civilization.

We ought, therefore, perhaps to rely where possible upon the earliest written observations of Europeans concerning American Indian belief. The accounts of the North American "savages" by sixteenth, seventeenth, and eighteenth-century Europeans, however, are invariably distorted by ethnocentrism, which to the cosmopolitan twentieth-century student appears so hopelessly abject as to be more entertaining than illuminating. The written observations of Europeans who first encountered American Indian cultures provide rather an instructive record of the implicit European metaphysic. Since Indians were not loyal to the Christian religion, it was assumed that they had to be mindfully servants of Satan, and that the spirits about which they talked and the powers which their shamans attempted to direct had to be so many demons from Hell. Concerning the Feast of the Dead among the Huron, Brebeuf wrote in 1636 that "nothing has ever better pictured for me the confusion among the damned."[3] His account, incidentally, is very informative and detailed concerning the physical requirements and artifacts of this ceremony, but the rigidity of his own system of belief makes it impossible for him to enter sympathetically that of the Huron.

Reconstructing the traditional Indian attitude toward nature is, therefore, to some extent a speculative matter. On the other hand, we must not abandon the inquiry as utterly hopeless. Post-contact American

Indians do tell of their traditions and their conceptual heritage. Among the best of these nostalgic memoirs is Neihardt's classic, *Black Elk Speaks*, one of the most important and authentic resources available for the reconstruction of an American Indian attitude toward nature. The explorers', missionaries', and fur traders' accounts of woodland Indian attitudes are also useful, despite their ethnocentrism, since we may correct for the distortion of their biases and prejudices. Using these two sorts of sources, first contact European records and transcribed personal recollections of tribal beliefs by spiritually favored Indians, plus disciplined and methodical modern ethnographic reports, we may achieve a fairly reliable reconstruction of traditional Indian attitudes toward nature. . . .

II

The late John Fire Lame Deer, a reflective Sioux Indian, comments, straight to the point, in his biographical and philosophical narrative, *Lame Deer: Seeker of Visions*, that although the whites (i.e., members of the European cultural tradition) imagine earth, rocks, water, and wind to be dead, they nevertheless "are very much alive."[4] In the previous section I tried to explain in what sense nature, as the *res extensa*, is conceived as "dead" in the mainstream of European natural thought. To say that rocks and rivers are dead is perhaps misleading since what is now dead once was alive. Rather in the usual European view of things such objects are considered inert. But what does Lame Deer mean when he says that they are "very much alive"?

He doesn't explain this provocative assertion as discursively as one might wish, but he provides examples, dozens of examples, of what he calls the "power" in various natural entities. According to Lame Deer, "Every man needs a stone. . . . You ask stones for aid to find things which are lost or missing. Stones can give warning of an enemy, of approaching misfortune."[5] Butterflies, coyotes, grasshoppers, eagles, owls, deer, especially elk and bear all talk and possess and convey power. "You have to listen to all these creatures, listen with your mind. They have secrets to tell."[6]

It would seem that for Lame Deer the "aliveness" of natural entities (including stones which to most Europeans are merely "material objects" and epitomize lifelessness) means that they have a share in the same consciousness that we human beings enjoy. Granted, animals and plants (if not stones and rivers) are recognized to be "alive" by conventional European conceptualization, but they lack awareness in a mode and degree comparable to human awareness. Among the Cartesians, even animal behavior was regarded as altogether automatic, resembling in every way the behavior of a machine. A somewhat more liberal and enlightened view allows that animals have a dim sort of consciousness, but get around largely by "instinct," a concept altogether lacking a clear definition and one very nearly as obscure as the notorious occult qualities (the "soporific virtues," and so on) of the Schoolmen. Of course, plants are regarded as, although alive, totally lacking in sentience. In any case, we hear that only human beings possess *self*-consciousness, that is, are aware that they are aware and can thus distinguish between themselves and everything else!

Every sophomore student of philosophy has learned, or should have, that solipsism is a redoubtable philosophical position, and corollary to that, that every characterization of other minds—human as well as nonhuman—is a matter of conjecture. The Indian attitude, as represented by Lame Deer, apparently was based upon the consideration that since human beings have a physical body *and* an associated consciousness (conceptually hypostatized or reified as "spirit"), all other bodily things, animals, plants, and, yes, even stones, were also similar in this respect. Indeed, this strikes me as an eminently reasonable assumption. I can no more directly perceive another human being's consciousness than I can that of an animal or plant. I *assume* that another human being is conscious since he or she is perceptibly very like me (in other respects) and I am conscious. To anyone not hopelessly prejudiced by the metaphysical *apartheid* policy of Christianity and Western thought generally, human beings closely resemble in anatomy, physiology, and behavior other forms of life. The variety of organic forms themselves are clearly closely related and the organic world, in turn, is continuous with the whole of nature. Virtually all things might be supposed, without the least strain upon credence, like ourselves, to be "alive," i.e., conscious, aware, or possessed of spirit.

Lame Deer offers a brief, but most revealing and suggestive metaphysical explanation:

> Nothing is so small and unimportant but it has a spirit given it by Wakan Tanka. Tunkan is what you might call a stone god, but he is also a part of the Great Spirit. The gods are separate beings, but they are all united in Wakan Tanka. It is hard to understand—something like the Holy Trinity. You can't explain it except by going back to the "circles within circles" idea, the spirit splitting itself up into stones, trees, tiny insects even, making them all *wakan* by his ever-presence. And in turn all these myriad of things which makes up the universe flowing back to their source, united in one Grandfather Spirit.[7]

This Lakota pantheism presents a conception of the world which is, to be sure, dualistic, but it is important to emphasize that, unlike the Pythagorean-Platonic-Cartesian tradition, it is not an *antagonistic* dualism in which body and spirit are conceived in contrary terms and pitted against one another in a moral struggle. Further, and most importantly for my subsequent remarks, the pervasiveness of spirit in nature, a spirit *in everything* which is a splinter of the Great Spirit, facilitates a perception of the human and natural realms as unified and akin.

Consider, complementary to this panpsychism, the basics of Siouan cosmogony. Black Elk rhetorically asks, "Is not the sky a father and the earth a mother, and are not all living things with feet or wings or roots their children?"[8] Accordingly, Black Elk prays, "Give me the strength to walk the soft earth, a relative to all that is!"[9] He speaks of the great natural kingdom as, simply, "green things," "the wings of the air," "the four-leggeds," and "the two-legged."[10] Not only does everything have a spirit, in the last analysis all things are related together as members of one universal family, born of one father, the sky, the Great Spirit, and one mother, the Earth herself.

More is popularly known about the Sioux metaphysical vision than about those of most other American Indian peoples. The concept of the Great Spirit and of the Earth Mother and the family-like relatedness of all creatures seems, however, to have been very nearly a universal American Indian idea, and likewise the concept of a spiritual dimension or aspect to all natural things. N. Scott Momaday remarked, "'The earth is our mother. The sky is our father.' This concept of nature, which is at the center of the Native American world view, is familiar to us all. But it may well be that we do not understand entirely what the concept is in its ethical and philosophical implications."[11] And Ruth Underhill has written that "for the old time Indian, the world did not consist of inanimate materials. . . . It was alive, and everything in it could help or harm him."[12]

Concerning the Ojibwa Indians, who speak an Algonkian language and at the time of first contact maintained only hostile relations with the Sioux, Diamond Jenness reports:

> Thus, then, the Parry Island Ojibwa interprets his own being; and exactly the same interpretation he applies to everything around him. Not only men, but animals, trees, even rocks and water are tripartite, possessing bodies, souls, and shadows. They all have a life like the life in human beings, even if they have all been gifted with different powers and attributes. Consider the animals which most closely resemble human beings; they see and hear as we do, and clearly they reason about what they observe. The tree must have a life somewhat like our own, although it lacks the power of locomotion. . . . Water runs; it too must possess life, it too must have a soul and a shadow.. Then observe how certain minerals cause the neighboring rocks to decompose and become loose and friable; evidently rocks too have power, and power means life, and life involves a soul and shadow. All things then have souls and shadows. And all things die. But their souls are reincarnated again, and what were dead return to life.[13]

Irving Hallowell has noted an especially significant consequence of the pan-spiritualism among the Ojibwa: "Not only animate properties," he writes, "but even 'person' attributes may be projected upon objects which to us clearly belong to a physical inanimate category."[14] Central to the concept of a person is the possibility of entering into social relations. Nonhuman persons may be spoken with, may be honored or insulted, may become allies or adversaries, no less than human persons.

The French fur traders and missionaries of the seventeenth century in the Great Lakes region were singularly impressed by the devotion of the savages with whom they lived to dreams. In 1648, Ragueneau speaking of the Huron, according to Kinietz, first suggested that dreams were "the language of the souls."[15] This expression lacks precision, but I think it goes very much to the core of the phenomenon. Through dreams and most dramatically through visions, one came into direct contact with the spirits of both human and nonhuman persons, as it were, naked of bodily vestments. In words somewhat reminiscent of Ragueneau's, Hallowell comments, "it is in dreams that the individual comes into direct communication with the *atiso'kanak*, the powerful 'persons' of the other-than-human class."[16] Given the animistic or pan-spiritualistic world view of the Indians, acute sensitivity and pragmatic response to dreaming makes perfectly good sense.

Dreams and waking experiences are sharply discriminated, but the theater of action disclosed in dreams and visions is continuous with and often the same as the ordinary world. In contrast to the psychologized contemporary Western view in which dreams are images of sorts (like after-images) existing only "in the mind," the American Indian while dreaming experiences reality, often the same reality as in waking experience, in another form of consciousness, as it were, by means of another sensory modality.

As one lies asleep and experiences people and other animals, places and so on, it is natural to suppose that one's spirit becomes temporarily dissociated from the body and moves about encountering other spirits. Or, as Hallowell says, "when a human being is asleep and dreaming his *otcatcakwin* (vital part, soul), which is the core of the self, may become detached from the body *(miyo)*. Viewed by another human being, a person's body may be easily located and observed in space. But his vital part may be somewhere else.[17] Dreaming indeed may be one element in the art of American Indian sorcery ("bear walking" among the Ojibwa). If the state of consciousness in dreams may be seized and controlled, and the phenomenal content of dreams volitionally directed, then the sorcerer may go where he wishes to spy upon his enemies or perhaps affect them in some malevolent way. It follows that dreams should have a higher degree of "truth" than ordinary waking experiences, since in the dream experience the person and everyone he meets is present in spirit, in essential self. This, notice, is precisely contrary to the European assumption that dreams are "false" or illusory and altogether private or subjective. E.g., in the second meditation Descartes, casting around for an example of the highest absurdity, says that it is, "as though I were to say 'I am awake now, and discern some truth; but I do not see it clearly enough; so I will set about going to sleep, so that my dreams may give me a truer and clearer picture of the fact.'" Yet this, in all seriousness, is precisely what the Indian does. The following episode from Hallowell's discussion may serve as illustration. A boy claimed that during a thunderstorm he saw a thunderbird. His elders were skeptical, since to see a thunderbird in such fashion, i.e., with the waking eye, was almost unheard of. He was believed, however, when a man who had dreamed of the thunderbird was consulted and the boy's description was "*verified!*"[18]

The Ojibwa, the Sioux, and if we may safely generalize, most American Indians, lived in a world which was peopled not only by human persons, but by persons and personalities associated with all natural phenomena. In one's practical dealings in such a world it is necessary to one's well-being and that of one's family and tribe to maintain good social relations not only with proximate human persons, one's immediate tribal neighbors, but also with the nonhuman persons abounding in the immediate environment. For example, Hallowell reports that among the Ojibwa "when bears were sought out in their dens in the spring they were addressed, asked to come out so that they could be killed, and an apology was offered to them."[19]

In characterizing the American Indian attitude toward nature with an eye to its eventual comparison to ecological attitudes and conservation values and precepts I have tried to limit the discussion to concepts so fundamental and pervasive as to be capable of generalization. In sum, I have claimed that the typical traditional American Indian attitude was to regard all features of the environment as enspirited. These entities possessed a consciousness, reason, and volition, no less intense and complete than a human being's. The Earth itself, the sky, the winds, rocks, streams, trees, insects, birds, and all other animals therefore had personalities and were thus as fully persons as other human beings. In dreams and visions the spirits of things were directly encountered and could become powerful allies to the dreamer or visionary. We may therefore say that the Indian's social circle, his community, included all the nonhuman natural entities in his locale as well as his fellow clansmen and tribesmen.

Now a most significant conceptual connection obtains in all cultures between the concept of a person, on the one hand, and certain behavioral restraints, on the other. Toward persons it is necessary, whether for genuinely ethical or purely prudential reasons, to act in a careful and circumspect manner. Among the Ojibwa, for example, according to Hallowell, "a moral distinction is drawn between the kind of conduct demanded by the primary necessities of securing a livelihood, or defending oneself against aggression, and unnecessary acts of cruelty. The moral values implied document the consistency of the principle of *mutual obligations* which is inherent in all interactions with 'persons' throughout the Ojibwa world."[20]

The implicit overall metaphysic of American Indian cultures locates human beings in a larger *social*, as well as physical, environment. People belong not only to a human community, but to a community of all nature as well. Existence in this larger society, just as existence in a family and tribal context, place people in an environment in which reciprocal responsibilities and mutual obligations are taken for granted and assumed without question or reflection. Moreover, a person's basic cosmological representations in moments of meditation or cosmic reflection place him or her in a world all parts of which are united through ties of kinship. All creatures, be they elemental, green, finned, winged, or legged, are children of one father and one mother. One blood flows through all; one spirit has divided itself and enlivened all things with a consciousness that is essentially the same. The world around, though immense and overwhelmingly diversified and complex, is bound together through bonds of kinship, mutuality, and reciprocity. It is a world in which a person might feel at home, a relative to all that is, comfortable and secure, as one feels as a child in the midst of a large family. As Brown reports:

> But very early in life the child began to realize that wisdom was all about and everywhere and that there were many things to know. There was no such thing as emptiness in the world. Even in the sky there were no vacant places. Everywhere there was life, visible and invisible, and every object gave us great interest to life. Even without human companionship one was never alone. The world teemed with life and wisdom, there was no complete solitude for the Lakota (Luther Standing Bear).[21]

III

I turn now to the claim made at the beginning of this discussion, viz., that in its practical consequences the American Indian view of nature is on the whole more productive of a cooperative symbiosis of people with their environment than is the view of nature predominant in the Western European tradition.

Respecting the latter, Ian McHarg writes that "it requires little effort to mobilize a sweeping indictment of the physical environment which is [Western] man's creation [and] it takes little more to identify the source of the value system which is the culprit."[22] According to McHarg, the culprit is "the Judeo-Christian-Humanist view which is so unknowing of nature and of man, which has bred and sustained his simple-minded anthropocentricism."[23]

Popular ecologists and environmentalists (perhaps most notably, Rachel Carson and Barry Commoner, along with McHarg and Lynn White, Jr.) have with almost loving attention recited a litany of environmental ills, spoken of "chlorinated hydrocarbons," "phosphate detergents," "nuclear tinkering," and "the gratified bulldozer" in language once reserved for detailing the precincts of Hell and abominating its seductive Prince. Given the frequency with which we are reminded of the symptoms of strain in the global biosphere and the apocalyptic rhetoric in which they are usually cast I may be excused if I omit this particular step from the present argument. Let us stipulate that modern technological civilization (European in its origins) has been neither restrained nor especially delicate in manipulating the natural world.

With somewhat more humor than other advocates of environmental reform Aldo Leopold characterized the modern Western approach to nature thus: "By and large our present problem is one of attitudes and implements. We are remodeling the Alhambra with a steam shovel, and we are proud of our yardage. We shall hardly relinquish the shovel, which after all has many good points, but we are in need of gentler and more objective criteria for its successful use."[24] So far as the historical roots of the environmental crisis are concerned, I have here suggested that the much maligned attitudes arising out of the Judeo-Christian tradition have not been so potent a force in the work of remodeling as the tradition of Western natural philosophy originating among the ancient Greeks and consolidated in modern scientific thought. At least the latter has been as formative of the cultural milieu, one artifact of which is the steam shovel itself, as the former; and together, mixed and blended, so to speak, they create a mentality in which unrestrained environmental exploitation and degradation could almost be predicted in advance.

It seems obvious (especially to philosophers and historians of ideas) that attitudes and values *do* directly "determine" behavior by setting goals (e.g., to subdue the Earth, to have dominion) and, through a conceptual representation of the world, providing means (e.g., mechanics and other applied sciences). Skepticism regarding this assumption, however, has been forthcoming. Yi-Fu Tuan says in "Discrepancies between Environmental Attitude and Behavior: Examples from Europe and China":

> We may *believe* that a world-view which puts nature in subservience to man will lead to the exploitation of nature by man; and one that regards man as simply a component in nature will entail a modest view of his rights and capabilities, and so lead to the establishment of a harmonious relationship between man and his natural environment. But is this correct?[25]

Yi-Fu Tuan thinks not. The evidence from Chinese experience which he cites, however, is ambiguous. Concerning European experience, he marshalls examples and cases in point of large scale transformations imposed, with serious ecological consequences, upon the Mediterranean environment by the Greeks and Romans. They were, of course, nominally pagans. He concludes this part of his discussion with the remark that "against this background of the vast transformations of nature in the pagan world, the inroads made in the early centuries of the Christian era were relatively modest."[26] I believe, nevertheless, that my discussion in part two of this paper has explained the environmental impact of Greek and Roman civilization consistently with the general thesis that world view substantially affects behavior! Among the Chinese before Westernization, the facts which Yi-Fu Tuan presents, indicate as many congruencies as discrepancies between the traditional Taoist and Buddhist attitude toward nature and Chinese environmental behavior.

A simple deterministic model will not suffice with respect to the question, do cultural attitudes and values really affect the collective behavior of a culture? On the one hand, it seems incredible to think that *all* our conceptualizations, our representations of the nature of nature, are, as it were, mere entertainment, sort of epiphenomena of the mind, while our actions proceed in some blind way from instinctive or genetically programmed sources. After all, our picture of nature defines our theater of action. It defines both the possibilities and limitations which circumscribe human endeavor. On the other hand, the facts of history and everyday experience do not support any simple cause and effect relationship between a given conceptual and valuational set and what people do. My own view is that it is basic to human nature to both consume and modify the natural environment. Representations of the order of nature and the proper relationship of people to that order may have either a tempering, restraining effect on manipulative and exploitative tendencies or they may have an accelerating, exacerbating effect. They also give form and direction to these inherently human drives and thus provide different cultures with their distinctive styles of doing things. It appears to me, further, that in the case of the predominant European mentality, shaped both by the Judeo-Christian and Greco-Roman images of nature and man, the effect was to accelerate the inherent human disposition to consume and modify surroundings. A kind of "take-off" or (to mix metaphors) "quantum leap" occurred, and Western European civilization was propelled for better or worse into its industrial, technological stage with a proportional increase in ecological and environmental distress. The decisive ingredient, the *sine qua non*, may have been the particulars of the European world view.

If the predominant traditional Chinese view of nature and man is, as it has been characterized by Yi-Fu Tuan, "quiescent" and "adaptive," the American Indian view of the world has been characterized as in essence "ecological," for example, by Stewart Udall, in the *Quiet Crisis*. In "First Americans, First Ecologists" Udall nostalgically invokes the memory of Thoreau and attributes to his ghost the opinion that "the Indians were, in truth, the pioneer ecologists of this country."[27] To assert without qualification that the American Indians were ecologists is, to say the least, overly bold. Ecology is a part of biology, just as organic chemistry is a part of chemistry. It is a methodic and *quantitative* study of organisms in a contextual, functional relationship to conditions of their several ranges and habitats. Udall, of course, disclaims that he means to suggest that Indians were scientists. One might prefer to say that American Indians intuitively acquired an essentially ecological "outlook," "perspective," or "habit of mind." That would be roughly to say that Indians viewed nature as a matrix of mutually dependent functional components integrated systematically into an organic whole. It would suggest a kind of global or holistic viewpoint; it would also imply an acute sensitivity to the complex factors influencing the life cycles of living things.

To attribute to American Indians, on the one hand, a highly abstract conceptual schematism and, on the other, disinterested, systematic, disciplined, and meticulous observation of minutiae is to press the romantic interpretation of American Indian thought much too far. Much of the material which I have already cited *does* indicate that both woodland and plains Indians were careful students of their natural surroundings. Knowledge of animals and their ways, particularly those of utilitarian value, and knowledge of plants, especially edible and medicinal ones, is a well-known and much respected dimension of traditional Indian cultures. The American Indian pharmacopoeia alone certainly testifies to Indian botanical acumen. My impression, nonetheless, is that the typically Indian representation of nature is more animistic and symbolic than mechanical and functional. The "rules" governing hunting and fishing seem more cast in the direction of achieving the correct etiquette toward game species than *consciously* achieving maximum sustained yield of protein "resources." Medicinal plants were sought as much for their magical, symbolic, and representational virtues as for their chemical effects. Of course, in the case of hunting and fishing, proper manners *are* behavioral restraints and, more often than not, the outcome of their being followed—of correct social forms in respect to bear, beaver, and so on, being observed—was to limit exploitation and, therefore, incidentally, to achieve sustained yield.

To suggest that the Indians were (intuitive or natural or pioneer or even primitive) ecologists, in other words, strikes me as being very much like saying that Indian healers, like Black Elk, were intuitive (etc.) physicians. Indian medicine was not at an earlier stage of development than European medicine, as if moving along the same path some distance behind. It followed a different path altogether. As Black Elk explains, "It is from understanding that power comes; and the power in the [curing] ceremony was in understanding what it meant; for nothing can live well except in a manner that is suited to the way the sacred Power of the World lives and moves."[28] The power that Black Elk employed was, *in his view*, ceremonial and symbolic—what it *meant*, not what it *did* to the patient. The cure, thus, was effected through symbolism, not biological mechanism.

The general American Indian world view (at least the one central part of it to which I have called attention) deflected the inertia of day-to-day, year-to-year, subsistence in a way that resulted, on the average, in conservation. Conservation of resources may have been, but probably was not, a *consciously* posited goal, neither a personal ideal nor a tribal policy. *Deliberate* conservation would indeed, ironically, appear to be inconsistent with the spiritual and personal attributes which the Indians regarded as belonging to nature and natural things, since these are represented by most conservationists in the predominant Pinchot tradition as only commodities, subject to scarcity, and therefore in need of prudent "development" and "management." The American Indian posture toward nature was, I suggest, neither ecological nor conservative in the modern scientific sense so much as it was moral or ethical. Animals, plants, and minerals were treated as persons, and conceived to be coequal members of a natural social order.

My cautious claim that American Indians were neither deliberate conservationists nor ecologists in the conventional sense of these terms, but manifested rather a distinctly ethical attitude toward nature and the myriad variety of natural entities is based upon the following basic points. The American Indians, on the whole, viewed the natural world as enspirited. Natural beings therefore felt, perceived, deliberated, and responded voluntarily as persons. Persons are members of a social order (i.e., part of the operational concept of a person is the capacity for social interaction). Social interaction is limited by (culturally variable) behavioral restraints, rules of conduct, which we call, in sum, good manners, morals, and ethics. The American Indians, therefore, in Aldo Leopold's turn of phrase lived in accordance with a "land ethic." This view is also maintained by Scott Momaday: "Very old in the Native American world view is the conviction that the earth is vital, that there is a spiritual dimension to it, a dimension in which man rightly exists. It follows logically that there are ethical imperatives in this matter."[29]

To point to examples of wastage—buffaloes rotting on the plains under high cliffs or beaver all but trapped-out during the fur trade—which are supposed to deliver the *coup de grace* to all romantic illusions of the American Indian's reverence for nature[30] is very much like pointing to examples of murder and war in European history and concluding therefrom that Europeans were altogether without a humanistic ethic of any sort. What is lacking is a useful understanding of the function of ethics in human affairs. Ethics bear, as philosophers point out, a normative relation to behavior; they do not describe how people actually behave, but rather set out how people ought to behave. Therefore, people are free either to act in accordance with a given ethic or not. The fact that on some occasions some do not scarcely proves that ethics are not on the whole influential and effective behavioral restraints. The familiar Christian ethic has exerted a decisive influence within European civilization; it has inspired noble and even heroic deeds both of individuals and whole societies. The documented influence of the

Christian ethic is not in the least diminished by monstrous crimes on the part of individuals. Nor do shameful episodes of national depravity, like the Spanish Inquisition, and genocide, as in Nazi Germany, refute the assertion that a humanistic ethic has palpably affected behavior among members of the European civilization and substantially shaped the character of that civilization itself. By parity of reasoning, examples of occasional destruction of nature on the pre-Columbian American continent and even the extirpation of species, especially during periods of enormous cultural stress, as in the fur trade era, do not, by themselves, refute the assertion that the American Indian lived not only by a tribal ethic but by a land ethic as well, the *overall* and *usual* effect of which was to establish a greater harmony between Indians and their environment than enjoyed by their European successors. . . .

NOTES

1. Joseph E. Brown, "Modes of Contemplation through Action: North American Indians," *Main Currents in Modern Thought* 30 (1973–74): 60.
2. Calvin Martin, *Keepers of the Game: Indian–Animal Relationships and the Fur Trade* (Berkeley and Los Angeles: University of California Press, 1978), p. 186.
3. W. Vernon Kinietz, *Indians of the Western Great Lakes, 1615–1760* (Ann Arbor: University of Michigan Press, 1965), p. 115.
4. Richard Erdoes, *Lame Deer: Seeker of Visions* (New York: Simon & Schuster, 1976), pp. 108–09.
5. Ibid., p. 101.
6. Ibid., p. 124.
7. Ibid., pp. 102–03.
8. John G. Neihardt, *Black Elk Speaks* (Lincoln: University of Nebraska Press, 1932), p. 3.
9. Ibid., p. 6.
10. Ibid., p. 7.
11. N. Scott Momaday, "A First American Views His Land," *National Geographic* 149 (1976): 14.
12. Ruth M. Underhill, *Red Man's Religion: Beliefs and Practices of the Indians North of Mexico* (Chicago: University of Chicago Press, 1965), p. 40.
13. Diamond Jenness, *The Ojibwa Indians of Parry Island, Their Social and Religious Life,* Canadian Department of Mines Bulletin no. 78, Museum of Canada Anthropological Series, no. 17 (Ottawa, 1935), pp. 20–21. The (Parry Island) Ojibwa, Jenness earlier details, divided spirit into two parts—soul and shadow—though, as Jenness admits, the distinction between the soul and shadow was far from clear and frequently confused by the people themselves.
14. A. Irving Hallowell, "Ojibwa Ontology, Behavior, and World View," *Culture in History: Essays in Honor of Paul Radin,* ed. S. Diamond (New York: Columbia University Press, 1960), p. 26.
15. Kinietz, *Indians of the Western Great Lakes,* p. 126.
16. Hallowell, "Ojibwa Ontology," p. 19.
17. Ibid., p. 41.
18. Ibid., p. 32.
19. Ibid., p. 35.
20. Ibid., p. 47 (emphasis added).
21. Brown, "Modes of Contemplation," p. 64.
22. Ian McHarg, "Values, Process, Form," from *The Fitness of Man's Environment* (Washington, D.C.: Smithsonian Institution Press, 1968) reprinted in Robert Disch, ed., *The Ecological Conscience* (Englewood Cliffs: Prentice-Hall, 1970), p. 25.
23. Ibid., p. 98.
24. Leopold, *Sand County Almanac,* pp. 225–26.
25. Yi-Fu Tuan, "Discrepancies between Environmental Attitude and Behavior," in *Ecology and Religion in History,* eds. Spring and Spring (New York: Harper and Row, 1974), p. 92.
26. Ibid., p. 98.
27. Stewart Udall, "First Americans, First Ecologists," *Look to the Mountain Top* (San Jose: Gousha Publications, 1972), p. 2.
28. Neihardt, *Black Elk Speaks,* p. 212.
29. Momaday, "First American Views," p. 18.
30. The most scurrilous example of this sort of argument with which I am acquainted is Daniel A. Guthre's "Primitive Man's Relationship to Nature," *BioScience* 21 (July 1971) : 721–23. In addition to rotting buffalo, Guthrie cites alleged extirpation of pleistocene megafauna by Paleo-Indians, c. 10,000 B. P. (as if that were relevant), and his cheapest shot of all, "the litter of bottles and junked cars to be found on Indian reservations today."

On the Environmental Ethics of the *Tao* and the *Ch'i*

Chung-ying Cheng

Chung-ying Cheng is a professor of philosophy at the University of Hawaii at Manoa, Hawaii. Cheng is the author of numerous articles and books on Chinese philosophy. He founded and edits Philosophical Review *and* The Journal of Chinese Philosophy, *and is editor of* Chinese Studies in Philosophy.

Cheng writes about how the Tao is applicable to our ecological understanding of the environment. Cheng states that the Tao is important to human well-being and complete ecological harmony with nature. The application of the Tao in this manner, he asserts, is important to both philosophers of the Tao and environmentalists. Cheng presents the ecological principle of nature, *from which comes the most important point about nature in the Tao: that the Tao does not impose itself on things, and stresses universal harmony, yet remains aware that there is constant flux and transformation. Cheng states that without an understanding of the Tao, the combination of technology and greed, among other things, will doom humans to self-slavery and eventual self-destruction.*

METHODOLOGICAL CONSIDERATIONS

Although environmental ethics is one of the applied ethics arising from contemporary interest in applying and exploring certain ethical concepts and positions in relation to a set of concrete situations which human persons confront in their life world,[1] a close reflection on this applied ethics leads to a metaphysical critique of certain basic ethical positions concerning relationships of human beings to nature, to other human beings, and to themselves. The fact is that ethics cannot be applied until we have a clear understanding of the underlying concepts of the human person and his/her end-values as well as a clear understanding of the objects or situations to which the applications pertain. Both understandings require a disclosure of presupposed reality and, therefore, a resolution on the order or scheme of things in which human persons find themselves.

Methodologically speaking, we could treat problems of applied ethics at three levels: the metaethical level, where meanings of ethical terms are clarified; the metaphysical level, where the fundamental premises of the nature of reality are examined; and finally,

Reprinted with permission of Chung-ying Cheng and *Environmental Ethics*, from *Environmental Ethics, Vol. 8,* No. 4, 1986. [Edited]

the normative level, where ethical norms of actions and attitudes are formulated. Environmental ethics apparently cannot be clearly understood until we come to grips with these three levels of understanding. This approach is particularly appropriate in consideration of the fact that environmental ethics is not a well-formed system of ethical concepts, and that no system of norms for this ethical concern has been fully formulated and agreed upon. The openness of this field is a feature not to be deplored, but to be commended, because inquiry into identifying its problems, not even to say resolving its problems, is a worthy methodological and metaphysical exercise and will be rewarding in terms of possible creative insights, not only into environmental-ethical issues, but also into a deeper foundation for ethics in general. We may indeed consider the three levels of understanding mentioned above as pertaining to the analytics of ethics, the teleology of ethics, and the deontology of ethics. In dealing with environmental ethics we must be concerned with its analytical, its teleological, as well as its deontological dimensions.[2]

ANALYTICAL CONSIDERATIONS

One central question for environmental ethics which must be raised before any other questions is what the term *environment* means or stands for. *Environment* is derived from *environs*, meaning "in circuit" or "turning around in" in Old French.[3] It is apparently a prepositional word, indicating an external relation without a context, also certainly devoid of a relationship of organic interdependence. Yet when we reflect on the experience of environment, we encounter many different things and different processes in the context of organic interdependence. We might say what we experience presupposes the existence of life and the living processes of many forms. This experience of environment is better expressed by the Chinese philosophical paradigm, *sheng-sheng-pu-yi* ("incessant activity of life creativity").[4] We must, therefore, make a distinction between a surface meaning and a depth meaning for environment. Without understanding life and the living process of life, we cannot understand the depth meaning of environment. On the other hand, without understanding the constituents and conditions of life, we cannot understand life and the living process of life. Hence, the very essence of environment requires an understanding of reality and the true identity of life in both its state and process aspects. This means we have to understand the *Tao* content and the *Tao* process in the environment, whereas Tao indicates the way of life-creativity in ceaseless movements and in a multitude of forms.

With the above analysis of the meaning of environment, it is clear that the essential depth meaning of environment was lost in modern man's conception of environment. The modern man's conception of environment is founded on the surface meaning of environment, which is typified by technology and science; with its underlying philosophy of modernday materialism. Cartesian dualism, and mechanistic naturalism, the concept of environment of modern man was very much objectified, mechanized, rigidified, dehumanized, and possibly even de-enlivened, and so de-environmentalized.[5] Environment is no longer an environment at all; environment becomes simply "the surroundings," the physical periphery, the material conditions and the transient circumstances. The environment is conceived as a passive deadwood, and very often as only visible and tangible externalia. In fact, as the depth meaning of environment suggested above, environment is active life; it is not necessarily visible or tangible, and certainly it cannot be simply a matter of externality. Hence, it cannot be treated as an object, the material conditions, a machine tool, or a transient feature. Environment is more than the visible, more than the tangible, more than the external, more than a matter of quantified period of time or a spread of space. It has a deep structure as well as a deep process, as the concept of *Tao* indicates.

The distinction between the surface meaning and the depth meaning of environment also suggests a distinction between the Western and the Chinese approach to environment. Whereas the West focuses on the external relation of man to his surroundings based upon a qualitative separation and confrontation between the human and nonhuman worlds, the Chinese focus on the internal relation of man to his surroundings based upon an integrative interdependence and a harmony between man and the world. For modern Western man after Descartes, the nonhuman world is to be rationally studied, researched, and then scientifically manipulated and exploited for the maximum utility of serving man. This will to conquer and dominate nature is, of course, premised on the externality of nature to man, but there are two other rational principles or assumptions involved in exercising this will to conquer and dominate.

First, it is assumed that nature is a completed work of mechanical forces with one-dimensional natural laws controlling its workings. The one-dimensional natural laws are revealed in the physical sciences and the reductionistic methodology of physicalism. Hence, biological laws are very often reduced to laws of physics and chemistry; no other laws are permitted to stand on their own. Yet the relationship between various forms of life in the totality of nature cannot be said to be fully captured by physicalistic laws; nor can the relationship between man and the world of things be said to be regulated by these laws. The very fact of the breakdown of the environment in industrialized societies, as reflected, for example, in the problems of water-air-noise pollution, precisely points to the lack of understanding of the relationship between various forms of life and man and his environment by way of modern science and technology.

There is a second assumption of the modern mechanical sciences: everything in the world forms an entity on its own as a closed system, and therefore can be individually and separately dealt with. This isolationist and atomistic assumption in the problem-solving methodology of modern science is strongly reflected in Western medical diagnostics and treatments. It was not until recent times that modern medical and health care researchers became aware of the potential limitations of this isolationist and atomistic approach, and became awakened to a holistic approach.

In contrast with the Western externalistic point of view on environment, the Chinese tradition, as represented by both Confucianism (with the *I Ching* as its metaphysical philosophy) and Taoism (with Chuang Tzu and Lao Tzu as its content), has developed an internalistic point of view on the environment. The internalistic point of view on the environment in Chinese philosophy focuses on man as the *consummator* of nature rather than man as the conqueror of nature, as a participant in nature rather than as a predator of nature. Man as the consummator of nature expresses continuously the beauty, truth, and goodness of nature; and articulates them in a moral or a natural cultivation of human life or human nature. This is paradigmatically well expressed in Confucius' saying, "Man can enlarge the Way *(Tao)* rather than the Way enlarging man."[6] It is also expressed in Chuang Tzu's saying, "The *Tao* penetrates and forms a Unity."[7] As part and parcel of nature, man does not stand opposite nature in a hostile way. On the contrary, man has profound concern and care for nature at large, as befitting his own nature. For his own growth and well-being, man has to cultivate the internal link in him between himself and Mother Nature. To conquer nature and exploit it is a form of self-destruction and self-abasement for man. The material consequence of the conquest and exploitation must be forestalled by an awakening to what man really is or in what his nature really consists.

In contrast with the two Western assumptions about the environment, Chinese philosophy clearly asserts that nature, and therefore man's environment, is not a complete work of production by a transcendent God, but rather is a process of continuous production and reproduction of life. In Bruno's words, nature is *Natura naturans,* not merely *Natura naturata*. In other words, nature is an organism of continuous growth and decay, but never devoid of internal life. With this understanding men cannot treat nature as an isolated and atomic part without regard for the totality involving a past and a future. This leads to the second understanding contrary to the Western methodology of atomism: man has to interact with nature in a totalistic manner, realizing that there is no single linear chain of causality. There is always a many-to-many relationship between cause and effect. Hence, man has to consider a many-to-many level approach to relate the potential needs of man to nature. Man has to naturalize man as well as to humanize nature, treating nature as his equal and as a member within the family of the *Tao*. This approach to nature is reflected in the holistic approach of Chinese medicine in both its diagnostic and medical/health care aspects.

The modern mandarin translation for *environment* is *huan-chin*, meaning "world of surroundings." This translation apparently reflects the surface meaning of *environment* correctly. But when embedded in the contexts of Chinese philosophy and Chinese cultural consciousness the "world of surroundings" does not simply denote individual things as entities in a microscopic structure: it also connotes a many-layered reality such as heaven and earth in a macroscopic enfoldment. This "world of surroundings" is generally conceived as something not static but dynamic, something not simply visible but invisible. It is in this sense of environment that we can speak of the *Tao* as the true environment of man: the true environment of man is also the true environment of nature or everything else in nature.

When asked about the presence of the *Tao*, Chuang Tzu had this to say: "(The *Tao* is) nowhere not present." Pressed as to where exactly the *Tao* lies. Chuang Tzu replied that the *Tao* is in the ants, in the weeds, in the ruins, and in the dungs.[8] The import of Chuang Tzu's message is that the *Tao* embraces everything, large or small, in the universe and imparts a unity of relationships in our environment, and that the *Tao* is a totality as well as a part of the totality pervading everything beyond our perception so that we cannot ignore what is hidden in our understanding of the environment. If understanding is the basis for action, this understanding of the environment in terms of the *Tao* is very essential for formulating an ethic of the environment, namely for articulating what human persons should do or attitudinize toward their world of surroundings. Two more observations have to be made in order to explicate the philosophy of the *Tao* for the purpose of the formulating an environmental ethics of the *Tao* or an ethics of the environment based on an understanding of the *Tao*.

The first observation concerns the *Tao* as the *tzu-jan*. *Tzu-jan* means "doing-something-on-its-own-accord," or natural spontaneity. In the *Tao Te Ching* it is said that "Man follows earth; earth follows heaven; heaven follows the *Tao* and the *Tao* follows *tzu-jan*."[9] But *tzu-jan* is not something beyond and above the *Tao*. It is the movement of the *Tao* as the *Tao*, namely as the underlying unity of all things as well as the underlying source of the life of all things. One important aspect of *tzu-jan* is that the movement of things must come from the *internal life* of things and never results from engineering or conditioning by an external power. That is why the life-creativity nature of the *Tao* is the only proper way of describing the nature of the movement of the *Tao*. However, to say this is not to say that only the *Tao* can have the movement of *tzu-jan*. In fact, all things can follow *tzu-jan* insofar as they follow the *Tao*, or in other words, act and move in the manner of the Tao and in unison and in accordance with the *Tao*. Perhaps a better way of expressing this is: things will move of their own accord (*tzu-jan*) insofar as they move by way of the *Tao* and the *Tao* moves by way of them. One has to distinguish between, on the one hand, *Tao*-oriented or *Tao*-founded movement and, on the other hand, thing-oriented or thing-founded movement. Only when the movement of a thing comes from the deep source of the thing—the *Tao* and its harmony with the totality of the movements of all other things—will the movement of things be genuinely of its own accord and, therefore, be spontaneous. Spontaneity (*tzu-jan*) is a matter of infinite depth and infinite breadth in an onto-cosmological sense.

One can, of course, speak of different degrees of *tzu-jan* in view of the different degrees of depth and breadth in harmonious relating and self-assertion among things. Just as things have their own histories and defining characteristics in form and substance, things also have their relative freedom of self-movement and life-creativity. Things, in fact, can be considered as conditions or preconditions of various forms of *tzu-jan* (spontaneity): insofar as things preserve their identity without destroying the identities of other things, and insofar as things change and transform without interfering with the process of change and transformation of other things, there is *tzu-jan*. This explains the mutual movement, rise and decline, ebb and flow, in things of nature.

For human beings, *tzu-jan* finds its rationale not only in the internal movement and life-creativity of human activity, but in the principle of least effort with maximum effect. Whatever produces maximum effect by minimum effort in human activity manifests natural spontaneity. One may, therefore, suggest that only in following natural spontaneity is there least effort and maximum effect. This can be called the *ecological principle of nature*.[10] Using this principle we can correctly interpret the most important point ever made about the nature of the *Tao*: "The *Tao* constantly does nothing and yet everything is being done" *(Tao-chang-wu-wei erh wu-pu-wei)*.[11] That the *Tao* constantly does nothing means that the *Tao* does not impose itself on things: the *Tao* only moves of its own accord. This also means that all things come into being on their own accord. The constant nonaction of the *Tao* is the ultimate cosmological principle of life-creativity and the only foundation for the evolution of the variety of life and the multitude of things. The nonaction of the *Tao* in this sense is an intrinsic principle of ultimate creativity; this intrinsic principle of ultimate creativity consists in an unlimitedness and an unlimitation of expression of life forms and life processes in a state of universal harmony and in a process of universal transformation.[12] In this ultimate sense of creativity, there is no effort made by the *Tao*, and yet there is an infinite effect, achieving life-creativity. The ecological principle reaches its ultimate limit in the principle of *chang-wu-wei*. Hence, we can conceive of the principle of least effort with maximum effect as an approximation to the *tzu-jan* of the *Tao* on the human plane.

With this principle correctly understood, we can resolve the dilemma and predicament arising from civilization and knowledge. The Taoist questions the value of knowledge and civilization, since they lead to greed, lust, and evil (tricks and treachery) in human society. In the same spirit, we can question the value of science and technology. In resolving many problems of man, do science and technology create more problems for man? Do science and technology seem to lead man to a purely pessimistic future? The Taoistic criticism here is that without an understanding of the *Tao* it is indeed possible and necessary that knowledge and civilization, science and technology, will doom man to self-slavery and self-destruction. Man simply falls into the bondage of his own conceptual prison and becomes a victim of his own desires. The Taoistic criticism of *wu-wei* is supposed to awaken man to self-examination and self-doubt; in this way man is awakened to a quest for self-surpassing and self-overcoming in an understanding of the totality of reality and its secret of creativity through *wu-wei* and reversion (*fan*).[13] With this awakening, man can still proceed with his knowledge and civilization, science and technology, if he is able to neutralize and temper his intellectual and intellectualistic efforts with a sense of the *Tao*. This means that man has to develop knowledge and civilization, science and technology, not out of pace with his efforts to relate to things, other humans and himself. His knowledge and civilization, science and technology, have to contribute to his relating to and integrating with the world of his surroundings. To do this he has to keep pace with his own growth as a sentient moral being, having regard and respect for his own identity and dignity as well as the identity and dignity of other beings, including his fellow man. Furthermore, he has to use his knowledge and, hence, science and technology, in keeping with the order of things, with his best interests conceived and deferred in harmony with life and in preservation or promotion of universal creativity. He also has to closely follow the principle of least effort, if not the principle of no effort, with maximum effect, if not infinite effect in terms of life and creativity—preservation and promotion—for his intellectual/scientific/technological/organizational activities.

As man is part and parcel of the *Tao*, it is only when man loses the sense of the *Tao* and respect for the *Tao* in his actual life that man becomes alienated from the *Tao* and his activities become a means of self-alienation which will inevitably result in losing the true identity of man by way of self-destruction. This is the natural and spontaneous reaction of the *Tao* to the self-alienation of man in his intellectual/scientific/exploitative en-grossment and obsession with himself. Hence, the remedy for knowledge and civilization, or for science and technology, is not more knowledge and more civilization, or more science and more technology, but a constant relating and integrating of these with the *Tao*. To do so is to naturalize as well as humanize knowledge and civilization, science and technology. It is to make these a part of the *Tao*. Although knowledge and civilization, science and technology, are man's forms for the appropriation of nature (the *Tao*), these forms should not remain apart: man should also let nature reappropriate them by integrating them into nature (the *Tao*). This is the essential point of an ethics of man's relation to the environment. To understand the *Tao* and to follow the *Tao* is the essence of the ethics of the environment; it is also the way to transform the artificiality and unnaturalness of knowledge and civilization, science and technology, into the spontaneity and naturalness of the *Tao*.

In light of this understanding, the conflict between the *Tao* and knowledge/civilization/science/technology can be resolved; the true ecology and life-creativity of nature can be restored with knowledge/civilization/science/technology. They can be seen as enhancing rather than obstructing, complementing rather than opposing, the actual spontaneity and harmony of the creativity of the *Tao*. This is the true wisdom of the Taoist critique of knowledge and civilization, science and technology. It is called *hsi-ming*, "hidden light," by Lao Tzu, and *liang-hsing*, "parallel understanding," by Chuang Tzu.[14] In this wisdom lies the most profound principle of both the ecology of nature and the ethics of the environment.

My second observation concerns the *Tao* as a process of the ramification and differentiation of the *ch'i*. Before I explain the meaning and reality of *ch'i* in Chinese philosophy, it is important to appreciate the significance of bringing in *ch'i* as an explanation of the depth structure and depth process of the environment. We have seen that the depth structure and depth process of the environment has been explained in terms of the *Tao* and its life-creativity (*sheng-sheng*). Even though this explanation is necessary in pinpointing the ontological being and becoming of the environment, it is not sufficient, on the one hand, to illuminate the dynamics and dialectics of the differentiation and ramifications of the *Tao* and, on the other hand, to manifest those dynamics and dialectics of the unification and integration of the *Tao*. In other words, there is a gap between the ontology of the *Tao* and the cosmology of the *Tao* which must be bridged.

It is when the *Tao* is seen in the form and activity of *ch'i* that this bridging takes place. It might be suggested that the *Tao* expresses itself in terms of three perspectives which result in three characterizations in the history of Chinese philosophy. The first perspective is derived from understanding the quality of the activity: it is the perspective of life-creativity as clearly formulated in the texts of the *I Ching*. This perspective has already been discussed above. The second perspective is derived from understanding the patterns of the activity: it is the perspective of the movement of internal spontaneity, reversion and return, as clearly formulated in the texts of the *Tao Te Ching* as well as those of the *Chuang Tzu*. In fact, a concentration on the patterns of the movement of the *Tao* may lead one to see the *Tao* in terms of principles and reasons. The Neo-Confucianist metaphysics of *li* ("principle") is a logical result of this development. This development also leads to an epistemology of the *Tao*. In both the ontology of the *Tao* (life-creativity) and epistemology of the *Tao* (principles of nonaction, etc.), the *Tao* is always conceived as a totality and a unity; the nature of the unity and totality of the *Tao* is stressed above all. In fact, the very concept of the *Tao* carries with it a reference to its unity and totality. Yet the *Tao* is as much a distribution and diversification of being and becoming as a unity and totality of being and becoming. Hence, we need another explanation of this former aspect of the *Tao* which will also serve the purpose of cosmologizing the ontology and epistemology of the *Tao*. This is how the *Tao*-as-the-*ch'i* paradigm comes in. This is also how the concept of *ch'i* based on experience of the *Tao* as *ch'i* develops. We might therefore suggest that to understand environment in its depth meaning, one has to focus on both the totalistic and distributive aspects of the environment. Hence, one must focus on both the *Tao* as *tzu-jan* and the *Tao* as *ch'i*.

Another consideration with regard to the importance of the *Tao* as the *ch'i* is that whereas the *Tao* focuses on reality as a passage of dynamic processes, the *ch'i* focuses on reality as a presence of material—stuff which leads to an actualization of things and the concretization of events. Hence, for understanding the formation and transformation of the environment in its substantive structure, one has to understand *ch'i.* It is in understanding *ch'i* that one can see and grasp the subtleties of the environment *vis-à-vis* human beings. It is only on this basis (i.e., understanding the *Tao* as *ch'i*) that one is capable of formulating an ethics of the environment or an ethics of the *Tao* toward the environment.[15] For this reason, we may consider the discussion of the nature of *ch'i* as constituting a metaphysical inquiry into the depth structure and depth process of the environment. As the goal of an ethics of the environment is to understand how human beings should relate to the environment *via* a true understanding of environment, we may see how a metaphysical inquiry into the structure and process of the environment also constitutes a teleological inquiry into the nature of the environment in relation to man. It is only when we are able to understand the nature of the environment in its true identity that we are able to see what the end-values of our thinking about and acting toward the environment are. The end-values are provided by our understanding of reality: to act in accordance with reality and our true nature will be our end and ultimately will be the criterion of value. . . .

NOTES

1. J. Baird Callicott has traced the beginning of the origin of environmental ethics in some of his papers. See "Conceptual Resources for Environmental Ethics in Asian Traditions of Thought: A Propaedeutic," *Philosophy East and West* 37, no 2 (1987) and "The Metaphysical Implications of Ecology," *Environmental Ethics*, this issue.
2. By *teleology* I actually mean the study of the metaphysics or ontology of ends or values for a given ethical concern. Therefore, the teleologial corresponds to the metaphysical level of consideration. Similarly the analytical corresponds to the metaethical level of consideration, whereas the deontological corresponds to the normative level of consideration.
3. Cf. Ernest Weekley, *An Etymological Dictionary of Modern English* (New York: Dover, 1967), p. 516 (*environ*), p. 1583 (*veer*).
4. *Sheng-sheng* is derived from the Great Appendix of the *I Ching,* sec. 5, where it is said that *"Sheng-sheng* is called the change." "*Pu-yi"* is derived from the *Book of Poetry* in "Chou Sung," where it is said that "The mandate of Heaven is indeed profound and incessant (*pu-yi*)." This stanza is quoted in *Chung Yung* to describe the depth and width of the reality of Heaven and Earth. It is quite clear that the incessant activity of life-creativity is precisely what the *Tao* is. As a life-experience based concept of reality, *Tao* was universally conceived by ancient philosophers as a universal process of change and transformation as well as the fountainhead of all forms of life in the world. Therefore, *Tao* can be said to be the in-depth foundation, background, and context of the so-called environment for any sentient being. We shall see a more metaphysical consideration of the *Tao* in the writings of Lao Tzu.
5. When I use the word *objectified,* I mean "being treated as an object"; when I use the word *mechanized,* I mean "being used merely as a machine"; when I use the word *rigidified,* I mean "being placed in the state of *rigor mortis*"; and when I use the word *de-enlivened,* I mean "being depleted of life and the living process"; when I use the word *dehumanized,* I mean "being given no consideration of human feeling and care"; finally, when I use the word *de-environmentalized,* I mean "being devalued as environment."
6. *Analects,* 15: 28.
7. *Chuang Tzu,* Chi Wu Lun.
8. See the Chih Pei Yu chapter of *Chuang Tzu.*
9. *Tao Te Ching,* 25.
10. *Ecology* originally meant the economy of nature; when nature acts, it acts ecologically. The production of life and all things in nature can be said to come from the ecological movement of nature. In understanding the ecology of nature, one would naturally understand the *Tao*; but only when one independently sees the universality, unity, and life-creativity of the *Tao,* will one truly understand the ecology of nature. Hence, the *Tao* can be said to be the metaphysical foundation of the ecology of nature, whereas the ecology of nature is one principle of movement manifesting the *Tao,* corresponding to its spontaneity.
11. Cf. *Tao Te Ching,* 37.
12. This principle can be indeed expressed as the following equivalence: *cheng-wu-wei* = *tzu-jan* = *sheng-sheng* = *wu-pu-wei,* i.e., the constant self-

restraining of externality = spontaneity = life-creativity = the natural harmony of all things.

13. *Jan* ("reversion") refers to the fact that the *Tao* reverses what is done against the nature of things. But *jan* is also *fu* ("return"). If things are done according to their nature and of their own accord, things will return to their origin and their identity will be recurrently assured. See the distinction in the context of the *Tao Te Ching*, 40. "Reversion is the movement of the *Tao*," 25, The distant is the reversion," and 16. "All ten thousand things take place concurrently. I observe their recurrence (*fu*) (*via* their origin)."
14. Cf. *Tao Te Ching*, 2; *Chuang Tzu*, Chi W'u Lun.
15. *Tao Te Ching*, 14.

The Power and the Promise of Ecological Feminism

Karen J. Warren

Karen J. Warren is a professor of philosophy at Macalester College in St. Paul, Minnesota. Warren is coauthoring a book entitled Ecological Feminism: What It Is and Why It Matters. *She edited a special issue of the journal* Hypatia *on ecological feminism.*

Ecological feminism asserts that there are important historical, theoretical, and symbolic connections between the control and domination of nonhuman nature and of women. Warren maintains that the conceptual connections between the domination of women and of nature are based in the conceptual framework of patriarchal oppression that operates on a logic of domination. She argues that the word "feminist" clarifies how the domination of nature is conceptually linked to patriarchy. Thus, ending the domination of nature requires ending patriarchy. Warren expands the feminist framework to include ecological feminism, which provides for a uniquely feminist environmental ethic. Warren concludes that any environmental ethic or feminist theory that does not take these connections into account is inadequate.

INTRODUCTION

Ecological feminism (ecofeminism) has begun to receive a fair amount of attention lately as an alternative feminism and environmental ethic.[1] Since Francoise d'Eaubonne introduced the term *ecofeminisme* in 1974 to bring attention to women's potential for bringing about an ecological revolution,[2] the term has been used in a variety of ways. As I use the term in this paper, ecological feminism is the position that there are important connections—historical, experiential, symbolic, theoretical—between the domination of women and the domination of nature, an understanding of which is crucial to both feminism and environmental ethics. I argue that the promise and power of ecological feminism is that *it provides a distinctive framework both for reconceiving feminism and for developing an environmental ethic which takes seriously connections between the domination of women and the domination of nature.* I do so by discussing the nature of a feminist ethic and the ways in which ecofeminism provides a feminist and environmental ethic. I conclude that any feminist theory *and* any environmental ethic which fails to take seriously the twin and interconnected dominations of women and nature is at best incomplete and at worst simply inadequate.

Reprinted with permission of Karen J. Warren and *Environmental Ethics,* from *Environmental Ethics, Vol. 12,* No. 2, 1990. [Edited]

FEMINISM, ECOLOGICAL FEMINISM, AND CONCEPTUAL FRAMEWORKS

Whatever else it is, feminism is at least the movement to end sexist oppression. It involves the elimination of any and all factors that contribute to the continued and systematic domination or subordination of women. While feminists disagree about the nature of and solutions to the subordination of women, all feminists agree that sexist oppression exists, is wrong, and must be abolished.

A "feminist issue" is any issue that contributes in some way to understanding the oppression of women. Equal rights, comparable pay for comparable work, and food production are feminist issues wherever and whenever an understanding of them contributes to an understanding of the continued exploitation or subjugation of women. Carrying water and searching for firewood are feminist issues wherever and whenever women's primary responsibility for these tasks contributes to their lack of full participation in decision making, income producing, or high status positions engaged in by men. What counts as a feminist issue, then, depends largely on context, particularly the historical and material conditions of women's lives.

Environmental degradation and exploitation are feminist issues because an understanding of them contributes to an understanding of the oppression of women. In India, for example, both deforestation and reforestation through the introduction of a monoculture species tree (e.g., eucalyptus) intended for commercial production are feminist issues because the loss of indigenous forests and multiple species of trees has drastically affected rural Indian women's ability to maintain a subsistence household. Indigenous forests provide a variety of trees for food, fuel, fodder, household utensils, dyes, medicines, and income-generating uses, while monoculture-species forests do not.[3] Although I do not argue for this claim here, a look at the global impact of environmental degradation on women's lives suggests important respects in which environmental degradation is a feminist issue.

Feminist philosophers claim that some of the most important feminist issues are *conceptual* ones: these issues concern how one conceptualizes such mainstay philosophical notions as reason and rationality, ethics, and what it is to be human. Ecofeminists extend this feminist philosophical concern to nature. They argue that, ultimately, some of the most important connections between the domination of women and the domination of nature are conceptual. To see this, consider the nature of conceptual frameworks.

A *conceptual framework* is a set of *basic* beliefs, values, attitudes, and assumptions which shape and reflect how one views oneself and one's world. It is a socially constructed lens through which we perceive ourselves and others. It is affected by such factors as gender, race, class, age, affectional orientation, nationality, and religious background.

Some conceptual frameworks are oppressive. An *oppressive conceptual framework* is one that explains, justifies, and maintains relationships of domination and subordination. When an oppressive conceptual framework is *patriarchal,* it explains, justifies, and maintains the subordination of women by men.

I have argued elsewhere that there are three significant features of oppressive conceptual frameworks: (1) value-hierarchical thinking, i.e., "up-down" thinking which places higher value, status, or prestige on what is "up" rather than on what is "down"; (2) value dualisms, i.e., disjunctive pairs in which the disjuncts are seen as oppositional (rather than as complementary) and exclusive (rather than as inclusive), and which place higher value (status, prestige) on one disjunct rather than the other (e.g., dualisms which give higher value or status to that which has historically been identified as "mind," "reason," and "male" than to that which has historically been identified as "body," "emotion," and "female"); and (3) logic of domination, i.e., a structure of argumentation which leads to a justification of subordination.[4]

The third feature of oppressive conceptual frameworks is the most significant. A logic of domination is not *just* a logical structure. It also involves a substantive value system, since an ethical premise is needed to permit or sanction the "just" subordination of that which is subordinate. This justification typically is given on grounds of some alleged characteristic (e.g., rationality) which the dominant (e.g., men) have and the subordinate (e.g., women) lack.

Contrary to what many feminists and ecofeminists have said or suggested, there may be nothing *inherently* problematic about "hierarchical thinking" or even "value-hierarchical thinking" in contexts other than contexts of oppression. Hierarchical thinking is important in daily living for classifying data, comparing information, and organizing material. Taxonomies (e.g., plant taxonomies) and biological nomenclatures seem to require *some* form of "hierarchical thinking." Even "value-hierarchical thinking" may be quite acceptable in certain contexts. (The same may be said of "value dualisms" in non-oppressive contexts.) For example, suppose it is true that what is unique about humans is our conscious capacity to radically reshape our social environments (or "societies"), as Murray Bookchin suggests.[5] Then one could truthfully say that humans are better equipped to radically reshape their environments than are rocks or plants—a "value-hierarchical" way of speaking.

The problem is not simply *that* value-hierarchical thinking and value dualisms are used, but *the way* in which each has been used *in oppressive conceptual frameworks* to establish inferiority and to justify subordination.[6] It is the logic of domination, *coupled with* value-hierarchical thinking and value dualisms, which "justifies" subordination. What is explanatorily basic, then, about the nature of oppressive conceptual frameworks is the logic of domination.

For ecofeminism, that a logic of domination is explanatorily basic is important for at least three reasons. First, without a logic of domination, a description of similarities and differences would be just that—a description of similarities and differences. Consider the claim "Humans are different from plants and rocks in that humans can (and plants and rocks cannot) consciously and radically reshape the communities in which they live; humans are similar to plants and rocks in that they are both members of an ecological community." Even if humans are "better" than plants and rocks with respect to the conscious ability of humans to radically transform communities, one does not *thereby* get any *morally* relevant distinction between humans and nonhumans, or an argument for the domination of plants and rocks by humans. To get *those* conclusions one needs to add at least two powerful assumptions, viz., (A2) and (A4) in argument A below:

(A1) humans do, and plants and rocks do not, have the capacity to consciously and radically change the community in which they live.

(A2) Whatever has the capacity to consciously and radically change the community in which it lives is morally superior to whatever lacks this capacity.

(A3) Thus, humans are morally superior to plants and rocks.

(A4) For any X and Y, if X is morally superior to Y, then X is morally justified in subordinating Y.

(A5) Thus, humans are morally justified in subordinating plants and rocks.

Without the two assumptions that *humans are morally superior* to (at least some) nonhumans, (A2), and that *superiority justifies subordination,* (A4), all one has is some difference between humans and some nonhumans. This is true *even if* that difference is given in terms of superiority. Thus, it is the logic of domination, (A4), which is the bottom line in ecofeminist discussions of oppression.

Second, ecofeminists argue that, at least in Western societies, the oppressive conceptual framework which sanctions the twin dominations of women and nature is a patriarchal one characterized by all three features of an oppressive conceptual framework. Many ecofeminists claim that, historically, within at least the dominant Western culture, a patriarchal conceptual framework has sanctioned the following argument B:

(B1) Women are identified with nature and the realm of the physical; men are identified with the "human" and the realm of the mental.
(B2) Whatever is identified with nature and the realm of the physical is inferior to ("below") whatever is identified with the "human" and the realm of the mental; or, conversely, the latter is superior to ("above") the former.
(B3) Thus, women are inferior to ("below") men; or, conversely, men are superior to ("above") women.
(B4) For any X and Y, if X is superior to Y, then X is justified in subordinating Y.
(B5) Thus, men are justified in subordinating women.

If sound, argument B establishes *patriarchy,* i.e., the conclusion given at (B5) that the systematic domination of women by men is justified. But according to ecofeminists, (B5) is justified by just those three features of an oppressive conceptual framework identified earlier: value-hierarchical thinking, the assumption at (B2); value dualisms, the assumed dualism of the mental and the physical at (B1) and the assumed inferiority of the physical vis-à-vis the mental at (B2); and a logic of domination, the assumption at (B4), the same as the previous premise (A4). Hence, according to ecofeminists, insofar as an oppressive patriarchal conceptual framework has functioned historically (within at least dominant Western culture) to sanction the twin dominations of women and nature (argument B), both argument B and the patriarchal conceptual framework, from whence it comes, ought to be rejected.

Of course, the preceding does not identify which premises of B are false. What is the status of premises (B1) and (B2)? Most, if not all, feminists claim that (B1), and many ecofeminists claim that (B2), have been assumed or asserted within the dominant Western philosophical and intellectual tradition.[7] As such, these feminists assert, as a matter of historical fact, that the dominant Western philosophical tradition has assumed the truth of (B1) and (B2). Ecofeminists, however, either deny (B2) or do not affirm (B2). Furthermore, because some ecofeminists are anxious to deny any ahistorical identification of women with nature, some ecofeminists deny (B1) when (B1) is used to support anything other than a strictly historical claim about what has been asserted or assumed to be true within patriarchal culture—e.g., when (B1) is used to assert that women properly are identified with the realm of nature and the physical.[8] Thus, from an ecofeminist perspective, (B1) and (B2) are properly viewed as problematic though historically sanctioned claims: they are problematic precisely because of the way they have functioned historically in a patriarchal conceptual framework and culture to sanction the dominations of women and nature.

What *all* ecofeminists agree about, then, is the way in which *the logic of domination* has functioned historically within patriarchy to sustain and justify the twin dominations of women and nature.[9] Since *all* feminists (and not just ecofeminists) oppose partriarchy, the conclusion given at (B5), all feminists (including ecofeminists) must oppose at least the logic of domination, premise (B4), on which argument B rests—whatever the truth-value status of (B1) and (B2) *outside of* a patriarchal context.

That *all* feminists must oppose the logic of domination shows the breadth and depth of the ecofeminist critique of B: it is a critique not only of the three assumptions on which this argument for the domination of women and nature rests, viz., the assumptions at (B1), (B2), and (B4); it is also a critique of patriarchal conceptual frameworks generally, i.e., of those oppressive conceptual frameworks which put men "up" and women "down," allege some way in which women are morally inferior to men, and use that alleged difference to justify the subordination of women by men. Therefore, ecofeminism is necessary to *any* feminist critique of patriarchy, and, hence, necessary to feminism (a point I discuss again later).

Third, ecofeminism clarifies why the logic of domination, and any conceptual framework which gives rise to it, must be abolished in order both to make possible a meaningful notion of difference which does not breed domination and to prevent feminism from becoming a "support" movement based primarily on shared experiences. In contemporary society, there is no one "woman's voice," no *woman* (or *human*) *simpliciter:* every woman (or human) is a woman (or human) of some race, class, age, affectional orientation, marital status, regional or national background, and so forth. Because there are no "monolithic experiences" that all women share, feminism must be a "solidarity movement" based on shared beliefs and interests rather than a "unity in sameness" movement based on shared experiences and shared victimization.[10] In the words of Maria Lugones, "Unity—not to be confused with solidarity—is understood as conceptually tied to domination."[11]

Ecofeminists insist that the sort of logic of domination used to justify the domination of humans by gender, racial or ethnic, or class status is also used to justify the domination of nature. Because eliminating a logic of domination is part of a feminist critique—whether a critique of patriarchy, white supremacist culture, or imperialism—ecofeminists insist that *naturism* is properly viewed as an integral part of any feminist solidarity movement to end sexist oppression and the logic of domination which conceptually grounds it. . . .

An ecofeminist ethic involves a reconception of what it means to be human, and in what human ethical behavior consists. Ecofeminism denies abstract individualism. Humans are who we are in large part by virtue of the historical and social contexts and the relationships we are in, including our relationships with nonhuman nature. Relationships are not something extrinsic to who we are, not an "add on" feature of human nature; they play an essential role in shaping what it is to be human. Relationships of humans to the nonhuman environment are, in part, constitutive of what it is to be a human.

By making visible the interconnections among the dominations of women and nature, ecofeminism shows that both are feminist issues and that explicit acknowledgement of both is vital to any responsible environmental ethic. Feminism *must* embrace ecological feminism if it is to end the domination of women because the domination of women is tied conceptually and historically to the domination of nature.

A responsible environmental ethic also *must* embrace feminism. Otherwise, even the seemingly most revolutionary, liberational, and holistic ecological ethic will fail to take seriously the interconnected dominations of nature and women that are so much a part of the historical legacy and conceptual framework that sanctions the exploitation of nonhuman nature. Failure to make visible these interconnected, twin dominations results in an inaccurate account of how it is that nature has been and continues to be dominated and exploited and produces an environmental ethic that lacks the depth necessary to be truly *inclusive* of the realities of persons who at least in dominant Western culture have been intimately tied with that exploitation, viz., women. Whatever else can be said in favor of such holistic ethics, a failure to make visible ecofeminist insights into the common denominators of the twin oppressions of women and nature is to perpetuate, rather than overcome, the source of that oppression.

This last point deserves further attention. It may be objected that as long as the end result is "the same"—the development of an environmental ethic which does not emerge out of or reinforce an oppressive conceptual framework—it does not matter whether that ethic (or the ethic endorsed in getting there) is feminist or not. Hence, it simply is *not* the case that any adequate environmental ethic must be feminist. My argument, in contrast, has been that it *does* matter, and for three important reasons. First, there is the scholarly issue of accurately representing historical reality, and that, ecofeminists claim, requires acknowledging the historical feminization of nature and naturalization of women as part of the exploitation of nature. Second, . . . the conceptual connections between the domination of women and the domination of nature are located in an oppressive and, at least in Western societies, patriarchal conceptual framework characterized by a logic of domination. Thus, . . . the failure to notice the nature of this connection leaves at best an incomplete, inaccurate, and partial account of what is required of a conceptually adequate environmental ethic. An ethic which *does not* acknowledge this is simply *not* the same as one that does, whatever else the similarities between them. Third, the claim that, in contemporary culture, one can have an adequate environmental ethic which is *not* feminist assumes that, in contemporary culture, the label *feminist* does not add anything crucial to the nature or description of environmental ethics. I have shown that at least in contemporary culture this is false, for the word *feminist* currently helps to clarify just *how* the domination of nature is conceptually linked to patriarchy and, hence, how the liberation of nature, is conceptually linked to the termination of patriarchy. Thus, because it has critical bite in contemporary culture, it serves as an important reminder that in contemporary sex-gendered, raced, classed, and naturist culture, an unlabeled position functions as a privileged and "unmarked" position. That is, without the addition of the word *feminist,* one presents environmental ethics as if it has no bias, including male-gender bias, which is just what ecofeminists deny: failure to notice the connections between the twin oppressions of women and nature *is* male-gender bias.

One of the goals of feminism is the eradication of all oppressive sex-gender (and related race, class, age, affectional preference) categories and the creation of a world in which *difference does not breed domination*—say, the world of 4001. If in 4001 an "adequate environmental ethic" is a "feminist environmental ethic," the word *feminist* may then be redundant and unnecessary. However, this is *not* 4001, and in terms of the current historical and conceptual reality the dominations of nature and of women are intimately connected. Failure to notice or make visible that connection in 1990 perpetuates the mistaken (and privileged) view that "environmental ethics" is *not* a feminist issue, and that *feminist* adds nothing to environmental ethics.[12]

CONCLUSION

I have argued in this paper that ecofeminism provides a framework for a distinctively feminist and environmental ethic. Ecofeminism grows out of the felt and theorized about connections between the domination of women and the domination of nature. As a contextualist ethic, ecofeminism refocuses environmental ethics on what nature might mean, morally speaking, *for* humans, and on how the relational attitudes of humans to others—humans as well as nonhumans—sculpt both what it is to be human and the nature and ground of human responsibilities to the nonhuman environment. Part of what this refocusing does is to take seriously the voices of women and other oppressed persons in the construction of that ethic. . . .

ACKNOWLEDGMENTS

Earlier versions of this paper were presented at the American Philosophical Association Meeting in New York City, December 1987, and at the University of Massachusetts, April 1988. The author wishes to thank the following people for their helpful comments and support: Bob Ackerman, Kim Brown, Jim Cheney, Mahmoud El-Kati, Eric Katz, Michael Keenan, Ruthanne Kurth-Schai, Greta Gaard, Roxanne Gudeman, Alison Jaggar, H. Warren Jones, Gareth Matthews, Michael McCall, Patrick Murphy, Bruce Nordstrom, Nancy Shea, Nancy Tuana, Bob Weinstock-Collins, Henry West, and the anonymous referees of *Environmental Ethics.*

NOTES

1. Explicit ecological feminist literature includes works from a variety of scholarly perspectives and sources. Some of these works are Leonie Caldecott and Stephanie Leland, eds., *Reclaim the Earth: Women Speak Out for Life on Earth* (London: The Women's Press, 1983); Jim Cheney, "Eco-Feminism and Deep Ecology," *Environmental Ethics* 9 (1987): 115–45; Andrée Collard with Joyce Contrucci, *Rape of the Wild: Man's Violence against Animals and the Earth* (Bloomington: Indiana University Press, 1988); Katherine Davies, "Historical Associations: Women and the Natural World," *Women & Environments* 9, no. 2 (Spring 1987): 4–6; Sharon Doubiago, "Deeper than Deep Ecology: Men Must Become Feminists," in *The New Catalyst Quarterly*, no. 10 (Winter 1987/88): 10–11; Brian Easlea, *Science and Sexual Oppression: Patriarchy's Confrontation with Women and Nature* (London: Weidenfeld & Nicholson, 1981); Elizabeth Dodson Gray, *Green Paradise Lost* (Wellesley, Mass.: Roundtable Press, 1979); Susan Griffin, *Women and Nature: The Roaring Inside Her* (San Francisco: Harper and Row, 1978); Joan L. Griscom, "On Healing the Nature/History Split in Feminist Thought," in *Heresies #13: Feminism and Ecology* 4, no. 1 (1981): 4–9; Ynestra King, "The Ecology of Feminism and the Feminism of Ecology," in *Healing Our Wounds: The Power of Ecological Feminism,* ed. Judith Plant (Boston: New Society Publishers, 1989), pp. 18–28, "The Eco-feminist Imperative," in *Reclaim the Earth,* ed. Caldecott and Leland (London: The Women's Press, 1983), pp. 12–16, "Feminism and the Revolt of Nature," in *Heresies #13: Feminism and Ecology* 4, no. 1 (1981):12–16, and "What is Ecofeminism?" *The Nation*, 12 December 1987; Marti Kheel, "Animal Liberation Is a Feminist Issue," *The New Catalyst Quarterly,* no. 10 (Winter 1987–88): 8–9; Carolyn Merchant, *The Death of Nature: Women, Ecology and the Scientific Revolution* (San Francisco, Harper and Row, 1980); Patrick Murphy, ed., "Feminism, Ecology, and the Future of the Humanities," special issue of *Studies in the Humanities* 15, no. 2 (December 1988); Abby Peterson and Carolyn Merchant, "Peace with the Earth: Women and the Environmental Movement in Sweden," *Women's Studies International Forum* 9, no. 5–6. (1986): 465–79; Judith Plant, "Searching for Common Ground: Ecofeminism and Bioregionalism," in *The New Catalyst Quarterly* no. 10 (Winter 1987/88): 6–7; Judith Plant, ed., *Healing Our Wounds: The Power of Ecological Feminism* (Boston: New Society Publishers, 1989); Val Plumwood, "Ecofeminism: An Overview and Discussion of Positions and Arguments," *Australasian Journal of Philosophy,* Supplement to vol. 64 (June 1986): 120–37; Rosemary Radford Ruether, *New Woman/ New Earth: Sexist Ideologies & Human Liberation* (New York: Seabury Press, 1975); Kirkpatrick Sale, "Ecofeminism—A New Perspective," *The Nation*, 26 September 1987: 302–05; Ariel Kay Salleh, "Deeper than Deep Ecology: The Eco-Feminist Connection,"

Environmental Ethics 6 (1984): 339–45, and "Epistemology and the Metaphors of Production: An Eco-Feminist Reading of Critical Theory," in *Studies in the Humanities* 15 (1988): 130–39; Vandana Shiva, *Staying Alive: Women, Ecology and Development* (London: Zed Books, 1988); Charlene Spretnak, "Ecofeminism: Our Roots and Flowering," *The Elmswood Newsletter*, Winter Solstice 1988; Karen J. Warren, "'Feminism and Ecology:' Making Connections," *Environmental Ethics* 9 (1987): 3–21; "Toward an Ecofeminist Ethic," *Studies in the Humanities* 15 (1988): 140–156; Miriam Wyman, "Explorations of Ecofeminism," *Women & Environments* (Spring 1987): 6–7; Iris Young, "'Feminism and Ecology' and 'Women and Life on Earth: Eco-Feminism in the 80's,'" *Environmental Ethics* 5 (1983): 173–80; Michael Zimmerman, "Feminism, Deep Ecology, and Environmental Ethics," *Environmental Ethics* 9 (1987): 21–44.

2. Francoise d'Eaubonne, *Le Feminisme ou la Mort* (Paris: Pierre Horay, 1974), pp. 213–52.
3. I discuss this in my paper, "Toward An Ecofeminist Ethic."
4. The account offered here is a revision of the account given earlier in my paper "Feminism and Ecology: Making Connections." I have changed the account to be about "oppressive" rather than strictly "patriarchal" conceptual frameworks in order to leave open the possibility that there may be some patriarchal conceptual frameworks (e.g., in non-Western cultures) which are *not* properly characterized as based on value dualisms.
5. Murray Bookchin, "Social Ecology versus 'Deep Ecology'," in *Green Perspectives: Newsletter of the Green Program Project*, no. 4–5 (Summer 1987): 9.
6. It may be that in contemporary Western society, which is so thoroughly structured by categories of gender, race, class, age, and affectional orientation, that there simply is no meaningful notion of "value-hierarchical thinking" which does not function in an oppressive context. For purposes of this paper, I leave that question open.
7. Many feminists who argue for the historical point that claims (B1) and (B2) have been asserted or assumed to be true within the dominant Western philosophical tradition do so by discussion of that tradition's conceptions of reason, rationality, and science. For a sampling of the sorts of claims made within that context, see "Reason, Rationality, and Gender," ed. Nancy Tuana and Karen J. Warren, a special issue of the American Philosophical Association's *Newsletter on Feminism and Philosophy* 88, no. 2 (March 1989): 17–71. Ecofeminists who claim that (B2) has been assumed to be true within the dominant Western philosophical tradition include: Gray, *Green Paradise Lost;* Griffin, *Woman and Nature: The Roaring Inside Her;* Merchant, *The Death of Nature;* Ruether, *New Woman/New Earth*. For a discussion of some of these ecofeminist historical accounts, see Plumwood, "Ecofeminism." While I agree that the historical connections between the domination of women and the domination of nature is a crucial one, I do not argue for that claim here.
8. Ecofeminists who deny (B1) when (B1) is offered as anything other than a true, descriptive, historical claim about patriarchal culture often do so on grounds that an objectionable sort of biological determinism, or at least harmful female sex-gender stereotypes, underlie (B1). For a discussion of this "split" among those ecofeminists ("nature feminists") who assert and those ecofeminists ("social feminists") who deny (B1) as anything other than a true historical claim about how women are described in patriarchal culture, see Griscom, "On Healing the Nature/History Split."
9. I make no attempt here to defend the historically sanctioned truth of these premises.
10. See, e.g., Bell Hooks, *Feminist Theory: From Margin to Center* (Boston: South End Press, 1984), pp. 51–52.
11. Maria Lugones, "Playfulness, 'World-Travelling,' and Loving Perception," *Hypatia* 2, no. 2 (Summer 1987): 3.
12. I offer the same sort of reply to critics of ecofeminism such as Warwick Fox who suggest that for the sort of ecofeminism I defend, the word *feminist* does not add anything significant to environmental ethics and, consequently, that an ecofeminist like myself might as well call herself a deep ecologist. He asks: "Why doesn't she just call it [i.e., Warren's vision of a transformative feminism] deep ecology? Why specifically attach the label *feminist* to it . . . ?" (Warwick Fox, "The Deep Ecology-Ecofeminism Debate and Its Parallels," *Environmental Ethics* 11, no. 1 [1989]: 14, n. 22). Whatever the important similarities between deep ecology and ecofeminism (or, specifically, my version of ecofeminism)—and, indeed, there are many—it is precisely my point here that the word *feminist* does add something significant to the conception of environmental ethics, and that any environmental ethic (including deep ecology) that fails to make explicit the different kinds of interconnections among the domination of nature and the domination of women will be, from a feminist (and ecofeminist) perspective such as mine, inadequate.

Radical American Environmentalism and Wilderness Preservation: A Third World Critique

Ramachandra Guha

Ramachandra Guha is at the Institute of Economic Growth in Delhi, India, where he is a reader in sociology. He has been a visiting lecturer at Yale, in the School of Forestry and Environmental Studies. Guha is the author of The Unquiet Woods: Ecological Change and Peasant Resistance in the Himalaya *(1990).*

From a Third World point of view, Guha critiques the American deep ecology approach to the environment. Guha focuses on four of deep ecology's tenets: the distinction between biocentrism and anthropocentrism; the emphasis on wilderness preservation; the embracing of Eastern philosophies and customs; and the claim of being the most radical view in environmentalism. Guha argues that the distinction between anthropocentrism and biocentrism does not help redress environmental degradation; that the preservation of wilderness causes further deprivation of human rights in the Third World; that the deep ecologists' understanding of Eastern traditions is incomplete; and that radical environmentalism, as in West Germany and India, needs to address the sociopolitical structure and integrate economic survival with ecological concerns. Guha concludes that deep ecology is inappropriate for application in the Third World.

> Even God dare not appear to the poor man except in the form of bread.
>
> —Mahatma Gandhi

INTRODUCTION

The respected radical journalist Kirkpatrick Sale recently celebrated "the passion of a new and growing movement that has become disenchanted with the environmental establishment and has in recent years mounted a serious and sweeping attack on it—style, substance, systems, sensibilities and all."[1] The vision of those whom Sale calls the "New Ecologists"—and what I refer to in this article as deep ecology—is a compelling one. Decrying the narrowly economic goals of mainstream environmentalism, this new movement aims at nothing less than a philosophical and cultural revolution in human attitudes toward nature. In contrast to the conventional lobbying efforts of environmental professionals based in Washington, it proposes a militant defense of "Mother Earth," an unflinching opposition to human attacks on undisturbed wilderness. With their goals ranging from the spiritual to the politi-

Reprinted with permission of Ramachandra Guha and *Environmental Ethics,* from *Environmental Ethics, Vol. 11,* No. 1, 1989. [Edited]

cal, the adherents of deep ecology span a wide spectrum of the American environmental movement. As Sale correctly notes, this emerging strand has in a matter of a few years made its presence felt in a number of fields: from academic philosophy (as in the journal *Environmental Ethics*) to popular environmentalism (for example, the group Earth First!).

In this article I develop a critique of deep ecology from the perspective of a sympathetic outsider. I critique deep ecology not as a general (or even a foot soldier) in the continuing struggle between the ghosts of Gifford Pinchot and John Muir over control of the U.S. environmental movement, but as an outsider to these battles. I speak admittedly as a partisan, but of the environmental movement in India, a country with an ecological diversity comparable to the U.S., but with a radically dissimilar cultural and social history.

My treatment of deep ecology is primarily historical and sociological, rather than philosophical, in nature. Specifically, I examine the cultural rootedness of a philosophy that likes to present itself in universalistic terms. I make two main arguments: first, that deep ecology is uniquely American, and despite superficial similarities in rhetorical style, the social and political goals of radical environmentalism in other cultural contexts (e.g., West Germany and India) are quite different; second, that the social consequences of putting deep ecology into practice on a worldwide basis (what its practitioners are aiming for) are very grave indeed.

THE TENETS OF DEEP ECOLOGY

While I am aware that the term *deep ecology* was coined by the Norwegian philosopher Arne Naess, this article refers specifically to the American variant.[2] Adherents of the deep ecological perspective in this country, while arguing intensely among themselves over its political and philosophical implications, share some fundamental premises about human–nature interactions. As I see it, the defining characteristics of deep ecology are fourfold:

First, deep ecology argues, that the environmental movement must shift from an "anthropocentric" to a "biocentric" perspective. In many respects, an acceptance of the primacy of this distinction constitutes the litmus test of deep ecology. A considerable effort is expended by deep ecologists in showing that the dominant motif in Western philosophy has been anthropocentric—i.e., the belief that man and his works are the center of the universe—and conversely, in identifying those lonely thinkers (Leopold, Thoreau, Muir, Aldous Huxley, Santayana, etc.) who, in assigning man a more humble place in the natural order, anticipated deep ecological thinking. In the political realm, meanwhile, establishment environmentalism (shallow ecology) is chided for casting its arguments in human-centered terms. Preserving nature, the deep ecologists say, has an intrinsic worth quite apart from any benefits preservation may convey to future human generations. The anthropocentric–biocentric distinction is accepted as axiomatic by deep ecologists, it structures their discourse, and much of the present discussion remains mired within it.

The second characteristic of deep ecology is its focus on the preservation of unspoilt wilderness—and the restoration of degraded areas to a more pristine condition—to the relative (and sometimes absolute) neglect of other issues on the environmental agenda. I later identify the cultural roots and portentous consequences of this obsession with wilderness. For the moment, let me indicate three distinct sources from which it springs. Historically, it represents a playing out of the preservationist (read *radical*) and utilitarian (read *reformist*) dichotomy that has plagued American environmentalism since the turn of the century. Morally, it is an imperative that follows from the biocentric perspective; other species of plants and animals, and nature itself, have an intrinsic right to exist. And finally, the preservation of wilderness also turns on a scientific argument—viz., the value of biological diversity in stabilizing ecological regimes and in retaining a gene pool for future generations. Truly radical policy proposals have been put forward by deep ecologists on the basis of these arguments. The influential poet Gary Snyder, for example, would like to see a 90 percent reduction in human populations to allow a restoration of pristine environments, while others have argued forcefully that a large portion of the globe must be immediately cordoned off from human beings.[3]

Third, there is a widespread invocation of Eastern spiritual traditions as forerunners of deep ecology. Deep ecology, it is suggested, was practiced both by major religious traditions and at a more popular level by "primal" peoples in non-Western settings. This complements the search for an authentic lineage in Western thought. At one level, the task is to recover those dissenting voices within the Judeo-Christian tradition; at another, to suggest that religious traditions in other cultures are, in contrast, dominantly if not exclusively "biocentric" in their orientation. This coupling of (ancient) Eastern and (modern) ecological wisdom seemingly helps consolidate the claim that deep ecology is a philosophy of universal significance.

Fourth, deep ecologists, whatever their internal differences, share the belief that they are the "leading edge" of the environmental movement. As the polarity of the shallow/deep and anthropocentric/biocentric distinctions makes clear, they see themselves as the spiritual, philosophical, and political vanguard of American and world environmentalism.

TOWARD A CRITIQUE

Although I analyze each of these tenets independently, it is important to recognize, as deep ecologists are fond of remarking in reference to nature, the interconnectedness and unity of these individual themes.

(1) Insofar as it has begun to act as a check on man's arrogance and ecological hubris, the transition from an anthropocentric (human-centered) to a biocentric (humans as only one element in the ecosystem) view in both religious and scientific traditions is only to be welcomed.[4] What is unacceptable are the radical conclusions drawn by deep ecology, in particular, that intervention in nature should be guided primarily by the need to preserve biotic integrity rather than by the needs of humans. The latter for deep ecologists is anthropocentric, the former biocentric. This dichotomy is, however, of very little use in understanding the dynamics of environmental degradation. The two fundamental ecological problems facing the globe are (i) overconsumption by the industrialized world and by urban elites in the Third World and (ii) growing militarization, both in a short-term sense (i.e., ongoing regional wars) and in a long-term sense (i.e., the arms race and the prospect of nuclear annihilation). Neither of these problems has any tangible connection to the anthropocentric–biocentric distinction. Indeed, the agents of these processes would barely comprehend this philosophical dichotomy. The proximate causes of the ecologically wasteful characteristics of industrial society and of militarization are far more mundane: at an aggregate level, the dialectic of economic and political structures, and at a micro-level, the life style choices of individuals. These causes cannot be reduced, whatever the level of analysis, to a deeper anthropocentric attitude toward nature; on the contrary, by constituting a grave threat to

human survival, the ecological degradation they cause does not even serve the best interests of human beings! If my identification of the major dangers to the integrity of the natural world is correct, invoking the bogy of anthropocentricism is at best irrelevant and at worst a dangerous obfuscation.

(2) If the above dichotomy is irrelevant, the emphasis on wilderness is positively harmful when applied to the Third World.. If in the U.S. the preservationist/utilitarian division is seen as mirroring the conflict between "people" and "interests," in countries such as India the situation is very nearly the reverse. Because India is a long settled and densely populated country in which agrarian populations have a finely balanced relationship with nature, the setting aside of wilderness areas has resulted in a direct transfer of resources from the poor to the rich. Thus, Project Tiger, a network of parks hailed by the international conservation community as an outstanding success, sharply posits the interests of the tiger against those of poor peasants living in and around the reserve. The designation of tiger reserves was made possible only by the physical displacement of existing villages and their inhabitants; their management requires the continuing exclusion of peasants and livestock. The initial impetus for setting up parks for the tiger and other large mammals such as the rhinoceros and elephant came from two social groups, first, a class of ex-hunters turned conservationists belonging mostly to the declining Indian feudal elite and second, representatives of international agencies, such as the World Wildlife Fund (WWF) and the International Union for the Conservation of Nature and Natural Resources (IUCN), seeking to transplant the American system of national parks onto Indian soil. In no case have the needs of the local population been taken into account, and as in many parts of Africa, the designated wildlands are managed primarily for the benefit of rich tourists. Until very recently, wildlands preservation has been identified with environmentalism by the state and the conservation elite; in consequence, environmental problems that impinge far more directly on the lives of the poor—e.g., fuel, fodder, water shortages, soil erosion, and air and water pollution—have not been adequately addressed.[5]

Deep ecology provides, perhaps unwittingly, a justification for the continuation of such narrow and inequitable conservation practices under a newly acquired radical guise. Increasingly, the international conservation elite is using the philosophical, moral, and scientific arguments used by deep ecologists in advancing their wilderness crusade. A striking but by no means atypical example is the recent plea by a prominent American biologist for the takeover of large portions of the globe by the author and his scientific colleagues. Writing in a prestigious scientific forum, the *Annual Review of Ecology and Systematics,* Daniel Janzen argues that only biologists have the competence to decide how the tropical landscape should be used. As "the representatives of the natural world," biologists are "in charge of the future of tropical ecology," and only they have the expertise and mandate to "determine whether the tropical agroscape is to be populated only by humans, their mutualists, commensals, and parasites, or whether it will also contain some islands of the greater nature—the nature that spawned humans, yet has been vanquished by them." Janzen exhorts his colleagues to advance their territorial claims on the tropical world more forcefully, warning that the very existence of these areas is at stake: "if biologists want a tropics in which to biologize, they are going to have to buy it with care, energy, effort, strategy, tactics, time, and cash."[6]

This frankly imperialist manifesto highlights the multiple dangers of the preoccupation with wilderness preservation that is characteristic of deep ecology. As I have suggested, it seriously compounds the neglect by the American movement of far more pressing environmental problems within the Third World. But perhaps more importantly, and in a more insidious fashion, it also provides an impetus to the imperialist yearning of Western biologists and their financial sponsors, organizations such as the WWF and IUCN. The wholesale transfer of a movement culturally rooted in American conservation history can only result in the social uprooting of human populations in other parts of the globe.

(3) I come now to the persistent invocation of Eastern philosophies as antecedent in point of time but convergent in their structure with deep ecology. Complex and internally differentiated religious traditions—Hinduism, Buddhism, and Taoism—are lumped together as holding a view of nature believed to be quintessentially biocentric. Individual philosophers such as the Taoist Lao Tzu are identified as being forerunners of deep ecology. Even an intensely political, pragmatic, and Christian influenced thinker such as Gandhi has been accorded a wholly undeserved place in the deep ecological pantheon. Thus the Zen teacher Robert Aitken Roshi makes the strange claim that Gandhi's thought was not human-centered and that he practiced an embryonic form of deep ecology which is "traditionally Eastern and is found with differing emphasis in Hinduism, Taoism and in Theravada and Mahayana Buddhism."[7] Moving away from the realm of high philosophy and scriptural religion, deep ecologists make the further claim that at the level of material and spiritual practice "primal" peoples subordinated themselves to the integrity of the biotic universe they inhabited.

I have indicated that this appropriation of Eastern traditions is in part dictated by the need to construct an authentic lineage and in part a desire to present deep ecology as a universalistic philosophy. Indeed, in his substantial and quixotic biography of John Muir, Michael Cohen goes so far as to suggest that Muir was the "Taoist of the [American] West."[8] This reading of Eastern traditions is selective and does not bother to differentiate between alternate (and changing) religious and cultural traditions; as it stands, it does considerable violence to the historical record. Throughout most recorded history the characteristic form of human activity in the "East" has been a finely tuned but nonetheless conscious and dynamic manipulation of nature. Although mystics such as Lao Tzu did reflect on the spiritual essence of human relations with nature, it must be recognized that such ascetics and their reflections were supported by a society of cultivators whose relationship with nature was a far more *active* one. Many agricultural communities do have a sophisticated knowledge of the natural environment that may equal (and sometimes surpass) codified "scientific" knowledge; yet, the elaboration of such traditional ecological knowledge (in both material and spiritual contexts) can hardly be said to rest on a mystical affinity with nature of a deep ecological kind. Nor is such knowledge infallible; as the archaeological record powerfully suggests, modern Western man has no monopoly on ecological disasters.

In a brilliant article, the Chicago historian Ronald Inden points out that this romantic and essentially positive view of the East is a mirror image of the scientific and essentially pejorative view normally upheld by Western scholars of the Orient. In either case, the East constitutes the Other, a body wholly separate and alien from the West; it is defined by a uniquely spiritual and nonrational "essence," even if this essence is valorized quite differently by the two schools. Eastern man exhibits a spiritual dependence with respect to nature—on the one hand, this is symptomatic of his prescientific and backward self, on the other, of his ecological wisdom and deep ecological consciousness. Both views are monolithic, simplistic, and have the characteristic effect—intended in one case, perhaps unintended in the other—of denying agency and reason to the East and making it the privileged orbit of Western thinkers.

The two apparently opposed perspectives have then a common underlying structure of discourse in which the East merely serves as a vehicle for Western projections. Varying images of the East are raw material for political and cultural battles being played out in the West; they tell us far more about the Western commentator and his desires than about the "East." Inden's remarks apply not merely to Western scholarship on India, but to Orientalist constructions of China and Japan as well:

> Although these two views appear to be strongly opposed, they often combine together. Both have a similar interest in sustaining the Otherness of India. The holders of the dominant view, best exemplified in the past in imperial administrative discourse (and today probably by that of "development economics"), would place a traditional, superstition-ridden India in a position of perpetual tutelage to a modern, rational West. The adherents of the romantic view, best exemplified academically in the discourses of Christian liberalism and analytic psychology, concede the realm of the public and impersonal to the positivist. Taking their succor not from governments and big business, but from a plethora of religious foundations and self-help institutes, and from allies in the "consciousness industry," not to mention the important industry of tourism, the romantics insist that India embodies a private realm of the imagination and the religious which modern, western man lacks but needs. They, therefore, like the positivists, but for just the opposite reason, have a vested interest in seeing that the Orientalist view of India as "spiritual," "mysterious," and "exotic" is perpetuated.[9]

(4) How radical, finally, are the deep ecologists? Notwithstanding their self-image and strident rhetoric (in which the label "shallow ecology" has an opprobrium similar to that reserved for "social democratic" by Marxist-Leninists), even within the American context their radicalism is limited and it manifests itself quite differently elsewhere.

To my mind, deep ecology is best viewed as a radical trend within the wilderness preservation movement. Although advancing philosophical rather than aesthetic arguments and encouraging political militancy rather than negotiation, its practical emphasis—viz., preservation of unspoilt nature—is virtually identical. For the mainstream movement, the function of wilderness is to provide a temporary antidote to modern civilization. As a special institution within an industrialized society, the national park "provides an opportunity for respite, contrast, contemplation, and affirmation of values for those who live most of their lives in the workaday world."[10] Indeed, the rapid increase in visitations to the national parks in postwar America is a direct consequence of economic expansion. The emergence of a popular interest in wilderness sites, the historian Samuel Hays points out, was "not a throwback to the primitive, but an integral part of the modern standard of living as people sought to add new 'amenity' and 'aesthetic' goals and desires to their earlier preoccupation with necessities and conveniences."[11]

Here, the enjoyment of nature is an integral part of the consumer society. The private automobile (and the life style it has spawned) is in many respects the ultimate ecological villain, and an untouched wilderness the prototype of ecological harmony; yet, for most Americans it is perfectly consistent to drive a thousand miles to spend a holiday in a national park. They possess a vast, beautiful, and sparsely populated continent and are also able to draw upon the natural resources of large portions of the globe by virtue of their economic and political dominance. In consequence, America can simultaneously enjoy the material benefits of an expanding economy and the aesthetic benefits of unspoilt nature. The two poles of "wilderness" and "civilization" mutually coexist in an internally coherent whole, and philosophers of both poles are assigned a prominent place in this culture. Paradoxically as it may seem, it is no accident that Star Wars technology and deep ecology both find their fullest expression in that leading sector of Western civilization, California.

Deep ecology runs parallel to the consumer society without seriously questioning its ecological and socio-political basis. In its celebration of American wilderness, it also displays an uncomfortable convergence with the prevailing climate of nationalism in the American wilderness movement. For spokesmen such as the historian Roderick Nash, the national park system is America's distinctive cultural contribution to the world, reflective not merely of its economic but of its philosophical and ecological maturity as well. In what Walter Lippman called the American century, the "American invention of national parks" must be exported worldwide. Betraying an economic determinism that would make even a Marxist shudder, Nash believes that environmental preservation is a "full stomach" phenomenon that is confined to the rich, urban, and sophisticated. Nonetheless, he hopes that "the less developed nations may eventually evolve economically and intellectually to the point where nature preservation is more than a business."[12]

The error which Nash makes (and which deep ecology in some respects encourages) is to equate environmental protection with the protection of wilderness. This is a distinctively American notion, born out of a unique social and environmental history. The archetypal concerns of radical enviromentalists in other cultural contexts are in fact quite different. The German Greens, for example, have elaborated a devastating critique of industrial society which turns on the acceptance of environmental limits to growth. Pointing to the intimate links between industrialization, militarization, and conquest, the Greens argue that economic growth in the West has historically rested on the economic and ecological exploitation of the Third World. Rudolf Bahro is characteristically blunt:

> The working class here [in the West] is the richest lower class in the world. And if I look at the problem from the point of view of the whole of humanity, not just from that of Europe, then I must say that the metropolitan working class is the worst exploiting class in history. . . . What made poverty bearable in eighteenth or nineteenth-century Europe was the prospect of escaping it through exploitation of the periphery. But this is no longer a possibility, and continued industrialism in the Third World will mean poverty for whole generations and hunger for millions.[13]

Here the roots of global ecological problems lie in the disproportionate share of resources consumed by the industrialized countries as a whole *and* the urban elite within the Third World. Since it is impossible to reproduce an industrial monoculture worldwide, the ecological movement in the West must begin by cleaning up its own act. The Greens advocate the creation of a "no growth" economy, to be achieved by scaling down current (and clearly unsustainable) consumption levels.[14] This radical shift in consumption and production patterns requires the creation of alternate economic and political structures—smaller in scale and more amenable to social participation—but it rests equally on a shift in cultural values. The expansionist character of modern Western man will have to give way to an ethic of renunciation and self-limitation, in which spiritual and communal values play an increasing role in sustaining social life. This revolution in cultural values, however, has as its point of departure an understanding of environmental processes quite different from deep ecology.

Many elements of the Green program find a strong resonance in countries such as India, where a history of Western colonialism and industrial development has benefited only a tiny elite while exacting tremendous social and environmental costs. The ecological battles presently being fought in India have as their epicenter the conflict over nature between the subsistence and largely rural sector and the vastly more powerful commercial-industrial sector. Perhaps the most celebrated of these battles concerns the Chipko (Hug the Tree) movement, a peasant movement against deforestation in the Himalayan foothills. Chipko is only one of several movements that have sharply questioned the nonsustainable demand being placed on the land and vegetative base by urban centers and industry. These include opposition to large dams by displaced peasants, the conflict between small artisan fishing and large-scale trawler fishing for export, the countrywide movements against commercial forest operations, and opposition to industrial pollution among downstream agricultural and fishing communities.[15]

Two features distinguish these environmental movements from their Western counterparts. First, for the sections of society most critically affected by environmental degradation—poor and landless peasants, women, and tribals—it is a question of sheer survival, not of enhancing the quality of life. Second, and as a consequence, the environmental solutions they articulate deeply involve questions of equity as well as economic and political redistribution. Highlighting these differences, a leading Indian environmentalist stresses that "environmental protection per se is of least concern to most of these groups. Their main concern is about the use of the environment and who should benefit from it."[16] They seek to wrest control of nature away from the state and the industrial sector and place it in the hands of rural communities who live within that environment but are increasingly denied access to it. These communities have far more basic needs, their demands on the environment are far less intense, and they can draw upon a reservoir of cooperative social institutions and local ecological knowledge in managing the "commons"—forests, grasslands, and the waters—on a sustainable basis. If colonial and capitalist expansion has both accentuated social inequalities and signaled a precipitous fall in ecological wisdom, an alternate ecology must rest on an alternate society and polity as well.

This brief overview of German and Indian environmentalism has some major implications for deep ecology. Both German and Indian environmental traditions allow for a greater integration of ecological concerns with livelihood and work. They also place a greater emphasis on equity and social justice (both within individual countries and on a global scale) on the grounds that in the absence of social regeneration environmental regeneration has very little chance of succeeding. Finally, and perhaps most significantly, they have escaped the preoccupation with wilderness preservation so characteristic of American cultural and environmental history.[17]

A HOMILY

In 1958, the economist J.K. Galbraith referred to overconsumption as the unasked question of the American conservation movement. There is a marked selectivity, he wrote, "in the conservationist's approach to materials consumption. If we are concerned about our great appetite for materials, it is plausible to seek to increase the supply, to decrease waste, to make better use of the stocks available, and to develop substitutes. But what of the appetite itself? Surely this is the ultimate source of the problem. If it continues its geometric course, will it not one day have to be restrained? Yet in the literature of the resource problem this is the forbidden question. Over it hangs a nearly total silence."[18]

The consumer economy and society have expanded tremendously in the three decades since Galbraith penned these words; yet his criticisms are nearly as valid today. I have said "nearly," for there are some hopeful signs. Within the environmental movement several dispersed groups are working to develop ecologically benign technologies and to encourage less wasteful life styles. Moreover, outside the self-defined boundaries of American environmentalism, opposition to the permanent war economy is being carried on by a peace movement that has a distinguished history and impeccable moral and political credentials.

It is precisely these (to my mind, most hopeful) components of the American social scene that are missing from deep ecology. In their widely noticed book, Bill Devall and George Sessions make no mention of militarization or the movements for peace, while activists whose practical focus is on developing ecologically responsible life styles (e.g., Wendell Berry) are derided as "falling short of deep ecological awareness."[19] A truly radical ecology in the American context ought to work toward a synthesis of the appropriate technology, alternate life style, and peace movements.[20] By making the (largely spurious) anthropocentric–biocentric distinction central to the debate, deep ecologists may have appropriated the moral high ground, but they are at the same time doing a serious disservice to American and global environmentalism.[21]

NOTES

1. Kirkpatrick Sale, "The Forest for the Trees: Can Today's Environmentalists Tell the Difference," *Mother Jones* 11, no. 8 (November 1986): 26.
2. One of the major criticisms I make in this essay concerns deep ecology's lack of concern with inequalities *within* human society. In the article in which he coined the term *deep ecology*, Naess himself expresses concerns about inequalities between and within nations. However, his concern with social cleavages and their impact on resource utilization patterns and ecological destruction is not very visible in the later writings of deep ecologists. See Arne Naess, "The Shallow and the Deep, Long-Range Ecology Movement: A Summary," *Inquiry* 16 (1973): 96 (I am grateful to Tom Birch for this reference).
3. Gary Snyder, quoted in Sale, "The Forest for the Trees," p. 32. See also Dave Foreman, "A Modest Proposal for a Wilderness System," *Whole Earth Review*, no. 53 (Winter 1986–87); 42–45.
4. See, for example, Donald Worster, *Nature's Economy: The Roots of Ecology* (San Francisco, Sierra Club Books, 1977).
5. See Centre for Science and Environment, *India: The State of the Environment 1982: A Citizens Report* (New Delhi: Centre for Science and Environment, 1982); R. Sukumar, "Elephant-Man Conflict in Karnataka," in Cecil Saldanha, ed., *The State of Karnataka's Environment* (Bangalore: Centre for Taxonomic Studies, 1985). For Africa, see the brilliant analysis by Helge Kjekshus, *Ecology Control and Economic Development in East African History* (Berkeley: University of California Press, 1977).
6. Daniel Janzen, "The Future of Tropical Ecology," *Annual Review of Ecology and Systematics* 17 (1986): 305–06; emphasis added.
7. Robert Aitken Roshi, "Gandhi, Dogen, and Deep Ecology," reprinted as appendix C in Bill Devall and George Sessions, *Deep Ecology: Living as if Nature Mattered* (Salt Lake City: Peregrine Smith Books, 1985). For Gandhi's own views on social reconstruction, see the excellent three volume collection edited by Raghavan Iyer, *The Moral and Political Writings of Mahatma Gandhi* (Oxford: Clarendon Press, 1986–87).
8. Michael Cohen, *The Pathless Way* (Madison: University of Wisconsin Press, 1984), p.120.
9. Ronald Inden, "Orientalist Constructions of India," *Modern Asian Studies* 20 (1986): 442. Inden draws inspiration from Edward Said's forceful polemic, *Orientalism* (New York: Basic Books, 1980). It must be noted, however, that there is a salient dif-

ference between Western perceptions of Middle Eastern and Far Eastern cultures respectively. Due perhaps to the long history of Christian conflict with Islam. Middle Eastern cultures (as Said documents) are consistently presented in pejorative terms. The juxtaposition of hostile and worshiping attitudes that Inden talks of applies only to Western attitudes toward Buddhist and Hindu societies.

10. Joseph Sax, *Mountains Without Handrails: Reflections on the National Parks* (Ann Arbor: University of Michigan Press, 1980), p. 42. Cf. also Peter Schmitt, *Back to Nature: The Arcadian Myth in Urban America* (New York: Oxford University Press, 1969), and Alfred Runte, *National Parks: The American Experience* (Lincoln: University of Nebraska Press, 1979).
11. Samuel Hays, "From Conservation to Environment: Environmental Politics in the United States since World War Two," *Environmental Review* 6 (1982): 21. See also the same author's book entitled *Beauty, Health and Permanence: Environmental Politics in the United States, 1955–85* (New York: Cambridge University Press, 1987).
12. Roderick Nash, *Wilderness and the American Mind,* 3rd ed. (New Haven: Yale University Press, 1982).
13. Rudolf Bahro, *From Red to Green* (London: Verso Books, 1984).
14. From time to time, American scholars have themselves criticized these imbalances in consumption patterns. In the 1950s, William Vogt made the charge that the United States, with one-sixteenth of the world's population, was utilizing one-third of the globe's resources. (Vogt, cited in E. F. Murphy, *Nature, Bureaucracy and the Rule of Property* [Amsterdam: North Holland, 1977, p. 29]). More recently, Zero Population Growth has estimated that each American consumes thirty-nine times as many resources as an Indian. See *Christian Science Monitor*, 2 March 1987.
15. For an excellent review, see Anil Agarwal and Sunita Narain, eds., *India: The State of the Environment 1984–85: A Citizens Report* (New Delhi: Centre for Science and Environment, 1985). Cf. also Ramachandra Guha, *The Unquiet Woods: Ecological Change and Peasant Resistance in the Indian Himalaya* (Berkeley: University of California Press, forthcoming).
16. Anil Agarwal, "Human–Nature Interactions in a Third World Country." *The Environmentalist* 6, no. 3 (1986): 167.
17. One strand in radical American environmentalism, the bioregional movement, by emphasizing a greater involvement with the bioregion people inhabit, does indirectly challenge consumerism. However, as yet bioregionalism has hardly raised the questions of equity and social justice (international, intranational, and intergenerational) which I argue must be a central plank of radical environmentalism. Moreover, its stress on (individual) *experience* as the key to involvement with nature is also somewhat at odds with the integration of nature with livelihood and work that I talk of in this paper. Cf. Kirkpatrick Sale, *Dwellers in the Land: The Bioregional Vision* (San Francisco: Sierra Club Books, 1985).
18. John Kenneth Galbraith, "How Much Should a Country Consume?" in Henry Jarrett, ed., *Perspectives on Conservation* (Baltimore: Johns Hopkins Press, 1958), pp. 91–92.
19. Devall and Sessions, *Deep Ecology*, p. 122. For Wendell Berry's own assessment of deep ecology, see his "Amplications: Preserving Wildness," *Wilderness* 50 (Spring 1987): 39–40, 50–54.
20. See the interesting recent contribution by one of the most influential spokesmen of appropriate technology—Barry Commoner, "A Reporter at Large: The Environment," *New Yorker*, 15 June 1987. While Commoner makes a forceful plea for the convergence of the environmental movement (viewed by him primarily as the opposition to air and water pollution and to the institutions that generate such pollution) and the peace movement, he significantly does not mention consumption patterns, implying that "limits to growth" do not exist.
21. In this sense, my critique of deep ecology, although that of an outsider, may facilitate the reassertion of those elements in the American environmental tradition for which there is a profound sympathy in other parts of the globe. A global perspective may also lead to a critical reassessment of figures such as Aldo Leopold and John Muir, the two patron saints of deep ecology. As Donald Worster has pointed out, the message of Muir (and, I would argue, of Leopold as well) makes sense only in an American context; he has very little to say to other cultures. See Worster's review of Stephen Fox's *John Muir and His Legacy,* in *Environmental Ethics* 5 (1983): 277–81.

ENVIRONMENTAL ETHICS—SUPPLEMENTARY READINGS

AMES, ROGER T. "Taoism and the Nature of Nature." *Environmental Ethics,* vol. 8, Winter 1986.

BOOTH, ANNIE, and WAYNE JACOBS. "Ties That Bind: Native American Beliefs as a Foundation for Environmental Consciousness." *Environmental Ethics,* vol. 12, Spring 1990.

CALLICOTT, J. BAIRD. "Conceptual Resources for Environmental Ethics in Asian Traditions of Thought: A Propaedeutic." *Philosophy East and West,* vol. 37(2), April 1987.

HALL, DAVID L. "On Seeking a Change of Environment, A Quasi-Taoist Proposal." *Philosophy East and West,* vol. 37(2), April 1987.

HARGROVE, EUGENE C. "Anglo-American Land Use Attitudes." *Environmental Ethics,* vol. 2, Summer 1980.

INADA, KENNETH K. "Environmental Problematics in the Buddhist Context." *Philosophy East and West,* vol. 37(2), April 1987.

MAGRAW, DANIEL, and JAMES NICKEL. "Can Today's International System Handle Transboundary Environmental Problems?" in *Upstream/Downstream,* Donald Scherer, editor. Philadelphia: Temple University Press, 1990.

MERCHANT, CAROLYN. "Women of the Progressive Conservation Movement." *Environmental Review,* vol. 8, Spring 1984.

OPHULS, WILLIAM. *Ecology and the Politics of Scarcity.* San Francisco: W. H. Freeman and Company, 1977.

SAGOFF, MARK. "Zuckerman's Dilemma: A Plea for Environmental Ethics." *Hastings Center Report,* September–October 1991.

SHRADER-FRECHETTE, KRISTIN. *Nuclear Power and Public Policy.* Dordrecht: D. Reidel Publishing Co., 1980.

ZAIDI, IQTIDAR H. "On the Ethics of Man's Interaction with the Environment: An Islamic Approach." *Environmental Ethics,* vol. 3, Spring 1980.

III

Hunger and Poverty

The "philanthropic" food relief programs that have aided many of the neediest countries are experiencing a decline in contributions, known as "famine fatigue." People of means are reportedly getting tired of providing economic assistance to deal with a problem that has not gone away and does not seem to be improving. The economic "famine fatigue" places hungry nations in even more peril.

In addition to giving money, there are other actions that a resident of the United States takes that may have far-reaching global effects. One example is eating beef. Consider:

> For every quarter-pound hamburger that comes from a steer raised in Central or South America, approximately 165 pounds of living matter have been destroyed, including some 20–30 different plant species, perhaps 100 insect species, and dozens of bird, mammal, and reptile species.[1]

Although the United States also has environmental pollution from beef production, the environmental costs of establishing beef production in Central and South America are coupled with human costs. For when cattle ranching is introduced into traditional agricultural societies, humans are also displaced.

> While peasant agriculture can often sustain a hundred people per square mile, the average rainforest cattle ranch "employs one person per 2,000 head of cattle and this . . . amounts at best to one person per twelve square miles." It has been the decision to use the land to create an artificial food chain, the most inequitable in history, that has resulted in misery for hundreds of millions of human beings around the world.[2]

As Jeremy Rifkin points out, the carrying capacity (or amount of life a specific area can sustain) of a square mile in the rain forest is drastically lessened when traditional agriculture is replaced with a cattle ranch. Where one square mile in the rain forest had previously sustained 100 people, after the intervention of cattle ranching, 12 square miles sustains one person. Considering that most of this beef is exported, local hunger is being *created* and the displaced 1,199 people must now find sustenance elsewhere. Those displaced may end up in cities with high unemployment, contributing to a cycle of poverty all too common in undeveloped countries. If this is the case, then a United States citizen's consumption of rain forest beef has many effects on people and the environment in areas far removed from that citizen.

Various situations in the Third World concerning hunger and poverty are affected by our actions, whether it be from our consumption habits or monetary donations (or lack thereof) to relief organizations. Some people assert that we have a *duty* to share with those in need. One example of people who assert that we have a duty to share are those in the Gabra tribe.

The Gabra are nomadic camel herders in Kenya's Chalbi Desert, who have adapted and survived for generations in their arid climate. The Gabra do not share Western assumptions about property, and do not even consider the milk from the animals they care for to "belong" to them. Furthermore, they lend camels to both their own people and outsiders, a practice that has strengthened their community.

The Gabra recognize that they must (that is, they have a moral obligation to) share such milk and camels with those who are in need. According to the Gabra perspective, a poor person shames them all.

What, then, are the limitations of our moral duties concerning situations such as hunger and poverty, both of particular urgency in the Third World? One could agree with William K. Reilly's assumptions (as put forth in the previous chapter) that education, proper economic growth, and population control are what is needed to change the situation. Or perhaps one believes there is a need for a more immediate answer and agrees with the Gabra of Kenya, that we must share what we have with those in need. Of concern in this chapter are the moral duties those of the developed nations have to those in the undeveloped nations concerning hunger and poverty, especially in light of the role the developed nations have played and continue to play in creating these problems.

Thomas Malthus (1766–1834) has long been cited as a voice of forewarning in the debate concerning population and food supplies. Malthus warned that because population grows geometrically and food production only increases arithmetically, the human race is endangered since population growth will always outrun food supplies. The only checks on this "law of population" are birth control and death. War, disease, and famine check the population by death, but to control birth, we must actively intervene. Although Malthus was mistaken on the *necessity* (at least in the short run in the "developed" countries) of population *always* outstripping food supplies, many still hold to his view that continued population growth cannot be sustained. Those who hold to his views concerning overpopulation and world hunger are called "neo-Malthusians," and they argue that overpopulation is the cause of world hunger. Garrett Hardin advocates this view.

According to Hardin, the problems encountered in countries such as India are the result of overpopulation. Overpopulation outruns the land's carrying capacity, and the end result is the *complete* inability to sustain life. Hardin points out that if we persist in feeding an overpopulated country, the results will be even more harmful than allowing those who are starving now to do so. Citing empirical evidence of the destruction that a minimally fed and overpopulated country wreaks on the land in the search for energy, he concludes that in order to provide adequate help, along with food we must send sufficient fuel (for warmth and cooking). Since this is nearly impossible, he argues that food-only policies must be abandoned. Hardin's moral argument is consequentialist and asserts that in looking to the most likely future, food-only programs do more harm than good, and our moral obligation is to refrain from causing harm.

Concerning those who are starving and those who are affluent, Peter Singer asserts a principle that states that if we can prevent suffering without sacrificing anything of comparable moral importance, then we are morally obligated to do so. Those with affluent lifestyles spend money on nonessential goods, and Singer finds this practice morally indefensible in view of the good the money could do when spent to alleviate suffering caused by starvation. Singer looks at the immediate consequences of suffering and does not focus on the long-range scenario that Hardin does. Singer makes a valuable contribution to the debate by considering the roles of the affluent nations in causing hunger in poverty-stricken nations. He argues that almost everyone is equally involved in the problems of overpopulation, pollution, and poverty, and hence moral obligations cannot be compartmentalized. Singer also points out that with our communications systems, we have become a "global village," and people may no longer justifiably claim ignorance of distant atrocities. Additionally, Singer argues, the principle of equality requires that we do not discriminate based on distance. In a later essay in this section Carlo Filice addresses this issue, including our duty to remain informed on distant atrocities.

John Arthur disagrees with Singer's conclusion that the affluent are morally obligated to give money, up to the point of sacrificing something of comparable moral importance. Arthur denies that Singer establishes that the affluent "few" have obligations to feed starving people. He argues that theories like Singer's fail to take into account the rights of the affluent. He states that there are cases where obligations of benevolence can override property rights; however, the fact that some are starving and some are affluent is not decisive in and of itself in settling the clash of rights. Arthur suggests that there is a duty of benevolence which *may* obligate those who are affluent not to exercise their consumption rights. Arthur further considers it a moral right to be able to pursue one's goals as one sees fit, as long as the rights of others are not violated. It is crucial, however, to determine precisely when our actions can be carried out without violating another's rights, in order to determine when we are obliged to act or not act.

In order to determine how our actions affect others, we need to become informed. What are our obligations for keeping informed, especially about distant atrocities? Carlo Filice addresses this question in his essay. As discussed above, Singer asserts that the fact that a starving person is in a distant part of the world does not excuse us from our moral duty to aid him or her. Filice agrees, especially for the "average" United States citizen. Filice reports the situation in East Timor as an example of a typical moral atrocity, particularly relevant because of the role the United States played. Most United States citizens are unaware of both the situation and the United States' role, although there is information (which must generally be sought out) in the public arena. Filice argues that most citizens are under a *prima facie* obligation (an authentic moral claim that may occasionally be overridden by another stronger moral claim) to keep informed of such distant atrocities. Indeed, Felice argues that being informed is a necessary condition for being able to fulfill one's moral obligation to help prevent a harm.

Concerning starvation, what models might we apply in order to help end current famines and prevent future occurrences? Lillian M. Li and J. D. Sethi address this question. Li argues that famines in Africa can be compared with those China experienced in the 1920s, and that the comparison may yield some possible solutions. Li points out that like the situation in China in the 1920s, the African famines occur in naturally vulnerable areas that are worsened by human behavior, including deforestation, overpopulation, poverty, ineffective agriculture, and political instability. The factors that allowed China to recover from famine include communal agriculture, grain rationing, and a powerful centralized government which gave famine relief high priority. Li considers the government actions of food production and distribution to be the most crucial in ending the famine, although she acknowledges that misuse of political power caused the famine of the Great Leap Forward. Li does make it clear that governmental policy will need to be culturally appropriate in order to be effective in Africa.

J. D. Sethi echoes the concern that government policy be culturally appropriate; however, he advocates a decentralization of power. Sethi asserts that any development strategy in the Third World must be compatible with the guarantee of basic rights, and must consist of two parts. First is the *below the line strategy,* wherein basic economic needs should be guaranteed and be consistent with legal and political rights. Second, rights may be expanded above the line, but this requires a different analysis and means of development.

Sethi argues that there are special problems of underemployment that plague Third World countries. He states that much of the debate about development and human rights is relevant only within the framework of mass prosperity. Developing countries often face problems of mass poverty, and thus the economic situations for the two worlds are quite disparate. Sethi argues that in order to address the great economic disparity, development cannot be had at the expense of human rights, as is often the focus when developed nations try to influence the developing nations. Sethi calls for the human being to be made the focus of development.

NOTES

1. Julie Denslow and Christine Padoch, *People of the Tropical Rainforest* (Berkeley: University of California Press, 1988), p. 169.
2. Jeremy Rifkin, *Beyond Beef: The Rise and Fall of the Cattle Culture* (New York: Dutton, 1992), p. 153.

Carrying Capacity as an Ethical Concept

Garrett Hardin

Garrett Hardin is a professor of biology at the University of California, Santa Barbara. His books include Population, Evolution, and Birth Control *(1969),* The Limits of Altruism: An Ecologist's View of Survival *(1977); and* Promethean Ethics: Living with Death, Competition, and Triage *(1980).*

Hardin supports a "lifeboat ethics" that is adapted from the notion of the tragedy of the commons. He argues that the developed countries should not help countries with starving people, such as those in India, by sending only food. He explains that the notion that those who are starving can be helped by food-only shipments is ill-founded because it assumes a fixed amount of people, and progress in conquering starvation. Hardin asserts that in sending food we are seriously harming *countries like India. He emphasizes that we can "never merely do one thing," and that supplying only food worsens political and economic strife, agricultural dependency, overpopulation, and environmental degradation.*

Lifeboat Ethics is merely a special application of the logic of the commons.[1] The classic paradigm is that of a pasture held as common property by a community and governed by the following rules: first, each herdsman may pasture as many cattle as he wishes on the commons; and second, the gain from the growth of cattle accrues to the individual owners of the cattle. In an underpopulated world the system of the commons may do no harm and may even be the most economic way to manage things, since management costs are kept to a minimum. In an overpopulated (or overexploited) world a system of the commons leads to ruin, because each herdsman has more to gain individually by increasing the size of his herd than he has to lose as a single member of the community guilty of lowering the carrying capacity of the environment. Consequently he (with others) overloads the commons.

Even if an individual fully perceives the ultimate consequences of his actions he is most unlikely to act in any other way, for he cannot count on the restraint *his* conscience might dictate being matched by a similar restraint on the part of *all* the others. (Anything less than all is not enough.) Since mutual ruin is inevitable, it is quite proper to speak of the *tragedy* of the commons.

Tragedy is the price of freedom in the commons. Only by changing to some other system (socialism or private enterprise, for example) can ruin be averted. In other

Reprinted by permission of *Soundings: An Interdisciplinary Journal, Volume 59,* No. 1, © 1976. [Edited]

words, in a crowded world survival requires that some freedom be given up. (We have, however, a choice in the freedom to be sacrificed.) Survival is possible under several different politico-economic systems—but not under the system of the commons. When we understand this point, we reject the ideal of distributive justice stated by Karl Marx a century ago. "From each according to his ability, to each according to his needs."[2] This ideal might be defensible if "needs" were defined by the larger community rather than by the individual (or individual political unit) *and if "needs" were static.*[3] But in the past quarter-century, with the best will in the world, some humanitarians have been asserting that rich populations must supply the needs of poor populations even though the recipient populations increase without restraint. At the United Nations conference on population in Bucharest in 1973 spokesmen for the poor nations repeatedly said in effect: "We poor people have the right to reproduce as much as we want to; you in the rich world have the responsibility of keeping us alive."

Such a Marxian disjunction of rights and responsibilities inevitably tends toward tragic ruin for all. It is almost incredible that this position is supported by thoughtful persons, but it is. How does this come about? In part, I think, because language deceives us. When a disastrous loss of life threatens, people speak of a "crisis," implying that the threat is temporary. More subtle is the implication of quantitative stability built into the pronoun "they" and its relatives. Let me illustrate this point with quantified prototype statements based on two different points of view.

Crisis analysis: "These poor people (1,000,000) are starving, because of a crisis (flood, drought, or the like). How can we refuse *them* (1,000,000)? Let us feed *them* (1,000,000). Once the crisis is past those who are still hungry are few (say 1,000) and there is no further need for our intervention."

Crunch analysis: "Those (1,000,000) who are hungry are reproducing. We send food to *them* (1,010,000). *Their* lives (1,020,000) are saved. But since the environment is still essentially the same, the next year *they* (1,030,000) ask for more food. We send it to *them* (1,045,000); and the next year *they* (1,068,000) ask for still more. Since the need has not gone away, it is a mistake to speak of a passing crisis: it is evidently a permanent crunch that this growing 'they' face—a growing disaster, not a passing state of affairs."

"They" increases in size. Rhetoric makes no allowance for a ballooning pronoun. Thus we can easily be deceived by language. We cannot deal adequately with ethical questions if we ignore quantitative matters. This attitude has been rejected by James Sellers, who dismisses prophets of doom from Malthus[4] to Meadows[5] as "chiliasts." Chiliasts (or millenialists, to use the Latin-derived equivalent of the Greek term) predict a catastrophic end of things a thousand years from some reference point. The classic example is the prediction of Judgment Day in the year 1000 anno Domini. Those who predicted it were wrong, of course; but the fact that this specific prediction was wrong is no valid criticism of the use of numbers in thinking. Millenialism is numerology, not science.

In science, most of the time, it is not so much exact numbers that are important as it is the relative size of numbers and the direction of change in the magnitude of them. Much productive analysis is accomplished with only the crude quantitation of "order of magnitude" thinking. First and second derivatives are often calculated with no finer aim than to find out if they are positive or negative. Survival can hinge on the crude issue of the sign of change, regardless of number. This is a far cry from the spurious precision of numerology. Unfortunately the chasm between the "two cultures," as C.P. Snow called them,[6] keeps many in the nonscientific culture from understanding the significance of the quantitative approach. One is tempted to wonder also whether an additional impediment to understanding may not be the mortal sin called Pride, which some theologians regard as the mother of all sins.

Returning to Marx, it is obvious that the *each* in "to each according to his needs" is not—despite the grammar—a unitary, stable entity: "each" is a place holder for a ballooning variable. Before we commit ourselves to saving the life of *each* and every person in need we had better ask this question: *"And then what?"* That is, what about tomorrow, what about posterity? As Hans Jonas has pointed out,[7] traditional ethics has almost entirely ignored the claims of posterity. In an overpopulated world humanity cannot long endure under a regime governed by posterity-blind ethics. It is the essence of ecological ethics that it pays attention to posterity.

Since "helping" starving people requires that we who are rich give up some of our wealth, any refusal to do so is almost sure to be attributed to selfishness. Selfishness there may be, but focusing on selfishness is likely to be non-productive. In truth, a selfish motive can be found in all policy proposals. The selfishness of *not* giving is obvious and need not be elaborated. But the selfishness of giving is no less real, though more subtle.[8] Consider the sources of support for Public Law 480, the act of Congress under which surplus foods were given to poor countries, or sold to them at bargain prices ("concessionary terms" is the euphemism). Why did we give food away? Conventional wisdom says it was because we momentarily transcended our normal selfishness. Is that the whole story?

It is not. The "we" of the above sentence needs to be subdivided. The farmers who grew the grain did not give it away. They sold it to the government (which then gave it away). Farmers received selfish benefits in two ways: the direct sale of grain, and the economic support to farm prices given by this governmental purchase in an otherwise free market. The operation of P.L. 480 during the past quarter-century brought American farmers to a level of prosperity never known before.

Who else benefited—in a selfish way? The stockholders and employees of the railroads that moved grain to seaports benefited. So also did freight-boat operators (U.S. "bottoms" were specified by law). So also did grain elevator operators. So also did agricultural research scientists who were financially supported in a burgeoning but futile effort "to feed a hungry world."[9] And so also did the large bureaucracy required to keep the P.L. 480 system working. In toto, probably several million people personally benefited from the P.L. 480 program. Their labors cannot be called wholly selfless.

Who *did* make a sacrifice for P.L. 480? The citizens generally, nearly two hundred million of them, paying directly or indirectly through taxes. But each of these many millions lost only a little: whereas each of the million or so gainers gained a great deal. The blunt truth is that *philanthropy pays*—if you are hired as a philanthropist. Those on the gaining side of P.L. 480 made a great deal of money and could afford to spend lavishly to persuade Congress to continue the program. Those on the sacrificing side sacrificed only a little bit per capita and could not afford to spend much protecting their pocketbooks against philanthropic inroads. And so P.L. 480 continued, year after year.

Should we condemn philanthropy when we discover that some of its roots are selfish? I think not, otherwise probably no philanthropy would be possible. The secret of practical success in large-scale public philanthropy is this: see to it that the losses are widely distributed so that the per captia loss is small, but concentrate the gains in a relatively few people so that these few will have the economic power needed to pressure the legislature into supporting the program.

I have spent some time on this issue because I would like to dispose once and for all of condemnatory arguments based on "selfishness." As a matter of principle we should always assume that selfishness is *part* of the motivation of every action. But what of it? If Smith proposes a certain public policy, it is far more important to know whether the policy will do public harm or public good than it is to know whether Smith's motives are selfish or selfless. Consequences ("ends") can be more objectively determined than motivations ("means"). Situational ethics wisely uses consequences as the measure of morality. "If the end does not justify the means, what does?" asked Joseph Fletcher.[10] The obsession of older ethical systems with means and motives is no doubt in part a consequence of envy, which has a thousand disguises.[11] (Though I am sure this is true, the situationist should not dwell on envy very long, for it is after all only a motive, and as such not directly verifiable. In any case public policy must be primarily concerned with consequences.)

Even judging an act by its consequences is not easy. We are limited by the basic theorem of ecology, "We can never do merely one thing."[12] The fact that an act has many consequences is all the more reason for deemphasizing motives as we carry out our ethical analyses. Motives by definition apply only to intended consequences. The multitudinous unintended ones are commonly denigrated by the term "side effects." But "The road to hell is paved with good intentions," so let's have done with motivational evaluations of public policy.

Even after we have agreed to eschew motivational analysis, foreign aid is a tough nut to crack. The literature is large and contradictory, but it all points to the inescapable conclusion that a quarter of a century of earnest effort has not conquered world poverty. To many observers the threat of future disasters is more convincing now than it was a quarter of a century ago—and the disasters are not all in the future either.[13] Where have we gone wrong in foreign aid?

We wanted to do good, of course. The question, "How can we help a poor country?" seems like a simple question, one that should have a simple answer. Our failure to answer it suggests that the question is not as simple as we thought. The variety of contradictory answers offered is disheartening.

How can we find our way through this thicket? I suggest we take a cue from a mathematician. The great algebraist Karl Jacobi (1804–1851) had a simple stratagem that he recommended to students who found themselves butting their heads against a stone wall. *Umkehren, immer umkehren*—"Invert, always invert." Don't just keep asking the same old question over and over: turn it upside down and ask the opposite question. The answer you get then may not be the one you want, but it may throw useful light on the question you started with.

Let's try a Jacobian inversion of the food/population problem. To sharpen the issue, let us take a particular example, say India. The question we want to answer is, "How can we help India?" But since that approach has repeatedly thrust us against a stone wall, let's pose the Jacobian invert, "How can we *harm* India?" After we've answered this perverse question we will return to the original (and proper) one.

As a matter of method, let us grant ourselves the most malevolent of motives: let us ask, "How can we harm India—*really* harm her?" Of course we might plaster the country with thermonuclear bombs, speedily wiping out most of the 600 million people. But, to the truly malevolent mind, that's not much fun: a dead man is beyond harming. Bacterial warfare could be a bit "better," but not much. No: we want something that will really make India suffer, not merely for a day or a week, but on and on and on. How can we achieve this inhumane goal?

Quite simply: by sending India a bounty of food, year after year. The United States exports about 80 million tons of grain a year. Most of it we sell: the foreign exchange it yields we use for such needed imports as petroleum (38 percent of our oil consumption in 1974), iron ore, bauxite, chromium, tin, etc. But in the pursuit of our malevolent goal let us "unselfishly" tighten our belts, make sacrifices, and do without that foreign exchange. Let us *give* all 80 million tons of grain to the Indians each year.

On a purely vegetable diet it takes about 400 pounds of grain to keep one person alive and healthy for a year. The 600 million Indians need 120 million tons per year; since their nutrition is less than adequate presumably they are getting a bit less than that now. So the 80 million tons we give them will almost double India's per capita supply of food. With a surplus, Indians can afford to vary their diet by growing some less efficient crops; they can also convert some of the grain into meat (pork and chickens for the Hindus, beef and chickens for the Moslems). The entire nation can then be supplied not only with plenty of calories, but also with an adequate supply of high quality protein. The people's eyes will sparkle, their steps will become more elastic; and they will be capable of more work. "Fatalism" will no doubt diminish. (Much so-called fatalism is merely a consequence of malnutrition.) Indians may even become a bit overweight, though they will still be getting only two-thirds as much food as the average inhabitant of a rich country. Surely—we think—surely a well-fed India would be better off?

Not so: *ceteris paribus,* they will ultimately be worse off. Remember, "We can never do merely one thing." A generous gift of food would have not only nutritional consequences: it would also have political and economic consequences. The difficulty of distributing free food to a poor people is well known. Harbor, storage, and transport inadequacies result in great losses of grain to rats and fungi. Political corruption diverts food from those who need it most to those who are more powerful. More abundant supplies depress free market prices and discourage native farmers from growing food in subsequent years. Research into better ways of agriculture is also discouraged. Why look for better ways to grow food when there is food enough already?

There are replies, of sorts, to all the above points. It may be maintained that all these evils are only temporary ones; in time, organizational sense will be brought into the distributional system and the government will crack down on corruption. Realizing the desirability of producing more food, for export if nothing else, a wise government will subsidize agricultural research in spite of an apparent surplus. Experience does not give much support to this optimistic view, but let us grant the conclusions for the sake of getting on to more important matters. Worse is to come.

The Indian unemployment rate is commonly reckoned at 30 percent, but it is acknowledged that this is a minimum figure. *Under*employment is rife. Check into a hotel in Calcutta with four small bags and four bearers will carry your luggage to the room—with another man to carry the key. Custom, and a knowledge of what the traffic will bear, decree this practice. In addition malnutrition justifies it in part. Adequately fed, half as many men would suffice. So one of the early consequences of achieving a higher level of nutrition in the Indian population would be to increase the number of unemployed.

India needs many things that food will not buy. Food will not diminish the unemployment rate (quite the contrary); nor will it increase the supply of minerals, bicycles, clothes, automobiles, gasoline, schools, books, movies, or television. All these things require energy for their manufacture and maintenance.

Of course, food is a form of energy, but it is convertible to other forms only with great loss; so we are practically justified in considering energy and food as mutually exclusive goods. On this basis the most striking difference between poor and rich countries is not in the food they eat but in the energy they use. On a per capita basis rich countries use about three times as much of the primary foods—grains and the like—as do poor countries. (To a large extent this is because the rich convert much of the grain to more "wasteful" animal meat.) But when it comes to energy, rich countries use ten times as much per capita. (Near the extremes Americans use 60 times as much per person as Indians.) By reasonable standards much of this energy may be wasted (e.g., in the manufacture of "exercycles" for sweating the fat off people who have eaten too much), but a large share of this energy supplies the goods we regard as civilized: effortless transportation, some luxury foods, a variety of sports, clean space-heating, more than adequate clothing, and energy-consuming arts—music, visual arts, electronic auxiliaries, etc. Merely giving food to a people does almost nothing to satisfy the appetite for any of these other goods.

But a well-nourished people is better fitted to try to wrest more energy from its environment. The question then is this: Is the native environment able to furnish more energy? And at what cost?

In India energy is already being gotten from the environment at a fearful cost. In the past two centuries millions of acres of India have been deforested in the struggle for fuel, with the usual environmental degradation. The Vale of Kashmir, once one of the garden spots of the world, has been denuded to such an extent that the hills no longer hold water as they once did, and the springs supplying the famous gardens are drying up. So desperate is the need for charcoal for fuel that the Kashmiri now make it out of tree leaves. This wasteful practice denies the soil of needed organic mulch.

Throughout India, as is well known, cow dung is burned to cook food. The minerals of the dung are not thereby lost, but the ability of dung to improve soil tilth is. Some of the nitrogen in the dung goes off into the air and does not return to Indian soil. Here we see a classic example of the "vicious circle": because Indians are poor they burn dung, depriving the soil of nitrogen and make themselves still poorer the following year. If we give them plenty of food, as they cook this food with cow dung they will lower still more the ability of their land to produce food.

Let us look at another example of this counter-productive behavior. Twenty-five years ago western countries brought food and medicine to Nepal. In the summer of 1974 a disastrous flood struck Bangladesh, killing tens of thousands of people, by government admission. (True losses in that part of the world are always greater than admitted losses.) Was there any connection between feeding Nepal and flooding Bangladesh? Indeed there was, and is.[14]

Nepal nestles amongst the Himalayas. Much of its land is precipitous, and winters are cold. The Nepalese need fuel, which they get from trees. Because more Nepalese are being kept alive now, the demand for timber is escalating. As trees are cut down, the soil under them is washed down the slopes into the rivers that run through India and Bangladesh. Once the absorption capacity of forest soil is gone, floods rise faster and to higher maxima. The flood of 1974 covered two-thirds of Bangladesh, twice the area of "normal" floods—which themselves are the consequence of deforestation in preceding centuries.

By bringing food and medicine to Nepal we intend only to save lives. But we can never do merely one thing, and the Nepalese lives we saved created a Nepalese energy-famine. The lives we saved from starvation in Nepal a quarter of a century ago were paid for in our time by lives lost to flooding and its attendant evils in Bangladesh. The saying, "Man does not live by bread alone," takes on new meaning.

Still we have not described what may be the worst consequence of a food-only policy: revolution and civil disorder. Many kindhearted people who support food aid programs solicit the cooperation of "hard-nosed" doubters by arguing that good nutrition is needed for world peace. Starving people will attack others, they say. Nothing could be further from the truth. The monumental studies of Ancel Keys and others have shown that starving people are completely selfish.[15] They are incapable of cooperating with others; and they are incapable of laying plans for tomorrow and carrying them out. Moreover, modern war is so expensive that even the richest countries can hardly afford it.

The thought that starving people can forcefully wrest subsistence from their richer brothers may appeal to our sense of justice, *but it just ain't so*. Starving people fight only among themselves, and that inefficiently.

So what would happen if we brought ample supplies of food to a population that was still poor in everything else? They would still be incapable of waging war at a distance, but their ability to fight among themselves would be vastly increased. With vigorous, well-nourished bodies and a keen sense of their impoverishment in other things, they would no doubt soon create massive disorder in their own land. Of course, they might create a strong and united country, but what is the probability of that? Remember how much trouble the thirteen colonies had in forming themselves into a United States. Then remember that India is divided by two major religions, many castes, fourteen major languages and a hundred dialects. A partial separation of peoples along religious lines in 1947, at the time of the formation of Pakistan and of independent India, cost untold millions of lives. The budding off of Bangladesh (formerly East Pakistan) from the rest of Pakistan in 1971 cost several million more. All these losses were achieved on a low level of nutrition. The possibilities of blood-letting in a population of 600 million well-nourished people of many languages and religions and no appreciable tradition of cooperation stagger the imagination. Philanthropists with any imagination at all should be stunned by the thought of 600 million well-fed Indians seeking to meet their energy needs from their own resources.

So the answer to our Jacobian questions, "How can we harm India?" is clear: send food *only*. Escaping the Jacobian by reinverting the question we now ask, "How can we *help* India?" Immediately we see that we must *never* send food without a matching gift of non-food energy. but before we go careening off on an intoxicating new program we had better look at some more quantities.

On a per capita basis, India uses the energy equivalent of one barrel of oil per year; the U.S. uses sixty. The world average of all countries, rich and poor, is ten. If we want to bring India only up to the present world average, we would have to send India about 9 x 600 million bbl. of oil per year (or its equivalent in coal, timber, gas or whatever). That would be more than five billion barrels of oil equivalent. What is the chance that we will make such a gift?

Surely it is nearly zero. For scale, note that our total yearly petroleum use is seven billion barrels (of which we import three billion). Of course we use (and have) a great deal of coal too. But these figures should suffice to give a feeling of scale.

More important is the undoubted psychological fact that a fall in income tends to dry up the springs of philanthropy. Despite wide disagreements about the future of energy it is obvious that from now on, for at least the next twenty years and possibly for centuries, our per capita supply of energy is going to fall, year after year. The food we gave in the past was "surplus." By no accounting do we have an energy surplus. In fact, the perceived deficit is rising year by year.

India has about one-third as much land as the United States. She has about three times as much population. If her people-to-land ratio were the same as ours she would have only about seventy million people (instead of 600 million). With the forested and relatively unspoiled farmlands of four centuries ago, seventy million people was probably well within the carrying capacity of the land. Even in today's India, seventy million people could probably make it in comfort and dignity—provided they didn't increase!

To send food only to a county already populated beyond the carrying capacity of its land is to collaborate in the further destruction of the land and the further impoverishment of its people.

Food plus energy is a recommendable policy; but for a large population under today's conditions this policy is defensible only by the logic of the old saying, "If wishes were horses, beggars would ride." The fantastic amount of energy needed for such a program is simply not in view. (We have mentioned nothing of the equally monumental "infrastructure" of political, technological, and educational machinery needed to handle unfamiliar forms and quantities of energy in the poor countries. In a short span of time this infrastructure is as difficult to bring into being as is an abundant supply of energy.)

In summary, then, here are the major foreign-aid possibilities that tender minds are willing to entertain:

a. Food plus energy—a conceivable, but practically impossible program.

b. Food alone—a conceivable and possible program, but one which would destroy the recipient.

In the light of this analysis the question of triage shrinks to negligible importance. If *any* gift of food to overpopulated countries does more harm than good, it is not necessary to decide which countries get the gift and which do not. For posterity's sake we should never send food to any population that is beyond the realistic carrying capacity of its land. The question of triage does not even arise. . .

NOTES

1. Garrett Hardin, 1968: "The Tragedy of the Commons," *Science*, 162: 1243–48.
2. Karl Marx, 1875: "Critique of the Gotha program." (Reprinted in *The Marx-Engels Reader*, Robert C. Tucker, editor. New York: Norton, 1972).
3. Garrett Hardin and John Baden, 1977. *Managing the Commons.* (San Francisco: W.H. Freeman.)
4. Thomas Robert Malthus, 1798: *An Essay on the Principle of Population, as It Affects the Future Improvement of Society.* (Reprinted, inter alia, by the University of Michigan Press, 1959, and The Modern Library, 1960).
5. Donella H. Meadows, Dennis L. Meadows, Jorgen Randers, and William H. Behrens, 1972: *The Limits to Growth* (New York: Universe Books).
6. C.P. Snow, 1963: *The Two Cultures; and a Second Look.* (New York: Mentor).

7. Hans Jonas, 1973: "Technology and Responsibility: Reflections on the New Task of Ethics," *Social Research,* 40:31–54.
8. William and Paul Paddock, 1967: *Famine—1975* (Boston: Little, Brown & Co.).
9. Garrett Hardin, 1975: "Gregg's Law," *BioScience,* 25:415.
10. Joseph Fletcher, 1966: *Situation Ethics* (Philadelphia: Westminster Press)
11. Helmut Schoeck, 1969: *Envy* (New York: Harcourt, Brace & World).
12. Garrett Hardin, 1972: *Exploring New Ethics for Survival* (New York: Viking).
13. Nicholas Wade, 1974: "Sahelian Drought: No Victory for Western Aid." *Science,* 185:234–37.
14. Erik P. Eckholm, 1975: "The Deterioration of Mountain Environments," *Science,* 189:764–70.
15. Ancel Keys, et al., 150: *The Biology of Human Starvation.* 2 vols. (Minneapolis: University of Minnesota Press).

Famine, Affluence, and Morality

Peter Singer

Peter Singer is a professor of philosophy and Director of the Centre for Human Bioethics at Monash University, in Victoria, Australia. His is the author of Animal Liberation *(1975) and* Practical Ethics *(1980) and the editor of* Applied Ethics *(1986).*

Singer considers it morally wrong for affluent people to spend money on nonessential goods while others are starving. Concerning the suffering of others, Singer asserts a principle we are moraly obligated to follow. The principle states that if we can prevent suffering without sacrificing anything of comparable moral importance, then we ought to do it. Giving monetary assistance to aid the starving is one way to prevent suffering. Those people who have the means are morally obligated to give money away until they sacrifice something of comparable moral importance, even if it requires them to radically alter and drastically reduce their standard of living.

As I write this, in November 1971, people are dying in East Bengal from lack of food, shelter, and medical care. The suffering and death that are occurring there now are not inevitable, not unavoidable in any fatalistic sense of the term. Constant poverty, a cyclone, and a civil war have turned at least nine million people into destitute refugees; nevertheless, it is not beyond the capacity of the richer nations to give enough assistance to reduce any further suffering to very small proportions. The decisions and actions of human beings can prevent this kind of suffering. Unfortunately, human beings have not made the necessary decisions. At the individual level, people have, with very few exceptions, not responded to the situation in any significant way. Generally speaking, people have not given large sums to relief funds; they have not written to their parliamentary representatives demanding increased government assistance; they have not demonstrated in the streets, held symbolic fasts, or done anything else directed toward providing the refugees with the means to satisfy their essential needs. At the government level, no government has given the sort of massive aid that would enable the refugees to survive for more than a few days. Britain, for instance, has given rather more than most countries. It has, to date, given £14,750,000. For comparative purposes, Britain's share of the nonrecoverable development costs of the Anglo-French Concorde project is already in excess of £275,000,000, and on present estimates will reach £440,000,000. The implication is that the British government values a super-

Singer, Peter; "Famine, Affluence; and Morality." *Philosophy and Public Afairs, Vol. 1,* No. 3, Spring 1972. Reprinted by permission of Princeton University Press.

sonic transport more than thirty times as highly as it values the lives of the nine million refugees. Australia is another country which, on a per capita basis, is well up in the "aid to Bengal" table. Australia's aid, however, amounts to less than one-twelfth of the cost of Sydney's new opera house. The total amount given, from all sources, now stands at about £65,000,000. The estimated cost of keeping the refugees alive for one year is £464,000,000. Most of the refugees have now been in the camps for more than six months. The World Bank has said that India needs a minimum of £300,000,000 in assistance from other countries before the end of the year. It seems obvious that assistance on this scale will not be forthcoming. India will be forced to choose between letting the refugees starve or diverting funds from her own development program, which will mean that more of her own people will starve in the future.[1]

These are the essential facts about the present situation in Bengal. So far as it concerns us here, there is nothing unique about this situation except its magnitude. The Bengal emergency is just the latest and most acute of a series of major emergencies in various parts of the world, arising both from natural and from man-made causes. There are also many parts of the world in which people die from malnutrition and lack of food independent of any special emergency. I take Bengal as my example only because it is the present concern, and because the size of the problem has ensured that it has been given adequate publicity. Neither individuals nor governments can claim to be unaware of what is happening there.

What are the moral implications of a situation like this? In what follows, I shall argue that the way people in relatively affluent countries react to a situation like that in Bengal cannot be justified; indeed, the whole way we look at moral issues—our moral conceptual scheme—needs to be altered, and with it, the way of life that has come to be taken for granted in our society.

In arguing for this conclusion I will not, or course, claim to be morally neutral. I shall, however, try to argue for the moral position that I take, so that anyone who accepts certain assumptions, to be made explicit, will, I hope, accept my conclusion.

I begin with the assumption that suffering and death from lack of food, shelter, and medical care are bad. I think most people will agree about this, although one may reach the same view by different routes. I shall not argue for this view. People can hold all sorts of eccentric positions, and perhaps for some of them it would not follow that death by starvation is in itself bad. It is difficult, perhaps impossible, to refute such positions, and so for brevity I will henceforth take this assumption as accepted. Those who disagree need read no further.

My next point is this: if it is in our power to prevent something bad from happening, without thereby sacrificing anything of comparable moral importance, we ought, morally, to do it. By "without sacrificing anything of comparable moral importance" I mean without causing anything else comparably bad to happen, or doing something that is wrong in itself, or failing to promote some moral good, comparable in significance to the bad thing that we can prevent. This principle seems almost as uncontroversial as the last one. It requires us only to prevent what is bad, and not to promote what is good, and it requires this of us only when we can do it without sacrificing anything that is, from the moral point of view, comparably important. I could even, as far as the application of my argument to the Bengal emergency is concerned, qualify the point so as to make it: if it is in our power to prevent something very bad from happening, without thereby sacrificing anything morally significant, we ought, morally, to do it. An application of this principle would be as follows: if I am walking past a shallow pond and see a child drowning in it, I ought to wade in and pull the child out. This will mean getting my clothes muddy, but this is insignificant, while the death of the child would presumably be a very bad thing.

The uncontroversial appearance of the principle just stated is deceptive. If it were acted upon, even in its qualified form, our lives, our society, and our world would be fundamentally changed. For the principle takes, firstly, no account of proximity or distance. It makes no moral difference whether the person I can help is a neighbor's child ten yards from me or a Bengali whose name I shall never know, ten thousand miles away. Secondly, the principle makes no distinction between cases in which I am the only person who could possibly do anything and cases in which I am just one among millions in the same position.

I do not think I need to say much in defense of the refusal to take proximity and distance into account. The fact that a person is physically near to us, so that we have personal contact with him, may make it more likely that we *shall* assist him, but this does not show that we *ought* to help him rather than another who happens to be further away. If we accept any principle of impartiality, universalizability, equality, or whatever, we cannot discriminate against someone merely because he is far away from us (or we are far away from him). Admittedly, it is possible that we are in a better position to judge what needs to be done to help a person near to us than one far away, and perhaps also to provide the assistance we judge to be necessary. If this were the case, it would be a reason for helping those near to us first. This may once have been a justification for being more concerned with the poor in one's own town than with famine victims in India. Unfortunately for those who like to keep their moral responsibilities limited, instant communication and swift transportation have changed the situation. From the moral point of view, the development of the world into a "global village" has made an important, though still unrecognized, difference to our moral situation. Expert observers and supervisors, sent out by famine relief organizations or permanently stationed in famine-prone areas, can direct our aid to a refugee in Bengal almost as effectively as we could get it to someone in our own block. There would seem, therefore, to be no possible justification for discriminating on geographical grounds.

There may be greater need to defend the second implication of my principle—that the fact that there are millions of other people in the same position, in respect to the Bengali refugees, as I am, does not make the situation significantly different from a situation in which I am the only person who can prevent something very bad from occurring. Again, of course, I admit that there is a psychological difference between the cases: one feels less guilty about doing nothing if one can point to others, similarly placed, who have also done nothing. Yet this can make no real difference to our moral obligations.[2] Should I consider that I am less obliged to pull the drowning child out of the pond if on looking around I see other people, no further away than I am, who have also noticed the child but are doing nothing? One has only to ask this question to see the absurdity of the view that numbers lessen obligation. It is a view that is an ideal excuse for inactivity; unfortunately most of the major evils—poverty, overpopulation, pollution—are problems in which everyone is almost equally involved.

The view that numbers do make a difference can be made plausible if stated in this way: if everyone in circumstances like mine gave £5 to the Bengal Relief Fund, there would be enough to provide food, shelter, and medical care for the refugees; there is no reason why I should give more than anyone else in the same circumstances as I am; therefore I have no obligation to give more than £5. Each premise in this argument is true, and the argument looks sound. It may convince us, unless we notice that it is based on a hypothetical premise, although the conclusion is not stated hypothetically. The argument would be sound if the conclusion were: if everyone in circumstances like mine were to give £5, I would have no obligation to give more than £5. If the conclusion were so stated, however, it would be obvious that the argument has no bearing on a situation in which it is not the case that everyone else gives £5. This, of course, is the actual situation. It is more or less certain that not everyone in circumstances like mine will give £5. So there will not be enough to provide the needed food, shelter, and medical care. Therefore by giving more than £5 I will prevent more suffering than I would if I gave just £5.

It might be thought that this argument has an absurd consequence. Since the situation appears to be that very few people are likely to give substantial amounts, it follows that I and everyone else in similar circumstances ought to give as much as possible, that is, at least up to the point at which by giving more one would begin to cause serious suffering for oneself and one's dependents—perhaps even beyond this point to the point of marginal utility, at which by giving more one would cause oneself and one's dependents as much suffering as one would prevent in Bengal. If everyone does this, however, there will be more than can be used for the benefit of the refugees, and some of the sacrifice will have been unnecessary. Thus, if everyone does what he ought to do, the result will not be as good as it would be if everyone did a little less than he ought to do, or if only some do all that they ought to do.

The paradox here arises only if we assume that the actions in question—sending money to the relief funds—are performed more or less simultaneously, and are also unexpected. For if it is to be expected that everyone is going to contribute something, then clearly each is not obliged to give as much as he would have been obliged to had others not been giving too. And if everyone is not acting more or less simultaneously, then those giving later will know how much more is needed, and will have no obligation to give more than is necessary to reach this amount. To say this is not to deny the principle that people in the same circumstances have the same obligations, but to point out that the fact that others have given or may be expected to give, is a relevant circumstance: those giving after it has become known that many others are giving and those giving before are not in the same circumstances. So the seemingly absurd consequence of the principle I have put forward can occur only if people are in error about the actual circumstances—that is, if they think they are giving when others are not, but in fact they are giving when others are. The result of everyone doing what he really ought to do cannot be worse than the result of everyone doing less than he ought to do, although the result of everyone doing what he reasonably believes he ought to do could be.

If my argument so far has been sound, neither our distance from a preventable evil nor the number of other people who, in respect to that evil, are in the same situation as we are, lessens our obligation to mitigate or prevent that evil. I shall therefore take as established the principle I asserted earlier. As I have already said, I need to assert it only in its qualified form: if it is in our power to prevent something very bad from happening, without thereby sacrificing anything else morally significant, we ought, morally, to do it.

The outcome of this argument is that our traditional moral categories are upset. The traditional distinction between duty and charity cannot be drawn, or at least, not in the place we normally draw it. Giving money to the Bengal Relief Fund is regarded as an act of charity in our society. The bodies which collect money are known as "charities." These organizations see themselves in this way—if you send them a check, you will be thanked for your "generosity." Because giving money is regarded as an act of charity, it is not thought that there is anything wrong with not giving. The charitable man may be praised, but the man who is not charitable is not condemned. People do not feel in any way ashamed or guilty about spending money on new clothes or a new car instead of giving it to famine relief. (Indeed, the alternative does not occur to them.) This way of looking at the matter cannot be justified. When we buy new clothes not to keep ourselves warm but to look "well-dressed" we are not providing for any important need. We would not be sacrificing anything significant if we were to continue to wear our old clothes, and give the money to famine relief. By doing so, we would be preventing another person from starving. It follows from what I have said earlier that we ought to give money away, rather than spend it on clothes which we do not need to keep us warm. To do so is not charitable, or generous. Nor is it the kind of act which philosophers and theologians have called "supererogatory"—an act which it would be good to do, but not wrong not to do. On the contrary, we ought to give the money away, and it is wrong not to do so.

I am not maintaining that there are no acts which are charitable, or that there are no acts which it would be good to do but not wrong not to do. It may be possible to redraw the distinction between duty and charity in some other place. All I am arguing here is that the present way of drawing the distinction, which makes it an act of charity for a man living at the level of affluence which most people in the "developed nations" enjoy to give money to save someone else from starvation, cannot be supported. It is beyond the scope of my argument to consider whether the distinction should be redrawn or abolished altogether. There would be many other possible ways of drawing the distinction—for instance, one might decide that it is good to make other people as happy as possible, but not wrong not to do so.

Despite the limited nature of the revision in our moral conceptual scheme which I am proposing, the revision would, given the extent of both affluence and famine in the world today, have radical implications. These implications may lead to further objections, distinct from those I have already considered. I shall discuss two of these.

One objection to the position I have taken might be simply that it is too drastic a revision of our moral scheme. People do not ordinarily judge in the way I have suggested they should. Most people reserve their moral condemnation for those who violate some moral norm, such as the norm against taking another person's property. They do not condemn those who indulge in luxury instead of giving to famine relief. But given that I did not set out to present a morally neutral description of the way people make moral judgments, the way people do in fact judge has nothing to do with the validity of my conclusion. My conclusion follows from the principle which I advanced earlier, and unless that principle is rejected, or the arguments shown to be unsound, I think the conclusion must stand, however strange it appears.

It might, nevertheless, be interesting to consider why our society, and most other societies, do judge differently from the way I have suggested they should. In a well-known article, J.O. Urmson suggests that the imperatives of duty, which tell us what we must do, as distinct from what it would be good to do but not wrong not to do, function so as to prohibit behavior that is intolerable if men are to live together in society.[3] This may explain the origin and continued existence of the present division between acts of duty and acts of charity. Moral attitudes are shaped by the needs of society, and no doubt society needs people who will observe the rules that make social existence tolerable. From the point of view of a particular society, it is essential to prevent violations of norms against killing, stealing, and so on. It is quite inessential, however, to help people outside one's own society.

If this is an explanation of our common distinction between duty and supererogation, however, it is not a justification of it. The moral point of view requires us to look beyond the interests of our own society. Previously, as I have already mentioned, this may hardly have been feasible, but it is quite feasible now. From the moral point of view, the prevention of the starvation of millions of people outside our society must be considered at least as pressing as the upholding of property norms within our society.

It has been argued by some writers, among them Sidgwick and Urmson, that we need to have a basic moral code which is not too far beyond the capacities of the ordinary man, for otherwise there will be a general breakdown of compliance with the moral code. Crudely stated, this argument suggests that if we tell people that they ought to refrain from murder and give everything they do not really need to famine relief, they will do neither, whereas if we tell them that they ought to refrain from murder and that it is good to give to famine relief but not wrong not to do so, they will at least refrain from murder. The issue here is: Where should we draw the line between conduct that is required and conduct that is good although not required, so as to get the best possible result? This would seem to be an empirical question, although a very difficult one. One objection to the Sidgwick-Urmson line of argument is that it takes insufficient account of the effect that moral standards can have on the decisions we make. Given a society in which a wealthy man who gives five percent of his income to famine relief is regarded as most generous, it is not surprising that a proposal that we all ought to give away half our incomes will be thought to be absurdly unrealistic. In a society which held that no man should have more than enough while others have less than they need, such a proposal might seem narrow-minded. What is is possible for a man to do and what he is likely to do are both, I think, very greatly influenced by what people around him are doing and expecting him to do. In any case, the possibility that by spreading the idea that we ought to be doing very much more than we are to relieve famine we shall bring about a general breakdown of moral behavior seems remote. If the stakes are an end to widespread starvation, it is worth the risk. Finally, it should be emphasized that these considerations are relevant only to the issue of what we should require from others, and not to what we ourselves ought to do.

The second objection to my attack on the present distinction between duty and charity is one which has from time to time been made against utilitarianism. It follows from some forms of utilitarian theory that we all ought, morally, to be working full time to increase the balance of happiness over misery. The position I have taken here would not lead to this conclusion in all circumstances, for if there were no bad occurrences that we could prevent without sacrificing something of comparable moral importance, my argument would have no application. Given the present conditions in many parts of the world, however, it does follow from my argument that we ought, morally, to be working full time to relieve great suffering of the sort that occurs as a result of famine or other disasters. Of course, mitigating circumstances can be adduced—for instance, that if we wear ourselves out through overwork, we shall be less effective than we would otherwise have been. Nevertheless, when all considerations of this sort have been taken into account, the conclusion remains: we ought to be preventing as much suffering as we can without sacrificing something else of comparable moral importance. This conclusion is one which we may be reluctant to face. I cannot see, though, why it should be regarded as a criticism of the position for which I have argued, rather than a criticism of our ordinary standards of behavior. Since most people are self-interested to some degree, very few of us are likely to do everything that we ought to do. It would, however, hardly be honest to take this as evidence that it is not the case that we ought to do it.

It may still be thought that my conclusions are so wildly out of line with what everyone else thinks and has always thought that there must be something wrong with the argument somewhere. In order to show that my conclusions, while certainly contrary to contemporary Western moral standards, would not have seemed so extraordinary at other times and in other places, I would like to quote a passage from a writer not normally thought of as a way-out radical, Thomas Aquinas.

> Now, according to the natural order instituted by divine providence, material goods are provided for the satisfaction of human needs. Therefore the division and appropriation of property, which proceeds from human law, must not hinder the satisfaction of man's necessity from such goods. Equally, whatever a man has in superabundance is owed, of natural right, to the poor for their sustenance. So Ambrosius says, and it is also to be found in the *Decretum Gratiani:* "The bread which you withhold belongs to the hungry; the clothing you shut away, to the naked; and the money you bury in the earth is the redemption and freedom of the penniless."[4]

I now want to consider a number of points, more practical than philosophical, which are relevant to the application of the moral conclusion we have reached. These points challenge not the idea that we ought to be doing all we can to prevent starvation, but the idea that giving away a great deal of money is the best means to this end.

It is sometimes said that overseas aid should be a government responsibility, and that therefore one ought not to give to privately run charities. Giving privately, it is said, allows the government and the noncontributing members of society to escape their responsibilities.

This argument seems to assume that the more people there are who give to privately organized famine relief funds, the less likely it is that the government will take over full responsibility for such aid. This assumption is unsupported, and does not strike me as at all plausible. The opposite view—that if no one gives voluntarily, a government will assume that its citizens are uninterested in famine relief and would not wish to be forced into giving aid—seems more plausible. In any case, unless there were a definite probability that by refusing to give one would be helping to bring about massive government assistance, people who do refuse to make voluntary contributions are refusing to prevent a certain amount of suffering without being able to point to any tangible beneficial consequence of their refusal. So the onus of showing how their refusal will bring about government action is on those who refuse to give.

I do not, of course, want to dispute the contention that governments of affluent nations should be giving many times the amount of genuine, no-strings-attached aid that they are giving now. I agree, too, that giving privately is not enough, and that we ought to be campaigning actively for entirely new standards for both public and private contributions to famine relief. Indeed, I would sympathize with someone who thought that campaigning was more important than giving oneself, although I doubt whether preaching what one does not practice would be very effective. Unfortunately, for many people the idea that "it's the government's responsibility" is a reason for not giving which does not appear to entail any political action either.

Another, more serious reason for not giving to famine relief funds is that until there is effective population control, relieving famine merely postpones starvation. If we save the Bengal refugees now, others, perhaps the children of these refugees, will face starvation in a few years' time. In support of this, one may cite the now well-known facts about the population explosion and the relatively limited scope for expanded production.

This point, like the previous one, is an argument against relieving suffering that is happening now, because of a belief about what might happen in the future; it is unlike the previous point in that very good evidence can be adduced in support of this belief about the future. I will not go into the evidence here. I accept that the earth cannot support indefinitely a population rising at the present rate. This certainly poses a problem for anyone who thinks it important to prevent famine. Again, however, one could accept the argument without drawing the conclusion that it absolves one from any obligation to do anything to prevent famine. The conclusion that should be drawn is that the best means of preventing famine, in the long run, is population control. It would then follow from the position reached earlier that one ought to be doing all one can to promote population control (unless one held that all forms of population control were wrong in themselves, or would have significantly bad consequences). Since there are organizations working specifically for population control, one would then support them rather than more orthodox methods of preventing famine.

A third point raised by the conclusion reached earlier relates to the question of just how much we all ought to be giving away. One possibility, which has already been mentioned, is that we ought to give until we reach the level of marginal utility—that is, the level at which, by giving more, I would cause as much suffering to myself or my dependents as I would relieve by my gift. This would mean, of course, that one would reduce oneself to very near the material circumstances of a Bengali refugee. It will be recalled that earlier I put forward both a strong and a moderate version of the principle of preventing bad occurrences. The strong version, which required us to prevent bad things from happening unless in doing so we would be sacrificing something of comparable moral significance, does seem to require reducing ourselves to the level of marginal utility. I should also say that the strong version seems to me to be the correct one. I proposed the more moderate version—that we should prevent bad occurrences unless to do so, we had to sacrifice something morally significant—only in order to show that even on this surely undeniable principle a great change in our way of life is required. On the more moderate principle, it may not follow that we ought to reduce ourselves to the level of marginal utility, for one might hold that to reduce oneself and one's family to this level is to cause something significantly bad to happen. Whether this is so I shall not discuss, since, as I have said, I can see no good reason for holding the moderate version of the principle rather than the strong version. Even if we accepted the principle only in its moderate form, however, it should be clear that we would have to give away enough to ensure that the consumer society, dependent as it is on people spending on trivia rather than giving famine relief, would slow down and perhaps disappear entirely. There are several reasons why this would be desirable in itself. The value and necessity of economic growth are now being questioned not only by conservationists, but by economists as well.[5] There is no doubt, too, that the consumer society has had a distorting effect on the goals and purposes of its members. Yet looking at the matter purely from the point of view of overseas aid, there must be a limit to the extent to which we should deliberately slow down our economy; for it might be the case that if we gave away, say forty percent of our Gross National Product, we would slow down the economy so much that in absolute terms we would be giving less than if we gave twenty-five percent of the much larger GNP that we would have if we limited our contribution to this smaller percentage.

I mention this only as an indication of the sort of factor that one would have to take into account in working out an ideal. Since Western societies generally consider one percent of the GNP an acceptable level for overseas aid, the matter is entirely academic. Nor does it affect the question of how much an individual should give in a society in which very few are giving substantial amounts.

It is sometimes said, though less often now than it used to be, that philosophers have no special role to play in public affairs, since most public issues depend primarily on an assessment of facts. On questions of fact, it is said, philosophers as such have no special expertise, and so it has been possible to engage in philosophy without committing oneself to any position on major public issues. No doubt there are some issues of social policy and foreign policy about which it can truly be said that a really expert assessment of the facts is required before taking sides or acting, but the issue of famine is surely not one of these. The facts about the existence of suffering are beyond dispute. Nor, I think, is it disputed that we can do something about it, either through orthodox methods of famine relief or through population control or both. This is therefore an issue on which philosophers are competent to take a position. The issue is one which faces everyone who has more money than he needs to support himself and his dependents, or who is in a position to take some sort of political action. These categories must include practically every teacher and student of philosophy in the universities of the Western world. If philosophy is to deal with matters that are relevant to both teachers and students, this is an issue that philosophers should discuss.

Discussion, though, is not enough. What is the point of relating philosophy to public (and personal) affairs if we do not take our conclusions seriously? In this instance, taking our conclusion seriously means acting upon it. The philosopher will not find it any easier than anyone else to alter his attitudes and way of life to the extent that, if I am right, is involved in doing everything that we ought to be doing. At the very least, though, one can make a start. The philosopher who does so will have to sacrifice some of the benefits of the consumer society, but he can find compensation in the satisfaction of a way of life in which theory and practice, if not yet in harmony, are at least coming together.

NOTES

1. There was also a third possibility: that India would go to war to enable the refugees to return to their lands. Since I wrote this paper, India has taken this way out. The situation is no longer that described above, but this does not affect my argument, as the next paragraph indicates.
2. In view of the special sense philosophers often give to the term, I should say that I use "obligation" simply as the abstract noun derived from "ought," so that "I have an obligation to" means no more, and no less, than "I ought to." This usage is in accordance with the definition of "ought" given by the *Shorter Oxford English Dictionary:* "the general verb to express duty or obligation." I do not think any issue of substance hangs on the way the term is used; sentences in which I use "obligation" could all be rewritten, although somewhat clumsily, as sentences in which a clause containing "ought" replaces the term "obligation."
3. J. O. Urmson, "Saints and Heroes," in *Essays in Moral Philosophy,* ed. Abraham I. Melden (Seattle and London, 1958), p. 214. For a related but significantly different view see also Henry Sidgwick, *The Methods of Ethics,* 7th ed. (London, 1907) pp. 220–221, 492–493.
4. *Summa Theologica,* II–II, Question 66, Article 7, in *Aquinas, Selected Political Writings,* ed. A. P. d'Entreves, trans J. G. Dawson (Oxford, 1948), p. 171.
5. See, for instance, John Kenneth Galbraith, *The New Industrial State* (Boston, 1967); and E. J. Mishan, *The Costs of Economic Growth* (London, 1967).

Rights and the Duty to Bring Aid

John Arthur

John Arthur is a professor of philosophy at State University of New York, Binghamton. He is the author of Justice and Economic Distribution *(1978) and* The Unfinished Constitution *(1989).*

Arthur asserts that views which are utilitarian in nature and hold that the affluent are morally obligated to help prevent starvation do not give the rights of the affluent adequate weight. Arthur takes issue with Peter Singer's principle which mandates that those who are affluent have a moral duty to give aid to the suffering if this aid does not cost the affluent anything of comparable moral importance. He places much weight on the importance of rights and denies that the rights of those suffering from starvation automatically outweigh the rights of the affluent in their quest for satisfaction of their interests. He argues instead for a duty of benevolence that may at times obligate the affluent to refrain from exercising their right to consume.

I

There is no doubt that the large and growing incidence of world hunger constitutes a major problem, both moral and practical, for the fortunate few who have surpluses of cheap food. Our habits regarding meat consumption exemplify the magnitude of the moral issue. Americans now consume about two and one-half times the meat they did in 1950 (currently about 125 lbs. per capita per year). Yet, meat is extremely inefficient as a source of food. Only a small portion of the total calories consumed by the animal remains to be eaten in the meat. As much as 95 percent of the food is lost by feeding and eating cattle rather than producing the grain for direct human consumption. Thus, the same amount of food consumed by Americans largely indirectly in meat form could feed one and a half billion persons on a (relatively meatless) Chinese diet. Much, if not all, of the world's food crisis could be resolved if Americans were simply to change their eating habits by moving toward direct consumption of grain and at the same time providing the surpluses for the hungry. Given this, plus the serious moral problems associated with animal suffering,[1] the overall case for vegetarianism seems strong.

I want to discuss here only one of these two related problems, the obligations of the affluent few to starving people. I begin by considering a recent article on the subject by Peter Singer, entitled "Famine, Affluence, and Morality."[2] I argue that Singer fails to establish the claim that such an obligation

John Arthur, "Rights and the Duty to Bring Aid" in *World Hunger and Moral Obligation*, Aiken/LaFollette, eds., © 1977, pp. 37–48. Reprinted by permission of John Arthur.

exists. This is the case for both the strong and weak interpretations of his view. I then go on to show that the role of rights needs to be given greater weight than utilitarian theories like Singer's allow. The rights of both the affluent and the starving are shown to be morally significant but not in themselves decisive, since obligations of benevolence can and often do override rights of others (e.g., property rights). Finally, I argue that under specific conditions the affluent are obligated not to exercise their rights to consume at the expense of others' lives.

II

Singer's argument is in two stages. First, he argues that two general moral principles are and ought to be accepted. Then he claims that the principles imply an obligation to eliminate starvation. The first principle is simply that "suffering and death from lack of food, shelter and medical care are bad."[3] This principle seems obviously true and I will have little to say about it. Some may be inclined to think that the existence of an evil in itself places an obligation on others, but that is, of course, the problem which Singer addresses. I take it that he is not begging the question in this obvious way and will argue from the existence of evil to the obligation of others to eliminate it. But how, exactly, does he establish the connection? It is the second principle which he thinks shows that connection.

The necessary link is provided by either of two versions of this principle. The first (strong) formulation which Singer offers of the second principle is as follows:

> if it is in our power to prevent something bad from happening, without thereby sacrificing anything of comparable moral importance, we ought, morally, to do it.[4]

The weaker principle simply substitutes for "comparable moral importance" the phrase "any moral significance." He goes on to develop these notions, saying that:

> By "without sacrificing anything of comparable moral importance" I mean without causing anything else comparably bad to happen, or doing something that is wrong in itself, or failing to promote some moral good, comparable in significance to the bad thing we can prevent.[5]

These remarks can be interpreted for the weaker principle by simply eliminating "comparable" in the statement.

One question is, of course, whether either of these two principles ought to be accepted. There are two ways in which this could be established. First, they could be shown, by philosophical argument, to follow from reasonably well established premises or from a general theory. Second, they might be justified because they are principles which underlie particular moral judgments the truth of which is accepted. Singer doesn't do either of these explicitly, although he seems to have the second in mind. He first speaks of what he takes to be the "uncontroversial appearance" of the principles. He then applies the principles to a similar case in which a drowning child requires help. Singer argues, in essence, that since the drowning is bad and it can be avoided without sacrificing something of moral significance, it is obligatory that the child be saved. He claims further that both the strong and weak versions are sufficient to establish the duty. Dirtying one's clothes, for example, is not of "moral significance" and so does not justify failure to act. The last part of his paper is devoted to the claim that the analogy between the case of the child and starving people is apt in that geographical distance and others' willingness to act are not acceptable excuses for inaction.

III

My concern here is not with these latter issues. Rather, I want to focus on the two versions of the second principle, discussing each in terms of (1) whether it is plausible, and (2) if true, whether it establishes the duty to provide aid. I will deal with the weak version first, arguing that it fails at step (2) in the argument.

This version reads, "if it is in our power to prevent something bad from happening without thereby sacrificing *anything* morally significant we ought morally to do it." Singer later claims that:

> Even if we accept the principle in its moderate form, however, it should be clear that we would have to give away enough to ensure that the consumer society, dependent as it is on people spending on trivia rather than giving to famine relief, would slow down and perhaps disappear entirely.[6]

The crucial idea of "morally significant" is left largely unanalyzed. Two examples are given: dirtying one's clothes and being "well dressed." Both are taken to be morally *in*significant.

It could perhaps be argued against Singer that these things *are* morally significant. Both, for example, would be cases of decreasing aesthetic value, and if you think aesthetic values are intrinsic you might well dispute the claim that being "well dressed" is without moral significance. There is, however, a more serious objection to be raised. To see this, we need to distinguish between the possible value of the *fact* of being "well dressed" and the value of the *enjoyment* some persons receive and create by being "well dressed" (and, of course, the unhappiness avoided by being "badly dressed").

That such enjoyment and unhappiness are of some moral significance can be seen by the following case. Suppose it were possible that, by simply singing a chorus of "Dixie" you could eliminate all the unhappiness and embarrassment that some people experience at being badly dressed. Surely, doing that would be an act of moral significance. It would be good for you to do so, perhaps even wrong not to. Similarly, throwing mud on people's clothes, though not a great wrong, is surely not "without *any* moral significance."

It seems then, that the weak principle (while perhaps true) does not generally establish a duty to provide aid to starving people. Whether it does in specific instances depends on the nature of the cost to the person providing the aid. If *either* the loss to the giver is in itself valuable or the loss results in increased unhappiness or decreased happiness to someone, then the principle does not require that the burden be accepted.

(It is interesting to ask just how much giving *would* be required by this principle. If we can assume that givers would benefit in some minimal way by giving—and that they are reasonable—then perhaps the best answer is that the level of giving required is the level that is actually given. Otherwise, why would people *not* give more if there is no value to them in things they choose to keep?)

In addition to the moral significance of the costs that I just described, there is a further problem which will become particularly significant in considering the strong principle. For many people it is part of their moral sense that they and others have a special relationship to their own goals or projects. That is, in making one's choices a person may properly weigh the outcome that one desires more heavily than the goals that others may have. Often this is expressed as a right or entitlement.[7] Thus, for example, if P acquires some good (x) in a just social arrangement without violating others' rights, then P has a special title to x that P is entitled to weigh against the desires of others. P need not, in determining whether he ought to give x to another, overlook the fact that x is his; he acquired it fairly, and so has special say in what happens to it. If this is correct, it is a fact of some moral significance and thus would also block the inference from the weak principle to the obligation to give what one has to others. I will pursue this line of argument in the following section while considering the strong version of the principle.

IV

Many people, especially those inclined toward utilitarianism, would probably accept the preceding, believing that it is the stronger of the two principles that should be used. "After all," they might argue, "the real issue is the great *disparity* between the amount of good which could be produced by resources of the rich if applied to problems of starvation as against the small amount of good produced by the resources if spent on second cars and houses, fancy clothes etc." I will assume that the facts are just as the claim suggests. That is, I will assume that it can *not* be plausibly argued that there are, for example, artistic or cultural values which (1) would be lost by such redistribution of wealth and (2) are equal in value to the starvation which would be eliminated. Thus, if the strong principle is true, then it (unlike the weak version) would require radical changes in our common understanding of the duties of the wealthy to starving people.

But is it true, as Singer suggests, that "if it is in our power to prevent something bad from happening without thereby sacrificing something of comparable moral significance we ought morally to do it"? Here the problem with the meaning of "moral significance" is even more acute than in the weak version. All that was required for the weak principle was that we be able to distinguish courses of action that have moral significance from those that do not. Here, however, the moral significance of alternative acts must be both *recognized* and *weighed*. And how is this to be done, according to Singer? Unfortunately, he provides little help here, though this is crucial in evaluating his argument.

I will discuss one obvious interpretation of "comparable moral significance," argue it is inadequate, and then suggest what I take to be some of the factors an adequate theory would consider.

Assuming that giving aid is not "bad in itself," the only other facts which Singer sees as morally significant in evaluating obligations are the good or bad consequences of actions. Singer's strong version obviously resembles the act utilitarian principle. With respect to starvation, this interpretation is open to the objection raised at the end of part III above, since it takes no account of a variety of important factors, such as the apparent right to give added weight to one's own choices and interests, and to ownership. I now wish to look at this claim in more detail.

Consider the following examples of moral problems which I take to be fairly common. One obvious means by which you could aid others is with your body. Many of your extra organs (eye, kidney) could be given to another with the result that there is more good than if you kept both. You wouldn't see as well or live as long, perhaps, but that is not of comparable significance to the benefit others would receive. Yet, surely the fact that it is your eye and you need it is not insignificant. Perhaps there could be cases where one is obligated to sacrifice one's health or sight, but what seems clear is that this is not true in every case where (slightly) more good would come of your doing so. Second, suppose a woman has a choice between remaining with her husband or leaving. As best she can determine, the morally relevant factors do not indicate which she should do (the consequences of each seem about equally good and there is no question of broken promises, deception, or whatever). But, suppose in addition to these facts, it is the case that by remaining with her husband the women will be unable to pursue important aspects of the plan of life she has set for herself. Perhaps by remaining she will be forced to sacrifice a career which she wishes to pursue. If the *only* facts that are of moral significance are the consequences of her choice, then she ought, presumably, to flip a coin (assuming there is some feature of her staying that is of equal importance to the unhappiness at the loss of the career *she* will experience). Surely, though, the fact that some goals are ones *she* chooses for herself (assuming she doesn't violate the others' rights) is of significance. It is, after all, *her* life and *her* future and she is entitled to treat it that way. In neither of these cases is the person required to accept as equal to his or her own goals and well-being the welfare of even his or her family, much less the whole world. The fact that others may benefit even slightly more from their pursuing another course is not in itself sufficient to show they ought to act other than they choose. Servility, though perhaps not a vice, is certainly not an obligation that all must fulfill.[8]

The above goes part way, I think, in explaining the importance we place on allowing people maximal latitude in pursuing their goals. Rights or entitlements to things that are our own reflect important facts about people. Each of us has only one life and it is uniquely valuable to each of us. Your choices do not constitute my life, nor do mine yours. The purely utilitarian interpretation of "moral significance" provides for assigning no special weight to the goals and interests of individuals in making their choices. It provides no basis for saying that though there may be greater total good done by one course, still a person could be entitled for some reason to pursue another.

It seems, then, that determining whether giving aid to starving persons would be sacrificing something of comparable moral significance demands weighing the fact that the persons are entitled to give special weight to their own interests where their future or (fairly acquired) property is at issue. Exactly *how much* weight may be given is a question that I will consider shortly. The point here is that the question of the extent of the obligation to eliminate starvation has not been answered. My argument was that however "moral significance" is best understood, it is far too simple to suggest that *only* the total good produced is relevant. If providing quality education for one's children is a goal, then (assuming the resources were acquired fairly) the fact that it is a goal *itself* provides additional weight against other ways the resources might be used, including the one that maximizes the total good. Further, if the resources to be used for the purpose are legitimately owned, then that too is something that the parent is entitled to consider.

Returning to the case of the drowning child, the same point may be made. Suppose it is an important part of a person's way of life that he not interfere. Perhaps the passer-by believes God's will is being manifested in this particular incident and strongly values noninterference with God's working out of His plan. Surely, this is especially relevant to the question of whether the person is obligated to intervene, even when the greatest good would be promoted by intervention. When saying that a person is obligated to act in some way, the significance *to the person* of the act must not only be considered along with all the other features of the act, but is also of special moral significance in determining that person's duty. More, however, needs to be said here.

Suppose, for instance, that the case were like this: A passer-by sees a child drowning but fails to help, not for the sake of another important goal but rather out of lack of interest. Such situations are not at all uncommon, as when people fail to report violent crimes they observe in progress. I assume that anyone who fails to act in such circumstances is acting wrongly. As with the case of the utilitarian principle discussed earlier, the drowning child also represents a limiting case. In the former, *no* significance is assigned to the woman's choice by virtue of its being *hers*. Here, however, the interests of *others* are not weighed. An acceptable principle of benevolence would fall between the two limiting cases. The relative moral significance of alternative acts could then be determined by applying the principle, distinguishing acts which are obligatory from charitable ones.

In summary, I have argued that neither the strong nor the weak principle advanced by Singer provides an adequate solution to the issue of affluence and hunger. The essential problem is with his notion of "moral significance." I argued that the weak principle fails to show any obligations, given the normal conception of factors which possess such significance. I then argued that the strong principle (which is close to act utilitarianism) is mistaken. The basic objection to this principle is that it fails to take account of certain aspects of the situation which must be considered in any adequate formulation of the principle.

V

As I suggested earlier, a fully adequate formulation of the principle of benevolence depends on a general theory of right. Such a theory would not only include a principle of benevolence but also give account of the whole range of rights and duties and a means to weigh conflicting claims. In this section, I discuss some of the various problems associated with benevolence, obligation, and rights. In the final section, I offer what I believe to be an adequate principle of benevolence.

One view, which has been criticized recently by Judith Thomson,[9] suggests that whenever there is a duty or obligation there must be a corresponding right. I presume we want to say that in some cases (e.g., the drowning child) there is an obligation to benevolence, but does this also mean that the child has a *right* to be aided? Perhaps there is only a semantic point here regarding "right," but perhaps also there is a deeper disagreement.

I suggest that, whether we call it a "right" or not, there are important differences between obligations based on benevolence and other obligations. Two differences are significant. First, the person who has the obligation to save the drowning child did not *do anything* that created the situation. But, compare this case with a similar one of a lifeguard who fails to save someone. Here there is a clear sense in which the drowning victim may claim a right to have another do his utmost to save him. An agreement was reached whereby the lifeguard *accepted* the responsibility for the victim's welfare. The guard, in a sense, took on the goals of the swimmers as his own. To fail to aid is a special sort of injustice that the passer-by does not do. It seems clearly appropriate to speak of the lifeguard's failure to act as a case of a right being violated.

A second important point regarding the drowning child example and rights is that the passer-by is not *taking positive steps* in reference to the child. This can be contrasted with an action that might be taken to drown a child who would not otherwise die. Here, again, it is appropriate to describe this act as a violation of a right (to life). Other violations of rights also seem to require that one act, not merely fail to take action—for example, property rights (theft) and privacy rights (listening without leave). The drowning child and starvation cases are wrong not because of acts but the failure to act.

Thus, there are important differences between duties of benevolence and others where a right is obviously at issue. Cases of failing to aid are not (unlike right violations) either instances of positive actions that are taken or ones in which the rich or the passer-by has taken responsibility by a previous act. It does not follow from this, however, that strong obligations are not present to save other persons. Obviously, one ought to aid a drowning child (at least) in cases where there is no serious risk or cost to the passer-by. This is true even though there is no obvious right that the child has to be aided.

Furthermore, if saving a drowning child requires using someone's boat without their permission (a violation of property right), then it still ought to be done. Duties to bring aid can override duties not to violate rights. The best thing to say here is that, depending on the circumstances, duties to aid and not to violate rights can each outweigh the other. Where actions involve both violation of rights and failing to meet duties to aid (the lifeguard's failing to save), the obligation is stronger than either would be by itself. Describing the situation in this way implies that although there is a sense in which the boat owner, the affluent spender, and the passer-by have a right to fail to act, still they are obligated not to exercise that right because there is a stronger duty to give aid.

Some may be inclined to say, against this, that in fact the passer-by does not have such a right not to help. But this claim is ambiguous. If what is meant is that they ought to help, then I agree. There is, however, still a point in saying owners of food have the right to use the food as they see fit. It serves to emphasize that there is a moral difference between these cases and ones where the object of need is *not* legitimately owned by anyone (as, for example, if it's not another's boat but a log that the drowning child needs). To say that the property right is *lost* where the principle of benevolence overrides is to hide this difference, though it is morally significant.

Other people might be inclined to say about these situations that the point of saying someone has a right to their food, time, boat or whatever is that others ought not to intervene to force them to bring aid. A person defending this view might accept my claim that in fact the person ought to help. It might then be argued that because they are not violating a right of another (to be saved) and they have a (property) right to the good, others can't, through state authority, force them to bring aid.

This claim obviously raises a variety of questions in legal and political philosophy, and is outside the scope of the present paper. My position does not preclude good samaritan laws, nor are they implied. This is a further question which requires further argument. That one has a moral right to x, but is obligated for other reasons not to exercise the right, leaves open the issue of whether others either can or should make that person fulfill the obligation.

If what I have said is correct, two general points should be made about starvation. First, even though it may be that the affluent have a right to use resources to pursue their own goals, and not provide aid, they may also be strongly obligated not to exercise the right. This is because, in the circumstances, the duty to benevolence is overriding. The existence and extent of such an obligation can be determined only by discovering the relative weight of these conflicting principles. In the final section, I consider how this should be done.

Second, even if it is also true that the passer-by and the affluent do not violate a right of another in failing to help, it may still be the case that they strongly ought not do so. Of course, their behavior could also be even worse than it is (by drowning the child or sending poisoned food to the hungry and thus violating their rights). All that shows, however, is that the failure to help is not the *most* morally objectionable course that can be imagined in the circumstances. This point hardly constitutes justification for failing to act.

VI

I argued earlier that neither Singer's weak principle nor the utilitarian one is what we are after. The former would imply (wrongly) little or no duty of benevolence, and the latter does not take seriously enough the rights and interests of the affluent. What is needed is a principle which we may use to determine the circumstances in which the needs of others create a duty to bring aid which is more stringent than the rights of the affluent to pursue their own interests and use their property as they desire.

The following principle, while similar to the utilitarian one, seems to be most adequate: "If it is in our power to prevent death of an innocent without sacrificing anything of *substantial* significance then we ought morally to do it." The problem, of course, is to determine exactly what is meant by "substantial significance." I assume there are no duties present that arise out of others' rights, as, for example, those of one's children to be provided for. Considerations of that sort would lead beyond the present paper. My concern here is limited to instances in which there is a question of bringing aid (where no obvious right to the aid is present) or using resources for other (preferred) ends.

There are two questions which are important in deciding whether what is being given up by the affluent is of substantial significance. First, we might specify *objectively* the needs which people have, and grant that the duty to bring aid is not present unless these needs have already been met. Included among the needs which are of substantial significance would be those things without which a person cannot continue to function physically—for example, food, clothing, health care, housing, and sufficient training to provide these for oneself.

It also, however, seems reasonable that certain psychological facts ought to be weighed before a person is obligated to help others meet their needs. For example, if you cannot have an even modestly happy life without some further good, then surely that, too, is something to which you are entitled. This suggests a second, *subjective* standard that should also be employed to determine whether something is of no substantial significance and so ought not be consumed at the expense of others' basic needs. The best way to put this, I believe, is to say that "if the lack of x would not affect the long-term happiness of a person, then x is of no substantial significance." By "long-term happiness" I mean to include anything which, if not acquired, will result in unhappiness over an extended period of one's life, not just something the lack of which is a source of momentary loss but soon forgotten. Thus, in a normal case, dirtying one's clothes to save a drowning child is of no substantial significance and so the duty of benevolence is overriding. If, however, selling some possession for famine relief would mean the person's life *really is* (for a long period) less happy, then the possessions are of substantial significance and so the person is not wrong in exercising the right of ownership instead of providing aid. If the possessions had been sold, it would have been an act of charity, not fulfillment of a duty. The same analysis can be provided for other choices we make—for example, how our time is spent and whether to donate organs. If doing so would result in your not seeing well and this would make your life less happy over time, then you are not obligated to do so.

If what I have said is correct, then duties of benevolence increase as one's dependence on possessions for living a happy life decreases. If a person's long-term happiness does not depend on (second?) cars and fancy clothes, then that person ought not to purchase those goods at the expense of others' basic needs being unfulfilled. Thus, depending on the psychological nature of persons, their duties of benevolence will vary.

The question of the actual effect of not buying a new car, house, clothes, or whatever on one's long-term happiness is of course a difficult one. My own feeling is that if the principle were to be applied honestly, those of us who are relatively affluent would discover that a substantial part of the resources and time we expend should be used to bring aid. The extent of the obligation must, finally, be determined by asking whether the lack of some good *really would* result in a need not being met or in a less happy life for its owner, and that is a question between each of us and our conscience.

In summary, I have argued that Singer's utilitarian principle is inadequate to establish the claim that acts to eliminate starvation are obligatory, but that such an obligation still exists. The rights of both the affluent and the hungry are considered, and a principle is defended which clarifies the circumstances in which it is a duty and not merely charitable to provide aid to others whose basic needs are not being met.

NOTES

1. Peter Singer, *Animal Liberation* (New York: New York Review of Books/Random House, 1975).
2. Peter Singer, "Famine, Affluence, and Morality," *Philosophy and Public Affairs,* I, no. 3 (Spring 1972).
3. Ibid., p. 149.
4. Ibid.
5. Ibid. I assume "importance" and "significance" are synonymous.
6. Ibid., p. 156.
7. In a recent book (*Anarchy, State, and Utopia,* New York: Basic Books, 1974), Robert Nozick argues that such rights are extensive against state authority.
8. For an argument that servility is wrong, see Thomas Hill, "Servility and Self-Respect," *The Monist,* VII, no. 4 (January 1973).
9. Judith Jarvis Thomson, "The Right to Privacy," *Philosophy and Public Affairs,* IV, no. 4 (Summer 1975).

On the Obligation to Keep Informed about Distant Atrocities

Carlo Filice

Carlo Filice is a professor of philosophy at the College at Geneseo, State University of New York.

Filice argues that we have a prima facie *duty to remain informed about distant atrocities. This duty is connected to our duty to help prevent major, avoidable harms such as suffering and death, whenever helping only requires us to make trivial sacrifices. He argues that in order for one to be truly helpful, one also has an obligation to place oneself in a position to be able to help prevent the harm. Felice states that the information necessary to judge one's ability to help end or prevent major harms is available to most people in developed countries and can be had without making major sacrifices. Given the conditions and guidelines Filice sets out, he concludes that it is morally wrong not to keep informed and not to help prevent all major, avoidable harm.*

One must know about faraway moral atrocities if one is to attempt to remedy them. Ignorance of these atrocities is at times a legitimate excuse for failure to make such attempts but not generally. It certainly is not a legitimate excuse when one deliberately keeps oneself uninformed of major atrocities; an example of such a person would be the well-educated, refined hedonist whose world revolves, by conscious choice, around private pleasure. On the other hand, it is a legitimate excuse in many cases when one simply lacks the means for being informed; an example of such would be the seriously underprivileged, culturally deprived, illiterate person.

But what about the cases of those people who fall somewhere between these two extremes? What about the single mother, working full-time as a nurse, who takes care of her children's needs most of the remainder of her hours? What about the young businessman almost wholly preoccupied with his struggle to make it in the business world? What about the medical student whose workload saps her of all desire to look at additional printed pages? What about the secretary whose after-work life is dedicated to cultivating her interest in French literature? What about the real estate agent in constant pursuit of new listings and loan agreements, who finds barely enough time to spend with her family? What about the small farmer in whose circle of friends and relatives questions about what might be happening in China, Brazil, or Mozambique do not come up? Is their relative ignorance of major moral atrocities excusable? Is their consequent inaction excusable?

Reprinted by permission of *Human Rights Quarterly, Vol. 12;* No. 3; August 1990. [Edited]

This is the issue I would like to explore in this essay. My claim will be that this type of ignorance is not excusable in most cases of "average" Westerners and of "average" U.S. citizens in particular. Consequently this ignorance does not excuse their doing nothing about large-scale abuses.

Consider the events in East Timor during the last fifteen years. They constitute a typical major moral atrocity. The choice of this example is recommended by a number of factors: (1) the relative magnitude of the evil; (2) the supportive (military, economic, diplomatic) role played by the U.S. government and others in this bloody episode; (3) the fact that most of us are unaware of this atrocity; (4) the fact that some sources of information concerning it can be found in the public arena, though they generally must be sought out.

The following are the basic facts of the East Timor situation as reported by Noam Chomsky and Edward S. Herman who gathered them from various uncontestable sources:

> On December 7, 1975 Indonesian armed forces invaded the former Portuguese colony of East Timor, only a few hours after the departure of President Gerald Ford and Henry Kissinger from a visit to Jakarta. Although Indonesia has effectively sealed off East Timor from the outside world, reports have filtered through indicating that there have been massive atrocities, with estimates running to 100,00 killed, about one-sixth of the population. An assessment by the Legislative Research Service of the Australian Parliament concluded that there is "mounting evidence that the Indonesians have been carrying out a brutal operation in East Timor," involving "indiscriminate killing on a scale unprecedented in post–World War II history."[1]

The above account reflects the number of dead as of 1979. A 1987 estimate as reported by the *New York Times* is 150,000. The entire population of East Timor was estimated by the *New York Times* in 1974 to be 620,000. That means that by now nearly one fourth of the population of this tiny, backward area has been killed. The main reason for the Indonesian invasion was the 1975 popular victory in East Timor (one year after East Timor was granted independence from Portugal) of a party named FRETILIN and the defeat of more conservative parties. FRETILIN's character is summarized by Chomsky and Herman on the basis of independent reports:

> FRETILIN was a moderate reformist national front, headed by a Catholic seminarian and initially involving largely urban intellectuals, among them young Lisbon-educated radical Timorese who "were most eager to search for their cultural origins" and who were "to lead the FRETILIN drive into the villages initiating consumer and agricultural cooperatives, and a literary campaign conducted in (the native language) along the lines used by Paulo Freire in Brazil. . . . It was "more reformist than revolutionary," calling for gradual steps towards complete independence, agrarian reform, transformation of uncultivated land and large farms to people's cooperatives, educational programs, steps towards producer-consumer cooperatives supplementing existing Chinese economic enterprises "for the purposes of supplying basic goods to the poor at low prices, controlled foreign aid and investment, and a foreign policy of non-alignment."[2]

This victorious party's platform did not please the Indonesian leadership which ten years earlier had carried out an internal purge of half a million suspected "communists." Thus, under a pretext to end a civil war in East Timor (there had in fact been some fighting between followers of FRETILIN and of UDT that had, however, quickly come to an end due to the former's preponderance of public support), Indonesia invaded and sealed the area from international observers and organizations, including the International Red Cross, and finding widespread indigenous resistance, proceeded to carry out the slaughter.

It is important to note that between 1973 and 1977 Indonesia received \$254 million of military aid (in arms, military aid grants, and military sales credit), and \$634 million in economic aid from the U.S.[3] Moreover, during this time 1,272 Indonesian military officers received

U.S. military training.[4] These facts, together with the timing of the invasion, (just after high-level consultations with Ford and Kissinger), the traditionally close ties between the Indonesian and the U.S. governments, and the lack of serious protests by the United States in the years since the invasion, show complicity on the part of the U.S. government and establishment, which included the media and the intellectual community.

The attempt by Indonesia to "pacify" East Timor has continued during the last thirteen years. While this was happening, the few books and reports on the massacre have generally escaped wide public attention in both the United States and in Europe. When mainstream publications such as the *New York Times* and *Newsweek* have reported on the invasion, they have generally distorted what actually occurred, by relying upon official Indonesian accounts, by ignoring reports offered by refugees in Portugal, and at least on one occasion, by deliberately altering the published version of events given by an Australian reporter who was in East Timor during the early weeks of the invasion.[5]

One could go on with such depressing details. One could also tell similar stories about other states within the U.S. sphere of influence such as Guatemala, Thailand, El Salvador, and Brazil. The point is that the case of East Timor is not an anomaly. The factors which make it an example of a slaughter relevant for the present essay apply to many other cases. In nearby El Salvador, for example, we find a regime which has permitted, or perhaps sponsored, the death-squad killing of tens of thousands during the last twelve years.[6] That same regime has received consistent U.S. economic, military, and diplomatic aid. Again, despite the magnitude of the evil, its proximity to the United States, and its greater news coverage, most of us are unable to locate El Salvador on a world map.

Because the "average" U.S. citizen does not know these massacres occur, nor of the government's relatively close ties to the regimes perpetrating them, the average citizen does nothing to help end the slaughters. Is this ignorance and resulting inaction morally excusable? The following is one line of argument in favor of a "no" answer. It tries to establish that most of us are under a prima facie obligation to keep informed about cases such as East Timor. What it maintains about U.S. citizens would also apply to citizens of other major powers whose governments play supportive roles in the atrocities of other governments.

1. One has a prima facie obligation to help prevent harm, especially major, avoidable suffering and death, whenever helping to do so requires only trivial sacrifices, such as buying fewer or no luxury items, spending less time watching television, etc., and whenever there is some chance that one's efforts will produce at least some success.[7]
2. One will not be in a position to help prevent harm if one is unaware of the occurrence of this harm.
3. One who has a prima facie obligation to help prevent X also has a prima facie obligation to attempt to position oneself so as to be able to help prevent X, particularly if these positional attempts are likely to be successful (e.g., if A has a prima facie duty to prevent his own violent behavior, A also has a prima facie duty to attempt to remain sober if drunkenness tends to make A violent, and if A's attempts to remain sober are not absolutely hopeless).
4. Therefore, each of us has a prima facie obligation to make serious attempts to become and remain informed about the occurrence of major, avoidable harm whenever these attempts at gaining the necessary information are likely to succeed and require small sacrifices, and whenever there is some chance for the prevention of at least some harm.
5. Major moral atrocities, such as the systematic and large-scale torture and killing by a government for political reasons, constitute one class of major avoidable harm.
6. Therefore, each of us has a prima facie obligation to make serious attempts to be informed about the occurrence of major moral atrocities (whenever the conditions in 4 above obtain).
7. Most people in developed countries who attempt to gain the necessary information are likely to succeed.

8. Most people in developed countries can make serious attempts to gain the necessary information about current moral atrocities without such attempts resulting in major sacrifices.
9. The preventive actions based on such information have some likelihood of leading to the prevention of at least some harm resulting from major moral atrocities.
10. Therefore, most people in developed countries have a prima facie obligation to make serious attempts to become informed about the current major moral atrocities, especially those occurring within their country's sphere of influence.

I will enlarge on this argument by considering a number of likely objections.

OBJECTION I: CITIZENS ARE POLITICALLY TOO NAIVE.

Attempting to seek information about ongoing atrocities taking place outside the sphere of most mainstream news coverage requires a prior decision to do so. This decision, in turn, cannot come about unless one has a considerable awareness of history and global politics. For example, one must know that mainstream national news services, even in "open" societies, tend to have blind spots concerning stories that would embarrass the fatherland and harm its perceived interests. One must know that there is a vast and complex world outside of one's own borders and that simple characterizations of this world, such as "Free World" versus "Communist World," are quite misleading. The average U.S. citizen, however, lacks this necessary historical and political astuteness, arguably through no fault of his or her own. Thus, since "ought" implies "can," and the average U.S. citizen lacks the cultural-motivational prerequisites to decide to seek information, he or she cannot really make such decisions, and thus cannot be morally obligated to seek such information. Similarly, naive creatures like young children cannot be under a moral obligation to decide to learn how to read so as to become responsible citizens.

This seems plausible, but consider a parallel argument. Johnny has grown up amidst people who perceive women as subservient to men. This assessment is reinforced by his sincere religious beliefs, which are also shared by his family and friends. It never occurs to Johnny to examine the validity of his view of women. Upon marrying, he bullies his wife into a subservient role, often through physical threats. He construes her complaints as symptoms of her rebellious and spoiled character. Shall we say that because Johnny is motivationally incapable of questioning his own assumptions about gender roles, he has no obligation to do so and consequently no obligation to change?[8]

Surely such an assertion would be problematic. There may be some extreme cases where a person, for example, a child, is absolutely incapable of examining his own morally dubious beliefs. In most cases, however, a person has some moments of doubt, even if briefly and rarely. At such times there is at least the possibility of serious probing. If most individuals who have such momentary doubts choose not to probe and instead slide back into blind self-righteousness, this does not show an absolute incapacity for change. It does show how difficult change is in these circumstances. Needless to say, however, fulfilling moral obligations is often quite difficult. While failure to do what one should may be understood and perhaps even forgiven, this does not lessen one's duty.

Similar things can be said about the alleged incapacity to decide to seek information about massive atrocities generally ignored or downplayed by mainstream media. Most people on at least some occasion do get hints that not all that is important is reported on television or in the local paper. These hints may come from some unusual public broadcasting program; or from one's own or an acquaintance's overseas trip which exposes one to slightly different and more skeptical points of view; or from one too many public confessions by government spokespersons about official lies; or from newsworthy events like Watergate and the Iran-contra affair. These occasional doubts concerning one's ordinary sources of information constitute tiny motivational openings which can lead to decisions to seek further and to see what additional matters are regularly being kept from one. The fact that on these occasions of doubt most individuals choose not to probe further does not show an absolute incapacity to do so. The additional fact that one's failing to do so can be understood and perhaps even forgiven does not lessen one's obligation to make such decisions.

OBJECTION II: CITIZENS ARE TOO POWERLESS TO FIND OUT.

Should the average U.S. citizen decide to seek the relevant information, are there not a number of factors which show that he or she most likely will not succeed in finding out about affairs such as the East Timor or the El Salvador bloodshed? Consider the following: large numbers of people are only semi-literate and would not walk into a library or bookstore or even read a newspaper. Others more literate lack knowledge of geography, history, international affairs, economics, and political and religious ideologies. They lack the general intellectual sophistication to know where to start looking and how to interpret what they find. Should this large majority of people not be exempt from the obligation to seek knowledge of matters beyond their intellectual reach?

My answer to this second objection is similar to my preceding reply. This second objection shows how difficult it is for most people to become informed about atrocities. Most people would first, or in the process, have to broaden themselves on many different fronts before they would be armed to do the requisite research. This intellectual broadening most people will choose not to do. However, I find it excessive to say that most people cannot do it.[9] Help can always be found, whether from the parish priest, the local librarian, or the college educated daughter-in-law. Naturally, sacrifices would have to be made.

But, our opponent might continue, most parish priest, librarians, and college educated daughters-in-law have never even heard of places like East Timor, and they may barely recognize names such as El Salvador, Indonesia, Guatemala, and Paraguay. How can they be counted on to inform the rest of us about what is going on there? If such information is available mainly in relatively obscure publications such as *The Nation* or Amnesty International reports which are not found in most libraries and bookstores, and they are not mentioned in most university courses, how can the average citizen be held morally accountable for being unaware of it? Should the blame not go to the mainstream press and to mainstream educators instead?

Undoubtedly, the press and the intellectual corps are preeminent bearers of moral responsibility for not taking sufficient measures to inform themselves and the public of various moral atrocities. But given that there are publications, albeit off the main media routes, which do report on these matters, is this responsibility not shared also by average middle-class literate citizens? Perhaps their responsibility is diminished due to their greater difficulty in attaining access to this information. But clearly one would not want to accept the principle that major wrongdoing can be ignored whenever information about it is hard to obtain, since such ignorance would have justified ignoring Nazi atrocities during the 1930s and 1940s.

The fact that difficulty of access can be overcome is shown by the success average citizens have had in pursuing their family "roots." The ingenuity in overcoming language, culture, and time barriers demonstrated by those seeking genealogical data belies attestations concerning the average person's research impotence. While one should not press the "roots" analogy too much, it is noteworthy that it, too, requires some prior preparatory work before the actual research can be undertaken. It may require learning to use libraries, to seek assistance, to consult with experts, and so on. The key point is that one does find ways when pursuing what is close to one's heart. The essential step, therefore, consists in bringing important moral matters close to one's heart. Failure to do so is not a failure due to research impotence. It is more like the unwillingness to take the moral point of view and thereby recognize "that objectively no one matters more than anyone else."[10]

OBJECTION III: HELP ONLY THOSE YOU CAN, I.E., YOUR NEIGHBORS.

The average individual's attempt to influence matters like the Indonesian policy vis-à-vis East Timor, runs this objection, is not likely to lead to the prevention of any harm. Perhaps if most individuals acted collectively, the likelihood of harm-prevention would be quite significant. But the effort of a lone individual is completely negligible, especially if one sets aside drastic options such as a public hunger strike. Would one not be more effectively beneficent by helping instead local charities, an alcoholic relative, or the neighborhood stray cats? And if so, why waste time and effort in trying to become informed about distant atrocities?

Naturally, there is some validity to this line of thinking. One's replies might include the following observations. First, one must concede that an individual alone will not generally accomplish visible results when speaking out on distant occurrences about which offical-dom—government, educational institutions, the press—is silent. But surely there are exceptions to this. If nothing else, the average individual may be heard by a few other individuals, each of whom, in turn, might reach a few others, generating a significant ripple effect. Perhaps, someone will be reached who has considerable power or access to the public ear.

Second, if likelihood of impact were an absolute moral prerequisite for action, then one could argue that a person should also not invest any effort in speaking out on those matters on which many others are already speaking out. Why? Because to add one more voice to a chorus of thousands would make no noticeable difference. Hence, the principle here presumed—i.e., that one should speak out only when one's voice is likely to have some nonnegligible effect—will justify a policy of almost never speaking out on large-scale affairs. Surely this consequence is objectionable, since such affairs are not what they could and should be. At the very least the magnitude of the preventable evil is an additional factor one should consider in deciding what to do.

Third, the ideal conditions for "local morality" cannot be obtained in the actual world. Perhaps in an ideal world where power and resources are somewhat equitably distributed, if each tends only to her own locality where a noticeable difference can be affected, the global result would probably be morally acceptable (though protection of common resources, such as the ozone layer, would require global and collective attention). But in a world like ours, where resources and power are disproportionately distributed, often through past and present injustice, the policy of each tending to her own property and community will not lead to morally acceptable global results. In this askew world, pursuing one's personal interests and community interests may mean keeping those in Timor or Brazil dispossessed; and one's power to do so is likely to more than offset another's power to improve his or her position. Any view that justifies the pursuit of ends benefiting only oneself and one's own, and that neglects to consider seriously the implications of such pursuits for "others," does not deserve the appellation "moral." Impartiality must be one of the essential features of the moral viewpoint. One aim of this viewpoint is the transcendence of the "one's own/others" dichotomy, hard as this may be.[11] Impartiality in an interconnected world implies a cosmopolitan outlook.

Thus, the principle at issue—only speak out on those issues where one's voice is *likely* to have a noticeable effect—must be rejected on moral grounds. It may be necessary, of course, to choose those ways of speaking out that are most likely to be productive, since the goal is not to attain some empty psychological and moral purity. Thus, one should, perhaps, write to those legislators, newspapers, and organizations which are most likely to listen and which can help publicize one's cause. There is no point in sending letters or articles to *The National Review* about East Timor or El Salvador and then expressing outrage when this material is not printed. As I have argued, however, the need for intelligence in one's efforts must not collapse into the need to limit one's focus to parochial matters.

Needless to say, having an obligation to find out about, and speak out on, distant matters does not exempt one from obligations to help the local indigent, alcoholic, or cat. Many of us can do both. In fact, since parochial and distant matters often causally interact, one may need to do both. But, one might ask, where does one draw the line? And where does one find the time? One does have to earn a living so as to be in a position to help both the local and the distant needy. One does have to fulfill one's family obligations. And one needs to take care of oneself, to do things for sheer pleasure, or to develop artistic and other skills, and not out of moral considerations.

Obviously these questions lead to immense complexities. One suggestion may be that in the interest of time and effectiveness what each individual should devote herself to, in addition to providing for self, family, and friends, depends on the individual's circumstances and expertise. For instance, the lawyer might most effectively use some of her time to defend the interests of the local disenfranchised and speak out about the misuses of the legal system in South Africa or about the U.S. government's selective and self-serving compliance with World Court decisions; the local radio announcer might best use her position to insert unusual and personally researched news items into ordinary broadcasts; the corporate employee might best explore the policies of the firm's international division, and if necessary blow the whistle on ethically dubious practices. Despite countless idiosyncrasies and complications, it remains a fact that most (or at least many) individuals can afford to sacrifice some of the time and resources ordinarily allotted for personal pleasure for the sake of those less fortunate.

These sacrifices need not result in significant "losses." One might, in fact, find that these "moral" pursuits will turn into creative and satisfying projects. These projects may even become replacements for some of one's more mindless leisure activities. Perhaps this is hoping for too much. At any rate, being embattled by myriad prima facie moral obligations, as well as by various practical exigencies, psychological addictions, and other demands, need not paralyze a person. To be sure, juggling all of these interests is quite a challenge; yet, given our present global interdependency and our wide informational access, it must be part of the condition of the average Westerner. As Sartre might say, choose one must. Such choices can be made intelligently and consciously, or nonreflectively and haphazardly. Morally speaking, there is no dilemma here. . . .

OBJECTION IV: IT WOULD BE GREAT TO HELP, BUT IS IT WRONG NOT TO HELP?

Philosophers of ethics distinguish between acts that are morally required and acts that, while commendable if done, are not obligatory, called "supererogatory" acts. Sharing one's salary with some group of destitute strangers constitutes a commendable but not an obligatory act. What about taking steps to broaden oneself culturally and intellectually in order to be able to keep abreast of foreign developments so as to help fight against major moral abuses? Wouldn't this also be a commendable but not required course of action? If so, the average citizen is not under any compelling obligation to engage in this course of action.

Let us assume that the commendable/obligatory distinction is valid. Even so, by appealing to certain considerations of compensatory justice it can be shown that the information-seeking course of action is obligatory. Consider the salary sharing example. While generally your sharing your salary with some poor strangers is not morally required (though some historical figures, like Jesus, have thought otherwise), what if you have contributed—even if only to a tiny degree—to their systematic impoverishment and have done so in some unfair way? One would think then that by way of compensation you owe them at least some help or some fraction of your possessions.

Has the average citizen contributed to a tiny degree, and in an unfair way, to the moral atrocities committed by foreign governments and the U.S. government in Vietnam? Those who would answer "yes" can advance the following argument:

1. In a democratic country, the government speaks for citizens and invests some of their tax money in foreign affairs. It performs this general function with their knowledge and approval. It is, thus, their agent or broker.
2. The U.S. government has helped, and continues to help, many brutal foreign regimes, often with some of its citizens' tax money.
3. Therefore, U.S. citizens' agent has clearly supported brutal foreign regimes.
4. A person shares responsibility with the agent for what the latter does while carrying out the duties with which it is charged; and the responsibility is shared even when the agent's actions are taken without the person's knowledge, so long as the agent is granted broad powers of action.
5. The U.S. government is given broad powers of action, especially in foreign affairs, and often does not fully inform the citizens about its foreign policies.
6. Therefore, the average U.S. citizen shares responsibility with the government for its foreign affairs policies which often support brutal foreign regimes.

Having thus contributed to moral atrocities, U.S. citizens are morally obligated to help the victims of such atrocities by way of compensation, if nothing else.[12]

But what about the case of those citizens who oppose the government's policies and vote for or otherwise support candidates and parties who call for an end to support to brutal regimes? Are these citizens not exempt from any complicity in these atrocities? Must they take further and more drastic actions, such as not paying a proportional share of their income taxes, in order to satisfy their moral obligations? Considered in its own right, this is a very difficult issue. For our purposes it suffices to say that this group constitutes a very small minority (most people, again, do not cast their votes and support on the basis of a candidate's position on foreign policy issues). Moreover, the type of person who is aware of and opposes these immoral foreign policies has thereby shown currency with the relevant world events and has already taken steps to help alleviate the atrocities. For most of the rest of us, the argument still stands.

But what if the government, as our agent, conceals from us or at least fails to explicitly inform us about its activities in other parts of the world? Would this not relieve us of the responsibility for the related atrocities despite our contribution to these atrocities through, for example, unwitting financial support? To answer this, we would have to know how actively we tend to seek the relevant information from our agent; how willing we are to close our eyes to its practices; and whether there are sources which can, if necessary, provide us with the relevant information. What has already been said on these issues shows that we can uncover our government's role in foreign atrocities.[13] In that case we, the citizens, remain partially responsible for its foreign deeds, and our compensatory obligation stands. In fact, once the moral obligation is seen as deriving from the principle of compensatory justice, our duty to help alleviate systematic human rights abuses becomes much stronger than would be the case if it derived merely from a general obligation to prevent harm to people we have in no way affected. Our actions and omissions have affected and do affect distant people, however unwitting we may be in this.

Because of this contribution to the harm, we have a particularly compelling duty to inform ourselves about these distant atrocities. Indeed, there are many other major sources of harm in our world, such as famines, diseases, environmental destruction, and the nuclear arms threat. My earlier argument, based on a general obligation to prevent harm, can also be used to spur us into keeping informed about these other evils. But if the demands upon our personal time and energy become too burdensome, and we must choose among subjects about which to keep informed, then we ought to inform ourselves first about those major evils to which we contribute—directly, through our actions, and indirectly, through the actions of our representative government. And while such major evils will not be confined to distant atrocities, some of these atrocities will surely fall under this most stringent category.

One must add that this argument has made no mention of the economic benefits that accrue to us through big business' exploitation of favorable foreign conditions (e.g., cheap labor, cheap resources, lenient safety regulations, low taxes, etc.). These favorable investment conditions are often systematically maintained by repressive regimes at steep human rights costs. Most of us benefit considerably from the success of these multinational firms. We benefit as consumers through cheaper products. We benefit as investors in stocks, banks, pension funds, and through greater dividends. And we benefit many other ways, given the support by multinationals for media organizations, hospitals, universities, and the arts. Accordingly, are we not obligated to compensate those who are violently repressed so that such benefits will continue to flow our way? . . .

The victims in El Salvador, East Timor, and elsewhere are not simply children, and perhaps they are not our "neighbors," but in our current global village, their cries can be heard by most of us, if we are willing to listen. And many of us unwittingly benefit from and contribute to their suffering. In such circumstances, one would think that the distance of the victims would not lessen our obligation to pay attention and take action.

NOTES

1. Noam Chomsky and Edward S. Herman, *The Washington Connection and Third World Fascism,* vol. 1 of *The Political Economy of Human Rights* (Boston: South End Press, 1979), 130.
2. Ibid., 134. The internal quotation quotes Jill Joliffe, *East Timor: Nationalism and Colonialism* (Australia: University of Queensland Press, 1978), 79.
3. Ibid., 45. The original sources of these data are the following: United States Department of Defense, *Foreign Military Sales and Military Assistance Facts* (Washington, 1976); U.S. Department of Defense, *Security Assistance Program, Presentation to Congress,* F.Y. 1978 (Washington, 1977); U.S. Agency for International Development, *U.S. Overseas Loans and Grants,* 1 July 1945–30 June 1975 (Washington, 1976).
4. Chomsky and Herman, 45.
5. Ibid., 136–38.
6. According to a 1985 Americas Watch Report these were the relevant statistics: "more than 40,000 civilian noncombatants killed—murdered by government forces and 'death squads' allied to them; another 3,000 disappeared; 750,000 or so (15 percent of the population, . . . homeless or 'displaced' within its borders." "With Friends Like These," in Cynthia Brown, ed., *Americas Watch Report on Human Rights and U.S. Policy in Latin America* (New York: Pantheon Books, 1985), 115.

   According to *New York Times* reporter James LeMoyne, "The Civil War has killed more than 70,000 people, most of them civilians shot by the army during the early 1980's." The victims have included nuns, priests, and an archbishop. No one has been successfully prosecuted and arrested for any of these thousands of killings. James LeMoyne, "The Guns of Salvador," *New York Times Magazine*, 5 Feb. 1989, 20.

7. The notion of "prima facie obligation" employed in this argument is most naturally derivative from consequentialist moral theories. However, I believe that it can also be grounded on deontological theories of rights and obligations. I would think that victims of torture and killing are entitled, by virtue of having basic "negative" rights, to receiving our help in avoiding being tortured and killed. However, this topic is too vast for it to be properly addressed here. I choose not to rely on the notion of rights generally, because I find rights to be metaphysically suspect unless they are taken as derived from more basic values such as harm and benefit.
8. Michael Slote correctly observes that the principle of "ought implies can" is vague because "(s)omeone might, for example, argue that since (a rich person), because of his given nature, is so selfish that he cannot bring himself to give away his money, he has no obligation to do so." The principle "claims the right to be as one oneself is because of one's nature. . . " Presumably these implications are quite objectionable. M. Slote, "The Morality of Wealth," in *World Hunger and Moral Obligations,* W. Aiken and H. LaFollette, eds. (Englewood Cliffs, New Jersey: Prentice Hall, 1977), 138.
9. Whether one has the right not to change and improve oneself is a complex issue. At the very least, however, such a right may conflict with the rights of others (to be given help in preventing their being tortured and killed) which may generate a duty that one keep informed on the condition of these others. I discuss this issue more fully in non-rights terms below. See note 11.
10. Recognizing this value parity constitutes the "basic moral insight," according to Thomas Nagel. T. Nagel, *The View From Nowhere* (New York, Oxford University Press, 1986, 205).
11. This claim has been contested by a number of contemporary philosophers: Philippa Foot, *Virtues and Vices and Other Essays in Moral Philosophy* (Berkeley: University of California Press, 1978); Bernard Williams, *Moral Luck* (Cambridge: Cambridge University Press, 1981); Susan Wolf, "Moral Saints," *Journal of Philosophy* 79 (1982): 419–31; Michael Slote, *Goods and Virtues* (Oxford: Clarendon Press, 1983); and Thomas Nagel, *The View From Nowhere*. In different ways each argues that it is not necessarily immoral to pursue personal, familial, or local goals at the expense of "common good" goals. The personal vs. impersonal dilemma is at the center of Nagel's moral and general philosophy. His opinion is that "the impartial standpoint of morality . . . will give to everyone a dispensation for a certain degree of partiality—in recognition of the fact that it is one aspect of the human perspective." In other words, an objective moral theory, in acknowledging all the facts in our universe, must take into account the fact that humans encounter the world from the subjective perspective of self, family, race, and nationality. The theory's moral demands cannot ignore this human fact. Consequently, an objective moral theory, such as utilitarianism, cannot be strickly impartial. I admit that the issue is profound and fascinating. But I would lean toward the hard line considered, but finally rejected, by Nagel: "One might take the severe line that moral requirements result from a correct assessment of the weight of good and evil, impersonally revealed, that it is our job to bring our motives into line with this, and that if we cannot do it because of personal weakness, this shows not that the requirements are excessive but that we are bad—though one might refrain from being too censorious about it." This view strikes me as rationally unavoidable once one grants the equal moral value of virtually every human. The partiality toward self that the above-mentioned philosophers defend goes directly against this moral axiom, particularly in a world of limited resources where my having x often deprives another or others. Were each of us insulated from others, the case might be different. Thomas Nagel, *The View From Nowhere*, 202–05.
12. A similar point is made by Slote in discussing whether wealthy individuals and nations who omit to share some of their wealth with the poor are justified in this omission. He observes that "(o)missions may not be permissible . . . if they in some sense preserve or perpetuate commissive wrongdoings." And since he thinks that in fact most wealthy individuals and nations become and remain wealthy by immoral means, they are obligated to share their wealth with those at whose expense this wealth becomes accumulated. M. Slote, "The Morality of Wealth," 141–45.
13. Note that here I am not relying on the conclusion of my earlier argument based on the general obligation to prevent harm. I am merely borrowing one premise from that argument.

Famine and Famine Relief: Viewing Africa in the 1980s from China in the 1920s

Lillian M. Li

Lillian M. Li is a professor of history at Swarthmore College in Pennsylvania. She is the author of China's Silk Trade: Traditional Industry in the Modern World, 1842–1937 *(1981), and co-editor of* China's History in Economic Perspective *(1992).*

Li suggests a model for relief from the famine in Africa based on the model that China instituted after 1949. Li points out that there are many apparent similarities between Africa and China. She argues that the most important factor that enabled China to overcome its famine problem was a strong centralized government which placed famine relief as the highest priority and strictly rationed the food supplies. Although such a policy is sure to be unpopular, Li argues that African countries must allow strong centralized (internal) governments to place famine relief as the highest priority. Li does acknowledge that this will be difficult because Africa lacks a tradition of political unity. However, until the danger is past, all other concerns, such as political divisions and economic growth, must take a back seat. For those interested in more of the details of the comparison between Africa and China, please see the original version of her essay.

During 1984 and 1985, as the tragedy of the Ethiopian famine has been played out in Africa, another human drama has unfolded in the United States and Europe. Although anticipated by experts for years, and in progress for months, the famine in Ethiopia did not reach the American public's attention until October 1984, when NBC evening news aired a BBC special about Ethiopia. As they ate dinner, Americans could watch with horror the specter of emaciated, fly-ridden bodies dying of starvation before their eyes. During the following winter and spring, millions of dollars poured into relief organizations such as Oxfam America and Catholic Relief Services, completely overwhelming their staffs. Rock stars, having already made a best-selling record, *We Are the World,* donated their talents to the ultimate transoceanic media event, "Live Aid"—grossing millions more for African relief.

A year later, the crisis in Ethiopia has peaked. Although several million remain "at risk," homeless and severely malnourished, summer rains in 1985 have brought the hope of a successful harvest in some areas. The flow of millions of dollars of international assistance has helped to limit the number of

Reprinted with permission of Lillian M. Li and Cambridge University Press from *Drought and Hunger in Africa,* edited by Michael H. Glantz (Cambridge, MA: Cambridge University Press, 1987). [Edited]

human fatalities. Yet, as Africans and African specialists know, the deep underlying causes of famine have not been addressed, and the deteriorating economic conditions in much of sub-Saharan Africa suggest that hunger and famine will continue to haunt Africa for the foreseeable future.

Just as Africa seems to be the "basket case" of the world today, half a century ago, it was China that was called "the land of famine." From the late nineteenth century, massive famines hit China like relentless waves, taking millions of lives. The 1876–79 drought-related famine in north China may have cost 9–13 million lives. Floods in the 1890s cost additional thousands. Each decade of the twentieth century brought major catastrophes. Nature seemed cruel and unforgiving, as droughts and floods alternated to create what seemed by the 1920s to be a chronic condition of famine in one part of China or another.

The American public was well aware of "the starving Chinese." Pictures of ragged and wide-eyed Chinese children filled the American newspapers. Unlike today, however, the real medium of fund-raising was neither journalists nor rock stars, but missionaries. In an era when thousands of young Americans went out to Asia to serve Christ, churches were the backbone of the relief effort. Collections were taken, sermons preached, relief stamps sold. The China Famine Fund of 1921 churned out slogan after slogan to nag the American conscience. "Famine relief is a sermon without words," the posters said, "Pick a Pal in China," "Give China a chance to live!" "15 million starving—Every minute counts." Articles explained, "How your dollar reaches a starving Chinese." "Self-Denial Week" was proclaimed. No contribution was too small. One could buy "Life-saving Stamps." "Each mercy stamp purchased for 3 cents provides food for one day for a Chinese" (Presbyterian Historical Society, 82/20/11).

In many respects the problems faced by Africa today resemble those experienced by China in the first half of this century. First, recurrent African famines take place in a physical environment whose natural instability and vulnerability have been exacerbated by human behavior. In the Sahel, the effect of drought has been greatly magnified by the spread of the desert southward, which, in turn has probably been caused by overgrazing of livestock, deforestation, and other land-use practices. In north China, similarly, since at least the mid-nineteenth century, the natural tendency of the Yellow River to overflow its banks had been greatly increased by neglect of dike repairs, and also by silting generated by continual deforestation of the upland areas.

Second, famine in Africa occurs in the context of a population explosion, which is sometime mistakenly taken to be the cause of the famine itself. Despite poverty and hunger—some would say because of them—Africa's population is growing faster than that of any other region of the world. Unlike Africa, China by the early twentieth century had already experienced centuries of high population density, but the rate of population growth seemed to many contemporary observers to have accelerated and to be creating Malthusian pressures on the land.

Third, the very low standard of living of large sectors of the population in Africa was also found in China in the 1920s and 1930s, and was frequently observed by foreigners. Chinese peasant life was characterized by malnutrition and poverty, high infant mortality, and low life expectancy.

Fourth, low productivity in agriculture is held largely responsible for Africa's increasing inability to feed itself, but the reasons for this low productivity are disputed. Similarly, both Chinese and foreigners in the 1920s and 1930s agreed that Chinese agriculture could be more productive but disagreed about the causes of agricultural stagnation.

Fifth, wide income inequalities in Africa are intensified by a growing urban–rural disparity in living standards and opportunities. In China before 1949, an ever-widening urban–rural gap seemed even more stark because most of the major cities were treaty ports where foreign privileges and the foreign presence were prominent.

Finally, Africa's serious economic problems are unfolding in a political context that is, in most African countries, quite unstable. In Ethiopia, of course, full-scale secessionist wars have greatly contributed to the severity of the famine. Likewise, China between 1911 and 1949 was in a state of political disorder, in which the major actors were militarists whose primary concern was their own survival.

Such apparent similarities—although on further examination they may be more apparent than real—strongly suggest that Africans may well wish to consider what lessons the Chinese experience with famine may contain for them. China has, after all, managed to avoid any major famine in the last 20 or more years. Although still a very poor country, China is proud of its self-sufficiency in food. With the recent economic reforms, there is every hope that the material life of the Chinese people will continue to improve. So far has China come from being "the land of famine" that last spring the Chinese Red Cross received donations from thousands of ordinary Chinese people, including school children, to aid famine victims in Africa (*China Daily,* 23 May 1985). . . .

"LESSONS" OF THE CHINESE EXPERIENCE

While it would be foolish for an outsider to pass judgment on the relative merits of these African issues, the Chinese conquest of famine over the past decades does, I believe, contain some lessons for Africa today. The appropriate lessons, I shall argue, are not the obvious ones.

There are several key aspects of the Chinese developmental experience in the period since 1949 that should be considered. First, with the establishment of the People's Republic of China (PRC), virtually all forms of Western assistance and trade that had been so prominent during the earlier Republican period were curtailed and, after about 1959, all forms of technical and financial assistance from the Soviet Union were also terminated, leaving China to pursue an independent path, free of foreign interference. Second, through rapid steps, the organization of agriculture became collectivized into large-scale communes. In this it was the mobilization of labor rather than new technology that was emphasized. Third, the distribution of grain was strictly controlled by the state through a system of rationing in the urban areas and a minimum guarantee in the countryside. Fourth, both food production and food distribution were managed by a highly centralized and powerful state apparatus that placed high priority on eliminating famine.

While it is the first three aspects that comprise the distinctive characteristics of the "Maoist" model of development, in my view it is the fourth characteristic—state policy—that may have been the most critical to the Chinese experience and that may be the most relevant to the African crisis. Almost complete economic self-sufficiency, as the ultimate expression of Chinese nationalism, may have been indispensable in establishing the legitimacy of the new national government, but it can hardly be said to have contributed directly to the elimination of hunger and famine. Collectivization may also have had greater political benefits than economic. Although grain output in China increased 75% from 1952 to 1977, agricultural growth barely kept pace with population growth (Tang & Stone, 1980, 13), and per capita grain output in 1980 was probably no greater than in the 1930s (Li, 1982, 701). Although it is too soon to evaluate the commune system definitively, the spectacular increases in output since the beginning of de-collectivization in 1978, strongly suggest that the communes may have inhibited growth by stifling individual initiative and motivation.

The system of food rationing, backed by a state reserve system, was probably the most important factor in the elimination of famine in China. Although the average per capita caloric availability of food in 1980 was probably no better than that in the 1930s, the critical difference between the two periods was that strict controls under the PRC assured the most equitable distribution of extremely meager resources. In a very real sense, then, the Maoist model gave higher priority to the *social* goal of equitable distribution than to the purely *economic* goal of growth. This degree of control over the distribution of food resources has probably never been achieved by any other government in world history, and it could not have been achieved in China without a highly powerful state system. Our growing understanding of China's state-granary and grain-price reporting system in the eighteenth and nineteenth centuries, moreover, permits us to understand that the food-distribution policies under the PRC represent an intensification of state policies from previous eras of Chinese history rather than a completely new direction (Li, 1982, 702).

The Maoist model has, of course, had a broad appeal to radical movements all over the world. Policies of isolation, at least from Western trade and aid, have been adopted in Cuba, Burma and other socialist countries, while land reform at least, if not collectivization, has been on the agenda in countries as distant and different as Ethiopia and Nicaragua. It is becoming painfully clear, however—at least to some observers—that such policies have often failed to raise the level of productivity. Even more painful should be the recognition that the Maoist model has now been repudiated by China, the very country that created it.

By contrast, the policy of strict rationing, which did work remarkably well in China to spread meager resources, is unlikely to be attempted on such an ambitious scale by any other country because it would be politically unpopular and, therefore, impossible to implement. The critical factor is not the type of ideology, political system or social policy, but a state policy that places the very highest priority on eliminating hunger and famine. It is state policy, together with the political capability to enforce it, that I believe are the transferable lessons of the Chinese experience.

Such a view is likely to meet serious objections. In Africa, many enlightened people regard the state and bureaucracy as the cause of the problem, not its solution. They see the clumsy manipulations of agricultural marketing boards and the corruption of their politicians as the very source of food distribution problems and, consequently, advocate a free market to eliminate the bottlenecks and disincentives that have occurred. To this, one can only respond that political control seems unavoidable in a situation crying for rapid solution. The relevant choice is between good government and bad, not between having political controls and not having them.

Second, there are those on the Chinese side who will surely object that in China, too, overcentralization of state power has had disastrous, indeed tragic, consequences. The Chinese government has now acknowledged that during the "three lean years" of the Great Leap Forward, 1959–61, a massive famine did occur in China. Some American demographers now calculate that as many as 30 million may have died of hunger and malnutrition during those years—making the Great Leap Forward the largest famine ever recorded in world history (Ashton *et al.*, 1984). Although bad weather certainly was a factor, this famine was primarily the result of overwhelming pressure put on communes to say they had fulfilled the unreasonable quotas of the Great Leap, when in fact they had not. It was, in short, truly a man-made famine (Bernstein, 1984).

State power can be a terrible force for evil, but whether it must necessarily be so, and whether the Great Leap famine was an inevitable consequence of overcentralization, or an aberration, is not yet clear. Here again, it seems that the choice must be between enlightened state policy and unenlightened policy, and not between policy or no policy.

Finally, some may object that the highly politicized model of famine prevention and control developed in China may be totally inappropriate for Africa and other areas of the world. China, after all, has had a unified state and culture for thousands of years, and bureaucratic centralization has not been difficult to achieve there. But African states lack the tradition of national unity and the political culture of bureaucratic rule.

Certainly, Africa has a great disadvantage in this respect, but it is not the Maoist model, or even a Chinese model, that I am advocating, but simply state policy that will place the highest priority on eliminating hunger and famine. Such policy must necessarily be appropriate for its culture. India may serve as an example of another populous and poor country that has eliminated famine through appropriate state policy, but a policy distinctly different from the Chinese model.

In the 1960s and earlier, it was India, not Africa, that was considered the most dangerously food-deficit area of the world, the "basket case" of its time, and among the largest recipients of grain from the United States under Public Law 480. Today, India is self-sufficient in food and even an exporter of rice. Although this happy turn of events has often been attributed to the recent successes of the Green Revolution, India has, in fact, succeeded in avoiding famine for a far longer period of time, virtually since its independence. The Bengal Famine of 1943 constituted such a psychological trauma, as well as a human tragedy, for the Indian people that, in the view of many observers, no Indian government since then could afford to permit famine to recur. To this end, India possesses a Public Distribution System for food, a key element of which is a system of fair price shops in urban areas (Chopra, 1981, chapters 1 & 27). In addition, as Michelle McAlpin's chapter illustrates, India has effective famine-warning and famine-relief systems. Despite devastating drought and severe crop shortages in Bihar in 1966–67, and again in Maharashtra in 1970–73, for example, no actual famine took place, if famine is measured by excess mortality.

Despite this commendable record in famine prevention, India is still tormented by widespread hunger, malnutrition and poverty. According to one estimate, perhaps one-third or more of India's population is malnourished (receiving fewer than 2100 calories a day; Sanderson & Roy, 1979, 107). As Amartya Sen has pointed out, there is a profound irony in the fact that India's life expectancy is much lower than China's (Sen, 1984, 501).[1] Measured by all standards of human welfare, life in China for the very poor is far more secure than life for India's poor. Yet, it is India that has completely avoided famines over at least the last 30 years, while China produced the Great Leap famine. In India, Sen asserts, a famine such as the Great Leap's could not have occurred because the more open political system would not have allowed it. Yet, from the African perspective today, what is most important is what the Indian and Chinese experiences share: a high priority assigned to the prevention of famine, and a state apparatus able to implement food control.

AFRICA'S PATH?

My emphasis on policy and politics has several implications. . . . First, it suggests that the emphasis given to economic development may be misplaced. Current economic development projects that stress local initiative and self-sufficiency assume a bottom-up type of development process, whereby economic development will be achieved gradually and political development will follow. The expectation that political democracy will necessarily emerge from economic development is based on Western liberal assumptions that may well prove to be disappointing. My stronger objection is that this model is too slow to address the immediate threat to millions of Africans of hunger, disease and starvation. To meet the African food crisis, strong and enlightened political leadership must take precedence over gradual economic planning.

Second, economic development models often bypass the very poor and ignore their immediate problems, a point stressed by Randall Baker. Like him, I believe that the urgent questions posed by hunger and famine must be addressed as issues separate from, and prior to, long-term economic development projects. Both the examples of China and India show—albeit in strikingly different ways—that even very poor countries can do what Baker has suggested: move national food security, especially for the very poorest, up to the highest priority and solve successfully that problem even before agricultural production "takes off." While the economic development of poor countries will eventually solve the problem of widespread hunger and malnutrition, the elimination of famine need not wait for that higher stage of development.

Third, the priority assigned to policy and political development places the question of international assistance, the original focus of this chapter, in its proper context. Foreign aid need not be summarily rejected by African nations as a precondition to their true political independence, but it can be used effectively if closely controlled by a responsible host government. China's use of foreign assistance after 1928, and its selective use of World Bank and other international financing at present, are two examples of use of foreign aid conditional on domestic Chinese political control.

In conclusion, an international perspective, and particularly a Chinese one, suggests that there is both good news for Africa and bad news. The good news is that famine in Africa *will* eventually end. In modern times each region of the world has, in turn, broken out of its famine cycle, and Africa will not be an exception. The experiences of China and India in particular should bring hope to Africa. The bad news, however, is that it may be much more difficult for Africa than for China or India, primarily because it lacks a tradition of political unity and bureaucratic experience. In addition, the militarization of politics and the superpower competition for influence in Africa greatly handicap the efforts of governments to implement a "food first" policy.[2] What is important for Africans is that their governments' political fortunes should be linked to their ability to put a stop to famine, not just for the urban middle class, but for the rural poor as well.

ACKNOWLEDGMENTS

I wish to thank the following people who generously shared their insights about various topics discussed in this chapter: Joel Charny, James Field, Shirley Holmes, Raymond Hopkins, John Kerr, James McCann, Michael Scott, Robert Snow, Subramanian Swamy, Deborah Toler and Homer Williams. None, however, should be held responsible for the views expressed. Swarthmore College and the National Endowment for the Humanities provided support during the period when I worked on this chapter.

NOTES

1. Sen states that life expectancy in India is 52 years, while life expectancy in China is 66-9 years. According to the *1984 World Population Data Sheet* (Population Reference Bureau, Washington, DC), life expectancy in India was 50 years, and in China 65 years.
2. This term is borrowed from the title *Food First* by Lappé & Collins (1977).

REFERENCES

ABCFM (American Board of Commissioners for Foreign Missions) (1860–1950). Archives at Houghton Library, Harvard University. ABC 16.3.12, North China Mission, 88 vols.

American National Red Cross (1929). *The Report of the American Red Cross Commission to China*. Washington, DC: American Red Cross.

Ashton, B., Hill, K., Piazza, A. & Zeitz, R. (1984). Famine in China, 1958–61. *Population and Development Review*, 10, 613–45.

Baker, J.E. (1943). *Fighting China's Famines*. Unpublished manuscript. New York: Burke Library, Union Theological Seminary.

Bernstein, T.P. (1984). Stalinism, famine and Chinese peasants: grain procurements during the Great Leap Forward. *Theory and Society*, 13(3), 339-77.

Blom, C.F. (1932). The values of famine relief work, *The Chinese Recorder*, 63(11), 696–99.

Bohr, P.R. (1972). *Famine in China and the Missionary: Timothy Richard as Relief Administrator & Advocate of National Reform*, 1876–1884. Cambridge, Mass.: East Asian Research Center, Harvard University.

China International Famine Relief Commission (1936). *The CIFRC Fifteenth Anniversary Book*, 1921–1936. Peiping: CIFRC.

China, National Flood Relief Commission (1932). *The Work of the National Flood Relief Commission of the National Government of China*, August 1931–June 1932. Shanghai: National Government of China.

Chopra, R. N. (1981). *Evolution of Food Policy in India*. New Delhi: Macmillan India Limited.
Edwards, D. W. (1932). The missionary and famine relief. *The Chinese Recorder*, 63(11), 689-96.

Jackson, T. (1982). *Against the Grain*. Oxford: OXFAM.

Johnson, W. R. Papers, deposited at Day Missions Library, Yale Divinity School, China Records Project, Record Group 6.

Lancaster, C. (1985). Africa's development challenges. *Current History*, April, 145–49.

Lappé, F. M. & Collins, J. (1977). *Food First: Beyond the Myth of Scarcity*. Boston: Houghton Mifflin.

Li, L. M. (1982). Introduction: Food, famine, and the Chinese state. *Journal of Asian Studies*, XLI, 687–707.

Nathan, A. J. (1965). *A History of the China International Famine Relief Commission*. Cambridge, Mass.: East Asian Research Center, Harvard University.

Presbyterian Historical Society. Philadelphia. Record Group 82. China Mission, 1890–1955. Box 20, Folders 11–12. China Famine Fund.

Sanderson, F. H. & Roy, S. (1979). *Food Trends and Prospects in India*. Washington, DC: The Brookings Institute.

Schwab, P. (1985). Political change and famine in Ethiopia. *Current History* (May), 221–23.

Sen, A. (1984). Development: which way now? In his *Resources, Values, and Development*, 485–508. Cambridge, Mass.: Harvard University Press.

Shawcross, W. (1984). *The Quality of Mercy: Cambodia, Holocaust and Modern Conscience*. New York: Simon & Schuster.

Shepherd, J. (1985a). When foreign aid fails. *The Atlantic Monthly*, April, 41–46.

Shepherd, J. (1985b). Ethiopia: the use of food as an instrument of US foreign policy. *Issue*, 14, 4–9.

Stroebe, G. G. (1932). The great central China flood of 1931. *The Chinese Recorder*, 63(11), 669–80.

Tang, A. M. & Stone, B. (1980). *Food Production in the People's Republic of China*. Washington, DC: International Food Policy Research Institute.

Thomson, J. C., Jr. (1969). *When China Faced West: American Reformers in Nationalist China, 1928–1937.* Cambridge, Mass.: Harvard University Press.

White, T. H. & Jacoby, A. (1946). *Thunder Out of China.* New York: William Sloan.

Human Rights and Development

J. D. Sethi

J. D. Sethi has been a member of the Planning Commission in New Delhi, India. He is the author of India's Static Power Structure *(1969),* India in Crisis *(1975), and* Gandhi Today *(1978).*

Sethi argues that the developing nations face mass poverty and this fact means that their problems are very different from those of the developed world. Sethi asserts that a "below the line strategy" *must be followed in which basic economic needs as well as political and legal rights are guaranteed. All too often, Sethi points out, developed nations address developing nations with plans that do not take into account basic human rights. In order to address the special needs of developing countries and guarantee human rights, Sethi asserts that the power of the political elite will have to be redistributed, and a decentralized, morally oriented model will need to be instituted. Sethi advocates the Gandhian model as the only one that combines the components necessary to simultaneously guarantee economic needs and human rights.*

The relationship between human rights and development is far too complex, varied, and sometimes inconsistent to be subject to a few neat generalizations. Most tested hypotheses of the relationship have been confronted with serious refutations. Cross-national analyses have proved to be equally meaningless, because they have been shown to have little bearing on specific situations prevailing in a given country. In the same country, at two different times, the relationship may be widely different. Even between two countries placed in more or less similar situations in the economic or the political fields, there may be divergent relationships.

Reprinted by permission of *Human Rights Quarterly, Vol. 3,* No. 3, Summer 1981. [Edited]

THEIR COMMON DENOMINATOR

If both human rights and development are desirable, but no generalizations are possible about their mutual relationship, how does one really approach the problem? As a first approximation, it would be appropriate to find the common denominator between the two, and insist on making that as a base line for further analysis. For example, some minimum political and legal rights will have to be linked with certain basic economic rights to make a single package of rights that ought to be ensured. Otherwise there will be no justification for relating the two. Liberty and democracy as well as provision of basic needs like food, clothing, and shelter should be considered the absolute minimum rights constituting this package. They each must be treated as basic rights.

A society which cannot meet some basic economic needs will always run the risk of the political rights of its citizens being eroded or extinguished. The reverse may not be always true, although there are far more numerous cases to support it than to oppose it. There are a large number of Third World countries in which the denial of human rights by authoritarian regimes has consistently accompanied a low level of development; people have been brutally exploited and denied minimum basic economic subsistence. Therefore, as a theoretical proposition, it has to be stressed that the development strategy of the Third World countries should consist of two parts. The first part should guarantee certain basic economic needs and also be consistent in guaranteeing political and legal rights. This may be called *below the line strategy*. If the Third World countries can resolve conflicts between human rights and development strategies at the level of what is called below the line, the second part of the strategy can be made more flexible and encompass a wide variety of experience and situations. Relating to the second part of the strategy, expansion of rights above the line will require a different kind of theoretical or conceptual analysis. Indeed there may be areas of conflict between the two, because of the role and the power that the state or the government assumes.

The irreducible minimum and the unsubstitutable method for providing for basic minimum economic needs below the line and judging its criterion would be to guarantee jobs to those able-bodied persons who are seeking jobs. The margin of tolerance for democracy and human rights is the availability of full employment at below the line development and the satisfaction of basic needs. The difficulty in most developing countries is that because of large scale underemployment, neither is there job security nor a guarantee of minimum economic needs. It is easier to evolve a strategy of development and employment for an economy in which there is open unemployment than for one which is suffering from underemployment. The basic needs strategies for these two situations are quite different.

MINIMUM NEEDS STRATEGY

The fact that the development strategies of the last two decades have failed to give benefits of development to the poor people has led to a search for alternative strategies. One of the strategies suggested is called the basic needs or the minimum needs strategy. Somehow, employment is not included in all definitions of this strategy. What has been included in it are areas or sectors which are of a social infrastructure kind which at best can be called investment in human capital. This minimum needs program strategy generally includes primary and adult education, primary health care, nutrition, family planning, and road and housing development.

The urgency and compulsion of the minimum needs strategy as distinct from employment has been provoked by the challenge of the appalling social and economic conditions of those who live below the poverty line. It is to be remembered that the very definition of the poverty line is in terms of per capita food consumption. The denial of these minimum needs, as defined above, to the common person is not an independent phenomenon, but a part of the employment situation on the one hand, and the distributive surplus sharing system of the economy on the other. In most developing countries it is the poor who finance the education and the health of the rich and the middle classes. In many countries the organization of the economic system just does not permit minimum needs being met among the common masses, and, therefore, is unlikely or unable to protect their political or legal rights.

A variety of reasons have been offered for this kind of minimum needs program. First, the minimum needs program (MNP) should be able to prepare underprivileged, undernourished, and uneducated persons to enter active employment. Second, since employment generation may take some time, these programs amount to a salvage operation for a very large number of people, a guarantee for them to live as human beings at subsistence level. Nevertheless, the central focus has still to be on employment. If employment is available to 95 percent of the people in the active labor force, the minimum needs strategy of the kind mentioned above may not be needed. However, if it is adopted it should help in sustaining peoples' interests in their political rights and their quality of life which creates consciousness about these rights as well as duties. In its absence there is always danger of people falling prey to the demogogues, populist leaders, dictators, or of becoming fatalists.

The third justification for the minimum needs program is for the removal of social poverty as distinguished from economic poverty. In many developing countries, particularly India, there is a serious discrimination against a large group of people on grounds of caste, religion, or race. In the final analysis, social poverty can be removed only if economic poverty is eliminated. However, in the intervening period, a set of social programs are needed to equalize opportunites or to create a support structure for increasing the competitive capabilities of the socially underprivileged.

The fourth reason for MNP is to create countervailing balancing forces against inequalities which are either historically given or are created by the development process itself. For many years inequality was suggested as a positive factor for development. Now all historical theories of inequality put forward as justification either for development or for the defense of human rights have been discredited. Today no one in the developing world is seriously prepared to consider such theories and rightly so. Even the principle of equality of opportunity which implicitly lay behind the creation of the social services has also been found to be perverse. The principle of equality of opportunity in a situation of gross inequalities and social backwardness always acts in favor of the privileged classes. It has been noticed that in the developing countries, particularly in India, health, education and other social services have been appropriated by a small minority even though in principle everyone is expected to benefit equally from them. If human rights and development are to be linked, then it is absolutely necessary that the principle of equality of opportunity be replaced by the principle of equality up to the point of below the line development. One way of doing this is to base all MNP on the principle of equality while other inequalities exist or are produced by development.

Therefore, a distinction need always be made between those minimum economic needs, such as food, clothing, and shelter, without which a human being cannot survive as a human being living at some acceptable level and which are tied to the right to employment, and those social minimum needs which make a person qualitatively better equipped as a member of the labor force, and a better human being who is capable of playing a political role. Human rights are connected with both kinds of needs. The first is the necessary condition without which no human rights can be sustained for long, and the second is the necessary condition for expanding the area of human rights once some minimum of these rights are guaranteed.

ECONOMIC VS. POLITICAL RIGHTS

In general, relationships between economic and political rights, and particularly between development and human rights are not the same in the developed world and the developing world. The former is much better equipped to meet the conditions mentioned above, to deal with the contradictions between the two, and to protect both human rights and the development process. "They differ for three general sets of reasons: (1) greater institutional and ideological safeguards, which can make any given negative pressure from market forces less likely to lead to political repression; (2) different economic structures which mitigate, though they probably do not reverse, negative pressures in the first place; and (3) a better established consensus on the need to keep market forces under restraint. The pressures are more manageable in the first place, but all industrialized countries which use democratic methods find it necessary to limit and manage market forces."

Common to all societies are three basic rights from which all other rights flow. They are: (1) the right to vote—elect—and to do so equally before the law; (2) the right to employment (subject to Marxian law of each according to his needs and not subject to the Keynesian law of each according to his demand); and (3) the right to free movement and assembly within a nation or transnational area. There is no point in overemphasizing the fact that none of these rights is absolute and that the rights of each individual are constrained by the rights enjoyed by others. More specifically, each of these rights are subject to numerous other constraints, of history, of society, of culture, of resources and development strategies, and of international situations. However, if all the three rights are guaranteed in a resonable degree, there is no reason why both human rights and proper development cannot go together.

What is important is that the demand for one right may put a constraint on the other and this is the point at which human rights and development goals diverge. For example, the right to vote and elect in a democratic system may be constrained by offering so few choices to the voters that the choices are between nearly indistinguishable candidates or issues. If elective choices are so few, then the right to employment may not be fully guaranteed, because the interest of the political elite may coincide with those whose control over the economic resources is such that employment guarantee is not given the proper priority. However, if everyone has to be given a job, there is no guarantee that the level of wages would be reasonable enough to sustain a family at a decent standard of living. However, over a period, the existence and defense of one right may reinforce the guarantee for some other right. The important point is that political and economic rights are mutually reinforcing.

For example, if the right to employment is guaranteed, then the right to elect may constitute a kind of political pressure which would guarantee a fair wage. Constraints on free movements of individuals between nations are far too many and are thus both the cause and the effect of international inequality and the perpetuation of the division of the world between the developed and the underdeveloped categories. It would be too much to expect a completely free movement of people from one nation to the other, but a relatively freer movement than what exists today will have a very large positive impact on the developmental and political processes of many countries. Since the developing countries are being asked to allow free movement of capital, commodities, and technology across nations, why not people? Human rights and development are as important internationally as they are nationally.

WESTERN VS. COMMUNIST SYSTEMS

Two intellectual pressures are being exerted on the Third World elite at the international level, one coming from the West and the other from the Communist world. Indeed, the elite in the developing world is caught in between the cross fire from the two. On the one hand, it is suggested that for liberty and democracy, the Third World must accept the Western political system. On the other hand, to speed up development and remove poverty, the use of some kind of a Marxist model is considered inescapable. The Western model, as it has historically evolved, requires a long time to achieve the economic goals; it also developed without the compulsion of guaranteeing human rights at the stage of development at which the poor nations are today. There are any number of romanticists—probably the largest number of them are in India—who believe that a semi-Marxist model of economic development can be easily married to Western political models. The results of such a marriage have been disastrous.

POLITICAL PLURALISM

The Western political system is based on one type of political pluralism, as distinguished from economic pluralism, although the two have some common areas of operation. However, there are also areas of conflict between human rights and development in the context of modern democratic theory. The conflicts originate from the restricted scope of the definition and institutions of democracy and not from any inherent conflict between the two. Political pluralism is considered as the basis and guarantee for democracy. But economic pluralism is neither a guarantee for human rights nor for development. Indeed economic pluralism beyond a point can be antidevelopmental and exploitative. This basic asymmetry between political and economic pluralism lies at the root of the contemporary conflict between the two. Economic pluralism in a backward society would permit conexistence of productive with unproductive classes, exploiters with the exploited, and those whose functions can be defined with those whose functions cannot be defined. Therefore, in the interest of economic development, economic pluralism as the guarantee of freedom and human rights emanates from the institutional character of modern democracies. Only if the institutions of representative democracies were to have, running parallel to these institutions, institutions of participatory democracy or direct democracy, could the internal balance and external limits of political pluralism be settled. In the absence of such a system of plural polity, economic pluralism merely defends the status quo and in situations of prolonged crisis can threaten political pluralism and thus democracy itself.

In developed countries the correspondence between the two has been ensured since the last quarter of the nineteenth century by two factors. First, capitalist economies have been quickly expanding on a long-term basis, eliminating feudal and other disfunctional elements, and groups from their systems. Second, different and conflicting economic interests have been crystalized into a few large identifiable groups. In the Third World, acceptance of economic pluralism has meant acceptance, along with functional class, of those economic classes which are either exploitative or antidevelopmental. Besides, pluralistic economic development has been proved to be rather slow in absorbing all the conflicts. The result has been erosion of political pluralism itself, and of liberty and democracy. If most of the Third World has fallen under the boots of dictators, it is because of attempts to maintain unlimited economic pluralism in order to justify, rather mistakenly, a loosely defined political pluralism.

An Emerging Political Crisis

Even in the developed world, trends have appeared to show that societies have become more complex and the crystalization of economic interests made more difficult since World War II. The result has been the rise of "overloaded" goverments which, after a quarter of a century of successful Keynesianism, have now been faced with the problems of unemployment, inflation, excessive taxation, and unproductive increases in public expenditure, all working together, to heighten economic pluralism. This new expanding economic pluralism is putting large pressures on the rights and liberties of the people. Human alienation, which created nihilism and ultimately eroded rights, liberties, and institutions that sustain these rights, has entered into individual relations and the social mores of the developed societies. In developed countries the political management of the human mind, human aspirations, and attitudes through technology and modern methods of control, have become ugly realities.

Political situations in these countries seem to face two new problems. First, Keynesianism is no longer a relevant economic solution, nor is monetarism which is its exact opposite. Both have gone bankrupt, although their respective gladiators are furiously engaged in shadow-boxing. Second, recent surveys have shown that the working classes and other less privileged groups in the developed world are preferring authoritarianism to democracy. The surveys may not actually result in the actualization of authoritarianism but they reflect alienation and indicate a situation of emerging political crisis from new economic pluralism.[1]

If the overloaded state is attempting to sustain unsustainable economic pluralism at the cost of abridgment of liberties, monetarism is pumping for a minimal state with a false promise of enlarging these liberties. Friedman and Nozick, the high priests of these philosophies, invite the debate about rights and development in the United States. They have their followers in other Western nations. Monetarism considers that unemployment, recession, and decline in standards of living will accompany it as nonissues. Therefore, those who are opting for monetarism in the name of liberty are ignoring the development and distribution problems. Not unexpectedly, the monetarists are opposed by those state bureaucracies, business, and other groups, the industrial-military complexes, that flourish in the overloaded state. Consequently, "the themes of debate which seemed, in the first two post-war decades, to have disappeared from the political landscape return with all their nineteenth century vigor: can individual liberty survive universal suffrage? Can the capitalist economy accommodate organized labor? How can the economy be put beyond politics? . . . arguments of this kind represent one of the few innovative contributions to political debate among political scientists outside the Marxist camp in 1970s"[2]

Keynesianism did lead to an increased expansion in the area of arbitrary action by government. With the failure of Keynesianism in the last decade there has emerged a new emphasis on putting limitations on this arbitrariness by dismantling part of the government and expanding the area of private market economy. The conservative government of Britain has tried to cut government's role and its expenditure levels but it has succeeded in doing so very marginally.

However, in many Third World countries of Africa, Asia, and Latin America it is political repression and denial of human rights that has been used to expand any private market mechanism or push forward monetarism. In some other Third World countries, political repression has come with overloaded governments, sometimes under monetarism and at others under Keynesianism, thus snapping the relationship between economic organization and human rights.

Corporatism

There is a difference between the criticism of big government by business and that by those, liberals or leftists, who believe big government, in the form in which it exists in the developed world, is a growing threat to human rights and inimical to structuring social security, antipoverty, or global-change programs. Their objection is to the corporate state which uses all kinds of power, business, bureaucracy, policy, and even the organized working class against the rest of society.

The problems of the so-called overloaded government and of the economic crisis in the developed world are related to the basic corporatist structure of the economy and society. Threats to human rights and liberties come from that structure itself. Since 1973, the decline in economic activity has strengthened both the corporatist trends in the capitalist countries and their counterparts, monopolist bureaucratic trends, in the Communist countries. Both trends have proved counterproductive to economic development, not to mention human rights.

According to Colin Crunch, "Corporatism is best regarded as a strategy pursued by capitalism when it cannot adequately subordinate labor by preventing its continuation and allowing market processes to work."[3] As a class concept, corporatism is the strategy of using capital to subordinate labor when the classic mode of control through the market becomes inoperative. As a nonclass concept, corporatism is the control of both capital and labor by the state in an attempt to create a balance of sharing wealth and power among all three. Whether a class or nonclass concept, corporatism becomes inevitable in a developed capitalist system when concentration in industry, technology, and power of technology, in economies of scale, state planning participation, and separation of ownership from control reach critical limits. The essential character of corporatism is that both labor and capital are powerful and the state has to be even more powerful to maintain an equilibrium between the power of labor and that of capital. The only new element in this long list of characteristics is the workers' participation in management, which is not yet a fully settled matter.

The relationship that exists is one between the corporate state and corporate economic culture. In this relationship dependence on or modification of market prices is irrelevant in every crucial respect except for efficiency. The control of markets by huge corporations has made market economics largely irrelevant. Small companies are being squeezed and along with them free enterprise is also. The oil industry in the United States is one example of this phenomenon. Therefore, the old liberal theory of linking political rights with free market mechanism has completely lost its empirical base.

The components of a corporate system have to bargain with other organized forces in the society, giving some semblance to pluralism or liberalism, but effective controls on human rights and even the human mind are maintained by the corporatist elements. This subsidiary bargaining itself depends on the primary bargaining system and framing of the rules of the game by the components of the corporate structure, the state, capital and labor. In authoritarian corporate regimes, there will be no rights guaranteed; whereas in democracies, the existence of these rights will remain contingent upon the stability and legitimization of the corporatist structure.

In many developing countries, the tendencies toward corporatism have taken firm ground in sectors of large scale industry and commerce, leaving the rest of the system totally atomized or feudal. That is why most developing countries have developed dual economies, the so-called modern and the so-called traditional. Sometimes, this dualism also takes the form of a rural–urban dichotomy, but more significantly and prominently, it marks the division between those who live below the poverty line and those who are above it. . . .

THE DEVELOPING WORLD

However, a large part of this aforementioned debate about development, equality, and human rights that is taking place in the West is irrelevant for the developing countries for one simple reason, namely: the debate is carried on within the framework of a certain degree of mass prosperity guaranteed for the people in the developed world. The developing countries on the other hand face problems of mass poverty. Political compulsions and economic situations of the two worlds are, therefore, widely different.

However, the developing world is not a world by itself. It is constantly subjected to economic, political, and intellectual pressures from the developed world, both capitalist and Communist. There may or may not be a theory of genuine interdependence, but there are certainly pressures exerted on the developing countries to make them dependent upon the developed world in one way or another. Nuclear deterrents, spheres of influence, internationalization of developmental strategies, and new protectionism are matters of concern to the developed world, and have a tremendous bearing on the problem of developed and political liberties of the developing countries.

Organizational overextension of the United Nations and the proliferation of its agencies has led to conceptual confusion, fragmentation of effort, and internal dissensions within the Third World about issues of development and human rights. Whether by design or by accident, this development has relegated into the background the U.N. struggle for human rights, and the development debate has reached a deadlock. Indeed, the link between human rights and development has been snapped. Each developed nation or group of them, in their attempt to influence the development pattern of the developing countries, has tended to ignore the abridgment or elimination of human rights.

The world is not divided between radicals and conservatives, not merely because yesterday's radicals are likely to be tomorrow's conservatives. The division is suspect, because those who are radicals in one area may be conservative in another. This applies as well to conservatives. Most significantly, however, the division is untenable because of the moral ambiguity of both. Neither has a definite value premise, although it would be wrong to say that neither has any values at all times.

However, the division between radicals and conservatives is very relevant when it comes to stating the relationship between rights and development. The conservatives believe that the existing system of distribution is just while the radicals call it basically unjust. The radicals also believe that the system of inequality is maintained by coercion and thus violates human rights whereas conservatives believe that equality can be imposed through coercion. The two have different views of society and hence of development. Conservatives view society as a social, plural system in which bargaining takes place whereas the radicals consider society as a system of conflicts and struggles.

Conservatives believe that rights and privileges are based on human nature, capabilities, and hard work, whereas radicals believe they are the result of inequalities of the social system itself. However, having said that, it is important to stress that the radicals have failed to formulate a model of development in politics which guarantees human rights. Whereas in theory, economics and politics may seem inseparable, in practice the radicals and the conservatives have taken positions that may snap the relationship between economics and politics.

Severing relations between the economic and the political is never complete. The link breaks when either development becomes an instrument of intolerable exploitation or democracy extends its limits beyond what current development can sustain, or when democracy tends toward its incapacity to maintain balanced pluralism or tends toward anarchy. A democratic system, if it is economically inefficient and is subjected to populist pressures, may pave the way for a repressive regime. Therefore, the relationship between development and human rights or generally between the economic and political is far more complex than is shown by a deterministic or causal theory. Within some areas of the operation, the two are autonomous. It is by protecting that area of autonomy that development of human rights can individually be defended when subjected to opposite pressures.

Both situations—the contradictions between political rights and development (in which the Third World elite believes it is caught) and the consonance between expanding political rights and the developed (as is claimed for the developed democracies)—are heading for a crisis. It seems that neither situation can guarantee an optimum combination of rights and development, because the human being is not made the focus of development. That is due to the absence of a moral dimension in the models of economic and political development. Implicitly, the dominant values in a society are those of the power elite; the masses simply follow those values. We return, then, to the role and responsibility of the power elite. It is that group's responsibility to identify its interests to some extent with those for whom below the line development has to be structured. The power elite maintains strong moral positions and links political rights and development with moral values. The power elite has to deny itself certain economic privileges in proportion to the power they exercise, in order to identify their interests with the nation in general and with those who live below the poverty line in particular.

This would require a tremendous decentralization of power from the center to the states and eventually to the local bodies. The organization of the poor is the crux of the matter. This restructuring task can be performed legitimately by political parties. But, since political parties in South Asia are largely urban based, the only alternative left is to structure minimum needs programs in such a way that these programs are handled by their intended recipients. Each program would require a certain awareness component so that rights are built into the development content. Such an approach is likely to be resisted by the local power structure. However, our experience is that resistance comes more from the urban power elite and less from the rural power elite, because currently the advantages from the social services largely benefit the urban elite.

The only model that I know of which combines all the components mentioned is the Gandhian model. In the Gandhian model development, political rights, democratic decentralization, and moral values are all interwoven into an organic whole. I have dealt with the Gandhian model elsewhere.[4] The central role in this model, is that of

Satyagrahis (those who insist on and struggle for the truth). They are the morally oriented, truth conscious elite, the elite which gets power from the people and also gives it back to them in running the programs of development and defending their rights.

NOTES

1. Both of these facts are also militating against any genuine assistance that the developed world may be required to give to the poor nations. The biggest opposition for this assistance comes from the working classes.
2. Colin Crunch, ed., *State and Capitalism in Contemporary Capitalism,* p. 16.
3. Ibid., p. 19.
4. J. D. Sethi, *Gandhi Today* (Durham, North Carolina: Carolina Academic Press, 1978); *India in Crisis* (New York: International Publication Service, 1975); and *India's Static Power Structure* (New York: Verry, 1969).

HUNGER AND POVERTY—SUPPLEMENTARY READINGS

AIKEN, WILLIAM. "The 'Carrying Capacity' Equivocation." *Social Theory and Practice,* vol. 6(1), Spring 1980.

DONNELLY, JACK. "Satisfying Basic Needs in Africa: Human Rights, Markets and the State," *Africa Today,* vol. 32(1 & 2), 1985.

EMMANUEL, ARGHIRI. "The Multinational Corporations and Inequality of Development," in *Multi-National Corporations and Third World Development,* Pradip Ghosh, editor. New York: Greenwood Press, 1984.

HARDIN, GARRETT. "Living on a Lifeboat." *BioScience* 24, October 1974.

HERNANDEZ, DONALD. "Fertility Reduction Policies and Poverty in Third World Countries: Ethical Issues." *Journal of Applied Behavioral Science,* vol. 20(4), 1984.

KAHN, HERMAN. "The Confucian Ethic and Economic Growth," in *The Gap Between Rich and Poor,* Mark Seligson, editor. Boulder, CO: Westview Press, 1984.

MAY, LARRY. "Minimal Justice and the World Hunger Problem," in *Agriculture, Change and Human Values.* Gainesville, FL: University of Florida, 1982.

NAGEL, THOMAS. "Poverty and Food: Why Charity Is Not Enough," in *Food Policy.* New York: The Free Press, 1977.

O'NEILL, ONORA. "Rights, Obligations and Needs." *Logos,* 1985.

PARPART, JANE L. "Women's Rights and the Lagos Plan of Action." *Human Rights Quarterly,* vol. 8(2), May 1986.

SEN, AMARTYA. "The Great Bengal Famine," in *Poverty and Famine.* England: Oxford University Press, 1981.

SIMON, LAURENCE. "Social Ethics and Land Reform: The Case of El Salvador." *Agriculture and Human Values,* Summer 1984.

IV

War and Violence

I observed that men rushed to arms for slight causes, or no cause at all, and that when arms have once been taken up there is no longer any respect for law, divine or human: it is as if in accordance with a general decree, frenzy had openly been let loose for the committing of all crimes. Confronted with such utter ruthlessness, many men who are the very furthest from being bad men, have come to the point of forbidding all use of arms . . .

—Hugo Grotius[1]

Most justifications for war begin with some reference to the principle of self-defense. Just as it is nearly uncontroversial that a person is morally justified in defending himself or herself from attack, so it is thought that nations are justified in defending themselves from attack by the use of violent force. Recourse is often made to another principle as well, namely, that we are all required to go to the aid of suffering innocent persons. As in the case of self-defense, it is often necessary to use violence to thwart an attack upon an innocent person. Finally, many people believe that it is justified to use force to prevent a greater evil than is had by the use of violence. This final view, much more controversial than the first two, is an important element in what has come to be known as the "just war" doctrine.

In sharp contrast to the just war doctrine is the doctrine called pacifism. Pacifists believe that all, or almost all, uses of violence are morally unjustified, especially in relations between nations. This doctrine often starts, as in our quotation from Grotius (who was not a pacifist), with the claim that individuals are corrupted by engaging in war and violence. In addition, violence is considered a direct affront to the humanity of the person against whom it is used. The use of violence, even to thwart violence, is always a form of disrespect that fails to treat the other as possessing intrinsic value and as having a life worthy of respect. Most pacifists believe that one need not be passive to be nonviolent; indeed, the most famous pacifists of recent times have also developed strategies of collective action and resistance, as we will see in several of the readings in this section.

Those who believe that war can be morally justified usually point to a paradigmatic case of a war waged for a just cause. Typically, World War II is cited as an example of a war which no reasonable person could have opposed since it had the highest of moral aims, namely, ending the Nazi attempt to exterminate all Jews and subjugate all of Europe. Indeed, some suggest that not only was it morally justified, but there was a strong moral obligation to fight in World War II. But even in such wars, pacifists will ask whether there were no alternative nonviolent courses of action that could have been pursued.

Just as the case for the moral justifiability of some wars is buttressed by the facts of World War II, so the case for pacifism is tremendously buttressed by the facts concerning the struggle for India's liberation from British colonial rule. Mohandas K. Gandhi led a successful mass revolution without the use of military arms or violence. And in more recent times, Martin Luther King ,Jr. led very successful nonviolent confrontations with state governments that engaged in unjust discriminatory practices against African Americans. In both cases, the leaders of these movements were philosophically committed to nonviolence and through their own successful efforts showed the effectiveness of collective political efforts that stop short of war.

There also are moral issues raised by the manner in which war is conducted. A controversy has raged about whether the United States conducted more bombing runs than it needed to in order to achieve its military objectives in the Gulf War. And even more people have claimed that the Iraqis engaged in immoral tactics in using Kuwaiti and American civilian hostages as shields to protect military targets during the same war. Indeed, many argue that the taking of hostages is always immoral, although it has been a tactic employed by both sides in most of the major wars of the last few hundred years. Even more persuasive arguments are made against the use of nuclear or chemical weapons.

One strand of revolutionary literature argues that most tactics, no matter how violent, are justifiable as long as the cause for which one fights is sufficiently honorable. Indeed, there is a long tradition of important political theorists, from Machiavelli through Lenin, who have argued that the goodness of the cause for which one fights justifies nearly any means one may employ to achieve that end. Such a position, sometimes referred to as "the ends justify the means," has also been roundly criticized for a similarly long period of time.

Our readings begin with an essay by Douglas Lackey, who provides a very careful summary of the main elements and problems of the traditional just war theory. The first part of his essay is devoted to the doctrine of *jus ad bellum*, the principles justifying engaging in war. The two most important considerations are whether the war is planned in defense of a just cause, and whether that war is planned for good intentions. The second half of the essay concerns the doctrine of *jus in bello*, the principles governing justified practices in wars. Here the two most important considerations are whether the violence inflicted is proportional to the just objective of the war, and whether the violent instruments of war are directed only at enemy soldiers, rather than at noncombatant civilians.

Gregory Kavka provides a critical examination of the applicability of just war theory to the recent war in the Persian Gulf. Among other things, Kavka examines the epistemological issue of how the intentions of the nation or of its leaders are to be known and assessed. He points out that it is terribly problematic whether collectivities such as nations have motives or intentions at all, and that this is especially difficult in applying the just war doctrine's "right intention" condition. Another important general point concerns the proportionality requirement: Should we be concerned only with actual outcomes, or also with outcomes that were intended, but did not, occur? This question, and a host of others, is ripe for philosophical analysis.

Mohandas K. Gandhi attempts to respond to some of the main critics of pacifism, especially those who criticized his own refusal to consider a resort to violence in the cause of confronting British oppression in India. Gandhi sets out his own views in the context of the principle of mutual love that most of the great religions of the East espouse. It is a violation of this principle, he argues, to use violence even to counter violence directed at oneself. But Gandhi was not an advocate of passive inaction. Rather he points us toward a form of nonviolent noncooperation that he has good reason to believe can be effective, especially when it is mounted on a very large scale. At the end of this selection, Gandhi attempts to explain why it was not morally justified for the British to go to war to stop Hitler—perhaps one of the most controversial of pacifist claims.

Some feminists have pointed out that they share with pacifists a condemnation of a predominantly male-aggressive manner of confronting instances of social injustice. Sara Ruddick sketches several cases of mass movements of resistance inspired by the values that have been traditionally cherished in women's lives. The traditional role of mother as maintainer of love and protector of the innocent has been used, she argues, to combat potentially harmful situations concerning war, state terrorism, and environmental destruction. The efforts of women's groups have resulted, she concludes, in new ways to invent peace.

Martin Luther King, Jr. defends a version of nonviolent civil disobedience by reference to several of the main principles of Judeo-Christian morality. Like Gandhi, King sees nonviolence as the expression of love, especially the biblical doctrine of "love thy neighbor as thyself." King outlines a strategy for confronting injustice that has proven to be the blueprint for many social movements of the last 25 years in the United States and Europe. He takes great pains to argue that there is nothing unpatriotic about civil disobedience. Indeed, he argues that civil disobedience can be one of the greatest expressions of concern for the laws of a nation.

Okwudibia Nnoli argues that some forms of injustice are so ingrained that nonviolent strategies have not and will not succeed. One is then faced with the predicament of either having to learn to live with the injustice or turning to a strategy of violence. Nnoli opts for violence because he believes that it is inhumane to allow people to be stunted in their development by oppressors who could be confronted if only enough people took up arms against these oppressors. Like the pacifists in this section, Nnoli believes that injustice needs to be confronted wherever it exists. But he differs from the pacifists in arguing that we should not be forced to stop short of success against oppressors merely because of a revulsion against the use of violence.

NOTE

1. Hugo Grotius, *Prolegomena to the Law of War and Peace*, Paragraph 29, 1625.

Just War Theory

Douglas P. Lackey

Douglas P. Lackey is a professor of philosophy at Baruch College and the Graduate Center of the City University of New York. He is the author of Moral Principles and Nuclear Weapons *(1984) and* The Ethics of War and Peace *(1989). He is the editor of* Ethics and Strategic Defense *(1989).*

Lackey surveys most of the important moral issues involved in the just war tradition. In addition to setting out the traditional justifications for engaging in war and the justifications for various forms of conduct during war, he focuses on several issues that have been quite problematic. For example, he points out that certain practices in the Vietnam War involved terrorist tactics but, according to the traditional doctrine of just war, these practices are justifiable. He also argues that attacks on a nation's citizens living abroad, or the seizure of their property, would not normally count as a just cause that would justify going to war.

WHEN TO FIGHT

Introduction

Rightly or wrongly, pacifism has always been a minority view. Most people believe that *some* wars are morally justifiable; the majority of Americans believe that World War II was a moral war. But though most people have clear-cut intuitions about the moral acceptability of World War II, the Vietnam War, and so forth, few people have a theory that justifies and organizes their intuitive judgments. If morally concerned nonpacifists are to defeat the pacifists to their moral left and the cynics to their moral right, they must develop a theory that will distinguish justifiable wars from unjustifiable wars, using a set of consistent and consistently applied rules.

From Douglas P. Lackey, *The Ethics of War and Peace,* ©1989, pp. 28–35 and 58–61. Reprinted by permission of Prentice-Hall, Inc., Englewood Cliffs, NJ. [Edited]

The work of specifying these rules, which dates at least from Aristotle's *Politics*, traditionally goes under the heading of "just war theory." The name is slightly misleading, since justice is only one of several primary moral concepts, all of which must be consulted in a complete moral evaluation of war. A just war—a morally good war—is not merely a war dictated by principles of justice. A just war is a morally justifiable war after justice, human rights, the common good, and all other relevant moral concepts have been consulted and weighed against the facts and against each other.

Just war theorists sometimes fail to notice that just war theory describes two sorts of just wars: wars that are morally permissible and wars that are morally obligatory. The distinction between the permissible and the obligatory is persuasively demonstrable at the personal level. If I am unjustly attacked, I have a right to use force in my own defense—assuming that I have no other recourse. But since it is always open for the holder of a right to waive that right, I am not *obliged* to use force in my own defense. But suppose that I have promised to defend Jones, that Jones is now exposed to unjust attack, and that Jones calls for my help. In such a case I am obliged to defend Jones. At the level of nations, the distinction between permissible war and obligatory war has important consequences for policy. Frequently policy analysts demonstrate that a certain use of force passes the tests of just war, and then infer that the war is obligatory, that "justice demands it." But it may well be that the use of force is merely permissible, in which case it is also permissible to forgo the use of force. Indeed, there may be powerful prudential considerations why such a merely permissible just war should not be fought.

Another little point in the logic of just war theory deserves attention. In just war theory, the terms "just" and "unjust" are logical contraries. It follows that in war one side at most can be the just side. But it is possible that both sides may be unjust, and it is fallacious to think that if one side is provably unjust, the other side must be provably just. If your enemy is evil, it does not follow that you are good.

In undertaking the moral evaluation of war, it is natural to distinguish rules that determine *when* it is permissible or obligatory to begin a war (*jus ad bellum*) from rules that determine *how* a war should be fought once it has begun (*jus in bello*). *Jus ad bellum* rules apply principally to political leaders; *jus in bello* rules apply principally to soldiers and their officers. The distinction is not ironclad, since there may be situations in which there is no morally permissible way to wage war, in which case it follows that the war should not be waged in the first place. (Some believe that American intervention in Vietnam was such a case.) In this section we take up *jus ad bellum*; the next section is devoted to *jus in bello*.

Competent Authority

From the time of Augustine, theorists have maintained that a just war can be prosecuted only by a "competent authority." Augustine, as we noted, considered the use of force by private persons to be immoral; consequently the only permissible uses of force were those sanctioned by public authorities. Medieval authors, with a watchful eye for peasant revolts, followed Augustine in confining the just use of force to princes, whose authority and patronage were divinely sanctioned. Given these scholastic roots, considerations of competent authority might appear archaic, but it is still helpful for purposes of moral judgment to distinguish wars from spontaneous uprisings, and soldiers and officers from pirates and brigands. Just war must, first of all, be war.

To begin, most scholars agree that war is a controlled use of force, undertaken by persons organized in a functioning chain of command. An isolated assassin cannot wage war; New York City's Mad Bomber in the 1950s only metaphorically waged war against Con Edison. In some sense, then, war is the contrary of violence. Second, the use of force in war must be directed to an identifiable political result, a requirement forever associated with the Prussian theorist Karl von Clauswitz. An "identifiable political result" is some change in a government's policy, some alteration in a form of government, or some extension or limitation of the scope of its authority. Since the extermination of a people is not an identifiable political result, most acts of genocide are not acts of war: the Turks did not wage war against the Armenians, nor did Hitler wage war on the Jews. (The American frontier cliché, "the only good Indian is a dead Indian" expresses the hopes of murderers, not soldiers.) And since the religious conversion of people is, in most cases, not a political result, many holy wars, by this definition, have not been wars.

Our definition of war as the controlled use of force for political purposes does not imply that wars can be waged only by the governments of nation-states. Many rebels and revolutionaries have used controlled force through a chain of command for political purposes, and there have been at least as many wars within states as there have been wars between states. If civil wars are genuine wars, the scope of "competent authority" must be extended from princes and political leaders to rebels and revolutionaries as well. But, as the case of Pancho Villa perhaps indicates, it is sometimes difficult to distinguish revolutionaries from bandits. In international law, this difficulty is described as the problem of determining when a rebel movement has obtained "belligerent status."

In the most recent international discussion of this issue, at the Geneva Conference of 1974–1977, delegates agreed that in the case of conflicts arising within a single nation-state between the government and "dissident armed forces or other organized groups," a state of war shall exist, provided the dissident forces are

> . . . under responsible command, exercise such control over part of its territory as to enable them to carry out sustained and concerted military operations and [to implement the laws of war]. (Protocol II, Article 1.1)

This recognition of belligerent status, however,

> shall not apply to situations of internal disturbances and tensions, such as riots, isolated and sporadic acts of violence, and other acts of similar nature, as not being armed conflicts. (Protocol I, Article 1.2)

According to these rules, the American Confederacy in 1860, by virtue of its military organization and control of territory, qualifies for belligerent status, whereas the Symbionese Liberation Army, which controlled no territory, and the Newark rioters of 1967, who obeyed no commands, fail to qualify. By this standard, the American Civil War was war but the Patty Hearst kidnapping was crime, verdicts with which most people would agree.

But the new Geneva standard does not always yield satisfactory results. The partisan movements in World War II—the resistance movements in France, Italy, and the Ukraine, and Tito's great movement in Yugoslavia—rarely could claim specific territory as their own, yet their struggles can hardly be dismissed as unjust on grounds of absence of competent authority. Different perplexities arise in the case of peasant movements, where frequently territory is controlled from the capital by day and by the revolutionaries at night. Perhaps the requirement of "territorial control" is too strong.

The new Geneva standard also requires that genuine belligerents must be capable of carrying out "sustained and concerted military operations." This proviso would deny belligerent status to revolutionary groups that engage primarily in terrorist attacks against civilians, and most people would happily classify such terrorists as international outlaws. But what of revolutionary groups that do not engage in "sustained and concerted military operations"—which, in many cases, would be suicidal for the revolutionaries—but engage in sustained acts of terror against government buildings and officials of the incumbent regime? The campaign of assassination directed by the National Liberation Front (NLF) in Vietnam against village chiefs and other officials siding with the Saigon government was, at one point, the main form of its revolutionary struggle, and it seems pointless to deny the NLF belligerent status on the ground that its members were not engaging in sustained and concerted military operations. Though it might be criticized on other grounds, the NLF assassination campaign was controlled use of force directed to political ends, not a riot and not sporadic violence. It was dirty, but it was war.

Right Intention

One can imagine cases in which a use of military force might satisfy all the external standards of just war while those who order this use of force have no concern for justice. Unpopular political leaders, for example, might choose to make war in order to stifle domestic dissent and win the next election. The traditional theory of just war insists that a just war be a war for the right, fought for the sake of the right.

In the modern climate of political realism, many authors are inclined to treat the standard of right intention as a quaint relic of a more idealistic age, either on the grounds that moral motives produce disastrous results in international politics or on the grounds that motives are subjective and unobservable. ("I will not speculate on the motives of the North Vietnamese," Henry Kissinger once remarked, "I have too much difficulty understanding our own.") But it is unfair to dismiss idealistic motives on the grounds that they produce disaster in international politics, since realistic motives have produced their own fair share of disasters. It is a mistake to dismiss motives as unobservable, when they are so often clearly exhibited in behavior. The real difficulty with the demand for idealistic motives is that people usually have more than one motive for each of their actions, which makes it difficult or impossible to specify *the* motive for the act.

Despite the difficulty of multiple motives, it is important to retain some version of the rule of right intention as part of the theory of just war. No thoughtful person can fail to be disturbed by current international practice, in which leaders make policy decisions without regard for moral considerations and then have their staffs cook up moral rationalizations after the fact. If it is too much to insist that political leaders make decisions solely on moral grounds or even primarily on moral grounds, we can insist that desire for what is morally right be at least *one* of their motives.

It follows from this qualified insistence on moral motivation in the political leadership that political leaders must be able to justify their decisions on moral grounds. They may not act primarily or solely for the right, but they must have some reason, producible on request, for thinking that they are acting for the right, among other things. For those who let slip the dogs of war, it is not sufficient that things turn out for the best. The evils of even a just war are sufficiently great that we can demand of leaders who initiate war that they understand the moral character of the results they seek.

If desire for the right must be included as one of the motives for just war, are there any motives that must be *excluded*? Various authors have insisted that a just war cannot be motivated by love of violence or hatred of the enemy. Even in the fifth century Augustine wrote, "The real evils in war are love of violence, vengeful cruelty, fierce and implacable enmity, wild resistance, lust for power, and the like" (*Contra Faustum*, XXII.75). Most people will agree that a leader who has love of violence or hatred of the enemy as his sole or chief motivation for war has a bad intention. But Augustine and other authors go further and argue that it is immoral to make war if hatred is just one of the many motivations one has for fighting. The rule is severe, but worth considering.

Consider the American campaign against Japan in World War II. By the usual standards, the American decision to fight against Japan satisfied the rules of just war. But as the war proceeded, many Americans, stirred up by wartime propaganda, were seized with racial animosity and came to hate all Japanese as such. The 4-year internment of 180,000 innocent Japanese Americans, the campaign of extermination against Japanese cities, and the attack on Hiroshima were all caused or rendered tolerable by this atmosphere of hate. Observing this, Augustine would condemn this hatred of the Japanese as sin and the war against Japan as unjust. Nevertheless, it would be unreasonable to tell the relatives of those who died at Pearl Harbor or on Bataan that they should not feel hatred toward those whose acts and decisions took the lives of those they loved.

The difficulties concerning hatred can perhaps be resolved by distinguishing justifiable from unjustifiable hatred. Hatred of leaders who choose to wage unjust war is justifiable; hatred of their compatriots and coracialists is not, since hatred of human beings as such—apart from their voluntary acts—is not a morally acceptable emotion. By this standard, American leaders who chose wartime policies as a result of race hatred toward the Japanese were not engaged in just war, even if their policies were acceptable by all other moral tests.

Just Cause

The most important of the *jus ad bellum* rules is the rule that the moral use of military force requires a just cause. From the earliest writings, just war theorists rejected love of war and love of conquest as morally acceptable causes for war: "We [should] wage war," Aristotle wrote, "for the sake of peace" (*Politics*, 1333A). Likewise, the seizure of plunder was always rejected as an acceptable cause for war. Beyond these elementary restrictions, however, a wide variety of "just causes" were recognized. The history of the subject is the history of how this repertoire of just causes was progressively cut down to the modern standard, which accepts only the single cause of self-defense.

As early as Cicero in the first century B.C., analysts of just war recognized that the only proper occasion for the use of force was a "wrong received." It follows from this that the condition or characteristics of potential enemies, apart from their actions, cannot supply a just cause for war. Aristotle's suggestion that a war is justified to enslave those who naturally deserve to be slaves, John Stuart Mill's claim that military intervention is justified in order to bestow the benefits of Western civilization on less advanced peoples, and the historically common view that forcible conversion to some true faith is justified as obedience to divine command are all invalidated by the absence of a "wrong received."

Obviously, the concept of a "wrong received" stands in need of considerable analysis. In the eighteenth century, the notion of wrong included the notion of insult, and sovereigns considered it legitimate to initiate war in response to verbal disrespect, desecrations of national symbols, and so forth. The nineteenth century, which saw the abolition of private duels, likewise saw national honor reduced to a secondary role in the moral justification of war. For most nineteenth century theorists, the primary wrongs were not insults, but acts or policies of a government resulting in violations of the rights of the nation waging just war.

By twentieth-century standards, this definition of international wrongs providing conditions of just war was both too restrictive and too loose. It was too restrictive in that it failed to recognize any rights of *peoples,* as opposed to *states*: rights to cultural integrity, national self-determination, and so forth. It was too loose in that it sanctioned the use of military force in response to wrongs the commission of which may not have involved military force, thus condoning, on occasion, the first use of arms.

These two excesses were abolished in twentieth-century international law. The right to national self-determination was a prevailing theme at the Versailles conference in 1919 and was repeatedly invoked in the period of decolonization following World War II. Prohibition of first use of force was attempted in drafting of the U.N. Charter in 1945:

> Article 2(4): All Members shall refrain in their international relations from the threat or use of force against the territorial integrity or political independence of any state or in any other manner inconsistent with the Purposes of the United Nations.
>
> Article 51: Nothing in the present Charter shall impair the inherent right of individual or collective self-defense if an armed attack occurs against a member of the United Nations, until the Security Council has taken the measures necessary to maintain international peace and security.

Strictly speaking, Article 51 does not prohibit first use of military force: to say that explicitly, the phrase "if an armed attack occurs" would have to be replaced by "if and only if an armed attack occurs." Nevertheless, Article 51, coupled with article 2(4), rules out anticipatory self-defense. Legitimate self-defense must be self-defense against an actual attack.

The U.N. Charter represents the most restrictive analysis of just cause in the history of the subject. In discussions since, members of the United Nations have continued to assume that just cause consists only in self-defense, but "self-defense" has come to be understood as a response to aggression. The definition of "aggression" thus becomes central to the analysis of just cause. In the United Nations, a special committee established to analyze the concept of aggression produced a definition adopted by the General Assembly on 14 December 1974:

> *Article 1.* Aggression is the use of armed force by a State against the sovereignty, territorial integrity, or political independence of another State, or in any other manner inconsistent with the Charter of the United Nations. . . .
>
> *Article 2.* The first use of armed force by a State in contravention of the Charter shall constitute *prima facie* evidence of an act of aggression [although the Security Council may come to determine that an act of aggression has not in fact been committed]. . . .
>
> *Article 3.* Any of the following acts regardless of a declaration of war shall . . . qualify as an act of aggression:
>
> (a) The invasion or attack by the armed force of a State on the territory of another State, or any military occupation, however temporary;
>
> (b) Bombardment by the armed forces of a State against the territory of another State;
>
> (c) The blockade of the ports or coasts of a State by the armed forces of another State;
>
> (d) An attack by the armed forces of a State on the land, sea, air, or marine and air fleets of another State; . . .
>
> (g) The sending by or on behalf of a State of armed bands, groups, irregulars, or mercenaries, which carry out acts of armed force against another State of such gravity as to amount to the acts listed above. . . .
>
> *Article 4.* The acts enumerated are not exhaustive.
>
> *Article 5.* No consideration of whatever nature, whether political, economic, military, or otherwise, may serve as a justification for aggression. . . .
>
> *Article 7.* Nothing in this definition . . . could in any way prejudice the right to self-determination, freedom, and independence, as derived from the Charter, of peoples forcibly deprived of that right . . . particularly peoples under colonial and racist regimes or other forms of alien domination; nor the right of these peoples to struggle to that end and to seek and receive support. . . .

By reading between the lines, the intent of the special committee can be easily discerned. In failing to enumerate under "acts of aggression" such traditional causes of war as attacks on citizens abroad, assaults on nonmilitary ships and aircraft on the high seas, and the seizure of property of aliens, the committee counted as aggression only military acts that might substantially affect the physical security of the nation suffering aggression. The only violation of rights that merits the unilateral use of force by nations is the physically threatening use of force by another state. . . .

HOW TO FIGHT

Introduction

People who believe that there are moral limits defining *when* wars should be fought naturally believe that there are moral limits defining *how* they should be fought. The idea that there are right and wrong ways to conduct war is an ancient one. In the Hebrew Bible, God states that though it may be necessary to kill one's enemy, it is never permissible to cut down his fruit trees (Deut. 20:19). In the sixth century B.C. the Hindu Laws of Manu specified, "When the King fights with his foes in battle, let him not strike with weapons concealed in wood, nor with barbed, poisoned, or flaming arrows."

Over the centuries, a vast array of rules and customs constituting *jus in bello* have been elaborated. There are rules that specify proper behavior toward neutral countries, toward the citizens of neutral countries, and toward neutral ships. There are rules governing what can and cannot be done to enemy civilians, to enemy soldiers on the battlefield, and to enemy soldiers when they are wounded and when they have surrendered. There are rules concerning proper and improper weapons of war, and proper and improper tactics on the battlefield.

In the late nineteenth and twentieth centuries, many of these "laws of war" were codified in a series of treaties, conventions, and protocols, signed and ratified by most of the principal nations of the world. Nations ratifying these sets of rules undertook to impose them on their own military establishments, pledging to prosecute violations and punish wrongdoers. When domestic enforcements have fallen short, nations victorious in war have undertaken the prosecution of violations perpetrated by defeated enemies. (Victorious nations are rarely prosecuted.)

With the exceptions of the Geneva Convention banning chemical warfare (1925) and the Second Protocol to the Fourth Geneva Convention (1977), the United States has ratified most of the principal international conventions regarding the laws of war. In their field manuals, the various military services of the United States consider themselves bound by the Hague Conventions of 1899 and 1907, by the Geneva Conventions of 1929, and by the four Geneva Conventions of 1949, which govern the sick and wounded on the battlefield (I), the sick and wounded at sea (II), prisoners of war (III), and the protection of civilian persons in time of war (IV).

Necessity, Proportionality, and Discrimination

For the student approaching the laws of war for the first time, the profusion of covenants, treaties, customs, and precedents can be bewildering. But fortunately there are a few leading ideas that have governed the development of the laws of war. The first is that the destruction of life and property, even enemy life and property, is inherently bad. It follows that military forces should cause no more destruction than is strictly necessary to achieve their objectives. (Notice that the principle does not say that whatever is necessary is permissible, but that everything permissible must be necessary.) This is the principle of necessity: that *wanton* destruction is forbidden. More precisely, the principle of necessity specifies that a military operation is forbidden if there is some alternative operation that causes less destruction but has the same probability of producing a successful military result.

The second leading idea is that the amount of destruction permitted in pursuit of a military objective must be proportionate to the importance of the objective. This is the *military* principle of proportionality (which must be distinguished from the *political* principle of proportionality in the *jus ad bellum*). It follows from the military principle of proportionality that certain objectives should be ruled out of consideration on the grounds that too much destruction would be caused in obtaining them.

The third leading idea, the principle of noncombatant immunity, is that civilian life and property should not be subjected to military force: military force must be directed only at military objectives. Obviously, the principle of noncombatant immunity is useful only if there is a consensus about what counts as "civilian" and what counts as "military." In the older Hague Conventions, a list of explicit nonmilitary targets is developed: "buildings dedicated to religion, art, science, or charitable purposes, historic monuments, hospitals . . . undefended towns, buildings, or dwellings." Anything that is not explicitly mentioned qualifies as a military target. But this list is overly restrictive, and the consensus of modern thought takes "military" targets to include servicemen, weapons, and supplies; the ships and vehicles that transport them; and the factories and workers that produce them. Anything that is not "military" is "civilian." Since, on either definition, the principle of noncombatant immunity distinguishes acceptable military objectives from unacceptable civilian objectives, it is often referred to as the principle of discrimination. (In the morality of war, discrimination is good, not evil.)

There is an objective and subjective version of the principle of noncombatant immunity. The objective version holds that if civilians are killed as a result of military operations, the principle is violated. The subjective version holds that if civilians are *intentionally* killed as a result of military operations, the principle is violated. The interpretation of "intentional" in the subjective version is disputed, but the general idea is that the killing of civilians is intentional if, and only if, they are the chosen *targets* of military force. It follows, on the subjective version, that if civilians are killed in the course of a military operation directed at a military target, the principle of discrimination has *not* been violated. Obviously, the objective version of the principle of discrimination is far more restrictive than the subjective.

The earlier Hague Conventions leaned toward the objective version of the principle of discrimination. The later Geneva Convention (IV), as interpreted in the Second Protocol of 1977, leans toward the subjective version:

> The civilian population as such, as well as individual civilians, shall not be the object of attack. . . . Indiscriminate attacks are prohibited, [including] those which are not directed at a specific military objective, those which employ a method or means which cannot be directed at a specific objective, or those which employ a method or means the effects of which cannot be limited or which are of a nature to strike military objectives and civilians or civilian objects without distinction.

If we adopt the subjective version of the principle of discrimination, it does not follow that any number of civilians may be permissibly killed so long as they are killed in pursuit of military objectives. The number of civilian deaths resulting from a military operation remains limited by the principle of proportionality. In sum,

> In all military operations, civilians should not be the target of attack. The deaths of civilians or damage to their property which are side-effects of military operations must be necessary for the achievement of the objective and proportionate to its importance.

The principles of necessity, proportionality, and discrimination apply with equal force to all sides in war. Violation of the rules cannot be justified or excused on the grounds that one is fighting on the side of justice. Those who developed the laws of war learned through experience that just causes must have moral limits.

Was the Gulf War a Just War?

Gregory S. Kavka

Gregory Kavka is professor of philosophy at the University of California, Irvine. He is the author of Hobbesian Moral and Political Theory *(1986) and* Moral Paradoxes of Nuclear Deterrence *(1987).*

Kavka applies the just war doctrine to the recent war in the Persian Gulf between the United States and Iraq. He pursues the following questions: Did the United States pursue war against Iraq with right intention? Was the good aimed at in fighting the war sufficient to outweigh the harm done in fighting that war? Were there any other means that the United States should have pursued first, before going to war? Were the specific practices of the United States military operation sufficiently aimed at military as opposed to civilian targets to justify the conduct of the Gulf War? Along the way, Kavka raises moral, epistemological, and practical problems with interpreting and applying the just war doctrine.

In the early months of 1991, the United States—in alliance with a number of other nations—fought a large scale air and ground war to evict Iraq's occupying army from the emirate of Kuwait. In this paper, I will consider the question of whether this U.S. military campaign was a just war according to the criteria of traditional just war theory[1]—the only developed moral theory of warfare that we have.[2] My aim, however, is not so much to reach a verdict about the morality of the Gulf War, as it is to identify relevant moral issues, and to reveal certain serious problems of application that are inherent in just war theory itself.

Just war theory divides into two parts concerning, respectively, the question of whether or not to fight a particular war (justice of war), and the question of how the war is conducted (justice in war). I begin by considering whether it was just, according to the justice of war criteria, for the U.S. to fight the Gulf War at all. I then turn to the question of whether the way the war was conducted satisfied the criteria of justice in war.

Reprinted by permission of *Journal of Social Philosophy, Vol. 22,* No. 1, Spring 1991. [Edited]

SHOULD THE WAR HAVE BEEN FOUGHT?

To be a just war, a military campaign must satisfy each of four criteria: it must be authorized by *competent authority,* fought for a *just cause,* motivated by the *right intentions,* and must not cause harms that are out of *proportion* with the goods achieved. I think it is fairly clear that the first two criteria were satisfied in the case of the Gulf War.

Although there was never a declaration of war by the U.S. Congress, the passage of resolutions by both houses of Congress—and the United Nations security council—which authorized the use of force to expel the Iraqi army from Kuwait, meant that U.S. President George Bush was acting as a competent authority in ordering U.S. troops into battle.[3] And the vindication of the rights of self-protection and self-determination of the Kuwaitis against the occupying Iraqi forces is a paradigm of a just cause. When we turn to the criteria of Right Intention and Proportionality, however, things get considerably more complicated.

Right Intention

The criterion of Right Intention concerns the subjective motivations of the war-making entities. One general difficulty with just war theory is that it is usually collective entities, like nations, that fight wars and there are two competing philosophical accounts of the nature of the motives and intentions of such collective entities. According to the *individualist account,* statements about the motives and intentions of collective entities are merely convenient abbreviations for more complex statements about the motives and intentions of the particular individual members of those entities. But the competing *collectivist account* says that motives and intentions can be attributed to corporate entities themselves if the actions of the entities' members express corporate policy and flow from corporate decision-procedures. As Peter French, a prominent collectivist, puts it: "[A] Corporation's Internal Decision Structure . . . licenses the prediction of corporate intentionality . . . [W]hen the corporate act is consistent with, an instantiation or an implementation of established corporate policy, then it is proper to describe it as having been done for corporate reasons, . . . as corporate intentional."[4] As we shall see, both the collectivist and individualist accounts pose serious problems of application when applied to a concrete situation such as U.S. actions in the Gulf War.

Consider first the collectivist account. Assuming that proper U.S. procedures were used in authorizing the war, the key question is what U.S. policy or policies the Gulf War implemented or instantiated. Doubtless there were many U.S. policies this war may be said to have implemented, and this fact points immediately to two sorts of problems. First, of the various policies implemented, must they *all* be morally good (or at least morally neutral) policies if the Right Intention criterion is to be satisfied? Or must this be true of only the majority of them, or of the most important ones? Second, at what level of specificity are the policies to be described and evaluated? U.S. policies, described at the most general levels (e.g., "do the right thing," "help friendly nations in trouble," "protect the national interest") are likely to be morally good or morally neutral. More specific descriptions of these policies that imply their immorality are likely to be controversial. Thus, while all might agree that "protect Middle East oil supplies to the West" was one policy implemented by the Gulf War, critics and friends of U.S. foreign policy are likely to disagree whether the implicit clause in the policy says "by any means necessary" or "by any proper means." The answer to this question is vital in determining the morality of the policy, and hence of the collective intention which implements it according to the collectivist account.

How, in principle, are such questions (about what the *real* collective policy is) to be answered? Presumably by looking at three sorts of evidence: past behavior of the collective, the nature of the collective's decision-procedures and the sorts of considerations that carry weight in that procedure, and the particular descriptions of policy that influenced decision-makers in the case at hand. The inclusion of the first two elements suggests that, according to the collectivist account, we cannot give a proper account of U.S. motives in the Gulf War without a more general determination of the morality of U.S. behavior in international relations, and the influence various considerations (including moral ones) have within the foreign-policy decision-making apparatus of the U.S. Since these matters are far beyond the scope of this paper, I turn instead to the individualist account which focuses exclusively on the third element: how the decision-makers involved thought of what they were doing and why they did it.

According to the individualist account, "collective motives and intentions" are simply agglomerations of individual motives and intentions among the collectives' members. Unfortunately, we have no good account that tells us how to determine (or accurately describe) the motives of a collective when the motives of its various members are diverse and various, as they typically are. Even among a small leadership group—say a head of state and her small circle of advisors—there are likely to be a variety of motives for embarking on a military campaign. Indeed, even if we focus on a single decision-maker like President Bush, there may be a number of motives present, and even the individual in question may not know what they all are and which are the most important ones. And even if we put aside epistemological questions about knowing people's motives, just war theory gives us no guidance as to how to deal with the multiplicity of motives. Whose motives count? Must they all be morally legitimate ones, or only the majority of them, or most of the important ones, or most of the important ones of the most influential decision-makers? In the absence of answers to these questions, we cannot—on the individualist account—really apply the criterion of Right Intention with great confidence.

Let us sidestep these problems in applying the individualist account to the Gulf War, together with epistemological problems about determining people's real motivations, by making two assumptions. First, it is the motives of President Bush and his top advisors that matter, and second, their publicly stated intention of promoting a new world order is really what motivated their actions in the gulf crisis. I am far from convinced that the second assumption is correct. But it would be wrong to dismiss it out of hand, on the grounds that some have, namely that previous U.S. failures to intervene militarily in situations as bad as the Kuwaiti one show that our leaders' motives in the Gulf War were imperialistic (control of the gulf), economic (cheap oil), or privately political (re-election). Just war theory, or any other plausible account of international morality (e.g., a rule-utilitarian one), does not require nations to intervene militarily in all situations of international injustice or aggression. It is perfectly permissible, indeed wise and desirable, for nations to limit their interventions to situations in which grave aggressions need to be prevented or reversed, the nation possesses the means to reliably bring this about, and the nation's interests would be significantly adversely affected if it did not do so. The mere fact that a nation picks and chooses its interventions to coincide with feasibility and national interest does not mean its motives are bad, nor that it has no concern for halting aggression. This is not to say that patterns of intervention may not constitute *evidence* about the motivations of a nation's leadership. It just says that a history of selective intervention, in itself, is no evidence of impure motives when there is an intervention, and we may not dismiss the second assumption solely on the grounds that the U.S. has failed to intervene when less oil-laden states have been the victims of aggression.

Similar points apply to two other common objections against U.S. intentions being proper in the gulf situation: that the U.S. has fought clearly unjust wars in the past (from the conquest of the American Indians to the recent invasion of Panama), and that previously it armed and encouraged the aggressors in this very war—the Saddam Hussein regime in Iraq. At most, on the individualist account, these facts form part of a complex pattern of evidence about U.S. motives and intentions in the current situation. They do not in themselves show that these motives and intentions are bad ones. As regards the first argument, in particular, it must be remembered that just war theory is designed to evaluate particular wars and the way they are conducted, it does not attempt to characterize a nation's history of involvement in wars in general. (Thus, the theory allows that just as a person of bad character may, on occasion, perform a right action, so a nation whose foreign policy is normally immoral may sometimes engage in just wars.) And while the second argument about our prior support for Iraq does have moral implications, they point toward—rather than away from—U.S. involvement in the Gulf War. For if the U.S. negligently created a danger by its prior coddling of the Iraqi regime, and the Kuwaitis suffered grievously as a result, the U.S. might bear a special responsibility to repair the effects of its negligence. On this line of reasoning, what would otherwise be a moral option for the United States—evicting the Iraqi army from Kuwait militarily—would become a moral responsibility or duty.[5]. . .

Proportionality

The criterion of Proportionality says that the good aimed at in fighting a war must outweigh the bads involved in, and caused by, the war itself.[6] There are three general difficulties with applying this criterion that make it difficult to determine whether the criterion was satisfied in the case of the Gulf War.

First, and most familiarly, there are enormous empirical difficulties in determining the effects of a war, even when it is over, together with possible disagreements about the scheme of value to be used in assessing the war and its consequences. Even if we waive the latter issue, the question about effects will remain largely unanswered for a very long time, since almost everyone agrees that it is the long-term effects on peace and stability in the Middle East that are most important, and they are not yet evident (if they ever will be).

Second, it is unclear whether we should apply the proportionality criterion with respect to actual outcomes or what the agents involved reasonably believed at the time they made their decisions.[7] The latter alternative has the advantage of taking the just war theory as a practical, action-guiding theory that is designed to help statesmen and citizens guide their deliberations about going to war, rather than a set of abstract formulas usable only by outsiders to praise or condemn after the fact. We would normally think of the subjective "reasonable belief" version of the criterion of Proportionality as being easier on decision-makers: it does not expect them to be prescient and does not subject them to Monday morning quarterbacking. But, in this case, using the "reasonable belief" version of the criterion may make it *harder* for the war in question to satisfy that criterion. For at least as regards the immediate effects, the Gulf War was shorter and involved fewer casualties (on both sides) than was reasonably expected ahead of time by top U.S. officials.

Third, evaluating a war in terms of its good and bad upshots is more complicated than simply observing its actual effects in the world. We must also compare the war and its effects to what the world would have been like had the war not occurred, i.e., to a *counterfactual* situation. But we cannot observe what would have happened, but did not; we can only hypothesize it based on what the world was like and our limited ability to identify and extrapolate trends.

Further, it is not obvious *which* counterfactual situation we are to consider in making our comparison: the one resulting from the nation in question doing nothing,[8] from its doing what it would most likely have done if it did not fight, or from its doing what (besides, possibly, fighting) would have maximized utility. This last way of identifying the relevant alternative may be too strong: it turns the Proportionality criterion into a requirement to maximize utility. But the first way seems too weak: it allows fighting when negotiations (or threats) would achieve the same ends more cheaply.[9] And the middle way can set the baseline of comparison too low. Suppose, for example, a nation would most likely turn its army to slaughtering a domestic minority if it did not fight the war in question. Then even a costly and unnecessary war might satisfy the Proportionality criterion.

Unable to solve this problem of picking out the relevant alternative in a satisfactory way, I will henceforth simply *assume* that the relevant alternative in the gulf situation was to continue the policy actually pursued prior to the outbreak of fighting: military defense of Saudi Arabia combined with economic sanctions against Iraq. Even given this assumption, however, and even if all the data were in about future actual developments in the region, we would not know for sure whether the war produced a favorable balance of good over evil. For we would not know what *would have happened* had the alliance not fought the war. Perhaps continuation of the economic sanctions would have worked to force Iraq from Kuwait or Saddam Hussein from power. Though I doubt this is likely to have occurred, if it had, it would have set a marvelous precedent for a new world order: cancellation of aggressive gains by united diplomatic and economic action rather than war. A more likely possibility is that a purely defensive force in Saudi Arabia would have sufficed to control Iraq's military ambitions, while Kuwaiti oil riches paid off Iraqi debts and provided the Iraqis with a new interest in regional stability. This outcome, sad as it would have been for Kuwait, would not necessarily have been intolerable for the world as a whole, nor worse than the actual consequences of the gulf conflict.

The fair conclusion to draw, I think, is that we do not know whether the Gulf War satisfied the criterion of Proportionality and may never know. This is due less to the peculiarities of the Gulf War, than to general problems concerning applicability of the Proportionality criterion: potentional disagreement about values, factual uncertainty and complexity, necessity of comparison with indeterminate counterfactual situations, and ambiguity between "actual outcomes" and "reasonable belief" interpretations of the criterion.[10] But even this agnostic conclusion suggests that the Gulf War fares better than most wars as regards proportionality. Most wars have clearly cost much and achieved little in terms of human well being. Supporters of the Gulf War can claim, without absurdity, that something humanly significant (the liberation of Kuwait and the removal of the Iraqi military threat) has been achieved at a reasonable cost.

Last Resort

Some interpretations of just war theory require, as a separate criterion, that all available peaceful alternatives be exhausted before a war can be justified.[11] I prefer to view this principle as a powerful rule of thumb to be used in applying the Proportionality criterion. Given the enormous costs of war, it is highly unlikely that it is proportionate to go to war before pursuing all peaceful alternatives for settling a dispute. But in the odd case where it is proportionate to fight before trying all alternatives that might conceivably work—for example, when an aggressor will use any extra time to make his military position unassailable—a nation is justified in doing so.

Though I do not endorse the last resort idea as a separate criterion that must be satisfied for a war to be just, I think it is instructive to look briefly at whether the U.S. went to war in the gulf as a last resort. Many members of the U.S. Congress apparently thought not; they voted in favor of continuing economic sanctions rather than going to war. But suppose the administration was right and the economic sanctions would not have been sufficient to force Iraq from Kuwait. (This view is credible in view of the fact that a tremendous air war did not suffice to make the Iraqis withdraw.[12]) Did the Bush Administration go the last mile for peace, as it claimed, by offering—and having—direct talks with Iraq at the highest level in order to prevent war?[13] Their apparent aim was to get Iraq to withdraw by credibly threatening to fight without actually fighting.[14] In this they failed.

But there was an alternative, potentially more effective, way of carrying out this strategy for avoiding war that was not attempted. The war occurred because the two Presidents—Bush and Hussein—looked at different precedents and drew different lessons. Bush looked at World War II, and saw Hussein as a Hitler-like tyrant who had to be stopped by superior military force.[15] Hussein looked at Viet Nam and the barracks-bombing in Lebanon and concluded that the U.S. would not sustain a military operation in which it suffered heavy casualties.[16] To get Iraq out of Kuwait without fighting, it was necessary to erase that conclusion from Hussein's mind, other than by verbal threats that he simply would not believe.

Suppose, however, that President Bush had publicly declared that he would not run for reelection in 1992 unless the Iraqi army was out of Kuwait and the original Kuwaiti government restored to power. This announcement would constitute the kind of precommitment to fight to the end in Kuwait that Hussein—a high political leader who is assumed to value political power above all else—would both believe and understand. If he had any doubts about the determination of top American leadership to drive him from Kuwait by force if necessary, this simple public act would have erased them. It would also erase any illusions that once the war began and there were casualties, American leaders would be inclined to pull back or compromise.

This course of action would have had its moral downside. If this last resort were tried but failed, the administration would have incentives to continue a stalemated war past the point of diminishing returns. Nonetheless, if President Bush had wished to walk the last mile for peace by maximizing his chances of expelling Iraq from Kuwait by threats rather than war, this is a policy he might have been well-advised to pursue. Whether his failure to do so renders the subsequent war "disproportionate" depends upon whether this maneuver would have significantly increased the chances of a peaceful settlement. One may reasonably doubt this if one believes that Iraq's behavior during the war indicates that nothing short of decisive military defeat would have driven them from Kuwait.

There is a further issue concerning satisfaction of the Last Resort criterion in the Gulf War. Just prior to the start of the coalition's brief and decisive ground campaign, the Soviet Union was apparently making some headway toward brokering a diplomatic solution that would involve Iraqi withdrawal from Kuwait. If the Last Resort criterion is regarded as a separate criterion that must be satisfied for war to be just, the gulf *ground* war would turn out to be unjust simply because the U.S. and its coalition partners passed up this opportunity to settle the dispute with Iraq without fighting a ground war.

On the other hand, if—as suggested above—we interpret the Last Resort criterion as a rule-of-thumb falling under the Proportionality criterion, the status of the ground war is harder to determine. Beneficial and legitimate objectives were achieved by the ground campaign: weakening of the dangerous Iraqi military, Iraq's commitment to paying reparations and its renunciation of its annexation of Kuwait, and strengthening of the "new world order" principle of nonaggression against one's neighbors. And casualties (especially civilian and coalition casualties) were light, because of the swiftness and one-sidedness of the campaign. Thus, unless we assume a "reasonable belief" interpretation of the proportionality criterion, and suppose that U.S. decision-makers expected much heavier casualties from the ground war even just before it commenced, the ground war might well satisfy the Proportionality criterion, despite the fact that the U.S. failed to pursue the Soviet peace initiative.

WAS THE WAR CONDUCTED IN A JUST MANNER?

The analysis of the previous section does not rule out the possibility that the Gulf War was a just one. Do the principles of Discrimination and Proportionality, which limit how a nation may fight a war (even one it is just to undertake) rule out that possibility? The principle of Discrimination requires not making civilian populations the object of attack. It allows the killing of civilians only as unintended (though possibly foreseen) consequences of attacking legitimate military targets.[17] Coalition policies of targeting only military assets, and ordering their pilots to withhold dropping their bombs when they could not hone in on assigned targets, taken together with the "relatively light" (given the amount of bombing) casualties suffered by Iraqi civilians, indicate general compliance with the principle of Discrimination by the coalition during the Gulf War.

Nonetheless, given the enormous number of powerful bombs dropped, and the targeting of military assets located in and near cities, there were still large numbers of civilian casualties—"collateral damage" in the euphemism used by the military briefers. These foreseeable Iraqi civilian casualties may not have been enough to render the entire war disproportionate. But the principle of Proportionality *within war* says that each operation or tactic must be proportionate, in terms of its costs and benefits (including, of course, the benefits of making overall victory more likely for the side fighting for justice).

This raises problems concerning the coalition's successful military strategy of postponing the ground war until the air war had reduced the effective capacity of resistance by the Iraqi military. This strategy was explicitly motivated by a legitimate desire to minimize coalition casualties. But even if Iraqi soldiers are eliminated from the calculations of proportionality due to being considered "guilty aggressors,"[18] Iraqi civilians cannot be eliminated from those same calculations. Their deaths may have only been unintended side-effects of the bombing of military targets, but to the extent that they were foreseeable, they must be included—at least on a par with coalition military deaths—in applications of the principle of proportionality.

Now it is possible that both civilian and military casualties were minimized by the coalition policy of continuing the air war for over a month before commencing the ground campaign. Perhaps a shorter air war would have led to a longer and fiercer ground war, with more casualties—civilian and military—on both sides. (At least their quick defeat on the ground allowed many Iraqi soldiers to surrender or flee. Even fewer might have survived a longer ground war.[19]) But if this is so, it is probably a lucky accident—there is no guarantee that it had to be so. The just war criterion of Proportionality in war implies that coalition war planners should have aimed at minimizing something different than they apparently did: innocent casualties (where this includes at least Iraqi civilians and neutrals caught on the field of battle) rather than simply coalition casualties.

CONCLUSION

Was the Gulf War a just war? The answer provided by the analysis of this paper is a resounding "maybe." It pretty clearly satisfied the criteria of Competent Authority, Just Cause, and Discrimination. It may or may not have satisfied the two Proportionality criteria and the Right Intention criterion. The difficulties with determining whether it did are not so much specific to this particular war, but are generic ones associated with applying just war theory in any real world situation. These include characterizing the nature of collective intentions, determining what the relevant motives and intentions of relevant decision-makers were, designating a scheme of value to evaluate outcomes, and making complex factual—and counterfactual—determinations about the effects of large-scale actions (like fighting a war) and their alternatives.

The fact that, after careful scrutiny, it remains at least possible that the Gulf War was a just war (according to the just war theory criteria), leaves that conflict in pretty select company. Even the Allies' effort in World War II, often taken as a paradigm of a moral war, clearly failed to satisfy at least one of the just war theory criteria: the principle of Discrimination. And it is not clear that World War II fares better than the Gulf War on the overall Proportionality criterion.

This is not (despite the analogy drawn in one of President Bush's speeches) because Saddam Hussein is another Hitler. He has not carried out a large-scale program of genocide justified by a racist ideology, nor—as the leader of Iraq—did he ever pose the threat to the world that was posed by Hitler astride the powerful German state. Nonetheless, in a space of a decade, he invaded—with aggressive intent—two neighboring states in a volatile and vital area of the world. Stopping him in a war with a few hundred thousand casualties may not have been disproportionate compared to stopping Hitler in a world conflict with tens of millions of casualties. Indeed, if over the next decade, the Middle East is more peaceful and stable than before the Gulf War, so that it seems likely that the war was after all a proportionate one, we may expect to see the Gulf War join (or even replace) World War II in common lore as the paradigm of a just war. If the analysis of this paper—based on traditional just war theory—is correct, this would not necessarily constitute a mistake.[20]

NOTES

1. There is no single canonical version of just war theory. The criteria used here to define that theory represent an attempt to distill the main elements of just war theory as portrayed in the recent philosophical literature.
2. The main alternative theories that are frequently applied to these issues are pacifism, which regards all wars as immoral, realism, which is a theory that denies the applicability of moral criteria to war, and utilitarianism, which is a general moral theory not specifically designed to deal with moral issues surrounding warfare.

3. Even the leaders of non-democratic allied nations were "competent authorities" in the relevant sense for just war theory, which is intended to rule out uses of force by private groups and individuals.
4. Peter A. French, "The Corporation as a Moral Person," in Peter A. French, ed., *The Spectrum of Responsibility* (New York: St. Martin's Press, 1991), pp. 298, 302.
5. This conclusion might not hold if, as some people suspect, the U.S. deliberately enticed Iraq into invading Kuwait in order to have an excuse to destroy its military power. But I do not find that suspicion very credible, despite the conflicting reports about what the U.S. Ambassador told Saddam Hussein in their July 25, 1991 meeting. (For one account, see Tom Mathews, "Road to War," *Newsweek*, January 28, 1991, pp. 54, 56.) U.S. diplomacy just prior to the invasion is better explained as bureaucratic fumbling and listening to the advice of the other Gulf states to appease Saddam, than it is by conspiracy theories. Nor does the fact that the U.S. government saw Saddam and his military as extremely dangerous *after* the invasion of Kuwait imply they saw them in the same light prior to that action.
6. The proportionality criterion takes account of probabilities: in the presence of uncertainty, good and bad effects are to be weighted by their probabilities. So, in principle, a particular good outcome (e.g., restoration of a legitimate government) may justify a small risk of causing a certain number of casualties, but not a large risk of causing the same number of casualties.
7. The notion of "reasonable belief" used here is intended to mean more than "beliefs that are reasonable given the agent's evidence." There are ways of being unreasonable in gathering evidence, such as deliberately avoiding evidence that might shift one's beliefs in an inconvenient way. Satisfying the "reasonable belief" version of the proportionality criterion requires having beliefs about outcomes that are "reasonable" in this strict sense.
8. Early in the crisis, President Bush apparently discussed the alternative of "doing nothing" with his top advisors. See Mathews, "The Road to War," p. 58.
9. This problem might be solved if, in contrast to what I propose below, we treat the Last Resort criterion as a separate criterion rather than a useful rule-of-thumb falling under the Proportionality criterion.
10. Of course, many of the same problems apply to competing theories that are consequentialist or have significant consequentialist elements, e.g., utilitarianism, patriotism (utilitarianism with one's scope of concern restricted to fellow citizens of one's country), and normative realism ("nations should act to best promote their own interests").
11. "Last Resort" is listed as a separate criterion, for example, in the American Catholic Bishops' famous pastoral letter on nuclear war. See U.S. Bishops, "The Challenge of Peace: God's Promise and Our Response," *Origins* 13 (May 19, 1983), pp. 10–11.
12. The fact that the air war was not sufficient to drive the Iraqis from Kuwait is strong, but not conclusive, evidence that sanctions alone would not have worked. It is not conclusive evidence because the air war may have stiffened resistance (or affected internal politics) so as to eliminate the withdrawal option for the Iraqis in ways sanctions would not have.
13. Here I assume, at least for the sake of argument, that the offer of direct talks was more than a play for domestic political support. Cf. Mathews, "The Road to War," p. 64.
14. Mathews, "The Road to War," pp. 63–65.
15. Mathews, "The Road to War," p. 64.
16. In the notorious July 25th meeting with U.S. Ambassador to Iraq, April Glaspie, Hussein is reported to have said, "Yours is a society which cannot accept 10,000 dead in one battle." (Mathews, "The Road to War," p. 56.)
17. It thus presupposes the problematic doctrine of double-effect, which ascribes enormous moral significance to the distinction between causing the deaths of innocent people intentionally and doing so non-intentionally. Whatever we may think of that doctrine, it is a central aspect of just war theory, and I will apply it here without questioning its validity.
18. It is unclear whether just war theory ascribes equal status to enemy soldiers under the proportionality criterion, for the notion of proportioning "good" to "evil" could include within it the idea that harm to the "innocent" counts more, where "innocence" is not moral innocence (which many Iraqi conscripts may have shared with their coalition counterparts), but innocence of participating in an unjust and threatening aggression. On the two notions of innocence, see, e.g., G.E.M. Anscombe, "War and Murder," in Richard Wasserstrom, ed., *War and Morality* (Belmont, CA: Wadsworth, 1970), pp. 42–53.
19. An alternative view is that the mass surrenders show the Iraqi would have surrendered as soon as attacked in any case. If this is so, the air war was an unnecessary, and therefore disproportionate, tactic.
20. An earlier version of this paper was presented on March 28, 1991, to a meeting of the Concerned Philosophers for Peace at the American Philosophical Association Pacific Division Meetings in San Francisco. I am grateful to the audience on that occasion, and to Edwin Curley, Peter French, Paul Graves, Ron Hirschbein, and Jeff McMahan for helpful discussion and suggestions.

The Practice of Satyagraha

Mohandas K. Gandhi

Mohandas K. Gandhi was a revolutionary political leader in India. He led a successful nonviolent revolt against British colonial rule that resulted in the creation of the independent state of India. He was the author of over 20 books, including The India of My Dreams *(1947),* Delhi Diary *(1948),* Satyagraha in South Africa *(1950), and* Women and Social Injustice *(1954).*

Gandhi presents the "classical" argument in favor of nonviolent resistance for a just cause. Gandhi argues that morality requires that all available means be attempted before recourse to violence can ever be justified. Nonviolent resistance must be attempted, he argues, and it can be such a successful alternative to violent war that its methods need to be taught to everyone. The main features of Gandhi's version of nonviolent resistance include respect for law; humility and lack of anger toward one's opponents; restraint not retaliation; and noncooperation rather than aggression. Gandhi justifies his views by reference to Hindu and Islamic traditions.

For the past thirty years, I have been preaching and practicing *satyagraha.* The principles of *satyagraha,* as I know it today, constitute a gradual evolution.[1]

Satyagraha differs from Passive Resistance as the North Pole from the South. The latter has been conceived as a weapon of the weak and does not exclude the use of physical force or violence for the purpose of gaining one's end, whereas the former has been conceived as a weapon of the strongest and excludes the use of violence in any shape or form.

The term *satyagraha* was coined by me in South Africa to express the force that the Indians there used for a full eight years, and it was coined in order to distinguish it from the movement then going on in the United Kingdom and South Africa under the name of Passive Resistance.

On the political field, the struggle on behalf of the people mostly consists in opposing error in the shape of unjust laws. When you have failed to bring the error home to the law-giver by way of petitions and the like, the only remedy open to you, if you do not wish to submit to error, is to compel him by physical force to yield to you or by suffering in your own person by inviting the penalty for the breach of the law. Hence *satyagraha* largely appears to the public as Civil Disobedience or Civil Resistance. It is civil in the sense that it is not criminal.

The law-breaker breaks the law surreptitiously and tries to avoid the penalty; not so the civil resister. He ever obeys the laws of the state to which he belongs, not out of fear of the sanctions, but because he considers them to be good for the welfare of society.

Mohandas K. Gandhi, "The Practice of Satyagraha," from *Gandhi: Selected Writings,* Ronald Duncan, editor (New York: Harper & Row, 1971). Reprinted with permission of the Navajivan Trust. [Edited]

But there come occasions, generally rare, when he considers certain laws to be so unjust as to render obedience to them a dishonor. He then openly and civilly breaks them and quietly suffers the penalty for their breach. And in order to register his protest against the action of the law-givers, it is open to him to withdraw his cooperation from the state by disobeying such other laws whose breach does not involve moral turpitude.

In my opinion, the beauty and efficacy of *satyagraha* are so great and the doctrine so simple that it can be preached even to children. It was preached by me to thousands of men, women, and children commonly called indentured Indians with excellent results.

The spirit of non-violence necessarily leads to humility. Non-violence means reliance on God, the Rock of Ages. If we would seek His aid, we must approach Him with a humble and a contrite heart. Non-cooperationists may not trade upon their amazing success at the Congress. We must act, even as the mango tree which droops as it bears fruit. Its grandeur lies in its majestic lowliness.

Non-cooperation is not a movement of brag, bluster, or bluff. It is a test of our sincerity. It requires solid and silent self-sacrifice. It challenges our honesty and our capacity for national work. It is a movement that aims at translating ideas into action. And the more we do, the more we find that much more must be done than we had expected. And this thought of our imperfection must make us humble.

A non-cooperationist strives to compel attention and to set an example not by his violence, but by his unobtrusive humility. He allows his solid action to speak for his creed. His strength lies in his reliance upon the correctness of his position. And the conviction of it grows most in his opponent when he least interposes his speech between his action and his opponent. Speech, especially when it is haughty, betrays want of confidence and it makes one's opponent skeptical about the reality of the act itself. Humility therefore is the key to quick success. I hope that every non-cooperationist will recognize the necessity of being humble and self-restrained. It is because so little is really required to be done and because all of that little depends entirely upon ourselves that I have ventured the belief that Swaraj is attainable in less than one year.

I am sorry that I find a nervous fear among some Hindus and Mohammedans that I am undermining their faith, and that I am even doing irreparable harm to India by my uncompromising preaching of non-violence. They seem almost to imply that violence is their creed. I touch a tender spot if I talk about extreme non-violence in their presence. They confound me with texts from the Mahabharata and the Koran eulogizing or permitting violence. Of the Mahabharata I can write without restraint, but the most devoted Mohammedan will not, I hope, deny me the privilege of understanding the message of the Prophet. I make bold to say that violence is the creed of no religion and that, whereas non-violence in most cases is obligatory in all, violence is merely permissible in some cases. But I have not put before India the final form of non-violence. The non-violence that I have preached from Congress platforms is non-violence as a policy. But even policies require honest adherence in thought, word and deed. If I believe that honesty is the best policy, surely whilst I so believe, I must be honest in thought, word and deed; otherwise I become an imposter. Non-violence being a policy means that it can upon due notice be given up when it proves unsuccessful or ineffective. But simple morality demands that, whilst a particular policy is pursued, it must be pursued with all one's heart. It is simple policy to march along a certain route, but the soldier who marches with an unsteady step along that route is liable to be summarily dismissed. I become therefore incredulous when people talk to me skeptically about non-violence or are seized with fright at the very mention of the word non-violence. If they do not believe in the expedient of non-violence, they must denounce it but not claim to believe in the expedient when their heart resists it. How disastrous it would be, if, not believing in violence even as an expedient, I joined, say a violence party and approached a gun with a perturbed heart! The reader will believe me when I say that I have the capacity for killing a fly. But I do not believe in killing even flies. Now suppose I joined an expedition for fly-killing as an expedient. Will I not be expected, before being permitted to join the expedition, to use all the available engines of destruction, whilst I remained in the army of fly-killers? If those who are in the Congress and the Khilafat committees will perceive this simple truth, we shall certainly either finish the struggle this year to a successful end, or be so sick of non-violence as to give up the pretension and set about devising some other program.

I hold that Swami Shraddhanandji has been needlessly criticized for the proposition he intended to move. His argument is absolutely honest. He thinks that we, as a body, do not really believe in non-violence even as a policy. Therefore, we shall never fulfill the program of non-violence. Therefore, he says, let us go to the councils and get what crumbs we may. He was trying to show the unreality of the position of those who believe in the policy with their lips, whereas they are looking forward to violence for final deliverance. I do say that, if Congressmen do not fully believe in the policy, they are doing an injury to the country by pretending to follow it. If violence is to be the basis of future government, the councillors are undoubtedly the wisest. For it is through the councils that, by the same devices by which the present administrators rule us, the councillors hope to seize power from the former's hands. I have little doubt that those who nurse violence in their bosoms will find no benefit from the lip-profession of non-violence. I urge, therefore, with all the vehemence at my command, that those who do not believe in non-violence should secede from the Congress and from noncooperation and prepare to seek election or rejoin law courts or Government colleges as the case may be. Let there be no manner of doubt that Swaraj established by non-violent means will be different in kind from the Swaraj that can be established by armed rebellion. Police and punishments there will be, even under such Swaraj. But there would be no room for brutalities such as we witness today both on the part of the people and the Government. And those, whether they call themselves Hindus or Mussulmans, who do not fully believe in the policy of non-violence, should abandon both noncooperation and non-violence.

For me, I am positive that neither in the Koran nor in the Mahabharata is there any sanction for and approval of the triumph of violence. Though there is repulsion enough in Nature, she lives by attraction. Mutual love enables Nature to persist. Man does not live by destruction. Self-love compels regard for others. Nations cohere, because there is mutual regard among the individuals composing them. Some day we must extend the national law to the universe, even as we have extended the family law to form nations—a larger family. God had ordained that India should be such a nation. For so far as reason can perceive, India cannot become free by armed rebellion for generations.

India can become free by refraining from national violence. India has now become tired of rule based upon violence. That to me is the message of the plains. The people of the plains do not know what it is to put up an organized armed fight. And they must become free, for they want freedom. They have realized that power seized by violence will only result in their greater grinding.

Such, at any rate, is the reasoning that has given birth to the policy, not the *dharma,* of non-violence. And even as a Mussulman or a Hindu, believing in violence, applies the creed of non-violence in his family, so are both called upon without question to apply the policy of non-violence in their mutual relations and in their relation to other races and classes, not excluding Englishmen. Those who do not believe in this policy and do not wish to live up to it in full, retard the movement by remaining in it.

When a person claims to be non-violent, he is expected not to be angry with one who has injured him. He will not wish him harm; he will wish him well; he will not swear at him; he will not cause him any physical hurt. He will put up with all the injury to which he is subjected by the wrong-doer. Thus non-violence is complete innocence. Complete non-violence is complete absence of ill-will against all that lives. It therefore embraces even sub-human life, not excluding noxious insects or beasts. They have not been created to feed our destructive propensities. If we only knew the mind of the Creator, we should find their proper place in His creation. Non-violence is therefore in its active form good will towards all life. It is pure Love. I read it in the Hindu scriptures, in the Bible, in the Koran.

Non-violence is a perfect state. It is a goal towards which all mankind moves naturally though unconsciously. Man does not become divine when he personifies innocence in himself. Only then does he become truly man. In our present state, we are partly men and partly beasts and in our ignorance and even arrogance say that we truly fulfill the purpose of our species, when we deliver blow for blow and develop the measure of anger required for the purpose. We pretend to believe that retaliation is the law of our being, whereas in every scripture we find that retaliation is nowhere obligatory. Retaliation is indulgence requiring elaborate regulating. Restraint is the law of our being. For highest perfection is unattainable without highest restraint. Suffering is thus the badge of the human tribe.

The goal ever recedes from us. The greater the progress, the greater the recognition of our unworthiness. Satisfaction lies in the effort, not in the attainment. Full effort is full victory. . . .

AN APPEAL TO EVERY BRITON

In 1896 I addressed an appeal to every Briton in South Africa on behalf of my countrymen who had gone there as laborers or traders and their assistants. It had its effect. However important it was from my viewpoint, the cause which I pleaded then was insignificant compared with the cause which prompts this appeal. I appeal to every Briton, wherever he may be now, to accept the method of non-violence instead of that of war, for the adjustment of relations between nations and other matters. Your statesmen have declared that this is a war on behalf of democracy. There are many other reasons given in justification. You know them all by heart. I suggest that, at the end of the war, whichever way it ends, there will be no democracy left to represent democracy. This war has descended upon mankind as a curse and a warning. It is a curse inasmuch as it is brutalizing man on a scale hitherto unknown. All distinctions between combatants and non-combatants have been abolished. No one and nothing is to be spared. Lying has been reduced to an art. Britain was to defend small nationalities. One by one they have vanished, at least for the time being. It is also a warning. It is a warning that, if nobody reads the writing on the wall, man will be reduced to the state of the beast, whom he is shaming by his manners. I read the writing when the hostilities broke out. But I had not the courage to say the word. God has given me the courage to say it before it is too late.

I appeal for cessation of hostilities, not because you are too exhausted to fight, but because war is bad in essence. You want to kill Nazism. You will never kill it by its indifferent adoption. Your soldiers are doing the same work of destruction as the Germans. The only difference is that perhaps yours are not as thorough as the Germans. If that be so, yours will soon acquire the same thoroughness as theirs, if not much greater. On no other condition can you win the war. In other words, you will have to be more ruthless than the Nazis. No cause, however just, can warrant the indiscriminate slaughter that is going on minute by minute. I suggest that a cause that demands the inhumanities that are being perpetrated today cannot be called just.

I do not want Britain to be defeated, nor do I want her to be victorious in a trial of brute strength, whether expressed through the muscle or the brain. Your muscular bravery is an established fact. Need you demonstrate that your brain is also as unrivaled in destructive power as your muscle? I hope you do not wish to enter into such an undignified competition with the Nazis. I venture to present you with a nobler and braver way, worthy of the bravest soldier. I want you to fight Nazism without arms, or, if I am to retain the military terminology, with non-violent arms. I would like you to lay down the arms you have as being useless for saving you or humanity. You will invite Herr Hitler and Signor Mussolini to take what they want of your beautiful island, with your many beautiful buildings. You will give all these but neither your souls, nor your minds. If these gentlemen choose to occupy your homes, you will vacate them. If they do not give you free passage out, you will allow yourselves man, woman, and child, to be slaughtered, but you will refuse to owe allegiance to them.

This process or method, which I have called non-violent non-cooperation, is not without considerable success in its use in India. Your representatives in India may deny my claim. If they do, I shall feel sorry for them. They may tell you that our non-cooperation was not wholly non-violent, that it was born of hatred. If they give that testimony, I will not deny it. Had it been wholly non-violent, if all the non-cooperators had been filled with goodwill towards you, I make bold to say that you who are India's masters would have become her pupils and, with much greater skill than we have, perfected this matchless weapon and met the German and Italian friends' menace with it. Indeed the history of Europe during the past few months would then have been written differently. Europe would have been spared seas of innocent blood, the rape of so many small nations, and the orgy of hatred.

This is no appeal made by a man who does not know his business. I have been practicing with scientific precision non-violence and its possibilities for an unbroken period of over fifty years. I have applied it in every walk of life, domestic, institutional, economic and political. I know of no single case in which it has failed. Where it has seemed sometimes to have failed, I have ascribed it to my imperfections. I claim no perfection for myself. But I do claim to be a passionate seeker after Truth, which is but another name for God. In the course of that search the discovery of non-violence came to me. Its spread is my life mission. I have no interest in living except for the prosecution of that mission.

I claim to have been a lifelong and wholly disinterested friend of the British people. At one time I used to be also a lover of your empire. I thought that it was doing good to India. When I saw that in the nature of things it could do no good, I used, and am still using, the non-violent method to fight imperialism. Whatever the ultimate fate of my country, my love for you remains, and will remain, undiminished. My non-violence demands universal love, and you are not a small part of it. It is that love which has prompted my appeal to you.

May God give power to every word of mine. In His name I began to write this, and in His name I close it. May your statesmen have the wisdom and courage to respond to my appeal. I am telling His Excellency the Viceroy that my services are at the disposal of His Majesty's Government, should they consider them of any practical use in advancing the object of my appeal.

(*Harijan*, 6th July 1940)

12th September 1947

Anger breeds revenge and the spirit of revenge is today responsible for all the horrible happenings here and elsewhere. What good will it do the Muslims to avenge the happenings in Delhi or for the Sikhs and the Hindus to avenge cruelties on our co-religionists in the Frontier and West Punjab? If a man or a group of men go mad, should everyone follow suit? I warn the Hindus and Sikhs that by killing and loot and arson they are destroying their own religions. I claim to be a student of religion and I know that no religion teaches madness. Islam is no exception. I implore you all to stop your insane actions at once. Let not future generations say that we lost the sweet bread of freedom because we could not digest it. Remember that unless we stop this madness the name of India will be mud in the eyes of the world.

21st October 1947

I have heard of another sad incident. It is not a communal murder. The victim is a Hindu government officer. A soldier shot him dead, because he would not act as he was directed. This tendency to use a gun on the slightest pretext is a grave portent. There are barbarous people in the world, to whom life has no value. They shoot dead human beings as they would shoot down birds or beasts. Is free India to be in this category? Man has not the power to create life, hence he has no right to take it. Yet the Muslims murder the Hindus and Sikhs and vice versa. When this cruel game is finished, the blood lust is bound to result in the Muslims slaughtering the Muslims, and the Hindus and Sikhs slaughtering themselves. I hope they will never reach that savage state. That is their fate unless both the states pull themselves together and set things right before it is too late.

NOTE

1. Extract from *Young India,* Vol. 1 by M.K. Gandhi, Madras, Ganesan Ltd. 1922.

A Women's Politics of Resistance

Sara Ruddick

Sara Ruddick teaches philosophy and women's studies at the New School for Social Research. She is the author of Maternal Thinking: Towards a Politics of Peace *(1989). She has also written a monograph entitled* Drafting Women *(1982).*

Ruddick discusses what she calls "a feminist maternal peace politics." The key dimension of her pacifist perspective is the use of feminine symbols as a model for organizing politically to resist various state practices and policies. She is especially interested in the symbolic role of the "mother" in providing for sustenance of children and family. Ruddick directly confronts one of the most common criticisms of pacifism, namely that it is unlikely to be effective over the long run. In drawing on examples from Argentina and Chile, Ruddick shows the power of largely nonviolent collective action taken by groups of women to oppose tyranny and military might.

A women's politics of resistance is identified by three characteristics: its participants are women, they explicitly invoke their culture's symbols of femininity, and their purpose is to resist certain practices or policies of their governors.

Women, like men, typically act out of social locations and political allegiances unconnected to their sex; women are socialists or capitalists, patriots or dissidents, colonialists or nationalists. Unlike other politics, a women's politics is organized and acted out by women. Women "riot" for bread, picket against alcohol, form peace camps outside missile bases, protect their schools from government interference, or sit in against nuclear testing. A women's politics often includes men: women call on men's physical strength or welcome the protection that powerful male allies offer. Nonetheless it is women who organize themselves self-consciously as women. The reasons women give for organizing range from an appreciation of the protection afforded by "womanliness" to men's unwillingness to participate in "sentimental" politics to the difficulty in speaking, much less being taken seriously, with men around. Typically, the point of women's politics is not to claim independence from men but, positively, to organize as women. Whatever the reasons for their separatism, the fact that women organize, direct, and enact a politics enables them to exploit their culture's symbols of femininity.

Women can also organize together without evoking common understandings of fem-

From *Maternal Thinking* by Sara Ruddick. Copyright ©1989 by Sara Ruddick. Reprinted by permission of Beacon Press. [Edited]

ininity. Feminist actions, for example, are often organized by women who explicitly repudiate the roles, behavior, and attitudes expected of "women." What I am calling a women's politics of resistance affirms obligations traditionally assigned to women and calls on the community to respect them. Women are responsible for their children's health; in the name of their maternal duty they call on the government to halt nuclear testing, which, epitomizing a general unhealthiness, leaves strontium-90 in nursing mothers' milk. If women are to be able to feed their families, then the community must produce sufficient food and sell it at prices homemakers can afford. If women are responsible for educating young children, then they resist government efforts to interfere with local schools.

Not all women's politics are politics of resistance. There are politics organized by women that celebrate women's roles and attitudes but that serve rather than resist the state. In almost every war, mothers of heroes and martyrs join together in support of military sons, knitting, writing, and then mourning, in the service of the military state. The best-known instance of women's politics is the organization of Nazi women in praise of *Kinder, Küche, Kirche*.[1] Today in Chile, a women's organization under the direction of the dictator Pinochet's wife celebrates "feminine power" (*el poder femenino*), which expresses itself through loyalty to family and fatherland.

A women's politics of *resistance* is composed of women who take responsibility for the tasks of caring labor and then find themselves confronted with policies or actions that interfere with their right or capacity to do their work. In the name of womanly duties that they have assumed and that their communities expect of them, they resist. This feminine resistance has made some philosophers and feminists uneasy. Much like organized violence, women's resistance is difficult to predict or control. Women in South Boston resist racial integration; mothers resist the conscription of their children in just wars.

Even where women aim to resist tyranny, their "feminine" protest seems too acceptable to be effective. As Dorothy Dinnerstein eloquently laments, women are *meant* to weep while men rule and fight:

> Women's resigned, implicitly collusive, ventilation of everybody's intuition that the world men rule is murderously crazy is a central theme in folklore, literature, drama [and women's politics of resistance].
>
> Think, for instance, of the proverb that groups woman with wine and song as a necessary counterpoint to battle, a counterpoint that makes it possible for men to draw back from their will to kill just long and far enough so that they can then take it up again with new vigor. Or think of the saying "Men must work and women must weep." Woman's tears over what is lethal in man's work, this saying implies, are part of the world's eternal, unalterable way. . . . [Her] tears serve not to deter man but to help him go on, for she is doing his weeping for him and he is doing what she weeps about for her.[2]

Christa Wolf expresses a related fear that women's resistance is as fragile as their dependence on individual men, loyalty to kin, and privileges of class:

> I was slow on the uptake. My privileges intruded between me and the most necessary insights; so did my attachment to my own family, which did not depend upon the privileges I enjoyed.[3]

For whatever reasons, feminists are apt to be disappointed in the sturdiness and extent of women's resistance. Dorothy Dinnerstein expresses this feminist disappointment:

> The absurd self-importance of his striving has been matched by the abject servility of her derision, which has on the whole been expressed only with his consent and within boundaries set by him, and which has on the

whole worked to support the stability of the realm he rules.[4]

While some people fear that "feminine" resistance is inevitably limited—and their fears seem to me not groundless—I place my hope in its unique potential effectiveness, namely, women's social position makes them inherently "disloyal to the civilization"[5] that depends on them. Thus Hegel worries, and I hope, that ostensibly compliant women are on the edge of dissidence. The state, whose most powerful governors depend on women's work and whose stability rests on the authority of the Fathers, "creates for itself in what it suppresses and what it depends upon an internal enemy—womankind in general."[6] Underlining as Hegel does women's exclusion from power, Julia Kristeva celebrates a woman who is "an eternal dissident in relation to social and political consensus, in exile from power, and therefore always singular, fragmentary, demonic, a witch."[7] Yet like Kristeva, I find that the dissident mother, perhaps unlike other witches, is not ony a potential critic of the order that excludes her but also and equally a conserver and legitimator of the order it is her duty to instill in her children. Kristeva expects from this dissident mother an "attentiveness to ethics" rooted in a collective experience and tradition of mothering. And I would expect from her the ambivalence that Jane Lazarre believes keeps the heart alive, even as it slows the trigger finger. This attentiveness to ethics can become effectively militant in a women's politics of resistance. Its ambivalence, while a spur to compassion, does not slow action if women are governed by principles of nonviolence that allow them to hate and frustrate oppressors they neither mutilate nor murder.

Women's politics of resistance are as various as the cultures from which they arise. Of the many examples I could choose, I select one, the resistance of Argentinian and Chilean women to military dictatorship, specifically to the policy of kidnapping, imprisonment, torture, and murder of the "disappeared." The resistance of the Madres (mothers) of Argentina to its military regime and the similar, ongoing resistance of Chilean women to the Pinochet dictatorshp politically exemplify central maternal concepts such as the primacy of bodily life and the connectedness of self and other. At the same time, these movements politically transform certain tendencies of maternal militarism such as cheery denial and parochialism.

Although women's work is always threatened by violence and although women in war always suffer the hunger, illness, mutilation, and loss of their loved ones, the crime of "disappearance" is especially haunting. Kidnapping and rumors of torture and murder destroy lives and families. Yet because the fate of the disappeared person is unclear, because no one in power acknowledges her or his existence, let alone disappearance, even mourning is impossible:

> *To disappear* means to be snatched off a street corner, or dragged from one's bed, or taken from a movie theater or cafe, either by police, or soldiers, or men in civilian clothes, and from that moment on to disappear from the face of the earth leaving not a single trace. It means that all knowledge of the *disappeared* is totally lost. Absolutely nothing is known about them. What was their fate? If they are alive, where are they? What are they enduring? If they are dead, where are their bones?[8]

Nathan Laks describes the Argentinian protest that began in Buenos Aires in 1976:

> Once in power [in Argentina in 1976], the military systematized and accelerated the campaign of terror, quickly annihilating the armed organizations of the Left and the unarmed ones, as well as many individuals with little or no connection to either. The indiscriminate nature of the kidnapping campaign and the

> impunity with which it was carried out spread terror—as intended. Relationships among friends and relatives were shattered by unprecedented fear. Perfectly decent individuals suddenly became afraid even to visit the parents of a kidnap victim, for any such gesture of compassion might condemn the visitor to a terrible fate. In this terrorized society, a small organization of women, mothers and other relatives of kidnapped Argentines staged a stunning act of defiance. One Thursday afternoon they gathered in the Plaza de Mayo, the main square in Buenos Aires and the site of countless historic incidents beginning in 1810 with the events that led to Argentina's separation from the Spanish Empire. In the center of the Plaza de Mayo, within clear sight of the presidential palace, the national cathedral, and several headquarters of ministries and corporations, the Mothers paraded in a closed circle.[9]

The Madres met each other outside hospitals or prisons, where they took food and other provisions and looked for traces of the disappeared, or outside government offices, where they tried, almost invariably without success, to get some accounting of their loved ones' whereabouts. When they marched, the Madres wore white kerchiefs with the names of the disappeared embroidered on them. Often they carried lighted candles and almost always they wore or carried photographs of the disappeared. In Chile, women chained themselves to the steps of the capitol, formed a human chain to a mine, Lonquen, where a mass grave was discovered, and took over a stadium where disappeared people had been rounded up, later to be tortured and killed.

The Latin American women's movements are clearly politics of resistance. The women who engage in them court imprisonment and torture and in some cases have become "disappeared" themselves. Knowing what fearful things could happen to them, women in Chile trained themselves to name and deal with what they feared:

> If they were afraid of facing police, they were told simply to find a policeman and stare at him until they could see him as a man and not as a representative of the state. [They] circled police vans on foot, until these symbols of the regime appeared as just another kind of motor vehicle. . . . The women also instructed one another how to deal with the tear gas . . . to stop eating two hours before demonstrations, to dress in casual clothing, to take off makeup but to put salt on their cheekbones to keep teargas powder from entering their eyes, . . . to carry lemon to avoid teargas sting and to get a jar with homemade smelling salts made up of salt and ammonia.[10]

The women talked among themselves about their terrors, found others who shared their fears, and marched with them in affinity groups. And thus they brought their bodies to bear against the state.

As in many women's politics of resistance, the Argentinian and Chilean women emphasize mothering among women's many relations. They are Madres, whether or not they are biological or adoptive mothers of individual disappeared; a later group is made up of Abuelas (grandmothers). Their presence and the character of their action, as well as the interviews they have given, invariably evoke an experience of mothering that is central to their lives, whatever other home work or wage labor they engage in. Repeatedly they remember and allude to ordinary tasks—clothing, feeding, sheltering, and most of all tending to extensive kin work. All these works, ordinarily taken for granted, are dramatically present just because they are interrupted; they are made starkly visible through the eerie "disappearance," the shattering mockery of a maternal and childlike "unchanging expectation of good in the heart."[11]

As these women honor mothering, they honor themselves. The destruction of the lives of their children, often just on the verge of adulthood, destroys years of their work; their loss and the impossibility of mourning it constitutes a violent outrage against them. Yet there is something misleading about this way of talking. The women do not speak of their work but of their children; they carry children's photographs, not their own. The distinctive structuring of the relation between self and other, symbolized in birth and enacted in mothering, is now politicized. The children, the absent ones, are *not* their mothers, who have decidedly *not* disappeared but are bodily present. The singular, irreplaceable children are lost. Yet as the pictures the Madres carry suggest, the children are not, even in disappearance, apart from their mothers but, in their absence, are still inseparable from them.

For these Argentinian and Chilean women, as for women in most cultures, mothering is intuitively or "naturally" connected to giving birth. The Abuelas, especially, have made a political point of the emotional significance of genetic continuity. Since the fall of the military regime, one of their projects has been to form a genetic bank to trace the biological parentage of children adopted by people close to the ruling class at the time the military was in power. The insistence on genetic connection is one aspect of a general affirmation of the body. Indeed, the vulnerability, promise, and power of human bodies is central to this women's politics of resistance, as it is to maternal practice:

> Together with the affirmation of life, the human body is a very important reference for these women. They often speak of physical pain, the wounds caused by the disappearnaces. It seems that wearing a photograph of the missing one attached to the clothing or in a locket around the neck is a way of feeling closer to them.[12]

Because they have suffered military violence—have been stripped naked, sexually humiliated, and tortured—children's bodies have become a locus of pain. Because the violation of bodies is meant to terrify the body itself becomes a place where terror is wrought. In resistance to this violation mothers' bodies become instruments of nonviolent power. Adorned with representations of bodies loved and violated, they express the necessity of love even amid terror, "in the teeth of all experience of crimes committed, suffered and witnessed."[13]

In their protests, these women fulfill traditional expectations of femininity and at the same time violate them. These are women who may well have expected to live out an ideology of "separate spheres" in which men and women had distinct but complementary tasks. Whatever ideology of the sexual division of labor they may have espoused, their political circumstances, as well as the appartently greater vulnerability and the apparently greater timidity and conventionality of the men they lived among, required that they act publicly as women. Women who bring to the public plazas of a police state pictures of their loved ones, like women who put pillowcases, toys, and other artifacts of attachment against the barbed wire fences of missile bases, translate the symbols of mothering into political speech. Preservative love, singularity in connection, the promise of birth and the resilience of hope, the irreplaceable treasure of vulnerable bodily being—these clichés of maternal work are enacted in public, by women insisting that their governors name and take responsibility for their crimes. They speak a "women's language" of loyalty, love, and outrage; but they speak with a public anger in a public place in ways they were never meant to do.

Although not a "peace politics" in a conventional sense, the Latin American protest undermines tendences of maternal practice and thinking that are identifiably militarist. To some extent, this is a matter of shifting a balance between tendencies in mothering that support militarism toward tendencies that subvert it. In this case, the balance shifts from denial to truthfulness, from parochialism to solidarity, and from inauthenticity to active responsibility. Writing about André Trocme and his parishioners in the French village of Le Chambon during World War II, Phillip Hallie identified three characteristics that enabled them to penetrate the confusion and misinformation with which Nazis covered their policy and then to act on their knowledge. "*Lucid knowledge, awareness of the pain of others,* and *stubborn decision* dissipated for the Chambonnais the Night and Fog that inhabited the minds of so many people in Europe, and the world at large, in 1942."[14] In the transformed maternal practice of the Argentinian and Chilean women, these same virtues of nonviolent resistance are at work.

Cheery denial is an endemic maternal temptation. A similar "willingness to be self-deceived," as the resistance leader André Trocme called it, also sustains many decent citizens' support of war policy. It is notorious that few people can bear, except very briefly, to acknowledge the dangers of nuclear weapons and the damage they have done and could still do. Similarly, few citizens really look at the political aims and material-emotional lives of people affected by their own country's interventionist war policies. By contrast, the Argentinian and Chilean women insist on, and then disseminate, "lucid knowledge" of military crimes. "What is so profoundly moving about them is their determination to find out the truth."[15] They insist that others, too, hear the truth. They are "ready to talk immediately; they need to talk, to make sure their story, so tragic and so common, . . . be told, be known."[16] In addition to talking, they make tapestries, "arpilleras," that tell stories of daily life including workers' organizing, police brutality, kidnapping, and resistance. The protests, tales, and arpilleras extend the maternal task of storytelling, maintaining ordinary maternal values of realism in the face of temptation to deny or distort. In this context, their ordinary extraordinary work becomes a politics of remembering.

After fighting in World War II the philosopher J. Glenn Gray wrote:

> The great god Mars tries to blind us when we enter his realm, and when we leave he gives us a generous cup of the waters of Lethe to drink. . . . When I consider how easily we forget the millions who suffered unbearably, either permanently maimed in body or mind, or who gave up their lives before they realized their purpose, I rebel at the whole insane spectacle of human existence.[17]

After the junta fell, Argentinian women insisted that violated bodies be *remembered*, which required that crimes be named, the men who committed them be brought to trial, and the bodies themselves, alive or dead, be accounted for and, where possible, returned.

"Awareness of the pain of others." The Argentinian and Chilean Madres spoke first of their own pain and the pain of relatives and friends of others disappeared. Similarly, maternal nonviolence is rooted, and typically limited by, a commitment to one's "own" children and the people they live among. . . . I spoke of this limitation as a principal source of maternal militarism; the parochialism of maternal practice can become the racialism that fuels organized violence. This tribal parochialism was also broken down in the Argentinian and Chilean protests.

As in mothering generally, women found it easiest to extend their concern for their own children to other mothers "like them"; only in this political context likeness had to do not with race or ethnicity but with common suffering. In Argentina, where protests are marked by the "singularity" of photographs, the women came to wear identical masks to mark their commonality. In Chile one woman said:

> Because of all this suffering we are united. I do not ask for justice for my child alone, or the other women just for their children. We are asking for justice for all. All of us are equal. If we find one disappeared one I will rejoice as much as if they had found mine.[18]

Concern for all victims then sometimes extended to collective concern for all the people of the nation:

> We are the women and mothers of this land, of the workers, of the professionals, of the students, and of future generations.[19]

This is still "nationalism," though of a noble sort. Many of the women went further as they explicitly identified with all victims of military or economic violence:

> In the beginning we only wanted to rescue our children. But as time passed we acquired a different comprehension. We understood better what is going on in the world. We know that when babies do not have enough to eat that, too, is a violation of human rights.[20]

> We should commit ourselves to make Lonquen [the mine where a mass grave was discovered] a blessed spot. May it be a revered spot, so that never again will a hostile hand be raised against any other person that lives on the earth.[21]

It would be foolish to believe that every woman in the Argentinian and Chilean protest movements extended concern from her own children to all the disappeared then to all of the nation, and finally to all victims everywhere. Why should women whose children and loved ones have been singularly persecuted extend sympathetic protection to all victims, an extension that is extraordinary even among women and men who do not suffer singular assault? Yet many of these women did so extend themselves—intellectually, politically, emotionally. They did not "transcend" their particular loss and love; particularity was the emotional root and source of their protest. It is through acting on that particularity that they extended mothering to include sustaining and protecting any people whose lives are blighted by violence.

"Stubborn decision." As children remind us, stubborn decision is a hallmark of maternity. And mothers reply: what looks like stubborn decision may well be a compound of timidity, vacillation, and desperation. Women in resistance are (almost certainly) not free from ordinary mothers' temptations to inauthenticity, to letting others—teachers, employers, generals, fathers, grandparents—establish standards of acceptablity and delegating to them responsibility for children's lives. And like ordinary mothers, women in resistance probably include in their ranks *individuals* who in ordinary times could speak back to the teacher or organize opposition to the local corporate polluter. But "stubborn decision" takes on a new and collective political meaning when women acting together walk out of their homes to appropriate spaces they never were meant to occupy.

Like their counterparts in resistance elsewhere, these stubbornly decisive Argentinian and Chilean women, whatever their personal timidities, publicly announce that they take responsibility for protecting the world in which they and their children must live. These women are the daughters, the heirs, of Kollwitz's *mater dolorosa*. As in Kollwitz's representations, a mother is victimized through the victimization of her children. These women are themselves victims; moreover, they bear witness to victimization first of loved ones, then of strangers; they stand against those in power, in solidarity with those who are hurt. Yet there is also a sense in which, by their active courage, they refuse victimization. More accurately, they mock dichotomies that still riddle political thought. There is no contradiction between "playing the role of victim" and taking responsibility for public policies. It is possible to act powerfully while standing with those who are hurt. It is neither weak nor passive to reveal one's own suffering while refusing to damage or mutilate in return. The Latin American *mater dolorosa* has learned how to fight as a victim for victims, not by joining the strong, but by resisting them.

A women's politics of resistance is not inherently a peace politics. Women can organize to sabotage peace treaties or to celebrate the heroes and martyrs of organized violence. During the Malvinas-Falklands war, Argentinian and English women sought each other out at a women's meeting in New York to denounce together their countries' militarism and imperialism. Yet during that same war, the Argentinian Madres were reported to use patriotic rhetoric to reinforce their own aims: "The Malvinas belong to us and so do our sons."

Nonetheless, in their own contexts, the Argentinian protest had and the Chilean protest still has antimilitarist implications. The regimes against which the women protest were and are militarist; the omnipresence of the soldier as oppressor and the general as the torturers' commander was—and in Chile still is—sufficient to symbolize a contrast between women and war. Moreover, the generals' actions have not been accidentally related to militarism. As Plato saw, when he rejected militarist rule in his totalitarian state, torture, kidnapping and other physical terrorism infect the rule of fearful tyrants, just as atrocities infect the best organized war. In their deliberately and increasingly brutal strategies to ensure absolute control, the generals exemplify the excesses inherent in militarized tyranny. Hence in the women's protests, not only a particular government but military rule is brought to trial.

Whatever their militarist sentiments or rhetoric, the Argentinian and Chilean protests express to the world the ideals of nonviolence. Although effective protest inevitably hurts its opponents and those associated with them, the protesters did not set out to injure but to end injuring. None of their actions even risked serious, lasting physical damage. Their aim was steadfastly one of reconnection and restoration of a just community, even though and because those responsible for violence were held accountable and were punished. By providing an example of persistent, stubborn action, the Argentinian and Chilean women have offered a model of nonviolent resistance to other Latin American countries and to the world. They have therefore contributed to collective efforts to invent peace, whatever their degree of effectiveness within their own countries. Like the maternal practice from which it grows, a women's politics of resistance may remain racial, tribal, or chauvinist; we cannot expect of women in resistance the rare human ability to stand in solidarity with all victims of violence. Yet if these Latin American protests are at all emblematic, they suggest that the peacefulness latent in maternal practice tends to be realized as participants act against, and therefore reflect on, violence itself.

NOTES

1. For a discussion of women's participation in (and occasional resistance to) the Nazi German government, see Claudia Koonz, *Mothers in the Fatherland: Women, the Family, and Nazi Politics* (New York: St. Martin's, 1987). Among the many virtues of this fascinating book is its tracing of the complex interconnections between women's separate spheres, the Nazi and feminist use of women's difference, and women's participation in but also disappointment in the Nazi state.
2. Dorothy Dinnerstein, *The Mermaid and the Minotaur* (New York: Harper & Row, 1976), p. 226.
3. Christa Wolf, *Cassandra* (New York: Farrar Straus & Giroux, 1984), p. 53.
4. Dorothy Dinnerstein, "The Mobilization of Eros," in *Face to Face* (Greenwood Press, 1982). Manuscript courtesy of the author. For an intellec-

tually sophisticated and high-spirited account of an American women's politics of resistance, see Amy Swerdlow's work on Women's Strike for Peace, forthcoming from the University of Chicago Press. For an example of her work, see "Pure Milk, Not Poison: Women's Strike for Peace and the Test Ban Treaty of 1963," in *Rocking the Ship of State: Toward a Feminist Peace Politics,* ed. Adrienne Harris and Ynestra King (Westview Press, 1989).

5. The title of a well-known essay by Adrienne Rich in *Lies, Secrets and Silence* (New York: Norton, 1979), pp. 275–310.
6. Hegel, *The Phenomenology of Mind,* part VI, A, b, "Ethical Action: Knowledge Human and Divine: Guilt and Destiny" (New York: Harper, 1967), p. 496.
7. Julia Kristeva, "Talking about *Polygoue*" (an interview with Francoise van Rossum-Guyon), in *French Feminist Thought,* ed. Toril Moi (Oxford: Basil Blackwell, 1987), p. 113.
8. Marjorie Agosin, "Emerging from the Shadows: Women of Chile," *Barnard Occasional Papers on Women's Issues,* vol. 2, no. 3, Fall 1987, p. 12. I am very grateful to Temma Kaplan, historian and director of the Barnard College Women's Center, whose interest in "motherist" and grass-roots womens' resistance movements inspired this section. Temma Kaplan provided me with material on the Madres and discussed an earlier draft of the chapter.
9. Nathan Laks, cited in Nora Amalia Femenia, "Argentina's Mothers of Plaza de Mayo: The Mourning Process from Junta to Democracy," *Feminist Studies*, vol. 13, no. 1, p. 10. The Argentinian Madres protested until the fall of the military regime and still exist today, though they are now divided in their political aims.
10. Marjorie Agosin, Temma Kaplan, Teresa Valduz, "The Politics of Spectacle in Chile," *Barnard Occasional Papers on Women's Issues,* vol. 2, no. 3, Fall 1987, p. 6.
11. Simone Weil, "Human Personality," in *Simone Weil Reader,* p. 315.
12. Agosin, "Emerging," p. 18.
13. Simone Weil, "Human Personality," in *Simone Weil Reader,* p. 315.
14. Phillip Hallie, *Lest Innocent Blood Be Shed* (New York: Harper & Row, 1979), p. 104. (Italics added.)
15. Agosin, "Emerging," p. 16.
16. Agosin, "Emerging," p. 14.
17. J. Glenn Gray, *The Warriors* (New York: Harper & Row, 1970), pp. 21, 23.
18. Agosin, "Emerging," p. 21.
19. Patricia M. Chuchryk, "Subversive Mothers: The Women's Opposition to the Military Regime in Chile," paper presented at the International Congress of the Latin American Studies Association, Boston, 1986, p. 9.
20. Rene Epelbaum, member of the Argentinian protest, in an interview with Jean Bethke Elshtain, personal communication.
21. Agosin, "Emerging," p. 18.

Letter from the Birmingham City Jail

Martin Luther King, Jr.

Martin Luther King, Jr. was a minister and one of the most important leaders of the civil rights movement in the United States. He was awarded the Nobel Peace Prize in 1964. He was the author of Strive Toward Freedom *(1958),* Why We Can't Wait *(1964) and* The Trumpet of Conscience *(1968).*

King provides another extremely influential account of nonviolent civil disobedience. He defines a nonviolent campaign as one that has four stages: (a) a determination that injustice is occurring; (b) negotiation to try to end the injustice; (c) a cleansing process that steels one against hatred and revenge; (d) nonviolent direct action. He offers a defense of this strategy, as opposed to a strategy of violence, by reference to traditional Judeo-Christian moral principles. Of central concern to King is the contention that we all share in responsibility for stopping injustice wherever it occurs. This contention is supported by reference to the principle of "love your neighbor," a principle which King believed to be strongly opposed to violence.

My dear Fellow Clergymen,

While confined here in the Birmingham City Jail, I came across your recent statement calling our present activities "unwise and untimely." Seldom, if ever, do I pause to answer criticisms of my work and ideas. If I sought to answer all of the criticisms that cross my desk, my secretaries would be engaged in little else in the course of the day, and I would have no time for constructive work. But since I feel that you are men of genuine goodwill and your criticisms are sincerely set forth, I would like to answer your statement in what I hope will be patient and reasonable terms.

I think I should give the reason for my being in Birmingham, since you have been influenced by the argument of "outsiders coming in." I have the honor of serving as president of the Southern Christian Leadership Conference, an organization operating in every Southern state, with headquarters in Atlanta, Georgia. We have some eighty-five affiliate organizations all across the South—one being the Alabama Christian Movement for Human Rights. Whenever necessary and possible we share staff, educational and financial resources with our affiliates. Several months ago our local affiliate here in Birmingham invited us to be on call to engage in a nonviolent direct action program if such were deemed necessary. We readily consented and when the hour came we lived up to our promises.

So I am here, along with several members of my staff, because we were invited here. I am here because I have basic organizational ties here.

Beyond this, I am in Birmingham because injustice is here. Just as the eighth century prophets left their little villages and carried their "thus saith the Lord" far beyond the boundaries of their home towns; and just as the Apostle Paul left his little village of Tarsus and carried the gospel of Jesus Christ to practically every hamlet and city of the Greco-Roman world, I too am compelled to carry the gospel of freedom beyond my particular home town. Like Paul, I must constantly respond to the Macedonian call for aid.

Moreover, I am cognizant of the interrelatedness of all communities and states. I cannot sit idly by in Atlanta and not be concerned about what happens in Birmingham. Injustice anywhere is a threat to justice everywhere. We are caught in an inescapable network of mutuality, tied in a single garment of destiny. Whatever affects one directly affects all indirectly. Never again can we afford to live with the narrow, provincial "outside agitator" idea. Anyone who lives inside the United States can never be considered an outsider anywhere in this country.

You deplore the demonstrations that are presently taking place in Birmingham. But I am sorry your statement did not express a similar concern for the conditions that brought the demonstrations into being. I am sure that each of you would want to go beyond the superficial social analyst who looks merely at effects, and does not grapple with underlying causes. I would not hesitate to say that it is unfortunate that so-called demonstrations are taking place in Birmingham at this time, but I would say in more emphatic terms that it is even more unfortunate that the white power structure of this city left the Negro community with no other alternative.

In any nonviolent campaign there are four basic steps: (1) Collection of the facts to determine whether injustices are alive, (2) Negotiation, (3) Self-purification and (4) Direct Action. We have gone through all of these steps in Birmingham. There can be no gainsaying of the fact that racial injustice engulfs this community.

Birmingham is probably the most thoroughly segregated city in the United States. Its ugly record of police brutality is known in every section of this country. Its unjust treatment of Negroes in the courts is a notorious reality. There have been more unsolved bombings of Negro homes and churches in Birmingham than any city in this nation. These are hard, brutal and unbelievable facts. On the basis of these conditions Negro leaders sought to negotiate with the city fathers. But the political leaders consistently refused to engage in good faith negotiation.

Then came the opportunity last September to talk with some of these leaders of the economic community. In the negotiating sessions certain promises were made by the merchants—such as the promise to remove the humiliating racial signs from the stores. On the basis of these promises Rev. Shuttlesworth and the leaders of the Alabama Christian Movement for Human Rights agreed to call a moratorium on any type of demonstrations. As the weeks and months unfolded we realized that we were the victims of a broken promise. The signs remained. Like so many experiences of the past we were confronted with blasted hopes, and the dark shadow of a deep disappointment settled upon us. So we had no alternative except that of preparing for direct action, whereby we would present our very bodies as a means of laying our case before the conscience of the local and national community. We were not unmindful of the difficulties involved. So we decided to go through a process of self-purification. We started having workshops on nonviolence and repeatedly asked ourselves the questions, "Are you able to accept blows without retaliating?" "Are you able to endure the ordeals of jail?" We decided to set our direct action program around the Easter season, realizing that with the exception of Christmas, this was the largest shopping period of the year. Knowing that a strong economic withdrawal program would be the by-product of direct action, we felt that this was the best time to bring pressure on the merchants for the needed changes. Then it occurred to us that the March election was ahead and so we speedily decided to postpone action until after election day. When we discovered that Mr. Connor was in the run-off, we decided again to postpone action so that the demonstrations could not be used to cloud the issues. At this time we agreed to begin our nonviolent witness the day after the run-off.

This reveals that we did not move irresponsibly into direct action. We too wanted to see Mr. Connor defeated; so we went through postponement after postponement to aid in this community need. After this we felt that direct action could be delayed no longer.

You may well ask, "Why direct action? Why sit-ins, marches etc.? Isn't negotiation a better path?" You are exactly right in your call for negotiation. Indeed, this is the purpose of direct action. Nonviolent direct action seeks to create such a crisis and establish such creative tension that a community that has constantly refused to negotiate is forced to confront the issue. It seeks so to dramatize the issue that it can no longer be ignored. I just referred to the creation of tension as a part of the work of the nonviolent resister. This may sound rather shocking. But I must confess that I am not afraid of the word tension. I have earnestly worked and preached against violent tension, but there is a type of constructive nonviolent tension that is necessary for growth. Just as Socrates felt that it was necessary to create a tension in the mind so that individuals could rise from the bondage of myths and half-truths to the unfettered realm of creative analysis and objective appraisal, we must see the need of having nonviolent gadflies to create the kind of tension in society that will help men to rise from the dark depths of prejudice and racism to the majestic heights of understanding and brotherhood. So the purpose of the direct action is to create a situation so crisis-packed that it will inevitably open the door to negotiation. We, therefore, concur with you in your call for negotiation. Too long has our beloved Southland been bogged down in the tragic attempt to live in monologue rather than dialogue.

One of the basic points in your statement is that our acts are untimely. Some have asked, "Why didn't you give the new administration time to act?" The only answer I can give to this inquiry is that the new administration must be prodded about as much as the outgoing one before it acts. We will be sadly mistaken if we feel the election of Mr. Boutwell will bring the millenium to Birmingham. While Mr. Boutwell is much more articulate and gentle than Mr. Connor, they are both segregationists, dedicated to the task of maintaining the status quo. The hope I see in Mr. Boutwell is that he will be reasonable enough to see the futility of massive resistance to desegregation. But he will not see this without pressure from the devotees of civil rights. My friends, I must say to you that we have not made a single gain in civil rights without determined legal and nonviolent pressure. History is the long and tragic story of the fact that privileged groups seldom give up their privileges voluntarily. Individuals may see the moral light and voluntarily give up this unjust posture; but as Reinhold Niebuhr has reminded us, groups are more immoral than individuals.

We know through painful experience that freedom is never voluntarily given by the oppressor; it must be demanded by the oppressed. Frankly, I have never yet engaged in a direct action movement that was "well timed," according to the timetable of those who have not suffered unduly from the disease of segregation. For years now I have heard the word "Wait!" It rings in the ear of every Negro with piercing familiarity. This "Wait" has almost always meant "Never." It has been a tranquilizing thalidomide, relieving the emotional stress for a moment, only to give birth to an ill-formed infant of frustration. We must come to see with the distinguished jurist of yesterday that "justice too long delayed is justice denied." We have waited for more that three hundred and forty years for our constitutional and God-given rights. The nations of Asia and Africa are moving with jet-like speed toward the goal of political independence, and we still creep at horse and buggy pace toward the gaining of a cup of coffee at a lunch counter. I guess it is easy for those who have never felt the stinging darts of segregation to say, "Wait." But when you have seen vicious mobs lynch your mothers and fathers at will and drown your sisters and brothers at whim; when you have seen hate-filled policemen curse, kick, brutalize and even kill your black brothers and sisters with impunity; when you see the vast majority of your twenty million Negro brothers smoldering in an air-tight cage of poverty in the midst of an affluent society; when you suddenly find your tongue twisted and your speech stammering as you seek to explain to your six-year-old daughter why she can't go to the public amusement park that has just been advertised on television, and see tears welling up in her little eyes when she is told that Funtown is closed to colored children, and see the depressing clouds of inferiority begin to form in her little mental sky, and see her begin to distort her little personality by unconsciously developing a bitterness toward white people; when you have to concoct an answer for a five-year-old son asking in agonizing pathos: "Daddy, why do white people treat colored people so mean?"; when you take a cross country drive and find it necessary to sleep night after night in the uncomfortable corners of your automobile because no motel will accept you; when you are humiliated day in and day out by nagging signs reading "white" and "colored"; when your first name becomes "nigger" and your middle name becomes "boy" (however old you are) and your last name becomes "John," and when your wife and mother are never given the respected title "Mrs."; when you are harried by day and haunted at night by the fact that you are a Negro, living constantly at tip-toe stance never quite knowing what to expect next, and plagued with inner fears and outer resentments; when you are forever fighting a degenerating sense of "nobodiness"; then you will understand why we find it difficult to wait. There comes a time when the cup of endurance runs over, and men are no longer willing to be plunged into an abyss of injustice where they experience the blackness of corroding despair. I hope, sirs, you can understand our legitimate and unavoidable impatience.

You express a great deal of anxiety over our willingness to break laws. This is certainly a legitimate concern. Since we so diligently urge people to obey the Supreme Court's decision of 1954 outlawing segregation in the public schools, it is rather strange and paradoxical to find us consciously breaking laws. One may well ask, "How can you advocate breaking some laws and obeying others?" The answer is found in the fact that there are two types of laws: There are *just* and there are *unjust* laws. I would agree with Saint Augustine that "An unjust law is no law at all."

Now what is the difference between the two? How does one determine when a law is just or unjust? A just law is a man-made code that squares with the moral law or the law of God. An unjust law is a code that is out of harmony with the moral law. To put it in the terms of Saint Thomas Aquinas, an unjust law is a human law that is not rooted in eternal and natural law. Any law that uplifts human personality is just. Any law that degrades human personality is unjust. All segregation statutes are unjust because segregation distorts the soul and damages the personality. It gives the segregator a false sense of superiority, and the segregated a false sense of inferiority. To use the words of Martin Buber, the great Jewish philosopher, segregation substitutes and "I-it" relationship for the "I-thou" relationship, and ends up relegating persons to the status of things. So segregation is not only politically, economically and sociologically unsound, but it is morally wrong and sinful. Paul Tillich has said that sin is separation. Isn't segregation an existential expression of man's tragic separation, an expression of his awful estrangement, his terrible sinfulness? So I can urge men to disobey segregation ordinances because they are morally wrong.

Let us turn to a more concrete example of just and unjust laws. An unjust law is a code that a majority inflicts on a minority that is not binding on itself. This is difference made legal. On the other hand a just law is a code that a majority compels a minority to follow that it is willing to follow itself. This is sameness made legal.

Let me give you another explanation. An unjust law is a code inflicted upon a minority which that minority had no part in enacting or creating because they did not have the unhampered right to vote. Who can say that the legislature of Alabama which set up the segregation laws was democratically elected? Throughout the state of Alabama all types of conniving methods are used to prevent Negroes from becoming registered voters and there are some counties without a single Negro registered to vote despite the fact that the Negro constitutes a majority of the population. Can any law set up in such a state be considered democratically structured?

These are just a few examples of unjust and just laws. There are some instances when a law is just on its face and unjust in its application. For instance, I was arrested Friday on a charge of parading without a permit. Now there is nothing wrong with an ordinance which requires a permit for a parade, but when the ordinance is used to preserve segregation and to deny citizens the First Amendment privilege of peaceful assembly and peaceful protest, then it becomes unjust.

I hope you can see the distinction I am trying to point out. In no sense do I advocate evading or defying the law as the rabid segregationist would do. This would lead to anarchy. One who breaks an unjust law must do it *openly, lovingly* (not hatefully as the white mothers did in New Orleans when they were seen on television screaming "nigger, nigger, nigger"), and with a willingness to accept the penalty. I submit that an individual who breaks a law that conscience tells him is unjust, and willingly accepts the penalty by staying in jail to arouse the conscience of the community over its injustice, is in reality expressing the very highest respect for law.

Of course, there is nothing new about this kind of civil disobedience. It was seen sublimely in the refusal of Shadrach, Meshach and Abednego to obey the laws of Nebuchadnezzar because a higher moral law was involved. It was practiced superbly by the early Christians who were willing to face hungry lions and the excruciating pain of chopping blocks, before submitting to certain unjust laws of the Roman empire. To a degree academic freedom is a reality today because Socrates practiced civil disobedience.

We can never forget that everything Hitler did in Germany was "legal" and everything the Hungarian freedom fighters did in Hungary was "illegal". It was "illegal" to aid and comfort a Jew in Hitler's Germany. But I am sure that if I had lived in Germany during that time I would have aided and comforted my Jewish brothers even though it was illegal. If I lived in a Communist country today where certain principles dear to the Christian faith are suppressed, I believe I would openly advocate disobeying these antireligious laws. I must make two honest confessions to you, my Christian and Jewish brothers. First, I must confess that over the last few years I have been gravely disappointed with the white moderate. I have almost reached the regrettable conclusion that the Negro's great stumbling block in the stride toward freedom is not the White Citizen's Council-er or the Ku Klux Klanner, but the white moderate who is more devoted to "order" than to justice; who prefers a negative peace which is the absence of tension to a positive peace which is the presence of justice; who constantly says, "I agree with you in the goal you seek, but I can't agree with your methods of direct action"; who paternalistically feels that he can set the timetable for another man's freedom; who lives by the myth of time and who constantly advises the Negro to wait until a "more convenient season." Shallow understanding from people of goodwill is more frustrating than absolute misunderstanding from people of ill will. Lukewarm acceptance is much more bewildering than outright rejection.

I had hoped that the white moderate would understand that law and order exist for the purpose of establishing justice, and that when they fail to do this they become dangerously structured dams that block the flow of social progress. I had hoped that the white moderate would understand that the present tension of the South is merely a necessary phase of the transition from an obnoxious negative peace, where the Negro passively accepted his unjust plight, to a substance-filled positive peace, where all men will respect the dignity and worth of human personality. Actually, we who engage in nonviolent direct action are not the creators of tension. We merely bring to the surface the hidden tension that is already alive. We bring it out in the open where it can be seen and dealt with. Like a boil that can never be cured as long as it is covered up but must be opened with all its pus-flowing ugliness to the natural medicines of air and light, injustice must likewise be exposed, with all of the tension its exposing creates, to the light of human conscience and the air of national opinion before it can be cured.

In your statement you asserted that our actions, even though peaceful, must be condemned because they precipitate violence. But can this assertion be logically made? Isn't this like condemning the robbed man because his possession of money precipitated the evil act of robbery? Isn't this like condemning Socrates because his unswerving commitment to truth and his philosophical delvings precipitated the misguided popular mind to make him drink the hemlock? Isn't this like condemning Jesus because His unique God-Consciousness and never-ceasing devotion to His will precipitated the evil act of crucifixion? We must come to see, as federal courts have consistently affirmed, that it is immoral to urge an individual to withdraw his efforts to gain his basic constitutional rights because the quest precipitates violence. Society must protect the robbed and punish the robber.

I had also hoped that the white moderate would reject the myth of time. I received a letter this morning from a white brother in Texas which said: "All Christians know that the colored people will receive equal rights eventually, but it is possible that you are in too great of a religious hurry. It has taken Christianity almost 2000 years to accomplish what it has. The teachings of Christ take time to come to earth." All that is said here grows out of a tragic misconception of time. It is the strangely irrational notion that there is something in the flow of time that will inevitably cure all ills. Actually time is neutral. It can be used either destructively or constructively. I am coming to feel that the people of ill will have used time much more effectively than the people of goodwill. We will have to repent in this generation not merely for the vitriolic words and actions of the bad people, but for the appalling silence of the good people. We must come to see that human progress never rolls in on wheels of inevitability. It comes through the tireless efforts and persistent work of men willing to be co-workers with God, and without this hard work time itself becomes an ally of the forces of social stagnation. We must use time creatively, and forever realize that the time is always ripe to do right. Now is the time to make real the promise of democracy, and transform our pending national elegy into a creative psalm of brotherhood. Now is the time to lift our national policy from the quicksand of racial injustice to the solid rock of human dignity.

You spoke of our activity in Birmingham as extreme. At first I was rather disappointed that fellow clergymen would see my nonviolent efforts as those of an extremist. I started thinking about the fact that I stand in the middle of two opposing forces in the Negro community. One is a force of complacency made up of Negroes who, as a result of long years of oppression, have been so completely drained of self-respect and a sense of "somebodiness" that they have adjusted to segregation, and, of a few Negroes in the middle class who, because of a degree of academic and economic security, and because at points they profit by segregation, have unconsciously become insensitive to the problems of the masses. The other force is one of bitterness and hatred, and comes perilously close to advocating violence. It is expressed in the various black nationalist groups that are springing up over the nation, the largest and best known being Elijah Muhammad's Muslim movement. This movement is nourished by the contemporary frustration over the continued existence of racial discrimination. It is made up of people who have lost faith in America, who have absolutely repudiated Christianity, and who have concluded that the white man is an incurable "devil." I have tried to stand between these two forces, saying that we need not follow the "do-nothingism" of the complacent or the hatred and despair of the black nationalist. There is the more excellent way of love and nonviolent protest. I'm grateful to God that, through the Negro church, the dimension of nonviolence entered our struggle. If this philosophy had not emerged, I am convinced that by now many streets in the South would be flowing with floods of blood. And I am further convinced that if our white brothers dismiss as "rabble rousers" and "outside agitators" those of us who are working through the channels of nonviolent direct action and refuse to support our nonviolent efforts, millions of Negroes, out of frustration and despair, will seek solace and security in black nationalist ideologies, a development that will inevitably lead to a frightening racial nightmare.

Oppressed people cannot remain oppressed forever. The urge for freedom will eventually come. This is what happened to the American Negro. Something within has reminded him of his birthright of freedom; something without has reminded him that he can gain it. Consciously and unconsciously, he has been swept in by what the Germans called the *Zeitgeist,* and with his black brothers of Africa, and his brown and yellow brothers of Asia, South America and the Caribbean, he is moving with a sense of cosmic urgency toward the promised land of racial justice. Recognizing this vital urge that has engulfed the Negro community, one should readily understand public demonstrations. The Negro has many pent-up resentments and latent frustrations. He has to get them out. So let him march sometime; let him have his prayer pilgrimages to the city hall; understand why he must have sit-ins and freedom rides. If his repressed emotions do not come out in these nonviolent ways, they will come out in ominous expressions of violence. This is not a threat; it is a fact of history. So I have not said to my people "get rid of your discontent." But I have tried to say that this normal and healthy discontent can be channelized through the creative outlet of nonviolent direct action. Now this approach is being dismissed as extremist. I must admit that I was initially disappointed in being so categorized.

But as I continued to think about the matter I gradually gained a bit of satisfaction from being considered an extremist. Was not Jesus an extremist in love—"Love your enemies, bless them that curse you, pray for them that despitefully use you." Was not Amos an extremist for justice—"Let justice roll down like waters and righteousness like a mighty stream." Was not Paul an extremist for the gospel of Jesus Christ—"I bear in my body the marks of the Lord Jesus." Was not Martin Luther an extremist—"Here I stand; I can do none other so help me God." Was not John Bunyan an extremist—"I will stay in jail to the end of my days before I make a butchery of my conscience." Was not Abraham Lincoln an extremist—"This nation cannot survive half slave and half free." Was not Thomas Jefferson an extremist—"We hold these truths to be self-evident, that all men are created equal." So the question is not whether we will be extremist but what kind of extremist will we be. Will we be extremists for hate or will we be extremists for love? Will we be extremists for the preservation of injustice—or will we be extremists for the cause of justice? In that dramatic scene on Calvary's hill, three men were crucified. We must not forget that all three men were crucified for the same crime—the crime of extremism. Two were extremists for immorality, and thusly fell below their environment. The other, Jesus Christ, was an extremist for love, truth and goodness, and thereby rose above his environment. So, after all, maybe the South, the nation and the world are in dire need of creative extremists.

I had hoped that the white moderate would see this. Maybe I was too optimistic. Maybe I expected too much. I guess I should have realized that few members of a race that has oppressed another race can understand or appreciate the deep groans and passionate yearnings of those that have been oppressed and still fewer have the vision to see that injustice must be rooted out by strong, persistent and determined action. I am thankful, however, that some of our white brothers have grasped the meaning of this social revolution and committed themselves to it. They are still all too small in quantity, but they are big in quality. Some like Ralph McGill, Lillian Smith, Harry Golden and James Dabbs have written about our struggle in eloquent, prophetic and understanding terms. Others have marched with us down nameless streets of the South. They have languished in filthy roach-infested jails, suffering the abuse and brutality of angry policemen who see them as "dirty nigger lovers." They, unlike so many of their moderate brothers and sisters, have recognized the urgency of the moment and sensed the need for powerful "action" antidotes to combat the disease of segregation.

Let me rush on to mention my other disappointment. I have been so greatly disappointed with the white church and its leadership. Of course, there are some notable exceptions. I am not unmindful of the fact that each of you has taken some significant stands on this issue. I commend you, Rev. Stallings, for your Christian stand on this past Sunday, in welcoming Negroes to your worship service on a non-segregated basis. I commend the Catholic leaders of this state for integrating Springhill College several years ago.

But despite these notable exceptions I must honestly reiterate that I have been disappointed with the church. I do not say that as one of the negative critics who can always find something wrong with the church. I say it as a minister of the gospel, who loves the church; who was nurtured in its bosom; who has been sustained by its spiritual blessings and who will remain true to it as long as the cord of life shall lengthen.

I had the strange feeling when I was suddenly catapulted into the leadership of the bus protest in Montgomery several years ago that we would have the support of the white church. I felt that the white ministers, priests and rabbis of the South would be some of our strongest allies. Instead, some have been outright opponents, refusing to understand the freedom movement and misrepresenting its leaders; all too many others have been more cautious than courageous and have remained silent behind the anesthetizing security of the stained-glass windows.

In spite of my shattered dreams of the past, I came to Birmingham with the hope that the white religious leadership of this community would see the justice of our cause, and with deep moral concern, serve as the channel through which our just grievances would get to the power structure. I had hoped that each of you would understand. But again I have been disappointed. I have heard numerous religious leaders of the South call upon their worshippers to comply with a desegregation decision because it is the *law,* but I have longed to hear white ministers say, "Follow this decree because integration is morally *right* and the Negro is your brother." In the midst of blatant injustices inflicted upon the Negro, I have watched white churches stand on the sideline and merely mouth pious irrelevancies and sanctimonious trivialities. In the midst of a mighty struggle to rid our nation of racial and economic injustice, I have heard so many ministers say "Those are social issues with which the gospel has no real concern," and I have watched so many churches commit themselves to a completely other-worldly religion which made a strange distinction between the body and soul, the sacred and the secular.

So here we are moving toward the exit of the twentieth century with a religious community largely adjusted to the status quo, standing as a tail-light behind other community agencies rather than a headlight leading men to higher levels of justice.

I have traveled the length and breadth of Alabama, Mississippi, and all the other southern states. On sweltering summer days and crisp autumn mornings I have looked at her beautiful churches with their lofty spires pointing heavenward. I have beheld the impressive outlay of her massive religious education buildings. Over and over again I have found myself asking: "What kind of people worship here? Who is their God? Where were their voices when the lips of Governor Barnett dripped the words of interposition and nullification? Where were they when Governor Wallace gave the clarion call for defiance and hatred? Where were their voices of support when tired, bruised and weary Negro men and women decided to rise from the dark dungeons of complacency to the bright hills of creative protest?"

Yes, these questions are still in my mind. In deep disappointment, I have swept over the laxity of the church. But be assured that my tears have been tears of love. There can be no deep disappointment where there is not deep love. Yes, I love the church; I love her sacred walls. How could I do otherwise? I am in the rather unique position of being the son, the grandson and the great-grandson of preachers. Yes, I see the church as the body of Christ. But, oh! How we have blemished and scarred that body through social neglect and fear of being nonconformists.

There was a time when the church was very powerful. It was during that period when the early Christians rejoiced when they were deemed worthy to suffer for what they believed. In those days the church was not merely a thermometer that recorded the ideas and principles of popular opinion; it was a thermostat that transformed the mores of society. Wherever the early Christians entered a town the power structure got disturbed and immediately sought to convict them for being "disturbers of the peace" and "outside agitators." But they went on with the conviction that they were "a colony of heaven," and had to obey God rather than man. They were small in number but big in commitment. They were too God-intoxicated to be "astronomically intimidated." They brought an end to such ancient evils as infanticide and gladiatorial contest.

Things are different now. The contemporary church is often a weak, ineffectual voice with an uncertain sound. It is so often the arch supporter of the status quo. Far from being disturbed by the presence of the church, the power structure of the average community is consoled by the church's silent and often vocal sanction of things as they are.

But the judgment of God is upon the church as never before. If the church of today does not recapture the sacrificial spirit of the early church, it will lose its authentic ring, forfeit the loyalty of millions, and be dismissed as an irrelevant social club with no meaning for the twentieth century. I am meeting young people every day whose disappointment with the church has risen to outright disgust.

Maybe again, I have been too optimistic. Is organized religion too inextricably bound to the status quo to save our nation and the world? Maybe I must turn my faith to the inner spiritual church, the church within the church, as the true *ecclesia* and the hope of the world. But again I am thankful to God that some noble souls from the ranks of organized religion have broken loose from the paralyzing chains of conformity and joined us as active partners in the struggle for freedom. They have left their secure congregations and walked the streets of Albany, Georgia, with us. They have gone through the highways of the South in tortuous rides for freedom. Yes, they have gone to jail with us. Some have been kicked out of their churches, and lost support of their bishops and fellow ministers. But they have gone with the faith that right defeated is stronger than evil triumphant. These men have been the leaven in the lump of the race. Their witness has been the spiritual salt that has preserved the true meaning of the Gospel in these troubled times. They have carved a tunnel of hope through the dark mountain of disappointment.

I hope the church as a whole will meet the challenge of this decisive hour. But even if the church does not come to the aid of justice, I have no despair about the future. I have no fear about the outcome of our struggle in Birmingham, even if our motives are presently misunderstood. We will reach the goal of freedom in Birmingham and all over the nation, because the goal of America is freedom. Abused and scorned though we may be, our destiny is tied up with the destiny of America. Before the pilgrims landed at Plymouth we were here. Before the pen of Jefferson etched across the pages of history the majestic words of the Declaration of Independence, we were here. For more than two centuries our foreparents labored in this country without wages; they made cotton king; and they built the homes of their masters in the midst of brutal injustice and shameful humiliation—and yet out of a bottomless vitality they continued to thrive and develop. If the inexpressible cruelties of slavery did not stop us, the opposition we now face will surely fail. We will win our freedom because the sacred heritage of our nation and the eternal will of God are embodied in our echoing demands.

I must close now. But before closing I am impelled to mention one other point in your statement that troubled me profoundly. You warmly commended the Birmingham police for keeping "order" and "preventing violence." I don't believe you would have so warmly commended the police force if you had seen its angry violent dogs literally biting six unarmed, nonviolent Negroes. I don't believe you would so quickly commend the policemen if you would observe their ugly and inhuman treatment of Negroes here in the city jail; if you would watch them push and curse old Negro women and young Negro girls; if you would see them slap and kick old Negro men and young boys; if you will observe them, as they did on two occasions, refuse to give us food because we wanted to sing our grace together. I'm sorry that I can't join you in your praise for the police department.

It is true that they have been rather disciplined in their public handling of the demonstrators. In this sense they have been rather publicly "nonviolent." But for what purpose? To preserve the evil system of segregation. Over the last few years I have consistently preached that nonviolence demands that the means we use must be as pure as the ends we seek. So I have tried to make it clear that it is wrong to use immoral means to attain moral ends. But now I must affirm that it is just as wrong or even more so, to use moral means to provide immoral ends. Maybe Mr. Connor and his policemen have been rather publicly nonviolent, as Chief Pritchett was in Albany, Georgia, but they have used the moral means of nonviolence to maintain the immoral end of flagrant racial injustice. T.S. Eliot has said that there is no greater treason than to do the right deed for the wrong reason.

I wish you had commended the Negro sit-inners and demonstrators of Birmingham for their sublime courage, their willingness to suffer and their amazing discipline in the midst of the most inhuman provocation. One day the South will recognize its real heroes. They will be the James Merediths, courageously and with a majestic sense of purpose facing jeering and hostile mobs and the agonizing loneliness that characterizes the life of the pioneer. They will be old, oppressed, battered Negro women, symbolized in a seventy-two year old woman of Montgomery, Alabama, who rose up with a sense of dignity and with her people decided not to ride the segregated buses, and responded to one who inquired about her tiredness with ungrammatical profundity: "My feet is tired, but my soul is rested." They will be the young high school and college students, young ministers of the Gospel and a host of their elders courageously and nonviolently sitting-in at lunch counters and willingly going to jail for conscience's sake. One day the South will know that when these disinherited children of God sat down at lunch counters they were in reality standing up for the best in the American dream and the most sacred values in our Judeo-Christian heritage, and thusly, carrying our whole nation back to those great wells of democracy which were dug deep by the founding fathers in the formulation of the Constitution and the Declaration of Independence.

Never before have I written a letter this long (or should I say a book?). I'm afraid that it is much too long to take your precious time. I can assure you that it would have been much shorter if I had been writing from a comfortable desk, but what else is there to do when you are alone for days in the dull monotony of a narrow jail cell other than to write long letters, think strange thoughts, and pray long prayers?

If I have said anything in this letter that is an overstatement of the truth and is indicative of an unreasonable impatience, I beg you to forgive me. If I have said anything in this letter that is an understatement of the truth and is indicative of my having a patience that makes me patient with anything less than brotherhood, I beg God to forgive me.

I hope this letter finds you strong in the faith. I also hope that circumstances will soon make it possible for me to meet each of you, not as an integrationist or a civil-rights leader, but as a fellow clergyman and a Christian brother. Let us all hope that the dark clouds of racial prejudice will soon pass away and the deep fog of misunderstanding will be lifted from our fear-drenched communities and in some not too distant tomorrow the radiant stars of love and brotherhood will shine over our great nation with all their scintillating beauty.

Yours for the cause of Peace and Brotherhood,

Martin Luther King, Jr.

Revolutionary Violence, Development, Equality, and Justice in South Africa

Okwudibia Nnoli

Okwudibia Nnoli is a professor of political science at the University of Nigeria. He is the author of Self Reliance and Foreign Policy in Tanzania *(1978) and* Path to Nigerian Development *(1981).*

Contrary to the views of the defenders of nonviolent resistance, Nnoli argues that violence, especially revolutionary violence, is often justified to confront the violence of domination. The oppressed are generally already at such a disadvantage in comparison with the ruling class that nothing short of violence will be effective in overcoming such conditions as poverty, hatred, and exploitation. Drawing on recent events in South Africa, Nnoli argues that nonviolence has been ineffective in ending apartheid. He advocates a form of revolutionary violence that stresses the necessity of liberating people from obstacles to their development as full-fledged equal human beings. This cause, he believes, is of the sort that justifies the use of violence.

Revolutionary violence is associated with a political program designed to effect a change in the social order. It usually occurs in the form of resistance against obvious social evils. Its goals are greater equality, justice, and freedom for the majority. It seeks the safety and freedom of both individual and group from threats to life and property and their protection from fear and doubt of all forms of danger.

Violence is often the result of the domination by the ruling class over the underprivileged classes, initially by force but sustained later by propaganda, intimidation, blackmail, bribery, and corruption. Usually visited by a dominant minority on a powerless majority, it is commonly based on a combination of exploitation, repression, and fragmentation of the majority which places them below a minimum level of existence and always at a disadvantage. Inevitably, confrontations ensue between spokespersons of the poor majority and those of the ruling class, including revolts, uprisings, and civil wars.

The objective of revolutionary violence is to pull the majority of the population above the minimum level of existence and to eliminate their disadvantage. When successful, it tends to move the socioeconomic and cultural system toward an ever larger measure of power to the people for conscious participation in building their own future; higher production for societal needs; nonexploitative relations of production and equitable principles of distribution; production that is

From *Emerging Human Rights,* edited by George W. Shephard and Mark Anikpo, © 1990, pp. III-128. Published by Greenwood Press, an imprint of Greenwood Publishing Group, Inc., Westport, CT. Reprinted with permission. [Edited]

oriented toward the reality, needs, and aspirations of the masses; and the maximum possible enjoyment of culture by the masses, as well as an aesthetically and ecologically sound environment.

Only pacifist liberals will deprecate such a humanizing violence. This is because they absolutize the concept of violence by avoiding the necessary distinction between aggressor and victim, predator and prey, exploiter and exploited. Such a view loses all practical meaning as well as all moral force. No contribution to peace and progress is likely to emanate from a lofty "even-handed" condemnation of all violence. It can only give aid and comfort to the subject of an aggressive war without deluding the victim of aggression. To eliminate war is essentially to eliminate aggressive war. To suggest that it can be done by eliminating wars of liberation conducted with revolutionary violence subverts both human logic and human values.

Violence that is used to hold a person down in poverty, ignorance, disease, prejudice, hate, and exploitation must be distinguished from violence used to free a person from these obstacles to human progress. The latter violence serves to remove impediments from the path of a person's realization of his or her potentialities as a morally autonomous agent. It implies the removal of a whole arsenal of restrictions on an oppressed person that had limited his or her area of choices and opportunities. In the process it removes the major obstacles to human creativity such as lack of self-confidence and self-respect, generates a new social and political consciousness that is regenerative, and frees the individual from despair, powerlessness, helplessness, and inaction. The individual becomes fearless, and in addition, acquires the consciousness of a common cause, national identity, and collective esprit de corps. Such a consciousness is vitally necessary for building a new society at a higher level of human creativity. It is a prerequisite for an assault on all forms of labor alienation, including those that arise from the odious system of apartheid. . . .

INEQUALITY, INJUSTICE, AND DEVELOPMENT

The inequality and injustice that pervade apartheid South Africa is inimical to the country's development. Although it enjoys a highly sophisticated industrial economy reputed to be the strongest in Africa, the nation's level of development falls far short of its potential. It is maintained by the unbridled exploitation of the black majority and their exclusion from the benefits of that economy. Under these conditions such a level of development cannot be sustained. Even if it could be sustained, its potential could not be maximized. The human rights implied by equality and justice are critical to a people's progress.

In fact, development is not possible without the full liberation of the creative energies of the individual in society. But such a liberation presupposes the enjoyment of certain rights implied by equality and justice such as the right to work, food, education, and health services; and freedom of speech, assembly, movement, privacy, and participation in the decision processes affecting one's life. In the absence of these rights, the people cannot be fully committed to the creation of new values and products, and the ability of the society to take care of its ever-increasing population is severely limited. Even when the society can cater to the social and economic needs of the population, the enjoyment of these rights is still necessary for full flowering of the people.

That conception of development in South Africa which equates development with economic growth and social welfare is faulty. It disregards such factors as inequality, injustice, exploitation, and oppression from the realm of analysis. In addition, it focuses on economic growth as reflected by increases in the GDP, industrialization, food, and capital formation, as well as welfare services addressed to basic needs, increased economic efficiency, and the construction of the infrastructure such as roads, railways, and electricity. Hence, a high premium is placed on capital formation and on the rate of growth of GDP and industrialization, and hardly any premium is placed on whether these are the result of foreign or indigenous creativity, the creativity of the minority or majority of the population; who benefits from this growth—foreigners, the rich or poor; and the consequences of this pattern of distribution for further development. The most dramatic form of human intervention in the development process, notably revolutions, cannot be entertained by analysis. The individual becomes mired in a mass of data. A person's role in the process and its consequences for that person as a human being are completely ignored. Under the circumstances reality cannot even be understood, let alone be transformed.

Development is first and foremost a phenomenon associated with changes in a person's humanity and creative energies, not in things. It is a dialectical phenomenon in which the individual and society interact with their physical, biological, and interhuman environments, transforming them for their own betterment and that of humanity at large, and being transformed in the process. The lesson learned and experiences acquired in this process are passed on to future generations, enabling them to improve their capacities to make further valuable changes in interhuman relations and their ability to transform nature. It is the unending improvement in the capacity of the individual and society to control and manipulate the forces of nature as well as themselves and other individuals and societies for their own benefit and that of humanity at large. As a process of actualizing the individual's inherent capacity to live a better life, development implies increasing skills and capacity to do things, greater freedom, self-confidence, creativity, self-discipline, responsibility, and material well-being.

Every society, whether developed or underdeveloped, forever struggles to realize fully its potential creativity. Development is a progressive process that probably has no end. Its goal at any particular time and place is circumscribed by the obstacles to realizing this potential. These obstacles vary from society to society, depending on their inherited level of production, the nature of their productive forces, the relations of production, patterns of social and cultural relations, the quality and creativity of the ruling circles, and the hostility or benignness of the physical environment and the neighboring societies. As old challenges are overcome, new and sometimes more intractable ones take their place. Therefore, development connotes training in the art of using local resources, including creative human energy, in the problem-solving rather than a wholesale imitation of the path to a good life that some societies have achieved. From this viewpoint it is possible for a people to accept the fact that they are not all that they ought to be without feeling inferior to other peoples.

Thus, development refers to the individual's progressive and qualitative self-improvement. This is brought about primarily by the cooperative use of his or her labor. In this way human beings have been able to tame the wild, build very complex structures, organize large populations, and extend their lifespan. Therefore, development occurs when labor conditions improve. Such an improvement varies directly with the elimination of all human and nonhuman impediments to the creative application of human labor. The most significant impediments are those that cause labor alienation.

In general there are two aspects to the alienation of labor, the one being psychological and the other, material. Psychologically, labor alienation is the consequence of the consignment of the individual to a low-level, menial, noncreative, and marginalized role in production. In this role people cannot take the initiative, are unable to comprehend the necessary interdependence of roles in the work process, and are the victims of a structural relationship of command and obedience. As human beings they are denied the opportunity to acquire self-confidence in the creative process. Workers lose all sense of initiative and creativity because their productive activities are in no way meaningfully connected in their minds with the general results of production or their basic needs. For them work is only a source of wages, not the extension of their social selves.

Materially, the alienation of labor arises when individuals are denied an adequate material compensation for their contribution to production. The same alienation results from poor health, ignorance, and in general the hostility of the physical and biological environment which reduces workers' productivity and consequently their material rewards. Therefore, the workers are also exploited and alienated from their labor when the funds that could be used in the public interest to provide them with social, health, and other welfare services are diverted to luxury consumption of a privileged minority of the population.

Although development thus centers on the individual, it has a social content. A particular state dominated by a particular ruling class always directs a particular form of development. In the process it may use direct violence or structural violence. Whether, when, and which types of violence will be used usually depends on whether it is unnecessary or impossible to use force to change or restore the balance between competing vital class interests. Therefore, violence is fundamental to the process of development. The form of development in a particular country is the product of a definite correlation of domestic class forces and international social forces. Structural violence represents a form of development organized by the dominant minority in the service of its psychological and material interests, and maintained in the final analysis by an intimidating system of armaments. It directly contradicts an alternative form of development meant to pull the majority above the minimum existence and eliminate their disadvantages. Thus, the link between violence and development may be reformulated in terms of the struggle to establish or sustain a particular form of development. In normative terms revolutionary violence is justifiable with respect to a concept of development formulated as the movement of the whole socioeconomic and cultural system toward greater progress on the basis of increased equality and justice in social relations.

REVOLUTIONARY VIOLENCE AND THE STRUGGLE AGAINST APARTHEID

South Africa has constructed a formidable shield of armor around apartheid. It has succeeded in doing so by employing its considerable foreign exchange earnings to purchase arms, luring Western powers to support its armament policy by its anti-Communist propaganda and by advertising its strategic location at the Cape of Good Hope. It has also been assisted by its easy access to external capitalist sources of technology for the expansion and modernization of its armed forces, the strong industrial base with which it manufactures modern arms and ammunition, and its devotion to give top priority to military expansion.

Thus, South Africa spent $2,510, $3,491, $2,971, and $2,982 million on arms in 1975, 1977, 1979 and 1982, respectively.[1] This expenditure is more than twice that of all the frontline states combined.[2] Even this does not properly reflect the military position of the racist regime. It does not include the cost of maintaining the enormous trained reserve, the citizen force, and the paramilitary forces such as Commando, Boss personnel, and the quasi-military police force. In addition, it excludes the expenditure on the forces deployed in Namibia. The truth is that white South Africa is a highly militarized society, and that militarization is not motivated by any present military threat from within or without the borders if the country. Instead, it is built around a single-minded pursuit of the antidevelopment policy of apartheid. The intention is to intimidate black South Africans and the frontline states into some accommodation with that odious policy and to lure the Western powers into a similar accommodation.

This overbearing arms posture of racist South Africa destroys the will of the white regime to compromise on apartheid. First, it creates the illusion that victory is around the corner. Consequently, the military establishment is more confident and arrogant. More emphasis is then placed on arms and more arms. This illusion is heightened by such events as the Nkomati Accords with Mozambique as well as the relatively unchallenged South African incursions into Angola, Lesotho, and Botswana. Nevertheless, the internal struggle against apartheid has intensified. People have exploded on an ever-increasing scale. The policy of scapegoating represented by the cross border raids and invasion has become less and less credible. It has become clear that the dynamics of the opposition to racism lie within South Africa itself.

Second, armaments have encouraged the racists to launch a policy of intimidating their opponents into making the most of the concessions in any bargaining situation. Thus, in negotiating with the frontline states, it agrees to give up nothing that is related to apartheid in return for concessions by these states on such fundamentals as support for the liberation movements. Even then, as the aftermath of the Nkomati Accords has shown, the racists have not lived up to their own side of the bargain.

Third, the will to compromise is often associated with cultural, economic, and social interests. In this way it is possible to separate it from the armaments system. As these interests are satisfied, the will is reinforced and the militarization is scaled down. In South Africa, however, there is a very close link between the sociocultural and the military. They are so intimately tied together by apartheid that the will to compromise is tied to the military and its armaments system. Apartheid thrives on violence, economic exploitation, socio political discrimination, and racial segregation. All these are held together by an escalating armaments system. Therefore, only a significant dent in this shield of armor will loosen these ties and provide the opportunities for the will to compromise to emerge from the socioeconomic and cultural level. Only revolutionary violence of all peoples and states oppressed by apartheid can do this.

Fourth, the history of the struggle against racism and colonialism in Southern Africa from Angola and Mozambique to Zimbabwe and now South Africa has shown that the racist's will to compromise has always been encouraged by the black majority's use of revolutionary violence against the structures of white racism. In the process, of course, the African states and peoples concerned have inevitably incurred some costs. But such sacrifices have often paled into insignificance with the achievement of their goal of freedom, equality, and justice.

Fifth, the arrogance associated with an overwhelming superiority in armaments has encouraged the racists to foreclose all avenues for peaceful change with South Africa. Consequently, the use of violence by the liberation movements and their moral and material support by the frontline states is inevitable. As noted earlier in this chapter, following the proscription of the African National Congress and the Pan-Africanist Congress, African political expression was manifested in workers' strikes and the spontaneous demonstrations and uprisings of the population at large. Each action has been met by violent police confrontation, brutality, and repression. The racists have even rebuffed their desire for a nonviolent solution by the frontline states as contained in such documents as the Lusaka Manifesto.

The implementation of apartheid is creating a serious financial burden for South Africa. President Botha admitted that the financial burden of the country's military presence in Namibia alone amounts to £800 million annually.[3] A number of countries have imposed economic sanctions following South Africa's declaration of a state of emergency in 1985. Economic boycott of white-owned businesses in black townships has created severe economic hardship for some white businesspeople. Apartheid is also to blame for the loss of markets for South African goods in many countries of Africa, Asia, and Latin America. And the racist regime is no longer able to disguise the severe economic crisis which its intransigence on apartheid is imposing on the country. "Inflation is on the march, unemployment is growing, the balance of payments is in disorder and there is no growth."[4] The cost of the Bantustanization of South Africa has become increasingly prohibitive. "Separate development was the most expensive economic method which could be used to solve South Africa's problems."[5]

Much property has been destroyed or damaged, and many lives have been lost as a result of apartheid. The number of people killed in political violence and sabotage in South Africa was six times greater in 1983 than in 1980. During the same period, the number of cases of violence increased sixfold.[6] While in 1983 about 214 people were killed in 395 cases of political violence, in 1984 over 1,000 were killed. The figure was much higher for 1985. In fact, 1984 and especially 1985 and 1986 have seen a general, massive and widespread uprising of the black population against apartheid. The white racist reaction has been to increase violence and brutality. As a result, the number of dead and wounded has escalated.

White South Africa remains intransigent over its policy of apartheid, even though the world community has repeatedly condemned it. The country has faced isolation by many members of that community, especially in cultural relations, though not in economic matters until 1986. Many countries and organizations now provide the ANC and PAC with moral and material support, thereby underlining their opposition to apartheid. The Lusaka Manifesto as well as many other African professions of good intentions toward the white community have been formulated to reassure the white community, but to no avail. All avenues for peaceful change have been closed.

During his later presidency, even Ronald Reagan abandoned his friendly posture of constructive engagement, and the American Congress imposed wide-ranging economic sanctions, threatening more if apartheid were not quickly dismantled. In the face of this increased hostility from the world community, the apartheid regime has become more adamant and hardened in its attitudes. In the face of the people's increased resistance, it has intensified state violence.

All efforts to use nonviolent means to overcome this South African intransigence have failed. Until very recently, the use of worldwide economic sanctions as a pressure on Pretoria has met with the disapproval of the Western powers. Limited sanctions were imposed following the state of emergency declared by the racists. It was designed to cause as little damage to the South African economy as possible. Until recently the West refused to disinvest in the racist enclave.

As a nonviolent pressure the arms embargo imposed on South Africa by the world community has remained ineffective. Today, in spite of the 1963 and 1977 embargoes, the racists have increased their armaments over the pre–1963 level in geometric proportion. Since then the country has emerged as a significant world power. All this has been made possible by Western shipments of arms to the country. South Africa now probably has nuclear weapons which it developed during the period of this embargo.

In the face of this South African intransigence over apartheid, revolutionary violence in the form of guerrilla war has become inevitable. Violence is being used to resolve the contradiction between apartheid and the development of the black community in South Africa. That violence is based on the idea that the people are the motivating force of all successful enterprises. It encourages not only their mobilization, but also reliance on them as the top priority in all national endeavors. Durable peace and success in development require the support of the population. In the absence of this support, ruling classes rely on arms or foreign assistance. In other words, they declare war on their own people or bypass them in the process of development.

The oppressed blacks have responded with revolutionary violence in the factories, in their communities, schools, and in the struggle against the South African Defense Force (SADF) occupying the black townships. They have seized the strategic initiative, with the state resorting to force and more force without being able to subdue them.[7] The emergence of street committees, people's courts, popular forms of defense, and other grass-roots forms of democracy have rendered the apartheid system ungovernable, eroded the conventional methods of administration, and compelled the military to use more force.[8]

REVOLUTIONARY VIOLENCE AND DEVELOPMENT IN SOUTH AFRICA

The current black resistance to apartheid using revolutionary violence has scored some success. This resistance has taken the form of increasing and more damaging attacks by the Umkhonto we Sizwe, industrial strikes, unionization of the workforce, formation of the Confederation of South Africa Trade Unions (COSATU) and its anti-apartheid demands, waves of school boycotts involving millions of students, attacks on those blacks who collaborate with the apartheid regime, and a successful consumer boycott of white-owned stores in black residential areas. These evident successes attest to the fact that even without arms an oppressed people will inevitably find a way of throwing off oppression.

> The significance of Soweto and the current wave of struggles is that a disarmed people, with nothing but their will to be free, harboring no illusion about the military and economic power of their adversary, nor about his intentions and resolve to kill as many as he could to subdue their will, have decided to fight, and if necessary die, rather than continue to live as slaves.[9]

Revolutionary violence against apartheid serves the cause of development not only because it removes the major obstacles to the progress of the black majority in South Africa. It also generates a new social and political consciousness among them that is regenerative. It frees them from their inferiority complex by destroying the myth of white superiority and invincibility, and from their despair and powerlessness. It makes the black man fearless, restoring his self-respect and self-confidence, values that are important for qualitative self-improvement or development. It promotes the mobilization of the masses, which introduces the ideas of a common cause, common struggle, and national identity. Such a consciousness is vitally necessary for building a new society at a higher level of human creativity. It is a prerequisite for an assault on all forms of the alienation of labor that arises from the odious system of apartheid.

Such mobilization of the popular forces enables the people to take the initiative economically and politically and to gain the necessary experiences in these areas of national life. In the process they acquire the capacity to make decisions about what is produced, how and why: and how the products are distributed. Similarly, they are able to assume responsibility for making the decisions which affect their lives. They are no longer the object but the subject of politics. And only the pressure of the vast number of the toiling black masses of South Africa applied through their mobilization and native participation in the organization and supervision of agricultural, commercial, industrial and political enterprises and supported by their organized power is capable of maximizing the development potential of the country.

The unorganized efforts of the people can only be a temporary dynamic in the development process. Neither stubborn courage nor fine slogans can be a substitute for organization. Revolutionary violence against apartheid enables the black masses to achieve organization. Through mobilization for violence against official racism, they have formed organizations that are seizing the initiative in politics and waging a relentless war against apartheid.

Finally, revolutionary violence also stimulates an increased technological capacity to transform and adapt the economy to changing demands and conditions. The struggle against apartheid provides a favorable condition for developing such a technological perspective. During times of war, the basic needs of the people come to the fore, especially the need for physical survival. When such needs are threatened, the creative energies of the people are galvanized and mobilized behind the survival effort. The population is often forced to improvise, to rely on local resources and initiatives, and to be innovative while maintaining the initiative. These factors are crucial to the development process.

CONCLUSIONS

The link between violence and development is often posed as the link between the armament system and development.[10] It appears in another form as the relationship between disarmament and development. The phenomenon of disarmament is the process of deflating the armaments dynamics, dismantling the stockpile of armaments, and eliminating the role of the armaments industry, including its research and development, in conflict resolution. Thus, it is significant in reducing violence, and disarmament is dialectically linked with direct violence.

The link between violence, armaments, or disarmament and development is often seen in terms of the relationship between expenditures on the armament system and increased productivity of the economy, with productivity tied to project construction. In this regard two schools of thought exist. One school believes that the link is positive because of the technological spinoffs of the armaments industry and nationalism of the armed forces, especially in the poor countries of the world.[11] The other school adopts a more moral posture. It decries the excessive expenditure of arms relative to that on the basic needs of the population. Therefore, it views the link as negative. Its assumption is that reduced spending on armaments would release more funds to be spent on development projects.[12] Both condemn violence from a pacifist liberal viewpoint and regard development in infrastructural terms.

Empirically, both schools have failed to justify their positions. The modernization of the Third World countries through the intervention of the arms industry in the economy, and the armed forces in politics, has not materialized. Instead, the resultant political instability has compounded the difficulties of improving the population's quality of life. The economy has also declined. Similarly, there is no evidence that resources released from cutbacks in arms spending would necessarily go into expenditure on development projects rather than to other forms of "waste" or unproductive spending.[13]

When a human-centered conception of development is linked to resistance against structural violence by means of revolutionary violence, then the positive impact of violence may be observed. The key lies in the impact of that means of action on self-confidence. Self-esteem is crucial for overcoming challenges. It prevents one from being subjectively overwhelmed by the magnitude of the problem, demoralized, or sapped of the will to succeed. Such self-confidence is incompatible with the state of acute and pervasive alienation of the South African black that is generated by apartheid. That policy is presently the major obstacle in the path of South Africa to a self-sustained creative transformation of the labor of the vast majority of its population and consequently the society's quality of life.

At the same time, a moral argument is sustainable because revolutionary violence and development are linked by the struggle for human rights without which the creative energies for development will be stunted and peace rendered ephemeral. Apartheid denies the black majority of South Africa the fundamental human rights, and it denies them easy access to employment, education, health care, and social welfare services generally. But these rights are crucial for a full moral existence of a society, and for the development process. Their realization improves the capacity of man to liberate himself from all forces that constrain his social self reproduction, self extension and the maximum release of his creative energy. A society that denies these rights to its majority has no moral claim to existence. And so the struggle continues.

NOTES

1. Sources: Sean Gervasi, "Breakdown of the United States Arms Embargo" in Western Massachusetts Association of Concerned African Scholars, ed., *U.S. Military Involvement in South Africa* (Boston: South End Press, 1978), p. 140; U.S. Arms Control and Disarmament Agency, *World Military Expenditures and Arms Transfers 1972–1982* (Washington, D.C.: ACADA Publication, 1984), p. 44.
2. Ibid.
3. Colin Legum, *African Contemporary Record* (New York and London: Africana, 1986), p. A9.
4. Quoted in Bernard Magubane, "South Africa: A Luta Continua," Paper presented at the biennial conference of the African Association of Political Science held in Addis Ababa, Ethiopia, May 13–15, 1985, p.34.
5. This quote in Magubane, "South Africa" is credited to Dr. Otto Count Lambsdorff who until 1986 was West Germany's minister for Economic Affairs.
6. Legum, *African Contemporary Record,* p. A5.
7. Horace Campbell, "The Dismantling of the Apartheid War Machine," *Third World Quarterly* 9, no. 2 (April 1987), p. 482.
8. Ibid., p. 488.
9. Magubane, "South Africa," p. 48.
10. Cf. United Nations General Assembly, *Study on the Relationship Between Disarmament and Development* (New York: United Nations, 1982);

Peter Lock, "Armaments Dynamics: An Issue in Development Strategies,"*Alternatives* 6, no. 2 (July 1980), pp.157—78; Nicole Ball and Milton Leitenberg, *Disarmament, Development and Their Interrelationship* (Los Angeles: Center for the Study of Armament and Disarmament, California State University, 1980).

11. Cf. Emile Benoit, *Defense and Economic Growth in Developing Countries* (Lexington, Mass,: Lexington Books, 1963); Emile Benoit, Max F. Millikan, and Everett E. Hagen, *Effect of Defense on Developing Economies,* Main Report, Vol. 2, ACDA/E–136 (Cambridge, Mass.: MIT Press, 1971).
12. Cf. Ruth L. Sivard, *World Military and Social Expenditures, 1977* (Leesburg, Va,: WNSE Publications, 1977); Nicole Ball, "Defense and Development: A Critique of the Benoit Study," *Economic Development and Social Change,* no. 31 (April 1983); Nicole Ball, "Military Expenditure, Economic Growth and Socio-Economic Development in the Third World," Conference paper no. 3, of the Swedish Institute of International Peace Research.
13. R.B. Duboff, "Converting Military Spending to Social Welfare: The Real Obstacles,"*Quarterly Review of Economics and Business* 12 (Spring 1972), pp. 7–22.

WAR AND VIOLENCE —SUPPLEMENTARY READINGS

BACK, ALLAN, and DAESHIK KIM. "Pacifism and the Eastern Martial Arts." *Philosophy East and West,* April 1982.

CHILDRESS, JAMES F. "Just War Theories." *Theological Studies* 1978.

DOMBROWSKI, DANIEL M. "Gandhi, Sainthood, and Nuclear Weapons." *Philosophy East and West,* vol. 33(4), October 1983.

FASHINA, OLADIPO. "Frantz Fanon and the Ethical Justification of Anti-Colonial Violence." *Social Theory and Practice,* Summer 1989.

GRAY, J GLENN . "The Enduring Appeals of Battle," in *The Warriors.* New York: Harcourt Brace, 1959.

HAJJAR, SAMI G., and R. KIERON SWAINE. "Social Justice: The Philosophical Justifications of Qadhafi's Construction." *Africa Today,* vol. 31(3), 1984.

HOLMES, ROBERT L. "Violence and the Perspective of Morality," in *On War and Morality.* Princeton, N.J.: Princeton University Press, 1989.

IHARA, CRAIG K. "Pacifism as a Moral Ideal," *Journal of Value Inquiry,* vol. 22, 1988.

LLOYD, GENEVIEVE. "Selfhood, War and Masculinity," in *Feminist Challenges,* Carole Pateman and Elizabeth Gross, editors. Boston: Northeastern University Press, 1986.

MAGNO, JOSEPH A. "Hinduism on the Morality of Violence." *International Philosophical Quarterly,* vol. 28(1), March 1988.

O'BRIEN, WILLIAM. "Just-War Theory," *The Conduct of Just and Limited War.* Praeger, 1981.

WALZER, MICHAEL. "War Crimes: Soldiers and Their Officers," in *Just and Unjust Wars.* New York: Harper Torchbooks, 1977.

V

Gender Roles and Morality

In many societies, being male means that one is thought to have different moral obligations as well as a different moral status than if one were female. Traditionally in the West, women were thought to be more emotional and less rational than men. Women were assigned the child-rearing and homemaking tasks while men were given, among other things, control of political affairs. In the West and elsewhere, as women become increasingly involved in all public realms, they have been subjected to discriminatory treatment in various forms, often explicitly rationalized by reference to the claim that they have different natures than men.

There are biological differences between men and women. Women menstruate, gestate, and lactate, whereas men do not. Men ejaculate, whereas women do not. Beyond the biological, there are other measurable differences between the two groups. Men, on the average, have greater upper body strength than women. Women in the West, on the average, score higher on verbal exams than men, while men score higher on mathematical exams than women. However, these statistical differences do have exceptions. The question to be raised is this: Do these natural and statistical differences between males and females call for differences in moral status? This chapter will address that question.

In many societies, natural and statistical differences between men and women are indeed thought to justify differential treatment of the sexes. Although it varies by degree, women are treated as if they are inferior to men in most cultures. In some Islamic societies, it is considered immoral for women to appear in public without being veiled, whereas this is not true for men. The preference for boys has resulted in excessive and disproportionate female mortality in Asian countries, with demographers placing estimates at over 50 million missing females in 1991 alone.[1] In the United States, parents continue to voice a strong preference for male over female children, and among other things, they invest more heavily in their sons' educations than in their daughters'.

Crimes that are gender-defined have also not been given equal status in many societies. Rape and sexual harassment in the United States are often not taken as seriously as are similar assault crimes that are not predominantly directed against women. One such example is Anita Hill's testimony in 1991 concerning sexual harassment she allegedly received from Clarence Thomas, a man who was legally responsible for enforcing the right he was accused of violating. Anita Hill was publicly and intensively grilled by the all-male Senate Judiciary Committee, while Clarence Thomas was never made to answer specific questions concerning the harassment. Sexual harassment, and even sexual slavery, are severe problems in many parts of the world, though not often considered as important as other crimes. In this chapter we will survey some varied viewpoints on the moral justifiability of differential treatment based on gender.

We begin with an essay by Carol Gilligan, a psychologist who has claimed to have discovered a difference that exists between the ways men and women engage in moral reasoning. She contends that women tend to reason according to what she calls a "care perspective," while men tend to reason according to a "justice perspective." Traditionally, the Western world has placed a premium on justice. The justice perspective stresses rights, impartiality, autonomy, and universalizability. The justice perspective has traditionally been considered the highest level in moral development and the highest approach to moral problems. These assumptions concerning the superiority of the justice approach are the focus of the studies of Jean Piaget and Lawrence Kohlberg.

Although she does not claim that all women reason according to the care perspective (nor that all men reason according to the justice perspective), Gilligan identified the care perspective in her studies of moral development as *part of women's moral reasoning*. Gilligan concluded from her studies of moral development and reasoning that women have a distinct moral voice. For Gilligan, and many others, an "ethics of care" stresses relationships and specific, actual situations people find themselves in (as opposed to the abstract hypotheticals so common in justice reasoning). These traits are also devalued on the traditional Western scale of moral reasoning. She argues that care and justice are two distinct perspectives, and although one may view a moral problem from one perspective or the other, the approaches cannot be integrated.

Marilyn Friedman challenges Gilligan's assertion that the care and justice perspectives are necessarily separate. Friedman argues that there is considerable overlap between the two, and that care, in particular, must take into account concerns of justice to be morally adequate. She points out that in practice, justice is relevant not only as traditionally conceived, but in close personal relationships. Justice serves relationships by putting constraints on the sharing of burdens and benefits, as well as the amount of caring that is appropriate. Justice is also relevant for redressing wrongs in relationships where one person has harmed another. Indeed, justice is essential since nurturing, caring, and connecting with others may place a person in a position with special vulnerability to harm. Friedman also points out that care is applicable in the public realm and is manifested in social programs such as welfare and famine relief. However, in the public realm care may also be taken to an extreme, as in partisanship and nepotism. Not only can harm result if either perspective is asserted to the exclusion of the other, but to exclude one position is morally inadequate. Friedman concludes that it would behoove us to move beyond gender stereotypes, "de-moralize the genders," and develop an integrated moral framework that can address all moral concerns.

Bruno Bettelheim argues that the genders are physiologically and socially determined to take on separate moral roles within the family. Although some of what Bettelheim writes seems quite dated, much of what he says is continually echoed by conservative social critics. Bettelheim wrote this piece in the 1950s, a time in United States history idealized by many as one when men and women knew and fulfilled their roles, the family was intact, and Mom stayed home properly fulfilling her "function" of meeting her family's needs. It is more than a little ironic that Bettelheim waxed nostalgic in the 1950s for just the things which some think the 1950s epitomized.

Bettelheim is specifically concerned with the father's role, but he also delineates the role of the mother. Bettelheim states that a woman is fulfilled through meeting her family's physical and emotional needs. In contrast, a man is fulfilled through protecting his family from and preparing his (male) children for the world. To expect men to share in the "women's" family duties not only goes against nature, but can cause the children harm. Bettelheim asserts that the child needs both a parent who will take his or her side no matter what (the mother), and a parent who will be able to give the child sound advice (even if it goes against the child's wishes) based on a broader perspective (the father). Bettelheim is thus an advocate for a moral division of labor based on gender.

Catherine MacKinnon's essay addresses the experience of sexual harassment. Although MacKinnon wrote this piece in the 1970s, it is still quite timely. MacKinnon mentions that in 1976 a sexual harassment study concluded that 81 percent of women on and around a U.S. naval base had experienced sexual harassment in some form. In 1992, widely reported incidents of U.S. naval personnel sexually harassing women led the Navy to institute mandatory sexual harassment education classes for all Navy personnel.

Sexual harassment is against United States federal law, primarily Title VII of the Civil Rights Act of 1964, as amended. Title VII violations fall under the Equal Employment Opportunity Commission (EEOC), the federal agency that is responsible for processing complaints of sexual harassment. Sexual harassment is defined as *unwelcome* behavior, sexual in nature, and can be verbal, physical, or visual. Physical sexual harassment ranges from blatant, overt behavior to a *single* incident of unwanted touching. Verbal sexual harassment ranges from "quid pro quo" (Latin, meaning "something for something") harassment to comments or lewd jokes. Quid pro quo harassment occurs when a supervisor, or someone with authority over the employee, makes unwelcome sexual advances such as "If you want to keep your job or get a raise, then go out with me." It is either an openly stated or an implied condition for getting benefits or raises, or for remaining employed. Visual sexual harassment encompasses the hostile work environment that results from the posting of pinups, pornographic photos, sexually oriented calendars, and so on.

Sexual harassment denies one's right to the opportunity to study or work without sexual extortion. Although federal law recognizes both genders as possible victims of sexual harassment, MacKinnon sees sexual harassment as predominantly an experience of women, as discrimination based on gender. In her essay, she argues that the claims that women "go along" or "want it" are myths that do not take into account the social, economic, and political power structure.

M. Annette Jaimes and Theresa Halsey address the myth that, American Indian women were always subordinate to the males in their tribes. As discussed above, Bettelheim insisted that the divisions of moral labor were necessitated by our physiological nature. Halsey and Jaimes challenge this, and present examples of different American Indian tribal cultures in which power was shared and was not gender-defined. They argue that the stereotype of women, particularly American Indian women, as docile, meek, and subordinate to males, is incorrect. They cite numerous tribal examples of women in key decision-making positions, and of women involved in all aspects of tribal culture, from war to economics to spiritual leadership. Halsey and Jaimes argue that the subsequent divestiture of American Indian women's status and power within the cultures was intentional, and was forced upon the tribes by the European colonizers.

Nayereh Tohidi's essay also deals with the imposition of Western values on traditional cultures. Tohidi writes about the situation in Iran following the Shah's ousting, and the failure of women's liberation to take hold. Although Iranian women were offered a Western "liberated" role, they (seemingly) rejected it in favor of traditional women's roles. She points out, however, that the picture of Western women given Iranian women was incomplete, since it only included superficial freedoms such as choice in dress. Further, the Western "choice" in dress was presented (some may argue quite accurately) as another form of oppression—women were seen as slaves to commercialized fashion who were told to make themselves attractive not only to the men in their lives, but to society as a whole. Furthermore, the current religious and political powers in Iran create an atmosphere in which women are often brutally kept "in their place" through the denial of basic human rights. Thus, Tohidi cautions that we must not conclude that Iranian women accept their role, for we must take into account the inadequate information available to them, and the severely oppressive atmosphere they live in.

As will become evident in the next section, many of the issues facing women overlap with those of racial and ethnic minorities, as both groups have been systematically denied economic, social, and political power.

NOTE

1. See Nicholas D. Kristof, "Stark Data on Women: 100 Million are Missing", *The New York Times,* November 5, 1991, p. B5–B9.

Moral Orientation and Moral Development

Carol Gilligan

Carol Gilligan is a developmental psychologist and a professor of education at the Harvard Graduate School of Education. She is the author of a much-discussed book, In a Different Voice *(1982). Gilligan's book has been a watershed in feminist theory. She is also the author of* Mapping the Moral Domain *(1988), and of numerous articles.*

Gilligan's research in moral development led her to identify a moral orientation that has care as its primary focus. Traditionally, justice is seen as the most important Western moral value. Gilligan claims that the studies of Jean Piaget and the early work of Lawrence Kohlberg have obscured and devalued the care perspective that was voiced by women she studied. Gilligan argues that one may consider a moral problem from either a justice or a care perspective, although the two perspectives cannot be integrated and the problem cannot be considered from both perspectives simultaneously. Gilligan traces the development of these moral orientations and considers the importance of the care perspective, as a perspective voiced by women.

When one looks at an ambiguous figure like the drawing that can be seen as a young or old woman, or the image of the vase and the faces, one initially sees it in only one way. Yet even after seeing it in both ways, one way often seems more compelling. This phenomenon reflects the laws of perceptual organization that favor certain modes of visual grouping. But it also suggests a tendency to view reality as unequivocal and thus to argue that there is one right or better way of seeing.

The experiments of the Gestalt psychologists on perceptual organization provide a series of demonstrations that the same proximal pattern can be organized in different ways so that, for example, the same figure can be seen as a square or a diamond, depending on its orientation in relation to a surrounding frame. Subsequent studies show that the context influencing which of two possible organizations will be chosen may depend not only on the features of the array presented but also on the perceiver's past experience or expectation. Thus, a bird-watcher and a rabbit-keeper are likely to see the duck-rabbit figure in different ways; yet this difference does not imply that one way is better or a higher form of perceptual organization. It does, however, call attention to the fact that the rabbit-keeper, perceiving the rabbit, may not see the ambiguity of the figure until someone points out that it can also be seen as a duck.

This paper presents a similar phenomenon with respect to moral judgment, describing two moral perspectives that organize thinking in different ways. The analogy to ambiguous figure perception arises from the observation that although people are aware of both perspectives, they tend to adopt one or the other in defining and resolving moral conflict. Since moral judgments organize thinking about choice in difficult situations, the adoption of a single perspective may facilitate clarity of decision. But the wish for clarity may also imply a compelling human need for resolution or closure, especially in the face of decisions that give rise to discomfort or unease. Thus, the search for clarity in seeing may blend with a search for justification, encouraging the position that there is one right or better way to think about moral problems. This question, which has been the subject of intense theological and philosophical debate, becomes of interest to the psychologist not only because of its psychological dimensions—the tendency to focus on one perspective and the wish for justification—but also because one moral perspective currently dominates psychological thinking and is embedded in the most widely used measure for assessing the maturity of moral reasoning.

In describing an alternative standpoint, I will reconstruct the account of moral development around two moral perspectives, grounded in different dimensions of relationship that give rise to moral concern. The justice perspective, often equated with moral reasoning, is recast as one way of seeing moral problems and a care perspective is brought forward as an alternate vision or frame. The distinction between justice and care as alternative perspectives or moral orientations is based empirically on the observation that a shift in the focus of attention from concerns about justice to concerns about care changes the definition of what constitutes a moral problem, and leads the same situation to be seen in different ways. Theoretically, the distinction between justice and care cuts across the familiar divisions between thinking and feeling, egoism and altruism, theoretical and practical reasoning. It calls attention to the fact that all human relationships, public and private, can be characterized *both* in terms of equality and in terms of attachment, and that both inequality and detachment constitute grounds for moral concern. Since everyone is vulnerable both to oppression and to abandonment, two moral visions—one of justice and one of care—recur in human experience. The moral injunctions, not to act unfairly toward others, and not to turn away from someone in need, capture these different concerns.

The conception of the moral domain as comprised of at least two moral orientations raises new questions about observed differences in moral judgment and the disagreements to which they give rise. Key to this revision is the distinction between differences in developmental stage (more or less adequate positions within a single orientation) and differences in orientation (alternative perspectives or frameworks). The findings reported in this paper of an association between moral orientation and gender speak directly to the continuing controversy over sex differences in moral reasoning. In doing so, however, they also offer an empirical explanation for why previous thinking about moral development has been organized largely within the justice framework.

My research on moral orientation derives from an observation made in the course of studying the relationship between moral judgment and action. Two studies, one of college students describing their experiences of moral conflict and choice, and one of pregnant women who were considering abortion, shifted the focus of attention from the ways people reason about hypothetical dilemmas to the ways people construct moral conflicts and choices in their lives. This change in approach made it possible to see what experiences people define in moral terms, and to explore the relationship between the understanding of moral problems and the reasoning strategies used and the actions taken in attempting to resolve them. In this context, I observed that women, especially when speaking about their own experiences of moral conflict and choice, often define moral problems in a way that eludes the categories of moral theory and is at odds with the assumptions that shape psychological thinking about morality and about the self.[1] This discovery, that a different voice often guides the moral judgments and the actions of women, called attention to a major design problem in previous moral judgment research: namely, the use of all-male samples as the empirical basis for theory construction.

The selection of an all-male sample as the basis for generalizations that are applied to both males and females is logically inconsistent. As a research strategy, the decision to begin with a single-sex sample is inherently problematic, since the categories of analysis will tend to be defined on the basis of the initial data gathered and subsequent studies will tend to be restricted to these categories. Piaget's work on the moral judgment of the child illustrates these problems since he defined the evolution of children's consciousness and practice of rules on the basis of his study of boys playing marbles, and then undertook a study of girls to assess the generality of his findings. Observing a series of differences both in the structure of girls' games and "in the actual mentality of little girls," he deemed these differences not of interest because "it was not this contrast which we proposed to study." Girls, Piaget found, "rather complicated our interrogatory in relation to what we know about boys," since the changes in their conception of rules, although following the same sequence observed in boys, did not stand in the same relation to social experience. Nevertheless, he concluded that "in spite of these differences in the structure of the game and apparently in the players' mentality, we find the same process at work as in the evolution of the game of marbles."[2]

Thus, girls were of interest insofar as they were similar to boys and confirmed the generality of Piaget's findings. The differences noted, which included a greater tolerance, a greater tendency toward innovation in solving conflicts, a greater willingness to make exceptions to rules, and a lesser concern with legal elaboration, were not seen as germane to "the psychology of rules," and therefore were regarded as insignificant for the study of children's moral judgment. Given the confusion that currently surrounds the discussion of sex differences in moral judgment, it is important to emphasize that the differences observed by Piaget did not pertain to girls' understanding of rules *per se* or to the development of the idea of justice in their thinking, but rather to the way girls structured their games and their approach to conflict resolution—that is, to their use rather than their understanding of the logic of rules and justice.

Kohlberg, in his research on moral development, did not encounter these problems since he equated moral development with the development of justice reasoning and initially used an all-male sample as the basis for theory and test construction. In response to his critics, Kohlberg has recently modified his claims, renaming his test a measure of "justice reasoning" rather than of "moral maturity" and acknowledging the presence of a care perspective in people's moral thinking.[3] But the widespread use of Kohlberg's measure as a measure of moral development together with his own continuing tendency to equate justice reasoning with moral judgment leaves the problem of orientation differences unsolved. More specifically, Kohlberg's efforts to assimilate thinking about care to the six-stage developmental sequence he derived and refined by analyzing changes in justice reasoning (relying centrally on his all-male longitudinal sample), underscores the continuing importance of the points raised in this paper concerning (1) the distinction between differences in developmental stage within a single orientation and differences in orientation, and (2) the fact that the moral thinking of girls and women was not examined in establishing either the meaning or the measurement of moral judgment within contemporary psychology.

An analysis of the language and logic of men's and women's moral reasoning about a range of hypothetical and real dilemmas underlies the distinction elaborated in this paper between a justice and a care perspective. The empirical association of care reasoning with women suggests that discrepancies observed between moral theory and the moral judgments of girls and women may reflect a shift in perspective, a change in moral orientation. Like the figure–ground shift in ambiguous figure perception, justice and care as moral perspectives are not opposites or mirror-images of one another, with justice uncaring and care unjust. Instead, these perspectives denote different ways of organizing the basic elements of moral judgment: self, others, and the relationship between them. With the shift in perspective from justice to care, the organizing dimension of relationship changes from inequality/equality to attachment/detachment, reorganizing thoughts, feelings and language so that words connoting relationship like "dependence" or "responsibility" or even moral terms such as "fairness" and "care" take on different meanings. To organize relationships in terms of attachment rather than in terms of equality changes the way human connection is imagined, so that the images or metaphors of relationship shift from hierarchy or balance to network or web. In addition, each organizing framework leads to a different way of imagining the self as a moral agent.

From a justice perspective, the self as moral agent stands as the figure against a ground of social relationships, judging the conflicting claims of self and others against a standard of equality or equal respect (the Categorical Imperative, the Golden Rule). From a care perspective, the relationship becomes the figure, defining self and others. Within the context of relationship, the self as a moral agent perceives and responds to the perception of need. The shift in moral perspective is manifest by a change in the moral question from "What is just?" to "How to respond?"

For example, adolescents asked to describe a moral dilemma often speak about peer or family pressure in which case the moral question becomes how to maintain moral principles or standards and resist the influence of one's parents or friends. "I have a right to my religious opinions," one teenager explains, referring to a religious difference with his parents. Yet, he adds, "I respect their views." The same dilemma, however, is also construed by adolescents as a problem of attachment, in which case the moral question becomes: how to respond both to oneself and to one's friends or one's parents, how to maintain or strengthen connection in the face of differences in belief. "I understand their fear of my new religious ideas," one teenager explains, referring to her religious disagreement with her parents, "but they really ought to listen to me and try to understand my beliefs."

One can see these two statements as two versions of essentially the same thing. Both teenagers present self-justifying arguments about religious disagreement; both address the claims of self and of others in a way that honors both. Yet each frames the problem in different terms, and the use of moral language points to different concerns. The first speaker casts the problem in terms of individual rights that must be respected within the relationship. In other words, the figure of the considering is the self looking on the disagreeing selves in relationship, and the aim is to get the other selves to acknowledge the right to disagree. In the case of the second speaker, figure and ground shift. The relationship becomes the figure of the considering, and relationships are seen to require listening and efforts at understanding differences in belief. Rather than the right to disagree, the speaker focuses on caring to hear and to be heard. Attention shifts from the grounds for agreement (rights and respect) to the grounds for understanding (listening and speaking, hearing and being heard). This shift is marked by a change in moral language from the stating of separate claims to rights and respect ("I have a right . . . I respect their views.") to the activities of relationship—the injunction to listen and try to understand ("I understand . . . they ought to listen . . . and try to understand."). The metaphor of moral voice itself carries the terms of the care perspective and reveals how the language chosen for moral theory is not orientation neutral.

The language of the public abortion debate, for example, reveals a justice perspective. Whether the abortion dilemma is cast as a conflict of rights or in terms of respect for human life, the claims of the fetus and of the pregnant woman are balanced or placed in opposition. The morality of abortion decisions thus construed hinges on the scholastic or metaphysical question as to whether the fetus is a life or a person, and whether its claims take precedence over those of the pregnant woman. Framed as a problem of care, the dilemma posed by abortion shifts. The connection between the fetus and the pregnant woman becomes the focus of attention and the question becomes whether it is responsible or irresponsible, caring or careless, to extend or to end this connection. In this construction, the abortion dilemma arises because there is no way not to act, and no way of acting that does not alter the connection between self and others. To ask what actions constitute care or are more caring directs attention to the parameters of connection and the costs of detachment, which become subjects of moral concern.

Finally, two medical students, each reporting a decision not to turn in someone who has violated the school rules against drinking, cast their decision in different terms. One student constructs the decision as an act of mercy, a decision to override justice in light of the fact that the violator has shown "the proper degrees of contrition." In addition, this student raises the question as to whether or not the alcohol policy is just, i.e., whether the school has the right to prohibit drinking. The other student explains the decision not to turn in a proctor who was drinking on the basis that turning him in is not a good way to respond to this problem, since it would dissolve the relationship between them and thus cut off an avenue for help. In addition, this student raises the question as to whether the proctor sees his drinking as a problem.

This example points to an important distinction, between care as understood or construed within a justice framework and care as a framework or a perspective on moral decision. Within a justice construction, care becomes the mercy that tempers justice; or connotes the special obligations or supererogatory duties that arise in personal relationships; or signifies altruism freely chosen—a decision to modulate the strict demands of justice by considering equity or showing forgiveness; or characterizes a choice to sacrifice the claims of the self. All of these interpretations of care leave the basic assumptions of a justice framework intact: the division between the self and others, the logic of reciprocity or equal respect.

As a moral perspective, care is less well elaborated, and there is no ready vocabulary in moral theory to describe its terms. As a framework for moral decision, care is grounded in the assumption that self and other are interdependent, an assumption reflected in a view of action as responsive and, therefore, as arising in relationship rather than the view of action as emanating from within the self and, therefore, "self governed." Seen as responsive, the self is by definition connected to others, responding to perceptions, interpreting events, and governed by the organizing tendencies of human interaction and human language. Within this framework, detachment, whether from self or from others, is morally problematic, since it breeds moral blindness or indifference—a failure to discern or respond to need. The question of what responses constitute care and what responses lead to hurt draws attention to the fact that one's own terms may differ from those of others. Justice in this context becomes understood as respect for people in their own terms.

The medical student's decision not to turn in the proctor for drinking reflects a judgment that turning him in is not the best way to respond to the drinking problem, itself seen as a sign of detachment or lack of concern. Caring for the proctor thus raises the question of what actions are most likely to ameliorate this problem, a decision that leads to the question of what are the proctor's terms.

The shift in organizing perspective here is marked by the fact that the first student does not consider the terms of the other as potentially different but instead assumes one set of terms. Thus the student alone becomes the arbiter of what is *the* proper degree of contribution. The second student, in turn, does not attend to the question of whether the alcohol policy itself is just or fair. Thus each student discusses an aspect of the problem that the other does not mention.

These examples are intended to illustrate two cross-cutting perspectives that do not negate one another but focus attention on different dimensions of the situation, creating a sense of ambiguity around the question of what is the problem to be solved. Systematic research on moral orientation as a dimension of moral judgment and action initially addressed three questions: (1) Do people articulate concerns about justice and concerns about care in discussing a moral dilemma? (2) Do people tend to focus their attention on one set of concerns and minimally represent the other? and (3) Is there an association between moral orientation and gender? Evidence from studies that included a common set of questions about actual experiences of moral conflict and matched samples of males and females provides affirmative answers to all three questions.

When asked to describe a moral conflict they had faced, 55 out of 80 (69 percent) educationally advantaged North American adolescents and adults raised considerations of both justice and care. Two-thirds (54 out of 80) however, focused their attention on one set of concerns, with focus defined as 75 percent or more of the considerations raised pertaining either to justice or to care. Thus the person who presented, say, two care considerations in discussing a moral conflict was more likely to give a third, fourth, and fifth than to balance care and justice concerns—a finding consonant with the assumption that justice and care constitute organizing frameworks for moral decision. The men and the women involved in this study (high school students, college students, medical students, and adult professionals) were equally likely to demonstrate the focus phenomenon (two-thirds of both sexes fell into the outlying focus categories). There were, however, sex differences in the direction of focus. With one exception, all of the men who focused, focused on justice. The women divided, with roughly one third focusing on justice and one third on care.[4]

These findings clarify the different voice phenomenon and its implications for moral theory and for women. First, it is notable that if women were eliminated from the research sample, care focus in moral reasoning would virtually disappear. Although care focus was by no means characteristic of all women, it was almost exclusively a female phenomenon in this sample of educationally advantaged North Americans. Second, the fact that the women were advantaged means that the focus on care cannot readily be attributed to educational deficit or occupational disadvantage—the explanation Kohlberg and others have given for findings of lower levels of justice reasoning in women.[5] Instead, the focus on care in women's moral reasoning draws attention to the limitations of a justice-focused moral theory and highlights the presence of care concerns in the moral thinking of both women and men. In this light, the Care/Justice group composed of one third of the women and one third of the men becomes of particular interest, pointing to the need for further research that attends to the way people organize justice and care in relation to one another—whether, for example, people alternate perspectives, like seeing the rabbit and the duck in the rabbit–duck figure, or integrate the two perspectives in a way that resolves or sustains ambiguity.

Third, if the moral domain is comprised of at least two moral orientations, the focus phenomenon suggests that people have a tendency to lose sight of one moral perspective in arriving at moral decision—a liability equally shared by both sexes. The present findings further suggest that men and women tend to lose sight of different perspectives. The most striking result is the virtual absence of care-focus reasoning among the men. Since the men raised concerns about care in discussing moral conflicts and thus presented care concerns as morally relevant, a question is why they did not elaborate these concerns to a greater extent.

In summary, it becomes clear why attention to women's moral thinking led to the identification of a different voice and raised questions about the place of justice and care within a comprehensive moral theory. It also is clear how the selection of an all-male sample for research on moral judgment fosters an equation of morality with justice, providing little data discrepant with this view. In the present study, data discrepant with a justice-focused moral theory comes from a third of the women. Previously, such women were seen as having a problem understanding "morality." Yet these women may also be seen as exposing the problem in a justice-focused moral theory. This may explain the decision of researchers to exclude girls and women at the initial stage of moral judgment research. If one begins with the premise that "all morality consists in respect for rules,"[6] or "virtue is one and its name is justice,"[7] then women are likely to appear problematic within moral theory. If one begins with women's moral judgments, the problem becomes how to construct a theory that encompasses care as a focus of moral attention rather than as a subsidiary moral concern.

The implications of moral orientation for moral theory and for research on moral development are extended by a study designed and conducted by Kay Johnston.[8] Johnston set out to explore the relationship between moral orientation and problem-solving strategies, creating a standard method using fables for assessing spontaneous moral orientation and orientation preference. She asked 60 eleven- and fifteen-year-olds to state and to solve the moral problem posed by the fable. Then she asked: "Is there another way to solve this problem?" Most of the children initially constructed the fable problems either in terms of justice or in terms of care; either they stood back from the situation and appealed to a rule or principle for adjudicating the conflicting claims or they entered the situation in an effort to discover or create a way of responding to all of the needs. About half of the children, slightly more fifteen- than eleven-year-olds, spontaneously switched moral orientation when asked whether there was another way to solve the problem. Others did so following an interviewer's cue as to the form such a switch might take. Finally, the children were asked which of the solutions they described was the best solution. Most of the children answered the question and explained why one way was preferable.

Johnston found gender differences parallel to those previously reported, with boys more often spontaneously using and preferring justice solutions and girls more often spontaneously using and preferring care solutions. In addition, she found differences between the two fables she used, confirming Langdale's finding that moral orientation is associated both with the gender of the reasoner and with the dilemma considered.[9] Finally, the fact that children, at least by the age of eleven, are able to shift moral orientation and can explain the logic of two moral perspectives, each associated with a different problem-solving strategy, heightens the analogy to ambiguous figure perception and further supports the conception of justice and care as organizing frameworks for moral decision.

The demonstration that children know both orientations and can frame and solve moral problems in at least two different ways means that the choice of moral standpoint is an element of moral decision. The role of the self in moral judgment thus includes the choice of moral standpoint, and this decision, whether implicit or explicit, may become linked with self-respect and self-definition. Especially in adolescence when choice becomes more self-conscious and self-reflective, moral standpoint may become entwined with identity and self-esteem. Johnston's finding that spontaneous moral orientation and preferred orientation are not always the same raises a number of questions as to why and under what conditions a person may adopt a problem-solving strategy that he or she sees as not the best way to solve the problem.

The way people chose to frame or solve a moral problem is clearly not the only way in which they can think about the problem, and is not necessarily the way they deem preferable. Moral judgments thus do not reveal *the* structure of moral thinking, since there are at least two ways in which people can structure moral problems. Johnston's demonstration of orientation-switch poses a serious challenge to the methods that have been used in moral judgment and moral development research, introducing a major interpretive caution. The fact that boys and girls at eleven and fifteen understand and distinguish the logics of justice and care reasoning directs attention to the origins and the development of both ways of thinking. In addition, the tendency for boys and girls to use and prefer different orientations when solving the same problem raises a number of questions about the relationship between these orientations and the factors influencing their representation. The different patterns of orientation use and preference, as well as the different conceptions of justice and of care implied or elaborated in the fable judgments, suggest that moral development cannot be mapped along a single linear stage sequence.

One way of explaining these findings, suggested by Johnston, joins Vygotsky's theory of cognitive development with Chodorow's analysis of sex differences in early childhood experiences of relationship.[10] Vygotsky posits that all of the higher cognitive functions originate as actual relations between individuals. Justice and care as moral ideas and as reasoning strategies thus would originate as relationships with others—an idea consonant with the derivation of justice and care reasoning from experiences of inequality and attachment in early childhood. All children are born into a situation of inequality in that they are less capable than the adults and older children around them and, in this sense, more helpless and less powerful. In addition, no child survives in the absence of some kind of adult attachment—or care, and through this experience of relationship children discover the responsiveness of human connection including their ability to move and affect one another.

Through the experience of inequality, of being in the less powerful position, children learn what it means to depend on the authority and the good will of others. As a result, they tend to strive for equality of greater power, and for freedom. Through the experience of attachment, children discover the ways in which people are able to care for and to hurt one another. The child's vulnerability to oppression and to abandonment thus can be seen to lay the groundwork for the moral visions of justice and care, conceived as ideals of human relationship and defining the ways in which people "should" act toward one another.

Chodorow's work then provides a way of explaining why care concerns tend to be minimally represented by men and why such concerns are less frequently elaborated in moral theory. Chodorow joins the dynamics of gender identity formation (the identification of oneself as male or female) to an analysis of early childhood relationships and examines the effects of maternal child care on the inner structuring of self in relation to others. Further, she differentiates a positional sense of self from a personal sense of self, contrasting a self defined in terms of role or position from a self known through the experience of connection. Her point is that maternal child care fosters the continuation of a relational sense of self in girls, since female gender identity is consonant with feeling connected with one's mother. For boys, gender identity is in tension with mother–child connection, unless that connection is structured in terms of sexual opposition (e.g., as an Oedipal drama). Thus, although boys experience responsiveness or care in relationships, knowledge of care or the need for care, when associated with mothers, poses a threat to masculine identity.[11]

Chodorow's work is limited by her reliance on object relations theory and problematic on that count. Object relations theory ties the formation of the self to the experience of separation, joining separation with individuation and thus counterposing the experience of self to the experience of connection with others. This is the line that Chodorow traces in explicating male development. Within this framework, girls' connections with their mothers can only be seen as problematic. Connection with others or the capacity to feel and think *with* others is, by definition, in tension with self-development when self-development or individuation is linked to separation. Thus, object-relations theory sustains a series of oppositions that have been central in Western thought and moral theory, including the opposition between thought and feelings, self and relationship, reason and compassion, justice and love. Object relations theory also continues the conventional division of psychological labor between women and men. Since the idea of a self, experienced in the context of attachment with others, is theoretically impossible, mothers, described as objects, are viewed as selfless, without a self. This view is essentially problematic for women, divorcing the activity of mothering from desire, knowledge, and agency, and implying that insofar as a mother experiences herself as a subject rather than as an object (a mirror reflecting her child), she is "selfish" and not a good mother. Winnicott's phrase "good-enough mother" represents an effort to temper this judgment.

Thus, psychologists and philosophers, aligning the self and morality with separation and autonomy—the ability to be self-governing—have associated care with self-sacrifice, or with feelings—a view at odds with the current position that care represents a way of knowing and a coherent moral perspective. This position, however, is well represented in literature written by women. For example the short story "A Jury of Her Peers," written by Susan Glaspell in 1917, a time when women ordinarily did not serve on juries, contrasts two ways of knowing that underlie two ways of interpreting and solving a crime.[12] The story centers on a murder; Minnie Foster is suspected of killing her husband.

A neighbor woman and the sheriff's wife accompany the sheriff and the prosecutor to the house of the accused woman. The men, representing the law, seek evidence that will convince a jury to convict the suspect. The women, collecting things to bring Minnie Foster in jail, enter in this way into the lives lived in the house. Taking in rather than taking apart, they begin to assemble observations and impressions, connecting them to past experience and observations until suddenly they compose a familiar pattern, like the log-cabin pattern they recognize in the quilt Minnie Foster was making. "Why do we *know*—what we know this minute?" one woman asks the other, but she also offers the following explanation:

> We live close together, and we live far apart. We all go through the same things—it's all just a different kind of the same thing! If it weren't—why do you and I *understand*.[13]

The activity of quilt-making—collecting odd scraps and piecing them together until they form a pattern—becomes the metaphor for this way of knowing. Discovering a strangled canary buried under pieces of quilting, the women make a series of connections that lead them to understand what happened.

The logic that says you don't kill a man because he has killed a bird, the judgment that finds these acts wildly incommensurate, is counterposed to the logic that sees both events as part of a larger pattern—a pattern of detachment and abandonment that led finally to the strangling. "I *wish* I'd come over here once in a while," Mrs. Hale, the neighbor, exclaims. "That was a crime! Who's going to punish that?" Mrs. Peters, the sheriff's wife, recalls that when she was a girl and a boy killed her cat, "If they hadn't held me back I would have—" and realizes that there had been no one to restrain Minnie Foster. John Foster was known as "a good man . . . He didn't drink, and he kept his word as well as most, I guess, and paid his debts." But he also was "a hard man," Mrs. Hale explains, "like a raw wind that gets to the bone."

Seeing detachment as the crime with murder as its ultimate extension, implicating themselves and also seeing the connection between their own and Minnie Foster's actions, the women solve the crime by attachment—by joining together, like the "knotting" that joins pieces of a quilt. In the decision to remove rather than to reveal the evidence, they separate themselves from a legal system in which they have no voice but also no way of voicing what they have come to understand. In choosing to connect themselves with one another and with Minnie, they separate themselves from the law that would use their understanding and their knowledge as grounds for further separation and killing.

In a law school class where a film-version of this story was shown, the students were divided in their assessment of the moral problem and in their evaluation of the various characters and actions. Some focused on the murder, the strangling of the husband. Some focused on the evidence of abandonment or indifference to others. Responses to a questionnaire showed a bi-modal distribution, indicating two ways of viewing the film. These different perspectives led to different ways of evaluating both the act of murder and the women's decision to remove the evidence. Responses to the film were not aligned with the sex of the viewer in an absolute way, thus dispelling any implication of biological determinism or of a stark division between the way women and men know or judge events. The knowledge gained inductively by the women in the film, however, was also gained more readily by women watching the film, who came in this way to see a logic in the women's actions and to articulate a rationale for their silence.

The analogy to ambiguous figure perception is useful here in several ways. First, it suggests that people can see a situation in more than one way, and even alternate ways of seeing, combining them without reducing them—like designating the rabbit–duck figure both duck and rabbit. Second, the analogy argues against the tendency to construe justice and care as opposites or mirror-images and also against the implication that these two perspectives are readily integrated or fused. The ambiguous figure directs attention to the way in which a change in perspective can reorganize perception and change understanding, without implying an underlying reality or pure form. What makes seeing both moral perspectives so difficult is precisely that the orientations are not opposites nor mirror images or better and worse representations of a single moral truth. The terms of one perspective do not contain the terms of the other. Instead, a shift in orientation denotes a restructuring of moral perception, changing the meaning of moral language and thus the definition of moral conflict and moral action. For example, detachment is considered the hallmark of mature moral thinking within a justice perspective, signifying the ability to judge dispassionately, to weigh evidence in an even-handed manner, balancing the claims of others and self. From a care perspective, detachment is *the* moral problem.

> "I could've come," retorted Mrs. Hale. . ."I wish I had come over to see Minnie Foster sometimes. I can see now . . . If there had been years and years of—nothing, then a bird to sing to you, it would be awful—still—after the bird was still . . . . I know what stillness is."

The difference between agreement and understanding captures the different logics of justice and care reasoning, one seeking grounds for agreement, one seeking grounds for understanding, one assuming separation and thus the need for some external structure of connection, one assuming connection and thus the potential for understanding. These assumptions run deep, generating and reflecting different views of human nature and the human condition. They also point to different vulnerabilities and different sources of error. The potential error in justice reasoning lies in its latent egocentrism, the tendency to confuse one's perspective with an objective standpoint or truth, the temptation to define others in one's own terms by putting oneself in their place. The potential error in care reasoning lies in the tendency to forget that one has terms, creating a tendency to enter into another's perspective and to see oneself as "selfless" by defining oneself in other's terms. These two types of error underlie two common equations that signify distortions or deformations of justice and care: the equation of human with male, unjust in its omission of women; and the equation of care with self-sacrifice, uncaring in its failure to represent the activity and the agency of care.

The equation of human with male was assumed in the Platonic and in the Enlightenment tradition as well as by psychologists who saw all-male samples as "representative" of human experience. The equation of care with self-sacrifice is in some ways more complex. The premise of self-interest assumes a conflict of interest between self and other manifest in the opposition of egoism and altruism. Together, the equations of male with human and of care with self-sacrifice form a circle that has had a powerful hold on moral philosophy and psychology. The conjunction of women and moral theory thus challenges the traditional definition of human and calls for a reconsideration of what is meant by both justice and care.

To trace moral development along two distinct although intersecting dimensions of relationship suggests the possibility of different permutations of justice and care reasoning, different ways these two moral perspectives can be understood and represented in relation to one another. For example, one perspective may overshadow or eclipse the other, so that one is brightly illuminated while the other is dimly remembered, familiar but for the most part forgotten. The way in which one story about relationship obscures another was evident in high-school girls' definitions of dependence. These definitions highlighted two meanings—one arising from the opposition between dependence and independence, and one from the opposition of dependence to isolation ("No woman," one student observed, "is an island.") As the word "dependence" connotes the experience of relationship, this shift in the implied opposite of dependence indicates how the valence of relationship changes, when connection with others is experienced as an impediment to autonomy or independence, and when it is experienced as a source of comfort and pleasure, and a protection against isolation. This essential ambivalence of human connection provides a powerful emotional grounding for two moral perspectives, and also may indicate what is at stake in the effort to reduce morality to a single perspective.

It is easy to understand the ascendance of justice reasoning and of justice-focused moral theories in a society where care is associated with personal vulnerability in the form of economic disadvantage. But another way of thinking about the ascendance of justice reasoning and also about sex differences in moral development is suggested in the novel *Masks*, written by Fumiko Enchi, a Japanese woman.[14] The subject is spirit possession, and the novel dramatizes what it means to be possessed by the spirits of others. Writing about the Rokujo lady in the *Tales of Genji*, Enchi's central character notes that:

> Her soul alternates uncertainly between lyricism and spirit possession, making no philosophical distinction between the self alone and in relation to others, and is unable to achieve the solace of a religious indifference.[15]

The option of transcendence, of a religious indifference or a philosophical detachment, may be less available to women because women are more likely to be possessed by the spirits and the stories of others. The strength of women's moral perceptions lies in the refusal of detachment and depersonalization, and insistence on making connections that can lead to seeing the person killed in war or living in poverty as someone's son or father or brother or sister, or mother, or daughter, or friend. But the liability of women's development is also underscored by Enchi's novel in that women, possessed by the spirits of others, also are more likely to be caught in a chain of false attachments. If women are at the present time the custodians of a story about human attachment and interdependence, not only within the family but also in the world at large, then questions arise as to how this story can be kept alive and how moral theory can sustain this story. In this sense, the relationship between women and moral theory itself becomes one of interdependence.

By rendering a care perspective more coherent and making its terms explicit, moral theory may facilitate women's ability to speak about their experiences and perceptions and may foster the ability of others to listen and to understand. At the same time, the evidence of care focus in women's moral thinking suggests that the study of women's development may provide a natural history of moral development in which care is ascendant, revealing the ways in which creating and sustaining responsive connection with others becomes or remains a central moral concern. The promise in joining women and moral theory lies in the fact that human survival, in the late twentieth century, may depend less on formal agreement than on human connection.

NOTES

1. Gilligan, C. (1977). "In a Different Voice: Women's Conceptions of Self and of Morality." *Harvard Educational Review* 47 (1982):481–517; *In a Different Voice: Psychological Theory and Women's Development.* Cambridge, Mass.: Harvard University Press.
2. Piaget, J. (1965). *The Moral Judgment of the Child.* New York, N.Y.: The Free Press Paperback Edition, pp. 76–84.
3. Kohlberg, L. (1984). *The Psychology of Moral Development.* San Francisco, Calif.: Harper & Row, Publishers, Inc.
4. Gilligan, C. and J. Attanucci. (1986). *Two Moral Orientations.* Harvard University, unpublished manuscript.
5. See Kohlberg, L. *op. cit.,* also Walker, L. (1984). "Sex Differences in the Development of Moral Reasoning: A Critical Review of the Literature." *Child Development* 55 (3):677–91.
6. Piaget, J., *op. cit.*
7. Kohlberg, L., *op. cit.*
8. Johnston, K. (1985). *Two Moral Orientations—Two Problem-solving Strategies: Adolescents' Solutions to Dilemmas in Fables.* Harvard University, unpublished doctoral dissertation.
9. Langdale, C. (1983). *Moral Orientation and Moral Development: The Analysis of Care and Justice Reasoning Across Different Dilemmas in Females and Males from Childhood through Adulthood.* Harvard University, unpublished doctoral dissertation.
10. Johnston, K., *op. cit.;* Vygotsky, L. (1978). *Mind in Society.* Cambridge, Mass.: Harvard University Press; Chodorow, N. (1974). "Family Structure and Feminine Personality" in *Women, Culture and Society,* L.M. Rosaldo and L. Lamphere, eds., Stanford, Calif.: Stanford University Press; see also Chodorow, N. (1978). *The Reproduction of Mothering: Psychoanalysis and the Sociology of Gender.* Berkeley, Calif.: University of California Press.
11. Chodorow, N., *op. cit.*
12. Glaspell, S. (1927). *A Jury of Her Peers.* London: E. Benn.
13. *Ibid.*
14. Fumiko, E. (1983). *Masks.* New York: Random House.
15. *Ibid.* p. 54.

Beyond Caring: The De-Moralization of Gender

Marilyn Friedman

Marilyn Friedman is a professor of philosophy at Washington University in St. Louis. Her emphasis is on feminist theory and social philosophy. Friedman is the author of What Are Friends For? Essays in Feminism, Personal Relationships, and Moral Theory *(1993).*

Friedman addresses the assertion in the writings of Carol Gilligan, among others, that a dichotomy exists between the justice and care perspectives. Friedman argues that care and justice overlap more than has been realized. She suggests that in order for the care perspective to be morally adequate, concerns of justice must be integrated within it. Friedman argues that justice is a manner of ensuring that people are treated fairly and according to what they are entitled to. In this way, adequate care must involve justice. Friedman argues that in practice, the moral problems that fall under the two categories of care and justice do not necessarily mandate distinct moral perspectives. Indeed, neither perspective taken alone will result in an appropriate standpoint for dealing with moral problems in practice.

Carol Gilligan heard a "distinct moral language" in the voices of women who were subjects in her studies of moral reasoning.[1] Though herself a developmental psychologist, Gilligan has put her mark on contemporary feminist moral philosophy by daring to claim the competence of this voice and the worth of its message. Her book, *In a Different Voice*, which one theorist has aptly described as a bestseller,[2] explored the concern with care and relationships which Gilligan discerned in the moral reasoning of women and contrasted it with the orientation toward justice and rights which she found to typify the moral reasoning of men.

According to Gilligan, the standard (or "male") moral voice articulated in moral psychology derives moral judgments about particular cases from abstract, universalized moral rules and principles which are substantively concerned with justice and rights. For justice reasoners: the major moral imperative enjoins respect for the rights of others (100); the concept of duty is limited to reciprocal noninterference (147); the motivating vision is one of the equal worth of self and other (63); and one important underlying presupposition is a highly individuated conception of persons.

By contrast, the other (or "female") moral voice which Gilligan heard in her studies

Reprinted with permission of *Canadian Journal of Philosophy* and Marilyn Friedman, from *Science, Morality, and Feminist Theory,* edited by M. Haner and K. Nielsen, *Canadian Journal of Philosophy, Supp. Vol. 13,* 1987, pp. 87–105. [Edited]

eschews abstract rules and principles. This moral voice derives moral judgments from the contextual detail of situations grasped as specific and unique (100). The substantive concern for this moral voice is care and responsibility, particularly as these arise in the context of interpersonal relationships (19). Moral judgments, for care reasoners, are tied to feelings of empathy and compassion (69); the major moral imperatives center around caring, not hurting others, and avoiding selfishness (90); and the motivating vision of this ethic is "that everyone will be responded to and included, that no one will be left alone or hurt" (63).

While these two voices are not necessarily contradictory in all respects, they seem, at the very least, to be different in their orientation. Gilligan's writings about the differences have stimulated extensive feminist reconsideration of various ethical themes.[3] In this paper, I use Gilligan's work as a springboard for extending certain of those themes in new directions . . . I will explore a different reason why actual women and men may not show a divergence of reasoning along the care–justice dichotomy, namely, that the notions of care and justice overlap more than Gilligan, among others, has realized. I will suggest, in particular, that morally adequate care involves considerations of justice. Thus, the concerns captured by these two moral categories do not define necessarily distinct moral perspectives, in practice. . . . People who treat each other justly can also care about each other. Conversely, personal relationships are arenas in which people have rights to certain forms of treatment, and in which fairness can be reflected in ongoing interpersonal mutuality. It is this latter insight—the relevance of justice to close personal relationships—which I will emphasize here.

Justice, at the most general level, is a matter of giving people their due, of treating them appropriately. Justice is relevant to personal relationships and to care precisely to the extent that considerations of justice itself determine appropriate ways to treat friends or intimates. Justice as it bears on relationships among friends or family, or on other close personal ties, might not involve duties which are universalizable, in the sense of being owed to all persons simply in virtue of shared moral personhood. But this does not entail the irrelevance of justice among friends or intimates.

Moral thinking has not always dissociated the domain of justice from that of close personal relationships. The earliest Greek code of justice placed friendship at the forefront of conditions for the realization of justice, and construed the rules of justice as being coextensive with the limits of friendship. The reader will recall that one of the first definitions of justice which Plato sought to contest, in the *Republic*, is that of "helping one's friends and harming one's enemies."[4] Although the ancient Greek model of justice among friends reserved that moral privilege for free-born Greek males, the conception is, nevertheless, instructive for its readiness to link the notion of justice to relationships based on affection and loyalty. This provides an important contrast to modern notions of justice which are often deliberately constructed so as to avoid presumptions of mutual concern on the parts of those to whom the conception is to apply.

As is well known, John Rawls, for one, requires that the parties to the original position in which justice is to be negotiated be mutually disinterested.[5] Each party is assumed, first and foremost, to be concerned for the advancement of her own interests, and to care about the interests of others only to the extent that her own interests require it. This postulate of mutual disinterestedness is intended by Rawls to ensure that the principles of justice do not depend on what he calls "strong assumptions," such as "extensive ties of natural sentiment."[6] Rawls is seeking principles of justice which apply to everyone in all their social interrelationships, *whether or not* characterized by affection and a concern for each other's well-being. While such an account promises to disclose duties of justice owed to all other parties to the social contract, it may fail to uncover *special* duties of justice which arise in close personal relationships the foundation of which is affection or kinship, rather than contract. The methodological device of assuming mutual disinterest might blind us to the role of justice among mutually interested and/or intimate parties.

Gilligan herself has suggested that mature reasoning about care incorporates considerations of justice and rights. But Gilligan's conception of what this means is highly limited. It appears to involve simply the recognition "that self and other are equal," a notion which serves to override the problematic tendency of the ethic of care to become *self-sacrificing* care in women's practices. However, important as it may be, this notion hardly does justice to justice.

There are several ways in which justice pertains to close personal relationships. The first two ways which I will mention are largely appropriate only among friends, relatives, or intimates who are of comparable development in their realization of moral personhood, for example, who are both mature responsible adults. The third sort of relevance of justice to close relationships, which I will discuss shortly, pertains to families, in which adults often interrelate with children—a more challenging domain for the application of justice. But first the easier task.

One sort of role for justice in close relationships among people of comparable moral personhood may be discerned by considering that a personal relationship is a miniature social system, which provides valued mutual intimacy, support, and concern for those who are involved. The maintenance of a relationship requires effort by the participants. One intimate may bear a much greater burden for sustaining a relationship than the other participant(s) and may derive less support, concern, and so forth than she deserves for her efforts. Justice sets a constraint on such relationships by calling for an appropriate sharing, among the participants, of the benefits and burdens which constitute their relationship.

Marilyn Frye, for example, has discussed what amounts to a pattern of *violation* of this requirement of justice in heterosexual relationships. She has argued that women of all races, social classes, and societies can be defined as a coherent group in terms of a distinctive function which is culturally assigned to them. This function is, in Frye's words, "the service of men and men's interests as men define them."[7] This service work includes personal service (satisfaction of routine bodily needs, such as hunger, and other mundane tasks), sexual and reproductive service, and ego service. Says Frye, ". . . at every race/class level and even across race/class lines men do not serve women as women serve men."[8] Frye is, of course, generalizing over society and culture, and the sweep of her generalization encompasses both ongoing close personal relationships as well as other relationships which are not close or are not carried on beyond specific transactions, for example, that of prostitute to client. By excluding those latter cases for the time being, and applying Frye's analysis to familial and other close ties between women and men, we may discern the sort of one-sided relational exploitation, often masquerading in the guise of love or care, which constitutes this first sort of injustice.

Justice is relevant to close personal relationships among comparable moral persons in a second way as well. The trust and intimacy which characterize special relationships create special vulnerabilities to harm. Commonly recognized harms, such as physical injury and sexual assault, become more feasible; and special relationships, in corrupt, abusive, or degenerate forms, make possible certain uncommon emotional harms not even possible in impersonal relationships. When someone is harmed in a personal relationship, she is owed a rectification of some sort, a righting of the wrong which has been done her. The notion of justice emerges, once again, as a relevant moral notion.

Thus, in a close relationship among persons of comparable moral personhood, care may degenerate into the injustices of exploitation, or oppression. Many such problems have been given wide public scrutiny recently as a result of feminist analysis of various aspects of family life and sexual relationships. Woman-battering, acquaintance rape, and sexual harassment are but a few of the many recently publicized injustices of "personal" life. The notion of distributive or corrective injustice seems almost too mild to capture these indignities, involving, as they do, violation of bodily integrity and an assumption of the right to assault and injure. But to call these harms injustices is certainly not to rule out impassioned moral criticism in other terms as well.

The two requirements of justice which I have just discussed exemplify the standard distinction between distributive and corrective justice. They illustrate the role of justice in personal relationships regarded in abstraction from a social context. Personal relationships may also be regarded in the context of their various institutional settings, such as marriage and family. Here justice emerges again as a relevant ideal, its role being to define appropriate institutions to structure interactions among family members, other household cohabitants, and intimates in general. The family, for example,[9] is a miniature society, exhibiting all the major facets of large-scale social life: decision-making affecting the whole unit; executive action; judgments of guilt and innocence; reward and punishment; allocation of responsibilities and privileges, of burdens and benefits; and monumental influences on the life-chances of both its maturing and its matured members. Any of these features *alone* would invoke the relevance of justice; together, they make the case overwhelming.

Women's historically paradigmatic role of mothering has provided a multitude of insights which can be reconstructed as insights about the importance of justice in family relationships, especially those relationships involving remarkable disparities in maturity, capability, and power.[10] In these familial relationships, one party grows into moral personhood over time, gradually acquiring the capacity to be a responsible moral agent. Considerations of justice pertain to the mothering of children in numerous ways. For one thing, there may be siblings to deal with, whose demands and conflicts create the context for parental arbitration and the need for a fair allotment of responsibilities and privileges. Then there are decisions to be made, involving the well-being of all persons in the family unit, whose immature members become increasingly capable over time of participating in such administrative affairs. Of special importance in the practice of raising children are the duties to nurture and to promote growth and maturation. These duties may be seen as counterparts to the welfare rights viewed by many as a matter of social justice.[11] Motherhood continually presents its practitioners with moral problems best seen in terms of a complex framework which integrates justice with care, even though the politico-legal discourse of justice has not shaped its domestic expression.[12]

I have been discussing the relevance of justice to close personal relationships. A few words about my companion thesis—the relevance of care to the public domain—is also in order.[13] In its more noble manifestation, care in the public realm would show itself, perhaps, in foreign aid, welfare programs, famine or disaster relief, or other social programs designed to relieve suffering and attend to human needs. If untempered by justice in the public domain, care degenerates precipitously. The infamous "boss" of Chicago's old-time Democratic machine, Mayor Richard J. Daley, was legendary for his nepotism and political partisanship; he cared extravagantly for his relatives, friends, and political cronies.[14]

In recounting the moral reasoning of one of her research subjects, Gilligan once wrote that the "justice" perspective fails "to take into account the reality of relationships" (147). What she meant is that the "justice" perspective emphasizes a self's various rights to noninterference by others. Gilligan worried that if this is all that a concern for justice involved, then such a perspective would disregard the moral value of positive interaction, connection, and commitment among persons.

However, Gilligan's interpretation of justice is far too limited. For one thing, it fails to recognize positive rights, such as welfare rights, which may be endorsed from a "justice" perspective. But beyond this minor point, a more important problem is Gilligan's failure to acknowledge the potential for *violence and harm* in human interrelationships and human community.[15] The concept of justice, in general, arises out of relational conditions in which most human beings have the capacity, and many have the inclination, to treat each other badly.

Thus, notions of distributive justice are impelled by the realization that people who together comprise a social system may not share fairly in the benefits and burdens of their social cooperation. Conceptions of rectificatory, or corrective, justice are founded on the concern that when harms are done, action should be taken either to restore those harmed as fully as possible to their previous state, or to prevent further similar harm, or both. And the specific rights which people are variously thought to have are just so many manifestations of our interest in identifying ways in which people deserve protection against harm by others. The complex reality of social life encompasses the human potential for helping, caring for, and nurturing others *as well as* the potential for harming, exploiting, and oppressing others. Thus, Gilligan is wrong to think that the justice perspective completely neglects "the reality of relationships." Rather, it arises from a more complex, and more realistic, estimate of the nature of human interrelationship.

In light of these reflections, it seems wise both to reconsider the seeming dichotomy of care and justice, and to question the moral adequacy of either orientation dissociated from the other. Our aim would be to advance "beyond caring," that is, beyond *mere* caring dissociated from a concern for justice. In addition, we would do well to progress beyond gender stereotypes which assign distinct and different moral roles to women and men. Our ultimate goal should be a non-gendered, non-dichotomized, moral framework in which all moral concerns could be expressed. We might, with intentional irony, call this project, "de-moralizing the genders."

NOTES

1. *In a Different Voice* (Cambridge, MA: Harvard University Press 1982), 73. More recently, the following works by Gilligan on related issues have also appeared: "Do the Social Sciences Have an Adequate Theory of Moral Development?" in Norma Haan, Robert N. Bellah, Paul Rabinow and William M. Sullivan, eds., *Social Science as Moral*

Inquiry (New York: Columbia University Press 1983), 33–51; "Reply," Signs 11 (1986), 324–33; and "Remapping the Moral Domain: New Images of the Self in Relationship," in Thomas C. Heller, Morton Sosna and David E. Wellberry, eds., *Reconstructing Individualism* (Stanford, CA: Stanford University Press 1986) 237–52. Throughout this paper, all page references inserted in the text are to *In a Different Voice*.

2. Frigga Haug, "Morals Also Have Two Genders," trans. Rodney Livingstone, *New Left Review* 143 (1984), 55.
3. These sources include: Owen J. Flanagan, Jr. and Jonathan E. Adler, "Impartiality and Particularity," *Social Research* 50 (1983), 576–96; Nel Noddings, *Caring* (Berkeley: University of California Press 1984); Claudia Card, "Virtues and Moral Luck" (unpublished paper presented at American Philosophical Association, Western Division Meetings, Chicago, IL, April 1985, and at the Conference on Virtue Theory, University of San Diego, San Diego, CA, February 1986); Marilyn Friedman, *Care and Context in Moral Reasoning*, MOSAIC Monograph #1 (Bath, England: University of Bath 1985), reprinted in Carol Harding, ed., *Moral Dilemmas* (Chicago: Precedent 1986), 25–42, and in Diana T. Meyers and Eva Feder Kittay, eds., *Women and Moral Theory* (Totowa, NJ: Rowman and Littlefield 1987), 190–204; all the papers in Meyers and Kittay; Linda K. Kerber, "Some Cautionary Words for Historians," *Signs* 11 (1986), 304–10; Catherine G. Greeno and Eleanor E. Maccoby, "How Different is the "Different Voice," *Signs* 11 (1986), 310-16; Zella Luria, "A Methodological Critique," *Signs* 11 (1986), 316-21; Carol B. Stack, "The Culture of Gender: Women and Men of Color," *Signs* 11 (1986), 321–4; Owen Flanagan and Kathryn Jackson, "Justice, Care, and Gender: The Kohlberg-Gilligan Debate Revisited," *Ethics* 97 (1987), 622–37. An analysis of this issue from an ambiguously feminist standpoint is to be found in: John M. Broughton, "Women's Rationality and Men's Virtues," *Social Research* 50 (1983), 597–642. For a helpful review of some of these issues, cf. Jean Grimshaw, *Philosophy and Feminist Thinking* (Minneapolis: University of Minnesota Press 1986), esp. chs. 7 and 8.
4. Book 1, 322–35. A thorough discussion of the Greek conception of justice in the context of friendship can be found in Horst Hutter, *Politics as Friendship* (Waterloo, ON: Wilfrid Laurier University Press 1978).
5. Rawls, *A Theory of Justice*, 13 and elsewhere.
6. Ibid., 129.
7. *The Politics of Reality* (Trumansburg, NY: The Crossing Press 1983) 9.
8. Ibid., 10.
9. For an important discussion of the relevance of justice to the family, cf. Susan Moller Okin, "Justice and Gender," *Philosophy and Public Affairs* 16 (1987), 42–72.
10. For insightful discussions of the distinctive modes of thought to which mothering gives rise, cf. Sara Ruddick, "Maternal Thinking," *Feminist Studies* 6 (1980) 342–67; and her "Preservative Love and Military Destruction: Some Reflections on Mothering and Peace," in Joyce Trebilcot, ed., *Mothering: Essays in Feminist Theory* (Totowa, NJ: Rowman & Allanheld 1983) 231–62; also Virginia Held, "The Obligations of Mothers and Fathers," in Trebilcot, ed. 7–20.
11. This point was suggested to me by L.W. Sumner.
12. John Broughton also discusses the concern for justice and rights which appears in women's moral reasoning as well as the concern for care and relationships featured in men's moral reasoning; "Women's Rationality and Men's Virtues," esp. 603–22. For a historical discussion of male theorists who have failed to hear the concern for justice in women's voices, cf. Carole Pateman, "'The Disorder of Women': Women, Love, and the Sense of Justice," *Ethics* 91 (1980), 20–34.
13. This discussion owes a debt to Francesca M. Cancian's warning that we should not narrow our conception of love to the recognized ways in which women love, which researchers find to center around the expression of feelings and verbal disclosure. Such a conception ignores forms of love which are stereotyped as characteristically male, including instrumental help and the sharing of activities. Cf. "The Feminization of Love," *Signs* 11 (1986), 692–709.
14. Cf. Mike Royko, *Boss: Richard J. Daley of Chicago* (New York: New American Library 1971).
15. Claudia Card has critiqued Gilligan's work for ignoring, in particular, the dismaying harms to which women have historically been subjected in heterosexual relationships, including, but by no means limited to, marriage ("Virtues and Moral Luck," 15–17).

Fathers Shouldn't Try to Be Mothers

Bruno Bettelheim

Bruno Bettelheim was a psychoanalyst and taught for many years in the Department of Education at the University of Chicago. He wrote 15 books, including Love is Not Enough *(1950),* Dialogues with Mothers *(1962),* and A Good Enough Parent *(1987).*

Bettelheim addresses the father's role in parenting in traditional families. He argues that it is a mistake for fathers to participate as much in infant care as mothers. Male physiology and psychology aren't adapted to the task of childrearing. Furthermore, he states, a woman's fulfillment is through motherhood, while a man's fulfillment is not through fatherhood, but through his moral, economic, and political *role in society. He warns that if both parents try to do both roles, the child will be denied security.*

What is Father's job? What should he stand for in his children's eyes?

Once the answers were quite clear. Today they're not so simple.

A very popular German verse goes: "It's as easy to become a father as it is difficult to be one." And this is said of the German father, who was at all times master of the house, whose word was law for wife and children. If being a father was difficult for him, how much more tenuous is the modern American father's position!

Being one myself and having had intimate experience with the inner feelings of many other fathers, I know of the confusion and utter bafflement which the modern father often feels. He does more for his children and with them, than his father did. Nevertheless, instead of feeling more of a father he feels less so. Nor are matters helped much by the many comic strips, radio and TV programs that either frankly ridicule fathers or depict them as silly boys. These things are not only damaging to the way his wife and children see the father, but also to the way he sees himself.

In the old-fashioned family the father, through his work, provided for the family's physical existence and, he hoped, its emotional well-being. He set an example for standards of behavior and enforced them. He was the protector and the breadwinner—in a time when the bread was harder to win and the family knew it.

Nowadays, with earning and living conditions improved, most children know no fear of want. This security, desirable as it is in itself, tends to obscure the importance of a father's contribution both in his own eyes and in those of his children. Though well aware himself of how hard he works, he no longer finds the recognition at home that used to be the reward of his efforts.

This is not all. When the father comes home and is tacitly expected (or openly asked) to take over the care of the children; when he is received with an account of what went wrong during the day, as if nothing could possibly have gone wrong during his day at work; or with the request to do things around the house—the impression is conveyed to the child that he has been more or less loafing all day and Mother now expects him to start on the serious tasks. That the father accepts this as the right order of things supports other notions the child gets from his storybooks and primers where the father's work, if depicted at all, is with rare and laudable exceptions shown as easy pleasure. The text sometimes says he is hardworking but the pictures which make a much deeper impression on the child, don't show it. The storybook farmers or mail carriers hardly ever work in sleet or rain, nor does sweat run down their foreheads or soak their shirts though the sun burns down strongly. There are never work accidents or any layoffs.

Furthermore, whether or not the father was a good provider used not to be questioned in the child's mind. If he did not provide as much as he might, the child probably did not know it. Nowadays all this is changed. The mass media see to that. They harass the child with how desirable it is to have a new car or dishwasher and how easy these are to get.

In many other ways, too, and in many families, the father's importance as a breadwinner is undermined. The general panacea that modern psychology seems to offer is that we now have better parent–child relationships. But how is a father to relate to his children?

Today's father is often advised to participate in infant care as much as the mother does, so that he, too, will be as emotionally enriched as she. Unfortunately, this is somewhat empty advice because the male physiology and that part of his psychology based on it are not geared to infant care.

Not that there is anything wrong in a father's giving the baby a bottle. Far from it. He should certainly do so whenever the situation requires it or he enjoys it. What is wrong is to think that this adds to his parenthood. What is wrong is a thinking based on what I can best term division of labor rather than on inherent function; a thinking that disregards physiology, denies that our emotions have their deepest roots in it; a thinking that separates activities from the emotions we bring to them.

Nowadays women assume, or have had thrust upon them by technological and social change, many roles in society which until recently were masculine prerogatives. Perhaps that is why they now expect men to assume some of the tasks once reserved for women, and men have become ready to accept such demands. But infant care and child-rearing, unlike choice of work, are not activities in which who should do what can be decided independently of physiology.

For example, just reviewing the mother's function reveals some of the reasons why fathers have a much harder time with their fatherhood than mothers do with motherhood. I believe it is due to the essential difference in their biological roles.

Nine months of growth and profound physiological changes in the mother precede the arrival of a baby, permitting her to prepare not only *physiologically, but emotionally* for the coming child. The birth act itself, *the dramatic changes in her body, all impress upon her what a momentous event has taken place.* Great as a father's desire for a child may be, there are certainly no physiological changes within him to accompany the arrival of the new family member. And afterwards, he has no close relationship with a child that can compare with that of a nursing mother. For her, nursing creates a cycle of tension and relief, of need and fulfillment that is directly connected with her bodily functions and gives her a wonderful feeling of importance and well-being. The father, on the other hand, simply continues to pursue his normal occupation, may even feel a need to do better at it. But he undergoes no physiological and emotional changes comparable to the mother's, has no comparable feelings of contributing intimately and directly to the baby's welfare. Probably he is dimly aware that the physiological underpinning for getting his own satisfaction by administering intimately to the needs of the infant is lacking. When he tries to find greater fulfillment of his fatherhood by doing more for the child along the lines only mothers used to follow, the result is that he finds less rather than more fulfillment, not only for his fatherhood, but also for his manhood.

The completion of womanhood is largely through motherhood, but fulfillment of manhood is not achieved largely through fatherhood. The fulfillment of manhood is achieved by making a contribution to society as a whole, an impulse which is quickened when a responsible man becomes a father. Without a child, there seems little reason why a man should wish to perpetuate society, to plan beyond the reaches of his life; why he should plant trees, the fruits of which will not ripen while he can still enjoy them. But the relationship between father and child never was and cannot now be built principally around child-caring experiences. It is built around a man's function in society: moral, economic, political.

The father who read the Scriptures to his family, impressed on his child that his interest was concentrated on matters transcending daily toil, matters that gave a meaning to life above and beyond the everyday experiences. Though the child did not understand the content of the Scriptures, his father's concern with them, and what the child dimly felt they stood for, made a lasting impression on him. This example of a deep concern for matters beyond the day-to-day struggle made the head of the family a father just as much as his providing the wherewithal for the family. Thus the old-fashioned father influenced the personality of his child not so much through what he did with the child as through the importance of what he, the father, was concerned with. It was the depth of his dedication to higher issues which gave a broader scope to the child's life. This the modern father can still contribute. How? Today much of a father's positive relationship to his child is built up around playing games, working around the house, fixing the car or other leisure-time activities—and not around the father's function in society. When these activities remain mere enjoyment, many modern fathers become play companions rather than parents. A meaningful parent is that father who manages to use such activities for conveying to the child what a man should be like in meeting life, in mastering it and its responsibilities.

When a father plays games and gets carried away by a childish desire to win, gets angry, upset or argumentative about rules, the child's confidence in him can be undermined. Also, in working together with their children, there are fathers who are more intent on getting done with the job than on using it to teach the child what it means to be a man.

For example, when a child watches his father slowly sawing through wood and even helps with his own little saw, the child may be daydreaming of how someday he will clear a large forest and build a city. The act of "doing together" shows the child the validity of his daydreams of future greatness because, while he dreamed them, something real was observed by his father. That the father's achievement required hard work, thinking, planning, is another important lesson that the child must learn, provided the work he has to do himself is not too hard.

So often it has been those men who have long and arduously daydreamed about a better world they would build who later become those best able to do it in reality. While those who were too soon made familiar with hardship as often as not learned to avoid it in later life, and to escape from it.

Contrary to such psychological facts, the opinion is widespread that hard work in childhood is the best training for meeting future hardships. The wish to get real work out of the child is often camouflaged behind high-sounding statements about its enhancing his self-respect. The child will recognize and resent our selfish motives.

These are some of the bad consequences of confused roles for the modern father who at one time is pal, at another the strict supervisor. The child can never be sure what attitude to expect. One of the most important factors contributing to the security of the child is the father's inner consistency. The father's attitude ought to be both strong and understanding, so that the child can afford to become angry and still feel secure nothing untoward will happen.

Provided such inner attitudes obtain, it is true that carefully planned and shared leisure-time activities—games, hikes, picnics, making things—can cement and add new enjoyment to a father and child relationship. They can be as satisfying for the father as the child. Although it has become fashionable for fathers to say they do not care what work their children choose to do when they grow up, many men hope that their sons will follow in their footsteps, take over the business, enter the same occupation, profession or company. Understandably, a father looks forward to the time when his child is grown enough so that he can teach him his craft. Unfortunately, a good many years are required by modern education, and by the time a child reaches the age at which he can learn a craft from his father, the child has also reached the developmental stage of late adolescence or early maturity, when his desire for independence from his parents stands in the way of such an undertaking. More often than not the father's dream that he will truly become a father by making a man out of his son through the handing down of a craft ends in deep disappointment for both of them. Actually no important teaching can take place once the child has reached maturity.

Most fathers realize this, at least to some degree. That is why we see efforts to build up a child's relation to his father at a much earlier age, and around paternal activities in which the child is better able to share. So intense has been the emphasis on "doing things together" that many fathers worry about the relatively short time they can spend with their children. This need not be a serious handicap. If a child sees his father for a few hours a day, he assumes that what his father is and how he acts during the time, is what he is and how he acts when he is away. When a father feels deeply for his child during the few hours he is with him the child is convinced he feels that way all the time. If the father is able to answer the child's questions about life, the child assumes he can answer all important questions. If the father remains calm and in command of himself in the small emergencies around the house the child will feel that, come hell or high water, his father can always control an emergency. And this gives the child the security he needs to meet life—a security far more important than just the act of playing ball or checkers or soldiers with his father.

The issue, as I see it, in this question of the modern father's role, is that in our society fathers have assumed too much the role of an "also ran." No longer is there one central figure in the home—the mother—whose sole or at least major function is to provide physical, physiological, emotionally intimate satisfaction to the members of the family and another equally important person—the father—whose role is clearly to protect against the outside world and to teach how to meet this world successfully. Since both parents try to do both, neither parent is experienced by the child as a secure haven for either. We all need both: someone who always takes our side and sees things our way, no matter what; and also someone who, though definitely on our side, can be relied on to give us sound advice even if it goes against our wishes, who responds to our needs by seeing them in a broader perspective.

Fathers will have to accept and be satisfied with the fact that their contribution will be less immediately obvious to the young child than the mother's. But how important to the child to have a father whose greater objectivity can be trusted in all emergencies just because he is not so immediately involved in the picayune squabbles; to be able to rely on the judgment of a father who is known to think beyond the problems of the moment to their far-reaching implications and consequences.

The child's view of the world and himself will be deeply influenced by the father's quiet confidence; the inner security which permits him freely and graciously to admit an error, which gives him freedom not to think poorly of himself if a colleague earns more money, which permits him not to blame his difficulties on others or to become defensive about them. In this matter of being a father, as in everything, it is not the externals that count, but the inner convictions and the ability to put them into practice.

Sexual Harassment: The Experience

Catherine A. MacKinnon

Catherine MacKinnon is an attorney and a professor of law at the University of Michigan Law School. Her books include, Sexual Harassment of Working Women *(1979) and* Feminism Unmodified *(1987). MacKinnon has also coauthored (with Andrea Dworkin) city ordinances concerning the recognition of pornography as a violation of sexual equality.*

MacKinnon analyzes sexual harassment from the perspective of women who have experienced it. Sexual harassment occurs in a relationship where there is a power imbalance; it is an unwelcome sexual advance that is one-sided and often comes with strings attached. MacKinnon states that sexual harassment denies one the opportunity (and right) to work or study without being subjected to sexual extortion. She argues that sexual harassment is the experience of a large and diverse group of women, cutting across all races, classes, ages, and marital statuses, and can be visual, verbal, or physical.

Most women wish to choose whether, when, where, and with whom to have sexual relationships, as one important part of exercising control over their lives. Sexual harassment denies this choice in the process of denying the opportunity to study or work without being subjected to sexual exactions. Objection to sexual harassment at work is not a neopuritan moral protest against signs of attraction, displays of affection, compliments, flirtation, or touching on the job. Instead, women

> are rattled and often angry about sex that is one-sided, unwelcome or comes with strings attached. When it's something a woman wants to turn off but can't (a co-worker or supervisor who refuses to stop) or when it's coming from someone with the economic power to hire or fire, help or hinder, reward or punish (an employer or client who mustn't be offended)—that's when [women] say it's a problem.[1]

Women who protest sexual harassment at work are resisting economically enforced sexual exploitation.

This chapter analyzes sexual harassment as women report experiencing it.[2] The analysis is necessarily preliminary and exploratory. These events have seldom been noticed, much less studied; they have almost never been studied *as* sexual harassment.[3] Although the available material is limited, it covers a considerably broader range of incidents than courts will (predictably) consider to be sex discrimination. Each incident or facet of the problem mentioned here will not have equal *legal* weight or go to the same legal issue; not every instance or aspect of

From Catherine A. MacKinnon, *Sexual Harassment of Working Women* (New Haven, CT: Yale University Press, 1979). Reprinted by permission of Yale University Press and Catherine A. MacKinnon. [Edited]

undesired sexual attention on the job is necessarily part of the legal cause of action. Some dimensions of the problem seem to contra-indicate legal action or to require determinations that courts are ill suited to make. The broader contextual approach is taken to avoid prematurely making women's experience of sexual harassment into a case of sex discrimination, no more and no less. For it is, at times, both more and less.

I envision a two-way process of interaction between the relevant legal concepts and women's experience. The strictures of the concept of sex discrimination will ultimately constrain those aspects of women's oppression that will be legally recognized as discriminatory. At the same time, women's experiences, expressed in their own way, can push to expand that concept. Such an approach not only enriches the law. It begins to shape it so that what *really* happens to women, not some male vision of what happens to women, is at the core of the legal prohibition. Women's lived-through experience, in as whole and truthful a fashion as can be approximated at this point, should begin to provide the starting point and context out of which is constructed the narrower forms of abuse that will be made illegal on their behalf. Now that a few women have the tools to address the legal system on its own terms, the law can begin to address women's experience on women's own terms.[4]

Although the precise extent and contours of sexual harassment await further and more exacting investigation, preliminary research indicates that the problem is extremely widespread. Certainly it is more common than almost anyone thought. In the pioneering survey by Working Women United Institute,[5] out of a sample of 55 food service workers and 100 women who attended a meeting on sexual harassment, from five to seven of every ten women reported experiencing sexual harassment in some form at some time in their work lives. Ninety-two percent of the total sample thought it a serious problem. In a study of all women employed at the United Nations, 49 percent said that sexual pressure currently existed on their jobs.[6] During the first eight months of 1976, the Division of Human Rights of the State of New York received approximately 45 complaints from women alleging sexual harassment on the job.[7] Of 9,000 women who responded voluntarily to a questionnaire in *Redbook Magazine*, "How do you handle sex on the job?" nine out of ten reported experiences of sexual harassment. Of course, those who experience the problem may be most likely to respond. Nevertheless, before this survey, it would have been difficult to convince a person of ordinary skepticism that 8,100 American women existed who would report experiencing sexual harassment at work.

Using the *Redbook* questionnaire, a naval officer found 81 percent of a sample of women on a navy base and in a nearby town reported employment-related sexual harassment in some form.[8] These frequency figures must, of course, be cautiously regarded. But even extrapolating conservatively, given that nine out of ten American women work outside the home some time in their lives[9] and that in April 1974, 45 percent of American women sixteen and over, or 35 million women, were employed in the labor force,[10] it is clear that a lot of women are potentially affected. As the problem begins to appear structural rather than individual, *Redbook's* conclusion that "the problem is not epidemic; it is pandemic—an everyday, everywhere occurrence"[11] does not seem incredible.

One need not show that sexual harassment is commonplace in order to argue that it is severe for those afflicted, or even that it is sex discrimination. However, if one shows that sexual harassment in employment systematically occurs between the persons and under the conditions that an analysis of it as discrimination suggests—that is, as a function of sex as gender—one undercuts the view that it occurs because of some unique chemistry between particular (or aberrant) individuals. That sexual harassment does occur to a large and diverse population of women supports an analysis that it occurs *because* of their group characteristic, that is, sex. Such a showing supports an analysis of the abuse as structural, and as such, worth legal attention as sex discrimination, not just as unfairness between two individuals, which might better be approached through private law.

If the problem is so common, one might ask why it has not been commonly analyzed or protested. Lack of public information, social awareness, and formal data probably reflects less its exceptionality than its specific pathology. Sexual subjects are generally sensitive and considered private; women feel embarrassed, demeaned, and intimidated by these incidents.[12] They feel afraid, despairing, utterly alone, and complicit. This is not the sort of experience one discusses readily. Even more to the point, sexual advances are often accompanied by threats of retaliation if exposed. Revealing these pressures enough to protest them thus risks the very employment consequences which sanctioned the advances in the first place.

It is not surprising either that women would not complain of an experience for which there has been no name. Until 1976,[13] lacking a term to express it, sexual harassment was literally unspeakable, which made a generalized, shared, and social definition of it inaccessible. The unnamed should not be mistaken for the nonexistent. Silence often speaks of pain and degradation so thorough that the situation cannot be conceived as other than it is:

> When the conception of change is beyond the limits of the possible, there are no words to articulate discontent, so it is sometimes held not to exist. This mistaken belief arises because we can only grasp silence in the moment in which it is breaking. The sound of silence breaking makes us understand what we could not hear before. But the fact we could not hear does not prove that no pain existed.[14]

As Adrienne Rich has said of this kind of silence, "Do not mistake it/for any kind of absence."[15] Until very recently issues analogous to sexual harassment, such as abortion, rape, and wife beating existed at the level of an open secret in public consciousness, supporting the (equally untrue) inference that these events were infrequent as well as shameful, and branding the victim with the stigma of deviance. In light of these factors, more worth explaining is the emergence of women's ability to break the silence.

Victimization by the practice of sexual harassment, so far as is currently known, occurs across the lines of age, marital status, physical appearance, race, class, occupation, pay range, and any other factor that distinguishes women from each other.[16] Frequency and type of incident may vary with specific vulnerabilities of the woman, or qualities of the job, employer, situation, or workplace, to an extent so far undetermined. To this point, the common denominator is that the perpetrators tend to be men, the victims women. Most of the perpetrators are employment superiors, although some are co-workers or clients. Of the 155 women in the Working Women United Institute sample, 40 percent were harassed by a male superior, 22 percent by a co-worker, 29 percent by a client, customer, or person who had no direct working relationship with them; 1 percent (N = 1) were harassed by a subordinate and 8 percent by "other."[17]

As to age and marital status, *Redbook* finds the most common story is of a woman in her twenties fending off a boss in his sixties, someone she would never choose as a sexual partner. The majority of women who responded to the survey, in which 92 percent reported incidents of sexual harassment, were in their twenties or thirties, and married. Adultery seems no deterrent. However, many women were single or formerly married and ranged in age from their teens to their sixties. In the Working Women United Institute speak-out, one woman mentioned an incident that occurred when she was working as a child model at age ten; another reported an experience at age 55.[18] The women in that sample ranged in age from 19 to 61. On further investigation, sexual harassment as a system may be found to affect women differentially by age, although it damages women regardless of age. That is, many older women may be excluded from jobs because they are considered unattractive sex objects, in order that younger women can be hired to be so treated. But many women preface their reports of sexual harassment with evaluations of their appearance such as, "I am fat and forty, but . . ."[19]

Sexual harassment takes both verbal and physical forms. In the Working Women United Institute sample, approximately a third of those who reported sexual harassment reported physical forms, nearly two-thirds verbal forms.[20] Verbal sexual harassment can include anything from passing but persistent comments on a woman's body or body parts to the experience of an eighteen-year-old file clerk whose boss regularly called her in to his office "to tell me the intimate details of his marriage and to ask what I thought about different sexual positions."[21] Pornography is sometimes used.[22] Physical forms range from repeated collisions that leave the impression of "accident" to outright rape. One woman reported unmistakable sexual molestation which fell between these extremes: "My boss . . . runs his hand up my leg or blouse. He hugs me to him and then tells me that he is 'just naturally affectionate.'"[23]

There is some suggestion in the data that working class women encounter physical as well as verbal forms of sexual harassment more often than middle class and/or professional women, who more often encounter only the verbal forms.[24] However, women's class status in the strict sense is often ambiguous. Is a secretary for a fancy law firm in a different class from a secretary for a struggling, small business? Is a nurse married to a doctor "working class" or "middle class" on her job? Is a lesbian factory worker from an advantaged background with a rich ex-husband who refuses to help support the children because of her sexual preference "upper class"? In any case, most women who responded to the *Redbook* survey, like most employed women, were working at white collar jobs earning between $5,000 and $10,000 a year. Many more were blue collar, professional, or managerial workers earning less than $5,000 or more than $25,000 a year. They report harassment by men independent of the class of those men.

The Working Women United Institute sample, in which approximately 70 percent reported incidents of sexual harassment, presented a strikingly typical profile of women's employment history. Almost all of the women had done office work of some kind in their work life. A quarter had done sales, a quarter had been teachers, a third file clerks, 42 percent had been either secretaries or receptionists, and 29 percent had done factory work. Currently, fifty-five were food service workers with the remainder scattered among a variety of occupations. The average income was $101–$125 per week. This is very close to, or a little below, the usual weekly earnings of most working women.[25]

Race is an important variable in sexual harassment in several different senses. Black women's reports of sexual harassment by white male superiors reflect a sense of impunity that resounds of slavery and colonization. Maxine Munford,* recently separated and with two children to support, claimed that on the first day at her new job she was asked by her employer "if she would make love to a white man, and if she would slap his face if he made a pass at her." She repeatedly refused such advances and was soon fired, the employer alleging she had inadequate knowledge and training for the job and lacked qualifications. His last statement before she left was: "If you would have intercourse with me seven days a week I might give you your job back."[26] Apparently, sexual harassment can be both a sexist way to express racism and a racist way to express sexism. However, black women also report sexual harassment by black men and white women complain of sexual harassment by black male superiors and co-workers. One complaint for slander and outrageous conduct accused the defendants of making statements including the following:

> warning customers about plaintiff's alleged desire to "get in his pants," pointing out that plaintiff had large breasts, stating "Anything over a handful is wasted," calling plaintiff "Momma Fuller" and "Big Momma," referring to her breasts, "Doesn't she have nice (or large) breasts?" "Watch out, she's very horny. She hasn't gotten any lately" "Have you ever seen a black man's penis?" "Do you know how large a black man's penis is?" "Have you ever slept with a black man" "Do you want to stop the car and screw in the middle of the street?"[27]

One might consider whether white women more readily perceive themselves as *sexually* degraded, or anticipate a supportive response when they complain, when they are sexually harassed by a black man than by a white man. Alternatively, some white women confide that they have consciously resisted reporting severe sexual harassment by black men to authorities because they feel the response would be supportive for racist reasons. Although racism is deeply involved in sexual harassment, the element common to these incidents is that the perpetrators are male, the victims female. Few women are in a position to harass men sexually, since they do not control men's employment destinies at work,[28] and female sexual initiative is culturally repressed in this society.[29]

As these experiences suggest, the specific injury of sexual harassment arises from the nexus between a sexual demand and the workplace. Anatomized, the situations can be seen to include a sexual incident or advance, some form of compliance or rejection, and some employment consequence. Sometimes these elements are telescoped, sometimes greatly attenuated, sometimes absent. All are variable: the type of incident or advance, the form of response, and the kind and degree of damage attributable to it. . . .

Women's feelings about their experiences of sexual harassment are a significant part of its social impact. Like women who are raped, sexually harassed women feel humiliated, degraded, ashamed, embarrassed, and cheap, as well as angry. When asked whether the experience had any emotional or physical effect, 78 percent of the Working Women United Institute sample answered affirmatively. Here are some of their comments:

> As I remember all the sexual abuse and negative work experiences I am left feeling sick and helpless and upset instead of angry. . . . Reinforced feelings of no control—sense of doom . . . I have difficulty dropping the emotion barrier I work behind when I come home from work. My husband turns into just another man. . . . Kept me in a constant state of emotional agitation and frustration; I drank a lot. . . .

*Her lawsuit, *Munford v. James T. Barnes & Co.*, 441 F. Supp. 459 (E.D. Mich. 1977), is discussed in chapter 4, *infra*, at 73 ff.

> Soured the essential delight in the work. . . . Stomachache, migraines, cried every night, no appetite.*[30]

In the Working Women United Institute study, 78 percent of the women reported feeling "angry," 48 percent "upset," 23 percent "frightened," 7 percent "indifferent," and an additional 27 percent mentioned feeling "alienated," "alone," "helpless," or other. They tend to feel the incident is their fault, that they must have done something, individually, to elicit or encourage the behavior, that it is "my problem."[31] Since they believe that no one else is subjected to it, they feel individually complicit as well as demeaned. Almost a quarter of the women in one survey reported feeling "guilty."

Judging from these responses, it does not seem as though women want to be sexually harassed at work. Nor do they, as a rule, find it flattering. As one explanation for women's apparent acquiescence, Sheila Rowbotham hypothesizes that (what amounts to) sexually harassed women are "subtly flattered that their sex is recognized. This makes them feel that they are not quite on the cash nexus, that they matter to their employer in the same way that they matter to men in their personal lifes."[32] While the parallel to home life lends plausibility to this analysis, only 10 percent of the women in the Working Women United Institute sample and 15 percent of the *Redbook* sample** reported feeling "flattered" by being on the sex nexus. Women do connect the harasser with other men in their lives, but with quite different results: "It made me think that the only reason other men don't do the same thing is that they don't have the power to." The view that women really want unwanted sex is similar to the equally self-serving view that women want to be raped. As Lynn Wehrli analyzes this:

> Since women seem to "go along" with sexual harassment, [the assumption is that] they must like it, and it is not really harassment at all. This constitutes little more than a simplistic denial of all we know about the ways in which socialization and economic dependence foster submissiveness and override free choice. . . . Those women who are able to speak out about sexual harassment use terms such as "humiliating," "intimidating," "frightening," "financially damaging," "embarrassing," "nerve-wracking," "awful," and "frustrating" to describe it. These words are hardly those used to describe a situation which one "likes."[33]

That women "go along" is partly a male perception and partly correct, a male-enforced reality. Women report being too intimidated to reject the advances unambivalently, regardless of how repulsed they feel. Women's most common response is to attempt to ignore the whole incident, letting the man's ego off the hook skillfully by *appearing* flattered in the hope he will be satisfied and stop. These responses may be interpreted as encouragement or even as provocation. One study found that 76 percent of ignored advances intensified.[34] Some women feel constrained to decline gently, but become frustrated when their subtle hints of lack of reciprocity are ignored. Even clear resistance is often interpreted as encouragement, which is frightening. As a matter of fact, any response or lack of response may be interpreted as encouragement. Ultimately women realize that they have their job only so long as they are pleasing to their male superior, so they try to be polite.[35]

Despite the feelings of guilt, self-loathing, and fear of others' responses, many women who have been sexually harassed do complain about it to someone—usually a woman friend, family member, or co-worker. About

*Ellipses separate different persons' responses.

**In both surveys, women could indicate as many feelings as they felt applied to them

a quarter of them complain to the perpetrator himself.[36] Those who complain, as well as those who do not, express fears that their complaints will be ignored, will not be believed, that they instead will be blamed, that they will be considered "unprofessional," or "asking for it," or told that this problem is too petty or trivial for a grown woman to worry about, and that they are blowing it all out of proportion. Carmita Wood's immediate supervisor, to whom she had reported incidents with her other superior at length, when asked to recall if she mentioned them, stated: "I don't remember specifically, but it was my impression, it was mentioned among a lot of things that I considered trivia. . . ."[37]

The instances of sexual harassment described present straightforward coercion: unwanted sex under the gun of a job or educational benefit. Courts can understand abuses in this form. It is important to remember that affirmatively desired instances of sexual relationships also exist which begin in the context of an employment or educational relationship. Although it is not always simple, courts regularly distinguish bona fide relationships from later attempts to read coercion back into them. Between the two, between the clear coercion and the clear mutuality, exists a murky area where power and caring converge. Here arise some of the most profound issues of sexual harassment, and those which courts are the least suited to resolve.

In education, the perceptive and initiating function of the teacher and the respect and openness of the student merge with the masculine role of sexual mastery and the feminine role of eager purity, especially where the life of the mind means everything. The same parallel between the relationship that one is supposed to be having and the conditions of sexual dominance and submission can be seen in the roles of secretary and boss. Rosabeth Kanter notes that the secretary comes to "feel for" the boss, "to care deeply about what happens to him and to do his feeling for him," giving the relationship a tone of emotional intensity.[38] Elsewhere, she sees that a large part of the secretary's job is to empathize with the boss's personal needs; she also observes that, since the secretary is part of the boss's private retinue, what happens to him determines what happens to her. Kanter does not consider that there may be a connection between the secretary's objective conditions and her feelings—sexual feelings included—about her boss.

Although the woman may, in fact, be and feel coerced in the sexual involvement in some instances of sexual harassment, she may not be entirely without regard for, or free from caring about, the perpetrator. Further investigation of what might be called "coerced caring," or, in the most complex cases, an "if this is sex, I must be in love" syndrome, is vital. It is becoming increasingly recognized that feelings of caring are not the only or even a direct cause of sexual desires in either sex.[39] In light of this, it cannot be assumed that if the woman cares about the man, the sex is not coerced. The difficulties of conceptualization and proof, however, are enormous. But since employed women are supposed to develop, and must demonstrate, regard for the man as a part of the job, and since women are taught to identify with men's feelings, men's evaluations of them, and with their sexual attractiveness to men, as a major component of their *own* identities and sense of worth,[40] it is often unclear and shifting whether the coercion or the caring is the weightier factor, or which "causes" which.

This is not the point at which the legal cause of action for sexual harassment unravels, but the point at which the less good legal case can be scrutinized for its social truths. The more general relationship in women between objective lack of choices and real feelings of love for men can be explored in this context. Plainly, the wooden dichotomy between "real love," which is supposed to be a matter of free choice, and coercion, which implies some form of the gun at the head, is revealed as inadequate to explain the social construction of women's sexuality and the conditions of its expression, including the economic ones. The initial attempts to establish sexual harassment as a cause of action should focus upon the clear cases, which exist in profusion. But the implications the less clear cases have for the tension between women's economic precariousness and dependency—which exists in the family as well as on the job—and the possibilities for freely chosen intimacy between unequals remain.

There is a unity in these apparently, and on the legal level actually, different cases. Taken as one, the sexual harassment of working women presents a closed system of social predation in which powerlessness builds powerlessness. Feelings are a material reality of it. Working women are defined, and survive by defining themselves, as sexually accessible and economically exploitable. Because they are economically vulnerable, they are sexually exposed; because they must be sexually accessible, they are always economically at risk. In this perspective, sexual harassment is less "epidemic" than endemic.

NOTES

1. Claire Safran, *Redbook Magazine* (November 1976), at 149 (hereinafter, *Redbook*). That respondents were self-selected is this study's most serious drawback. Its questions are perceptively designed to elicit impressionistic data. (The questionnaire was published in the January 1976 issue.) When the results are interpreted with these characteristics in mind, the study is highly valuable. Scholars who look down upon such popular journalistic forays into policy research (especially by "women's magazines") should ask themselves why *Redbook* noticed sexual harassment before they did.
2. Much of the information in this chapter is based upon discussions with ten women who shared their experiences of sexual harassment with me from five to twenty or more hours apiece. In addition, I have studied lengthy first person written accounts by five other women. Several women reported the situations and feelings of other women who were being sexually harassed by the same man they were discussing with me. Where permission has been sought and obtained, some of this material will be quoted or referenced throughout. Where quotations in this chapter are unattributed, or statements of fact (such as the racial characteristics of victims and perpetrators) or feelings (such as caring about the man involved) are not otherwise footnoted, they are derived from one or several women from my own research.
   Finally, although the context was education rather than employment, much of my grasp of sexual harassment as an experience is owed to the extensive investigation conducted at Yale from 1976 to 1978 by the plaintiffs and the Yale Undergraduate Women's Caucus Grievance Committee in connection with *Alexander v. Yale*, 459 F. Supp. 1 (D. Conn. 1977). In this research, incidents involving at least half a dozen faculty members or administrators and a total of about fifty women were systematically uncovered and pursued, to the extent the victims were willing.
3. Sex on the job has not gone entirely unnoticed; it is only sexual harassment conceived as such that has been ignored. Two examples illustrate. One study entitled "Rape at Work" reports rapes of women on their jobs by hospital or prison inmates, students or clients; employers, superiors, or co-workers are not mentioned. Carroll M. Brodsky, "Rape at Work," in Marcia J. Walker and Stanley L. Brodsky, eds., *Sexual Assault, the Victim and the Rapist* (Lexington, Mass.: D.C. Heath & Company, 1976), at 35–52. This study is useful, however, for observing dynamics of on-the-job rape that are also true for sexual harassment, whether it includes rape or not. Rape at work was experienced as worse than at other places because it had been seen as a safe place, where the woman did not have to be constantly on guard (at 43–44). And the site of the assault is difficult to avoid (at 44). In another study of "occupations and sex," the examination is divided between jobs "where the occupation involves sex"—cab driving, vice squad duty, and gynecology—and jobs "where the occupation is sex"—stripteasing and prostitution. James M. Henslin *Studies in the Sociology of Sex* (New York: Appleton-Century-Crofts, 1971). This defines as the universe for study the rarified extremes of the convergence of sexuality with work to the neglect of the common experience of thousands of women. See, however, Carroll M. Brodsky, *The Harassed Worker*

(Lexington, Mass.: Heath, 1976), at 27–28 for a useful if brief discussion.

4. Recent attempts to understand women's experience from women's point of view have produced upheavals in standard conceptions in many academic disciplines. One clear example is in the field of history. See Gerda Lerner, *The Female Experience: An American Documentary* (Indianapolis: Bobbs-Merrill, 1977), especially the introduction; Joan Kelly-Gadol, "The Social Relation of the Sexes: Methodological Implications of Women's History," *Signs: Journal of Women in Culture and Society*, vol. 1, no. 4 (1976), at 809–824; Hilda Smith, "Feminism and the Methodology of Women's History," in Berenice A. Carroll, ed., *Liberating Women's History* (Chicago: University of Illinois Press, 1976), at 369–384.
5. References to this survey come from three sources. One is my own interpretation of a simple collation of the marginals from the survey, generously provided by Working Women United Institute (hereinafter, WWUI). The total is 145 women, because 5 women both attended the speak-out and worked in Binghamton. Whenever possible, I will refer to the published article which reports some of the data and provides some analysis. Dierdre Silverman, "Sexual Harassment: Working Women's Dilemma," *Quest: A Feminist Quarterly*, vol. III, no. 3 (1976–1977), at 15–24 (hereinafter, Silverman). Finally, Lin Farley's testimony before the Commission on Human Rights of the City of New York, Hearings on Women in Blue-Collar, Service and Clerical Occupations, "Special Disadvantages of Women in Male-Dominated Work Settings" (April 21, 1975) (mimeograph) refers to the same study.
6. United Nations Ad Hoc Group on Equal Rights for Women, Report on the Questionnaire xxxvi, Report on file at the New York University Law Review, reported in Note, 51 *New York U.L. Rev.* 148, 149, n. 6.
7. Letter of December 8, 1976, from Marie Shear, public information officer of the division, to Lynn Wehrli, copy in author's file.
8. *Redbook*, at 217, 219.
9. Nancy Seifer, "Absent from the Majority: Working Class Women in America" (New York: Institute of Human Relations, National Project on Ethnic America of the American Jewish Committee, 1973), at 11.
10. *1975 Handbook*, at 28.
11. *Redbook*, at 217. The only study I have found that sheds further light upon the statistical prevalence of sexual harassment of women is Diana E.H. Russell's 1978 pretest interviews of ninety-two women randomly selected from San Francisco households. The general purpose of the study was to investigate sexual assault and rape. Her question #46a was: "Some people have experienced unwanted sexual advances by someone who had authority over them such as a doctor, teacher, employer, minister, or therapist. Did you ever have any kind of unwanted sexual experience with someone who had authority over you?" Responses to this question were 16.9 percent yes, 83.1 percent no. From an examination of the rest of the marginals, it seems possible that these results are low. The more specific and detailed the questions became, the higher the affirmative responses tended to be. A woman who was sexually harassed by more than one authority figure would be counted only once. The percentage of affirmative responses to this question is about the same as to the question about sexual experiences with close relatives, but lower than to those about rape. Several questions were asked about rape. Perhaps more questions on authority figures would have increased the prevalence figures. Since the sampling was done by households, the incidence of sexual harassment might not be as high as it would be in subsamples, for instance, of employed women only. Nevertheless, nearly one-fifth of *all women* is a lot of women. The most startling result of the pretest is that thirty-four respondents reported a total of sixty-five incidents of rape and attempted rape in the course of their lives, with a pair or group assault counted as one attack. This means that approximately one-third of all women have been raped, or experienced an attempted rape. The preliminary analysis of the full sample of 935 interviews will be available April 1, 1979. Information from Diana E.H. Russell, "The Prevalence of Rape and Sexual Assault," *Summary Progress Report*, March 31, 1978; Appendix IV: Edited Interview Schedule with Marginals. This research was sponsored by the National Institute of Mental Health and funded through the Center for the Prevention and Control of Rape.
12. *Redbook*, at 217; Silverman, at 18.
13. Working Women United Institute (now at 593 Park Ave., New York, N.Y. 10021) seems to have been the first to use these words as anything approaching a term of art, at first in connection with the case of Carmita Wood in October, 1975 (*infra*, note 61). The concept was also used and developed by the Alliance Against Sexual Coercion (P.O. Box 1, Cambridge, Mass. 02139), for example in their "Position Paper #1" (September 1976) and appears in Carroll Brodsky, *The Harassed Worker* (Lexington, Mass.: Heath, 1976), at 27–28.
14. Sheila Rowbotham, *Woman's Consciousness, Man's World* (London: Penguin, 1973), at 29–30.
15. Adrienne Rich, *The Dream of a Common Language, Poems 1974–1977* (New York: W.W. Norton & Co., 1978), "Cartographies of Silence," at 17.
16. This statement is supported by every study to date and by my own research. These dimensions of sexual harassment were further documented at a

speak-out by Women Office Workers, 600 Lexington Avenue, New York, N.Y., in October 1975. Accounts of the event, and WOW's complaint to the Human Rights Commission, can be found in *Majority Report*, November 1–15, 1975; Paula Bernstein, "Sexual Harassment on the Job," *Harper's Bazaar* (August 1976); *New York Daily News*, April 22, 1976; *New York Post*, April 22, 1976.

17. WWUI.
18. Silverman, at 18.
19. The information from the *Redbook* study in this paragraph is at 217, 149.
20. WWUI.
21. *Redbook*, at 217.
22. The use of pornographic videotapes is reported in "2 Phone Executives Called Promiscuous—Witnesses Tell of Sex in Offices as Trial on Wrongful Death Nears End in Texas," *New York Times*, September 3, 1977. The legal action is for the wrongful death of the man who committed suicide on being accused of a fact pattern seeming to amount to sexual harassment of many women employees.
23. *Redbook*, at 149.
24. Silverman, at 18; *Redbook*, at 217, 219.
25. WWUI; in May 1974, the median weekly earning for women working full time was $124.00. *1975 Handbook*, at 126.
26. The quotations are Ms. Munford's allegations from the Joint Pre-Trial Statement in her case, at 7 and 8, respectively. The decision in the case is *Munford v. James T. Barnes & Co.*, 441 F. Supp. 459 (E.D. Mich. 1977). In addition to Munford, the plaintiffs in *Alexander* (Price), *Barnes*, and *Miller* (see chap. 1, *supra*, note 5) are black women charging sexual harassment by white men. (Diane Williams is a black woman charging sexual harassment by a black man.)
27. First Amended Complaint for Outrageous Conduct and Slander; Law Action for Unpaid Wages; Demand for Jury Trial, Count IX, *Fuller v. Williames* No. A7703-04001 (Ore. Cir. Ct. 1977).
28. See the discussion of vertical stratification in chap. 2.
29. See the discussion of sex roles and sexuality, in chap. 5.
30. Silverman, at 18, 19.
31. *Redbook*, at 149; WWUI; *all* my own cases.
32. Rowbotham, *supra*, note 14, a 90.
33. Lynn Wehrli, "Sexual Harassment at the Workplace: A Feminist Analysis and Strategy for Social Change" (M.A. thesis, Massachusetts Institute of Technology, December 1976).
34. Silverman, at 19.
35. All my cases and all the studies comment upon a need to be polite during the incident, or to exit politely.
36. WWUI; Silverman, at 19.
37. Statement by [Mr. X], Lab. of Nuclear Studies, Transcript at 37, *In re Carmita Wood*, Case No. 75-92437, New York State Department of Labor, Unemployment Insurance Division (Referee).
38. Kanter, *supra*, note 55, at 88.
39. See discussion at 156–58, *infra*.
40. For commentary on this point written by men, see Jack Litewka, "The Socialized Penis," and other articles in *For Men Against Sexism*, Jon Snodgrass, ed. (Albion, Cal.: Times Change Press, 1977), at 16–35.

American Indian Women At the Center of Indigenous Resistance in Contemporary North America

M. Annette Jaimes with Theresa Halsey

M. Annette Jaimes (Juaneño/Yaqui), is a lecturer in American Indian studies with the Center for Studies of Ethnicity and Race in America (CESRA). Jaimes has edited The State of Native America: Genocide, Colonization and Resistance *(1992), and* Fantasies of the Master Race *(1992). Theresa Halsey (Standing Rock Sioux) is the director of the Title V American Indian Education Program of the Boulder Valley School District in Colorado. A longtime activist, she works primarily on community educational issues.*

Jaimes and Halsey argue that historically, American Indian women were not meek, docile and subordinate to males, as they have often been portrayed. Furthermore, American Indian women formed, and continue to form, the core of resistance in the conflict between tribal peoples and Euro-Americans. Citing many historically documented examples, they argue that traditional American Indian societies were not male-dominated. Indeed, female "warriors" were not uncommon, women held key decision-making positions concerning all aspects of socioeconomic existence, and most tribal cultures were matrilineal, placing property ownership in women. Jaimes and Halsey attribute the changes in women's tribal status to the European colonizers' direct intervention in indigenous cultures.

> A people is not defeated until the hearts of its women are on the ground.
>
> Traditional Cheyenne Saying

> The United States has not shown me the terms of my surrender.
>
> Marie Lego
> Pit River Nation, 1970

Reprinted by permission of the South End Press, 116 St. Botolph Street, Boston, MA 02115, from *The State of Native America* by M. Annette Jaimes with Theresa Halsey, 1992. [Edited]

The two brief quotations forming the epigraph of this chapter were selected to represent a constant pattern of reality within Native North American life from the earliest times. This is that women have always formed the backbone of indigenous nations on this continent. Contrary to those images of meekness, docility, and subordination to males with which we women typically have been portrayed by the dominant culture's books and movies, anthropology, and political ideologues of both rightist and leftist persuasions, it is women who have formed the very core of indigenous resistance to genocide and colonization since the first moment of conflict between Indians and invaders. . . .

MYTHS OF MALE DOMINANCE

A significant factor militating against fruitful alliances—or even dialogue—between Indians and non-Indians is the vast and complex set of myths imposed and stubbornly defended by the dominant culture as a means of "understanding" Native America both historically and topically. . . . As concerns indigenous women in particular, this fantastical lexicon includes what anthropologist Eleanor Burke Leacock has termed the "myths of male dominance."[1] Adherence to its main tenets of the stereotypes involved seems to be entirely trans-ideological within the "mainstream" of American life, a matter readily witnessed by recent offerings in the mass media by Paul Valentine, a remarkably reactionary critic for the *Washington Post*, and Barbara Ehrenreich, an ostensibly socialist-feminist columnist for *Time* Magazine and several more progressive publications.

In a hostile review of the film *Dances with Wolves* published in April 1991, Valentine denounces producer-director Kevin Costner for having "romanticized" American Indians.[2] He then sets forth a series of outlandish contentions designed to show how nasty things really were in North America before Europeans came along to set things right. An example of the sheer absurdity with which his polemic is laced is a passage in which he has "the Arapaho of eastern Colorado . . . igniting uncontrolled grass fires on the prairies" which remained barren of grass "for many years afterward," causing mass starvation among the buffalo (as any high school botany student might have pointed out, a fall burn-off actually *stimulates* spring growth of most grasses, prairie grasses included). He then proceeds to explain the lot of native women in precontact times as being the haulers of "the clumsy two stick travois used to transport a family's belongings on the nomadic seasonal treks" (there were virtually no precontact "nomads" in North America, and dogs were used to drag travois prior to the advent of horses).[3]

Ehrenreich, for her part, had earlier adopted a similar posture in a *Time* Magazine column arguing against the rampant militarism engulfing the United States during the fall of 1990. In her first paragraph, while taking a couple of gratuitous and utterly uninformed shots at the culture of the southeast African Masai and indigenous Solomon Islanders, she implies America's jingoist policies in the Persian Gulf had "descended" to the level of such "primitive"—and male dominated—"warrior cultures" as "the Plains Indian societies," where "the passage to manhood allowing young males to marry required the blooding of the spear, the taking of a scalp or head."[4] Ehrenreich's thoroughly arrogant use of indigenous cultures as a springboard upon which to launch into the imagined superiority of her own culture and views is no more factually supportable than Valentine's, and is every bit as degrading to native people of *both* genders. Worse, she extends her "analysis" as a self-proclaimed "friend of the oppressed" rather than as an unabashed apologist for the status quo.

The truth of things was, of course, rather different. Contra Ehrenreich's thesis, the Salish/Kootenai scholar D'Arcy McNickle long ago published the results of lengthy and painstaking research which showed that 70 percent or more of all precontact societies in North America practiced no form of warfare at all. . . .[5] This may have been due in part to the fact that, as Laguna researcher Paula Gunn Allen has compellingly demonstrated in her recent book, *The Sacred Hoop*, traditional native societies were never "male dominated" and there were likely no "warrior cultures" worthy of the name before the European invasion.[6] There is no record of *any* American Indian society, even after the invasion, requiring a man to kill in war before he could marry. To the contrary, military activity—including being a literal warrior—was never an exclusively male sphere of endeavor.

Although it is true that women were typically accorded a greater social value in indigenous tradition—both because of their biological ability to bear children, and for reasons which will be discussed below—and therefore tended to be noncombatant to a much greater degree than men, female fighters were never uncommon once the necessity of real warfare was imposed by Euroamericans.[7] These included military commanders like Cousaponakeesa—Mary Matthews Musgrove Bosomworth, the "Creek Mary" of Dee Brown's 1981 novel—who led her people in a successful campaign against the British at Savannah during the 1750s.[8] Lakota women traditionally maintained at least four warrior societies of their own, entities which are presently being resurrected.[9] Among the Cherokees, there was Da'nawa-gasta, or "Sharp War," an especially tough warrior and head of a women's military society.[10] The Piegans maintained what has been mistranslated as "Manly-Hearted Women," more accurately understood as being "Strong-Hearted Women," a permanent warrior society.[11] The Cheyennes in particular fielded a number of strong women fighters, such as Buffalo Calf Road (who distinguished herself at both the Battle of the Rosebud in 1876 and during the 1878 "Cheyenne Breakout"), amidst the worst period of the wars of annihilation waged against them by the United States.[12] Many other native cultures produced comparable figures, a tradition into which the women of the preceding section fit well, and which serves to debunk the tidy (if grossly misleading and divisive) male/female, warlike/peaceful dichotomies deployed by such Euroamerican feminist thinkers as Ehrenreich and Robin Morgan.[13]

More important than their direct participation in military activities was native women's role in making key decisions, not only about matters of peace and war, but in all other aspects of socioeconomic existence. Although Gunn Allen's conclusion that traditional indigenous societies added up to "gynocracies" is undoubtedly overstated and misleading, this is not to say that Native American women were not politically powerful. Creek Mary was not a general *per se*, but essentially head of state within the Creek Confederacy. Her status was that of "Beloved Woman," a position better recorded with regard to the system of governance developed among the Cherokees slightly to the north of Creek domain:

> Cherokee women had the right to decide the fate of captives, decisions that were made by vote of the Women's Council and relayed to the district at large by the War Woman or Pretty Woman. The decisions had to be made by female clan heads because a captive who was to live would be adopted into one of the families whose affairs were directed by the clan-mothers. The clan-mothers also had the right to wage war, and as Henry Timberlake wrote, the stories about Amazon women warriors were not so farfetched considering how many Indian women were famous warriors and powerful voices in the councils. . . . The war women carried the titled Beloved Women, and their power was great. . . . The Women's Council, as distinguished from the District, village, or Confederacy councils, was powerful in a number of political and socio-spiritual ways, and may have had the deciding voice on which males would serve on the Councils. . . . Certainly the Women's Council was influential in tribal decisions, and its spokeswomen served as War Women and Peace Women, presumably holding offices in the towns designated as red towns and white towns, respectively. Their other powers included the right to

speak in the men's Council [although men lacked a reciprocal right, under most circumstances], the right to choose whom and whether to marry, the right to bear arms, and the right to choose their extramarital occupations.[14]

While Creek and Cherokee women "may" have held the right to select which males assumed positions of political responsibility, this was unquestionably the case within the Haudenosaunee (Six Nations Iroquois Confederacy) of New York state. Among the "Sixers," each of the fifty extended families (clans) was headed by a clan mother. These women formed a council within the confederacy which selected the males who would hold positions on a second council, composed of men, representing the confederacy's interests, both in formulation of internal policies and in conduct of external relations. If at any time, particular male council members adopted positions or undertook policies perceived by the women's council as being contrary to the people's interests, their respective clan mothers retained the right to replace them. Although much diminished after two centuries of U.S. colonial domination, this "Longhouse" form of government is ongoing today.[15]

The Haudenosaunee were hardly alone among northeastern peoples in according women such a measure of power. At the time of the European arrival in North America, the Narragansett of what is now Rhode Island were headed by a "sunksquaw," or female chief. The last of these, a woman named Magnus, was executed along with ninety other members of the Narragansett government after their defeat by English Major James Talcot in 1675.[16] During the same period, the Esopus Confederacy was led, at least in part, by a woman named Mamanuchqua (also known as Mamareoktwe, Mamaroch, and Mamaprocht).[17] The Delawares *generically* referred to themselves as "women," considering the term to be supremely complementary.[18] Among other Algonquin peoples of the Atlantic Coast region—e.g., the Wampanoag and Massachusetts Confederacies, and the Niaticks, Scaticooks, Niantics, Pictaways, Powhatans, and Caconnets—much the same pattern prevailed:

> From before 1620 until her death in 1677, a squaw-sachem known as the "Massachusetts Queen" by the Virginia colonizers governed the Massachusetts Confederacy. It was her fortune to preside over the Confederacy's destruction as the people were decimated by disease, war, and colonial manipulations. . . . Others include the Pocasett sunksquaw Weetamoo, who was King Philip's ally and "served as a war chief commanding over 300 warriors" during his war with the British. . . . Awashonks, another [woman head of state] of the Mid-Atlantic region, was squaw-sachem of the Sakonnet, a [nation] allied with the Wampanoag Confederacy. She [held her office] in the latter part of the seventeenth century. After fighting for a time against the British during King Philip's War, she was forced to surrender. Because she then convinced her warriors to fight with the British, she was able to save them from enslavement in the West Indies.[19]

Women's power within traditional Indian societies was also grounded in other ways. While patrilineal/patrilocal cultures did exist, most precontact North American civilizations functioned on the basis of matrilineage and matrilocality. Insofar as family structures centered upon the identities of wives rather than husbands—men joined women's families, not the other way around—and because men were usually expected to relocate to join the women they married, the context of native social life was radically different from that which prevailed (and prevails) in European and Euro-derived cultures.[20]

> Many of the largest and most important Indian peoples were matrilineal. . . . Among these were: in the East, the Iroquois, the Siouan

[nations] of the Piedmont and Atlantic coastal plain, the Mohegan, the Delaware, various other [nations] of southern New England, and the divisions of the Powhatan Confederacy in Virginia; in the South, the Creek, the Choctaw, the Chickasaw, the Seminole, and the [nations] of the Caddoan linguistic family; in the Great Plains, the Pawnee, the Hidatsa, the Mandan, the Oto, the Missouri, and the Crow and other Siouan [nations]; in the southwest, the Navajo, and the numerous so-called Pueblo [nations], including the well known Hopi, Laguna, Acoma, and Zuñi.[21]

In many indigenous societies, the position of women was further strengthened economically, by virtue of their owning all or most property. Haudenosaunee women, for example, owned the fields which produced about two-thirds of their people's diet.[22] Among the Lakota, men owned nothing but their clothing, a horse for hunting, weapons and spiritual items; homes, furnishings, and the like were the property of their wives. All a Lakota woman needed to do in order to divorce her husband was to set his meager personal possessions outside the door of their lodge, an action against which he had no appeal under traditional law.[23] Much the same system prevailed among the Anishinabé and numerous other native cultures. As Mary Oshana, an Anishinabé activist, has explained it:

> Matrilineal [nations] provided the greatest opportunities for women: women in these [nations] owned houses, furnishings, fields, gardens, agricultural tools, art objects, livestock and horses. Furthermore, these items were passed down through female lines. Regardless of their marital status, women had the right to own and control property. The woman had control of the children and if marital problems developed the man would leave the home.[24]

Additional reinforcement of native women's status accrues from the spiritual traditions of most of North America's indigenous cultures. First, contrary to the Euroamerican myth that American Indian spiritual leaders are invariably something called "medicine men," women have always held important positions in this regard. Prime examples include Coocoochee of the Mohawks, Sanapia of the Comanches, and Pretty Shield of the Crows.[25] Among the Zuñi and other Puebloan cultures, women were members of the Rain Priesthood, the most important of that society's religious entities.[26] Women are also known to have played crucial leadership roles within Anishinabé, Blackfeet, Chilula, and Diné spiritual practices, as well as those of many other native societies.[27]

More important in some ways, virtually all indigenous religions on this continent exhibit an abundant presence of feminine elements within their cosmologies.[28] When contrasted to the hegemonic masculinity of the deities embraced by such "world religions" as Judaism, Christianity, and Islam—and the corresponding male supremacism marking those societies which adhere to them—the real significance of concepts like Mother Earth (universal), Spider woman (Hopi and Diné), White Buffalo Calf Woman (Lakota), Grandmother Turtle (Iroquois), Sky Woman (Iroquois), Hard Beings Woman and Sand Altar Woman (Hopi), First Woman (Abanaki), Thought Woman (Laguna), Corn Woman (Cherokee), and Changing Woman (Diné) becomes rather obvious.[29] So too does the real rather than the mythical status of women in traditional Native American life. Indeed, as Diné artist Mary Morez has put it, "In [our] society, the woman is the dominant figure who becomes the wise one with old age. It's a [matrilineal/matrilocal] society, you know. But the Navajo woman never demands her status. She achieves, earns, accomplishes it through maturity. That maturing process is psychological. It has to do with one's feelings for the land and being part of the whole cycle of nature. It's difficult to describe to a non-Indian."[30]

Bea Medicine, a Hunkpapa Lakota scholar, concurs, noting that "Our power is obvious. [Women] are primary socializers of our children. Culture is transmitted primarily through the mother. The mother teaches languages, attitudes, beliefs, behavior patterns, etc."[31] Anishinabé writer and activitist Winona LaDuke concludes, "Traditionally, American Indian women were never subordinate to men. Or vice versa, for that matter. What native societies have always been about is achieving balance in all things, gender relations no less than any other. Nobody needs to tell us how to do it. We've had that all worked out for thousands of years. And, left to our own devices, that's exactly how we'd be living right now."[32] Or, as Priscilla K. Buffalohead, another Anishinabé scholar, has put it, "[We] stem from egalitarian cultural traditions. These traditions are concerned less with equality of the sexes and more with the dignity of the individual and their inherent right—whether they be women, men or children—to make their own choices and decisions.[33]

DISEMPOWERMENT

The reduction of the status held by women within indigenous nations was a first priority for European colonizers eager to weaken and destabilize target societies. With regard to the Montagnais and Naskapi of the St. Lawrence River Valley, for example, the French, who first entered the area in the 1550s, encountered a people among whom "women have great power. . . . A man may promise you something and if he does not keep his promise, he thinks he is sufficiently excused when he tells you that his wife did not wish him to do it."[34] They responded, beginning in 1633, by sending Jesuit missionaries to show the natives a "better and more enlightened way" of comporting themselves, a matter well-chronicled by the priest, Paul Le Jeune:

> Though some observers saw women as drudges, Le Jeune saw women as holding "great power" and having "in every instance . . . the choice of plans, of undertakings, of journeys, of winterings." Indeed, independence of women was considered a problem by the Jesuits, who lectured the men about "allowing" their wives sexual and other freedom and sought to introduce European principles of obedience.[35]

Most likely, the Jesuit program would have gone nowhere had the sharp end of colonization not undercut the Montagnais-Naskapi traditional economy, replacing it with a system far more reliant upon fur trapping and traders by the latter part of the 17th century.[36] As their dependence upon their colonizers increased, the Indians were compelled to accept more and more of the European brand of "morality." The Jesuits imposed a form of monogamy in which divorce was forbidden, implemented a system of compulsory Catholic education, and refused to deal with anyone other than selected male "representatives" of the Montagnais and Naskapi in political or economic affairs (thus deforming the Indian structure of governance beyond recognition).[37]

> Positions of formal power such as political leadership, [spiritual leadership], and matrilocality, which placed the economic dependence of a woman with children in the hands of her mother's family. . .shifted. [Spiritual and political] leadership were male [by 1750], and matrilocality had become patrilocality. This is not so strange given the economics of the situation and the fact that over the years the Montagnais became entirely Catholicized.[38]

Among the Haudenosaunee, who were not militarily defeated until after the American Revolution, such changes took much longer. It was not until the early 19th century that, in an attempt to adjust to the new circumstances of subordination to the

United States, the Seneca prophet Handsome Lake promulgated a new code of law and social organization which replaced their old "petticoat government" with a male-centered model more acceptable to the colonizers.[39] In attempting to shift power from "the meddling old women" of Iroquois society,

> Handsome Lake advocated that young women cleave to their husbands rather than to their mothers and abandon the clan-mother controlled Longhouse in favor of a patriarchal, nuclear family arrangement. . . . While the shift was never complete, it was sufficient. Under the Code of Handsome Lake, which was the tribal version of the white man's way, the Longhouse declined in importance, and eventually Iroquois women were firmly under the thumb of Christian patriarchy.[40]

To the south, "the British worked hard to lessen the power of women in Cherokee affairs. They took Cherokee men to England and educated them in European ways. These men returned to Cherokee country and exerted great influence on behalf of the British in the region.[41] Intermarriage was also encouraged, with markedly privileged treatment accorded mixed-blood offspring of such unions with English colonialists. In time, when combined with increasing Cherokee dependence on the British trade economy, these advantages resulted in a situation where "men with little Cherokee blood [and even less loyalty] wielded considerable power over the nation's policies.[42] Aping the English, this new male leadership set out to establish a plantation economy devoted to the growing of cotton and tobacco.

> The male leadership bought and sold not only black men and women but men and women from neighboring tribes, the women of the leadership retreated to Bible classes, sewing circles, and petticoats that rivaled those of their white sisters. Many of these upper-strata Cherokee women married white ministers and other opportunists, as the men of their class married white women, often the daughters of white ministers. . . . Cherokee society became rigid and modeled on Christian white social organization of upper, middle, and impoverished classes usually composed of very traditional clans.[43]

This situation, of course, greatly weakened the Cherokee Nation, creating sharp divisions within it which have not completely healed even to the present day. Moreover, it caused Euroamericans in surrounding areas to covet not only Cherokee land *per se*, but the lucrative farming enterprises built up by the mixed-blood male caste. This was a powerful incentive for the U.S. to undertake the compulsory removal of the Cherokees and other indigenous nations from east of the Mississippi to points west during the first half of the 19th century.[44] The reaction of assimilated Cherokees was an attempt to show their "worth" by becoming even more ostentatiously Europeanized.

> In an effort to stave off removal, the Cherokee in the early 1800s, under the leadership of men such as Elias Boudinot, Major Ridge, and John Ross (later Principal Chief of the Cherokee in Oklahoma Territory), and others, drafted a constitution that disenfranchised women and blacks. Modeled after the Constitution of the United Sates, whose favor they were attempting to curry, and in conjunction with Christian sympathizers to the Cherokee cause, the new Cherokee constitution relegated women to the position of chattel. . . . [Under such conditions], the last Beloved Woman, Nancy Ward, resigned her office in 1817, sending her cane and her vote on important questions to the Cherokee Council.[45]

Despite much groveling by the "sellouts," Andrew Jackson ordered removal of the Cherokees—as well as the Creeks, Choctaws, Chickasaws, and Seminoles—to begin in 1832.[46] By 1839, the "Trail of Tears" was complete, with catastrophic population loss for the indigenous nations involved.[47] By the latter stage, traditionalist Cherokees had overcome sanctions against killing other tribal members in a desperate attempt to restore some semblance of order within their nation: Major Ridge, his eldest son, John, and Elias Boudinot were assassinated on June 22, 1839.[48] Attempts were made to eliminate other members of the "Ridge Faction" such as Stand Watie, John A. Bell, James Starr, and George W. Adair, but these failed, and the assimilationist faction continued to do substantial damage to Cherokee sovereignty.[49] Although John Rollin Ridge, the Major's grandson, was forced to flee to California in 1850 and was unable to return to Cherokee Country until after the Civil War.[50] Stand Watie (Boudinot's younger brother) managed to lead a portion of the Cherokees into a disastrous alliance with the Confederacy from which the nation never recovered.[51]

Across the continent, the story was the same in every case. In *not one* of the more than 370 ratified and perhaps 300 unratified treaties negotiated by the United States with indigenous nations was the federal government willing to allow participation by native women. In *none* of the several thousand non-treaty agreements reached between the United States and these same nations were federal representatives prepared to discuss anything at all with women. In *no* instance was the United States open to recognizing a female as representing her people's interests when it came to administering the reservations onto which American Indians were ultimately forced; always, men were required to do what was necessary to secure delivery of rations, argue for water rights, and all the rest.[52] Meanwhile, . . . the best and most patriotic of the indigenous male leadership—men like Tecumseh, Osceola, Crazy Horse, and Sitting Bull—were systematically assassinated or sent to far-away prisons for extended periods. The male leadership of the native resistance was then replaced with men selected on the basis of their willingness to cooperate with their oppressors. Exactly how native women coped with this vast alteration of their circumstances, and those of their people more generally, is a bit mysterious:

> If a generalization may be made, it is that female roles of mother, sister, and wife were ongoing because of the continued care they were supposed to provide for the family. But what of the role of women in relationship to agents, to soldiers guarding the "hostiles," and to their general physical deprivation in societies whose livelihood and way of life had been destroyed along with the bison? We are very nearly bereft of data and statements which could clarify the transitional status of women during this period. The strategies adopted for cultural survival and the means of transmitting these to daughters and nieces are valuable adaptive mechanisms which cannot be even partially reconstructed.[53]

These practical realities, imposed quite uniformly by the conquerors, were steadily reinforced by officially sponsored missionizing and mandatory education in boarding schools, processes designed to inculcate the notion that such disempowerment of Indian women and liquidation of "recalcitrant" males was "natural, right, and inevitable."[54]. . .

NOTES

1. Burke Leacock, Eleanor, *Myths of Male Dominance: Collected Articles on Women Cross-Culturally,* Monthly Review Press, New York, 1981.
2. Valentine, Paul, "Dances with Myths," *Washington Post;* reprinted in the *Boulder* [Colorado] *Daily Camera,* April 7, 1991.
3. Valentine also informs us that these "nomadic hunters and gatherers moved from spot to spot, strewing refuse in their wake" (What sort of "refuse"? Plastic? Aluminum cans? Polyvinyl Chlorides?) before running down the usual litany of imagined native defects: "[Indians] were totalitarian, warlike and extremely brutal. Some practiced slavery, torture, human sacrifice and cannibalism, and imposed rigid social dictatorships." That there is not one shred of solid evidence supporting *any* of this is no bother. Valentine and his ilk simply condemn anyone bothering with the facts as a "politically correct . . . revisionist." Left unexplained is why anyone might deliberately seek to be politically *in*correct, or why blatant inaccuracies

or lies—such as those in which they trade—shouldn't be revised and corrected.

4. Ehrenreich, Barbara, "The Warrior Culture," *Time,* October 15, 1990. It should be noted that the practice of scalping, derived from the taking of heads, was introduced to North America by the British, who had earlier developed the technique during the conquest and colonization of Ireland (see Canny, Nicholas P., "The Ideology of English Colonization: From Ireland to America," *William and Mary Quarterly,* 3rd Ser., No. 30, 1973, pp. 575–98). For a more detailed response, see Ward Churchill's letter on the article (frozen out of *Time*) in *Z Magazine,* November 1990.
5. McNickle, D'Arcy, *The Surrounded,* University of New Mexico Press, Albuquerque (2nd edition), 1978.
6. Gunn Allen, Paula, *The Sacred Hoop: Recovering the Feminine in American Indian Traditions,* Beacon Press, Boston, 1986, p. 266.
7. Indication of the relatively higher valuation placed upon women may be found in the fact that among the Iroquois, Susquehannahs, and Abenakis ("Hurons"), for example, the penalty for killing a woman was double that for killing a man (see Thomas Foreman, Caroline, *American Indian Women Chiefs,* Hoffman Printing Co., Muskogee, OK (1954, p. 9). On the diversity of native women's social functions and activities, see Shirer Mathes, Valerie, "A New Look at the Role of Women in Indian Societies," *American Indian Quarterly,* Vol. 2, No. 2, 1975, pp. 131–39.
8. See Thomas Foreman, op. cit., pp. 85–7. Also see Coulter, E. Merton, "Mary Musgrove, Queen of the Creeks: A Chapter of the Early Georgia Troubles," *Georgia Historical Quarterly,* Vol. 11, no. 1, 1927, pp. 1–30, and Corry, John Pitts, "Some New Light on the Bosworth Claims," *Georgia Historical Quarterly,* No. 25, 1941, pp. 195–224. The novel in question is Brown, Dee, *Creek Mary's Blood,* Simon and Schuster Publishers, New York, 1981.
9. Discussion with Madonna Thunderhawk (Hunkpapa Lakota), April 1985; discussion with Robert Grey Eagle (Oglala Lakota), July 1991.
10. Thomas Foreman, op. cit., p. 85.
11. See Lewis, Oscar, "Manly-Hearted Women Among the Northern Piegan," *American Anthropologist,* No. 43, 1941, pp. 173–87.
12. On Buffalo Calf Road, see Agonito, Rosemary, and Joseph Agonito, "Resurrecting History's Forgotten Women: A Case Study from the Cheyenne Indians," *Frontiers: A Journal of Women's Studies,* No. 6, Fall 1981, pp. 8–9; and Sandoz, Mari, *Cheyenne Autumn,* Avon Books, New York, 1964). Information on four other 19th-century warrior women may be found in Ewers, John C., "Deadlier than the Male," *American Heritage,* No. 16, 1965, pp. 10–13. More generally, see Medicine, Bea, "'Warrior Women': Sex Role Alternatives for Plains Indian Women," in Patricia Albers and Beatrice Medicine, eds., *The Hidden Half: Studies of Plains Indian Women,* University Press of America, Lanham, MD, 1983, pp. 267–80.
13. Robin Morgan's *The Demon Lover: On the Sexuality of Terrorism* (W.W. Norton Publishers, New York, 1989), in which any female engaged in physical combat is found to be the mere pawn of some man (or at least "male energy") is the most extraordinarily insulting and demeaning treatise possible, not only for Native American women, but for African Americans like Assata Shakur, Latinas like Lolita Labrón and Alejandrina Torres, Europeans like Ingrid Barabass and Monica Helbing, Euroamericans like Susan Rosenberg and Linda Evans, and perhaps a quarter of the female populations of Africa, Asia, and Palestine.
14. Gunn Allen, op. cit., pp. 36–37. She is drawing on Timberlake, Lt. Henry, *Lieutenant Henry Timberlake's Memoirs,* Marietta, GA, 1948, p. 94.
15. Concerning the ongoing nature of the Longhouse government, and women's role in it, see Anonymous, "A Woman's Ways: An Interview with Judy Swamp," *Parabola,* Vol. 5, No. 4, 1980, pp. 52–61. Also see Cook, Katsi, "The Women's Dance: Reclaiming Our Powers on the Women's Side of Life," *Native Self-Sufficiency,* No. 6, 1981, pp. 17–19.
16. See Grumet, Robert Steven, "Sunksquaws, Shamans, and Tradeswomen: Middle-Atlantic Coastal Algonkian Women During the 17th and 18th Centuries," in Mona Etienne and Eleanor Burke Leacock, eds., *Women and Colonization: Anthropological Perspectives,* Praeger Publishers, New York, 1980.
17. Ibid., pp. 51–2.
18. See Wallace, Anthony F.C., "Women, Land, and Society: Three Aspects of Aboriginal Delaware Life," *Pennsylvania Archaeologist,* No. 17, 1947, pp. 1–35; and Weslager, C.S., "The Delaware Indians as Women," *Journal of the Washington Academy of Science,* No. 37, September 15, 1947, pp. 298–304.
19. Gunn Allen, op. cit., p. 35. She relies heavily on Grumet, op. cit.
20. For further information on these customs, see Niethammer, Carolyn, *Daughters of the Earth: The Lives and Legends of Native American Women,* Macmillan Publishers, New York, 1977. Also see Kidwell, Clara Sue, "The Power of Women in Three American Indian Societies," *Journal of Ethnic Studies,* Vol. 6, No. 3, 1979, pp. 113–21. An overview of the extent to which matrilineal/matrilocal societies predominated in precontact Native North America, see Lowie, Robert H., "The Matrilineal Complex," *University of California Publications in Archaeology and Ethnology,* No. 16, 1919–1920, pp. 29–45.
21. Terrell, John Upton, and Donna M. Terrell, *Indian Women of the Western Morning: Their Life in Early America,* Anchor Books, New York, 1974, p. 24.

22. See Brown, Judith K., "Economic Organization and the Position of Women Among the Iroquois," *Ethnohistory,* Vol. 17, Nos. 3–4, Summer–Fall 1970, pp. 151–67. Also see Trigger, Bruce G. "Iroquoian Matriliny," *Pennsylvania Archaeologist,* No. 48, 1978, pp. 55–65.
23. See Powers, Marla N., *Oglala Women: Myth, Ritual and Reality,* University of Chicago Press, Chicago, 1986, p. 89.
24. Oshana, Mary, "Native American Women in Westerns: Reality and Myth," *Frontiers: A Journal of Women's Studies,* No. 6, Fall 1981, p. 46.
25. See Hornbeck Tanner, Helen, "Coocoochee: Mohawk Medicine Woman," *American Indian Culture and Research Journal,* Vol. 3, No. 3, 1979, pp. 23–42; Jones, David, *Sanapia: A Comanche Medicine Woman,* Holt, Rinehart and Winston Publishers, New York, 1968; and Linderman, Frank, *Pretty Shield: Medicine Woman of the Crows,* John Day Publishers, New York, 1932; reprinted 1974.
26. Terrell and Terrell, op. cit., p. 25.
27. See Landes, Ruth, *The Ojibwa Religion and the Midewiwin,* University of Wisconsin Press, Madison, 1968; Kent, Susan, "Hogans, Sacred Circles and Symbols: The Navajo Use of Space," in David Brugge and Charlotte J. Frisbie, eds., *Essays in Honor of Leland Wyman,* Museum of New Mexico Press, Santa Fe, 1982; Lake, Robert G., "Chilula Religion and Ideology: A Discussion of Native American Humanistic Concepts and Processes," *Humbolt Journal of Social Relations,* Vol. 7, No. 2, 1980, pp. 113–34; and Kehoe, Alice, "Old Woman Had Great Power," *Western Canadian Journal of Anthropology,* Vol. 6, No. 3, 1976, pp. 68–76. Also see Thrift Nelson, Ann, "Native American Women's Ritual Sodalities in Native North America," *Western Canadian Journal of Anthropology,* Vol. 6, No. 3, 1976, pp. 29–67.
28. For a thorough analysis of the metatheological precepts embodied in indigenous American spirituality, see Deloria, Vine Jr., *God Is Red,* Grossett and Dunlap Publishers, New York, 1973; reprinted by Dell Books, New York, 1983. Further elaboration is provided in his *Metaphysics of Modern Existence,* Harper and Row Publishers, New York, 1979.
29. Contrary to the contentions of University of Colorado Professor of Religious Studies Sam Gill, the idea of Mother Earth—which is quite universal among Native North Americans—was not imported from Europe (Gill, Sam D., *Mother Earth: An American Story,* University of Chicago Press, Chicago, 1987). For detailed refutation, see the special section of *Bloomsbury Review* (Vol. 8, No. 5, September–October 1988) edited by M. Annette Jaimes and devoted to critique of Gill's thesis and methods.
30. Quoted in Katz, op. cit., p. 126. For further background on the status of Diné women, see Stewart, Irene, *A Voice in Her Tribe: A Navajo Woman's Own Story,* Ballena Press, Socorro, NM, 1980; and Roessel, Ruth, *Women in Navajo Society,* Navajo Resource Center, Rough Rock, AZ, 1981.
31. Quoted in Katz, op. cit., p. 123.
32. From a talk delivered during International Women's Week, University of Colorado at Boulder, April 1985 (tape on file).
33. Buffalohead, Priscilla K., "Farmers, Warriors, Traders: A Fresh Look at Ojibway Women," *Minnesota History,* No. 48, Summer 1983, p. 236.
34. Thwaites, Rubin Gold, ed., *The Jesuit Relations and Allied Documents,* Vol. 5 (of 71 Volumes), Burrow Brothers Publishers, Cleveland, 1906, p. 179.
35. Leacock, op. cit., p. 35.
36. For a broader examination of the impact of the fur trade upon the internal structures of indigenous societies, see Van Kirk, Sylvia, *Many Tender ties: Women in Fur-Trade Society, 1670–1870,* University of Oklahoma Press, Norman, 1980.
37. Leacock, "Montagnais Women and the Jesuit Program for Colonization," in ibid., pp. 43–62.
38. Gunn Allen, op. cit., p. 40.
39. The expression "petticoat government" comes from the British colonialist John Adair in regard to the Cherokee Nation. See Brown, John P., *Old Frontiers,* State Historical Society of Wisconsin, Madison, 1938, p. 20.
40. Gunn Allen, op. cit., p. 33. She relies upon Brandon, William, *The Last Americans: The Indian in American Culture,* McGraw-Hill Publishers, New York, 1974, p. 214.
41. Gunn Allen, op. cit., p. 37.
42. Ibid. It should be noted that this calculated and vicious colonialist use of mixed-bloods as a means to undercut traditional societies, a tactic which is ongoing in the present day, is a primary cause of the sort of racially-oriented infighting among Indians which continues to confuse the questions of Indian identity addressed in Chapter Four.
43. Ibid.
44. For a solid sample of the avaricious sentiments involved in this federal policy, see U.S. Congress, *Speeches on the Passage of the Bill for Removal of the Indians, Delivered in the Congress of the United States, April and May, 1830,* Perkins and Marvin Publishers, Boston, 1830; Kraus Reprint Co., Millwood, NY, 1973.
45. Gunn Allen, op. cit., pp. 37–8. It should be noted that the three men named did not share the same position on Cherokee removal. John Ross, "despite his large degree of white blood," was an ardent Cherokee patriot and fought mightily against U.S. policy (see Eaton, Rachel E., *John Ross and the Cherokee People,* Cherokee National Museum, Muskogee, OK, 1921). Boudinot and Major Ridge (or "The Ridge"), were devout assimilationists who worked—for a fee—to further U.S. interests by engineering an appearance of acceptance of

removal among their own people (see Wilkins, Thurman, *Cherokee Tragedy: The Ridge Family and the Decimation of a People*, University of Oklahoma Press, Norman [2nd edition, revised], 1986). On Nancy Ward, see Tucker, Norma, "Nancy Ward: Gighau of the Cherokees," *Georgia Historical Quarterly*, No. 53, June 1969, pp. 192–200.

46. On the forced relocation, see Pirtle, Caleb III, *The Trail of Broken Promises: Removal of the Five Civilized Tribes to Oklahoma*, Eakin Press, Austin, TX, 1987.
47. Cherokee demographer Russell Thornton estimates that about 10,000 Cherokees—approximately half the nation's population—perished as a result of the Trail of Tears. See Thornton, Russell, *The Cherokees: A Population History*, University of Nebraska Press, Lincoln, 1990, pp. 73–7.
48. Starr, Emmet McDonald, *Starr's History of the Cherokee Indians*, Indian Heritage Association, Fayetteville, AK, 1922; reprinted 1967, p. 113.
49. Wardell, Morris L., *A Political History of the Cherokee Nation* 1838–1907, University of Oklahoma Press, Norman, 1938; reprinted 1977, p. 17.
50. See Parins, James W., *John Rollin Ridge: His Life and Works*, University of Nebraska Press, Lincoln, 1991.
51. See Franks, Kenny A., *Stand Watie and the Agony of the Cherokee Nation*, Memphis State University Press, Memphis, TN, 1979.
52. The author has been through hundreds of the relevant documents—all of them engineered in Washington, D.C.—without ever coming across a single reference to federal negotiators dealing with a native woman responsibly. Instead, they appear to have been quite uniformly barred from meetings and other proceedings, these being "men's work" in the Euroamerican view. Early reservation records are replete with the same attitude.
53. Medicine, Bea, "The Interaction of Culture and Sex Roles in Schools," in U.S. Department of Education, Office of Educational Research and Development. National Institute of Education, *Conference on Educational and Occupational Needs of American Indian Women*, October 1976, U.S. Government Printing Office, Washington, D.C., 1980, p. 149.
54. For an excellent first-hand recounting of the process, see Lindsey, Lilah Denton, "Memories of the Indian Territory Mission Field," *Chronicles of Oklahoma*, No. 36, Summer 1958, p. 181–98.

Gender and Islamic Fundamentalism: Feminist Politics in Iran

Nayereh Tohidi

Nayereh Tohidi is a professor of women's studies at Harvard University. She was a leading member of the Iranian Womens' Movement in the 1970s, and is the author of Women and Struggle in Iran.

Tohidi addresses the situation of women in Iran after Khomeini's rise, following the Shah's defeat. Following Khomeini's takeover, women were required to fully cover their bodies in public, schools were sex-segregated, and women were forbidden to enter many fields of study. In addition, the legal age of marriage for girls was reduced to nine; women convicted of adultery were stoned to death; and under the Law of Retribution, a woman's life was devalued to half the value of a man's. Tohidi argues that although women in Iran may appear to have accepted the revival of traditional roles, this acceptance is based on inadequate information and has taken place in an atmosphere of severe oppression.

Millions of Iranian women boldly stepped out from behind the four walls of their homes into the public arena in the Revolution of 1979. Their involvement in the revolution took many forms: some collected and disseminated news or distributed leaflets; others gave shelter to the wounded or to political activists under attack. Many actively marched and demonstrated in the streets, some went so far as to help erect barricades against the police, and a few even took up arms and went underground as members of a guerrilla movement.

Reprinted with permission of Indiana University Press and Nayereh Tohidi, from *Third World Women and the Politics of Feminism,* edited by Chandra Mohanty, Indiana University Press, 1991. [Edited]

During the early months of 1979, some women activists, particularly the university-educated and middle-class women, while opposing the Shah as the symbol of tyranny, gradually grew suspicious of the movement as they noted that many of the women participating in the demonstrations wore veils. Their anxiety increased as Khomeini took over the leadership of the revolution and as the streets filled with repetitive cries of "Islamic Rule!" and "God's Party Is the Only Party!" Nevertheless, like many of their male friends, these women dismissed their anxiety by assuming that Khomeini was simply playing a spiritual role, and that clerical rule would be incompatible with Iran's developing capitalist system. They felt that the dynamic process so inherent in the revolution would eventually expose and eliminate the retrogressive and reactionary factions from the leadership. Or so they thought.

Many Iranian activists at the time, both women and men, considered the veil a part of the superstructure or a secondary phenomenon which bothered only Western feminists or a few Iranian women intellectuals. The immediate concern was to rid the country of the Shah's regime and his imperialist supporters. Thus, as contradictory as it might seem to Western feminists, many women, even nonreligious, nontraditional, and highly educated women, took up the veil as a symbol of solidarity and opposition to the Shah (AZ 1981). At rallies and demonstrations, chadors (veils) and roosaries (large scarves) were extended to the unveiled women, who felt obliged to show their solidarity with the majority. Many university-educated, middeclass and leftist women, who may not have worn the veil before or usually would have seen it as nonprogressive, considered it a minor concession for the sake of unity against the common enemy.

During the early months of 1979, amid the exhilaration at the Shah's defeat, the active organization of several women's groups provided an encouraging sign for women's emancipation. For the first time in many women's lives, after years of repression, women were organizing for women. As March 8, 1979, approached—International Women's Day (IWD)—women's groups worked hard to mobilize thousands of Iranian women to commemorate the event. The days of optimism and euphoria did not last long, however. Two days before the event was to take place, Khomeini began to announce restrictive measures against women. His ultimatums enraged the women. Instead of causing them to abandon their plans to rally, they resulted in an outburst of spontaneous militant demonstrations. Women were outraged that the veil was once again becoming compulsory and that the government would dare to try to eliminate women from serving as judges in the courts. Women refused to accept the repeal of the Family Protection Law of 1975 which restricted polygyny and men's unilateral right to divorce and to child custody. Instead of the planned one-day rally, the storm raged for nearly a week. It was the first and most open confrontation that Iranian women were able to mount against the fundamentalist rulers.

Although the government cautiously restrained itself from immediately imposing these new measures, the forward march of the popular movement was, for all practical purposes, brought to a grinding halt. The quest for social justice, democracy, and independence had to be unwillingly abandoned as the revolution was coercively aborted. Women, members of national ethnic minorities, popular and progressive organizations, workers and newly formed labor councils, intellectuals, journalists, publishers—one by one, all became victims of the waves of terror imposed by a theocracy that showed itself to be more and more regressive. Of all these groups that actively participated in the revolution, the Iranian women played perhaps the least understood and most enigmatic role.

How regrettable that most of those who identified with the left and other democratic movements and those who were progressive in their thinking could not have perceived the hateful misogynist character of the newly imposed religious law and the fundamentalist and reactionary regime. In this essay, I would like to suggest the results of such a misperception and the possible reasons for it.

PRESENT SITUATION OF WOMEN IN IRAN

Today, in spite of the massive participation of Iranian women in the revolution, women's position has worsened rather than improved. Women experience the same subjugations as before—except in most cases, they have increased in scope. The official rights and duties of women along with the expected behavior patterns and sex roles that accompany them have progressed no further than during the oppressive Pahlavi rule. In many cases, the situation more closely mirrors Iran's precapitalist days. Some of the most blatant violations of women's rights by the Islamic regime are as follows:

Under the civil code currently practiced in Iran, all women, including non-Muslims and foreigners, are required to wear the veil and observe Islamic *Hejab* (complete covering of a woman). As Khomeini commanded, "no part of a woman's body may be seen except her face and the part of her hand between the wrist to the tip of her fingers." Appearing without *Hejab* is considered a crime punishable by seventy-five lashes or up to a year's imprisonment. Bands of club-wielders, employed by the "Center to Fight the Undesired," impose *Hejab* upon women. Slogans such as "Death to Those without *Hejab*" cover the walls in cities, inciting action against unveiled women.[1]

Many public areas are now sex-segregated, including schools and universities. A number of girls' schools have had to close because of the shortage of women teachers. The illiteracy rate among women, particularly in the rural areas, has been increasing. In higher education, women are banned from entering certain fields of study, such as law, agriculture, geology, archaeology, and mining engineering. Married women are prohibited from attending public school altogether.

The legal age for marriage has also changed, a further reflection of the regressive attitude toward women and young girls. When Khomeini first came to power, he lowered the minimum legal age for girls to marry from eighteen to thirteen years, and in certain cases to as low as nine. Polygyny, previously restricted by the Family Protection Law, has been reinstated: a man may have up to four wives officially, as well as others on a temporary basis (*sigh'a or Mut'a)*. Under the *Shari'a* (Islamic Code of Ethics), as interpreted by Iranian *Shi'a* clergy, temporary marriage can be contracted for a fixed period of time—ranging from a few minutes to ninety-nine years—after a nominal fee is paid to the woman and a verse is repeated. This type of marriage takes place for the sole purpose of men's sexual pleasure (Haeri 1983). By relegitimizing and officially encouraging *Mut'a*, the Islamic regime has, in reality, endorsed a form of prostitution.

Except in extremely unusual circumstances, women cannot seek a divorce. If a woman is divorced, she loses the custody rights of her children automatically to the father (after the age of seven for girl children, and after the age of two for boy children). A woman does not have the right of guardianship over her children during marriage, after divorce, or even after the death of her husband.

In terms of control over their bodies, sexually and reproductively, women have few rights. Abortion is illegal. Women convicted of adultery are stoned to death; and acts of homosexuality are punishable by death if the "offense" is repeated. Thousands of women imprisoned for their political beliefs have been tortured and executed.

With regard to mobility and occupational choices, women's lives are very restricted. For instance, a woman is legally not allowed to leave the house without her husband's permission, and she must get written permission before traveling abroad. Besides having to get her husband's written permission before taking a job, a woman is officially discouraged from gaining employment outside the home. Of those who are employed, many are fired under the pretense of failure to observe Islamic *Hejab*, are laid off, or are made to retire early. According to a bill passed by the Islamic parliament, full-time women employees are restricted to part-time employment. The government announced that "in order to promote motherhood and family life, the salary of any male employee will be raised 40 percent if his wife quits her job."

In keeping with the above measures, the Law of Retribution (*Quasas*) was passed in 1982 which states that the value of a woman's life is only half that of a man's. The testimony of two women equals that of one man; and in the case of major crimes, such as murder, a woman's testimony is not considered at all.

Finally, the eight-year-long genocidal war between Iran and Iraq has further compounded the effects of economic deterioration, high unemployment, high rate of inflation, brain drain, and the exodus of professionals from the country. There are a vastly increasing number of widowed, displaced, and refugee women who are all undergoing unbearable economic hardship and emotional suffering.

It is important to note that, on the other hand, the Islamic government has not been totally successful in implementing all of its ideological objectives. Some of the patriarchal demands of the clergy are, inevitably, in contradiction with the structural imperatives of the Iranian capitalist economy. Contemporary Iranian women's social role, their literacy level (35 percent), the participation rate of urban women in the labor force (12 percent), and, particularly, their recent massive political participation in the revolution have made it difficult for the present ruling clergy to radically transform women's socioeconomic roles and return all women back to the domestic sphere. Economic necessities, for example, force many women into low-paid jobs in the formal and informal sector and domestic wage labor. Some educated women with prior work experience are self-employed. Thus, the mere participation of women in public economic activities and the violations of the Islamic code of *Hejab* on their part have undermined the fundamentalist notion of women's role and have worked in resistance to total subjection.

WHY DID WOMEN RALLY BEHIND KHOMEINI?

Considering the extent to which so many Iranian women wholeheartedly endorsed and involved themselves in the revolution, one must seek to explain the present tragic fate of women in Iran. A major question is, Why haven't women continued to vehemently protest against the Islamic government's imposition of the veil and other oppressive measures? Do women of all social strata perceive their present situation as devastating and deteriorating? And finally, why do some groups of women still support the Islamic Republic of Khomeini?

The postrevolutionary changes that have affected women negatively can be overemphasized if they are not seen in the context of past and present laws and if class differences and social context are ignored (Higgins 1985, 483). The historical, socioeconomic, political, cultural, and psychological factors behind the revolution all must be considered in the analysis of women's situation. In Iran, as in most other "Third World" countries, women's issues and organizations have been related to the national anticolonial and antiimperialist movements. Consequently, the fate of the women's movement and women's social status have been closely intertwined with the general course of national and class struggles.

The historical precedent and social tradition for massive participation of women in the Iranian Revolution of 1977–79 go back to the 1905–1911 constitutional movement. This movement never managed to overthrow feudalism and neocolonial domination, and did not succeed in implementing its bourgeois-democratic goals for women. However, the seeds were planted for future struggle and consciousness raising.[2]

Iran, under the Pahlavi reign (1922–1979) and through neocolonialist imposition, was changing rapidly from a semifeudal Asiatic society to a centralized capitalist state dependent mainly upon the United States. However, the uneven process of capitalist development and the restricted character of industrialization, along with an absolutist and corrupt monarchy, tended to reinforce the persistence of precapitalist modes of production to a considerable extent (Jazani 1980). This in turn continued to reproduce traditional social relationships, values, attitudes, and behavior patterns, including gender roles and family arrangements.

While the process of modernization, i.e., capitalist development and Westernization, was advantageous to an important sector of the upper class and the emerging middle class, it was often harmful to the traditional segment of the middle class (the merchant [bazaar] bourgeoisie and petite bourgeoisie), as well as their historical ally the clergy. Bazaar merchants and artisans often suffered ruinous competition from Western goods, and later on from larger commercial and industrial enterprises of their own Westernized upper class. Therefore, conflict and friction were set in motion between the growing "modernized" social strata, who imitated and aspired to a Western lifestyle, and the powerful clergy and traditional bazaaries, who perceived the cultural and economic changes as jeopardizing their very existence.

It was the women who belonged to the latter strata, of traders, merchants, shopkeepers, and artisans, whose lifestyle, religious beliefs, and cultural identity were being challenged, negated, ridiculed, and sometimes coercively taken away by the Westernization process of the Shah's state.[3] In the 1970s, the younger generation of women from this strata were caught up in two conflicting and competing value systems—the traditional one reinforcing their families and the religious standards of public morality, and the more modern one aligning them with a Westernized imported culture reinforced by the state. To resolve this dilemma, many fell back on their "traditional roots," intrigued by the Islamic model of womanhood presented by ideologues such as Ali Shariati or even the more conservative fundamentalists opposing the Shah. And it was they who, later on, made up the core of veiled militant contingents who demonstrated in the streets.

One reason for the appeal of the more traditional image is that the rapid changes imposed by the Shah did not serve the needs of the majority of women. The emergence of a new market which attracted cheap female labor was just one inevitable process of capitalist development, industrialization, and land reform in Iran. As a consequence of the restricted character of industrialization and proletarianization, however, women were, for the most part, absorbed by the growing sector of services and state employment. While the number of literate, highly educated, and wage-earning women in urban centers increased, no genuine change or fundamental process took place in the status, social relations, and/or conditions of everyday life for the majority of Iranian women. A few reforms pertaining to the legal rights of women, e.g., the Family Protection Law (1975), while positive and progressive on paper, did not affect the majority of women. Similarly, peasant women did not noticeably benefit from the Shah's land reform (Tabari and Yeganeh 1982). As in many "Third World" countries, development was directed and manipulated by multinational corporations and resulted in a sharp deterioration in the conditions of women's daily lives, intensifying their exploitation and degraded status.

On the other hand, the very act of leaving behind the old traditions and of participating in social production in the public sphere was a step forward for urban working women in terms of gaining autonomy. Yet the lack of corresponding supportive social provisions, and effective legal reforms, made working outside the home a perpetual struggle. Women were subject to continual exploitation. Besides receiving low wages, they were exposed to constant sexual harassment on the workplace, and were discouraged by resentful negative attitudes from relatives and family members at home.

The model for the "new woman" proposed by the Shah's regime did not appeal to many Iranians. According to traditional norms, a woman was to hide her body in public and submit herself like an obedient servant or piece of property, first to her father, and later to her husband. The "new woman," on the other hand, was expected to ornament and show herself in order to please both the public and her husband, while at the same time serve as a cheap commodity in the labor force (AZ 1981).

The constant exposure of women to the modernized version of "woman" and the corresponding values of Western culture, and the deliberate efforts made to cultivate a mass-consumption consciousness—slavish imitation of European fashions, preoccupation with self-presentation, and, in short, commercialization of women—created a confused and, in part, "alien" model of womanhood, thus hardly preferable to the traditional one. The resultant dual value system, with its constant dilemmas and the alienation it caused many women, manifested itself in the formation of two distinct groups: one group, made up of the highly educated and professional women, modified their traditional attitudes and adapted to the new environment; and the other group, often under great pressure from their families, resisted the "imposed, alien, corrupt, and non-Islamic" standards and embraced the traditional forms. The latter group, made up of members of the bazaar merchants and traditional petite bourgeoisie, felt excluded, isolated, and put down by the Western dominant culture. This, in turn, resulted in resentment, distrust, and hidden hostility toward unveiled "modern" women.[4]

Traditional models of womanhood were reintroduced by the leaders and ideologues of the Islamic opposition, such as Ali Shariati, Taleghani, and Motahari.[5] Fatimeh, the daughter of the Prophet Mohammad and the wife of Ali, the first Imam, became the personification of virtue and obedience; and Zeinab, sister of Hossein, the Third Imam, who was martyred by the corrupt rulers of the day, became the symbol of outspoken, aggressive, and militant women. These role models, while they were reintroduced in deliberately modified political portraits, provided women with an identity and a much-needed defense mechanism. In such a situation, and given the factors enumerated above, the clergy found a climate ripe for channeling the genuine grievances of women into a puritanical Islamic movement.

Other sociopolitical factors also contributed to the acceptance of fundamental Islam as an alternative to the Shah. Specifically, a history of failure of nationalist and communist forces in Iran and the subsequent distrust and disillusionment with the left, combined with the Shah's systematic and ruthless repression of newly forming democratic and leftist organizations, created a vacuum of progressive alternatives for the anti-Shah movement. Unlike Islamic groups, the left lacked a national network to communicate effectively with the majority of people in Iran, and they were unable to offer a vocabulary more familiar to the populace. As a result, progressive ideas did not find their appropriate place in society. The leftist forces were under constant suppression and, thus, could only offer the image of an underground guerrilla woman (such as that of Ashraf Dehghani and Marzieh Oskooei, two well-known Fedaee), and such a model could not be adopted by the majority of women.

Furthermore, the left relied mostly on an economic deterministic analysis of Iranian society, and this limited its perspective on the situation of women. Analysis of the oppression of women and a more general democratic and cultural evaluation of Iranian society required a more thorough analysis which the left failed to initiate and develop (Azari 1983). Moreover, illiteracy (65 percent) and political inexperience prevailed, especially among women. Historically, women had no outside public associations except with the mosques. There were no popular women's groups that were solely and truly organized to raise feminist consciousness. It was in such a social and political context that Islam became the expected and familiar vent for protest. Fundamentalists in countries such as Iran, Lebanon, Morocco, and Pakistan gain control by channeling people's frustration and anger into a familiar language, ideology, and value system.

It is clear that the changes and policies implemented by the Islamic Republic of Iran (IRI) have generally had a negative and retrogressive impact on the economic and cultural conditions of the majority of the population, both women and men. But while the IRI has restricted the rights and opportunities of women in most aspects, there is still a group of women (supportive of the Islamic regime) who, because of their social class and cultural background, have gained certain privileges, as well as a positive self-concept and a sense of power, dignity, and pride (Higgins 1985). Although their role in community politics has remained indirect, protected, and secondary to that of men, they have managed to retain their subsequently gained activism in the public sphere (Hegland 1986). However, as far as the women's movement and feminism are concerned, the activism, ideology, and point of view of this group of Iranian women resemble those of Phyllis Schlafy in the United States, except that she does not wear a veil!

At the same time, Islam should not be conceptualized as an autonomous, monolithic, and static structure that has shaped the socioeconomic process and all social relationships, including women's status (Moghadam 1983). Iran's present predicament, and that of Iranian women in particular, cannot be explained by focusing exclusively on the compulsory veil, the *Shari'a*-based restrictive legal rights, or the Islamic fundamentalism of the present regime. The prevailing conditions of women in Iran are not the overnight result of Khomeini's regime with its Islamic rules. Nor is it Islam that subjugates women any more than fundamentalist Catholicism does in Latin America. As el Saadawi (1980) writes, "the great religions of the world uphold similar principles in so far as the submission of women to men is concerned."

Like many other Middle Eastern countries, Iranian society is characterized by the uneven development of capitalism and industrialization. Therefore, the persistence of the traditional orthodox school of Islam and its formidable laws and regulations in terms of sex roles correspond to the persistence of precapitalistic modes of production. The direct and indirect consequences of years of patriarchy, repression, dictatorial monarchy, and cultural and economic penetration of imperialist forces have all contributed to the present backlash in Iran.

Yet it is very important to realize the place and function of Islamic ideology in the struggle for social change. To view the Islamic fundamentalist revival in the Middle East as an ostensibly "antiimperialist," radical, and militant trend has the potential for great deception, as it continues to influence both women and men and their approach to politics in the Middle East. It obscures and distorts the objectives and direction of the national liberation movements. Furthermore, local and international reactionary forces have been indirectly and covertly reinforcing the pan-Islamic and fundamentalist revival in the Middle East; for instance, by redirecting the aims of the movement and by dividing people into religious factions, they have been building a strong and subtle "barrier against communism."[6] Consider, for instance, the role of fundamentalist forces such as *Amal, Aldaawa, Ekhwan al Muslemin*, and *Hezbollah* in Lebanon, Iraq, Egypt, and Iran. These forces must be more adequately dealt with rather than passively accepted as part of the revolution which will go away later.

With regard to women's movements, especially in Iran, Egypt, Pakistan, Lebanon, and Palestine, there is an urgent need to fight back and reverse the fundamentalist trend, in terms of both educating and organizing people. The ideological significance of Islam as a political alternative to which the masses have turned must be understood, and appropriate measures must be drawn up in response to it (Tabari and Yeganeh 1982). A call for separation of the state from religion as a democratic principle should be included in any progressive platform of political groups faced with the threat of fundamentalism. Women must insist on holding out for this principle more than ever.

"Third World" women's movements and their people's national democratic and anti-imperialist struggles are closely interrelated theoretically and empirically (Chinchilla 1977; Sen and Grown 1987). Alone, a woman's movement can never transform the foundations of sexism and sexual oppression. Neither can a revolution which seeks to transform class relationships meet its goals if it does not incorporate the question of women's oppression. Specific demands of women must be incorporated into the national antiimperialist movement and class struggle right from the beginning. *The women's question should not be relegated to the days after the revolution*—as has been, unfortunately, the tendency of many left and revolutionary movements. Cases such as the Algerian and Iranian revolutions have proven that the success of a nationalist or even a socialist revolution does not automatically lead to liberation for women.

In the case of Middle Eastern women, in particular because of the recent spread of religious fundamentalism, it is more important than ever to raise women's issues and integrate the women's question into the national and class struggle. Therefore, mobilization of women in democratic and autonomous organizations through the process of revolution must utilize women's political power inside the revolution. Otherwise, "women may be used by the revolution as tools, as cheap labor, cheap fighters—to die first and be liberated last!" (el Saadawi 1980).

NOTES

1. One of the methods of reprisal against unveiled women was formulated by Hashemi Rafsanjani, one of the most influential clergy, who serves as speaker of the Islamic parliament and the commander in chief. In one of his Friday sermons (May 4, 1986) broadcast by radio, TV, and print media, Mr. Rafsanjani announced that those women who are still not in perfect compliance with the Islamic *Hejab* (categorized in Farsi as *Bad Hejab*), meaning those who are not covered properly, e.g., revealing some hair beneath their headscarves and wearing bright colors, will be arrested and put in a concentration camp to

undergo reindoctrination and do forced labor. Unlike regular or political prisoners, these women must have their daily expenses paid by husbands or male kinsmen.

It should be noted, however, that recently, following the end of the Iran–Iraq war (August 1988), there has appeared a shift toward moderation in the regime's policy with respect to women's dress code. Ironically, Rafsanjani himself is one of those who have started speaking in favor of a less rigid policy and attitude toward women and men's clothing, as well as other restrictions against arts and music. The seriousness and consistency of the Islamic regime's recent move toward openness remain to be seen. But despite the present uncertainty, one needs to explore the reasons behind such a shift and its subsequent implications, particularly since it has coincided with a renewed wave of persecution and execution of political opponents.

For a review and analysis of the latest developments in the women's situation under the Islamic Republic of Iran, see Nayereh Tohidi, "Gender, Modernization and Identity Politics in Iran" in *Gender and National Identity: The Woman Question in Algeria, Iran, Afghanistan, and Palestine,* V. Moghadam, editor, London: Zed Books, 1993.

2. For a comprehensive historical account of the Iranian women's movement, see Sanasarian (1982) and *Women and Struggle in Iran,* no. 4 (1985):5–15.
3. For example, women were forced to remove their veils in 1935 under Reza Shah (the late deposed Shah's father). This measure was designed to help "modernize" Iran. To enforce the idea, police were ordered to physically remove the veil from any woman wearing it in public. Undoubtedly, this would have been a progressive step if women had chosen to do it themselves. Instead, it humiliated and alienated many Iranian women, who resorted to staying behind closed doors and not venturing into the streets in order to avoid this embarrassing confrontation.

   Consequently, the veil became politicized. Not to wear it became associated with identifying with the West, and the abusive and brutal policies of the Pahlavi regime. This partially explains why the adoption of the veil became a symbolic protest against the Shah. For further discussion on politicization of the veil in Iran, see Sanasarian (1982, 137–39).
4. It is interesting and revealing to note that the present harsh and aggressive punishment and surveillance of women who fail to observe Islamic *Hejab* are usually carried out by women from the very same traditional groups who call themselves "*Hezbollahee* women," i.e., "Partisans of God" or "Zeinab's Sisters." Their deeply rooted hostility toward unveiled women can be explained in part by their previous sociopsychological experiences under the Shah.
5. For further elaboration, see Azari (1983, 66).
6. Note the issue of Reagan's secret deals and support of the Iranian fundamentalist government, as well as overt support of Afghanistan's Islamic fundamentalists fighting the Afghan government. In both cases, Reagan's justification is that these forces—no matter how repressive, backward, and reactionary they are—should be supported and deserve to be called "moderate" or "freedom fighters as long as they are anti-communist."

REFERENCES

AZ. 1981. "The Women's Struggle in Iran." *Monthly Review* (March):22–30.

AZARI, F. 1983. *Women of Iran: The Conflict with Fundamentalist Islam.* London: Ithaca Press.

CHINCHILLA, NORMA S. 1977. "Mobilizing Women: Revolution in the Revolution." *Latin American Perspectives* 4, no. 4 (Issue 15):83–101.

EL SAADAWI, NAWAL. 1980. *The Hidden Face of Eve: Women in the Arab World.* London: Zed Press.

HAERI, S. 1983. "The Institution of *Mut'a* Marriage in Iran: A Formal and Historical Perspective." In G. Nashat, ed. *Women and Revolution in Iran.* Boulder, Colo.: Westview Press.

HEGLAND, MARY E. 1986. "Political Roles of Iranian Village Women." *Middle East Report (MERIP)*, no. 138, pp. 14–19.

HIGGINS, PATRICIA J. 1985. "Women in the Islamic Republic of Iran: Legal, Social, and Ideological Changes." *Signs: Journal of Women in Culture and Society* 10, no. 3:477–94.

JAZANI, B. 1980. *Capitalism and Revolution in Iran.* London: Zed Press.

MOGHADAM, V. 1983. "Peripheral Capitalism and Feminism." *Women and Struggle in Iran,* no. 3, pp. 20–25.

———.1988. "Women, Work, and Ideology in the Islamic Republic." *International Journal of Middle East Studies* 20:221–43.

SANASARIAN, E. 1982. *The Women's Rights Movement in Iran: Mutiny, Appeasement, and Repression from 1900 to Khomeini.* New York: Praeger.

SEN, G., and C. GROWN. 1987. *Development, Crisis, and Alternative Visions: Third World Women's Perspectives.* New York: Monthly Review Press.

TABARI, A, and N. YEGANEH. 1982. *In the Shadow of Islam: The Women's Movement in Iran.* London: Zed Press.

GENDER ROLES AND MORALITY—SUPPLEMENTARY READINGS

ACCAD, EVELYNE. "Sexuality and Sexual Politics: Conflicts and Contradictions for Contemporary Women in the Middle East," in *Third World Women and the Politics of Feminism*, Mohanty, Russo, and Torres, editors. Bloomington, IN: Indiana University Press, 1991.

ALEXANDER, M. JACQUI. "Redrafting Morality: The Postcolonial State and the Sexual Offenses Bill of Trinidad and Tobago," in *Third World Women and the Politics of Feminism*, Mohanty, Russo, and Torres, editors. Bloomington, IN: Indiana University Press, 1991.

BAIER, ANNETTE. "Whom Can Women Trust," in *Feminist Ethics*, Claudia Card, editor. Lawrence, KS: University of Kansas Press, 1991.

BARRY, KATHLEEN. "Female Sexual Slavery: Understanding the International Dimensions of Women's Oppression." *Human Rights Quarterly*, vol. 3(2), Spring 1981.

DILLON, ROBIN S. "Care and Respect," in *Explorations in Feminist Ethics*, Cole and Coultrap-McQuin, editors. Bloomington, IN: Indiana University Press, 1992.

EL MERNISSI, FATIMA. "Democracy as Moral Disintegration: The Contradiction Between Religious Belief and Citizenship as a Manifestation of the Ahistoricity of the Arab Identity," in *Women of the Arab World*, Nahid Toubia, editor. London: Zed Books, 1988.

HARDING, SANDRA. "The Curious Coincidence of Feminine and African Moralities," in *Women and Moral Theory*, Eva Kittay and Diana Meyers, editors. Totowa, NJ: Rowman & Littlefield, 1987.

HOAGLAND, SARAH LUCIA. "Lesbian Ethics and Female Agency," in *Explorations in Feminist Ethics*, Cole and Coultrap-McQuin, editors. Bloomington, IN: Indiana University Press, 1992.

JAGGAR, ALISON. "On Sexual Equality." *Ethics*, 1974.

MOODY-ADAMS, MICHELLE. "Gender and the Complexity of Moral Voices," in *Feminist Ethics*, Claudia Card, editor. Lawrence, KS: University of Kansas Press, 1991.

SWANTON, CHRISTINE, Viviane Robinson, and Jan Crosthwaite. "Treating Women as Sex-Objects." *Journal of Social Philosophy*, vol. 20(3), Winter 1989.

TONG, ROSEMARY. "Sexual Harassment," in *Women, Sex and the Law*. Totowa, NJ: Rowman and Allenheld, 1984.

VI

Racial and Ethnic Discrimination

Prejudice is the reason of fools.

—Voltaire

Racial and ethnic discrimination is a fact of life for many people. Although the more blatant forms may have declined in certain countries within the last 30 years or so, discrimination persists in many areas of life. Economically, in the United States, there is still unequal pay. In 1992, women and minorities earned an average of 75 cents for every dollar earned by white men for the same job. Furthermore, many desirable jobs are still without any minority or women employees. This situation is referred to as the "glass ceiling" and is an invisible barrier in the job market which keeps women and minorities "in their place" on the job. Low pay is a particularly effective tool for keeping groups of people fixed at a lower societal position and precluding their equal access to political, social, and economic power.

There is far-reaching agreement that discrimination against women and minorities, based on the trait of gender or ethnic origin, is morally wrong. These practices of discrimination violate the *principle of equality.* Although not universally accepted, this principle mandates that equals be treated equally, and that unequals be treated unequally. The treatment should be based on relevant similarities or differences among individuals. Relevant differences in job hiring are those that have to do with job performance. For example, for a mechanic's position, one needs proper training and education to meet the requirements for certification. Sex and race are not relevant traits for the job, and to deny anyone a job based on these traits is to violate the principle of equality. Normally, the principle of equality is not violated when discrimination is based on relevant differences such as training or ability. Furthermore, it does not always violate the principle of equality to discriminate based on race—as, for example, only auditioning a black man to play Othello, since the part calls for a black man. What is morally objectionable is to discriminate based on irrelevant traits.

However, there is no such far-reaching agreement on how to correct past and present practices that systematically discriminate against women and minorities. The principle of equality requires that equals be treated equally in the matters of hiring, promotion, and pay. If the principle of equality entails a moral right, employers are morally obligated not to violate this principle. Furthermore, there is a legal obligation in the United States not to discriminate based on irrelevant traits such as racial or ethnic origin. However, it is controversial whether or not a business must go beyond this obligation and adopt a policy actively favoring minorities or women. Affirmative action is one such policy.

Affirmative action programs range from actively recruiting qualified minorities and women, to favoring qualified, though unequally qualified minority and women applicants, to establishing quota systems whereby a certain number of minorities or women *must* be hired. Although all three are preferential treatment programs, the last two provoke the most controversy. Affirmative action is often criticized as perpetuating the harms which it hopes to cure, and for this reason some of its opponents call affirmative action "reverse discrimination." They argue that affirmative action uses the same morally irrelevant traits used in unjust racial discrimination, and thus it is inconsistent and not morally justifiable. Proponents of affirmative action argue that it is fair and consistent, as well as necessary to correct past injustices. Proponents also argue that without active intervention, minority applicants will not have access to their fair share of the prized jobs in society. In the United States, hard quotas have been ruled unconstitutional; however, the shortage of minorities in some professions may constitute a "compelling state interest," and active recruitment to correct this imbalance would then be legally acceptable.

Bernard Boxill addresses such a compelling interest and argues in favor of color-conscious policies such as affirmative action. Boxill addresses the need of minorities to have representation in the professions, such as the need for black attorneys. Boxill asserts that a doctor or lawyer with black skin is more likely to provide services to those who otherwise would not have access to them. He contends that colorblind policies involve a grave cost to self-esteem, as they imply that people should not be treated differently just because they are born with qualities such as dark skin color. However, society does not value dark skin, and discriminates accordingly, further aggravating the shortage of black professionals. Concerned that blacks receive fair consideration, he argues for a type of merit in color-conscious policies wherein differences in color and talent are equally weighted. He concludes that color-conscious policies can be justifiable in the same way that talent-based policies can be.

Lisa Newton argues that color-conscious policies such as affirmative action are *prima facie* unjustified because they involve reverse discrimination. She appeals to the principle of equality, and argues that affirmative action violates the very same principle of equality used to assert that sexual and racial discrimination are wrong. Justice requires that we treat citizens equally under the law, and injustice is the violation of equality. She argues that it is equally wrong to favor a group with special privileges and to disfavor a group by denying their members basic rights that are granted to others. Newton concludes that programs favoring minorities are thus *prima facie* wrong as they violate the fundamental principle of equality. Newton is further concerned with the practical problems that will result if a policy of affirmative action is adopted. Reverse discrimination, she concludes, will result in complete destruction of "justice, law, equality, and citizenship itself."

Kwame Anthony Appiah addresses the concept of racism. Appiah distinguishes between racialism, intrinsic racism, and extrinsic racism. Racialism, he states, is the belief that there are intrinsic and specific characteristics of the races which are not shared among the races. These characteristics allow races to be distinguished from one another. Extrinsic racism asserts that the races warrant morally different treatment because of their inherent traits. Intrinsic racism is the belief that each race has a different moral status, regardless of the characteristics of the race. Intrinsic racism is often associated with partiality for those of one's own race. Appiah asserts that holding racist dispositions involves self-deception, for it requires that one believe that there are morally relevant differences between the races. Appiah denounces all forms of racism as morally wrong, because racism violates the imperative to utilize only morally relevant bases in making moral distinctions, and allows one to escape universal moral demands.

Laurence Thomas questions the commonly held assumption that racism and sexism are similar. Although women and minorities have been treated similarly, he states that there are fundamental conceptual differences between racism and sexism. One example Thomas raises is that since women are required for the perpetuation of the species, men will not completely exclude themselves from women, but there is no such natural basis for whites to keep blacks around.

Thomas argues that the identity of men is fundamentally tied to their sexist views of women, while the identity of whites has no fundamental tie to being racists. For example, Thomas claims that the women's movement has led men to form groups to deal with the challenges to their masculine identities, while the civil rights movement did not result in a similar action by whites. Thomas labels his thesis—that sexism is more central to identity than racism—the racial and sexual identity thesis (RSI thesis). Thomas concludes that racism and sexism are two different and distinct social aberrations, and that in light of the RSI thesis, racist views are easier to eliminate than sexist views. While acknowledging that racism does not exclusively apply to blacks, Thomas limits his discussion of racism to that against blacks. Thomas thus epitomizes the traditional approach to racism that Vine Deloria, Jr. brings into question.

Deloria asserts that racism is much more than a matter of white–black relations. He charges that the forms of racism against African Americans and American Indians are very different. African Americans were ignored and systematically kept out of the dominant society, while American Indians were forced to assimilate. One such example is that blacks did not have their children taken from their homes and sent to white schools where they were forced to learn the white culture, as Indian children were. American Indians are still being forced to assimilate, as is exemplified in the recent Supreme Court ruling denying the use of peyote in American Indian religion, and the continuing refusal to honor the sanctity of burial grounds. Furthermore, black–white segregation is still very much a part of our experience. Deloria asserts that solving the racial problem requires that the white man (his words) must understand and take responsibility for the past by facing racism as a problem he has created within himself and others.

Taking responsibility for one's racist attitudes is one such starting point in understanding the racial question. Larry May argues for such a moral accountability. He addresses the role racist attitudes play in facilitating racially motivated harms. May asserts that a racist climate increases the likelihood of racially motivated harm. This climate is produced by people who share racist attitudes, and even though these people may not directly cause racial harms, their attitudes often contribute to a type of joint venture in which all members share in moral responsibility for that harm. May argues that continuing to hold racist attitudes that are known to contribute to a moral climate that permits racial harms is a form of reckless behavior. People who exhibit reckless behavior share responsibility for the risk for and the actual harm. Although those who actually cause the harm are legally culpable, the moral responsibility does not lie with them alone. To begin to understand one's share in responsibility for racism requires one to take steps to eliminate one's racist attitudes and to refuse to contribute to a racist climate.

The Color-Blind Principle

Bernard Boxill

Bernard Boxill is a professor of philosophy at the University of North Carolina at Chapel Hill. He is the author of Blacks and Social Justice *(1984).*

Boxill attempts to defend affirmative action plans by arguing that there is no reason for selection plans to be strictly colorblind, that is, for race never to be a criterion of selection. He asserts that some theorists misinterpret the reasons why it is unjust to discriminate based on race. Although he acknowledges that color-conscious policies, such as Jim Crow laws, can be heinous, he contends that it may be perfectly justified to discriminate among people according to traits or skills they are not responsible for possessing. He argues that it is just as bad to completely ignore race as it is to completely ignore talent. He concludes that either color or talent may be the foundation of just discrimination.

PLESSY

In 1892, Homer Plessy, an octoroon, was arrested in Louisiana for taking a seat in a train car reserved for whites. He was testing a state law which required the "white and colored races" to ride in "equal but separate" accommodations, and his case eventually reached the Supreme Court.

Part of Plessy's defense, though it must be considered mainly a snare for the opposition, was that he was "seven-eighths Caucasian and one-eighth African blood," and that the "mixture of colored blood was not discernible in him." The bulwark of his argument was, however, that he was "entitled to every right, privilege and immunity secured to citizens of the white race," and that the law violated the Fourteenth Amendment's prohibition against unequal protection of the laws.[1] Cannily, the court refused the snare. Perhaps it feared—and with reason—that the ancestry of too many white Louisianans held dark secrets. But it attacked boldly enough Plessy's main argument that the Louisiana law was unconstitutional. That argument, Justice Henry Billings Brown wrote for the majority, was unsound. "Its underlying fallacy," he averred, was its "assumption that the enforced separation of the two races stamps the colored race with a badge of inferiority." "If this be so," Brown concluded, "it is not by reason of anything found in the act, but solely because the colored race chooses to put that construction upon it."[2]

Only one judge dissented from the court majority—Justice John Marshall Harlan. It was the occasion on which he pronounced his famous maxim: "Our Constitution is color-blind." In opposition to Justice Brown, Justice Harlan found that the "separation of citizens on the basis of race [was a] badge of servitude . . . wholly inconsistent [with] equality before the law."[3]

Plessy's is the kind of case which makes the color-blind principle seem indubitably right as a basis for action and policy, and its contemporary opponents appear unprincipled, motivated by expediency, and opportunistic. This impression is only strengthened by a reading of Justice Brown's tortuously preposterous defense of the "equal but separate" doctrine. It should make every advocate of color-conscious policy wary of the power of arguments of expediency to beguile moral sense and subvert logic. Yet I argue that color-conscious policy can still be justified. The belief that it cannot is the result of a mistaken generalization from *Plessy.* There is no warrant for the idea that the color-blind principle should hold in some general and absolute way.

"I DIDN'T NOTICE" LIBERALS

In his book *Second Wind*, Bill Russell recalls how amazed he used to be by the behavior of what he called "I didn't notice" liberals. These were individuals who claimed not to notice people's color. If they mentioned someone Russell could not place, and Russell asked whether she was black or white, they would answer, "I didn't notice." "Sweet and innocent," Russell recalls, "sometimes a little proud."[4] Now, the kind of color-blindness the "I didn't notice" liberals claim to have may be a worthy ideal—Richard Wasserstrom, for example, argues that society should aim toward it—but it is absolutely different from the color-blind principle which functions as a basis for policy.[5] Thus, while Wasserstrom supports color-conscious policies to secure the ideal of people not noticing each others' color, the principle of color-blindness in the law opposes color-conscious policies and does not necessarily involve any hope that people will not notice each others' color. Its thesis is simple: that no *law* or *public policy* be designed to treat people differently because they are of a different color.

COLOR-BLIND AND COLOR-CONSCIOUS POLICIES

The essential thing about a color-conscious policy is that it is designed to treat people differently because of their race. But there are many different kinds of color-conscious policies. Some, for example the Jim Crow policies now in the main abolished, aim to subordinate blacks, while others, such as busing and preferential treatment, aim at elevating blacks.

Some color-conscious policies explicitly state that persons should be treated differently because of their race, for example the segregation laws at issue in *Plessy;* others make no mention of race, but are still designed so that blacks and whites are treated differently, for example, the "grandfather clauses" in voting laws that many states adopted at the turn of the century. To give one instance, in Louisiana this clause stated that those who had had the right to vote before or on 1 January 1867, or their lineal descendants, did not have to meet the educational, property, or tax requirements for voting. Since no blacks had had the right to vote by that time, this law worked effectively to keep blacks from voting while at the same time allowing many impoverished and illiterate whites to vote—yet it made no mention of race.

My object in this chapter is to demonstrate that the color-blind principle, which considers all color-conscious policies to be invalid, is mistaken. I do not deny that many color-conscious policies are wrong. Jim Crow was certainly wrong, and, for different reasons, proposals for black control of inner cities and inner city schools are probably wrong. But this is not because they are color-conscious, but for reasons which indicate that color-conscious policies like busing and affirmative action could be correct.

Advocates of the belief that the law should be color-blind often argue that this would be the best means to an ideal state in which people are color-blind. They appeal to the notion that, only if people notice each other's color can they discriminate on the basis of color and, with considerable plausibility, they argue that color-conscious laws and policies can only heighten people's awareness of each other's color, and exacerbate racial conflict. They maintain that only if the law, with all its weight and influence, sets the example of color-blindness, can there be a realistic hope that people will see through the superficial distinctions of color and become themselves color-blind.

But this argument is not the main thesis of the advocates of legal color-blindness. Generally, they eschew it because of its dependency on the empirical. Their favorite argument, one that is more direct and intuitively appealing, is simply that it is wicked, unfair, and unreasonable to penalize a person for what he cannot help being. Not only does this seem undeniably true, but it can be immediately applied to the issue of race. No one can help being white or being black, and so it seems to follow that it is wicked, unfair, and unreasonable to disqualify a person from any consideration just because he is white or black. This, the advocates of color-blindness declare, is what made Jim Crow law heinous, and it is what makes affirmative action just as heinous.

The force of this consideration is enhanced because it seems to account for one peculiar harmfulness of racial discrimination—its effect on self-respect and self-esteem. For racial discrimination makes some black people hate their color, and succeeds in doing so because color cannot be changed. Furthermore, a racially conscious society has made color seem an important part of the individual's very essence, and since color is immutable it is easily susceptible to this approach. As a result, the black individual may come, in the end, to hate even himself. Even religion is here a dubious consolation. For if God makes us black or white, to the religious black that by which he is marked may come to seem a curse by the Almighty, and he himself therefore essentially evil.

Of course, there are strategies that attempt to circumvent these effects of racial discrimination, but their weaknesses seem to confirm the need for color-blindness. For example, some black people concede that black is bad and ugly, but attempt to soften the effects of this concession by insisting that black is only "skin deep," we are all brothers beneath the skin, and the body, which is black and ugly, is no part of and does not sully the soul, which is the real self and is good. Thus, black people sometimes protested that although their skins were black, their souls were white, which is to say, good. There is truth to this feeling, in that nothing is more certain than that neither a black nor a white skin can make a person good or bad. Yet it is not a wholly successful approach to the problem of color. It requires that the black person believe that he is in some sense a ghost, which he can believe only if he is a lunatic. Another strategy is put forth by Black Nationalism. The black nationalist agrees with the racists' view that his color is an important and integral part of his self, but affirms, in opposition to the racists, that it has value. This strategy, which is exemplified by the slogans "black is beautiful" and "black and proud," has the obvious advantage of stimulating pride and self-confidence. Nevertheless, it is no panacea. For one thing, it has to contend with the powerful propaganda stating that black is *not* beautiful. And there is a more subtle problem. Since the black cannot choose *not* to be black, he cannot be altogether confident that he would choose to *be* black, nor, consequently, does he really place a special value in being black. Thus, some people, black and white, have expressed the suspicion that the slogan "black is beautiful" rings hollow, like the words of the man who protests too loudly that he loves the chains he cannot escape. In this respect the black who can pass as white has an advantage over the black who cannot. For, though he cannot choose not to be black, he can choose not to be *known* to be black.

THE RESPONSIBILITY CRITERION

A final argument in favor of legal color-blindness is related to, and further develops, the point that people do not choose to be, and cannot avoid being, black or white. This links the question of color-blindness to the protean idea of individual responsibility. Thus, William Frankena writes, that to use color as a fundamental basis for distributing "opportunities, offices, etc." to persons is "unjust in itself," because it is to distribute goods on the basis of a feature "which the individual has not done, and can do nothing about; we are treating people differently in ways that profoundly affect their lives because of differences for which they have no responsibility."[6] Since this argument requires that people be treated differently in ways which profoundly affect their lives only on the basis of features for which they are responsible, I call it the responsibility criterion.

The responsibility criterion also seems to make the principle of color-blindness follow from principles of equal opportunity. Joel Feinberg takes it to be equivalent to the claim that "properties can be the grounds of just discrimination between persons only if those persons had a fair opportunity to acquire or avoid them."[7] This implies that to discriminate between persons on the basis of a feature for which they can have no responsibility is to violate the principle of fair opportunity. But color (or sex) is a feature of persons for which they can have no responsibility.

The responsibility criterion may seem innocuous because, though, strictly interpreted it supports the case for color-blindness, loosely interpreted it leaves open the possibility that color-conscious policies are justifiable. Thus, Frankena himself allows that color could be an important basis of distribution of goods and offices if it served "as [a] reliable sign[s] of some Q, like ability or merit, which is more justly employed as a touchstone for the treatment of individuals."[8] This sounds like a reasonable compromise and is enough to support some arguments for color-conscious policies. For example, it could support the argument that black and white children should go to the same schools because being white is a reliable sign of being middle-class, and black children, who are often lower-class, learn better when their peers are middle-class. Similarly, it might support the argument that preferential hiring is compensation for the harm of being discriminated against on the basis of color, and that being black is a reliable sign of having been harmed by that discrimination.

But however loosely it is interpreted, the responsibility criterion cannot be adduced in support of all reasons behind color-conscious policies. It cannot, for example, sustain the following argument, sketched by Ronald Dworkin, for preferential admission of blacks to medical school. "If quick hands count as 'merit' in the case of a prospective surgeon this is because quick hands will enable him to serve the public better and for no other reason. If a black skin will, as a matter of regrettable fact, enable another doctor to do a different medical job better, then that black skin is by the same token 'merit' as well."[9] What is proposed here is not that a black skin is a justifiable basis of discrimination because it is a reliable sign of merit or some other factor Q. A closely related argument does make such a proposal, viz., that blacks should be preferentially admitted to medical school because being black is a reliable sign of a desire to serve the black community. But this is not the argument that Dworkin poses. In the example quoted above what he suggests is that being black is in *itself* merit, or, at least, something very like merit.

According to the responsibility criterion, we ought not to give A a job in surgery rather than B, if A is a better surgeon than B only because he was born with quicker hands. For if we do, we treat A and B "differently in ways that profoundly affect their lives because of differences for which they have no responsibility." This is the kind of result which puts egalitarianism in disrepute. It entails the idea that we might be required to let fumblers do surgery and in general give jobs and offices to incompetents, and this is surely intolerable. But, as I plan to show, true egalitarianism has no such consequences. They are the result of applying the responsibility criterion, not egalitarian principles. Indeed, egalitarianism must scout the responsibility criterion as false and confused.

Egalitarians should notice first, that, while it invalidates the merit-based theories of distribution that they oppose, it also invalidates the need-based theories of distribution they favor. For, if people are born with special talents for which they are not responsible, they are also born with special needs for which they are not responsible. Consequently, if the responsibility criterion forbids choosing A over B to do surgery because A is a better surgeon because he was born with quicker hands, it also forbids choosing C rather than D for remedial education because C needs it more than D only because he was born with a learning disability and D was not.

At this point there may be objections. First, that the responsibility criterion was intended to govern only the distribution of income, not jobs and offices—in Feinberg's discussion, for example, this is made explicit. Second, that it does not mean that people should not be treated differently because of differences, good or bad, which they cannot help, but rather that people should not get less just because they are born without the qualities their society prizes or finds useful. This seems to be implied in Frankena's claim that justice should make the "same proportionate contribution to the best life for everyone" and that this may require spending more on those who are "harder to help"—probably the untalented—than on others. Qualified in these ways, the responsibility criterion becomes more plausible. It no longer implies, for example, that fumblers should be allowed to practice surgery, or that the blind be treated just like the sighted. But with these qualifications it also becomes almost irrelevant to the color-blind issue. For that issue is not only about how income should be distributed. It is also about how jobs and offices should be distributed.

Most jobs and offices are distributed to people in order to produce goods and services to a larger public. To that end, the responsibility criterion is irrelevant. For example, the purpose of admitting people to medical schools and law schools is to provide the community with good medical and legal service. It does not matter whether those who provide them are responsible for having the skills by virtue of which they provide the goods, or whether the positions they occupy are "goods" to them. No just society makes a person a surgeon just because he is responsible for his skills or because making him a surgeon will be good for him. It makes him a surgeon because he will do good surgery.

Accordingly, it may be perfectly just to discriminate between persons on the basis of distinctions they are not responsible for having. It depends on whether or not the discrimination serves a worthy end. It may be permissible for the admissions policies of professional schools to give preference to those with higher scores, even if their scores are higher than others only because they have higher native ability (for which they cannot, of course, be considered responsible), if the object is to provide the community with good professional service. And, given the same object, if for some reason a black skin, whether or not it can be defined as merit, helps a black lawyer or doctor to provide good legal or medical service to black people who would otherwise not have access to it, or avail themselves of it, it is difficult to see how there can be a principled objection to admissions policies which prefer people with black skins—though, again, they are not responsible for the quality by virtue of which they are preferred.

JUSTICE AND THE RESPONSIBILITY CRITERION

A further point needs to be made in order to vindicate color-conscious policies. The principles of justice are distributive: Justice is concerned not only with increasing the total amount of a good a society enjoys, but also with how that good should be distributed among individuals. Generally, judicial principles dictate that people who are similar in ways deemed relevant to the issue of justice, such as in needs or rights, should get equal amounts of a good, and people who are dissimilar in these regards should get unequal amounts of the good. In terms of these principles certain laws and rules must be considered unjust which would not otherwise be thought unjust. Consider, for example, a policy for admitting persons to medical school which resulted in better and better medical service for white people, but worse and worse medical service for black people. This policy would be unjust, however great the medical expertise—certainly a good—it produced, unless color is relevant to the receiving of good medical attention.

In a case like this, where it is not, the theoretical circumstance outlined by Dworkin, in which black skin might be considered a "merit," becomes viable. It is true, of course, that color is not, precisely, merit. But to insist on strict definition in this context is to cavil. The point is that if black clients tend to trust and confide more in black lawyers and doctors, then color—functioning as merit—enables a good to be produced and distributed according to some principle of justice.

If these considerations are sound, then the responsibility criterion thoroughly misconstrues the reasons for which racial discrimination is unjust. Racial discrimination against blacks is unjust because it does not enable goods to be produced and distributed according to principles of justice. It is not unjust because black people do not choose to be black, cannot *not* be black, or are not responsible for being black. This is completely irrelevant. For example, a policy denying university admission to people who parted their hair on the right side would be unjust because the way in which people part their hair is irrelevant to a just policy of school admission. It does not matter in the least, in relation to the nature and object of education, that they choose how they part their hair. Similarly, even if black people could choose to become white, or could all easily pass as white, a law school or medical school that excluded blacks because they were black would still act unjustly. Nothing would have changed.

The arguments in support of color-blindness tend to make the harmfulness of discrimination depend on the difficulty of avoiding it. This is misleading. It diverts attention from the potential harmfulness of discrimination that *can* be avoided and brings the specious responsibility criterion into play. Suppose again, for example, that a person is denied admission to law school because he parts his hair on the right side. Though he, far more easily than the black person, can avoid being unfairly discriminated *against*, he does not thereby more easily avoid being the object, indeed, in a deeper sense, the victim, of unfair discrimination. If he parts his hair on the left side he will presumably be admitted to law school. But then he will have knowingly complied with a foolish and unjust rule and this may well make him expedient and servile. Of course, he will not be harmed to the same extent and in the same way as the victim of racial discrimination. For example, he probably will not hate himself. Unlike color, the cause of his ill-treatment is too easily changed for him to conceive of it as essential to himself. Moreover, if he chooses to keep his hair parted on the right side and thus to forego law school, he *knows* that he is not going to law school because he freely chose to place a greater value on his integrity or on his taste in hairstyles than on a legal education. He knows this because he knows he could have chosen to change his hairstyle. As I noted earlier, this opportunity for self-assertion, and thus for self-knowledge and self-confidence, is denied the black who is discriminated against on the basis of his color.

Nevertheless, as I stated earlier, the considerations that stem from applying the responsibility criterion to a judgment of racial discrimination are secondary to understanding its peculiar harmfulness. Suppose, for example, that a person is not admitted to medical school to train to be a surgeon because he was born without fingers. If all the things he wants require that he have fingers, he may conceivably come to suffer the same self-hatred and self-doubt as the victim of racial discrimination. Yet his case is different, and if he attends to the difference, he will not suffer as the victim of racial discrimination suffers. The discrimination that excludes him from the practice of surgery is not denigrating his interests because they are his. It is a policy that takes into account a just object—the needs of others in the community for competent surgery. Allowing him to be a surgeon would rate other, equally important, interests below his. But racial discrimination excludes its victims from opportunities on the basis of a belief that their interests are ipso facto less important than the interests of whites. The man without fingers may regret not being born differently, but he cannot resent how he is treated. Though his ambitions may be thwarted, he himself is still treated as a moral equal. There is no attack on his self-respect. Racial discrimination, however, undermines its victims' self-respect through their awareness that they are considered morally inferior. The fact that racial discrimination, or any color-conscious policy, is difficult to avoid through personal choice merely adds to its basic harmfulness if it is in the first place unjust, but is not the *reason* for its being unjust.

It remains to consider Feinberg's claim that if people are discriminated for or against on the basis of factors for which they are not responsible the equal opportunity principle is contravened. This I concede. In particular, I concede that color-conscious policies giving preference to blacks place an insurmountable obstacle in the path of whites, and since such obstacles reduce opportunities, such policies may make opportunities unequal. But this gives no advantage to the advocates of color-blind policies. For giving preference to the competent has exactly the same implications as giving preference to blacks. It, too, places obstacles in the paths of some people, this time the untalented, and just as surely makes opportunities unequal. Consequently, an advocate of color-blindness cannot consistently oppose color-conscious policies on the grounds that they contravene equal opportunity and at the same time support talent-conscious policies. Nor, finally, does my concession raise any further difficulty with the issue of equal opportunity. As I argue later, equal opportunity is not a fundamental principle of justice, but is derived from its basic principles. Often these basic principles require that opportunities be made more equal. Invariably, however, these same principles require that the process of equalization stop before a condition of perfect equality of opportunity is reached.

To conclude, adopting a color-blind principle entails adopting a talent-blind principle, and since the latter is absurd, so also is the former. Or, in other words, differences in talent, and differences in color, are, from the point of view of justice, on a par. Either, with equal propriety, can be the basis of a just discrimination. Consequently, the color-blind principle is not as simple, straightforward, or self-evident as many of its advocates seem to feel it is. Color-conscious policies can conceivably be just, just as talent-conscious policies can conceivably be—and often are—just. It depends on the circumstances.

NOTES

1. Derrick A. Bell, Jr., ed., *Plessy v. Ferguson* in *Civil Rights: Leading Cases* (Boston: Little, Brown, 1980), 64–77.
2. Ibid., 71.
3. Ibid., 71–77.
4. Bill Russell and Taylor Brand, *Second Wind* (New York: Random House, 1979), 187.
5. Richard A. Wasserstrom, "Racism and Sexism," in Richard A. Wasserstrom, *Philosophy and Social Issues* (Notre Dame, Ind.: University of Notre Dame Press, 1980), 24, 25.
6. William Frankena, "Some Beliefs About Justice," in *Justice,* ed. Joel Feinberg and Hyman Gross (Encino, Calif.: Dickenson, 1977), 49.
7. Joel Feinberg, *Social Philosophy* (Englewood Cliffs, N.J.: Prentice-Hall, 1973), 49.
8. Frankena, "Some Beliefs About Justice," 49.
9. Ronald Dworkin, "Why Bakke Has No Case," *New York Review of Books*, 10 Nov. 1977, 14.

Reverse Discrimination As Unjustified

Lisa H. Newton

Lisa H. Newton is a professor of philosophy at Fairfield University in Connecticut. She is the editor of Ethics in America: Source Reader *(1989), the book used for the PBS series which was the first television series concerning contemporary applied ethics.*

Newton argues that policies such as affirmative action are unjustified because they are forms of reverse discrimination, and this violates the principle of justice. Justice, she states, is treating each citizen equally under the law. Conversely, injustice is the violation of the principle of equality. Injustice results from favoring a group with special licenses or disfavoring a group by denying them what is guaranteed to others. Any discrimination is prima facie *wrong if it violates the principle of justice. Thus, favoring women and blacks is an injustice. Newton argues that in the end, adopting a policy of discrimination destroys our citizenship, and makes us instead "petitioners for favors."*

I have heard it argued that "simple justice" requires that we favor women and blacks in employment and educational opportunities, since women and blacks were "unjustly" excluded from such opportunities for so many years in the not so distant past. It is a strange argument, an example of a possible implication of a true proposition advanced to dispute the proposition itself, like an octopus absentmindedly slicing off his head with a stray tentacle. A fatal confusion underlies this argument, a confusion fundamentally relevant to our understanding of the notion of the rule of law.

Two senses of justice and equality are involved in this confusion. The root notion of justice, progenitor of the other, is the one that Aristotle (*Nichomachean Ethics* 5. 6; *Politics* 1. 2; 3. 1) assumes to be the foundation and proper virtue of the political association. It is the condition which free men establish among themselves when they "share a common life in order that their association bring them self-sufficiency"—the regulation of their relationship by law, and the establishment, by law, of equality before the law. Rule of law is the name and pattern of this justice; its equality stands against the inequalities—of wealth, talent, etc.—otherwise obtaining among its participants, who by virtue of that equality are called "citizens." It is an achievement—complete, or, more frequently, partial—of certain people in certain concrete situations. It is fragile and easily disrupted by powerful individuals who discover that the blind equality of rule of law is inconvenient for their interests. Despite its

Lisa Newton, "Reverse Discrimination as Unjustified" in *Ethics, Vol. 83*, July 1973, published by The University of Chicago Press. Reprinted by permission.

obvious instability, Aristotle assumed that the establishment of justice in this sense, the creation of citizenship, was a permanent possibility for men and that the resultant association of citizens was the natural home of the species. At levels below the political association, this rule-governed equality is easily found; it is exemplified by any group of children agreeing together to play a game. At the level of the political association, the attainment of this justice is more difficult, simply because the stakes are so much higher for each participant. The equality of citizenship is not something that happens of its own accord, and without the expenditure of a fair amount of effort it will collapse into the rule of a powerful few over an apathetic many. But at least it has been achieved, at some times in some places; it is always worth trying to achieve, and eminently worth trying to maintain, wherever and to whatever degree it has been brought into being.

Aristotle's parochialism is notorious; he really did not imagine that persons other than Greeks could associate freely in justice, and the only form of association he had in mind was the Greek *polis.* With the decline of the *polis* and the shift in the center of political thought, his notion of justice underwent a sea change. To be exact, it ceased to represent a political type and became a moral ideal: the ideal of equality as we know it. This ideal demands that all men be included in citizenship—that one Law govern all equally, that all men regard all other men as fellow citizens, with the same guarantees, rights, and protections. Briefly, it demands that the circle of citizenship achieved by any group be extended to include the entire human race. Properly understood, its effect on our associations can be excellent: it congratulates us on our achievement of rule of law as a process of government but refuses to let us remain complacent until we have expanded the associations to include others within the ambit of the rules, as often and as far as possible. While one man is a slave, none of us may feel truly free. We are constantly prodded by this ideal to look for possible unjustifiable discrimination, for inequalities not absolutely required for the functioning of the society and advantageous to all. And after twenty centuries of pressure, not at all constant, from this ideal, it might be said that some progress has been made. To take the cases in point for this problem, we are now prepared to assert, as Aristotle would never have been, the equality of sexes and of persons of different colors. The ambit of American citizenship, once restricted to white males of property, has been extended to include all adult free men, then all adult males including ex-slaves, then all women. The process of acquisition of full citizenship was for these groups a sporadic trail of half-measures, even now not complete; the steps on the road to full equality are marked by legislation and judicial decisions which are only recently concluded and still often not enforced. But the fact that we can now discuss the possibility of favoring such groups in hiring shows that over the area that concerns us, at least, full equality is presupposed as a basis for discussion. To that extent they are full citizens, fully protected by the law of the land.

It is important for my argument that the moral ideal of equality be recognized as logically distinct from the condition (or virtue) of justice in the political sense. Justice in this sense exists *among* a citizenry, irrespective of the number of the populace included in that citizenry. Further, the moral ideal is parasitic upon the political virtue, for "equality" is unspecified—it means nothing until we are told in what respect that equality is to be realized. In a political context, "equality" is specified as "equal rights"—equal access to the public realm, public goods and offices, equal treatment under the law—in brief, the equality of citizenship. If citizenship is not a possibility, political equality is unintelligible. The ideal emerges as a generalization of the real condition and refers back to that condition for its content.

Now, if justice (Aristotle's justice in the political sense) is equal treatment under law for all citizens, what is injustice? Clearly, injustice is the violation of that equality, discriminating for or against a group of citizens, favoring them with special immunities and privileges or depriving them of those guaranteed to the others. When the southern employer refuses to hire blacks in white-collar jobs, when Wall Street will only hire women as secretaries with new titles, when Mississippi high schools routinely flunk all black boys above ninth grade, we have examples of injustice, and we work to restore the equality of the public realm by ensuring that equal opportunity will be provided in such cases in the future. But of course, when the employers and the schools *favor* women and blacks, the same injustice is done. Just as the previous discrimination did, this reverse discrimination violates the public equality which defines citizenship and destroys the rule of law for the areas in which these favors are granted. To the extent that we adopt a program of discrimination, reverse or otherwise, justice in the political sense is destroyed, and none of us, specifically affected or not, is a citizen, a bearer of rights—we are all petitioners for favors. And to the same extent, the ideal of equality is undermined, for it has content only where justice obtains, and by destroying justice we render the ideal meaningless. It is, then, an ironic paradox, if not a contradiction in terms, to assert that the ideal of equality justifies the violation of justice; it is as if one should argue, with William Buckley, that an ideal of humanity can justify the destruction of the human race.

Logically, the conclusion is simple enough: all discrimination is wrong *prima facie* because it violates justice, and that goes for reverse discrimination too. No violation of justice among the citizens may be justified (may overcome the *prima facie* objection) by appeal to the ideal of equality, for that ideal is logically dependent upon the notion of justice. Reverse discrimination, then, which attempts no other justification than an appeal to equality, is wrong. But let us try to make the conclusion more plausible by suggesting some of the implications of the suggested practice of reverse discrimination in employment and education. My argument will be that the problems raised there are insoluble, not only in practice but in principle.

We may argue, if we like, about what "discrimination" consists of. Do I discriminate against blacks if I admit none to my school when none of the black applicants are qualified by the tests I always give? How far must I go to root out cultural bias from my application forms and tests before I can say that I have not discriminated against those of different cultures? Can I assume that women are not strong enough to be roughnecks on my oil rigs, or must I test them individually? But this controversy, the most popular and well-argued aspect of the issue, is not as fatal as two others which cannot be avoided: if we are regarding the blacks as a "minority" victimized by discrimination, what is a "minority"? And for any group—blacks, women, whatever—that has been discriminated against, what amount of reverse discrimination wipes out the initial discrimination? Let us grant as true that women and blacks were discriminated against, even where laws forbade such discrimination, and grant for the sake of argument that a history of discrimination must be wiped out by reverse discrimination. What follows?

First, are there other groups which have been discriminated against? For they should have the same right of restitution. What about American Indians, Chicanos, Appalachian Mountain whites, Puerto Ricans, Jews, Cajuns, and Orientals? And if these are to be included, the principle according to which we specify a "minority" is simply the criterion of "ethnic (sub) group," and we're stuck with every hyphenated American in the lower-middle class clamoring for special privileges for *his* group—and with equal justification. For be it noted, when we run down the Harvard roster, we find not only a scarcity of blacks (in comparison with the proportion in the population) but an even more striking scarcity of those second-, third-, and fourth-generation ethnics who make up the loudest voice of Middle America. Shouldn't they demand *their* share? And eventually, the WASPs will have to form their own lobby, for they too are a minority. The point is simply this: there is no "majority" in America who will not mind giving up just a bit of their rights to make room for a favored minority. There are only other minorities, each of which is discriminated against by the favoring. The initial injustice is then repeated dozens of times, and if each minority is granted the same right of restitution as the others, an entire area of rule governance is dissolved into a pushing and shoving match between self-interested groups. Each works to catch the public eye and political popularity by whatever means of advertising and power politics lend themselves to the effort, to capitalize as much as possible on temporary popularity until the restless mob picks another group to feel sorry for. Hardly an edifying spectacle, and in the long run no one can benefit: the pie is no larger—it's just that instead of setting up and enforcing rules for getting a piece, we've turned the contest into a free-for-all, requiring much more effort for no larger a reward. It would be in the interests of all the participants to reestablish an objective rule to govern the process, carefully enforced and the same for all.

Second, supposing that we do manage to agree in general that women and blacks (and all the others) have some right of restitution, some right to a privileged place in the structure of opportunities for a while, how will we know when that while is up? How much privilege is enough? When will the guilt be gone, the price paid, the balance restored? What recompense is right for centuries of exclusion? What criterion tells us when we are done? Our experience with the Civil Rights movement shows us that agreement on these terms cannot be presupposed: a process that appears to some to be going at a mad gallop into a black takeover appears to the rest of us to be at a standstill. Should a practice of reverse discrimination be adopted, we may safely predict that just as some of us begin to see "a satisfactory start toward righting the balance," others of us will see that we "have already gone too far in the other direction" and will suggest that the discrimination ought to be reversed again. And such disagreement is inevitable, for the point is that we could not *possibly* have any criteria for evaluating the kind of recompense we have in mind. The context presumed by any discussion of restitution is the context of rule of law: law sets the rights of men and simultaneously sets the method for remedying the violation of those rights. You may exact suffering from others and/or damage payments for yourself if and only if the others have violated your rights; the suffering you have endured is not sufficient reason for them to suffer. And remedial rights exist only where there is law: primary human rights are useful guides to legislation but cannot stand as reasons for awarding remedies for injuries sustained. But then, the context presupposed by any discussion of restitution is the context of preexistent full citizenship. No remedial rights could exist for the excluded; neither in law nor in logic does there exist a right to *sue* for a standing to sue.

From these two considerations, then, the difficulties with reverse discrimination become evident. Restitution for a disadvantaged group whose rights under the law have been violated is possible by legal means, but restitution for a disadvantaged group whose grievance is that there was no law to protect them simply is not. First, outside of the area of justice defined by the law, no sense can be made of "the group's rights," for no law recognizes that group or the individuals in it, *qua* members, as bearers of rights (hence *any* group can constitute itself as a disadvantaged minority in some sense and demand similar restitution). Second, outside of the area of protection of law, no sense can be made of the violation of rights (hence the amount of the recompense cannot be decided by any objective criterion). For both reasons, the practice of reverse discrimination undermines the foundation of the very ideal in whose name it is advocated; it destroys justice, law, equality, and citizenship itself, and replaces them with power struggles and popularity contests.

NOTE

A version of this paper was read at a meeting of the Society for Women in Philosophy in Amherst, Massachusetts, 5 November 1972.

Racisms

Kwame Anthony Appiah

Kwame Anthony Appiah was raised in Ghana and is a professor of philosophy and African-American studies at Harvard University. He is the author of several books, including In My Father's House *(1992). He is currently editing* The Oxford Book of African Literature.

Appiah distinguishes various aspects of racism, including racialism, as well as intrinsic and extrinsic racism. Racialism is the view that there are inherent traits and tendencies of each race that are not shared with members of other races, and which allow us to divide people into distinct races. Extrinsic racism is the view that the races inherently have different essences that entail different morally relevant traits. Intrinsic racism is the view that moral differentiation between races is justified because each race has a different moral status, irrespective of its racial essence. The disposition he calls "racial prejudice" is the tendency to subscribe to false moral and theoretical propositions about races. Appiah asserts that racialism is false, and that both kinds of racism are theoretically and morally wrong.

If the people I talk to and the newspapers I read are representative and reliable, there is a good deal of racism about. People and policies in the United States, in Eastern and Western Europe, in Asia and Africa and Latin America are regularly described as "racist." Australia had, until recently, a racist immigration policy; Britain still has one; racism is on the rise in France; many Israelis support Meir Kahane, an anti-Arab racist; many Arabs, according to a leading authority, are anti-Semitic racists;[1] and the movement to establish English as the "official language" of the United States is motivated by racism. Or, at least, so many of the people I talk to and many of the journalists with the newspapers I read believe.

But visitors from Mars—or from Malawi—unfamiliar with the Western concept of racism could be excused if they had some difficulty in identifying what exactly racism was. We see it everywhere, but rarely does anyone stop to say what it is, or to explain what is wrong with it. Our visitors from Mars would soon grasp that it had become at least conventional in recent years to express abhorrence for racism. They might even notice that those most often accused of it—members of the South African Nationalist party, for example—may officially abhor it also. But if they sought in the popular media of our day—in newspapers and magazines, on television or radio, in novels or films—for an explicit definition of this thing "we" all abhor, they would very likely be disappointed.

Now, of course, this would be true of many of our most familiar concepts. *Sister, chair, tomato*—none of these gets defined in

Kwame Anthony Appiah, "Racisms," in *Anatomy of Racism,* edited by David Theo Goldberg (Minneapolis, MN: University of Minnesota Press, 1990).

the course of our daily business. But the concept of racism is in worse shape than these. For much of what we say about it is, on the face of it, inconsistent.

It is, for example, held by many to be racist to refuse entry to a university to an otherwise qualified "Negro" candidate, but not to be so to refuse entry to an equally qualified "Caucasian" one. But "Negro" and "Caucasian" are both alleged to be names of races, and invidious discrimination on the basis of race is usually held to be a paradigm case of racism. Or, to take another example, it is widely believed to be evidence of an unacceptable racism to exclude people from clubs on the basis of race; yet most people, even those who think of "Jewish" as a racial term, seem to think that there is nothing wrong with Jewish clubs, whose members do not share any particular religious beliefs, or Afro-American societies, whose members share the juridical characteristic of American citizenship and the "racial" characteristic of being black.

I say that these are inconsistencies "on the face of it," because, for example, affirmative action in university admissions is importantly different from the earlier refusal to admit blacks or Jews (or other "Others") that it is meant, in part, to correct. Deep enough analysis may reveal it to be quite consistent with the abhorrence of racism; even a shallow analysis suggests that it is intended to be so. Similarly, justifications can be offered for "racial" associations in a plural society that are not available for the racial exclusivism of the country club. But if we take racism seriously we ought to be concerned about the adequacy of these justifications.

In this essay, then, I propose to take our ordinary ways of thinking about race and racism and point up some of their presuppositions. And since popular concepts are, of course, usually fairly fuzzily and untheoretically conceived, much of what I have to say will seem to be both more theoretically and more precisely committed than the talk of racism and racists in our newspapers and on television. My claim is that these theoretical claims are required to make sense of racism as the practice of reasoning human beings. If anyone were to suggest that much, perhaps most, of what goes under the name "racism" in our world cannot be given such a rationalized foundation, I should not disagree: but to the extent that a practice cannot be rationally reconstructed it ought, surely, to be given up by reasonable people. The right tactic with racism, if you really want to oppose it, is to object to it rationally in the form in which it stands the best chance of meeting objections. The doctrines I want to discuss can be rationally articulated: and they are worth articulating rationally in order that we can rationally say what we object to in them.

RACIST PROPOSITIONS

There are at least three distinct doctrines that might be held to express the theoretical content of what we call "racism." One is the view—which I shall call *racialism*[2]—that there are heritable characteristics, possessed by members of our species, that allow us to divide them into a small set of races, in such a way that all the members of these races share certain traits and tendencies with each other that they do not share with members of any other race. These traits and tendencies characteristic of a race constitute, on the racialist view, a sort of racial essence; and it is part of the content of racialism that the essential heritable characteristics of what the nineteenth century called the "Races of Man" account for more than the visible morphological characteristics—skin color, hair type, facial features—on the basis of which we make our informal classifications. Racialism is at the heart of nineteenth-century Western attempts to develop a science of racial difference; but it appears to have been believed by others—for example, Hegel, before then, and many in other parts of the non-Western world since—who have had no interest in developing scientific theories.

Racialism is not, in itself, a doctrine that must be dangerous, even if the racial essence is thought to entail moral and intellectual dispositions. Provided positive moral qualities are distributed across the races, each can be respected, can have its "separate but equal" place. Unlike most Western-educated people, I believe—and I have argued elsewhere[3]—that racialism is false; but by itself, it seems to be a cognitive rather than a moral problem. The issue is how the world is, not how we would want it to be.

Racialism is, however, a presupposition of other doctrines that have been called "racism," and these other doctrines have been, in the last few centuries, the basis of a great deal of human suffering and the source of a great deal of moral error.

One such doctrine we might call "extrinsic racism": extrinsic racists make moral distinctions between members of different races because they believe that the racial essence entails certain morally relevant qualities. The basis for the extrinsic racists' discrimination between people is their belief that members of different races differ in respects that *warrant* the differential treatment, respects—such as honesty or courage or intelligence—that are uncontroversially held (at least in most contemporary cultures) to be acceptable as a basis for treating people differently. Evidence that there are no such differences in morally relevant characteristics—that Negroes do not necessarily lack intellectual capacities, that Jews are not especially avaricious—should thus lead people out of their racism if it is purely extrinsic. As we know, such evidence often fails to change an extrinsic racist's attitudes substantially, for some of the extrinsic racist's best friends have always been Jewish. But at this point—if the racist is sincere—what we have is no longer a false doctrine but a cognitive incapacity, one whose significance I shall discuss later in this essay.

I say that the *sincere* extrinsic racist may suffer from a cognitive incapacity. But some who espouse extrinsic racist doctrines are simply insincere intrinsic racists. For *intrinsic racists*, on my definition, are people who differentiate morally between members of different races because they believe that each race has a different moral status, quite independent of the moral characteristics entailed by its racial essence. Just as, for example, many people assume that the fact that they are biologically related to another person—a brother, an aunt, a cousin—gives them a moral interest in that person,[4] so an intrinsic racist holds that the bare fact of being of the same race is a reason for preferring one person to another. (I shall return to this parallel later as well.)

For an intrinsic racist, no amount of evidence that a member of another race is capable of great moral, intellectual, or cultural achievements, or has characteristics that, in members of one's own race, would make them admirable or attractive, offers any ground for treating that person as he or she would treat similarly endowed members of his or her own race. Just so, some sexists are "intrinsic sexists," holding that the bare fact that someone is a woman (or man) is a reason for treating her (or him) in certain ways.

There are interesting possibilities for complicating these distinctions: some racists, for example, claim, as the Mormons once did, that they discriminate between people because they believe that God requires them to do so. Is this an extrinsic racism, predicated on the combination of God's being an intrinsic racist and the belief that it is right to do what God wills? Or is it intrinsic racism because it is based on the belief that God requires these discriminations because they are right? (Is an act pious because the gods love it, or do they love it because it is pious?) Nevertheless, the distinctions between racialism and racism and between two potentially overlapping kinds of racism provide us with the skeleton of an anatomy of the propositional contents of racial attitudes.

RACIST DISPOSITIONS

Most people will want to object already that this discussion of the propositional content of racist moral and factual beliefs misses something absolutely crucial to the character of the psychological and sociological reality of racism, something I touched on when I mentioned that extrinsic racist utterances are often made by people who suffer from what I called a "cognitive incapacity." Part of the standard force of accusations of racism is that their objects are in some way *irrational.* The objection to Professor Shockley's claims about the intelligence of blacks is not just that they are false; it is rather that Professor Shockley seems, like many people we call "racist," to be unable to see that the evidence does not support his factual claims and that the connection between his factual claims and his policy prescriptions involves a series of non sequiturs.

What makes these cognitive incapacities especially troubling—something we should respond to with more than a recommendation that the individual, Professor Shockley, be offered psychotherapy—is that they conform to a certain pattern: namely, that it is especially where beliefs and policies are to the disadvantage of nonwhite people that he shows the sorts of disturbing failure that have made his views both notorious and notoriously unreliable. Indeed, Professor Shockley's reasoning works extremely well in some other areas: that he is a Nobel Laureate in physics is part of what makes him so interesting an example.

This cognitive incapacity is not, of course, a rare one. Many of us are unable to give up beliefs that play a part in justifying the special advantages we gain (or hope to gain) from our positions in the social order—in particular, beliefs about the positive characters of the class of people who share that position. Many people who express extrinsic racist beliefs—many white South Africans, for example—are beneficiaries of social orders that deliver advantages to them by virtue of their "race," so that their disinclination to accept evidence that would deprive them of a justification for those advantages is just an instance of this general phenomenon.

So too, evidence that access to higher education is as largely determined by the quality of our earlier educations as by our own innate talents, does not, on the whole, undermine the confidence of college entrants from private schools in England or the United States or Ghana. Many of them continue to believe in the face of this evidence that their acceptance at "good" universities shows them to be intellectually better endowed (and not just better prepared) than those who are rejected. It is facts such as these that give sense to the notion of false consciousness, the idea that an ideology can prevent us from acknowledging facts that would threaten our position.

The most interesting cases of this sort of ideological resistance to the truth are not, perhaps, the ones I have just mentioned. On the whole, it is less surprising, once we accept the admittedly problematic notion of self-deception, that people who think that certain attitudes or beliefs advantage them or those they care about should be able, as we say, to "persuade" themselves to ignore evidence that undermines those beliefs or attitudes. What is more interesting is the existence of people who resist the truth of a proposition while thinking that its wider acceptance would in no way disadvantage them or those individuals about whom they care—this might be thought to describe Professor Shockley; or who resist the truth when they recognize that its acceptance would actually advantage them—this might be the case with some black people who have internalized negative racist stereotypes; or who fail, by virtue of their ideological attachments, to recognize what is in their own best interests at all.

My business here is not with the psychological or social processes by which these forms of ideological resistance operate, but it is important, I think, to see the refusal on the part of some extrinsic racists to accept evidence against the beliefs as an instance of a widespread phenomenon in human affairs. It is a plain fact, to which theories of ideology must address themselves, that our species is prone both morally and intellectually to such distortions of judgment, in particular to distortions of judgment that reflect partiality. An inability to change your mind in the face of appropriate[5] evidence is a cognitive incapacity; but it is one that all of us surely suffer from in some areas of belief; especially in areas where our own interests or self-images are (or seem to be) at stake.

It is not, however, as some have held, a tendency that we are powerless to resist. No one, no doubt, can be impartial about everything—even about everything to which the notion of partiality applies; but there is no subject matter about which most sane people cannot, in the end, be persuaded to avoid partiality in judgment. And it may help to shake the convictions of those whose incapacity derives from this sort of ideological defense if we show them how their reaction fits into this general pattern. It is, indeed, because it generally *does* fit this pattern that we call such views "racism"—the suffix "-ism" indicating that what we have in mind is not simply a theory but an ideology. It would be odd to call someone brought up in a remote corner of the world with false and demeaning views about white people a "racist" if that person gave up these beliefs quite easily in the face of appropriate evidence.

Real live racists, then, exhibit a systematically distorted rationality, the kind of systematically distorted rationality that we are likely to call "ideological." And it is a distortion that is especially striking in the cognitive domain: extrinsic racists, as I said earlier, however intelligent or otherwise well informed, often fail to treat evidence against the theoretical propositions of extrinsic racism dispassionately. Like extrinsic racism, intrinsic racism can also often be seen as ideological; but since scientific evidence is not going to settle the issue, a failure to see that it is wrong represents a cognitive incapacity only on controversially realist views about morality. What makes intrinsic racism similarly ideological is not so much the failure of inductive or deductive rationality that is so striking in someone like Professor Shockley but rather the connection that it, like extrinsic racism, has with the interests—real or perceived—of the dominant group.[6] Shockley's racism is in a certain sense directed *against* nonwhite people: many believe that his views would, if accepted, operate against their objective interests, and he certainly presents the black "race" in a less than flattering light.

I propose to use the old-fashioned term "racial prejudice" in the rest of this essay to refer to the deformation of rationality in judgment that characterizes those whose racism is more than a theoretical attachment to certain propositions about race.

RACIAL PREJUDICE

It is hardly necessary to raise objections to what I am calling "racial prejudice"; someone who exhibits such deformations of rationality is plainly in trouble. But it is important to remember that propositional racists in a racist culture have false moral beliefs but may not suffer from racial prejudice. Once we show them how society has enforced extrinsic racist stereotypes, once we ask them whether they really believe that race in itself, independently of those extrinsic racist beliefs, justifies differential treatment, many will come to give up racist propositions, although we must remember how powerful a weight of authority our arguments have to overcome. Reasonable people may insist on substantial evidence if they are to give up beliefs that are central to their cultures.

Still, in the end, many will resist such reasoning; and to the extent that their prejudices are really not subject to any kind of rational control, we may wonder whether it is right to treat such people as morally responsible for the acts their racial prejudice motivates, or morally reprehensible for holding the views to which their prejudice leads them. It is a bad thing that such people exist; they are, in a certain sense, bad people. But it is not clear to me that they are responsible for the fact that they are bad. Racial prejudice, like prejudice generally, may threaten an agent's autonomy, making it appropriate to treat or train rather than to reason with them.

But once someone has been offered evidence both (1) that their reasoning in a certain domain is distorted by prejudice, and (2) that the distortions conform to a pattern that suggests a lack of impartiality, they ought to take special care in articulating views and proposing policies in that domain. They ought to do so because, as I have already said, the phenomenon of partiality in judgment is well attested in human affairs. Even if you are not immediately persuaded that you are yourself a victim of such a distorted rationality in a certain domain, you should keep in mind always that this is the usual position of those who suffer from such prejudices. To the extent that this line of thought is not one that itself falls within the domain in question, one can be held responsible for not subjecting judgments that *are* within that domain to an especially extended scrutiny; and this is a fortiori true if the policies one is recommending are plainly of enormous consequence.

If it is clear that racial prejudice is regrettable, it is also clear in the nature of the case that providing even a superabundance of reasons and evidence will often not be a successful way of removing it. Nevertheless, the racist's prejudice will be articulated through the sorts of theoretical propositions I dubbed extrinsic and intrinsic racism. And we should certainly be able to say something reasonable about why these theoretical propositions should be rejected.

Part of the reason that this is worth doing is precisely the fact that many of those who assent to the propositional content of racism do not suffer from racial prejudice. In a country like the United States, where racist propositions were once part of the national ideology, there will be many who assent to racist propositions simply because they were raised to do so. Rational objection to racist propositions has a fair chance of changing such people's beliefs.

EXTRINSIC AND INTRINSIC RACISM

It is not always clear whether someone's theoretical racism is intrinsic or extrinsic, and there is certainly no reason why we should expect to be able to settle the question. Since the issue probably never occurs to most people in these terms, we cannot suppose that they must have an answer. In fact, given the definition of the terms I offered, there is nothing barring someone from being both an intrinsic and an extrinsic racist, holding both that the bare fact of race provides a basis for treating members of his or her own race differently from others and that there are morally relevant characteristics that are differentially distributed among the races. Indeed, for reasons I shall discuss in a moment, *most* intrinsic racists are likely to express extrinsic racist beliefs, so that we should not be surprised that many people seem, in fact, to be committed to both forms of racism.

The Holocaust made unreservedly clear the threat that racism poses to human decency. But it also blurred our thinking because in focusing our attention on the racist character of the Nazi atrocities, it obscured their character as atrocities. What is appalling about Nazi racism is not just that it presupposes, as all racism does, false (racialist) beliefs—not simply that it involves a moral incapacity (the inability to extend our moral sentiments to all our fellow creatures) and a moral failing (the making of moral distinctions without moral differences)—but that it leads, first, to oppression and then to mass slaughter. In recent years, South African racism has had a similar distorting effect. For although South African racism has not led to killings on the scale of the Holocaust—even
s both left South Africa judicially exe-
more (mostly black) people per head
ulation than most other countries and
massive differences between the life
es of white and nonwhite South
s—it *has* led to the systematic oppres-
nd economic exploitation of people
e not classified as "white," and to the
n of suffering on citizens of all racial
cations, not least by the police state
required to maintain that exploitation
pression.

... of our resistance, therefore, to calling the racial ideas of those, such as the Black Nationalists of the 1960s, who advocate racial solidarity, by the same term that we use to describe the attitudes of Nazis or of members of the South African Nationalist party, surely resides in the fact that they largely did not contemplate using race as a basis for inflicting harm. Indeed, it seems to me that there is a significant pattern in the modern rhetoric of race, such that the discourse of racial solidarity is usually expressed through the language of *intrinsic* racism, while those who have used race as the basis for oppression and hatred have appealed to *extrinsic* racist ideas. This point is important for understanding the character of contemporary racial attitudes.

The two major uses of race as a basis for moral solidarity that are most familiar in the West are varieties of Pan-Africanism and Zionism. In each case it is presupposed that a "people," Negroes or Jews, has the basis for shared political life in the fact of being of the same race. There are varieties of each form of "nationalism" that make the basis lie in shared traditions; but however plausible this may be in the case of Zionism, which has in Judaism, the religion, a realistic candidate for a common and nonracial focus for nationality, the peoples of Africa have a good deal less in common culturally than is usually assumed. I discuss this issue at length in *In My Father's House: Essays in the Philosophy of African Culture,* but let me say here that I believe the central fact is this: what blacks in the West, like secularized Jews, have mostly in common is that they are perceived—both by themselves and by others—as belonging to the same race, and that this common race is used by others as the basis for discriminating against them. "If you ever forget you're a Jew, a goy will remind you." The Black Nationalists, like some Zionists, responded to their experience of racial discrimination by accepting the racialism it presupposed.[7]

Although race is indeed at the heart of Black Nationalism, however, it seems that it is the fact of a shared race, not the fact of a shared racial character, that provides the basis for solidarity. Where racism is implicated in the basis for national solidarity, it is intrinsic, not (or not only) extrinsic. It is this that makes the idea of fraternity one that is naturally applied in nationalist discourse. For, as I have already observed, the moral status of close family members is not normally thought of in most cultures as depending on qualities of character; we are supposed to love our brothers and sisters in spite of their faults and not because of their virtues. Alexander Crummell, one of the founding fathers of Black Nationalism, literalizes the metaphor of family in these startling words:

> Races, like families, are the organisms and ordinances of God; and race feeling, like family feeling, is of divine origin. The extinction of race feeling is just as possible as the extinction of family feeling. Indeed, a race *is* a family.[8]

It is the assimilation of "race feeling" to "family feeling" that makes intrinsic racism seem so much less objectionable than extrinsic racism. For this metaphorical identification reflects the fact that, in the modern world (unlike the nineteenth century), intrinsic racism is acknowledged almost exclusively as the basis of feelings of community. We can surely, then, share a sense of what Crummell's friend and co-worker Edward Blyden called "the poetry of politics," that is, "the feeling of race," the feeling of "people with whom we are connected."[9] The racism here is the basis of acts of supererogation, the treatment of others better than we otherwise might, better than moral duty demands of us.

This is a contingent fact. There is no logical impossibility in the idea of racialists whose moral beliefs lead them to feelings of hatred for other races while leaving no room for love of members of their own. Nevertheless most racial hatred is in fact expressed through extrinsic racism: most people who have used race as the basis for causing harm to others have felt the need to see the others as independently morally flawed. It is one thing to espouse fraternity without claiming that your brothers and sisters have any special qualities that deserve recognition, and another to espouse hatred of others who have done nothing to deserve it.[10]

Many Afrikaners—like many in the American South until recently—have a long list of extrinsic racist answers to the question why blacks should not have full civil rights. Extrinsic racism has usually been the basis for treating people worse than we otherwise might, for giving them less than their humanity entitles them to. But this too is a contingent fact. Indeed, Crummell's guarded respect for white people derived from a belief in the superior moral qualities of the Anglo-Saxon race.

Intrinsic racism is, in my view, a moral error. Even if racialism were correct, the bare fact that someone was of another race would be no reason to treat them worse—or better—than someone of my race. In our public lives, people are owed treatment independently of their biological characters: if they are to be differently treated there must be some morally relevant difference between them. In our private lives, we are morally free to have aesthetic preferences between people, but once our treatment of people raises moral issues, we may not make arbitrary distinctions. Using race in itself as a morally relevant distinction strikes most of us as obviously arbitrary. Without associated moral characteristics, why should race provide a better basis than hair color or height or timbre of voice? And if two people share all the properties morally relevant to some action we ought to do, it will be an error—a failure to apply the Kantian injunction to universalize our moral judgments—to use the bare facts of race as the basis for treating them differently. No one should deny that a common ancestry might, in particular cases, account for similarities in moral character. But then it would be the moral similarities that justified the different treatment.

It is presumably because most people—outside the South African Nationalist party and the Ku Klux Klan—share the sense that intrinsic racism requires arbitrary distinctions that they are largely unwilling to express it in situations that invite moral criticism. But I do not know how I would argue with someone who was willing to announce an intrinsic racism as a basic moral idea; the best one can do, perhaps, is to provide objections to possible lines of defense of it.

DE GUSTIBUS

It might be thought that intrinsic racism should be regarded not so much as an adherence to a (moral) proposition as the expression of a taste, analogous, say, to the food prejudice that makes most English people unwilling to eat horse meat, and most Westerners unwilling to eat the insect grubs that the !Kung people find so appetizing. The analogy does at least this much for us, namely, to provide a model of the way that *extrinsic* racist propositions can be a reflection of an underlying prejudice. For, of course, in most cultures food prejudices are rationalized: we say insects are unhygienic and cats taste horrible. Yet a cooked insect is no more health-threatening than a cooked carrot, and the unpleasant taste of cat meat, far from justifying our prejudice against it, probably derives from that prejudice.

But there the usefulness of the analogy ends. For intrinsic racism, as I have defined it, is not simply a taste for the company of one's "own kind," but a moral doctrine, one that is supposed to underlie differences in the treatment of people in contexts where moral evaluation is appropriate. And for moral distinctions we cannot accept that "de gustibus non est disputandum." We do not need the full apparatus of Kantian ethics to require that public morality be constrained by reason.

A proper analogy would be with someone who thought that we could continue to kill cattle for beef, even if cattle exercised all the complex cultural skills of human beings. I think it is obvious that creatures that shared our capacity for understanding as well as our capacity for pain should not be treated the way we actually treat cattle—that "intrinsic speciesism" would be as wrong as racism. And the fact that most people think it is worse to be cruel to chimpanzees than to frogs suggests that they may agree with me. The distinction in attitudes surely reflects a belief in the greater richness of the mental life of chimps. Still, I do not know how I would *argue* against someone who could not see this; someone who continued to act on the contrary belief might, in the end, simply have to be locked up.

THE FAMILY MODEL

I have suggested that intrinsic racism is, at least sometimes, a metaphorical extension of the moral priority of one's family; it might, therefore, be suggested that a defense of intrinsic racism could proceed along the same lines as a defense of the family as a center of moral interest. The possibility of a defense of family relations as morally relevant—or, more precisely, of the claim that one may be morally entitled (or even obliged) to make distinctions between two otherwise morally indistinguishable people because one is related to one and not to the other—is theoretically important for the prospects of a philosophical defense of intrinsic racism. This is because such a defense of the family involves—like intrinsic racism—a denial of the basic claim, expressed so clearly by Kant, that from the perspective of morality, it is as rational agents *simpliciter* that we are to assess and be assessed. For anyone who follows Kant in this, what matters, as we might say, is not who you are but how you try to live. Intrinsic racism denies this fundamental claim also. And, in so doing, as I have argued elsewhere, it runs against the mainstream of the history of Western moral theory.[11]

The importance of drawing attention to the similarities between the defense of the family and the defense of the race, then, is not merely that the metaphor of family is often invoked by racism; it is that each of them offers the same general challenge to the Kantian stream of our moral thought. And the parallel with the defense of the family should be especially appealing to an intrinsic racist, since many of us who have little time for racism would hope that the family is susceptible to some such defense.

The problem in generalizing the defense of the family, however, is that such defenses standardly begin at a point that makes the argument for intrinsic racism immediately implausible: namely, with the family as the unit through which we live what is most intimate, as the center of private life. If we distinguish, with Bernard Williams, between ethical thought, which takes seriously "the demands, needs, claims, desires, and generally, the lives of other people,"[12] and morality, which focuses more narrowly on obligation, it may well be that private life matters to us precisely because it is altogether unsuited to the universalizing tendencies of morality.

The functioning family unit has contracted substantially with industrialization, the disappearance of the family as the unit of production, and the increasing mobility of labor, but there remains that irreducible minimum: the parent or parents with the child or children. In this "nuclear" family, there is, of course, a substantial body of shared experience, shared attitudes, shared knowledge and beliefs; and the mutual psychological investment that exists within this group is, for most of us, one of the things that gives meaning to our lives. It is a natural enough confusion—which we find again and again in discussions of adoption in the popular media—that identifies the relevant group with the biological unit of *genitor, genetrix,* and *offspring* rather than with the social unit of those who share a common domestic life.

The relations of parent and their biological children are of moral importance, of course, in part because children are standardly the product of behavior voluntarily undertaken by their biological parents. But the moral relations between biological siblings and half-siblings cannot, as I have already pointed out, be accounted for in such terms. A rational defense of the family ought to appeal to the causal responsibility of the biological parent and the common life of the domestic unit, and not to the brute fact of biological relatedness, even if the former pair of considerations defines groups that are often coextensive with the groups generated by the latter. For brute biological relatedness bears no necessary connection to the sorts of human purposes that seem likely to be relevant at the most basic level of ethical thought.

An argument that such a central group is bound to be crucially important in the lives of most human beings in societies like ours is not, of course, an argument for any specific mode of organization of the "family": feminism and the gay liberation movement have offered candidate groups that could (and sometimes do) occupy the same sort of role in the lives of those whose sexualities or whose dispositions otherwise make the nuclear family uncongenial; and these candidates have been offered specifically in the course of defenses of a move toward societies that are agreeably beyond patriarchy and homophobia. The central thought of these feminist and gay critiques of the nuclear family is that we cannot continue to view any one organization of private life as "natural," once we have seen even the broadest outlines of the archaeology of the family concept.

If that is right, then the argument for the family must be an argument for a mode of organization of life and feeling that subserves certain positive functions; and however the details of such an argument would proceed it is highly unlikely that the same functions could be served by groups on the scale of races, simply because, as I say, the family is attractive in part exactly for reasons of its personal scale.

I need hardly say that rational defenses of intrinsic racism along the lines I have been considering are not easily found. In the absence of detailed defenses to consider, I can only offer these general reasons for doubting that they can succeed: the generally Kantian tenor of much of our moral thought threatens the project from the start; and the essentially unintimate nature of relations within "races" suggests that there is little prospect that the defense of the family—which seems an attractive and plausible project that extends ethical life beyond the narrow range of a universalizing morality—can be applied to a defense of races.

CONCLUSIONS

I have suggested that what we call "racism" involves both propositions and dispositions.

The propositions were, first, that there are races (this was *racialism*) and, second, that these races are morally significant either (a) because they are contingently correlated with morally relevant properties (this was *extrinsic racism*) or (b) because they are intrinsically morally significant (this was *intrinsic racism*).

The disposition was a tendency to assent to false propositions, both moral and theoretical, about races—propositions that support policies or beliefs that are to the disadvantage of some race (or races) as opposed to others, and to do so even in the face of evidence and argument that should appropriately lead to giving those propositions up. This disposition I called "racial prejudice."

I suggested that intrinsic racism had tended in our own time to be the natural expression of feelings of community, and this is, of course, one of the reasons why we are not inclined to call it racist. For, to the extent that a theoretical position is not associated with irrationally held beliefs that tend to the *dis*advantage of some group, it fails to display the *directedness* of the distortions of rationality characteristic of racial prejudice. Intrinsic racism may be as irrationally held as any other view, but it does not *have* to be directed *against* anyone.

So far as theory is concerned I believe racialism to be false: since theoretical racism of both kinds presupposes racialism, I could not logically support racism of either variety. But even if racialism were true, both forms of theoretical racism would be incorrect. Extrinsic racism is false because the genes that account for the gross morphological differences that underlie our standard racial categories are not linked to those genes that determine, to whatever degree such matters are determined genetically, our moral and intellectual characters. Intrinsic racism is mistaken because it breaches the Kantian imperative to make moral distinctions only on morally relevant grounds—granted that there is no reason to believe that race, *in se*, is morally relevant, and also no reason to suppose that races are like families in providing a sphere of ethical life that legitimately escapes the demands of a universalizing morality.

NOTES

1. Bernard Lewis, *Semites and Anti-Semites* (New York: Norton, 1986).
2. I shall be using th words "racism" and "racialism" with the meanings I stipulate: in some dialects of English they are synonyms, and in most dialects their definition is less than precise. For discussion of recent biological evidence see M. Nei and A. K. Roychoudhury, "Genetic Relationship and Evolution of Human Races," *Evolutionary Biology,* vol. 14 (New York: Plenum, 1983) pp. 1–59; for useful background see also M. Nei and A.K. Roychoudhury, "Gene Differences between Caucasian, Negro, and Japanese Populations," *Science,* 177 (August 1972), pp. 434–35.
3. See my "The Uncompleted Argument: Du Bois and the Illusion of Race," *Critical Inquiry,* 12 (Autumn 1985); reprinted in Henry Louis Gates (ed.), *"Race," Writing, and Difference* (Chicago: University of Chicago Press, 1986), pp. 21–37.
4. This fact shows up most obviously in the assumption that adopted children intelligibly make claims against their natural siblings: natural parents are, of course, causally responsible for their child's existence and that could be the basis of moral claims, without any sense that biological relatedness entailed rights or responsibilities. But no such basis exists for an interest in natural *siblings*; my sisters are not causally responsible for my existence. See "The Family Model," later in this essay.
5. Obviously what evidence should *appropriately* change your beliefs is not independent of your social or historical situation. In mid-nineteenth-century America, in New England quite as much as in the heart of Dixie, the pervasiveness of the institutional support for the prevailing system of racist belief—the fact that it was reinforced by religion and state, and defended by people in the universities and colleges, who had the greatest cognitive authority—meant that it would have been appropriate to insist on a substantial body of evidence and argument before giving up assent to racist propositions. In California in the 1980s, of course, matters stand rather differently. To acknowledge this is not to admit to a cognitive relativism; rather, it is to hold that, at least in some domains, the fact that a belief is widely held—and especially by people in positions of cognitive authority—may be a good prima facie reason for believing it.
6. Ideologies, as most theorists of ideology have admitted, standardly outlive the period in which they conform to the objective interests of the dominant group in a society; so even someone who thinks that the dominant group in our society no longer needs racism to buttress its position can see racism as the persisting ideology of an earlier phase of society. (I say "group" to keep the claim appropriately general; it seems to me a substantial further claim that the dominant group whose interests an ideology serves is always a class.) I have argued, however, in "The Conservation of 'Race'" that racism continues to serve the interests of the ruling classes in the West; in *Black American Literature Forum,* 23 (Spring 1989), pp. 37–60.
7. As I argued in "The Uncompleted Argument: Du Bois and the Illusion of Race." The reactive (or dialectical) character of this move explains why Sartre calls its manifestations in Négritude an "antiracist racism"; see "Orphée Noir," his preface to Senghor's *Anthologie de la nouvelle poésie nègre et malagache de langue française* (Paris: PUF, 1948). Sartre believed, of course, that the synthesis of this dialectic would be transcendence of racism; and it was his view of it as a stage—the antithesis—in that process that allowed him to see it as a positive advance over the original "thesis" of European racism. I suspect that the reactive character of antiracist racism accounts for the tolerance that is regularly extended to it in liberal circles; but this tolerance is surely hard to justify unless one shares Sartre's optimistic interpretation of it as a stage in a process that leads to the end of all racisms. (And unless your view of this dialectic is deterministic, you should in any case want to play an argumentative role in moving to this next stage.)

   For a similar Zionist response see Horace Kallen's "The Ethics of Zionism," *Maccabean,* August 1906.
8. "The Race Problem in America," in Brotz's *Negro Social and Political Thought* (New York: Basic Books, 1966), p. 184.
9. *Christianity, Islam and the Negro Race* (1887; reprinted Edinburgh: Edinburgh University Press, 1967), p. 197.
10. This is in part a reflection of an important asymmetry: loathing, unlike love, needs justifying; and this, I would argue, is because loathing usually leads to acts that are *in se* undesirable, whereas love leads to acts that are largely *in se* desirable—indeed, supererogatorily so.
11. See my "Racism and Moral Pollution," *Philosophical Forum,* 18 (Winter–Spring 1986–87), pp. 185–202.
12. *Ethics and the Limits of Philosophy* (Cambridge, Mass.: Harvard University Press, 1985). p. 12. I do not, as is obvious, share Williams's skepticism about morality.

Sexism and Racism: Some Conceptual Differences

Laurence Thomas

Laurence Thomas is a professor of philosophy at Syracuse University in New York. He is the author of Living Morally: A Psychology of Moral Character *(1989).*

Thomas addresses what he considers to be conceptual differences between sexism and racism. He argues that the positive self-concept of men is chiefly tied to their being sexists, and thus is central to their being, while the self-concept of being white is not inextricably tied to being racist. Thomas asserts that the way men perceive women is fundamental to men's conception of who they are, while the way whites conceive of blacks is not fundamental to their identity as whites. He therefore concludes that sexism is more difficult to end than racism.

How should we understand the difference between sexism and racism? Is the difference merely that we have women as victims of the former and blacks (or some other minority group) as victims of the latter? Or, are there differences of a deeper sort?

Consider: If a black were to report to his colleagues (all of whom are white) that he had just been called a "nigger," one could be reasonably certain that, since he is black, his colleagues would convey considerable sympathy toward him for having been subjected to such extreme verbal abuse. But if a woman were to report to her colleagues (all of whom are male) that she had just been called a "chick," "fox," or even a "dumb broad," I suspect that her colleagues—and it is the reaction of her male colleagues which should concern us—would not be likely to suppose that she had been subjected to equally extreme verbal abuse;[1] and, therefore, they would be less inclined to view her as deserving of or in need of sympathy, let alone considerable sympathy. I believe that the different reactions that we would get here are indicative of some fundamental differences between sexism and racism. In this essay, I shall argue that the following are two such differences: *(a)* Sexism, unlike racism, readily lends itself to morally unobjectionable description. *(b)* The positive self-concept of men has been more centrally tied to their being sexists than has been the positive self-concept of whites to their being racists. An unfortunate consequence of *a* and *b*, I am afraid, is that racist attitudes are relatively easier to give up than sexist ones. This perhaps is what one would expect given the different reactions that we would get from the two parallel situations which I have just described. Before getting underway, though, I want to make a few preliminary remarks.

1. Sexism and racism are obviously very large topics to try to cover in a single

Laurence Thomas, "Sexism and Racism: Some Conceptual Differences" in *Ethics, Vol. 90,* January 1980, published by the University of Chicago Press. Reprinted by permission.

essay. My discussion, therefore, will be extremely one sided in that I shall be concerned with the attitude of the sexist and the racist qua perpetrator only and not qua victim. This, of course, is not to say that a person cannot be on both sides of the fence.[2] Thus, I shall make no attempt, except in passing, to give an account of the self-concept which a victim of either sexism or racism has. It seems to be a fact that women are less likely to see themselves as victims of sexism than blacks (say) are to see themselves as victims of racism.[3] I believe that what I shall have to say on these two topics will be compatible with this fact.

2. Undoubtedly, there are different conceptions of sexism and racism, just as there are different conceptions of justice.[4] However, my aim is not to defend a particular conception of either social phenomenon; instead, I shall offer only a skeletal account of both which others, no doubt, will flesh out in different ways.
3. I mean only to be explaining the difference between sexism and racism. I do not in any way suppose that either can be morally justified. Moreover, I shall not be concerned with whether one is more morally objectionable than the other. For both are sufficiently objectionable, on moral grounds, that everyone should be equally concerned to perpetuate neither.
4. Finally, although I hardly think that blacks constitute the only ethnic group which has been the victim of racism, I am going to limit the discussion to blacks nonetheless. Not only will this make the discussion more manageable; I am, for the most part, concerned with racism (and sexism) in the United States—and it is fair to say that, because of both their physical features and numbers, blacks have been the primary target of racism in the United States.

I

Obviously enough, if *a* and *b* are true, then sexism and racism must differ in the way in which each views its victims. The following social phenomenon sheds some light on the matter. In response to the demands of liberated women, men are forming groups in order to come to grips with their conception of themselves as men, that is, in order to understand what the male role comes to.[5] However, whereas the struggle against sexism has sent men back to the drawing board, as it were, in order to redefine their maleness, the struggle against racism has not resulted in a similar reaction on the part of whites. Whites have not found themselves at a loss to understand themselves qua white persons. The point here is not that the lives of whites have gone unaffected in this regard. Rather, it is that, although men often perceive the women's movement as an affront to their masculinity, the black movement has not been perceived in a similar vein by whites. Whites have not taken being less of a racist to mean being less of a white in the way that men have taken being less of a sexist to mean being less of a man (see Section III). Why is this? The answer which readily recommends itself is that the conception which men have of women is much more central to the conception which men have of themselves than is the case for whites with respect to blacks. I shall refer to this view as the racial and sexual identity (RSI) thesis. Lest there be any misunderstanding, I should note that it no more follows from the truth of this thesis that sexism exists than it does that racism does not.

The truth of the RSI thesis is, I believe, well supported by the following considerations: (1) Since the beginning of humanity, women and men have had to interact for the purpose of procreation in order for the human species to survive. (2) There are male and female members of every race; hence, no race is dependent upon the members of any other race for its survival. (3) Any male and female member of any race can have offspring. (4) Whereas one can be racially mixed, one's gender is an all-or-nothing matter. A person is either male or female, taking the sexual organs to be the determining factor.[6] (5) The races are not regarded as biological complementaries of one another, but the two sexes are. Thus, it suffices that there exists some race or other which is different from a person's own race in order for it to be possible for that person to have a racial identity; such identity does not require the existence of a particular race. Our sexual identity, however, is clearly predicated upon the existence of a particular sex, namely, the opposite one. I shall assume that the RSI thesis is well supported by these five considerations. The thesis will be central to the account which I shall give of the way in which sexism and racism each conceives of its object: women and blacks, respectively.

Now, I should note that sexism and racism are commonly taken to be quite similar. This is because both racist and sexist attitudes rest upon the view that, respectively, there are innate differences between whites and blacks, on the one hand, and men and women, on the other, which in each case make it natural for the latter to be subordinate to the former.[7] For instance, blacks and women have been stereotyped as being both intellectually and emotionally inferior to whites and men, respectively. But closer inspection reveals that even this similarity is not without a fundamental difference. For whereas the woman's lack turns out to make her naturally suited for the home and raising children and, therefore, natural for her to be around, the conclusion that it is natural for blacks to be around is not forthcoming. Indeed, it has been said by blacks and whites alike that things would be better if all blacks were back in Africa.[8] So we encounter a difference between sexism and racism even in the respect in which they are thought to be most similar. It takes only a moment of reflection to see that this difference can be explained by reference to the considerations offered in support of the RSI thesis. There is no biological role for blacks to play in the reproduction of white offspring, however much whites may find it desirable to have blacks around for other reasons. It is in this light that the remarks of this paragraph must be understood.

Taking my cue from the preceding discussion, the way in which sexism and racism each conceives of its object can be put as follows: Sexism entails the view that, although *(a)* women are inferior to men in some sense, *(b)* biological considerations dictate that women ought to be around in order to insure the survival of the human species. Moreover, in view of *a* and *b*, *(c)* it is appropriate for women to cater to the wants and needs of men; indeed, women are understood as complementing men. Racism entails the view that *(a)* blacks are in some sense inferior to whites and that, in view of this, *(b)* it is appropriate for blacks to cater to the wants and needs of whites, but not the view that *(c)* biological considerations dictate that blacks ought to be around whites and, therefore, that blacks complement whites. It goes without saying that I am merely stating what I take to be the core of a sexist conception of women and a racist conception of blacks; in no way do I mean to be endorsing either.

Some explanatory remarks are in order. What I mean by the claim that women complement men is aptly expressed by the saying, "Behind every man there is a good woman." Women are supposed to possess or excel at those virtues which make them naturally suited for being supportive of and bringing out the best in men.[9] For instance, women are supposed to possess a greater capacity than men for being understanding, encouraging, and sympathetic. (The first capacity, which has to do with patience and tolerance, is not to be confused with the capacity to understand, which has to do with intellectual ability.) Thus, it is thought to be to a man's benefit to associate himself with the right woman, since the right woman, so the view goes, will be a man's constant source of support and encouragement, thereby enabling him to excel at what he does. Women, then, are thought to play a central role in the self-development of men and, thus, in men having a positive conception of themselves. Nothing of the sort is thought to be true of blacks vis-à-vis whites. There are no time-honored sayings to the effect that "behind every white there is a good black." It has not been thought that by associating with the right black whites will enhance their chances of excelling at whatever they do, of being their best as whites.[10]

We now have before us a skeletal account of the way in which sexism and racism construe women and blacks, respectively. As I have remarked, others may wish to flesh out these accounts in different ways. In any event, we are in the position to make good the claim that the following are two of the fundamental differences between sexism and racism: *(a)* Sexism, unlike racism, readily lends itself to a morally unobjectionable description. *(b)* The positive self-concept of men has been more centrally tied to their being sexists than has been the positive self-concept of whites to their being racists. In the order mentioned, I turn to these two claims in the sections which follow.

II

I shall proceed in this section by arguing first that sexism readily lends itself to a morally unobjectionable description and then for the claim that racism does not.

A major aspect of the traditional male role is what I shall call the benefactor role. It is the role of men to protect women and to provide them with the comforts of life. That men should be the benefactors of women (in the sense described) is, it should be observed, a natural outcome of a sexist conception of women. For it will be recalled that, according to that conception, women play a central role in the self-development of men. And, of course, any person has good reasons to protect and provide for that which plays a central role in her or his self-development. But it goes without saying that this aspect of the traditional male role hardly seems morally objectionable.[11] For we do not normally suppose that a person does that which is morally wrong in benefiting someone. And on the face of it, surely, providing a person with the comforts of life would hardly seem to be a morally objectionable thing to do. After all, are they not desired by nearly everyone? At first blush, then, the traditional male role seems quite immune to moral criticism, which explains why the charge of sexism often seems to be lacking in moral force. Indeed, it is not uncommon to hear a man boast of being a sexist—even nowadays!

Now, of course, an arrangement where men benefit women is not morally objectionable—in and of itself, that is. What is morally objectionable, though, are the presuppositions behind it, one of the most important of them being that this sort of arrangement is ordained by nature.[12] From this presupposition, a number of things are thought to follow, such as that men should earn more money than women (period) and that the work which women do around the home is not as important as the work which men do on the job. These matters could be pursued at length, but I shall not do so here. For my concern has been to show that sexism, readily lends itself to a morally unobjectionable description. And to show that it is a natural outcome of a sexist conception of women that men should be the benefactors of women (in the sense described) is to show this much.

Let us now look at racism. The first thing we should observe is that a racist conception of blacks does not naturally give rise to the view that whites should be the benefactors of blacks. This should come as no surprise, for it will be remembered (*a*) that blacks and whites alike have thought that things would be better if all blacks were back in Africa and (*b*) that blacks have not been thought to play a central role in the self-development of whites. For blacks were thought to be too inferior for that. Whites, then, have never conceived of it as their role qua whites to be the benefactor of blacks. And, as history shows,[13] the benefit of blacks has hardly been the concern of racist arrangements. For the most part, the benefit of blacks was incidental to (an unintended side effect of) such arrangements or, in any case, up to the whim of those responsible for such arrangements. These facts, alone, make it very difficult for racism to be viewed in a morally unobjectionable light.

Now it might be objected that racism can be so viewed if we suppose that whites held blacks to be inferior in their moral status to whites.[14] But not so. For one thing, the case of women shows that persons can have what I called the benefactor role even with respect to living things presumed to be of inferior moral status. After all, it is impossible to understand the doctrine of coverture (e.g.) without supposing that according to it women are inferior in their moral status to men.[15] For another, the cruel treatment of living things of inferior moral status is morally wrong in any event, as the case of animals shows. Racism, though, has often called for the cruel treatment of blacks, whose moral status has most certainly not been thought to be inferior to the moral status of animals. So the objection fails.

A satisfactory case, I believe, has been made for the claims that sexism unlike racism, readily admits of a morally unobjectionable description.

III

The task of this section is to show that the positive self-concept of men has been more centrally tied to their being sexists than has been the positive self-concept of whites to their being racists. I shall first say a few words about what a person's positive self-concept comes to.

There are various aspects of a person's positive self-concept. However, the one which is germane to our discussion is what is called self-esteem.[16] It is the attitude which we have toward ourselves regarding our ability to interact effectively with our social environment, to achieve the goals which we set for ourselves. Respectively, our self-esteem is positive or negative if we have a reasonably favorable or unfavorable attitude toward ourselves in this regard. No person without deep psychological problems desires to have a negative conception of her- or himself. Thus, those activities which we believe will enhance our self-esteem have a natural attraction for us. So we are disinclined to give up those activities the successful pursuit of which enhances our self-esteem unless we have reason to believe that we can maintain our self-esteem by engaging in other activities. Obviously enough, the range of our abilities is very relevant here. The wider it is the more options there are that are open to us.

But now it is our values which determine the sorts of activities whose successful pursuit will enhance our self-esteem. Hence, having an excellent voice for classical music will do little to enhance our self-esteem if we have no interest in such music. On the other hand, if being able to sing classical music well is very important to us, then our self-esteem will suffer a severe blow if we are told by someone whose opinion we highly respect that this is an end which is beyond our reach. In large measure the social institutions among which we live determine the sorts of values which we come to have. And those values which have been instilled in us since childhood by our familial, educational, and religious institutions may have such a tenacious hold upon us that we find ourselves unable to give them up even when the ends which they call for prove to be beyond our reach. These few remarks about self-esteem, as sketchy as they are, should give us enough of a handle on the concept to permit us to proceed with the task of showing that the positive self-concept (self-esteem) of sexists is more centrally tied to the fact that they are sexists than is the positive self-concept (self-esteem) of racists to the fact that they are racists. (Throughout the remainder of this essay, I shall use the term "self-esteem" instead of "self-concept.")

If the RSI thesis is sound, then our sexual identity is clearly central to the conception which we have of ourselves. As things stand, though, while our gender is clearly relevant to our sexual identity, it is far from being the sole determiner of it.[17] Our beliefs about the sorts of roles we should play have a most powerful influence in this regard. There is, we might say, as much a social sense of the terms "woman" and "man" as there is a biological one. A person is a woman or man in the biological sense merely in virtue of having the appropriate biological properties. But to be a woman or man in the social sense not only must one have the appropriate biological properties; one must also have the appropriate aspirations and social behavior. The traditional female and male roles define a social sense of the terms "woman" and "man." Hence, a woman's self-esteem can turn upon the fact that she measures up to the traditional female role; a man's self-esteem can turn upon the fact that he measures up to the traditional male role.

Now we have seen that, according to the traditional male role, men have what I have called the benefactor role with respect to women: they are supposed to protect women and provide them with the comforts of life. That men should have this role with respect to women is, without a doubt, one of the most deeply entrenched views of our society. A "real" man is one who "wears the pants around the house." He is the breadwinner. Indeed, the benefactor role is not an optional feature of the traditional male role—something which a man may take or leave as it pleases him. For it will be remembered that it is supposedly ordained by nature that men should have the benefactor role with respect to women. Unless there is some excuse, such as that of being a priest, it follows, according to the traditional male role, that men ought to be the benefactors of women. Thus, men believe that it is appropriate for their conception of themselves to turn upon how well they live up to the benefactor role. And, in the cases of those men who do so reasonably well, their self-esteem is enhanced precisely because their success in this regard constitutes an affirmation of their ability to be men in the social sense of the term. In view of the considerations advanced in this and the preceding paragraph, there is no getting around the fact that the positive self-esteem of men has been centrally tied to their being sexists.

We do not encounter an analogous situation between the black and white races. One very important reason why this is so is that there is only a biological sense of the races and, so, the black and white races. Thus, racial identity for whites, and any other race, is something which has been more or less entirely settled by biological considerations. To be a full-fledged white person one has never had to own black slaves or even to hate blacks. This latter point is well illustrated by the case of the nigger lover. To be sure, many whites looked rather disparagingly upon the nigger lover. But this is not because whites considered her or him to be a white person *manqué*. The nigger lover was not a mulatto! A mulatto can no more be a nigger lover than a male a tomboy or a female a sissy. As for the first point, suffice it to say that American slaveowners were hardly of the opinion that European whites were less than full-fledged whites on account of the fact that black slavery was not a very prominent feature of European white societies.

Of course, I do not mean to deny the obvious fact that whites have perceived there to be fundamental differences among themselves, as, for example, class differences.[18] Nor do I mean to deny that whites have thought certain forms of conduct to be inappropriate for them, as, for example, the conduct of a nigger lover. What I do mean to deny, however, is that the racial identity of whites turned upon any of these differences. And if I am right about this, then it follows with impeccable logic that the racial identity of whites has not turned upon their being racists.

Now, to be sure, there have been many whites whose self-esteem has been enhanced by the fact that they were racists. At one point in his life George Wallace was certainly such an individual. It is significant to note, though, that the word "racist" is not the name of an institutional role, as are, say, the words "teacher," "governor," and "spouse."[19] Moreover, the definitions of such roles do not make any reference to the sorts of activities which, under some description or other, are properly characterized as racist. No one, for instance, supposes that a person cannot be a teacher, governor, or spouse unless she or he is a racist,[20] though, to be sure, many may think that only racists should occupy such roles. If, therefore, it is true that for any institutional role K a person S can perform K without being a racist, under some description or other, then it has to be equally true that, if S were a racist, then S could cease to be one without S's self-esteem being jeopardized with respect to the performance of K. When this consideration is coupled with the fact that the racial identity of whites has not turned upon their being racists, what follows most straightforwardly is that the self-esteem of whites has not been centrally tied to their being racists.

Now, the word "sexist" is not the name of an institutional role either. However, there is at least one institutional role, namely that of being a spouse (traditionally understood), which by definition makes reference to the sorts of activities which are sexist under at least some description. For the attitudes which the traditional male spouse has toward women (his wife, in particular) are, needless to say, dictated by the traditional male role, as what I have called the benefactor role should make clear. And, as we have seen, in their endeavors to measure up to the benefactor role, the self-esteem of men has been centrally tied to their being sexists.

I should conclude this section by noting that nothing I have said implies that the self-esteem of slavemasters did not or could not have turned upon their owning slaves. For their slaves were their property; and one's self-esteem can turn upon how much property one owns, whether that property is land, cattle, houses, or black slaves. Thus, it would be a mistake to suppose that the fact that the self-esteem of slaveowners turned upon their owning slaves militates against the arguments of this section. For being a slave holder was not, surely, a defining characteristic of either a racist or a white person during the times of slavery; and so, a fortiori, it has not been since the passing of slavery.

IV

Throughout this essay, I have assumed that the traditional male role can be described in a morally objectionable way. I do not now want to argue the case. Rather, I would like for the reader to engage in a brief thought experiment with me. Suppose that men were the victims of sexism and that

> [everything a man] wore, said, or did had to be justified by reference to female approval; if he were compelled to regard himself, day in day out, not as a member of society, but merely . . . as a virile member of society. If the center of his dress-consciousness were the cod-piece, his education directed to making him a spirited lover and meek paterfamilias; his interests held to be natural only in so far as they were sexual. If from school and lecture-room, press and pulpit, he heard the persistent outpouring of a shrill and scolding voice, bidding him remember his biological function. If he were vexed by continual advice how to add a rough male touch to his typing, how to be learned without losing his masculine appeal, how to combine chemical research with education, how to play bridge without incurring the suspicion of impotence. If, instead of allowing with a smile that "women prefer cavemen," he felt the unrelenting pressure of a whole social structure forcing him to order all his goings in conformity with that pronouncement.[21]

I have no doubt that most men would find a world thus described quite objectionable—and on moral grounds. If so, then there is indeed a morally objectionable way of describing the traditional male role in this world.

The differences between sexism and racism go much deeper than, as is commonly supposed, the fact that women are victims of the former and blacks of the latter. If I have argued soundly in this essay, then we have seen that sexism and racism are not two ways of referring to the same social monster, but two rather different ones.

V

My objective in this essay has been to show that there are at least two fundamental differences between sexism and racism: *(a)* Sexism, unlike racism, readily lends itself to a morally unobjectionable description. *(b)* The positive self-concept of men has been more centrally tied to their being sexists than has been the positive self-concept of whites to their being racists. As I said at the outset of this essay, it is, I believe, a consequence of the truth of *a* and *b* that racist attitudes are relatively easier to give up than sexist ones. I shall not attempt a defense of this claim at this point. Suffice to say, first of all, that persons must see that something is morally objectionable before they take themselves to have a moral reason for giving it up. We have seen that sexism presents a greater difficulty than racism in this regard. Second, it is a fact that people are disinclined to alter their behavior if they have reason to believe that in doing so they would jeopardize their self-esteem.[22] And we have seen that sexism presents a greater difficulty than racism in this regard as well.

In this essay, I have argued that there are some fundamental differences between sexism and racism. I have not denied that there are any similarities between the two; nor have I meant to do so.

ACKNOWLEDGMENT

I was first prompted to think about the topic of this paper in the fall of 1976 when I received an invitation from Stanley M. Browne, on behalf of Talladega College (Alabama), to give a talk on it. Versions of this paper have since been read at Georgia State University, Tuskegee Institute, Union College, Western Michigan University, and the American Philosophical Association meetings (Pacific Division). Lawrence Alexander saved me from a number of slips and stylistic infelicities. Lyla H. O'Driscoll and Alison M. Jagger forced me to be more careful than I would have been in my remarks about the sexual identity of men. Section III of this paper was extensively revised in the light of the very forthright criticisms of my APA commentator, Robert C. Williams. Among others who have been kind enough to offer extensive comments are: C. Freeland, D. Jamieson, H. McGary, J. Narveson, J. Nickel, and A. Soble. A special word of thanks goes to Sandra Bartky and Connie Price for their encouragement in writing this paper from the very start. The completion of later drafts of this paper was facilitated by my having an A. W. Mellon Faculty Fellowship at Harvard University for the 1978–79 academic year.

NOTES

1. A sexual parallel here would have to be denigrating, but not vulgar. Thus, words such as "bitch" and "cunt" do not parallel the racial epithet "nigger." Indeed, in certain contexts, the word "nigger" is not even denigrating: a black woman may call a black man with whom she is in love her "sweet nigger." Of the three expressions mentioned in the text, I suspect that "dumb broad," suggested to me by A. Soble, is the closest parallel to "nigger," though it still misses the mark.
2. Marabel Morgan, it would seem, is a woman who is on both sides of the fence. The "total woman" classes organized by her are based on the view that for a married woman "love is *unconditional* acceptance of him [her husband] and his feelings" (emphasis added) (see *The Total Woman* [New York: Pocket Books, 1975], p. 161).
3. See Eugene D. Genovese, *Roll, Jordan, Roll: The World Slaves Made* (New York: Pantheon Books, 1974).
4. On the difference between the concept and a conception of justice, see John Rawls, *A Theory of Justice* (Cambridge, Mass.: Harvard University Press, 1971), pp. 5–11.
5. Cf. David Gelman et al., "How Men Are Changing," *Newsweek* (January 16, 1978), and Peter Knobler, "Is It More Difficult to Be a Man Today?" *New York Times* (May 27, 1978). Also, there is Gene Marine, *A Male Guide to Women's Liberation* (New York: Avon Books, 1972), and many other books of this genre.
6. Among persons and other higher animals, there can only be what is called pseudohermaphroditism, i.e., genetic abnormalities or hormonal imbalances (see *The Encyclopedia Americana*, international ed., s.v. "hermaphrodite").
7. In connection with sexism, two of the most sophisticated writers whom I have come across are Mary Wollstonecraft, *A Vindication of the Rights of Women* (first published in 1792), and Dorothy L. Sayers, *Unpopular Opinions* (New York: Harcourt Brace & Co., 1947).
8. Among blacks who have held this view, Marcus Garvey comes foremost to mind (see Edmund David Cronon, *Black Moses: The Story of Marcus Garvey and the Universal Negro Improvement Association* [Madison: University of Wisconsin Press, 1969]).
9. Cf. Morgan. Wollstonecraft speaks of men having the pleasure of commanding flattering sycophants (see p. 13 of the edition of *A Vindication of the Rights of Women* edited by Carol H. Post [New York: W.W. Norton & Co., 1975]). Wollstonecraft's point is developed in a contemporary vein by L. Blum et al., "Altruism and Women's Oppression," *Philosophical Forum* 5 (1973): 196–221.
10. During the times of slavery American whites did not think that European whites needed to find themselves the right black in order to better themselves.
11. In order to keep down the length of this essay, I have deliberately not said anything about the traditional male role in connection with sex. The sexual exploitation of women is surely one of the worst aspects of the traditional male role. In the work compiled by the Sex Information and Educational Council of the United States, *Sexuality and Man* (New York: Charles Scribner's Sons, 1970), we find the following remarks: "Four major premarital sexual standards exist today: Abstinence, the formal standard of forbidding intercourse to both sexes; the Double Standard, the Western world's oldest standard, which allows males to have greater access to coitus than females; Permissiveness with Affection . . . ; and

Permissiveness without Affection . . ." (p. 40). And this is to say nothing of the humiliation to which women have been subjected in connection with rape. It was once common practice for men to sexually abuse the women they captured. And, even today, many rapes go unreported because of the humiliation to which the victims are subjected (See Gerda Lerna, *The Female Experience: An American Documentary* [Indianapolis: Bobbs-Merrill Co., 1977], pp. 433 ff.). It goes without saying that I have also left aside the traditional female role in connection with sex and childbearing. For an excellent discussion in connection with the former, see Christopher Lasch, "The Flight From Feeling: Sociopsychology of Sexual Conflict," *Marxist Perspectives* 1 (1978): 74–95. This essay was brought to my attention by Eugene Rivers.

12. I am indebted to Linda Patrik (Union College) for much of the way that I have put this paragraph.
13. See Genovese.
14. In my "Rawlsian Self-Respect and the Black Consciousness Movement" *(Philosophical Form* 9 [1978]: 303–14), I have distinguished between having full, partial, and no moral status. A thing has no moral status (e.g. stones) if there are no rights which it can have and there are no duties which it can have or which can be owed to it. A thing has only partial moral status (e.g., animals) if there are duties which can be owed to it, but there are no duties which it can have. A thing has full moral status (e.g., persons) if there are rights and duties which it can have. As for whether or not animals can have rights, suffice it to say that they cannot, unlike persons, have rights against one another. A dog does not violate any rights of the squirrel which it catches and kills or hurts.
15. The doctrine reads thus: "By marriage the husband and the wife are one person in law; that is, the very being or legal existence of the woman is suspended during the marriage, or at least incorporated and consolidated into that of the husband; under whose wing, protection, and cover, she performs everything" (see William Blackstone, *Commentaries on the Laws of England,* reprint ed. [London: Dawsons of Pall Mall, 1966], p. 430).
16. See, among others, Stanley Coopersmith, *The Antecedents of Self-Esteem* (San Francisco: W. H. Freeman & Co., 1967): L. Edward Well and Gerald Marwell, *Self-Esteem: Its Conceptualization and Measurement* (Beverly Hills, Calif.: Sage Publications, 1976); and Robert W. White, "Ego and Reality in Psychoanalytic Theory," *Psychological Issues,* vol. 3, monograph 11 (1963). I have tried to show the importance of distinguishing between self-esteem and self-respect, which I have defined in terms of having the conviction that one has and is deserving of full moral status (see my "Morality and Our Self-Concept," *Journal of Value Inquiry* 12 [1978]: 258–68).
17. In a nonsexist society, perhaps the difference between gender identity and sexual identity would collapse (see Richard Wasserstrom, "Racism, Sexism, and Preferential Treatment: An Approach to the Topics," *UCLA Law Review* 24 [1977]: 581–622). For some illuminating discussions concerning the roles of women, see the collection of articles in Jo Freeman, ed., *Woman: A Feminist Perspective* (Palo Alto, Calif.: Mayfield Publishing Co., 1975); and Michele Garskof, ed., *Roles Women Play* (Belmont, Calif.: Brooks/Cole Publishing Co., 1971).
18. See, e.g., Patricia Hollis, ed., *Class and Conflict in Nineteenth-Century England, 1815–1850* (London: Routledge & Kegan Paul, 1973).
19. In the use of the word "institutional," I follow John Rawls, "Two Concepts of Rules," *Philosophical Review* 64 (1955): 3–32.
20. Indeed, it would seem that this is true even of the role of slavemaster. Aristotle thought it natural that there should be slaves. I do not see, though, that he thought it natural that the slaves should be black (see *Politics*, bk. 1).
21. Sayers (n. 7 above), pp. 143–45. A later paragraph reads as follows: "If, after a few centuries of this kind of treatment, the male was a little self-conscious, a little on the defensive, I should not blame him. If he traded a little upon his sex, I could forgive him. If he presented the world with a major social problem, I would scarcely be surprised. It would be more surprising if he retained any rag of sanity and self-respect."
22. The fact that a person's self-esteem may be enhanced by the successful pursuit of morally unacceptable ends is often proferred as an explanation as to why those for whom street crime is a way of life do not accept the more traditional moral values (see, e.g., Charles Silberman, *Criminal Violence, Criminal Justice* [New York: Random House, 1978], chaps. 2 and 3).

The Red and the Black

Vine Deloria, Jr.

Vine Deloria, Jr. (Standing Rock Sioux) is a professor of American Indian studies, political science, and law at the University of Colorado at Boulder. Deloria has authored numerous books, including Custer Died for Your Sins *(1969);* God Is Red *(1973);* Behind the Trail of Broken Treaties *(1974); and* American Indian Policy in the Twentieth Century *(1985).*

Deloria criticizes the tradition of viewing civil rights issues as applying solely to African Americans, and broadens our discussion to include American Indians. Deloria distinguishes between the types of conflicts that American Indians and African Americans have had with the federal government. He states that American Indians need to adjust the legal relationship between the various tribes and the government, while African Americans need to work on socioeconomic relations with the government. Deloria suggests that the ultimate understanding of and solution to the racial question lies with the white majority. Whites must examine the past and come to see that they have created the racism dilemma, and must take responsibility to cease projecting their fears and their way of life onto other races.

Civil Rights has been the most important and least understood movement of our generation. To some it has seemed to be a simple matter of fulfilling rights outlined by the Constitutional amendments after the Civil War. To others, particularly church people, Civil Rights has appeared to be a fulfillment of the brotherhood of man and the determination of humanity's relationship to God. To those opposing the movement, Civil Rights has been a foreign conspiracy which has threatened the fabric of our society.

For many years the movement to give the black people rights equal to those of their white neighbors was called Race Relations. The preoccupation with race obscured the real issues that were developing and meant that programs devised to explore the area of race always had a black orientation.

To the Indian people it has seemed quite unfair that churches and government agencies concentrated their efforts primarily on the blacks. By defining the problem as one of race and making race refer solely to black, Indians were systematically excluded from consideration. National church groups have particularly used race as a means of exploring minority-group relations. Whatever programs or policies outlined from national churches to their affiliates and parishes were generally black-oriented programs which had been adapted to include Indians.

There was probably a historical basis for this type of thinking. In many states in the last century, Indians were classified as white by laws passed to exclude blacks. So there was a connotation that Indians might in some way be like whites. But in other areas, particularly marriage laws, Indians were classified as blacks and this connotation really determined the role into which the white man forced the red man. Consequently, as far as most Race Relations were concerned, Indians were classified as non-whites.

There has been no way to positively determine in which category Indians belong when it comes to federal agencies. The Bureau of Indian Affairs consistently defined Indians as good guys who have too much dignity to demonstrate, hoping to keep the Indian people separate from the ongoing Civil Rights movement. Other agencies generally adopted a semi-black orientation. Sometimes Indians were treated as if they were blacks and other times not.

The Civil Rights Commission and the Community Relations Service always gave only lip service to Indians until it was necessary for them to write an annual report. At that time they always sought out some means of including Indians as a group with which they had worked the previous fiscal year. That was the extent of Indian relationship with the agency: a paragraph in the annual report and a promise to do something next year.

Older Indians, as a rule, have been content to play the passive role outlined for them by the bureau. They have wanted to avoid the rejection and bad publicity given activists.

The Indian people have generally avoided confrontations between the different minority groups and confrontations with the American public at large. They have felt that any publicity would inevitably have bad results and since the press seemed dedicated to the perpetuation of sensationalism rather than straight reporting of the facts, great care has been taken to avoid the spotlight. Because of this attitude, Indian people have not become well known in the field of intergroup and race relations. Consequently they have suffered from the attitudes of people who have only a superficial knowledge of minority groups and have attached a certain stigma to them.

The most common attitude Indians have faced has been the unthoughtful Johnny-come-lately liberal who equates certain goals with a dark skin. This type of individual generally defines the goals of all groups by the way he understands what he wants for the blacks. Foremost in this category have been younger social workers and clergymen entering the field directly out of college or seminary. For the most part they have been book-fed and lack experience in life. They depend primarily upon labels and categories of academic import rather than on any direct experience. Too often they have achieved positions of prominence as programs have been expanded to meet needs of people. In exercising their discretionary powers administratively, they have run roughshod over Indian people. They have not wanted to show their ignorance about Indians. Instead, they prefer to place all people with darker skin in the same category of basic goals, then develop their programs to fit these preconceived ideas.

Since the most numerous group has been the blacks, programs designed for blacks were thought adequate for all needs of all groups. When one asks a liberal about minority groups, he unconsciously seems to categorize them all together for purposes of problem solving. Hence, dark-skinned and minority group as categorical concepts have brought about the same basic results—the Indian is defined as a subcategory of black.

Cultural differences have only seemed to emphasize the white liberal's point of view in lumping the different communities together. When Indians have pointed out real differences that do exist, liberals have tended to dismiss the differences as only minor aberrations which distinguish different racial groups.

At one conference on education of minority groups, I once mentioned the existence of some three hundred Indian languages which made bicultural and bilingual education a necessity. I was immediately challenged by several white educators who attempted to prove that blacks also have a language problem. I was never able to make the difference real to them. For the conference people the point had again been established that minority groups all had the same basic problems.

Recently, blacks and some Indians have defined racial problems as having one focal point—the White Man. This concept is a vast oversimplification of the real problem, as it centers on a racial theme rather than on specific facts. And it is simply the reversal of the old prejudicial attitude of the white who continues to define minority groups as problems of his—that is, Indian problem, Negro problem, and so on.

Rather than race or minority grouping, non-whites have often been defined according to their function within the American society. Negroes, as we have said, were considered draft animals, Indians wild animals. So too, Orientals were considered domestic animals and Mexicans humorous lazy animals. The white world has responded to the non-white groups in a number of ways, but primarily according to the manner in which it believed the non-whites could be rescued from their situation.

Thus Orientals were left alone once whites were convinced that they preferred to remain together and presented no basic threat to white social mores. Mexicans were similarly discarded and neglected when whites felt that they preferred to remain by themselves. In both cases there was no direct confrontation between whites and the two groups because there was no way that a significant number of them could be exploited. They owned little; they provided little which the white world coveted.

With the black and the Indian, however, tensions increased over the years. Both groups had been defined as animals with which the white had to have some relation and around whom some attitude must be formed. Blacks were ex-draft animals who somehow were required to become non-black. Indeed, respectability was possible for a black only by emphasizing characteristics and features that were non-black. Indians were the ex-wild animals who had provided the constant danger for the civilizing tendencies of the invading white. They always presented a foreign aspect to whites unfamiliar with the western hemisphere.

The white man adopted two basic approaches in handling blacks and Indians. He systematically excluded blacks from all programs, policies, social events, and economic schemes. He could not allow blacks to rise from their position because it would mean that the evolutionary scheme had superseded the Christian scheme and that man had perhaps truly descended from the ape.

With the Indian the process was simply reversed. The white man had been forced to deal with the Indian in treaties and agreements. It was difficult, therefore, to completely overlook the historical antecedents such as Thanksgiving, the plight of the early Pilgrims, and the desperate straits from which various Indian tribes had often rescued the whites. Indians were therefore subjected to the most intense pressure to become white. Laws passed by Congress had but one goal—the Anglo-Saxonization of the Indian. The antelope had to become a white man.

Between these two basic attitudes, the apelike draft animal and the wild free-running antelope, the white man was impaled on the horns of a dilemma he had created within himself.

It is well to keep these distinctions clearly in mind when talking about Indians and blacks. When the liberals equate the two they are overlooking obvious historical facts. Never did the white man systematically exclude Indians from his schools and meeting places. Nor did the white man ever kidnap black children from their homes and take them off to a government boarding school to be educated as whites. The white man signed no treaties with the black. Nor did he pass any amendments to the Constitution to guarantee the treaties of the Indian.

The basic problem which has existed between the various racial groups has not been one of race but of culture and legal status. The white man systematically destroyed Indian culture where it existed, but separated blacks from his midst so that they were forced to attempt the creation of their own culture.

The white man forbade the black to enter his own social and economic system and at the same time force-fed the Indian what he was denying the black. Yet the white man demanded that the black conform to white standards and insisted that the Indian don feathers and beads periodically to perform for him.

The white man presented the *problem* of each group in contradictory ways so that neither black nor Indian could understand exactly where the problem existed or how to solve it. The Indian was always told that his problem was one of conflicting cultures. Yet, when solutions were offered by the white man, they turned out to be a reordering of the legal relationship between red and white. There was never a time when the white man said he was trying to help the Indian get into the mainstream of American life that he did not also demand that the Indian give up land, water, minerals, timber, and other resources which would enrich the white men.

The black also suffered from the same basic lie. Time after time legislation was introduced which purported to give the black equal rights with the white but which ultimately restricted his life and opportunities, even his acceptance by white people. The initial Civil Rights Act following the thirteenth, fourteenth, and fifteenth amendments was assumed to give the blacks equal rights with "white citizens." In fact, it was so twisted that it took nearly a century to bring about additional legislation to confirm black rights.

In June of 1968 the Supreme Court finally interpreted an ancient statute in favor of blacks in the matter of purchasing a house. Had the right existed for nearly a century without anyone knowing it? Of course not, the white had simply been unwilling to give in to the black. Can one blame the black athletes at the recent Olympic Games for their rebellion against the role cast for them by white society? Should they be considered as specially trained athletic animals suitable only for hauling away tons of gold medals for the United States every four years while equality remains as distant as it ever was?

It is time for both black and red to understand the ways of the white man. The white is after Indian lands and resources. He always has been and always will be. For Indians to continue to think of their basic conflict with the white man as cultural is the height of folly. The problem is and always has been the adjustment of the legal relationship between the Indian tribes and the federal government, between the true owners of the land and the usurpers.

The black must understand that whites are determined to keep him out of their society. No matter how many Civil Rights laws are passed or how many are on the drawing board, the basic thrust is to keep the black out of society and harmless. The problem, therefore, is not one of legal status, it is one of culture and social and economic mobility. It is foolish for a black to depend upon a law to make acceptance of him by the white possible. Nor should he react to the rejection. His problem is social, and economic, and cultural, not one of adjusting the legal relationship between the two groups.

When the black seeks to change his role by adjusting the laws of the nation, he merely raises the hope that progress is being made. But for the majority of blacks progress is not being made. Simply because a middle-class black can eat at the Holiday Inn is not a gain. People who can afford the best generally get it. A socioeconomic, rather than legal adjustment must consequently be the goal.

But the understanding of the racial question does not ultimately involve understanding by either blacks or Indians. It involves the white man himself. He must examine his past. He must face the problems he has created within himself and within others. The white man must no longer project his fears and insecurities onto other groups, races, and countries. Before the white man can relate to others he must forego the pleasure of defining them. The white man must learn to stop viewing history as a plot against himself.

It was more than religious intolerance that drove the early colonists across the ocean. More than a thousand years before Columbus, the barbaric tribes destroyed the Roman Empire. With utter lack of grace, they ignorantly obliterated classical civilization. Christianity swept across the conquerors like the white man later swept across North America, destroying native religions and leaving paralyzed groups of disoriented individuals in its wake. Then the combination of Christian theology, superstition, and forms of the old Roman civil government began to control the tamed barbaric tribes. Gone were the religious rites of the white tribesmen. Only the Gothic arches in the great cathedrals, symbolizing the oaks under which their ancestors worshiped, remained to remind them of the glories that had been.

Not only did the European tribes lose their religion, they were subjected to a new form of economics which totally destroyed them: feudalism. The freedom that had formerly been theirs became only the freedom to toil on the massive estates. Even their efforts to maintain their ancient ways fell to the requirements of the feudal state as power centered in a few royal houses.

Feudalism saw man as a function of land and not as something in himself. The European tribes, unable to withstand the chaos of medieval social and political forces, were eliminated as power consolidated in a few hands. Far easier than the Indian tribes of this continent, the Europeans gave up the ghost and accepted their fate without questioning it. And they remained in subjection for nearly a millenium.

The religious monolith which Christianity had deviously constructed over the Indo-European peasants eventually showed cracks in its foundations. The revolution in religious thought triggered by Martin Luther's challenge to Papal authority was merely an afterthought. It did no more than acknowledge that the gates had been opened a long time and that it was perfectly natural to walk through them into the new era.

In the sixteenth century Europe opened up the can of worms which had been carefully laid to rest a millenium earlier. The Reformation again brought up the question of the place of Western man in God's scheme of events. Because there was no way the individual could relate to the past, he was told to relate to the other world, leaving this world free for nationalistic exploitation—the real forger of identity.

Because tribes and groups had been unable to survive, the common denominator, the individual, became the focal point of the revolt. Instead of socially oriented individuals, the Reformation produced self-centered individuals. Social and economic Darwinism, the survival of the fittest at any cost, replaced the insipid brotherhood of Christianity not because Christianity's basic thrust was invalid, but because it had been corrupted for so long that it was no longer recognizable.

The centuries following the Reformation were marked with incredible turmoil. But the turmoil was not so much over religious issues as it was over interpretation of religious doctrines. Correctness of belief was preferred over truth itself. Man charged back into the historical mists to devise systems of thought which would connect him with the greats of the past. Fear of the unfamiliar became standard operating procedure.

Today Europe is still feeling the effects of the submersion of its original tribes following the demise of the Roman Empire. Western man smashes that which he does not understand because he never had the opportunity to evolve his own culture. Instead ancient cultures were thrust upon him while he was yet unprepared for them.

There lingers still the unsolved question of the primacy of the Roman Empire as contrasted with the simpler more relaxed life of the Goths, Celts, Franks, and Vikings.

Where feudalism conceived man as a function of land, the early colonists reversed the situation in their efforts to create "new" versions of their motherlands. Early settlers made land a function of man, and with a plentitude of land, democracy appeared to be the inevitable desire of God. It was relatively simple, once they had made this juxtaposition, to define Indians, blacks, and other groups in relation to land.

The first organizing efforts of the new immigrants were directed toward the process of transplanting European social and political systems in the new areas they settled. Thus New England, New France, New Spain, New Sweden, New Haven, New London, New York, New Jersey, Troy, Ithaca, and other names expressed their desire to relive the life they had known on the other side of the Atlantic—but to relive it on their own terms. No one seriously wanted to return to the status of peasant, but people certainly entertained the idea of indigenous royalty. If your ancestor got off the boat, you were one step up the ladder of respectability. Many Indians, of course, believe it would have been better if Plymouth Rock had landed on the Pilgrims than the Pilgrims on Plymouth Rock.

The early colonists did not flee religious persecution so much as they wished to perpetuate religious persecution under circumstances more favorable to them. They wanted to be the persecutors. The rigorous theocracies which quickly originated in New England certainly belie the myth that the first settlers wanted only religious freedom. Nothing was more destructive of man than the early settlements on this continent.

It would have been far better for the development of this continent had the first settlers had no illusions as to their motives. We have seen nearly five centuries of white settlement on this continent, yet the problems brought over from Europe remain unsolved and grow in basic intensity daily. And violence as an answer to the problem of identity has only covered discussion of the problem. . . .

Shared Responsibility for Racism

Larry May

Larry May is a professor of philosophy at Washington University in St. Louis. He is the author of The Morality of Groups *(1987) and* Sharing Responsibility *(1992). May is also the coeditor of* Collective Responsibility *(1991) and* Rethinking Masculinity *(1992).*

May investigates the conceptual legitimacy of asserting that one shares moral responsibility for harms that one did not directly cause, particularly harms related to attitudes held in common with those who cause harm. Attitudes, May states, are not merely cognitive states, but affect how a person will behave. Our attitudes often contribute to an atmosphere in which harms are more likely to occur. May argues that moral responsibility for racial harms is to be shared by all members of the community who hold racist attitudes, even those who did not directly perpetrate the harm. Those who hold racist attitudes are like those who risk harm by holding a loaded gun.

At large state universities like the one where I used to teach, there has been an increase in racism. Not only have racial epithets been scrawled on bathroom stalls, but cross burnings and other more violent acts of racism are again occurring. Over the last ten years there has been a steady rise in racist attitudes among white students, faculty, and administrators. Yet the response of members of these academic communities to racially motivated violence is often to say that they do not share in responsibility for these events since they have played no causal role in the incidents. On February 4, 1988, Steven Beering, president of Purdue University, issued a public statement which read, in part: "The recent cross-burning incident at the Black Cultural Center was outrageous and deplorable. It brings shame to the responsible person, but we must not allow it to bring shame to our community."[1] This is a common response to incidents of racism in America. The individuals who directly perpetrated a harmful act are held to be responsible, to be worthy of shame, but the members of the community, many of whom share the attitudes of the perpetrators, are not held to share in the responsibility. I want to investigate the conceptual legitimacy of claiming that a person shares responsibility for harms that he or she has not directly caused, especially harms that are correlated with certain kinds of attitudes. . . .

Reprinted by permission of the University of Chicago Press from *Sharing Responsibility* by Larry May, ©1992 by the University of Chicago. All rights reserved. [Edited]

OMISSIONS AND RISKS

Negligent omissions concern things left undone that a person had a duty to do.

Those who have such duties are responsible for their omissions in ways not true of other people who omitted the same actions but had no duty to do them. The salesperson who sold you your car and omitted to warn you about the danger of operating it in a certain way may well be responsible for the harm resulting from your operating it in that way, even though such harm was not intended by the salesperson and the salesperson's behavior did not directly produce the harm. On the other hand, if I as your neighbor omitted to warn you about the danger of operating your car in that particular way, my omission is not connected to your harm in the way that the car salesperson's is, since I do not stand in a special relationship with you.

Omissions can facilitate and even enhance the ability of others to do certain kinds of things. If I have been designated to supervise your conduct, it will take an omission on my part to allow you to act in ways that my supervisory veto could have negated. By omitting to block your proposed action, I facilitate your behavior, and my action is similar to my contribution to a type of joint venture. Consider a case in which I am supposed to supervise your operation of a forklift truck on a loading dock. If after giving the keys to you, I leave the premises, then any harm caused by your use of the forklift truck is a harm that I facilitated as supervisor. When it is true that I have supervisory duty to block certain of your actions, then my omitting to block your action is similar to my contribution to a joint venture. Hence, it is commonly recognized in law and morality that those who fail in their supervisory duties share in responsibility for harms resulting from such omissions.

When a person's negligent omission contributes to the production of a harmful effect, then it is reasonable to consider that person to be partly responsible for that harm. The reason is that negligent omissions create a situation in which there is much greater likelihood that harmful effects will be produced. Negligence generally creates risks because due care is not being exercised in the prevention of harm. Negligent omissions are a kind of risky behavior even when no harm is actually produced. In all such cases, it does not make much sense to assign full responsibility to each participant since the roles of the participants vary so greatly. Also, negligent omissions do not clearly contribute to a discrete part of the harmful result.

Let us turn now to three cases of risky behavior, in an attempt to assess the plausibility of the claim that risk takers should share in responsibility for certain harms even though their behaviors and attitudes do not directly cause these harms. First of all, consider the case of someone who does not remove the snow from his sidewalk, knowing that his omission risks harm to delivery people; in fact one such person slips and hurts himself. Even if there is no intent to bring about the harm, it is generally thought that the taking of a risk itself renders a person responsible for any harms reasonably expected to follow from the risky omission or commission. This is a key assumption for my analysis and one quite commonly recognized. Such a premise is recognized in tort and criminal law. Certain risk takers are considered liable for various harms because of their recklessness, even though the harm is an unintended consequence of their behavior.

Consider next the case of two people, each of whom does not remove the snow from his or her portion of a common sidewalk, although each knows that harm to delivery people and others is risked. The first person's omission actually results in an accident on his portion of the sidewalk; the second person's omission does not result in harm. If both displayed the same knowledgeability and lack of due care, then the first person is unlucky and the second is lucky. And in law only one, the first person, will have his omission viewed as legally actionable, since only on his portion of the sidewalk was there any harm to be remedied. But it seems that both are at fault for having knowingly engaged in a risky enterprise. From a moral perspective, as I will argue below, both people have engaged in risky omissions and the fact that one of them was unlucky does not seem relevant.[2] One party may be more guilty than the other, but neither should be fully relieved of responsibility for the harm.

As is well known, one of the problems with allowing luck to be considered morally relevant is that a person's moral responsibility then turns on a factor which is completely beyond the control of the person in question. I will later argue for expanding the range of things for which it is relevant to hold people morally responsible, in particular to our attitudes and beliefs. But in arguing for the view that the attitudes and beliefs we choose, not just our overt behaviors, are relevant to judgments of responsibility, I remain committed to the view that people should only be judged morally responsible for those things that are under their control; but control does not necessarily mean that one could have made the world a different place. Here it remains true that whether one shoveled one's part of the sidewalk or not, the harm on the other part would still have occurred.

The importance of stressing control in moral responsibility is that it correctly puts the emphasis on what people have chosen (to do or to be). But if it should be true, in the cases we are here considering, that a person is relieved of responsibility merely due to good luck, even though her choices are faulty, then the notion of being a moral agent, which includes our choices of who we are and not just of what we do, ceases to have the high moral importance it is normally afforded. I'll return to this point in the final section of this chapter.

Consider finally the case of someone who owns a portion of a common sidewalk and who observes another person fail to remove the snow from his portion of the sidewalk. The first person then sees that a delivery person is harmed by this omission. Having made this observation, during the next snowstorm the observer nonetheless then decides not to remove the snow from her portion of the sidewalk. Again, due to good luck, the observer's action does not result in harm, even though the similar behavior of another neighbor does result in harm. Yet it seems that the observer is perhaps even more at fault than the person whose behavior resulted in harm. The observer has engaged in omissions in a way that she has already observed to produce harm. Such behavior is best described as morally reckless and probably also blameworthy.

Yet the reckless observer's behavior did not seem to contribute to the perpetration of a harmful result at all. Indeed, it might be claimed that since no harm was produced there is no causal responsibility for harm either. It thus seems odd to say that the reckless observer is morally at fault, since there is no harm of which this person is even partially causally responsible. However, the reckless observer did initiate a causal process that she recognized as likely to result in harm, even though the causal process did not actually result in harm. Following the model of criminal law we might think of this act as involving an attempted harm. In order to be at fault (or guilty) of an attempted harm a person must knowingly initiate a causal process which is likely to produce harm.

It is my contention that those who knowingly risk harm to others, even when their behavior does not directly cause any harm, share responsibility for the harm caused by those whose similar actions directly produce that harm. The reason for this is quite straightforward: the person who merely risks harm and the person who risks *and* actually causes harm have both acted in morally similar ways. When two people both have increased the likelihood of harm and both are equally knowledgeable that their actions increased the likelihood of harm, then their risky behavior creates a greater likelihood than previously existed that harm will occur, and they should share in the responsibility for the harms that result. In the remainder of this chapter I will expand on one particular sort of risk taking, namely, contributing to a climate of racist attitudes in a community.

RACIST ATTITUDES AND RISKS

Various attempts can lead to an increased likelihood of harm. For example, a parent's careless attitude regarding the safety of his children can easily lead to behavior likely to produce harm. Such a careless attitude could lead the parent to operate a car in an area where his children are playing, thereby increasing the likelihood that the automobile will strike and harm one of the children. But the attitude of carelessness can also increase the risk of harm by others. The careless parent is likely to omit taking various precautions, such as removing rusty objects and matches from proximity to children's toys; he thereby increases the likelihood that children would harm themselves.

In discussing potentially harmful attitudes, I am not interested in what may be described as *mere* thoughts. Attitudes are not mere cognitive states, but they are also affective states in which a person is, under normal circumstances, moved to behave in various ways as a result of having a particular attitude. The test for whether someone actually has a particular attitude or not is a behavioral test, or at least a counterfactual behavioral analysis, based on the assumption that if a person really does have a certain attitude, then certain behavior normally results. In this section, I will discuss cases in which a person has an attitude likely to result in harm, in situations in which others with similar attitudes are causing harm.

Certain cultural attitudes, such as racism, can have an effect similar to that produced by the careless parent. Those who have racist attitudes, as opposed to those who do not, create a climate of attitudes in which harm is more likely to occur. We come now to the central applied concern of this chapter, namely, to show that the members of a community who share racist attitudes also share in responsibility for racially motivated harms produced by some of the members because of this climate of racist attitudes. Here is a more extreme case of sharing responsibility for effects one has not directly caused than those previously discussed. Indeed, in the case of cultural racism, it may happen that only a small number of the members of such a community directly perpetrate harm, yet most or all of the members share in responsibility for these harms.

The members of a group who hold racist attitudes, both those who have directly caused harm and those who could directly cause harm but haven't done so yet, share in responsibility for racially motivated harms in their communities by sharing in the attitude that risks harm to others. Consider again the case of racial violence on college campuses. When administrators and faculty condone racist attitudes, sometimes adopting those attitudes themselves, a risk of racial violence is created. The individual racist attitudes considered as an aggregate constitute a climate of attitude and disposition that increases the likelihood of racially motivated harm. The climate of racist attitudes creates an atmosphere in which the members of a community become risk takers concerning racial violence.[3]

My thesis is that insofar as people share in the production of an attitudinal climate, they participate in something like a joint venture that increases the likelihood of harm. Those who hold racist attitudes, but who do not themselves cause harm directly, participate in the racial harms of their societies in two distinct ways: first, by causally contributing to the production of racial violence by others; and second, by becoming, like the reckless observer discussed above, people who choose to risk harm and yet do nothing to offset this risk. I will take up each of these points in turn.

First, those who hold racist attitudes may participate in racial violence by causally contributing to a climate that influences others to cause harm. There are several distinct ways in which having contributed to a climate of opinion may make a person responsible for the harms perpetrated by others who are influenced by that climate. In some cases there may be a straightforward causal connection between those who contribute to a climate of opinion and those who perpetrate a harm. Think of Thomas Becket, archbishop of Canterbury, who was murdered by Henry II's knights after the king created a climate of opinion simply by asking aloud why he had no followers loyal enough to rid him of the false priest. Here one person's expressed attitudes created in others a hatred that causally contributed to a harm, just as if that person had contributed to a common undertaking. Henry II's attitudes, once publicly known, had a strong impact on the attitudes and behaviors of the members of his court. Even though Henry did not direct his knights to murder Thomas (and may not have intended that his behavior be interpreted as his knights did), few would dispute that Henry shared in the responsibility for the murder of Thomas. Such judgments rely on the causal connection between Henry's attitudes and behavior and the attitudes and behavior of those who murdered Thomas.

In other cases a person's contribution to a climate of opinion has a much less straightforward causal connection with the perpetration of a harm. Consider someone who is a member of a group of people who voice public disapproval of another group of people, knowing that their acts are likely to incite still others to violence against the disapproved group. Such a person may be responsible for the harms that occur even though, due to good luck, his own public disapproval was not the act of disapproval that *directly* provoked the violence. Rather, his contribution was a bit more remote; perhaps he provided the first straw, but not the proverbial last straw that broke the camel's back. Both of these cases concern attitudes that are publicly expressed and that at least indirectly contribute to the production of harm. I turn next to situations in which the resultant harm does not depend on the public expression of racist attitudes.

The second main group of cases concerns members of a group who continue to hold racist attitudes even after similar attitudes in others are known to have produced racially motivated violence. These members share in responsibility for the racially motivated harm even if their attitudes have not been publicly expressed and have not straightforwardly contributed to the harm. If having a certain attitude leads some people to cause harm, then each person who holds that attitude risks being a producer of harm. To do that which risks harm to another, especially if it is known that the harm is highly likely and not merely possible, implicates the risk taker in these harms. And while the share in the responsibility may be greater for one who holds the risky attitude and directly causes harm than it is for one who does not directly cause harm, nonetheless there is a sharing in the responsibility for harm by all those who share the potentially harm-producing attitudes.

In some of these cases, those who hold racist attitudes should share in responsibility for racially motivated violence because their racist attitudes may reinforce, or even contribute, to the legitimation of the racist attitudes of those who do produce racially motivated violence. On college campuses, the racist attitudes of faculty members or administrators often have a clear impact on students who actually engage in racially motivated violence. Here the racist attitudes of the faculty members and administrators might stand in a causal chain, but that chain is tenuous and not normally the kind of causal contribution that makes someone responsible for a harm. What is important is *not* any direct causal connection but the fact that these attitudes indirectly contribute to a climate of opinion that makes racially motivated violence more likely. Because of this, I believe these faculty members and administrators share in responsibility for the racially motivated harms in their communities.

In other cases, those who hold racist attitudes do not *do* anything that could be said to stand in the causal chain leading to racially motivated violence. But insofar as these people do not try to decrease the chances of such violence by changing their own attitudes, given that similar attitudes in others have produced harm, they demonstrate a kind of moral recklessness, similar to that of the reckless observer, which implicates them in the racially motivated violence. In these cases, the person with racist attitudes is like someone who aims a gun at another person and pulls the trigger but, unbeknownst to him, there is no bullet in the chamber. The fact that the gun does not go off in his hands, but it does go off in the hands of the next person to pull the trigger, does not eliminate his share in the responsibility for the harm. Both people who act recklessly share responsibility not just for the risk but for the actual harm. While it is true that the one who actually caused the harm is the one who is generally taken to court, the matter is different if we are not primarily interested in choosing who is the most guilty person.

In American law there is a famous case involving a drug, DES which was taken by pregnant women to prevent miscarriages.[4] It turned out that DES caused cancer in a number of the daughters of the women who had taken it. Because of the length of time it took for the harm to manifest itself, it was not clear in a particular woman's case which of several manufacturers had produced the dose of the drug that had caused the cancer. The court decided to apportion damages among all the manufacturers based on the likelihood that each company had produced the dose of DES in question (as determined by each company's share of the market at the time the dose was sold). The manufacturers of DES had each contributed to what had turned out to be a hazardous environment for pregnant women and their daughters. When it is unclear who actually perpetrated a harm, it seems acceptable to apportion responsibility according to likelihood of having been a harm producer. This is especially true when all the members of a group act in identical or relevantly similar ways. I want to suggest that this strategy is equally valid in some cases even when we do have knowledge of which member actually produced the harm in question. To return to the example of pulling the trigger of a partially loaded gun, someone who takes such risks with the health and safety of others should not be relieved of responsibility due to good luck, nor should all of the responsibility fall on the person who has the bad luck to pull the trigger when a bullet has come into the chamber.

It might be objected that having racist attitudes is not like pulling the trigger of a gun that may or may not be loaded.[5] Such an objection might be based on the claim that there is a significant difference between those who act on their attitudes and those who do not, which is not captured in the analogy of two people who both clearly act on the basis of their motivations. I would respond by again emphasizing that there is a difference between those who have mere thoughts or beliefs and those who have attitudes. Attitudes involve dispositions to behave in various ways. And while it is possible to override these dispositions, the cases I am considering involve those who do nothing to prevent their attitudes from leading to behavior that could cause harm. The failure to do anything to prevent one's racist attitudes from leading to racially motivated violence is similar to the failure of the person who aims a loaded gun to do anything to make sure that the gun will not go off. I take it that most people who have racist attitudes have not done anything to make sure that their attitudes do not lead them to racially motivated violence. I would agree that a person who is aware of having racist attitudes and who chooses to suppress them or to allow them to be overridden by other motivations is not like the person who pulls the trigger of a gun that may or may not be loaded. The first person's precautions against violent behavior will normally mitigate his or her responsibility.

The racist who does not directly cause harm, but who chooses to maintain unsuppressed attitudes not significantly different from those of other racists whose attitudes he or she knows, or should know, directly cause harm, should share in responsibility for the racial harms perpetrated by those in society who share the racist attitudes. The racist who directly causes harm, and those racists I have described who do not, are both responsible for racially motivated harm. The racist who does not cause harm is responsible because he or she shares in the attitudes and dispositions that, but for good luck, would cause harm.

In *On Guilt and Innocence*, Herbert Morris tries to make sense of Karl Jasper's claim that all Germans shared guilt for the Holocaust. Morris describes a type of shared guilt concerning

> the deeds and characteristics of others. We connect ourselves in some way with these others and when they act we see it not just reflected on them but on us. . . . We are not at fault, but we still see their conduct as reflecting on us, reflecting perhaps on deficiencies we share with them.[6]

Morris correctly identifies one of the sources of shared guilt: a feeling that another's deficiency has produced a harm and that I share this deficiency. Each person with the deficiency shares the risk of harm because each is negligent for risking the harm that the deficiency is known to have produced. The shared risk of being a harm producer is the element which links the members to the harm caused by other members.

All those who hold racist attitudes and have done nothing significant to make it less likely that they will directly cause racial violence, even though they could have, share in responsibility for that violence. This is similar to my claim about those who engage in negligent omissions. But this is not to say that all those who hold racist attitudes share to the same degree in the responsibility as all others who hold these attitudes and have also directly caused racially motivated harm as a result. Those who have not actually caused harm may often find that shame rather than blame or punishment is the proper category to describe what should follow from their sharing responsibility for various harms. Indeed it is often true that *feeling* guilty or responsible is what should properly be the response of those who have these attitudes, rather than being held guilty or responsible. It will also often make sense to employ categories of responsibility here that do not involve the kind of accusatory stance toward the person in question that is involved in talk of guilt or blame. This is why, I take it, Morris talks of a "deficiency" rather than a fault. . . . As I have argued, all those people who hold racist attitudes in communities where racially motivated violence occurs share in the responsibility for these harms. . . .

NOTES

1. President Beering's statement was issued as a memorandum to the entire Purdue faculty.
2. Bernard Williams has argued that luck does matter in the moral assessment of people's behavior and character. See his *Moral Luck*, especially pp. 20–39. Williams is mainly concerned about the kind of case in which luck leads to good consequences that the agent could not have known would occur. In such cases, Williams argues that our moral assessment will be affected by whether these good consequences result or not. But in the cases I am examining, people are not taking risks out of a hope that greatly beneficial consequences for self or others will occur. Rather, they are taking risks hoping, if hoping at all, merely that greatly harmful consequences to others will not occur. Whether or not Williams's position is plausible (I do not find it so), the difference in our cases should lead to different intuitive judgments. In my cases people are taking risks with the lives of others, and without the consent of these others. On this point, Judith Jarvis Thomson provides a basis for seeing the intuitive difference. See her essay "Imposing Risks," in her book *Rights, Restitution and Risk,* ed. William Parent (Cambridge: Harvard University Press, 1986).
3. Judith Jarvis Thomson provides an interesting analysis of the relationship between this case and other examples of risks in "Imposing Risks," especially pp. 181–83, ibid.
4. See Sindell v. Abbott Laboratories, 26 Cal. 3d 588, 163 Cal. Rptr. 132, 607 P. 2d 924 (1980). The *Chicago Tribune* reported that in DES cases the theory of "market-share liability had been adopted in one form or another by the supreme courts of four states—California, Washington, Wisconsin, and New York. But the Illinois Supreme Court rejected the idea in a 5–2 decision." See *Chicago Tribune*, July 4, 1990, sec. 1, p. 7.
5. This was one of many excellent objections raised by Patricia Greenspan, my commentator at the APA Eastern Division meetings, December 1988, where I read a shortened version of this chapter. The point has also been pushed with great vigor by Roger Gardner, to whom I am indebted for lengthy discussions of possible rejoinders.
6. Herbert Morris, *On Guilt and Innocence* (Berkeley and Los Angeles: University of California Press, 1976), p. 135.

RACIAL AND ETHNIC DISCRIMINATION—SUPPLEMENTARY READINGS

BANTON, MICHAEL. "The International Defense of Racial Equality." *Ethnic and Racial Studies,* vol. 13(4), October 1990.

BOXILL, BERNARD. "Self-Respect and Protest," in *Philosophy Born of Struggle,* Leonard Harris, editor. Dubuque, IA: Kendall/Hunt, 1983.

CORNELL, STEPHEN. "Land, Labour and Group Formation: Blacks and Indians in the United States." *Ethnic and Racial Studies,* vol. 13(3), July 1990.

HARRIS, LEONARD. "The Concept of Racism," in *Exploitation and Exclusion,* Zegeye, Harris, and Maxted, editors. London: Hans Zell, 1991.

KARENGA, MAULANA. "Society, Culture and the Problem of Self-Consciousness: A Kawaida Analysis." in *Philosophy Born of Struggle,* Leonard Harris, editor, Dubuque, IA: Kendall/Hunt, 1983.

LAWSON, BILL. "Nobody Knows Our Plight: Moral Discourse, Slavery and Social Progress." *Social Theory and Practice,* vol. 18(1), Spring 1992.

MAPHAI, VINCENT. "Prisoners' Dilemmas: Black Resistance—Government Response." *The Philosophical Forum* (Special Issue on Apartheid), Winter–Spring 1987.

MCGARY, HOWARD. "Race and Class Exploitation," in *Exploitation and Exclusion*, Zegeye, Harris, and Maxted, editors. London: Hans Zell, 1991.

NAILS, DEBRA. "A Human Being Like Any Other: Like No Other." *The Philosophical Forum,* Winter–Spring 1987.

OUTLAW, LUCIUS. "Toward a Critical Theory of Race," in *Anatomy of Racism,* David Theo Goldberg, editor. Minneapolis: University of Minnesota Press, 1990.

SAID, EDWARD W. "Zionism from the Standpoint of its Victims," in *Anatomy of Racism,* David Goldberg, editor. Minneapolis: University of Minnesota Press, 1990.

VII

The Aids Epidemic

Because AIDS was first discovered among gay men in New York, Los Angeles, and San Francisco, society has externalized its anxiety over AIDS by directing it toward an enemy, and that enemy has been homosexuality. Meanwhile gay men have had to deal with death not only in terms of physical and psychological terrors, but also within a context of social alienation and invisibility.

—Christine Pierce and Donald Van DeVeer.[1]

AIDS is the plague of the latter half of the twentieth century. AIDS is the acronym for "acquired immune deficiency syndrome." We think we know what causes AIDS, which is more than could be said of the great plagues of earlier centuries. It is believed to be caused by the human immunodeficiency virus (HIV). But as of now, we do not have an effective medicine to counteract HIV. And as with many such viruses, more people have the virus than have the AIDS disease. So testing for the virus does not necessarily tell us who has the disease AIDS. Yet, tragically, those who have AIDS do not survive the disease, for they will die of other ailments caused when their immune systems break down.

The AIDS virus is transmitted through blood or semen (or other bodily fluids). Most people contract AIDS from anal or vaginal intercourse, from intravenous injections or blood transfusions, or from their infected mothers at birth. In the recent past, the most discussed cases in the West were those that were caused by male homosexual contact. Many conservative commentators have sought to portray AIDS as just revenge on those who choose the "unacceptable" lifestyle of homosexuality. Presently, heterosexuals have the fastest growing infection rate. Many health-care workers worry that the disease will reach epidemic proportions if policies are not adopted to curtail its spread.

Curtailing AIDS would seemingly require the identification of those who carry the virus and the isolation of those people from the rest of the population. To identify all of those who have the virus would require massive testing. Furthermore, isolating those individuals would require quarantining in numbers unheard of in the history of modern medicine. Both of these practices are the subject of the bulk of the essays in this section. Ethical questions of confidentiality. coercion, and fairness are raised and considered. In addition, several essays attempt to discuss the controversy surrounding AIDS in Europe and Africa.

The question of unjustified coercion of those suspected of having, or known to have, AIDS raises the important philosophical question of paternalism. Paternalism is the practice of restricting the liberty of a person for that person's own good, yet doing so against the person's will. One of the most commonly cited cases of paternalism concerns legal requirements that motorcycle operators wear helmets. One way to justify this requirement is by reference to the good that will be done to the motorcyclist. Of course, there are many other ways of justifying the requirement, since it turns out that motorcyclists who do not wear helmets are involved in a larger number of, and more serious, accidents, than those who wear helmets. There is greater loss of other's lives and more damage to property in cases where people do not wear helmets than in cases where they do.

Another important philosophical issue concerns privacy and confidentiality. Any plan to curtail AIDS must either be voluntary or it must forcibly identify those who have the AIDS virus. Yet any forcible attempt to obtain information about those who carry the virus would involve either a breach of patient–physician confidentiality or a violation of the privacy rights of the AIDS virus carrier. Both of these strategies are difficult to justify, although the enormity and seriousness of the AIDS crisis surely cannot be easily dismissed.

Our first selection is from Richard Mohr. In arguing that AIDS testing is a form of discrimination against gays, Mohr pushes us to see the underlying homophobia (fear of homosexuals) that underlies many calls for AIDS testing and quarantining. Mohr contends that in the United States there is such a close identification between AIDS and homosexuality, and such a negative association with homosexuality, that people are blindly discriminating against those who have, or might have AIDS. He contends that this is like the policies that tried to separate blacks from the rest of the population for fear of what they might do to the fabric of white society.

Karen Clifford and Russel Iuculano counter Mohr's arguments with a relatively simple economic argument. Since insurance companies will often be the ones who pay the huge medical bills run up by AIDS victims, surely they should be allowed to test for the virus before deciding whether and at what level to insure, just as is true for all other health conditions. To deny insurance companies the right to test for AIDS would be a violation of their property rights. Of course, such testing must conform to the same standards of fair testing that apply to all other medical screening. They conclude that there is no reason in principle to prohibit testing for the AIDS virus.

Many popular defenders of AIDS testing and quarantining begin with the assumption that homosexuality is unnatural and can be legitimately curtailed, especially if it is connected to the spread of AIDS. Christine Pierce characterizes such an argument as a natural law argument. In her essay she tries to show that such arguments run against the grain of pluralistic viewpoints on ethics that are employed in law and legislation. Pierce points out that in some forms the restrictions on homosexuals' lives countenanced by AIDS legislation amount to paternalism, since they try, supposedly out of a concern for their own good, to force people to change their sexual practices against their wills.

David Conway takes up the same issue by attempting to construct nonpaternalistic arguments in favor of quarantining or closing gay bathhouses. He first considers a justification that would simply urge that we punish those who engage in what are sometimes classified as immoral practices. But here he points out that quarantining AIDS victims would sweep much more broadly than just punishing homosexuals. Secondly, he attacks a rationale such as that proposed by Clifford and Iuculano by pointing out that society may wish to bear the increased costs that result from not violating the privacy rights of AIDS victims. Consent is also a part of his argument against seeing AIDS as a harm to individual members of society. After all, he argues, if individuals do not want to risk the harm of AIDS they need only refrain from having sexual contact. Conway admits that the issue is more complicated than this argument would indicate, but he nonetheless feels that it is not clear that society and its individual members are straightforwardly harmed by the AIDS epidemic.

Carol Tauer enters this debate to point out that in France there is such a high regard for patient confidentiality that France has not even engaged in much data collection, let alone restrictions, on AIDS victims. In Great Britain, paternalism still runs very deep, but there are signs that this is changing. And in the United States, Tauer argues, the individualistic emphasis that favored nearly absolute individual rights is also changing. In all three societies, the AIDS crisis has called into question long-standing traditions of medical ethics. There is a tension between the needs, or felt needs, of the community and the rights of AIDS patients, a tension that has resulted in inconsistent public policies in several countries.

Nicholas Christakis considers a culture with quite a different set of moral traditions from those of Western Europe and the United States. There has never been a strong tradition of individual rights in Africa, and hence questions of informed consent and patient confidentiality have not been given the priority they have received in Western countries. But this is quite troubling, says Christakis, because it opens the African continent up for possible exploitation by Western scientific interests that want drugs and vaccines tested. Christakis worries about what he calls "medical imperialism" in Africa, and argues that precautions need to be taken so that the rights of Africans are not violated in the rush to find and test an AIDS vaccine.

NOTE

1. Christine Pierce and Donald VanDeVeer, *AIDS: Ethics and Public Policy,* 1988, p. 2. Belmont, CA: Wadsworth Publishing Co.

Policy, Ritual, Purity: Mandatory AIDS Testing

Richard Mohr

Richard Mohr is a professor of philosophy at the University of Illinois at Champaign/Urbana. He is the author of Gays/Justice: A Study of Ethics, Society and Law *(1988) and* Gay Ideas *(1992). He founded and edited a series of books on gay and lesbian studies for Columbia University Press.*

Mohr argues that such practices as mandatory AIDS testing are a form of discrimination against gays that is akin to the discrimination suffered by African Americans who were subjected to segregation in the American South. In both cases, discriminatory practices were a form of ritual by which the larger society defined those discriminated against as aberrant, thereby degrading the individuals in society's eyes. Testing separates the population into two groups, us and them, and breeds intolerance. Mohr concludes that AIDS testing is not merely a panicked response to a legitimate medical crisis, but rather one more instance of unjust discrimination against a minority by a majority.

"There is not a good word to be said for anybody's behavior in this whole mess."

—Larry Kramer, *The Normal Heart*

A TALE OF THE SOUTH AND A THESIS

Well after *Brown v. the Board of Education,* Jackson, Mississippi maintained racially segregated public swimming pools, claiming that only through segregation could violence and social chaos be avoided there.[1] The federal courts saw through this stratagem, noting that it was a variant of the heckler's veto thinly masking racial animus.[2] But they did not tell Jackson to integrate its swimming pools—only that it could not maintain segregated ones. Did Jackson integrate its pools? No. The city council voted instead to close them all. This time out, the courts were not so wise.

In 1971, the Supreme Court upheld the constitutionality of the pool closings.[3] The Court was snookered by the surface similarity of the policy's treatment of blacks and whites—neither could, after all, use the swimming pools. The practice appeared to treat similar cases similarly. And indeed the pool closing statute did not refer in any way to blacks. However, shallow formalism aside, the pool closing was an even more inequitable treatment of blacks than was the original policy of segregation. Segregation merely perpetuated custom, but the closings were a social ritual that elevated pervasive

Reprinted with permission of Richard D. Mohr, from his *Gays/Justice* (New York: Columbia University Press, 1988). [Edited]

custom to the level of a sacred value. For the white city council's action told blacks that whites view them as so disgusting and polluting that white solidarity will be maintained even if to do so requires of whites the loss of comfort, joy, and the pleasures of the season. Happiness is as nothing when social identity is challenged—racial purity is not a value that the South was willing to sell; it was priceless. The Court could not see that the point of the legislative act of closing the swimming pools was to stigmatize blacks, even though the act made no mention of them.[4]

Similarly, I will argue here that the point of mandatory AIDS antibody testing is the degradation of gays and the reconsecration of heterosexual supremacy as a sacred value, even though mandatory testing, to date, has not been directly aimed at gays nor indeed has made any mention of them. AIDS testing legislation is not to be understood as business-as-usual public policy making aimed at maximizing overall social utility or realizing public goods;[5] it can be adequately understood only in terms of the nature and function of social rituals, in particular, purification rituals.

SOME SOCIAL STRUCTURES

Six years into the AIDS crisis the nation's civic leader and moral paterfamilias gave his first speech on AIDS. Without ever mentioning gays, he entrusted the moral evaluation of the disease's possessors to the future estate and its judgment of God, while resting present judgment in an awkwardness-dodging silence.[6]

In marked contrast, the speech carefully attended to recommended statute, administrative policy, and government practice, which he announced ought chiefly to take the form of mandatory testing for AIDS antibodies among certain segments of society: marriage license applicants, prisoners, and immigrants applying for permanent U.S. residency.[7] Subsequently, the latter two forms of testing were formally instituted at the national level through administrative rule[8] and the Illinois legislature has passed mandatory marital testing—the first state legislature to do so.[9] Other groups already subject to mandatory federal AIDS testing are military recruits and active duty personnel, Foreign Service officers, and employees of the Job Corps.[10]

Doctors, social workers, government health agencies, medical ethics think tanks, AIDS support groups, gay and civil rights groups and the like have done a passable, if mixed and modest, job—sometimes marred by phony patriotism[11]—in showing that mandatory testing policies are not justified on traditional public health grounds. They have shown in particular that coerced testing is unlikely to do much to stop the spread of the disease but is likely to drive the disease underground. They have also shown it to be a very poor investment of social dollars, incapable of justification on a cost-benefit analysis, and having consequences that are tragic when producing false test results and absurd considering that the funds for the tests' administration could be going into desperately needed research and patient care.[12]

However, this public health community, in showing that mandatory testing is nonsensical from the point of view of social utility and in opposing it on that ground, has completely missed the social point of the statutes and rules mandating antibody testing; indeed in its very claims (though true) that the laws are inefficient, it actually sustains the evil of the laws' real purposes. For legislative and administrative actions mandating AIDS testing are not miscalculations, merely misdirected attempts to maximize utility, nor are they failed attempts to provide the things that everyone wants but can only get through the intervention and coercive coordinations of the state—the admitted aims of most legitimate legislation. Rather they are social rituals through which the nation expresses and strengthens its highest values, its sacred values—the values, that is, for which it will pay any price.[13]

Such rituals and their values are the means by which and the forms in which the nation identifies itself to itself, and through which it maintains, largely unconsciously, its group solidarity. But group solidarity comes with a price—or as anthropologist and social theorist Mary Douglas has summarized the main finding of her lifework: "Solidarity is only gesturing when it involves no sacrifice."[14] The social inefficiency of AIDS testing demonstrated by the public health community is the sacrifice that society has accepted to express and reconfigure its solidarity around its central sacred value. An examination of cases—especially that of marital testing—will show that the chief sacred value wrought by various AIDS testing laws is what Adrienne Rich has called compulsory heterosexuality.[15]

Mandatory AIDS antibody testing laws are social purification rituals through which, by calling for sacrifices of and by the dominant culture, that culture reaffirms the sanctity of compulsory heterosexuality and rededicates heterosexuality's central and controlling place in society. The imprecatory counterpoint of such sanctification is the degradation of gays, even though in part for social convenience and moral salve the laws make no mention of them.

But even setting aside attempts to skirt possible political ugliness and taboos on speaking of sex, it is still probable that gays would not be mentioned in AIDS legislation—at least for now. For typically, especially when all goes passably well, a society does not have a foreground cognition of what its highest values are. They are not the object of its active concern but a filter through which all social structures are projected and, in turn, through which social behavior is perceived.[16] The latter filtering explains, for instance, the leaden density of most people's inability to see even openly gay people.

Paradoxically, then, in the case at hand, that which is most degraded—the gay person—goes entirely unmentioned, while the most carefully articulated values and best justified actions—those of the public health community—actually contribute to overall social evil.

If I am anywhere near the mark, then we shall unhappily have broached a justifiable skepticism about the nature and existence of human goodness and the worth of democracies, even constitutionally restrained ones. . . .

PROGNOSIS

Testing discovers and divides. Testing discovers the invisible and mysterious and it divides "us" from "them." It is the perfect vehicle for a civilization in need of reasserting its most basic values under challenge. It casts lurking threats into the light so that they may be exiled or committed to the flames. At the same time, testing regroups the dominant culture by showing that it is willing not only to sacrifice others to its values but sacrifice itself *for the sake of* them as well.

This sacrifice by and of the dominant culture may be understood on an analogy to civil disobedience on which an individual sacrifices his interests or at least puts them imminently at risk for the sake of his central values, his personal integrity. With AIDS testing and other purification rituals the body politic sacrifices its interests for the sake of a higher goal, that of preserving and solidifying its identity and integrity. The difference between civil disobedience and social purification rituals of course is that in civil disobedience the state is resisted, while in purification rituals the state is blindly affirmed and strengthened as the instrument and vehicle of purification.

When a government uses coercion to express a society's deepest values and establish or rededicate them as sacred, there will be no stopping it however odious and immoral its acts, for these values are already or come to be embedded in a pre-institutional social knowledge which serves as a lens through which all else is judged. The pairing of coercion and sacred values will simply short circuit the usual procedures that put limits on tyranny. Through the filter of sacred values, what is zany as social policy and might be discovered as such through, say, careful legislative hearings, will be seen rather as natural, necessary, and good—not in need of any articulated or particularized justification. And any hint of attack on the values themselves must and will be dealt with as through expiation—prayer in action, holy war—a cleansing of taint and a rededication through self-sacrifice of purity restored.

If we now ask what is to be done and what is to become of things, I fear my social interpretation of AIDS testing counsels little, if any, hope—and perhaps it will be resisted for that very reason. As we have seen in the transfiguration of sexual values worked by the AIDS crisis, people yearn for purpose in their lives to such an extent that they will even scan the universe looking for it when they fail to find it in themselves or hereabout. This tendency of the human mind, while in a way admirable—for it shows a certain intrepidness of the human spirit even among human weaklings—is nevertheless scary—for it means that people will try anything and they rarely, especially if weak, just stop at trying it on and for themselves. One sees this in people who have voluntarily taken the antibody test, come up negative, and then mount a pretty high horse call for coerced testing of others. The political right is counting on the large number of recently married body-negatives to serve as the advance troops for universal mandatory testing.

Even if mandatory testing were to take its most severe forms, the Supreme Court, which Martin Luther King Jr. always paired with God and which in our society is structurally the chief dispenser of rights, will be of no help in blunting the coercive state.[17] Compulsory heterosexuality need not have been mentioned in the nation's constitution, for all that is in it would be interpreted through that filter. Thus the Supreme Court could rule that gays have no privacy right to have sex, without even discussing gays or privacy or sex.[18] Under the filter of heterosexuality, the configuration of gays, sex, and privacy was completely invisible, not even a mote on the field of rights. Yet when glitches in custom have legally burdened traditional family structures, the Court has come to the rescue with the constitutional magic of Substantive Due Process—voiding laws in order to assert and restore familial sanctity as beyond calculations of social utility.[19] The Courts will be of no help addressing mandatory AIDS testing for similar reasons. The legislation in its social function—as the expression of sacred values—asserts the very values that make up the Court's interpretative lens.

The picture is gloomier still. If the courts will not work, what of trying to educate society? If my interpretation is anywhere near the mark, then many liberals (and I include myself here) have been mistaken to suppose that society's response to the AIDS crisis is a panicked response caused largely by ignorance. Rather the coercive legislation which society is now enacting in response to AIDS is simply the expected working out of the country's governing social knowledge as it has become aware of new facts. Mary Douglas might as well have had the AIDS crisis specifically in mind when she wrote quite generally:

> The conclusion [is] that individuals in crises do not make life and death decisions on their own. Who shall be saved and who shall die is settled by institutions. Putting it even more strongly, individual ratiocination cannot solve such problems. An answer is only seen to be the right one if it sustains the institutional thinking that is already in the minds of individuals as they try to decide.[20]

Society's response to the AIDS crisis could be changed only if the culture itself were changed, and that is not going to occur, if ever, twixt now and Vaccine Day, should it come. Societies are even less likely than individuals to change behavior through education and we have seen that traditional educational efforts have had no significant effect in stopping the spread of AIDS among gays; urban gay centers where educational efforts were most intense now have AIDS-saturated gay male populations.[21] Such change as has occurred in gay male behavior patterns is not the result of safe-sex pamphlets broadcasting, as they do, mixed and confusing messages about sex and sexuality. No, the educator was death. And we know from the history of war that death wins no teaching awards. And we should remember too that when death is the social educator, society responds not with new ideas and liberality but with fear and retrenchment.

Still less likely are educational efforts going to be effective because AIDS social coercion has become a body accelerated under the gravitational pull of our anxieties over nuclear destruction. Doing anything significant to alleviate the prospects of the collective death of everything that can die is effectively out of reach of any ordinary individual and indeed of any political group now in existence. So individuals transfer the focus of their anxieties from nuclear omnicide to AIDS, by which they feel equally and similarly threatened, but about which they think they can do something—at least through government. AIDS coercion is doing double duty as a source of sacred values and as a vent for universal anxieties over universal destruction. Against this daunting combination, no educational efforts will have any significant effects.

What of the public health community? Here the paradox is that the more the public health community points up the irrationality of mandatory testing by its own criteria, the more it underscores and contributes to the true public function of the testing, which is the assertion of group solidarity through self-sacrifice. In this crisis, the good intentions, good will, sometimes good arguments, and even some good actions of the public health community all inadvertently contribute to evil. Theodicy is here inverted. The public health community in the crisis is the lone lit candle in Kafka's cathedral: its singular flame simply makes the darkness darker.

Well-intended gay leaders and theorists, particularly of a socialist stripe,[22] have, I fear, also inadvertently contributed to this evil. Gays—for reasons as diverse as self-hatred and hoped-for society collegiality—have played a shell game of statistics in order to claim that AIDS is not a gay disease. In doing so, they simply misunderstand the operative social dynamics of the crisis and reinforce irrelevant public health thinking on AIDS. As gays indulge the discomforts of nongays in the crisis by denying these dynamics, they act as abused children do who try to comfort their parent even while he is beating them. When gays fail to oppose marital testing, because they think it does not affect them, and hope thereby to score a few social points by appearing patriotic, they are as aware of social realities as

European Jewry of the 1930s allowed itself to be when it failed to oppose anti-miscegenation laws on the ground that Jews were supposed to marry Jews anyway.

When gays are not busy indulging worldly heterosexuals, they are scampering off to God, the big heterosexual in the sky. Instead of thus shooting into the void their ability to generate value through reverence, gays should begin to establish rituals by which they value and honor themselves. Some recent gay AIDS burial rituals, though marred by religiosity, have been a step in the right direction.[23] The ritualistic dimensions of old-fashioned consciousness-raising groups are another. Finally, by laying hearthstones together, gays would help return sacred values to their most proper place, the sanctities of the home and the privacies of life.[24] And instead of pinning their hopes on answered prayer from Masses or on compassion from the masses, gays should prepare to resist. Now when The Good is receding from gays with all the speed and brilliance of quasars, it is time to stop looking for silver linings.

I fully expect though that gay self-hatred, exacerbated as it has been by the AIDS crisis and its concomitant transvaluation of sex and sexuality, will defeat both efforts—not a promising picture, but then it should be beginning to become clear that we have grossly underestimated the evil of men and the cussedness of things.

NOTE

1. This paper was written for and delivered to the Chicago Area AIDS Task Force, a private-sector, umbrella organization of the various public and private Cook County agencies and organizations addressing the AIDS crisis, July 14, 1987.
2. *Brown v. Board of Education* 347 U.S. 483 (1954); *Clark v. Thompson,* 206 F. Supp. 539 (S.D. Miss. 1962), aff'd, 313 F. 2d 637 (5th Cir), cert. denied, 375 U.S. 951 (1963).
3. *Palmer v. Thompson,* 403 U.S. 217, 219–21, 226 (1971).
4. The Supreme Court has made little progress on this front. See *McCleskey v. Kemp,* 107 S. Ct. 1756 (1987), in which the Supreme Court rejected as constitutionally irrelevant statistical evidence—twice as strong as that causally linking smoking to heart disease—showing that the lives of white murder victims are valued many times more than the lives of black murder victims. Both the equal protection of the laws and the bar to cruel and unusual punishment require (so the Court declared) particularized showings of an intent to discriminate against a specific individual—showings which, given speech taboos now covering racism, can never be met.
5. Examples of the "public goods" which I mean here include national defense, water purification, and equal opportunity. By "public good" I mean a good which everyone wants but cannot get or get efficiently through voluntary arrangements and which thus for its realization requires coercive coordination from the state—typically to circumvent "free riders"—so that *each* person gets what he wants.

   Public health can be a public good in this sense, when for instance a measure carried out in the name of public health takes the form of the funding of research for vaccines against airborne viruses. But in this paper I use "public health" in an operational, nonnormative, adjectival sense simply to designate people, actions, institutions, and the like which are typically referred to in ordinary English usage as elements of the public health community and its behavior.
6. *The Advocate* [Los Angeles], July 7, 1987, no. 476, p. 11.
7. "President Calls for Widespread Testing," *The New York Times,* June 1, 1987, p 1.
8. "AIDS Test Ordered for U.S. Prisoners and Immigration," *The New York Times,* June 9, 1987, p. 1.
9. "Illinois Backs AIDS Tracing," *The New York Times,* July 1, 1987, p. Y9; "Veto of AIDS Bills Urged in Illinois," *The New York Times,* July 7, 1987, p. Y11. Illinois was the first state to have its legislature pass mandatory marital AIDS-antibody testing. Between the passage of the bill and its signing by Illinois' governor several months later, Louisiana's legislature passed and its governor signed such legislation; the bills in both states went into effect on January 1, 1988. "Broad Laws on AIDS Signed in Illinois," *The New York Times,* September 22, 1987, p. Y15; "AIDS Bills Focus on Education," *Chicago Tribune,* September 22, 1987, p. 1.

   When the implementation of the Illinois Testing law proved socially unwieldy, its senate sponsor claimed that "the cost of implementing the law was not a consideration in creating it." "Prenuptial AIDS Screening a Strain in Illinois," *The New York Times,* January 26, 1988, p. 1.

10. "AIDS Test Ordered for U.S. Prisoners and Immigration," *The New York Times,* June 9, 1987, p. 1. Popular support for all forms of testing is overwhelming. A Gallup poll shows that 90 percent of people favor testing immigrants, 88 percent federal prisoners, 83 percent military personnel, 80 percent marriage license applicants and 52 percent all Americans. "Widespread Tests for AIDS Virus Favored by Most, Gallup Reports," *The New York Times,* July 13, 1987, p. Y11.
11. The American Medical Association, for example, is on record as supporting testing of prisoners and immigrants. "Doctors' Panel Suggests Limited AIDS Testing," *The New York Times,* June 21, 1987, p. Y19.
12. "Need to Widen [Voluntary] AIDS Testing Seen as Health Forum Ends" and "Homosexuals Applaud Rejection of Mandatory Test for AIDS: Advocates Express Relief over Consensus," *The New York Times,* February 26, 1987, p. Y13.
13. For an analysis of sacred or priceless values in government deliberations, see Douglas MacLean, "Social Values and the Distribution of Risk," in Douglas MacLean, ed., *Values at Risk,* pp. 85–93 (Totowa, N.J.: Rowan and Allanheld, 1986).
14. Mary Douglas, *How Institutions Think* (Syracuse: Syracuse University Press, 1986), p. 4.
15. Adrienne Rich, "Compulsory Heterosexuality and Lesbian Existence," *Signs: Journal of Women in Culture and Society* (Summer 1980) 5 (4):631–60.
16. Mary Douglas explains:

> For Fleck, the thought style [of society] sets the preconditions of any cognition, and determines what can be counted as a reasonable question and a true or false answer. It provides the context and sets the limits for any judgment about objective reality. Its essential feature is to be hidden from the members of the thought collective.

How Institutions Think, p. 13.

17. See Deborah Jonês Merritt, "Communicable Disease and Constitutional Law: Controlling AIDS," *New York University Law Review* (1986) 61:739—99.
18. *Bowers v. Hardwick,* 106 S. Ct. 2841 (1986).
19. See, for example, *Meyer v. Nebraska,* 262 U.S. 390, 399–401 (1923) (giving parents a constitutional right of Substantive Due Process to have their children taught German), *Pierce v. Society of Sisters,* 268 U.S. 510, 534–35 (1925) (Substantive Due Process used to strike down a Ku Klux Klan inspired Oregon law requiring parents to send their children to public schools), and *Moore v. City of East Cleveland,* 431 U.S. 494 (1977) (Substantive Due Process used to void a zoning ordinance barring grandchildren from living with their grandparents). *Moore* provided the constitutional standard that was used in *Bowers,* 106 S. Ct. at 2844, to claim basically that gays have no place in the constitutional scheme of the United States: "Our decisions establish that the Constitution protects the sanctity of the family precisely because the institution of the family is deeply rooted in this Nation's history and tradition. It is through the family that we inculcate and pass down many of our most cherished values, moral and cultural." *Moore,* at 503–4, footnotes omitted.
20. Douglas, *How Institutions Think,* p. 4.
21. "Five-Year Plan to Fight AIDS Drafted by New York," *The New York Times,* May 25, 1987, p. Y11.
22. See, for example, Dennis Altman, *AIDS in the Mind of America* (Garden City, N.Y.: Doubleday, 1986), chapter 3.
23. "New Rituals Ease Grief as AIDS Toll Increases," *The New York Times,* May 11, 1987, p. C11.
24. I do not think that rituals and sacred values have no role in public life or even government actions. The use of public funds for government-sponsored voluntary initiatives that enhance the value which people in general place on the particularized lifeplans of individuals is quite unobjectionable and actually will tend to put breaks on governmental tyranny, by asserting the value of the right of individuals to live out their own distinctive lives and to not be viewed socially and legally as merely filling socially assigned functions. Rescue missions are clear cases of such admirable social ritual:

> Startling examples of ritualized behavior are common in our dealings with hazard and risks. We need only to consider our willingness to engage in rescue missions when identified individuals are involved: saving crash victims, fliers lost at sea, or an astronaut; retrieving the wounded or dead in battle; diverting resources from making mines safer in order to mount rescue missions for trapped miners; or even supporting individual medical treatment rather than more public health research. These actions and policies defy economic or even risk-minimizing sense.

MacLean, "Social Values", p. 87.

AIDS and Insurance: The Rationale for AIDS-Related Testing

Karen A. Clifford and Russel P. Iuculano

Karen Clifford is Assistant Counsel, Health Insurance Association of America.
Russel Iuculano is Senior Counsel, American Council of Life Insurance.

These authors argue that AIDS testing is a quite legitimate and necessary strategy for the insurance industry to pursue in order to protect its economic interests. They begin by pointing out that America's economic health, not merely its medical well-being, is threatened by the AIDS epidemic. The health-care system and the medical insurance industry may be put in jeopardy by the tremendously escalating costs involved in treating AIDS patients. AIDS testing will allow insurers to regain their predictive abilities and plan in a rational way. They argue that such testing is not unfair as long as it is conducted according to objective standards. Indeed, if insurers are prohibited from testing for the AIDS virus, this would itself constitute an unfair infringement of their economic rights.

Acquired Immune Deficiency Syndrome (AIDS) is potentially the most serious health threat the United States has ever faced. The disease, although unknown in this nation until 1981, may afflict as many as 270,000 Americans by 1991, causing an estimated 179,000 deaths.[1] Most of these deaths will occur among the 1 to 1.5 millions Americans already infected with the virus, many of whom do not yet show signs of illness.[2]

Although the immediate danger posed by AIDS to Americans has understandably attracted a great deal of attention, the epidemic also threatens the country's economic well-being and the solvency of its health care system. In the rush to ensure that persons with AIDS are treated fairly, some legislatures have enacted and others are considering laws which, by mandating the abandonment of time-honored and sensible underwriting principles, endanger the financial stability of many insurers.

The United States Public Health Service estimates that the annual direct cost of health care for the estimated 171,000 AIDS patients expected to be alive in 1991 will be between eight billion and sixteen billion dollars.[3] This figure assumes a per case cost of $46,000 to $92,000.[4] Some studies predict considerably higher costs.[5] A large portion of these health care costs will be borne by insurance companies. Yet, high as they are, these figures underestimate the total impact of AIDS on the insurance industry because they do not

Reprinted by permission of *The Harvard Law Review*, Karen Clifford, and Russel P. Iuculano, from *The Harvard Law Review*, 1987. [Edited]

include the cost of outpatient health care, including counseling and home health care costs. Moreover, these studies do not reflect claims incurred for loss of income due to disability, and they do not in any way measure the impact on the life insurance business. Insurers expect to pay billions of dollars for AIDS-related claims over the next several years as they fulfill contractual responsibilities to policyholders who are or become AIDS patients.[6] Estimates indicate that the insurance community has already paid a significant portion of the health care costs associated with AIDS, from thirteen to sixty-five percent in some hospitals.[7]

Insurance is founded on the principle that policyholders with the same expected risk of loss should be treated equally. Infection with the AIDS virus is now known to be a highly significant factor, one that cannot be ignored by any actuarially sound insurance system. Yet some lawmakers, understandably motivated by sympathy for persons with AIDS, are giving serious consideration to a prohibition on any use of AIDS-related testing for insurance purposes, a ban that would seriously distort the fair and equitable functioning of the insurance pricing system.

This commentary argues that insurers must be allowed to continue using AIDS-related testing to determine insurability. Part I begins with an explanation of some fundamental principles of insurance and examines how these principles might apply to individuals at risk for developing AIDS. Parts II and III then review both the legal and medical rationales behind testing by insurers and set forth recent actions by several jurisdictions that have prohibited AIDS-related testing for insurance purposes. [We] conclude that such actions present potential dangers to both insurers and the insurance-buying public. Finally, [We] suggest an alternative means of financing the AIDS-related costs of individuals who are denied insurance.

I. BASICS OF INSURANCE UNDERWRITING

Even a cursory review of the fundamentals of insurance underwriting underscores the unprecedented challenges and implications the AIDS crisis holds for the life and health insurance industry. Underwriting is generally defined as the "process by which an insurer determines whether or not and on what basis it will accept an application for insurance."[8] The primary goal of underwriting is the accurate prediction of future mortality and morbidity costs.[9] An insurance company has the responsibility to treat all its policyholders fairly by establishing premiums at a level consistent with the risk represented by each individual policy holder. As one ob-server has noted, "[b]asic to the concept of providing insurance to persons of different ages, sexes, . . . occupations and health histories . . . [is] the right of the insurer to create classifications to recognize the many differences which exist among individuals."[10] Individual characteristics that have an impact on risk assessment, such as age, health history and general physical condition, gender,[11] occupation, and use of alcohol and tobacco, are analyzed separately and in combination to determine their effects on mortality.[12] "It is the understanding of the way these various [characteristics] influence mortality that enables companies to classify applicants into groups or classes with comparable mortality risks to be charged appropriate premium rates."[13]

At last count, some 158 million Americans under the age of sixty-five were covered by some form of group health insurance, and nine million more were covered solely by individual health insurance.[14] About ninety percent of the insured population is covered by group health insurance and forty-seven percent is covered by group life insurance.[15] Group insurance underwriting involves an evaluation of the risk of a *group*—for example, employees, members of a labor union, or members of an association—to determine the terms on which the insurance contract will be acceptable to the insurer.[16]

In contrast to underwriting for individual insurance, insurers underwriting group life insurance and health insurance consider only the relevant characteristics of the *group,* not of the individuals who comprise the group. Such an approach operates "on the premise that in any large group of individuals there will only be a few individuals who have medical conditions of [significant] severity and frequency which would, using individual underwriting standards, make them either a substandard or noninsurable risk,"[17] Thus, the issue of testing for the presence of the AIDS virus, its antibodies, AIDS-related complex (ARC), or the active presence of AIDS relates only to new coverage for which evidence of insurability is required.[18]

II. FAIRNESS AND EQUITY REQUIRED BY INSURANCE LAW

The insurance industry has long been subject to statutory rules requiring the fair and equitable treatment of insured parties in the underwriting process. The Unfair Trade Practices Act (UTPA), developed by the National Association of Insurance Commissioners (NAIC), was, by 1960, enacted in some form in all states and the District of Columbia.[19] The central tenet of the UTPA is its distinction between fair and unfair discrimination. State insurance laws modeled on the NAIC Act both compel discrimination in certain situations and prohibit unfair discrimination in others.[20] For example, the Act deems it inequitable to charge identical premiums for life insurance to a sixty-year-old man in poor health and a twenty-year-old woman in good health.[21] In such a case, an insurer must differentiate between the two to determine an equitable premium: "[r]ates should be adequate but not excessive and should discriminate fairly between insureds . . . so that each insured will pay in accordance with the quality of his risk."[22]

Likewise, section 4(7)(a) of the UTPA prohibits any insurer from "making or permitting any *unfair* discrimination between individuals of the same class and equal expectation of life in the rates charged for any contract of life insurance." Section 4(7)(b) contains a similar provision for health insurance that proscribes "unfair discrimination between individuals of the same class and having essentially the same hazard."[23] We contend that persons who have been infected by the AIDS virus are not of the same class and risk as those who have not been infected.

The proper definition of "fairness" in the underwriting context has been the subject of litigation. In *Physicians Mutual Insurance Co. v. Denenberg,*[24] for example, the Pennsylvania Insurance Commissioner had revoked his approval of several of Physicians Mutual's health insurance policy forms.[25] Each of the policy forms in question provided for an initial premium of one dollar, regardless of the type of risk insured.[26] The Commissioner's action was based on his determination that the policy forms "effected unfair discrimination and . . . were not in accord with sound actuarial principles."[27] Agreeing with the Commissioner's ruling, a Pennsylvania state court found that "[t]he $1.00 premium in the first month in no way relate[d] actuarially to the risk involved and [was] discriminatory."[28] To underwrite within the spirit of state antidiscrimination laws, an insurer is bound to accord similar treatment in the underwriting process to those representing similar health risks.[29]

Last year, Washington became the first state to address the practical application of its Unfair Trade Practices Act to the underwriting of AIDS. The state's insurance department had promulgated a rule establishing minimum standards to be met by insurers in underwriting the AIDS risk. The regulation construed the state's UTPA "to *require* grouping of insureds into classes of like risk and exposure" and the "charg[ing of] a premium commensurate with the risk and exposure."[30] The department's rule stresses the Act's mandate that underwriting considerations for AIDS be consistent with underwriting considerations for other diseases. It notes, by way of example, that "policies issued on a standard basis should not be surcharged to support those issued to insureds suffering from an ailment."[31]

The Washington regulation illustrates that although, on its face, the UTPA seems to impose only a negative duty on insurers, closer examination reveals that under the Act insurers have a positive duty to separate insureds with identifiable, serious health risks from the pool of insureds without those risks. Failure to do so represents a forced subsidy from the healthy to the less healthy. To meet the fundamental fairness requirements of the UTPA and to address the concern for unfair discrimination, insurers must continue to use objective, accurate, and fair standards for appraising the risk of AIDS. As will be shown below, the tests for infection by the AIDS virus indisputably identify an actuarially significant risk of developing AIDS. If the insuring process is to remain fair to other applicants and policyholders, insurers must be permitted to treat tests for infection by the AIDS virus in the same manner as they treat medical tests for other diseases.[32] To ignore risk levels associated with infection and treat a seropositive individual on the same terms as one not similarly infected would constitute unfair discrimination against noninfected insureds and, therefore, violate the state's Unfair Trade Practices Acts.[33]

III. AIDS Antibody Tests Are Valid Underwriting Tools

AIDS is caused by a virus that has been given various scientific designations but is chiefly known as HTLV-III. When the HTLV-III virus enters the bloodstream, it begins to attack certain white blood cells (T-lymphocytes) which are vital to the body's immune defenses. In response to infection with the virus, the white blood cells produce antibodies. A person generally develops antibodies two weeks to three months after infection.[34]

A protocol of tests, known as the ELISA-ELISA-Western blot (WB) series, is considered highly accurate for determining the presence of infection with the HTLV-III virus. A person with two positive ELISA tests and a positive WB is a true confirmed positive with 99.9% reliability.[35] The insurance industry and the medical profession commonly administer the ELISA-ELISA-WB series of tests.[36]

Several developments have established the reliability of the series of AIDS antibody tests used by insurers. The blood test series is consistent with the Centers for Disease Control's (CDC) definition of HTLV-III infection, which provides that "[f]or public health purposes, patients with repeatedly reactive screening tests for HTLV-III/LAV antibody (e.g. [ELISA]) in whom antibody is also identified by the use of supplemental tests [including the Western blot test] should be considered both infected and infective."[37]

Further evidence of the reliability of these tests comes from the findings of the Wisconsin State Epidemiologist, who was recently directed by state law to determine whether any test or series of tests was "medically significant and sufficiently reliable" for detecting the presence of antibodies to HTLV-III.[38] The epidemiologist concluded, after a comprehensive review of the relevant medical literature, that two positive ELISA tests followed by a positive WB are "medically significant and sufficiently reliable" for detecting the presence of HTLV-III antibody.[39]

Nonetheless, when analyzing a test's validity for underwriting purposes, reliability, in and of itself, is not sufficient. A test must also be established as an effective and accurate predictor of future morality and morbidity costs. In June 1986, the CDC estimated that 20% to 30% of those infected will develop the invariably fatal disease over the next five years.[40] In July of the same year, the National Institutes of Health predicted that, over the next six to eight years, as many as 35% of HTLV-III antibody positive persons may develop AIDS.[41] On October 29, 1986, the Institute of Medicine of the National Academy of Sciences issued a 374-page report, *Confronting AIDS,* which estimated that up to 50% of all those infected with the virus might develop full-scale AIDS within ten years.[42]

Quite apart from signaling the risk of developing AIDS itself, HTLV-III infection may herald the onset of other illnesses such as ARC or neurological disease. Studies cited by the CDC found that 25% of those who were confirmed positive with the HTLV-III antibody developed ARC within two to five years.[43] An individual suffering from ARC may have a weakened immune system and manifest such symptoms as night sweats, weight loss, fatigue, fever, gastrointestinal symptoms, and enlargement of the lymph nodes, and may become disabled as a result.[44] Due to the chronic nature of these ailments, ARC may, in and of itself, give rise to substantial medical expenses.

Despite the wealth of medical data that lends support to AIDS-related testing for insurance purposes, utilization of such tests is sometimes questioned because there are a significant number of individuals who have tested positive but have not yet developed AIDS. This viewpoint, however, demonstrates a fundamental lack of familiarity with basic insurance principles. Underwriting is, by its very nature, concerned with probabilities, not certainties; no one knows how many infected people will eventually develop AIDS. Even assuming that "only" twenty percent will contract AIDS during the first five years, there is a demonstrable risk that a large percentage of infected individuals will develop AIDS in year six and beyond.

A twenty percent assumption implies that 200 of each 1000 applicants testing positive on the ELISA-ELISA-WB series will develop AIDS within five years and, therefore, die within approximately seven years.[45] In comparison, life insurance mortality tables estimate that, of a standard group of 1000 persons aged thirty-four, only about seven and one-half (as opposed to 200 in 1000) will die within the first seven years from any cause.[46]

The substantially greater risk represented by persons who test positive for HTLV-III infection is obvious. The comparison of 200 deaths to seven and one-half deaths indicates that a person infected with the AIDS virus is, over a seven-year period, twenty-six times more likely to die than is someone in "standard health"[47] The actuarial significance of these percentages is overwhelming and cannot be ignored. Because such tests are reliable, accurate, and effective predictors of risk, they must be considered appropriate as underwriting tools. . . .

CONCLUSION

To operate in a voluntary market, insurance underwriting must appraise the risk of an unknown and unanticipated occurrence and spread that risk over a large number of individuals. The risk must be assessed as accurately as possible because the whole price structure of insurance depends on the principle that individuals who present the same expected risk of loss pay the same premium. When an insurer is able to estimate accurately the risk to which it is exposed, it can, in turn, be more precise in pricing the cost of the insurance.

Contrary to this principle, several jurisdictions have imposed legal constraints which place AIDS outside the normal medical and regulatory rules pertaining to underwriting for other diseases. Although it is legally permissible for an insurer to obtain medical information about an applicant who may contract any other disease, such as heart disease or cancer, some states grant AIDS carriers special treatment by completely exempting them from relevant tests.

The tests for infection by the AIDS virus are extremely accurate in the same sense that any tests used in the insurance business can be accurate: they provide a basis for an objective determination of significantly higher risks and, hence, risk-based pricing. Legislation intended to force life and health insurers to ignore reliable, scientific evidence of a person's increased risk of contracting a fatal disease will result in significant inequities to policyholders. Given the potential magnitude of the AIDS epidemic and the substantial likelihood that gay rights advocates will seek additional legal constraints on AIDS-related testing by insurers, the financial consequences of AIDS to all involved—insurers, policyholders, and the public—will become even more severe.

Because the life and health insurance industry's livelihood is dependent on insuring persons against premature death and the costs of disability, it is as concerned as the public health community with curbing this tragic disease. Although the industry is fully cognizant of the concerns of those who have been infected with the AIDS virus, it must also consider its responsibility to those who have not been infected. If projections of AIDS cases materialize, public policy makers will be faced with an increasingly pressing need to achieve a balance between competing concerns. This balance need not, and indeed should not, be achieved at the expense of an industry that will inevitably bear a substantial amount of the costs associated with the AIDS crisis.

ACKNOWLEDGMENT

The authors would like to acknowledge, with gratitude, the able assistance of J. Bruce Ferguson, Editor, Law Publications, ACLI.

NOTES

1. See *U.S. Public Health Service, Public Health Service Plan for the Prevention and Control of AIDS and the Aids Virus* 5 (Report of the Coolfont Planning Conference, June 4–6, 1986) [hereinafter *Public Health Service Plan].*
2. See *id.*
3. See Institute of Medicine, National Academy of Sciences, *Confronting AIDS, Directions for Public Health, Health Care,and Research* 21 (1986) [hereinafter *Confronting AIDS*]. This figure substantially underestimates actual expenses associated with AIDS because it does not include aggregate medical expenses associated with AIDS-related complex (ARC) patients or infected individuals. These expenses may outstrip all other costs associated with AIDS because of the large number of ARC or seropositive individuals and because of the length of treatment they undergo. One study estimated that the average hospital stay for AIDS patients to be between 13 and 25 days, at an average charge of from $740 to $950 per hospital day. See Scitovsky and Rice, "Estimates of the Direct and Indirect Costs of Acquired Immunodeficiency Syndrome in the United States, 1985, 1986, & 1991," 102 *Pub. Health Rep.* 10 (1987).
4. See *Public Health Service Plan, supra* note I. at 15.
5. See, eg. Hardy, Rauch, Echenberg, Morgan & Curran, "The Economic Impact of the First 10,000 Cases of Acquired Immunodeficiency Syndrome in the United States," 255 *J. Am. Med. Ass'n*. 209, 210 (1986) (estimating hospitalization costs of approximately $147,000 per case for the first 10,000 AIDS cases).
6. If, in the year 1991, 54,000 people die of AIDS, as has been projected by the United States Public Health Service, see *Public Health Service Plan, supra* note I, at 5, and if one-half of those people owned $50,000 of individual life insurance—a

conservative estimate—the resulting claim liability of the insurance industry would be $2.7 billion.

7. See *Confronting AIDS, supra* note 3, at 165.
8. Health Insurance Association Of America, *A Course In Group Life and Health Insurance* pt. A, at 379 (1985) [hereinafter] HIAA 1985 ed.].
9. "Mortality" is defined as "the death rate at each age as determined from prior experience." "Morbidity" is the "incidence and severity of sickness and accidents in a well-defined class or classes of persons." *Id.* at 366.
10. Bailey, Hutchison & Narber, "The Regulatory Challenge to Life Insurance Classification," 25 *Drake L. Rev.* 779, 780 (1976) (footnote omitted).
11. In *Manufacturers Hanover Trust Co. v. United States,* 775 F.2d 459 (2nd Cir. 1985), *cert. denied,* 106 S. Ct. 1490 (1986), the Second Circuit upheld the Internal Revenue Service's use of gender-based mortality tables to compute the value of reversionary trust interests. The court concluded that categorizing individuals by gender and calculating different costs and benefits on the basis of this group characteristic did not discriminate against individuals and did not involve any intent to discriminate against men and women. See *id.* at 465, 469.
12. See R. Mehr, E. Cammack & T. Rose, *Principles of Insurance* 657–59 (8th ed. 1985), C. Will, *Life Company Underwriting* 6, 8–19 (1974); Bailey, Hutchison & Narber, *supra* note 10, at 785.
13. C. Will, *supra* note 12, at 6.
14. See Letter from Thomas D. Musco, HIAA Director of Statistics, to the *Harvard Law Review* (Mar. 31, 1987) (citing unpublished 1986 Health Insurance Association of America Survey) (on file at Harvard Law School Library).
15. See Public Relations Division, Health Insurance Association of America, *Source Book of Health Insurance Data:* 1986 Update 6; Letter from Suzanne K. Sternnock, ACLI Program Director, to the *Harvard Law Review* (Apr. 16, 1987) (citing a forthcoming 1984 Life Insurance Marketing and Research Association Survey) (on file at Harvard Law School Library).
16. Groups must have characteristics that permit the insurance company to predict, within reasonable limits, the probable claim costs under the contracts issued. The underwriting of a new group involves a general assimilation and evaluation of all the relevant factors to be considered. Common factors include, but are not limited to, the size of the group, type of industry, number of eligible lives, cost sharing involved, type of insurance plan, and previous coverage and experience. See *HIAA* 1985 ed., *supra* note 8, at 153.
17. *Id.* Although no screening takes place in most group situations, there are at least three instances in which a group plan may require evidence of insurability. These exceptions include: (1)small groups, (2) late entrants to a group plan, and (3) large amounts of life insurance that are used to supplement basic coverage. It is common to use individual underwriting standards in these situations due to the increased danger of adverse selection—the tendency of persons with poorer than average health expectations to apply for insurance to a greater extent than persons with average or better health expectations. Underwriting standards are stricter for small groups, for example, because the size of the group is insufficient to spread the risk broadly enough to absorb the effect of adverse selection. The same rationale supports the use of evidence of insurability in the group area for "late entrants." These are employees who decline coverage when first eligible but later seek to be covered. Finally, every group life insurer has a "guaranteed issue" amount, the maximum face amount it will approve without requiring evidence of insurability. Individuals seeking coverage above the guaranteed issue amount may be required to furnish a statement of health or to undergo a medical examination. See *id.* at 204–7.
18. In the United States, individual health insurance accounts for 10% of the health insurance in force, see Health Insurance Association of America, *HIAA Annual Survey of Health Insurance Coverage* (1984) [hereinafter *HIAA Annual Survey*], and individual life insurance approximately 58% of the life insurance in force, *see* American Council of Life Insurance, *1986 Life Insurance Fact Book* 30.
19. See Bailey, Hutchison & Narber, *supra* note 10, at 782.
20. See *id.* at 782.
21. See *id.*
22. *Id.* quoting A. Mowbray, R. Blanchard & C. Williams, *Insurance* 411 (6th ed. 1969) (emphasis omitted); accord *Thompson* v. *IDS Life Ins. Co.,* 274 Or. 649, 654, 549 P.2d 510, 512, (1976) (en banc) ("[I]nsurance, to some extent, always involves discrimination, to a large degree based on statistical differences and actuarial tables. The legislature specifically intended . . . to only prohibit *unfair* discrimination in the sale of insurance policies." (emphasis in original) [footnote omitted]).
23. National Association of Insurance Commissioners, *An Act Relating to Unfair Methods of Competition and Unfair and Deceptive Acts and Practices in the Business of Insurance,* 1972 Proc. NAIC I 493, 495 (as amended).
24. 15 Pa. Commw. 509, 327 A.2d 415 (1974).
25. See *id.* at 511, 327 A.2d at 416.
26. See *id.*
27. *Id.* at 515, 327 A.2d at 418.
28. *Id.* at 516, 327 A.2d at 419.
29. *Cf.* S. Huebner & K. Black, *Life Insurance* 4 (10th ed. 1982) (stating that equitable principles require those with more serious health risks to be charged higher premiums).
30. *Wash. Admin. Code ?* 284-90-010(2) (effective Nov. 14, 1986) (emphasis added).

31. *Id.*
32. In opposing AIDS-related testing by insurers, gay rights advocates have placed particular emphasis on laws prohibiting consideration of the sickle cell trait. Sickle cell *trait,* however—as opposed to the disease of sickle cell *anemia*—presents only a minimal increased risk of mortality or morbidity. As a study prepared by the National Academy of Sciences noted, "[s]ickle-cell trait (AS) has been considered—except in situations that involve exposure to significant hypoxia, dehydration, or acidosis—as a benign and relatively innocuous condition." National Research Council, National Academy of Sciences, *The S-Hemoglobinopathies: An Evaluation of Their Status in the Armed Forces* 1–2 (1973) (footnote omitted).
33. A different interpretation of the Unfair Trade Practices Act was made in Massachusetts when the Commissioner of Insurance, on December 12, 1986, issued a "Policy Statement,"which announced that the use of AIDS antibody tests by life and health insurers constituted an unfair trade practice under that state's version of the Act, see *Mass. Gen. L.* ch. 176D, §3(7) (1984), and that violators would be subject to an enforcement action. See Letter from Peter Hiam, Commissioner of Insurance to All Life/Health Insurance Companies (Dec. 12, 1986) (Policy Statement Re: Application Form Questions Inquiring About AIDS and ARC). The validity of the Policy Statement may be subject to legal challenge because the Massachusetts Legislature expressly declined to enact legislation in 1986 that would have prohibited life and health insurers from requiring AIDS antibody tests as a condition of insurability. See S. 489, Reg. Sess., §2(1986). Moreover, the Policy Statement was issued without any prior notice, opportunity for comment, or public hearing as required by the Massachusetts Administrative Procedures Act, See Mass. Gen. L. ch. 31 §4 (1984).
34. See U.S. Dep't of Health and Human Services, *Surgeon General's Report on Acquired Immune Deficiency Syndrome* 10 (1986).
35. See J. Slaff & J. Brubaker, *The AIDS Epidemic* 201 (1985) (citing Dr. Robert Gallo, National Institutes of Health researcher and a co-discoverer of the HTLV-III virus).
36. See American Council of Life Insurance & The Health Insurance Association of America, *AIDS Survey of Member Companies* 2 (Aug. 19, 1986) (unpublished survey) [hereinafter AIDS Survey of Member Companies].
37. "CDC Classification System for HIV Infections," 35 *Morbidity & Mortality Weekly Rep.* 334, 335 (1986).
38. *Wis. Stat. Ann.* §631.90(3)(a) (West Supp. 1986).
39. J. Davis, *Seriologic Tests for the Presence of Antibody to Human T-Lymphotropic Virus Type III: Information Pursant to the Purposes of Wisconsin Statute §631.90 Regarding Their Use in Underwriting Individual Life, Accident and Health Insurance Policies* 22(Wis, Dep't of Health and Social Servs., 1986) [hereinafter Report of Wisconsin Epidemiologist].
40. See *Public Health Insurance Plan, supra* note 1, at 5. In 1985, the CDC cited studies in which 5% to 19% of those infected with the AIDS virus were found to develop AIDS over a period of two to five years. See "Provisional Public Health Service Inter-Agency Recommendations for Screening Donated Blood and Plasma for Antibody to the Virus Causing Acquired Immunodeficiency Syndrome," 34 *Morbidity & Morality Weekly Rep.* 5 (1985) [hereinafter] *Recommendations for Screening.*
41. See National Institutes of Health, "The Impact of Routine HTLV-III Antibody Testing on Public Health," 6 *Consensus Development Conference Statement* 10 (1986).
42. See *Confronting AIDS, supra* note 3, at 7.
43. See *Recommendations for Screening, supra* note 40, at 5.
44. See *Report of Wisconsin Epidemiologist, supra* note 39, at 3.
45. See *Confronting AIDS, supra* note 3, at 7. ("Most patients die within two years of the appearance of clinical disease; few survive longer than 3 years.").
46. *See* Society of Actuaries, Transactions: 1982 *Reports of Mortality and Morbidity Experience* 55 (1985). That is the approximate mortality upon which the premium cost of an individual standard class life insurance policy for such a person is based.
47. See Affidavit of Warren L. Kleinsasser, M.D. at 6, American Council of Life Ins. v. District of Columbia, 645 F. Supp. 84 (D.D.C. 1986).

AIDS and *Bowers v. Hardwick*

Christine Pierce

Christine Pierce is an associate professor of philosophy at North Carolina State University. She has coedited People, Penguins and Plastic Trees *(1986) and* AIDS: Ethics and Public Policy *(1988).*

Pierce examines natural law arguments in the debate about AIDS. She argues that there is little basis for thinking that AIDS is naturally transmitted more readily in homosexual relations than in heterosexual relations. Pierce also carefully examines a recent Supreme Court opinion to show the widespread use of natural law arguments to suppress gay rights. She argues that such arguments are incompatible with deontological positions such as those supporting human rights, as well as with consequentialist positions that are espoused by many policy makers. She concludes that laws regulating homosexuality that are supported by natural law arguments are examples of unjustified paternalism.

During the AIDS crisis, natural law arguments have turned up again not only in relation to anti-sodomy arguments, but even as parts of important claims about AIDS prevention made by the medical and scientific community. Such arguments were invoked by the state of Georgia in the 1986 Supreme Court case, *Bowers v. Hardwick,*[1] in which the Court held that the Constitution does not confer a fundamental right upon homosexuals to engage in sodomy. As we shall see, the Court accepted a version of legal moralism ignoring both the relevance of a right to privacy and two friend-of-the-Court briefs urging them to consider public health implications of prohibiting homosexual sodomy. I want to argue against legal moralism both in its standard form and in a more sophisticated version that permits natural law arguments a place in legal reasoning. Natural law arguments have aggravated the AIDS crisis by contributing not only to bad law but to bad science.

Natural law arguments which attempt to fix blame for AIDS on gay sex are variants of arguments from design. For example, Representative William Dannemeyer (R-California), a leading proponent of AIDS legislation, stated on the House floor that "God's plan for man was Adam and Eve, not Adam and Steve."[2] Ken Kesey, author of *One Flew Over the Cuckoo's Nest,* recently remarked: "It seems to me it's one's job to put sperm in a place that's designed for it. You don't put crankcase oil in your power steering system. And when God says, 'Do not put crankcase oil in your power steering system,' he's not saying, 'if you do, you'll go to hell,' he's saying, 'if you do, you'll blow

Reprinted by permission of *Journal of Social Philosophy, Vol. 20,* No. 3, Winter 1989.

the seals out of your power steering.'"[3] If blowing the seals out of one's power steering system is analogous to getting AIDS or any sexually transmitted disease, then the only well-designed sex between or among human beings is lesbian sex. As physician Barbara Herbert put it, "Only nuns have less incidence of sexually transmitted diseases (STD's) than lesbians . . . where you see an STD there's been a penis in the picture."[4]

I want now to examine some serious attempts on the part of the contemporary medical and scientific community to use natural law arguments in their effort to show that AIDS will not spread in any significant way into the heterosexual population. The first is the popular so-called efficiency thesis.

The efficiency thesis is important. Understandably, it has been incorporated into safe sex guidelines, for such guidelines need to be explicit as to who is at risk. Some scientists maintain that HIV is more *efficiently* transmitted through anal sex than vaginal sex with the implication that heterosexuals who practice only vaginal intercourse are at very low risk. However, the fact of heterosexual transmission is not in question. *The New England Journal of Medicine* reports an example of sexual transmission of HIV from a man to a woman to a man.[5] A 37-year-old married man engaged in homosexual activity while on business trips to New York. He and his 33-year-old wife had vaginal intercourse accompanied by heavy mouth kissing about twice a month. After her husband died from pneumocystis carinii pneumonia (PCP), she had a sexual relationship with a 26-year-old male neighbor. She too died from PCP. The neighbor, who developed AIDS related complex (ARC), reported no drug use and no sexual contact except the above mentioned relationship which included only vaginal intercourse and deep kissing. Comparatively few cases of vaginal transmission (particularly woman to man) exist today. The efficiency thesis attempts to explain this fact. It is thought that the lining of the anus is easily torn, thus facilitating the entry of infected semen into the bloodstream. "The rugged vagina," in the words of John Langone, unlike "the vulnerable rectum," is *designed* to withstand the trauma of intercourse. . . . "[6] Although it may be true that rectums and vaginas are respectively tender and tough, it has not been demonstrated that a traumatic event is necessary for the transmission of HIV. For example, artificial insemination[7] is not a traumatic procedure and yet women can get AIDS from undergoing this process if the sperm is contaminated. Moreover, if it turns out that HIV can cross mucous membranes, no trauma will be required to transmit AIDS.

Although scientific research already points to the possibility of direct infection of cells without trauma or tears, conventional assumptions about the proper sexuality continue to influence both the design of experiments and the interpretation of results. For instance, in late 1986, a team of federal scientists headed by Dr. Malcolm Martin found that HIV can directly infect cells from the colon and rectum in the test tube, suggesting that AIDS could spread in anal intercourse without any breakage in tissue. Dr. Martin's team tested 13 other types of cells representing a wide range of human tissues such as breast, lung, pancreas and ovary, none of which proved to be susceptible to the AIDS virus. Though he neglected even to test vaginal cells for any susceptibility to HIV, the new finding, according to *The New York Times* interpretation, "may help to explain the high incidence of AIDS among male homosexuals practicing anal intercourse."[8]

Scientist or science reporter, heterosexuals have a vested interest in believing that AIDS will be largely confined to the gay male population—that AIDS really is the "gay plague." Moreover, the efficiency thesis relies, as does the next argument under consideration, on beliefs about the proper place for depositing sperm that historically have been used to support the view that heterosexuality is good and homosexuality is bad.

Steve Witkin and a team of researchers from Cornell conducted experiments intended to show that the mere introduction of semen into the bloodstream during anal intercourse—not the trauma—adversely affects the immune systems of males. Witkin theorized that in order for the species to continue, "females have evolved immunological mechanisms to deal with exposure to sperm."[9] A woman, he thought, was not at risk for AIDS even if her partner ejaculated inside her rectum. Men, however, have not evolved such mechanisms, hence, the implication that gay anal sex from an evolutionary point of view is biologically unnatural. Witkin's thesis explains why rabbits described in the following experiments were male. The researchers engaged in what David Black, author of *The Plague Years,* calls "bunny bondage." In an effort to test the thesis that depositing semen from one male into the rectum of another might cause the receiver to produce antibodies to foreign semen and in turn suppress the immune system, researchers . . . ."took rabbits and gave them rabbit semen rectally once a week. . . . Healthy males were restrained and 1 ml of fresh semen. . . was deposited . . . to a depth of 5 cm with a No. 7 French rubber catheter."[10]

Like so many religious explanations for disease, says Richard Goldstein, a reviewer of David Black's book, Witkin's theory "not only wrongly fixes blame but falsely reassures."[11] Views like Witkin's including the efficiency thesis suggest that "prevention may ultimately be a matter of harmonizing with natural order."[12]

In *Bowers,* the court was presented by the petitioner with natural law arguments which were admissible because the Court embraced legal moralism, rejecting, to the surprise of many, the rights approach it had been developing in sex-related cases over the past twenty years. A brief review of the facts surrounding the Bowers case follows:

Michael Hardwick was arrested for sodomy in his own bedroom.[13] Police arrived at Hardwick's door to see him about an unrelated charge—a ticket for public drunkenness which Hardwick claims he had long since paid. Hardwick, a gay bartender, received the ticket as he was leaving his place of work. According to Hardwick, he left at 6:00 a.m. because he had been working on a sound system. Although he did not pay the fine on the appointed date, he did settle the matter in person at a later time. Thus, Hardwick was not expecting to be visited by the police. A house guest answered the door and let the officer in. Not knowing that Hardwick had company, the guest said Hardwick was in his room. The officer went to Hardwick's bedroom, caught him in the act of consensual fellatio, and arrested him. Although the charges were later dropped, Hardwick sued Michael J. Bowers, the attorney general of Georgia, in hopes of achieving Supreme Court review of a law that had, he thought, "inadequate rationale." According to the Georgia statute:

> A person commits the offense of sodomy when he performs or submits to any sexual act involving the sex organs of one person and the mouth or anus of another.

It is important to note at the outset that the issue before the Court in *Bowers v. Hardwick* was whether to affirm a lower court ruling that Georgia, in order to keep its sodomy statute, would have to demonstrate that it promoted a compelling state interest. Michael Hardwick's winning the case would not have made Georgia's sodomy law unconstitutional; it simply would have required Georgia to show that its sodomy statute serves some legitimate state objective and is the most narrowly drawn means of achieving that end.

Bowers is an example of legal moralism par excellence. Legal moralism, as characterized by Joel Feinberg, is the view that "it can be morally legitimate to prohibit conduct on the ground that it is inherently immoral, even though it causes neither harm nor offense to the actor or to others."[14] A view often associated with Patrick Devlin, legal moralism is also put forward in a more sophisticated form by Ronald Dworkin in an article critical of Devlin. I want to argue against Dworkin's proposal that legal moralism might be acceptable as long as certain minimal rational requirements are met. Dworkin distinguishes between moral views that ought not to be legally enforced because they are based on prejudice, emotional reaction, false claims or arguments from authority (what Dworkin calls parroting) and genuine moral convictions that might be legally enforced. As Dworkin puts it, "Not every reason I might give will do."[15] Among the reasons that will do, however, as a legitimate basis for prohibiting *X*, is "*X* is unnatural." As we shall see, the reasoning in *Bowers* arguably meets neither the minimal standards outlined by Dworkin, nor even the lower requirements advocated by Devlin.

Patrick Devlin takes the view that, ultimately, morality is a matter of feeling, in particular, feelings of disgust, indignation, and intolerance on the part of ordinary people. Moreover, he claims that moral views should be legally enforced if these feelings are sufficiently intense (reach "concert pitch," as H.L.A. Hart puts it). These feelings need not be based on any rational considerations. In essence, the majority of the Court said that there is no fundamental right to homosexual sodomy because people have strongly disapproved of it and have done so for a very long time.

For example, the majority says, "Sodomy was a criminal offense at common law and was forbidden by the laws of the original thirteen States. . . . In fact, until 1961, all 50 States outlawed sodomy, and today, 24 States and the District of Columbia continue to provide criminal penalties for sodomy performed in private and between consenting adults."[16] Chief Justice Burger says, "Decisions of individuals relating to homosexual conduct have been subject to state intervention throughout the history of Western civilization."[17]

The Court, in *Bowers,* does not take a critical view of history. It does not consider the possibility that popular prejudices can undermine individual rights in societies that are deeply rooted in sexism, heterosexism and racism. However, the Court has not always thought of history as buttressing moral claims. Twenty years ago, section 20-59 of the Virginia law stated:

> If any white person intermarry with a colored person, or any colored person intermarry with a white person, he shall be guilty of a felony and shall be punished by confinement in the penitentiary for not less than one nor more than five years.[18]

In *Loving v. Virginia*[19] a unanimous Court found Virginia's ban on interracial marriages a product of "invidious racism." In that case, the Court was unpersuaded either by tradition or by the trial court's argument from design that "Almighty God created the races white, black, yellow, malay, and red, and he placed them on separate continents. And but for their interference with his arrangement there would be no cause for such marriages. The fact that he separated the races shows that he did not intend for the races to mix."[20] The Court was also unpersuaded by the fact that anti-miscegenation statutes had been common in Virginia since colonial times and that Virginia was one of 16 states that prohibited interracial marriage. Nonetheless, when

Michael Hardwick claimed that "the presumed belief of a majority of the electorate in Georgia that homosexual sodomy is immoral and unacceptable" is an "inadequate rationale to support the law," the Court said simply, "we do not agree."[21]

There is an important feature of Devlin's legal moralism that is relevant to the outcome of *Bowers*. Devlin notes that "the limits of tolerance shift." Although, on his view, we are justified in passing laws on no other basis than deeply held feelings of disapproval, when the limits of tolerance shift, we should change the laws. Polls in 1986 conducted by *Time* and *Newsweek* magazines show an absence of majority approval for the outlawing of any of a variety of specific sexual practices, including oral and anal sex, between consenting adults.[22] Thus, one might argue that the Supreme Court does not even realistically apply legal moralism of the sort articulated by Devlin.

It is also important to note, for example, that the trend of States to repeal laws against sodomy or interracial marriage has been interpreted as cutting both ways. Virginia, as we have seen, was one of the 16 States to prohibit interracial marriage in 1967. Fifteen years earlier 30 States prohibited interracial marriage. This data was taken by the Court as showing that the limits of tolerance shift. A similar trend vis-a-vis sodomy laws was used by the Court to show that many people still oppose sodomy.[23]

Natural law arguments figure into the case since the petitioner, Bowers, appeals to the beliefs of Western philosophers who thought that homosexuality was unnatural. As Bowers argues, "No universal principle of morality teaches that homosexual sodomy is acceptable conduct. To the contrary, traditional Judeo-Christian values proscribe such conduct. Indeed, there is no validation for sodomy found in the teaching of the ancient Greek philosophers Plato or Aristotle. More recent thinkers, such as Immanuel Kant, have found homosexual sodomy no less unnatural."[24]

In the *Laws* (the work of Plato's cited by Bowers), Plato, himself a homosexual, characterizes homosexual sex as unnatural, whereas in earlier dialogues he portrayed the intensity and delights of homosexuality,[25] even suggesting that homoerotic experience is an important prerequisite for knowing the essence of Beauty.[26] In the *Laws,* Plato's last work, he maintained that heterosexuality—with its procreative end—was inherently orderly; he approved of the use of the law to enforce what he saw as natural, i.e., orderly sexuality. Some commentators on Plato have charged him with inconsistency. Others have said Plato got increasingly conservative in his old age. However, there is another possible interpretation here. Plato, in the *Laws,* was legislating for a public which, by and large, did not consist of philosophers. Not above considerable elitism and (some say) a bit of totalitarianism, Plato thought—as does Petitioner Bowers—that marriage, family and procreation were institutions designed to promote social control. Bowers says that

> . . . homosexual sodomy is the anathema of the basic units of our society—marriage and the family. To decriminalize or artificially withdraw the public's expression of its disdain for this conduct does not uplift sodomy, but rather demotes these sacred institutions to merely other alternative lifestyles. One author has described that result as the promotion of indifference toward these foundations of social order, where historically there has been endorsement.[27]

Unlike the Attorney General of Georgia, Plato made an honorable pederastic exception for philosophers—an exception not needed (in the *Laws*) for members of the general public who lived their lives in the realm of opinion, not the realm of knowledge.

Although Bowers cites Kant as a philosopher who disapproved of sodomy,[28] other legal scholars such as David Richards have found support in Kant for the opposite point of view. Richards cites Kant as an author of the idea of human rights, as one "who best articulated its radical implications for the significance of respect for moral personality."[29] Extending the Kantian notion of autonomy to sexuality, Richards says: "Sexuality . . . is not a spiritually empty experience that the state may compulsorily legitimize only in the form of rigid, marital procreational sex, but one of the fundamental experiences through which, as an end in itself, people define the meaning of their lives."[30] Rights, typically, protect certain basic interests or desires of persons even if so doing makes the majority unhappy. Being able to love, according to Richards, is central to human lives. Moreover, "[f]reedom to love means that a mature individual must have the autonomy to decide how and whether to love another."[31]

Despite Kant's talk about rights as guarantees of proper respect for moral personality or rational autonomy, Kant did not see the implications of his theory for sexual autonomy. Of course, whenever one is developing a new theory, one may fail to see the whole range of its possible applications. Kant, for example, never asked whether non-human animals were capable of rational autonomy. In the *Lectures,* he referred to them as "man's instruments."[32] Kant also thought women quite lacking in rational ability and therefore did not see that they had any need for the rights of "man." Thus, in citing Kant, both Bowers and Richards are right. Kant was a very conventional man. He was also one of the originators of a theory of rights with radical implications for moral and social thought.

On a view like Devlin's, there is no theoretical limit to the legal enforcement of morality. Principles—such as Mill's principle of liberty or a right to privacy—are designed to function as just such limits. Blackmun, in his dissent, laments the "overall refusal" of the Court to "consider the broad principles that have informed our treatment of privacy in specific cases."[33]

The word "privacy" does not appear in the Constitution. Nonetheless, a series of Supreme Court decisions has established a right of privacy. It is said to exist in the penumbra of certain Amendments and, more philosophically, in the concept of liberty itself. (The word "liberty" is in the Constitution.)

A number of cases have established the constitutional status of a right of privacy.[34] *Griswold v. Connecticut*[35] held that a right of privacy protects the use of contraceptives by married persons. In this case, much was made of the fact that if contraceptives were illegal, police could enter the bedroom and search for them. *Eisenstadt v. Baird*[36] held that unmarried persons, under the equal protection clause, also have the right to use contraceptives. *Roe v. Wade*[37] held that the right of privacy encompasses a woman's decision to have an abortion. *Stanley v. Georgia,*[38] upheld the right to private possession of obscene material. Although a First Amendment case, the Court stressed the importance of the privacy of one's own home. In the words of Justice Marshall, "[Stanley] is asserting the right to read or observe what he pleases—the right to satisfy his intellectual and emotional needs in the privacy of his own home."[39]

One way to explain a connection between the concepts of privacy and liberty is to borrow some thoughts from J.S. Mill. Mill advances roughly the following principle of liberty: People (competent adults, not children) should be allowed to voice their opinion and direct their lives as they see fit as long as no one else is wrongfully harmed. It follows from this principle that what one does to oneself, as long as no harm comes to another, is one's own business. A private action then is one that concerns oneself and does not wrongly harm others. Mill adds that if more than one party is involved, all parties must give their consent. Thus, what consenting adults do, as long as others are not wrongly harmed, is private, i.e., their own business and not the business of the law. On such a view, it would be natural to suppose that a right of privacy would include sexual intimacies between consenting adults in their bedroom. The recognition of a right to sexual autonomy—something very much like Mill's view—was believed by many, including David Richards and dissenting Justice Blackmun, to be the Court's view in its development of privacy law. Thus, many were surprised that the Court did not extend the right of privacy to the facts in *Bowers*.

With respect to prior cases in privacy, the Court said, "None of the rights announced in these cases bears any resemblance to the claimed constitutional right of homosexuals to engage in acts of sodomy. . . . No connection between family, marriage, or procreation on the one hand and homosexual activity on the other has been demonstrated."[40] The majority produced no principle for this distinction. Nan D. Hunter, an ACLU attorney, calls the Court's statement one of "unmasked contempt . . . as if gay people don't create families, belong in families, raise children, or have the staying power for those 9.4-year-long average marriages that are the bedrock of civilized society."[41] It is not insignificant that the majority here aligned itself with Bowers who in turn sided with Plato in thinking it a legitimate function of the law to bolster the conventional institutions of marriage, family, and procreation.

The complaint here is not simply that the Court did not extend the right of privacy to consensual sexual conduct between adults in their bedroom, but that the Court did not even recognize the right of privacy as the fundamental right at issue. Blackmun, in the opening sentence of his dissent, says: "This case is no more about 'a fundamental right to engage in homosexual sodomy,' as the Court purports to declare, than *Stanley v. Georgia*, . . . was about a fundamental right to watch obscene movies . . ."[42] To push the point, in Kansas, in 1986, the legislature passed a law banning sex toys in general and vibrators in particular.[43] If a challenge to this law should ever reach the Supreme Court, no one would expect the Court to find in the Constitution a fundamental right to own a vibrator.[44] Since the legislation was part of a pornography package, we might anticipate that the right of freedom of expression and/or the right of privacy would count as a fundamental right at issue.

Recognition of a fundamental right by the courts triggers heightened judicial scrutiny. Very good reasons (a "compelling interest," in the language of law) must be given by a State if a law is to survive this heightened scrutiny. In a case where no fundamental right is recognized, almost any reason, however weak, will do. As we have seen in *Bowers*, moral beliefs were used as reasons without meeting any rational requirements such as those suggested by Ronald Dworkin. For example, Dworkin would not count as genuine moral convictions those claims based only on arguments from authority such as appeals to the beliefs of Plato, Kant and the Judeo-Christian tradition. Interestingly, in citing Kant as an authority, Bowers also stated Kant's reason for opposing homosexuality by noting that Kant thought homosexuality unnatural. It is unclear, I think, whether one has committed the fallacy of argument from authority if in appealing to an authority one cites as well the authority's reason for opposing whatever is at issue.

Assuming the man on the bus does produce a reason that is not disqualified on Dworkin's grounds, that reason, Dworkin says, "will presuppose some general moral principle or theory even though [the man on the bus] may not be able to state that principle or theory . . .[45] Presumably, it is unreasonable to make everyone who rides the bus take a course in moral philosophy, hence, Dworkin's standards of rationality are minimal, requiring only that one be able to produce a reason for one's view and use it consistently. "*X* has harmful consequences," "*X* violates my rights," "*X* is unnatural," even "The Bible forbids *X*" count as genuine reasons, and if used consistently, constitute a genuine moral conviction. Joel Feinberg objects to Dworkin's version of legal moralism when he says, "Even if there is a *genuine* moral consensus in a community that certain sorts of 'harmless' activities are wrong, I see no reason why that consensus should be enforced by the criminal law . . . even a genuine 'discriminatory' popular morality might, for all that, be *mistaken* . . . "[46] Undoubtedly, mistaken moralities and bad reasons will find their way into the criminal law on Dworkin's view. To illustrate the point, reasons of the sort "*X* is unnatural" are bad reasons and yet such reasons surely would pass Dworkin's test for they have a principled form and presuppose a general moral theory. In not requiring the ordinary person to recognize moral reasons in their principle form or to know anything about the moral theories to which the reasons are attached, Dworkin does not and cannot require a citizen to have a *good* reason for his moral point of view, for without a knowledge of ethical theory or metatheory, there is no basis for judging between competing kinds of reason.

It is easy to think that in adopting legal moralism one simply adds a principle of legal moralism to the harm principle, the offense principle, etc., in an effort to sanction increasingly invasive restrictions on personal liberty. In some instances, however, endorsing legal moralism is costly to society, i.e., personal liberty is not the only cost. E.g., a friend-of-the-court brief accompanying *Bowers* filed jointly by the American Psychological Association and the American Public Health Association argued, correctly, I believe, that "from a public health standpoint, the [Georgia] statute is simply counterproductive . . . the statute does not deter conduct that spreads AIDS, but it may deter conduct essential to combating it."[47] Briefly, the Associations of Psychology and Public Health argued that sodomy statutes adversely affect scientific investigation directed toward containing AIDS and finding a cure and interfere with health education efforts designed to encourage safer sexual practices. Specifically, the Associations supported their claims in the following way:

> A statutory scheme that creates a realistic fear of punishment if certain behavior is disclosed runs the risk of obscuring important data, as individuals simply refuse to volunteer for studies or provide needed information, and of creating false data, as individuals try to conform what they reveal to what they believe is legal. . . . With respect to at least two important issues—the existence of potentially high risk to recent immigrants from Haiti and the transmissibility of the AIDS virus from women to men—there is reason to believe that falsification of information, caused by fear of punishment, have distorted the epidemiological picture. Finding these and other crucial pieces of the AIDS puzzle should not have to depend on the ability of the epidemiologists to guess whether patients are not telling the truth because they fear being punished . . . community effort and support [for major educational efforts] are made more difficult in an environment in which a concomitant of participating in educational efforts is self-incrimination. Attending an educational presentation on "safe sex", for example, could be seen as an admission of engaging in sexual practices prohibited by the statute. Criminalization is likely to compromise the efficacy of informal educational networks by making people more cautious about what they reveal about themselves to acquaintances. It also presents state public

> health officials with the awkward choice of appearing to suppress information about safe sex techniques or appearing to condone felonious conduct.[48]

The Associations also point out that the Georgia statute does not further any mental health objectives and causes substantial psychological harm by fostering homophobia among heterosexuals and internalized homophobia among gay people. Roy Cohn, a queer-baiter in the McCarthy era who recently died of AIDS, is a classic case of the destructive behavior that results from internalized homophobia. It is worthy of note that Cohn's medical records showed him "reluctant to be celibate"[49] and his public statements showed him reluctant to tell the truth.

Rather than relinquish the idea that homosexual sex is wicked, some would even deny condoms to those who need them, preferring to see people die of AIDS. E.g., the Corrections Department in New York State made condoms available to married prisoners enrolled in a family visitation program, whereas condoms were not made available to prisoners not enrolled in the program even though officials realized some prisoners engaged in homosexual sex and could use the condoms to protect themselves against AIDS.[50] Of course, if natural sex is procreative sex, then the use of condoms by heterosexuals is equally unnatural. However, somewhere between Aquinas and Bowers, a new use of "natural" has emerged for convienence-oriented consumers. In defense of a company decision not to portray gay users of condoms in television commercials, Susan Smirnoff, spokesperson for Trojan, recently said "[Condoms] are effective against infection when used properly. A condom's proper use is for vaginal intercourse."[51]

The point I want to make here is that natural law arguments and consequentialist arguments are incompatible. Aquinas said that rape is not as bad as consensual sodomy or interrupting heterosexual intercourse, because (heterosexual) rape allows for the possibility of fulfilling the purpose of sexuality, namely, procreation. At the very least, it seems somewhat peculiar to prefer sexual acts which are by definition unloving, violent abuses of persons to acts which need not be, and may be quite the contrary. Consequences, however destructive of individuals or society, do not matter a whit in the face of what is claimed to be the natural order. To those who care nothing about real consequences, Richard Goldstein says, "Better you should wear a condom. But if a layer of latex is all it takes to still the winds of doom, what kind of moral mystery does AIDS pose?"[52]

Regardless of one's assessment of the foregoing arguments regarding the social costs of prohibiting homosexual sodomy, the fact remains that to advocate the prohibition of homosexual sodomy because it is believed to be wicked or unnatural is to dispense with any discussion of harmful consequences that may result from the prohibition. Had the Court ruled in Hardwick's favor, Georgia could have made its case—on the basis of public health or whatever—for its sodomy statute. But, Georgia did not have to give any good reasons for its law nor did the Court concern itself with arguments to the effect that the public health is ill-served by the prohibition of sodomy. The Court, as we have seen, dismissed these arguments in favor of traditional views that were poorly supported or wholly unsupported: Bowers said that Kant said that homosexuality is unnatural.

NOTES

1. *Bowers v. Hardwick,* 106 S.Ct. 2841 (1986).
2. Note: "The Constitutional Rights of AIDS Carriers," *Harvard Law Review* 99 (1986), p. 1274.
3. Richard Goldstein, "A Plague on All Our Houses,"

The Village Voice, Literary Supplement, September 1986, p. 17.

4. Barbara Herbert, M.D., quoted in "Lesbian/Gay Health Conference," *Off Our Backs,* May 1986, p. 3.
5. *The New England Journal of Medicine,* vol. 314, no. 15, 1986, p. 987.
6. John Langone, "AIDS," *Discover,* December 1985, pp. 40–41.
7. Some prefer the term "alternative insemination" for the obvious and good reason that "artificial" is in opposition to "natural."
8. *The New York Times,* December 14, 1986.
9. David Black, *The Plague Years: A Chronicle of AIDS, The Epidemic of Our Times* (New York: Simon and Schuster, 1986), p. 99.
10. Ibid., p. 97.
11. Goldstein, p. 17.
12. Ibid.
13. The facts surrounding Hardwick's arrest are found in an interview with him in *The Advocate,* September 2, 1986, pp. 38–41, 110. See also Donahue Transcript #07116 (Cincinnati: Multimedia Entertainment, Inc., 1986).
14. Joel Feinberg, *Offense to Others* (Oxford University Press, 1985,) p. xiii.
15. Ronald Dworkin, "Lord Devlin and the Enforcement of Morals," *Morality and the Law,* edited by Richard Wasserstrom (Belmont, CA: Wadsworth Publishing Company, 1971), p. 63.
16. 106 S.Ct. 2841, 2844, 2845 (1986).
17. 106 S.Ct. 2841, 2847 (1986).
18. *Loving v. Virginia,* 388 U.S. 1 (1967).
19. 388 U.S. 1, 3 (1967).
20. Ibid.
21. 106 S.Ct. 2841, 2846 (1986).
22. "Sex Busters," *Time,* July 21, 1986, p. 22. See also "Poll Shows Americans Disapprove of Ruling," *The Advocate,* August 5, 1986, p. 11.
23. In a footnote, Justice Stevens comments, "Interestingly, miscegenation was once treated as a crime similar to sodomy." 106 S.Ct. 2841, 2857 (1986).
24. Petitioner's Brief, p. 20.
25. See, for example, the *Symposium* and the *Phaedrus.*
26. Gregory Vlastos. foremost authority on Plato, gives this interpretation. See "The Individual as an Object of Love in Plato," *Platonic Studies* (Princeton: Princeton University Press, 1973). See, in particular, Appendix II *(Sex in Platonic Love),* pp. 38–42.
27. Petitioner's Brief, pp. 37–38.
28. Immanuel Kant, *Lectures on Ethics,* trans. Louis Infield (Cambridge: Hackett Publishing Company, n.d., reprint of the 1979 ed. published by Methuen, London), p. 170.
29. David A.J. Richards, *Sex, Drugs, Death and the Law: An Essay on Human Rights and Overcriminalization* (Totowa, N.J.: Rowman and Littlefield, 1982), p. 31.
30. Ibid., p. 52.
31. Ibid., p. 55.
32. Kant, p. 240.
33. 106 S.Ct. 2841, 2852 (1986).
34. The following sketch of the constitutional status of privacy serves only the limited functions of explaining why Blackmun and others thought the Court in earlier cases was developing a right to sexual autonomy and providing some background for the ensuing critical discussion of Dworkin.
35. 381 U.S. 479 (1965).
36. 405 U.S. 438 (1972).
37. 410 U.S. 113 (1973).
38. 394 U.S. 557 (1969).
39. 394 U.S. 557, 565 (1969).
40. 106 S.Ct. 2841, 2844 (1986).
41. Nan D. Hunter, "Banned in the U.S.A.: What the Sodomy Ruling Will Mean," *The Village Voice,* July 22, 1986, pp. 15–16.
42. 106 S.Ct. 2841, 2848 (1986).
43. "Sex Busters," *Time,* p. 21.
44. Thanks to Beth Timson for this point.
45. Ronald Dworkin, p. 64.
46. Joel Feinberg, "'Harmless Immoralities' and Offensive Nuisances," *Rights, Justice, and the Bounds of Liberty* (Princeton: Princeton University Press, 1980), p. 83.
47. Brief of Amici Curiae, American Psychological Association and American Public Health Association in Support of Respondents, pp. 27, 22. A friend-of-the-court brief supporting the petitioners was filed by Professor David Robinson, Jr., George Washington Law School.
48. Ibid., pp. 24–27. The following footnote in the brief explains the Associations' claim that the transmissibility of the AIDS virus from women to men is an area where falsification of information may have occurred: "A study of military personnel done at Walter Reed Army Medical Center shows a much higher incidence of female-to-male transmission of HTLV-III/LAV virus than most other United States reports. The question of the incidence of female-to-male transmission is an important area of current inquiry. It is possible that the other reports show an artificially low incidence of such transmission. But another explanation for the disparity is that the military personnel in the Walter Reed study were reluctant to admit to homosexual activity or intravenous drug use, either of which could lead to discharge."
49. Dale Van Atta, "Faint Light, Dark Point: Roy Cohn, AIDS, and the question of privacy," *Harper's* (November 1986), pp. 56–57.
50. *The Citizen,* Auburn, NY, December 23, 1986.
51. *Gay Community News,* Feb. 1–7, 1987.
52. Goldstein, p. 17.

AIDS and Legal Paternalism

David A. Conway

David A. Conway is an associate professor of philosophy at the University of Missouri in St. Louis. He is the author of A Farewell to Marx *(1987).*

Conway examines a number of arguments that would provide a nonpaternalistic basis to testing or quarantining AIDS carriers. Most of his essay is concerned with the question: Is it true that not quarantining AIDS carriers poses a serious threat to the society at large? Conway concludes that there are serious risks that are run by members of the population at large due to the non-quarantining of AIDS carriers. But while this provides a possible basis for nonpaternalistic arguments to quarantine AIDS carriers, there are many other factors that would make it unlikely that this argument would work given the specific facts of the current AIDS crisis.

The great majority of the known cases of Acquired Immune Deficiency Syndrome (AIDS) in the United States are believed to have been contracted through homosexual activities.[1] As a result there have been calls for, and in some instances passage of, laws whose purpose is to decrease the number of homosexual contacts and thus at least to slow the spread of this lethal ailment. These actual or suggested laws include those that would close bars and baths where meetings and sexual activities are likely to take place, and those that would provide for the quarantine of carriers of the AIDS virus.[2]

It is frequently maintained, however, that laws such as these provide for unwarranted paternalistic intrusion on the chosen actions of consenting adults. For instance, faced with the threat of being closed down by local government, proprietors of baths and bars have maintained that the men who choose to frequent their establishments and to engage in sexual activities there are well aware of the dangers of doing so. If these people are willing to risk their own health and even lives by frequenting the bars and baths, that is "their own business." It is not the business of the law to interfere with those free choices.

Philosopher Jonathan Lieberson argues in the same vein:

> The New York Post has called the civil rights of bathhouse patrons "irrelevant banter." But AIDS in bathhouses is contracted through consensual acts. . . . While the state government has in principle the right to intervene in private sex activity in order to protect people from an epidemic of highly contagious disease, it . . . has not been shown that AIDS is very contagious. . . .[3]

And widely syndicated columnist Charles Krauthammer says this about the notion that AIDS carriers should be quarantined:

David A. Conway, "AIDS and Legal Paternalism" in *Social Theory and Practice, Vol. 13,* No. 3, Fall 1987.

> The fact is plain: AIDS is hard to transmit. It stubbornly sticks to certain high-risk groups engaged in sexual promiscuity and intravenous drug abuse. . . . [B]oth are voluntary. . . . Quarantine is justified when it is the only way to protect citizens from involuntary infection. If Jones can give you his tuberculosis by sneezing on you in a subway car, then society must protect you by locking him up. But if Jones needs your full cooperation in a rather complicated act to give you his AIDS, what possible reason can society have for locking up Jones in the name of protecting you?[4]

The principle that lies behind these positions would seem to be Mill's: "There is no room for [even considering a prohibition] when a person's conduct affects the interests of no persons besides himself, *or needs not affect them unless they like*. . . . In all such cases, there should be perfect freedom, legal and social, to do the action and stand the consequences."[5] Mill's principle clearly entails that it is illegitimate to close baths and bars and to quarantine AIDS carriers to protect their potential patrons and lovers from contracting AIDS, since the patrons and lovers consent to take the risks of getting the disease. The opposing doctrine—the one that would have it that it is a proper function of the law to protect the individual from making unwise choices that may bring him harm—has come to be called "legal paternalism." In these terms, Mill's position is that of principled anti-paternalism, and arguments such as those given by Lieberson and Krauthammer against the legitimacy of closing the baths or quarantining carriers appear to rest on anti-paternalistic presuppositions.[6]

It has often been claimed that the sort of anti-paternalism defended by Mill is much too radical to be plausible, since, for instance, it would (so say Mill and others) make it illegitimate to interfere even with the sale of dangerous drugs.[7] Nonetheless, Mill's position has considerable plausibility. If the only reason that can be given for preventing me from riding a motorcycle without wearing a helmet or from playing the commodities market or from handling poisonous snakes is that the action may bring me harm, then it is hardly far-fetched to think that you do not have adequate reason for interfering with my informed deliberate decision to perform that action. This indicates that paternalistic justifications for interference with individual liberty are, at best, inherently weak, and so non-paternalistic justifications are almost always to be preferred.

The question that I now want to consider is whether the threat posed by AIDS actually does somehow provide the basis for a coherent non-paternalistic rationale for actions such as closing baths and bars and quarantining carriers of the virus. Here are some possible rationales.

1. The homosexual acts that spread AIDS are immoral in themselves. The aim of laws which would close meeting places or quarantine homosexual carriers is to prevent people from behaving immorally or to punish them for having done so.

This sort of rationale is not paternalistic in our sense, for the purpose here is not the prevention of harm to self but rather the enforcement of morality as such.[8] Many quite understandably find this function of law considerably less palatable than paternalism.[9] While it would justify the closings and quarantines, it also could justify a general repressive anti-gay campaign that would appeal to only the most diligent of moralists. More basic to present purposes, even though AIDS and homosexuality are understandably closely connected in the public mind (it would be naive to think that the recent AIDS panic would have been so severe were it not for fear and loathing of homosexuality), AIDS is one thing and homosexuality is another. Our question is whether the threat of AIDS, not homosexuality itself, can be the basis of a non-paternalistic justification for the closings and quarantines. And so this proposed justification is not really to the point.

2. Many AIDS victims will require protracted hospital or hospice care for which they cannot pay from their own resources. This means that they will be dependent on public funds for support. The aim of closing the baths and quarantining carriers is to protect society from the monetary burden of providing such support.

Reasoning of this sort is common enough in legal cases (for example, as justification for requiring motorcyclists to wear helmets), but it is not at all clear that it can actually provide a non-paternalistic rationale for actions that might slow the spread of AIDS (or, for that matter, for requiring the helmets). If someone is seriously in need of health care which he cannot afford, it may be that society should see to it that the care is provided. But the fact that society should do this does not mean that it does not have a genuine choice as to whether to do it. (Even if I really should give the change in my pocket to the blind street musician, I still have the choice of whether or not to do so. It would, in general, be ethically peculiar to hold that having an obligation to do *A* interferes with my freedom of choice whether to do *A*.) If society provides care for AIDS patients and incurs the attendant expenses of doing so, that is something that society consents to do. Thus, a person becoming sick with AIDS (or falling off a motorcycle while not wearing a helmet) and then needing medical care beyond his ability to pay does not force a harmful financial burden on any unwilling party.

It may yet be possible to develop a non-paternalistic, "burden on society" rationale for closing baths and quarantining carriers.[10] In particular, even given that having an obligation to help someone leaves a person free to help or not to help, it still seems that there should be something more to be said for the view that if I have an obligation to take care of you when you get into trouble (fall off a motorcycle, contract AIDS), than I have some right to prevent you from getting into that trouble (to make you wear a helmet, to prevent you from visiting bathhouses). One form of that "something more" will be suggested below. For now let us just note that any financial "burden on society" rationale would not get to the heart of the matter. For the intuition that there are non-paternalistic grounds for closing the baths and quarantining carriers surely turns on the harm of suffering and dying of AIDS, whereas the relevant harm in the "burden on society" rationale is the quite different harm of monetary loss to those who do not have the disease. Thus, the most that might be said for the "burden on society" rationale is that it would make it possible to get the "right" result albeit for the "wrong" reason. There would be, perhaps, a certain value in this (better to send the gangland dope importer and murderer to jail for non-payment of income taxes than not to send him at all), but it remains unsatisfying.[11] What we really want to know is whether there is anything behind the intuitive conviction that there are legitimate grounds for closings and quarantines *and* that those grounds are those given in (3).

3. The point of closing the baths or quarantining AIDS carriers is not to protect society from the financial burden of caring for AIDS sufferers. Nor is it to protect those individuals who would deliberately take the risk of visiting a bath or of having sex with an acknowledged carrier. The point is to protect society at large from involuntarily being subjected to the threat of AIDS.

Despite the intuitive appeal that this has, we have to wonder just how society at large is threatened by AIDS.

(*a*) The greater the number of people there are who have a highly contagious disease the greater is the threat to those who might become its unwilling victims. Everyone knows, for instance, that the more people there are around with a cold the more likely I am to catch it by being sneezed on. Thus there is clearly a non-paternalistic rationale for laws that would prevent Smith from consenting to engage in an act that could well result in his contracting a highly contagious disease from Jones. The rationale is not paternalistic since the aim is not to protect Smith's welfare but rather to protect society at large from Smith becoming a carrier of a disease that will make him a danger to others.

As cogent as this reasoning is, it is predicated on the disease in question being highly contagious, and AIDS is certainly not that. It is not transmitted by shaking hands, sharing a drinking glass, or even by being sneezed on. Aids is virtually always passed from one person to another by actions that require the active participation of the potential victim (in the case of homosexual transmission, by participation in what Krauthammer interestingly refers to as "a rather complicated act"). This means that just as the man who would visit the baths chooses to take the risks involved in doing so, anyone "further down the line" who contracts AIDS (such as someone who decides to enter into a homosexual relationship with the person who frequents the baths) also has consented to engage in the risky conduct that has this unfortunate result. Thus at each stage those who are harmed are harmed as a result of choosing actively to cooperate in the acts that result in this happening. And since no one is harmed without consenting to take the risks, any interference in the process, for instance by closing the baths, must be intended to protect individuals from their own deliberate choices. There is nothing in the process analogous to being sneezed on by a cold carrier. And so any justification that there may be here for closing the baths or for quarantining an AIDS carrier still appears to be a paternalistic one.[12]

(*b*) It would be far to soon to give up on (3). For while it is both correct and important to realize that AIDS is not spread by casual everyday contact, it is still a mistake to think that only those who consent to take a risk are in fact put at risk by the presence of the AIDS virus in some other individuals. Consider, for instance, a woman "Alice," who does not know that her lover is bisexual and that he visits the baths a dozen or more times each year. In choosing to engage in sexual activities with him she is not deliberately choosing to take the risk of contracting AIDS, for she is unaware that this is a real possibility. In this respect she is in a very different position from the man who must know the AIDS risk of engaging in multiple sex acts in a gay bath. Perhaps the rationale for closing the baths is to protect members of "the public at large" like Alice from the unknown threat of contracting AIDS.

There are certainly non-paternalistic grounds for doing something on Alice's behalf. Even Mill's reputedly extreme anti-paternalism explicitly allows for intervention when the agent is not aware of the risks involved in a choice. "If either a public officer or anyone else saw a person attempting to cross a bridge which had been ascertained to be unsafe, and there was no time to warn him of his danger, they might seize him and turn him back, without any real infringement on his liberty; for liberty consists in doing what one desires, and he does not desire to fall into the river."[13] Since the point of opposition to paternalism is that one should not be prevented from bringing harm or the risk of harm to oneself if one freely chooses to do so; since one is not freely choosing to bring on or to risk a harm one does not know about; and finally, since the interference with the action continues only until the agent is made aware of the risks involved, there is clearly nothing in Mill's position that any anti-paternalist should object to.[14]

Nor, however, is there anything in Mill's position that would justify closing the baths or quarantining AIDS carriers. At most it would be justified to restrict certain activities until requisite information could be disseminated. For instance, the baths could be closed until signs could be printed and posted regarding the danger of AIDS and the precautions necessary for "safe sex." (Such signs have in fact been posted in many establishments.) If Alice's friends knew specifically of her new lover's sexual habits, they could be sure that she had this information, and they might even do what they could to interrupt the relationship until they could bring this about. The role of society in regard to Alice would be that it should come to her aid by promulgating information about whatever dangers there might be in certain sorts of sexual activities.[15]

One may well think that if this is all that an anti-paternalist could allow to be done on Alice's behalf then there is something quite wrong with anti-paternalism. For we should all feel a considerable sympathy for anyone in Alice's position, and yet the information that society would normally be able to supply is not in fact going to be a great deal of help to Alice. Essentially what she is going to learn is that there is such a disease as AIDS but that only a small percentage of men who have regular relationships with women carry the AIDS virus and that the virus appears to be difficult to transmit through conventional heterosexual activities.[16] Unfortunately, such information would lead Alice to underestimate the actual danger of contracting AIDS from this particular lover who, unknown to her, is a bisexual and a frequenter of the baths. Of course society could see to it that Alice received much more complete information. Detailed records about just who visits baths and who their friends are could be compiled and published on a regular basis. Laws could be enacted requiring that everyone provide any potential partner with the particulars of one's sexual history. But while these are things that could be done, it is unlikely that any of us would want to live in that sort of Draconian society.

So the case of Alice seems to lead the opponent of paternalism to some unhappy alternatives. In the name of anti-paternalism the baths will not be closed, and either Alice will face a much greater possibility of contracting a lethal disease than she realizes or society must intrude upon the private lives of its citizens in order to get the information needed to enlighten Alice about the real risks in her specific case.

The anti-paternalist may simply deny that the first of these alternatives is intolerable. We all have to make many decisions with less than ideal information. The fact that Alice must do so does not justify infringing on liberty by closing baths and bars or quarantining carriers. (Of the many "Alice's" facing the decision of whether to have sex with a friend, the vast majority in fact will not be in danger of contracting AIDS.) But perhaps the anti-paternalist need not take this possibly "heroic" position, for there is still another way in which we might be able to make a non-paternalistic case for closings or quarantines.

(*c*) To contract AIDS is to suffer harm. If this is the only harm that persons might suffer as the result of the presence of the AIDS virus in the community, then it is difficult to imagine that any non-paternalistic justification for closing the baths or for quarantining carriers of the virus might be successful, given that the disease is contracted by consensual acts. But actually contracting AIDS is not the only way in which one can be harmed by the presence of the virus in the community. A "desert island" scenario should help to explain why this is so.

> Suppose there exists a certain Harvey, benevolent dictator of a small and entirely isolated society made up of a few thousand highly sensual persons. Some of these prefer their own sex, some the other, but they are all capable of intense enjoyment with anyone else. On the whole their sex lives are extremely satisfying, and they regard this as necessary not only for happiness but for their most basic psychological well-being. One day (as you might have guessed) trouble intrudes into this world in the form of a new and lethal disease. Christening it "The Lethal Ailment," the official doctor quickly determines that just a small handful of inhabitants actually have the disease, that it is transmitted only by sexual activity, and that it is rather hard to transmit at all but it is far more readily transmitted through certain activities preferred by a minority of the population.
>
> Harvey is not only benevolent; he is also wise enough to rely on a staff of skilled advisors when expertise is needed. This time he turns to Jeremy, his resident source of wisdom on matters legal and philosophical. As it happens, Jeremy is a devoted follower of Mill, and so he advises Harvey in this way: "Everybody on the island knows the disease is here and how one can get it. You could lock up the people who have it or close down the places where they are likely to do the things that transmit it, but the only reason for your doing things like this would be to protect the folks from their own choices. If old Smith there chooses to take the risk of contracting this disease it is his own business. You stay out of it."
>
> Harvey follows Jeremy's advice and stays out of it. Shortly thereafter he takes the opportunity for a balloon trip to the outside world. Returning twenty years later he finds a society considerably reduced in number and happiness . Many people have died of the disease, and a very large number of those who are still alive suffer from it. Jeremy, as sick as he is, is sanguine. "It is true that the results have not been too good, but we avoided paternalism. Mill would have been proud of us. No one contracted the disease who did not deliberately choose to take the risk of contracting it. No one who did not consent to do so was ever threatened with the harm of the disease. What we have here is the triumph of a principle of liberty."
>
> "What we have here is an idiot of an advisor."
>
> "But all I did was follow Mill's precepts. I just told you. No one was harmed who did not consent to be harmed."
>
> "What about me?"
>
> "You?"
>
> "I came back from the outside world to my homeland of loving sensuality only to find myself faced with nothing better than a choice between a killer disease and celibacy. No one is harmed who did not consent to be harmed, you say? What greater harm could there be than being faced with those two miserable alternatives? I am getting in my balloon and going back to the outside world."
>
> But Harvey's balloon had burst. He couldn't go anywhere. There are no records of what happened after that on Harvey's Island.

The inhabitants of Harvey's unfortunate island are threatened with a harm: contracting The Lethal Ailment. But they also come to face a related but different harm, having a choice between alternatives each of which is so undesirable that to have to choose between them is itself to be harmed. When the point is reached that everybody else carries the disease or any other person is quite likely to be a carrier, each individual faces the alternatives of celibacy or the likelihood of contracting a disease from which he will not recover. Having to choose between these alternatives is a very real harm, and it is not one to which the individual in any way consents to be subjected. In short, *anyone who gets The Lethal Ailment does so as a result of consenting to take the risk of getting it rather than choosing to be celibate. But no one consents to the harm of being faced with only these miserable alternatives.* Thus, insofar as the aim was to prevent this harm, Harvey did have, despite Jeremy's misguided advice, a non-paternalistic rationale for locking up carriers and closing places where people were likely to engage in the sexual activities by which the disease was most easily transmitted.

Both the "burden on society" and "Alice" discussions above were left with the suggestion that there might be more to be said. The Harvey story enables us to see what this would be. Obviously that story suggests a way of reconceptualizing the "Alice" situation so that it really might provide a non-paternalistic rationale for closing the baths. Given that Alice has all the information that could reasonably be made available to her, when she chooses to have sexual relations with her lover she is consenting in as enlightened a way as practically possible to take whatever AIDS risks there may be. She did not, however, consent to having to face just the alternatives of rejecting her lover or taking those risks, and the existence of the baths contributes to her having to face these alternatives. If having to face them does indeed constitute a harm, then in the Alice case we really do have a non-paternalistic rationale for the closings.

Perhaps the "burden on society" rationale can be reformulated in a similar though not so obvious way. Understood on the model of the story of Harvey, there may well be a legitimate basis for the intuitive conviction that if I have an obligation to take care of you when you get into trouble, then I have some right to prevent you from getting into that trouble. It is not that your getting into trouble and my resulting obligation forces on me the harm of taking care of you. Obligation or no, I am quite free, after all, just to leave you to fend for yourself. What your getting into trouble does force on me is this set of alternatives: either I neglect my obligation to take care of you or I shoulder the financial burden of your care. If being faced with just these alternatives is counted a harm, then the "burden on society" argument would provide a genuinely non-paternalistic reason for closing the baths or quarantining carriers of the AIDS virus.[17]

What all this tells us is that there *can be* non-paternalistic reasons for closing gay bathhouses and quarantining AIDS virus carriers even though everyone who might get the disease consents to take the risk of doing so. It does not, however, tell us that there really *are* such reasons. That latter point depends on whether the activities of the bath patrons and carriers will actually make it likely that persons (or society) will have to face alternatives so thoroughly unacceptable that having to face them is to be harmed.

Whether in fact this happens depends, first, on what the actual consequences of not closing the baths or quarantining the carriers are likely to be. For instance, is it likely that we would all come to find ourselves, like Harvey, facing a choice between celibacy or a near certainty of contracting a killing disease? Or, perhaps, is the virus so difficult to transmit by heterosexual activity that there is no genuine risk in heterosexual relationships? In this event AIDS would not force a choice between celibacy and the risk of death on anyone but it would force the choice between celibacy, exclusive heterosexuality, and the risk of death on everyone, including homosexuals.

Here questions of a second, a more conceptual/evaluative, nature become crucial. What consequences would constitute a genuine *harm?* While it is clear (at least it seems to me that it would be incredible to deny) that a person is harmed by being faced with a choice between celibacy and contracting a lethal disease, would a homosexual be harmed by being restricted to choosing between celibacy, heterosexual activity, and contracting the disease? If one sees sexual orientation as a matter of (as current terminology often has it) sexual *preference,* being so restricted may not appear to be a harm. (If my *preference* is for blond pudgy sexual partners, am I *harmed* if I am somehow limited to a choice between celibacy and a generous selection of slender dark-haired partners?) On the other hand, most heterosexuals would think it a very great harm indeed to be limited to a choice between celibacy, homosexuality, and contracting a fatal disease. Does not parity dictate that the homosexual is equally harmed by being restricted to a choice between celibacy, heterosexuality and the disease?

Further, it is clearly artificial to think that any activities would absolutely ensure contracting AIDS. Thus, the alternatives posed by the presence of the AIDS virus are not likely to be as simple as celibacy or contracting the disease (or celibacy, heterosexuality, or contracting the disease). They will instead be something more like celibacy or *X* amount of risk of contracting the disease (or celibacy, heterosexuality, or *Y* amount of risk of contracting the disease). And so, in considering whether or not having to face some particular set of alternatives constitutes a harm, we must consider not only what the "safe choices" are (celibacy, exclusive heterosexuality, and so on.) but also how great a risk there is in deviating from the safe choices. Harvey is clearly harmed because his choices are celibacy and the *practical certainty* of getting The Lethal Ailment. But if one's choices were between celibacy and a chance of getting AIDS approximately equal to the chance of being devoured by a runaway zoo lion, then only the most paranoid would think herself harmed by having to face those alternatives. Sorting out such conceptual/evaluative considerations is entirely necessary if we are to determine whether the presence of the AIDS virus does indeed threaten members of the community with a harm to which they do not consent.

Suppose that it finally does turn out (as it quite likely will) that not closing the baths and not quarantining carriers brings some degree of harm to unconsenting parties, that not doing these things contributes to people being limited to alternatives so undesirable that having to face them is a harm. In this event, Mill's anti-paternalistic principle that "there is no room for [even considering a prohibition] when a person's conduct affects the interests of no person besides himself, or needs not affect simply does not come into play. Anti-paternalism does not dictate that it would be in principle illegitimate to close the baths or to quarantine carriers of the AIDS virus. But the fact that closings and quarantines are not in principle illegitimate does not mean that they are warranted overall. For whatever non-paternalistic reasons there may be for closing baths and quarantining carriers, there may be stronger reasons against such actions. For instance, it might be wise to leave the baths open because they serve as locations for educating gays on sexual safety. And quarantining all carriers of the AIDS virus—which some say, could be as many as two million people—would most likely be completely unworkable even if it were somehow desirable.

There are difficult issues of substance here. My aim has not been to argue that they should be resolved in any particular way. It has been to show that even if AIDS is spread exclusively through consensual acts there can be non-paternalistic grounds for closing the baths or quarantining the carriers. Without question there is a great deal of plausibility in the claim that it is no one's business but Smith's if he freely chooses to frequent the baths or even to have a homosexual relationship with a known carrier. But in spite of the plausibility of this position, it is altogether too simple. The hard social issues posed by AIDS cannot be so easily disposed of by appeal to an anti-paternalistic principle.

NOTES

1. It is often said that approximately 73% of AIDS cases have been contracted through homosexual activities. This figure may be somewhat high, however, since the disease can be and often is spread through the sharing of drug needles, and AIDS victims who are both homosexual and drug users have been classified as homosexual rather than intravenous drug users. This is pointed out by Jonathan Lieberson in "The Reality of AIDS," *The New York Review of Books* (January 16, 1986), p.44. Insofar as engaging in particular sexual activities and sharing drug needles are equally consensual acts, the relative percentage of cases contracted in these two ways has no bearing on any issues discussed in this paper.
2. Similar reasoning would support closing "shooting galleries," places where there is widespread sharing of drug needles. The issues regarding paternalism and AIDS discussed here could be equally well discussed in terms of this possibility.
3. Lieberson, "The Reality of AIDS," p.48.
4. *St. Louis Post Dispatch* (November 5, 1985), p. 3b.
5. John Stuart Mill, *On Liberty* (Indianapolis: Hackett, 1978), pp. 73–74, italics added.
6. Richard D. Mohr also seems to take the position that any rationale for closing gay baths must be an illegitimate paternalistic one. ("AIDS: What to Do—And What Not to Do," *Report from the Center for Philosophy and Public Policy* (Fall 1985): 6–7.) *Newsweek* quotes Dr. Dean F. Echenberg, director of San Francisco's Bureau of Communicable Diseases, to a similar effect regarding quarantines (September 23, 1985, p. 23).
7. Mill, *On Liberty,* p.p. 94–96; H.L.A. Hart, *Law Liberty, and Mortality* (New York: Random House, 1966), pp. 32–33.
8. Hart (*Law Liberty, Mortality,* pp. 30–34), Joel Feinberg (*Social Philosophy*) [Englewood Cliffs: Prentice Hall, 1973] Ch. 2–3), and others take it (rightly I should think) that there is a clear enough distinction between moralism and paternalism. (Lord Devlin, however, rejects the distinction, and John Kleinig questions both its clarity and moral importance. See Kleinig's *Paternalism* [Totowa: Rowan & Allanheld, 1983], pp. 14–16).
9. For instance, Hart, *Law, Liberty, and Morality.*
10. On this question, see Kleinig, *Paternalism,* pp. 92–95.
11. I am not suggesting here that a financial burden is not a harm. Nor am I suggesting that it would not be a harm of the relevant kind to justify non-paternalistic interference. Rather, I am suggesting that any rationale for closings and quarantines in terms of this harm does not explicate our sense that the harm of AIDS itself ought to supply a non-paternalistic rationale for such actions. (Imagine a society in which, somehow, medical care were entirely cost-free on every level. This stipulation does not rid us of our intuition that AIDS poses a threat of harm to society.)
12. The line of reasoning in this paragraph makes explicit what is at least implicit in Lieberson and Krauthammer. In other words they seem to mean not just that the person who visits the bath or has sex with a carrier consents to his action but also anyone further down the line also consents to anything that could result in his getting the disease.
13. Mill, *On Liberty,* p. 95.
14. The view that even such temporary interference with action is justified has been called "weak paternalism." I take it, however, that this is far too weak a doctrine of interference to be called "paternalism" at all, and so my "anti-paternalist" is not opposed to this sort of interference. (Cf. Feinberg, *Social Philosophy* pp. 49–50; Tom L. Beauchamp, "Paternalism and Biobehavioral Control," *The Monist* 60 (1977): 67–68.
15. Cf. Mohr, "AIDS: What to Do . . . And What Not to Do," p. 6. Rejecting paternalism, he maintains that education is the only appropriate response when a person is unable to assess the AIDS-risks involved in a course of action.
16. Despite the frequently heard alarms that AIDS can be and is rapidly being spread into and through the heterosexual community, "there is no clear evidence that AIDS in the United States has yet spread beyond the known risk groups. notably homosexuals and drug addicts." (*New York Times* editorial, "AIDS Alarms, False Alarms, "February 4, 1987, p. 26.) The editorial backs up this claim and gives an extraordinarily sensible analysis of the reasons behind the well-intended alarms to the contrary. (But the actual extent of the risk to heterosexuals is not crucial here. "Alice," in other words, heterosexuals, should be informed of the degree of risk, whatever that might be.)
17. This is not to say that having to face just these alternatives (or those that Alice faces) really should be counted as harm. Whether it should be is a further question. Some of the considerations this further question involves are discussed in the paragraphs that follow above.

AIDS and Human Rights: An Intercontinental Perspective

Carol A. Tauer

Carol Tauer is a professor of philosophy at the College of St. Catherine in Minnesota.

Tauer discusses the different responses to the AIDS crisis in France and Great Britain, as compared with the United States. Among the issues she examines in her comparative study are these: confidentiality, paternalistic intervention, education about AIDS, testing for AIDS antibodies, quarantining, and protection of the civil rights of the AIDS carriers. She argues that France is much more resistant to collecting data on those who are AIDS carriers, and Great Britain is much more resistant to engaging in testing for AIDS, than is the United States. Tauer links these differences with the different ways in which these countries understand medical ethics issues.

BACKGROUND: INTERCONTINENTAL DIMENSIONS

Persons who suffer from AIDS or AIDS-related conditions fear not only the disease but also violations or deprivations of basic rights. They are concerned about invasions of their personal privacy and possible restrictions on their freedom of movement and activity. They worry that they may be denied employment, health or life insurance, housing, and even health care.

The United States and the various nations of western Europe differ in their responses to the social and ethical problems posed by AIDS. While all of these nations basically subscribe to the same international declarations of human rights (for example, the *Universal Declaration of Human Rights*, the *European Convention on Human Rights)*, there are both conceptual and practical differences in their understanding of these statements.

In the international documents on human rights, we find support for three categories of rights which measures to control AIDS may threaten:[1] (1) the right of personal privacy and confidentiality regarding medical and sexual information; (2) the right to free movement within one's country and to associate where and how one chooses; (3) the right to pursue one's economic good, without limitation based on irrelevant grounds ([for example], sex, sexual preference). Providing some contrast to this perspective, the World Health Organization takes a more utilitarian stance in relation to its goal of promoting health as the right of all people. For WHO, health is fundamental to the attainment of international peace and security, and so cooperation in the control of disease, especially communicable disease, is essential.[2]

Reprinted by permission of the author.

In its 1976 document, *Health Aspects of Human Rights,* WHO explicitly adopts "the Benthamite principle of 'the greatest happiness of the greatest number' " and advocates curtailing personal liberty not only for the sake of the common good, but also to promote the health of the individual in question.[3]

Here we see exemplified in statements from one international forum, the United Nations, the underlying tension found in discussions of public policy on AIDS. What is the appropriate balance between the common good, in this case the public health, and the rights and liberties of individual persons? Each member nation is attempting to answer this question in the light of its own laws and traditions, and, as a result, a variety of different practices and policies are emerging.

But it is not only this question, complex as it is, which contributes to differing approaches to the AIDS crisis. A second crucial issue concerns the practice of medicine itself. Since AIDS is a disease, it is handled within a medical model, not only one of civil liberties. Thus, one's conception of the role and duties of the physician, the nature of the physician–patient relationship, and the physician's responsibility for the health of the individual and the public, will affect one's approach to AIDS. Again, each nation has different traditions and codes on these matters, which will influence its policy regarding AIDS.

In considering human rights and AIDS, this paper will focus on France and Great Britain, relating significant aspects of their responses to that of the United States. As of November 13, 1986, the largest number of AIDS cases reported in European countries were in France (997, not including the overseas departments), the Federal Republic of Germany (715), and the United Kingdom (512).[4] At this time, there had been over 26,500 cases in the U.S.; and the rate of infection in any European country (less than 20 per million population) was still low compared to the U.S. rate (greater than 110 per million).

In both France and Great Britain—in contrast to Italy, for example—very few of the AIDS patients are IV drug abusers. The overwhelming majority are homosexual or bisexual men, as in the United States; hence this paper will focus on the potential for violations of rights within that population.

While the approaches of these three countries illustrate cultural and political divergences rooted in history, two new trends also emerge: As an international bioethical community develops, engaging in discussion and sharing documents, there is movement toward a greater uniformity of response to bioethical problems. And secondly, in the United States there are signs of a movement away from the almost single-minded focus on individual rights and liberties of the recent past. Both of these factors will undoubtedly affect the AIDS debate in the coming years.

CONFIDENTIALITY

Among the human rights which have a traditional link to medical ethics is the right of privacy. While privacy has many dimensions, the aspect of personal control of private information is perhaps the greatest concern of those at risk for AIDS and AIDS-related conditions. Violations of the confidentiality of private information not only trespass on an intimate domain, involving both medical data and information about sexual behavior but, because of the nature of AIDS, they may also lead to denial of employment, insurance, and housing.

Medical professionals of all western societies have traditionally regarded confidentiality of information as a serious obligation. However, within the modern hospital in the United States, it is not unusual for as many as 100 people to have access to the medical records of the patient,[5] in addition to third–party payers of whatever sort. This situation is not unique to the U.S.; a dean of the Newcastle Faculty of Medicine observed that as many as 150 different people could have access to patient notes in hospital![6] Moreover, when a disease is reportable by law to either local or national health authorities, the cases (however they are identified) become part of a data bank, most likely computerized, over which no individual health professional has control.

The Centers for Disease Control, which mandate national reporting of AIDS cases in the United States, have developed a system for coding the identifications of the individuals involved. While authorities say there is no way to reconstruct a person's name from the coded identification, some members of the homosexual or gay community are dubious.[7] Furthermore, local departments of health at the state level have their own reporting regulations. Colorado and several other states even require the results of positive antibody tests to be identified by name, whereas California law explicitly prohibits such reporting unless there is written consent of the person tested.[8] The state of Minnesota, which predicts a major increase in cases, is experimenting with a curious policy: According to state law, positive antibody tests are to be reported by name; however, individuals may circumvent this requirement by being tested at an "alternative testing site" where they may remain anonymous.[9]

As of March 22, 1985, Great Britain included AIDS under some of the provisions of the law governing "notifiable diseases," but decided not to require the reporting of AIDS cases themselves.[10] Health officials said that a policy of voluntary reporting (without names) was operating effectively and was all that was needed.[11] British law gives particular legal protection to all records of sexually transmitted diseases which are held by National Health Service authorities. These records "shall not be disclosed" except to a medical practitioner for purposes of treatment or prevention,[12] In hospitals, records relating to venereal diseases are "locked away separate from the main hospital records,"[13] a unique provision which shows a high degree of sensitivity to the implications of disclosure.

French physicians invest medical confidences with a sacredness linked to a religious tradition, somewhat like the secrecy of the Catholic confessional. This view is expressed in French law, which protects "the professional secret" from disclosure in a court of law and does not even permit the patient to waive confidentiality in his own interest.[14] The duty of confidentiality with respect to all third parties is strongly asserted as part of "Code de déontologie médicale," the statement of medical ethics which is imposed by law on French physicians.[15]

While French law and practice seem to provide essentially absolute protection for medical confidentiality, British and American codes allow exceptions, either to protect a third party or for the sake of the common good. American case law contains precedents of a "duty to warn" a third party who is in danger of harm;[16] and currently there is much discussion as to how this duty would apply to the physician of a person who is infectious for the AIDS virus. The codes of both the British Medical Association and the General Medical Council permit disclosure for the sake of the public interest and, somewhat surprisingly, for purposes of approved medical research.[17] There appears to be quite a bit of leeway for the British physician to determine what may ethically be revealed, apart from special provisions such as the statutes on sexually transmitted diseases.

Physicians, like other professionals, customarily devise their own ethical codes and enforce them through self-regulation. Even when a professional code is included within statutory law, as in France, the duties are those already recognized by members of the profession in that country. Confidentiality, traditionally one of the most cherished values of the profession of medicine, is challenged today by public policy decisions which mandate its abrogation for a cause which is viewed as a greater good. Thus, required reporting of medical information implies that the good consequences which will follow as a result of gathering this information justify both overriding the patient's privacy right and endangering his related interests (for example, his interest in nondiscriminatory treatment when he seeks insurance).

There are two distinct purposes for which public health agencies may use the data they gather about cases of a communicable disease. Both purposes are preventive, but in different ways. The first purpose is epidemiological research, the tracing of patterns of a disease in order to identify causal agents, modes of transmission, ebbs and flows in the history of the disease. As a result of such research, recommendations on disease control are provided to the public, to physicians, and to local government agencies. The U.S. Centers for Disease Control and the British Communicable Disease Surveillance Centre gather their case data for this purpose. Much epidemiological study can be done without specific information of the individuals involved, but some research requires that at least one investigator have this information. The protection of confidentiality in epidemiological research has been a topic of ethical concern for many years.[18]

But while continuing questions are raised, both Britain and the U.S. show a substantial history of epidemiological research. (See Gordis *et al.* for an impressive listing of results achieved by this work.) Because of its strong insistence on confidentiality, France has been slow to gather the data needed for studies of this type. French investigation of AIDS has therefore focused on virological and immunological research, while epidemiological work has been centered in the U.S. Recently, however, there have been signs of a convergence in bioethical standards. For example, a 1985 recommendation of the French national committee on bioethics, "Recommendations on Medical Registers for Epidemiologic Study and Prevention,"[19] stimulated a detailed response from the National Medical Council, . . . incorporating many of the confidentiality precautions suggested nine years ago by Gordis *et al.*[20] While France is clearly learning from the Anglo-American experience, its cautiousness and discretion can also be instructive to that tradition.

The second purpose for gathering case data is the exercise of direct intervention into the person-to-person transmission of a communicable disease. This intervention may involve the tracing and warning of contacts of an infectious person and/or surveillance of the activities of this person so as to prevent further possible transmission. While the epidemiological use of data presents a speculative danger of violation of confidentiality, its use for direct intervention (which requires a noncoded record of a person's identity) seems to present an immediate ethical dilemma. Whether this abrogation of confidentiality is justified by the lethal and catastrophic nature of AIDS is hotly contested in the U.S., while such measures seem generally to have been rejected in Great Britain and hardly even considered in France. In the U.S., state and local jurisdictions are in the process of developing a tangle of reporting regulations based on their perceptions of this second function for public health data.

INFORMED CONSENT AND THE RIGHT TO KNOW

The practice of medicine has traditionally been a paternalistic enterprise. In the past few decades it has become much less so in the United States, and there is now a clearer public recognition of patients' rights, both morally and legally. While the statutory assertions of these rights differ somewhat from state to state, as does case law, the American Hospital Association has promulgated a general statement which is universally accepted by hospitals. Among accepted rights are the right to informed consent to treatment, the right to know one's diagnosis and prognosis, and the right to refuse treatment, even life-sustaining treatment. In competent patients, these rights may not be overridden even for what a professional perceives to be the best interests of the patient.

In contrast, Great Britain and France have retained a more paternalistic view of the role of the physician, so that the physician's duty to promote the best interests of the patient generally takes precedence over the patient's rights related to autonomy. Correlatively, the standard for whether a physician has done his or her duty is established almost exclusively by the medical profession in France and Britain, and lawyers and judges defer to medical judgment and testimony in these matters. In the U.S., the courts often exercise an independent function on behalf of patients' rights, and standards such as that of "the reasonable patient" may be applied.

While the French code of medical ethics is part of statutory law, its formulation is entirely the work of the Conseil National de l'Ordre des Médecins.[21] This "Code de déontologie médicale" is expressed in terms of physician duties, and the only right the patient is specifically granted is that of choosing his or her own physician. While the physician is instructed to respect the wishes of the sick person as far as possible, an extraordinary control over information is retained: "For legitimate reasons, which the physician recognizes in conscience, a sick person may be left in ignorance of a grave diagnosis or prognosis."[22]

Although there is now a multidisciplinary national committee on bioehtics in France, the charge of this committee restricts it to matters related to biomedical research; clinical issues remain under the jurisdiction of the medical council.[23] Since the committee interprets its charge rather broadly, its documents show substantive interchange with the medical council ([for example], see above on confidentiality and epidemiological research). Another currently debated issue involves phase I drug trials, in which drugs are given their initial testing for toxicity, dosage, and mode of administration. In the United States, these trials are customarily conducted with healthy volunteers (usually paid). Such a practice has been repugnant to the French medical profession: "There is no justifiable scientific or medical reason for exposing to risk a subject who has no medical reason to participate in a trial and who can expect no benefit from it. Hence, we condemn . . . all phase I trials conducted on subjects."[24] Most French jurists have also supported the view that a healthy normal subject does not have the right to consent to such involvement, even with full information, understanding, and voluntariness.[25] But the national ethics committee is providing a forum for consideration of a change in this stance; and there is evidence that such trials, with careful safeguards, may become ethically acceptable, as they are in the U.S.[26]

In his perceptive study *The Unmasking of Medicine,* Ian Kennedy has detailed the paternalistic bias of the British medical profession, ranging from control of the "sick note," by which the physician certifies that an absent worker truly was ill, to permission for an abortion, where physicians are unavoidably involved in psychosocial judgements.[27] A recent legal case in Britain has thoroughly examined American case law on informed consent and rejected some of its conclusions. The case, that of Mrs. Amy Sidaway, involved her complaint that her physician had not told her the risks of her surgery. The Court of Appeal decided against her, stating that "the doctrine of informed consent [forms] no part of English law," and that "most [people] prefer to put themselves unreservedly in the hands of their doctors. . . . [This] is simply an acceptance of the doctor–patient relationship as it has developed in this country." Final appeal to the House of Lords supported this view; the Lords determined that what to volunteer to disclose was a matter for the physician's clinical judgment. However, they did allow for a court finding contrary to medical testimony in extreme or blatant cases of nondisclosure, and they also stressed the physician's obligation to answer fully and truthfully any questions which the patient actually asked.[28]

Paternalistic practice in France and Britain represents not only the way the doctor–patient relationship has developed in each country, but, in general, the way the class structure has developed. In Britain, social classes 1 to 5 are defined on the basis of occupational and educational level, with class 1 the professional class. A camaraderie among doctors, lawyers, and professors results from their having enjoyed basically the same background and education; hence they are supposedly able to understand each other's language. On the other hand, those who belong to classes 4 or 5 could not be expected to understand technical information, so are assumed to put their trust in the professional's judgment.[29] In France the class structure is also much more clearly defined than in the U.S., and the rural and working classes have a standard of living and level of culture well below those of the bourgeoisie, which includes the professional class.

European notions of the status and role of the professional have had the practical consequence of determining who controls certain types of information. In *Un Virus Étrange Venu d'Ailleurs,* Jacques Leibowitch describes the current openness of information and discussion about AIDS as the Americanization of the disease. It is not merely that the U.S. Centers for Disease Control have decided what is to count worldwide as AIDS, a matter complained of by a variety of European scientists and clinicians.[30] But also socioculturally, "the disease carries the cultural insignia of its origin," presumably the United States.[31] Continuing in Leibowitch's words:

> To tell, to make known, to announce the disease and death—to inform the patient of the medical procedures that will follow, to obtain his informed consent, to expose and to discuss while exposing—North America has its cultural features. In France, we had another tradition. To say nothing, to know nothing; a father protects us with his mysteries. . . . [Now] everyone will know: Good-bye, mystery; hello, terror.[32]

TESTING OR SCREENING FOR AIDS ANTIBODIES

The American patient's "right to know" is an enunciated extension of a general right claimed by the U.S. citizen. With regard to health matters, this claim is supported by U.S. public health officials, who take the position that full knowledge contributes to prudent personal health decisions. The Centers for Disease Control have based their recommendations regarding such general testing for AIDS antibodies on that assumption.

Emphasizing that such tests should be voluntary and accompanied by thorough counseling, the CDC recommends that serologic testing "be routinely offered to all persons at increased risk when they present [themselves] to health-care settings." These recommendations enumerate first the behaviors counseled for those who test negative, and, second, the behaviors counseled for those who test positive.[33] While these behaviors are similar in many respects, the CDC seems to imply that knowledge of one's antibody status will be determininative if one needs to make changes in life-style and behavior.

Local health authorities have made similar recommendations. For example, the Minnesota State Department of Health has published notices with the heading, "Don't Guess about It," encouraging persons who may be infected to take advantage of free testing and counseling. In many localities of the U.S., general testing sites were first made available in order to dissuade persons seeking serologic testing from using blood donation centers for this purpose. But presently, the use of these testing sites is being encouraged on the typically American presupposition that more information is better than less in making the individual medical or life-style decisions.

In contrast to the United States, British public health authorities are not urging general serum antibody tests, even for members of high-risk groups. The value of routine testing is questioned by the Chief Medical Officer, Department of Health and Social Security, as well as by staff of the National AIDS Counseling Training Unit.[34] After considering the purposes for which such test results might legitimately be used, these authorities conclude that the possible benefits are highly speculative. There is no concrete evidence that knowledge of test results actually leads to greater behavior change than mass education and focused counseling programs, nor that it would in any other way contribute to halting the spread of the disease. Thus these officials believe that there is no justification for risking the harms ([for example], stigmatization, loss of employment or insurance) to which the test might lead.

Here British health authorities take a position similar to that of many gay organizations in the United States. For example, the Gay Men's Health Crisis (New York City) nationally distributed an advertisement with the headline, "The Test Can Be Almost as Devastating as the Disease."[35] But there is disagreement within the gay community, and some gay groups, especially in urban centers of continental Europe, are urging use of the test.[36]

Lack of British enthusiasm for routine testing does not mean that there is indifference in the situations in which a confirmed positive test result would call for a clear response. Miller *et al.* . . . list settings within which screening ought to be done: with donors of blood and blood products, organs for transplant, semen, and growth hormone[s]; before and during the pregnancy of a woman at risk; and probably with hemodialysis patients. The slowness with which Britain instituted screening of blood donations (not widely introduced until October 1985) should not be attributed to lack of concern. Rather, the delay was due to great care and extensive investigation in order to locate, among available testing methods, the best one,([that is, the method] with the fewest false positives and with nearly zero false negatives).[37]

Discussion of serological testing in official sources in France is largely limited to its use with blood donors. The national committee on bioethics has proposed a policy on screening blood donors, noting the absolute necessity of such screening to ferret out infection of blood with SIDA (AIDS).[38] The proposal carefully delineates the counseling which must accompany a positive finding: The physician of the blood center must impress upon the seropositive person that he has a heavy responsibility to his family and/or other sexual contacts in order to stop the spread of the disease. The document shows the expected French discretion regarding intimate information; the physician must adjust his discourse to each individual situation, and no reporting requirement is mentioned or recommended.

GOVERNMENT-SPONSORED EDUCATION PROGRAMS

Given their decision not to promote identification of cases of AIDS infections, British health authorities have been consistent in putting resources into mass education and focused counseling programs instead. Chief Medical Officer Acheson specifically includes adolescents, undeclared homosexual and bisexual men, and, in fact, all sexually active men and women among those whom government-sponsored educational programs must reach. He also notes that the national press, radio, and television will provide sexually explicit information if necessary, and that public response (to effectiveness and offensiveness) will be periodically evaluated.[39]

The first stage in the government's educational campaign included full-page advertisements in the national newspapers on March 16 and 17, 1986, advertisements in the gay press, and posters and leaflets provided to groups like the Terrence Higgins Trust (a gay organization formed to deal with AIDS), at a total cost of £2.5 million.[40] The national press advertisements were highly explicit, stating that "rectal sex . . . should be avoided," that "using a sheath [condom] reduces the risk of AIDS and other diseases," and that "any act that damages the penis, vagina, anus, or mouth is dangerous."[41]

While U.S. public health authorities have consistently advocated mass educational programs, their efforts have generally had to be more restrained. They have been able to provide some funding to those who work with the gay community and with IV drug users for the development of clear and direct educational programs. But material provided for mass consumption is directed either at those who will read fairly technical explanations of the disease and its transmission, or at those who are sophisticated enough to read between the lines of a vague, generalized warning. Adolescent, disadvantaged, and semiliterate persons are not apt to be informed by scientific or euphemistic discussions.

Several reasons for this restraint may be cited: (1) The Reagan administration has objections to government funding for sexually explicit materials, particularly regarding homosexual activity, and, as a result, a number of CDC programs have not been implemented.[42] (2) There is a strong antipornography movement, and some citizens are highly vocal about educational materials which they view as too explicit sexually.[43] (3) There is a widespread but unconfirmed belief that informing young people about sexual practices will only lead them to experiment with them. (4) Activities which are described in educational materials are often illegal; for example, sodomy is criminal by the laws of about half the states.

One may expect that the tide will turn as a result of Surgeon General C. Everett Koop's report on AIDS, issued October 22, 1986. In this report, Koop calls for AIDS sex education, beginning in the elementary grades, as the central focus of public health efforts against AIDS.[44] This focus is strongly supported by the study of the Institute of Medicine, National Academy of Sciences, which was made public one week later.[45] It is too early, however, to assess the effects of these recommendations.

In France, the reluctance to expose the disease is almost universal. While the gay community in the United States has been a leader in the educational effort there, in France there has been a tendency among gay people to deny the seriousness of the disease. An American reporter describes Parisian gays as "charmed by what they perceive to be the *vraiment New Yorkaise* overreaction to the situation. . . . Eyebrows arched wryly at the discussion of safe sex."[46] Association AIDES has found great resistance in its efforts to institute programs to educate patrons of gay bars and bathhouses in Paris.[47]

Gay people of other countries, however, have been particularly critical of French authorities for their meager financial commitment to AIDS education (while France is the European country hardest hit). It was not until late 1985 that the government allocated its first $30,000 for AIDS education, an amount less than one San Francisco foundation spends locally in a month.[48] When Dr. Luc Montagnier of the Pasteur Institute recently wrote an informational pamphlet, the decision was made to produce it as a glossy 94-page pamphlet which would be sold for $4, thus excluding many people who needed the information but would not or could not pay that sum.[49]

A country which has been most highly praised for its government's commitment to education on AIDS, as well as for its national office to coordinate all AIDS policy decisions, is the Netherlands. The director of this office, Jan Van Wijngaarden, attributes its success to the integration of homosexuality into Dutch society and the lack of bigotry among the Dutch public.[50]

Reports have also been received about imaginative educational efforts in Norway. For example, an Oslo billboard shows a cartoon face drawn on the top of a male organ to illustrate a text about using condoms to prevent the transmission of AIDS. Publicity of this type shows a realization that masses of people will only be attracted, hence informed and affected, by media presentations which are clever, contemporary, and graphic.[51]

QUARANTINE AND OTHER RESTRICTIVE POLICIES

The ethical conflict between the common good and the rights or freedoms of individuals is perhaps illustrated most clearly in the situation where a restriction on movement or association is imposed or contemplated by public authorities. The quarantine, with its long and controversial history, provides an example of a public health measure which can be highly restrictive, and which in some forms is being proposed for the control of AIDS.

In Britain, the Public Health Act of 1984 has been interpreted specifically for its application to AIDS. The section on detention was amended thus:

> A justice of the peace may on the application of any local authority make an order for the detention in hospital of an inmate of that hospital suffering from acquired immune deficiency syndrome if the justice is satisfied that on his leaving . . . proper precautions to prevent the spread of the disease would not be taken by him.[52]

Two applications of the statute have been reported in British journals, both involving rather unusual circumstances. In one case, a hospitalized AIDS patient was put under detention orders for three weeks by Manchester magistrates. The Manchester medical officer described this man as "bleeding copiously and trying to discharge himself [from hospital]." The legal correspondent reporting to the *British Medical Journal* raised the obvious question: What if it were risky sexual behavior rather than bleeding, which endangered others? Detention for such cause would seem to be within the intent of the law. Yet, as the correspondent notes, "To apply the law in this way would clearly raise grave political difficulties for the central government as well as for any local authority concerned."[53]

Interestingly, the other reported case of detention in England also involved bleeding. In this case, the patient was on a psychiatric ward, and at one point he cut his hands and deliberately smeared blood around his room and into the corridor. The police were called, and the person is now being detained in a prison setting.[54]

Thus far in the United States, actual quarantine or isolation has been seriously considered only in relation to prostitutes who are AIDS carriers. A restrictive measure which has had more impact on the gay community in general involves the closing or regulation of gay bathhouses or other meeting places where casual or anonymous sex is a common activity. San Francisco experienced a series of orders and injunctions; in the end, the California Superior Court prohibited legal closing of such establishments, but ordered safeguards like removal of cubicle doors, inspection by monitors every ten minutes, and expulsion of patrons observed in acts of high-risk sex.[55] New York has adopted an emergency regulation which provides for closing establishments which allow anal or oral sex acts on their premises.[56] While gay rights groups are most incensed at this ruling, it has also been applied to heterosexual gathering places.

French public policy has not yet confronted the issue of quarantine or even of regulation of bathhouse activity. In Paris, the police are reportedly engaging in increased harassment of the gay community, using the threat of AIDS as their justification, but apparently on legitimate grounds (for example, to identify minors practicing prostitution or frequenting bathhouses.)[57]

Perhaps the most comprehensive policy among European nations has been established by Sweden. By including AIDS under the provisions of its venereal disease laws, as it did in late 1985, Sweden could be interpreted to require compulsory testing of persons in high-risk groups, and for those with seropositive tests, reporting to health authorities, naming of all sexual partners, prohibition of risky conduct (sexual or drug–related), and, in certain cases, confinement to hospitals. At least one person with a seropositive test has been so confined because he continued to share needles with other drug users and to have sex without taking necessary protective precautions.[58]

Clearly a common thread in laws about AIDS, among states in the U.S., Great Britain, and Sweden, is *some* explicit provision for the mandatory restriction of persons who are judged to be an imminent threat to the health of others. However, major problems exist concerning not only the implementation but also the efficacy of such laws. As with [that of] some American states, British law focuses on persons who actually have AIDS, while scientists believe that those who have been infected with the virus, but have not (yet) developed the disease, may actually be more infectious than those who are ill. One must ask whether a policy calling for legal restriction has any meaning without required testing of large population groups; and since that sort of program is not seriously contemplated by public health officials (except perhaps in Sweden), the legal enactments may be more token than efficacious. At most, they seem to provide legal protection for government officials who may wish to restrain an individual whose behavior is particularly blatant, harmful, and perhaps malicious.

PROTECTIONS FOR CIVIL RIGHTS

Each nation has its own tradition with respect to the protection of civil rights. Both the role of the law, whether constitutional, statutory, or case law, and the attitudes of the citizens, differ from country to country; and these differences engender subtle variations in the national concern for the civil rights of AIDS victims.

As members of the European Community, both France and Great Britain have subscribed to its *Convention on Human Rights* and have accepted the provision whereby an individual citizen may appeal to the Commission of Human Rights in Strasbourg if the citizen believes his or her rights under the Convention have been violated by his or her State. It has been suggested that grievances against the National Health Service with regard to confidentiality could be brought before this body, and cases on detention for psychiatric illness have already been decided.[59]

In Article 8, the *European Convention* gives explicit protection to the individual's private and family life, home and correspondence, and states that public authorities may not interfere with the exercise of this right unless it is necessary for some greater social good.[60] This privacy right has been applied by the European Court against national laws prohibiting homosexual acts between consensual adults in private. Although the rest of the United Kingdom had decriminalized such activity in 1967 (Sexual Offenses Act), Northern Ireland had not. An individual's appeal to the European Commission in the early 1980s resulted in the Court's judgment that the law in Northern Ireland did, in fact, violate Article 8 of the Convention and had to be changed.[61]

It has been noted that persons at risk for AIDS in European countries display a relative lack of concern about the possible loss of their civil rights. This phenomenon could perhaps be linked to the fact that homosexual activity is not illegal in these countries, and also perhaps to the national health care systems by which full medical coverage is provided to citizens of most European nations.[62]

While a privacy right is not specifically enunciated in the United States Constitution, it has been found to be implicit in other protections asserted there. Thus, it has been applied to issues in child-rearing and education, marriage, contraception, abortion (*Roe* v. *Wade)*, and termination of medical treatment (*In re Karen Ann Quinlan)*. However, recently the U.S. Supreme Court rendered a decision specifying a point beyond which the privacy right did not apply. On June 30, 1986, the Court asserted that individual states were entitled to make laws which prohibit sodomy. While most such state laws apply to both homosexual and heterosexual acts (anal and possibly oral sex acts), the Court's opinion clearly focuses on a possible state interest in prohibiting homosexual sodomy.[63] Although the ruling makes no mention of AIDS, it is possible that the majority justices had this disease in mind, for they seem concerned about decisions states may wish to make to safeguard public welfare. And it is known that at least one amicus brief urged the Court to consider AIDS as a good reason for states to have laws against sodomy.[64]

Though the rights of gay persons are protected in some jurisdictions of the U.S., particularly in liberal urban centers, there is no general protection for the homosexual person as such, as there is for the person of a minority race as such. Until recently, however, there was a belief that the rights of those with AIDS or AIDS-related conditions would be safeguarded under the federal Rehabilitation Act of 1973. Under this law, it is illegal for agencies and programs which receive any federal funds to discriminate against those who are handicapped or perceived to be handicapped, provided these persons are otherwise qualified (for example, to do a particular job). As of June 7, 1986, civil rights lawyers in the Justice Department supported a broad application of the Act to AIDS victims.[65] But shortly thereafter, a different position was taken by the Justice Department itself.

In a ruling of June 22, 1986, the Justice Department asserted that a person may not be excluded from a job or a program on grounds that he or she suffers from the disabling effects of the disease AIDS, but may be excluded if there is a concern that he or she might spread the disease.[66] While adverting to the U.S. Public Health Service's assurances that AIDS is not spread by casual contact, the ruling calls the weight of this opinion into question by putting the burden of proof on the person who claims to have been dismissed unfairly. This decision is currently binding on the executive branch, which is the executor of regulations for federally funded agencies and programs.

However, the ruling will have little effect in cities and states which have already ruled that persons with AIDS or positive antibody tests are protected by local antidiscrimination laws. For example, Minnesota and its two major cities have indicated that the Justice Department ruling is irrelevant there.[67] Nonetheless, the Justice Department's conservative interpretation of the application of the Rehabilitation Act presages a national scenario of inconsistent policies, with discrimination excusable in some jurisdictions if an employer is irrationally fearful regarding the transmission of AIDS.

NOTES

1. See I. Brownlie, Ed., *Basic Documents on Human Rights,* 2nd ed. (Oxford: Clarendon Press, 1981).
2. World Health Organization, "Preamble to the Constitution of the World Health Organization" (1946), in *The First Ten Years of the World Health Organization* (Geneva: WHO, 1958).
3. World Health Organization, *Health Aspects of Human Rights* (Geneva: WHO, 1976), p. 42.
4. Information provided by the WHO Control Program on AIDS, Geneva.
5. Mark Siegler, "Confidentiality in Medicine: A Decrepit Concept," *New England Journal of Medicine* 307 (1982), pp. 1518–21.
6. Alexander W. Macara, "Confidentiality—A Decrepit Concept? Discussion Paper," *Journal of the Royal Society of Medicine* 77 (1984), p. 579.
7. Charles Marwick, "'Confidentiality' Issues May Cloud Epidemiologic Studies of AIDS," *Journal of the American Medical Association* 250 (1983), pp. 1945–46.
8. Michael Mills, Constance Wofsy, and John Mills, "The Acquired Immunodeficiency Syndrome: Infection Control and Public Health Law," *New England Journal of Medicine* 314 (April 3, 1986), pp. 931–36.
9. Department of Health (Minnesota), "Rules Governing Communicable Diseases," *Disease Control Newsletter,* Insert 12, No. 5 (June, 1985); Walter Parker, "AIDS Screening Tests Offered Anonymously," *St. Paul Pioneer Press and Dispatch* (November 13, 1985), pp. 1A and 4A.
10. The Public Health (Infectious Diseases) Regulations 1985 (Statutory Instrument 1985, No. 434), England and Wales.
11. Rodney Deitch, "Government's Response to Fears about Acquired Immunodeficiency Syndrome," *Lancet* (March 2, 1985), pp. 530–31.
12. The National Health Service (Venereal Diseases) Regulations 1974 (Statutory Instrument 1974, No. 29), England and Wales.
13. E.D. Acheson, "AIDS: A Challenge for the Public Health," *Lancet* (March 22, 1986), p. 665.
14. John Harvard, "Medical Confidence," *Journal of Medical Ethics* 11 (1985), pp. 8–11; Daniel W. Shuman, "The Privilege Study: The Psychotherapist–Patient Privilege in Civil and Common Law Countries," *Proceedings, Sixth World Congress on Medical Law* (Ghent, Belgium, 1984), pp.73–77.
15. "Code de déontologie médicale," Décret No. 79–506 du Juin 1979, *Journal Officiel de la Republique Française* (June 30, 1979).
16. California Supreme Court, *Tarasoff* v. *Regents of the University of California,* 131 Cal. Rptr. 14 (decided July 1, 1976).
17. Raanan Gillon, "Confidentiality," *British Medical Journal* 291 (185), pp. 1634–36; Huw. W.S. Francis, "Of Gossips, Eavesdroppers, and Peeping Toms," *Journal of Medical Ethics* 8 (1982), pp. 134–43.
18. Leon Gordis, Ellen Gold, and Raymond Seltser, "Privacy Protection in Epidemiologic and Medical Research: A Challenge and a Responsibility," *American Journal of Epidemiology* 105 (1977), pp.163–68; Charles Marwick, "Epidemiologists Strive to Maintain Confidentiality of Some Health Data," *Journal of the American Medical Association* 252 (1984), pp. 2377–83; W.E. Waters, "Ethics and Epidemiological Research," *International Journal of Epidemiology* 14 (1985), pp. 48–51.
19. Comité Consultatif National d'Éthique pour les Sciences de la Vie et de la Santé, Avis sur les registres médicaux poor études épidémiologiques et de prévention." *Journées Annuelles d'Éthique 1985* (Paris: INSERM, 1985), pp. 13–14.
20. Louis René, "Secret médical et collecte de renseigenments médicaux à usage épidémiologique," *Lettre d'Information du Comité Consultatif* No. 4 (April 1986, p. 3.
21. Conversation with Catherine Labrusse-Riou, member of the Comité Consultatif National d'Éthique (June 25, 1986).
22. "Code de déontologie médicale," Titre I, Articles 6 and 7: Titre II, Article 42: "Pous des raisons légitimes que le médicin apprécie en conscience, un malade peut être laissé dans l'ignorance d'un diagnostic ou un pronostic grave."
23. Conversation with Catherine LaBrusse-Riou.
24. Pierre Arpaillange, Sophie Dion, and Georges Mathe, "Proposal for Ethical Standards in Therapuetic Trials," *British Medical Journal* 291 (1985), pp. 887–89.
25. *Ibid.*, p. 887.
26. Assistance Publique Hôpitaux de Paris, "Recommendations concernant les essais therapuetiques sur des voluntaires sains, *Lettre d'Information du Comité Consultatif* No. 3 (January 1986), p. 2.
27. Ian Kennedy, *The Unmasking of Medicine* (London: Granada, 1983).
28. Robert Schwartz and Andrew Grubb, "Why Britain Can't Afford Informed Consent," *Hastings Center Report* 15, No. 4 (August 1985), pp. 19–25; Diana

Brahams, "Doctor's Duty to Inform Patient of Substantial or Special Risks When Offering Treatment," *Lancet* (March 2, 1985), pp. 528–30.
29. Schwartz and Grubb, *op. cit.*, p. 22.
30. J. Seale, "AIDS Virus Infection: Prognosis and Transmission," *Journal of the Royal Society of Medicine* 79 (February 1986), p. 122; Jean-Baptiste Brunet *et al.* "Epidemiological Aspects of Acquired Immune Deficiency Syndrome in France," *Annals of the New York Academy of Sciences (A.I.D.S.)*, Vol. 437, p. 334.
31. Jacques Leibowitch, *A Strange Virus of Unknown Origin,* trans. by Richard Howard, introduction by Robert C. Gallo (New York: Ballantine Books, 1985), p. 93.
32. *Ibid.*, pp. 92–94.
33. Centers for Disease Control, "Additional Recommendations to Reduce Sexual and Drug Abuse-Related Transmission of Human T-Lymphotropic Virus Type III/Lymphadenopathy-Associated Virus," *Morbidity and Mortality Weekly Report* 35 (March 14, 1986), pp. 152–55.
34. Acheson, *op. cit.* pp. 662–66; David Miller *et al.* "HTLV-III: Should Testing Ever Be Routine? *British Medical Journal* 292 (April 5, 1986), pp. 941–43.
35. Advertisement in *GLC Voice* (Minneapolis, November 4, 1985), p. 10.
36. Michael Helquist, "The State of the Science: Taking the Test in Europe," *Coming Up!* 7, No. 4 (January 1986).
37. See, for example. "Notes and News: HTLV-III Antibody Screening," *Lancet* (August 31, 1985), p. 513.
38. Comité Consultatif National d'Éthique pour les Sciences de la Vie et de la Santé, "Avis concernant les problèmes éthiques posés par l'appréciation des risques du SIDA par la recherche d'anticorps spécifiques chez les donneurs de sang," *Lettre d'Information du Comité Consultatif* No. 1 (July 1985), p. 1.
39. Acheson, *op. cit.*, p. 664.
40. "Notes and News: Public Information Campaign on AIDS," *Lancet* (March 22, 1986), p. 694.
41. Are You At Risk from AIDS?" full page notice in the *Observer* (March 16–17, 1986).
42. Marlene Cimons, "AIDS Education Plans Halted to Avoid Uproar over Explicit Advice," *Minneapolis Star and Tribune* (December 4, 1985), p. 11A.
43. See, for example, Joe Kimball, "Officials Balk at Paying for AIDS Ad with Unclothed Man," *Minneapolis Star and Tribune* (June 17, 1986), pp. 1B and 5B; Lewis Cope, "Ad Blitz about AIDS Begins," *Minneapolis Star and Tribune* (August 9, 1986), pp. 1C and 6C.
44. "Surgeon General Calls for Early AIDS Education, Opposes Compulsory Tests," *Minneapolis Star and Tribune* (October 22, 1986).
45. "Huge AIDS Effort Urged," *St. Paul Pioneer and Dispatch* (October 30, 1986), pp. 1A and 4A.
46. Otis Stuart, "Ghosts," *New York Native* No. 139 (December 16–22, 1985), pp. 33 and 37.
47. Gerald Koskovich, "Letter from Paris," *The Advocate* No. 441 (March 4, 1986), pp. 31–32.
48. Randy Shilts, "Dutch Speedy, Others Lag on AIDS Warnings," *San Francisco Chronicle* (January 3, 1986).
49. "Lack of Funds Hampers European Efforts to Halt Spread of AIDS," *New York Times* (November 11, 1985).
50. Shilts, *op. cit.*
51. Jim Klobuchar, "Sermonette Would Play Well in Oslo," *Minneapolis Star and Tribune* (July 31, 1986), p. 1B. For an illustration of the use of advertising techniques to educate physicians about control of staph infection when standard educational efforts failed, see "When Wonder Drugs Don't Work," NOVA Broadcast (London: BBC-TV, 1986).
52. The Public Health (Infectious Diseases) Regulations 1985 (Statutory Instrument 1985) No. 434, Section 3.
53. "Detaining Patients with AIDS," *British Medical Journal* 291 (October 19, 1985), p. 1,102.
54. C. Thompson *et al.*, "AIDS: Dilemmas for the Psychiatrist," *Lancet* (February 1, 1986), pp. 269–70; responses in *Lancet* (March 1, 1986), pp. 496–97.
55. Mills, Wofsy. and Mills, *op.cit.*, p. 935.
56. "N.Y. Rule Curbing Gay Sex Practices Becomes Law," *Minneapolis Star and Tribune* (December 21, 1985).
57. "In Search of 'Moral Danger'" *The Body Politic* (July 1985), p. 25.
58. "Swedish Government Considering Drastic Action to Stop AIDS," *Equal Time* (November 13, 1985) (reprinted from *New York Native*); Shilts, *op. cit.;* "HTLV-III Carrier Detained in Swedish Hospital," *American Medical News* (February 7, 1986), p. 8.
59. A.H. Robertson, *Human Rights in Europe* (Manchester: Manchester University Press, 1977); Paul Sieghart, *The International Law of Human Rights* (Oxford: Clarendon Press, 1983),
60. Brownlie, *op. cit.*, p. 343.
61. "Just Satisfaction under the Convention: Dudgeon Case," *European Law Review* 8 (1983), p. 205.
62. Helquist, *op. cit.*
63. "Excerpts from the Court Opinions on Homosexual Relations," *New York Times* (July 1, 1986), p. A18.
64. William F. Woo, "AIDS Epidemic and the Georgia Ruling," *St. Louis Post–Dispatch* (July 6, 1986). For a full discussion of this issue, see Chris D. Nichols, "AIDS—A New Reason to Regulate Homosexuality?" *Journal of Contemporary Law* 11 (1984), pp. 315–43.
65. Robert Pear, "AIDS Victims Gain in Fight on Rights," *New York Times* (June 8, 1986), pp. 1 and 19.
66. Robert Pear, "Rights Laws Offer Only Limited Help on AIDS, U.S. Rules," *New York Times* (June 23, 1986), pp. A1 and A13.
67. "AIDS Decision Scorned", *Minneapolis Star and Tribune* (June 22, 1986), p. 10B.

The Ethical Design of an AIDS Vaccine Trial in Africa

Nicholas A. Christakis

Nicholas A. Christakis is a Robert Wood Johnson Clinical Scholar at the University of Pennsylvania's Medical School. He has published many essays on cross-cultural medical ethics, clinical decision-making and medical sociology.

Christakis is interested in the ethical justifiability of testing an AIDS vaccine in Africa. He considers various safeguards that must be employed to guarantee that Africans are not treated as guinea pigs to help medical authorities in the West come to an understanding of the AIDS virus. Among other things, he argues that subjects need to be fully informed of the risks. Given the way some African societies are structured and the traditions involved in those societies, obtaining consent may involve significant interaction with community leaders and a substitution of the leader's consent for that of the individual. But the difficulties in obtaining consent should not make Western scientists lax in their pursuit of a test that is respectful of the trial participants.

On March 19, 1987, a group of French and Zairian scientists published a report in *Nature* stating that one of the investigators, Dr. Daniel Zagury of the Pierre and Marie Curie University in Paris, had immunized himself with an investigational AIDS vaccine.[1] With "the full support of the Zairian Ethics Committee," the investigators also immunized "a small group of Zairians, all of whom were HIV-seronegative volunteers and immunologically normal."

The fact that this first trial of an AIDS vaccine took place in Africa leads to a variety of concerns. Most troubling is the possibility that Africans might serve as "guinea pigs" for clinical trials that would not be allowed in the U.S. or Europe, particularly in view of past cases of disregard for the rights of human subjects of research in Third World countries. Africans, feeling that "Western science often comes to Africa with dirty hands," have been concerned that Western investigators, unchecked by foreign or local supervision, might conduct "savage experiments."[2] Indeed, an unidentified source close to the Zagury group informed a *New York Times* reporter that a major reason they conducted the trial in Zaire was that "It was easier to get official permission [in Zaire] than in France."[3]

Differences in permissibility of trials in developed versus developing countries, however, are not supposed to occur.

Reprinted with permission of *The Hastings Center Report*, June/July 1988.

According to the guidelines for human subjects research established jointly by the World Health Organization (WHO) and the Council for International Organizations of Medical Sciences (CIOMS), when research is conducted by investigators of one country on subjects of another, "the research protocol should be submitted to ethical review by the initiating agency. The ethical standards applied should be no less exacting than they would be for research carried out within the initiating country."[4] Yet the great complexity, varied presentation, and wide distribution of HIV infection challenge this stance. When the epidemiologic and scientific aspects of HIV infection and vaccination are coupled with the cultural differences throughout areas of the world where AIDS is prevalent and AIDS research is conducted, the uniform application of ethical principles in the conduct of an AIDS vaccine trial becomes considerably more complicated.

To some extent, the CIOMS guidelines anticipate this. Their stated purpose is to amend the principles of the Declaration of Helsinki "to suggest how [these principles] may be applied in the special circumstances of many technologically developing countries."[5] There is a tension in the guidelines, however, between the desire for culturally relevant application of ethical principles on the one hand and the belief that "the ethical implications of research involving human subjects are identical in principle wherever the work is undertaken" on the other. If trials of HIV vaccines are to take place worldwide, this tension must be resolved. Are there justifiable differences in research ethics in different sociocultural settings? How are ethical concerns to be met in the face of a pandemic? Is it possible to distinguish "medical imperialism" from legitimate reasons for conducting an AIDS vaccine trial in Africa?

DESIGN OF AN AIDS VACCINE TRIAL

Though several types of AIDS vaccines are being considered, investigation has been largely directed towards using recombinant DNA technology to produce HIV proteins or insert portions of the HIV genome into other viruses (such as the vaccinia virus used by the Zagury group).[6] A protocol for evaluating candidate vaccines would involve: (1) preparing the vaccine in sufficient quantity and purity; (2) testing in animals to see if it results in antibodies able to neutralize HIV *in vitro;* (3) testing in nonhuman primates to establish the ability of the vaccine to protect against subsequent challenge with HIV; (4) testing in a small group of humans (members of AIDS risk groups or others) to evaluate short-term safety and immunogenicity (a phase I trial); (5) determining ideal dose and spacing of the vaccine through larger safety and immunogenicity trials (phase II); and (6) determining protection against HIV infection through large scale efficacy trials involving as many as 1,000 to 2,0000 subjects (phase III).[7] A phase III trial would be of the randomized, double-blind, controlled type.

The epidemiology of HIV in Africa will raise special considerations in the scientific design of a trial that will, in turn, affect its ethical design. The ethical design of an AIDS vaccine trial in Africa, that is, must be informed by the scientific parameters of the research and of the study population in the familiar interaction between science and ethics.

As we shall see, however, attention must be focused on specific ethical and cultural constraints prevailing in settings where AIDS research is conducted. Even if the epidemiological and scientific parameters of HIV infection were the same in research settings throughout the world, the proper ethical design of AIDS vaccine trials would still vary with the ethical and cultural parameters of the research populations.

ASSEMBLING A SUITABLE STUDY GROUP

Participants in a phase III trial would have to be followed and assessed for HIV infection through serial testing and examination. Such follow-up is time-consuming and expensive because of the variable expression and long latency period of HIV infection. Proper evaluation of a vaccine will require a large number of subjects drawn from a suitable population. The ease of assembling the requisite number of appropriate subjects and the relatively low cost of conducting a trial in Africa (because of typically low wages) have been explicitly identified by some investigators as benefits of conducting AIDS research in Africa.[8]

Africa has also been offered as a vaccine test site on the basis of certain scientific considerations. Specifically, subjects in a phase III trial would have to meet two important technical requirements: they would have to be free of HIV infection at the beginning of the trial, and they would nevertheless have to be *at risk* for HIV infection.

Subjects must initially be free of HIV infection to assess the vaccine's ability to prevent subsequent infection; a person already infected with HIV who received the vaccine would falsely be identified as a vaccine "failure," that is, as someone in whom the vaccine was ineffective. In addition, absence of HIV infection is necessary to avoid the possibility of serious complications that might arise if an HIV-infected individual were given a recombinant viral vaccine. An individual infected with HIV and suffering from subtle immunocompromise could develop a serious infection with the non-HIV virus used in the vaccine (such as generalized vaccinia).

At present, determining freedom from HIV infection would be accomplished through testing for HIV antibodies. But freedom from infection is not guaranteed by a single test showing absence of HIV antibodies: the test result may simply be inaccurate—scientific tests are not infallible and there will be false negative results—or the research subject may, in fact, be infected with HIV, but have not yet developed antibodies.[9] Most people infected with HIV develop antibodies within six to twelve months if they are to develop them at all. Research subjects would thus have to be retested at a six to twelve-month interval to assure lack of prior exposure. Of course, during this interval, the study population would ideally need to avoid further exposure to HIV, which could lead to infection that might escape detection at the second testing.

The second requirement, being at risk for HIV infection, is necessary to assess the vaccine's ability to prevent HIV infection: a study population at no risk of infection whatsoever would not permit evaluation of vaccine efficacy since no one at all, in either the vaccine or control groups, would become infected.

Two aspects of the epidemiology of HIV infection in Africa facilitate meeting this requirement. First, the predominant mode of transmission of HIV in Africa is thought to be via heterosexual sex; the identified risk factors include having a large number of sexual partners, having sex with prostitutes, being a prostitute, or being a sexual partner of an infected person.[10] Second, estimates of HIV antibody seroprevalence for various sub-Saharan countries range from 0.5 percent to 8.8 percent for healthy controls and 14.6 percent to 55.6 percent for risk groups such as prostitutes.[11] This high prevalence implies high risk of infection for uninfected members of the society that would allow a trial to detect a difference between the vaccinated and unvaccinated (control) study groups with greater ease in less time. Moreover, the substantial prevalence of HIV infection in the general heterosexual population further facilitates assembling an approximately large study group.

Thus, the benefit of conducting a phase III AIDS vaccine trial in Africa (because of the high risk) would be at least partially offset by the likely increase in adverse affects attributable to vaccination (because of the high prevalence and consequent increase in the number of falsely negative individuals included in the trial).

Of course, the benefit here is to the conduct of the investigation in the form of a speedier, more accurate trial, and hence to the investigators and society-at-large. The cost, however, is borne by the research subjects. This problem could be minimized—but not eliminated—by a scrupulous testing policy aimed at excluding HIV-seropositve individuals from the study. However, achieving this objective would require a certain degree of intrusion upon the privacy of study subjects to ensure that they abstain from risky behaviors in the six-month interval between the two required HIV tests. Moreover, a degree of accuracy in testing beyond that traditionally seen in laboratories in the developing world would have to be assured.

A final scientific concern in assembling a suitable study group regards the applicability of the findings. The pattern of infection in Africa may reflect as yet unknown biological factors in the population at risk or in the virus that may require testing a vaccine in Africa simply to evaluate vaccine efficacy in circumstances that may be unique. Since an effective vaccine efficacy would be of great utility in this continent, some trials in Africa would presumably be essential.

RISKS AND CONSENTS

Eligible research subjects would have to consent to participation in the trial, which would require researchers to provide information regarding both benefits and risks. The salient personal benefit to participation in an AIDS vaccine trial is the possibility of gaining immunity to a deadly infection. An effective vaccine would be very beneficial for society-at-large, but this is not ordinarily seen as a direct benefit to the individual.

The risks involved in trial participation are significant, however. For HIV subunit or recombinant viral vaccines, possible direct adverse consequences of participation in a vaccine trial include: (1) serious infection (generalized vaccinia, for example) in the case of undetected HIV infection in recipients of a viral vaccine; (2) mild or severe systemic reactions to the vaccine (headache, severe febrile reactions, convulsions); and (3) hypersensitivity reactions. A further hazard of such research is the possible increase in risky behaviors because participants feel relatively protected. Finally, it is theoretically possible that receiving one type of an AIDS vaccine might preclude immunization with a more effective vaccine developed subsequently.

The need to test for HIV infection both at the onset and during the conduct of the trial creates a further problem peculiar to participating in an AIDS vaccine trial: that of learning one's antibody status. Some have argued that being HIV positive is burdensome knowledge that should not be imposed.[12] Thus, people *excluded* from vaccine trial participation because of HIV antibody positivity might suffer through acquiring knowledge of their status. For persons *enrolled* in the trial, the necessary surveillance of HIV antibody status might also ultimately result in knowledge of HIV infection that the subject would otherwise have avoided.

Research subjects would also have to be advised that as a consequence of participation they will become HIV seropositive by conventional screening methods. Serocon-version may, in turn, lead to discrimination against the subject. This eventuality has led to some innovative measures. In a trial approved but not yet under way in the U.S., subjects will be issued both a certificate testifying to their participation in the trial and a copy of their Western blot results showing a characteristic pattern identified as being a result of participation and not infection.[13]

BENEFICENT TREATMENT OF SUBJECTS

The risks involved in the trial of an AIDS vaccine mandate beneficent treatment of participants. In the context of human subjects research, beneficence has found two complementary expressions: "(1) do not harm, and (2) maximize possible benefits and minimize possible harms,"[14] For the benefits to outweigh the risks in the trial of an AIDS vaccine, an individual would have to be at some risk of HIV infection. The necessity of being at risk thus has both scientific and ethical import.

But beneficent treatment of AIDS vaccine trial subjects has several aspects beyond a suitable risk/benefit ratio. Volunteers must be informed that vaccination does not provide license to engage in risky behavior, and must be counseled regarding "safe sex" practices. In Africa, counseling should at a minimum consist of strong advice to decrease the number of sexual partners, to avoid prostitutes, and to abstain from sex with individuals known to be infected. Counseling, along with informing participants of their negative antibody status, would likely result in a decrease in risky behavior.[15]

In advanced trials to test vaccine efficacy, however, these interventions could diminish the ability of the study to detect a difference between true vaccine recipients and controls by decreasing the incidence of HIV infection in *all* participants for reasons *unrelated* to vaccine status. To circumvent this problem, a larger study group would be required to detect the relatively smaller measured influence of the vaccine. But increasing the size of the study group has attendant adverse consequences, including the increased risk of exposing more individuals to the experimental vaccine and increased cost. Thus, there will be unavoidable conflict between research design and ethics. This conflict should be resolved in favor of beneficent treatment of subjects: to minimize risk to individual research subjects, study size should be increased and all participants should be counseled to avoid risky behaviors.

Deliberately counseling all participants to avoid risky behaviors will likely also increase the time required to complete the study since researchers would have to wait longer to detect sufficient cases of HIV infection for the results to be significant. This necessity must be seen in light of the considerable pressure to develop an effective HIV vaccine rapidly.

The interpersonal nature of HIV transmission may create an additional ethical problem pertaining to the beneficent treatment of research subjects. The unit of analysis in AIDS vaccine trials, some have suggested, should *not* be the individual.[16] Given that simply participating in AIDS research may offer some benefits, especially if participation serves to lower risky behavior, researchers may be obliged to recruit, insofar as possible, the sexual—and where applicable, needle-sharing—partners of research subjects.

Indeed, there is presently a study under way in Africa that involves deliberate tracking of HIV-discordant couples to determine the natural history and transmissibility of the disease where condom use is the sole preventive measure.[17] The ethics of such a study are questionable, *unless* the seronegative member the couple is properly informed of the risk continued sex with his or her partner poses despite condom use. The argument that researchers studying progression of HIV infection in groups of individuals are merely observing events that would have taken place regardless of the researchers' presence—a so-called study in nature—is untenable. The mere presence of the researchers disturbs the "natural setting" (certainly it does so in this case since condoms and recommendations regarding their use are distributed). Moreover, physician researchers have incumbent upon them the duty to protect the health of their subjects, even if in so doing they compromise their research.[18]

ETHICAL STANDARDS IN CROSS-CULTURAL PERSPECTIVE

Consideration of Africa as a test site should transcend the standard scientific and ethical concerns outlined above and should incorporate broader concern arising from the conduct of research in disparate sociocultural settings. The conduct of a vaccine trial in Africa will highlight not only practical and scientific differences, but also ethical and cultural differences between Africa and the West.

Soliciting informed consent to participate in research is one of the major areas where variation in ethical standards will be encountered. The Western principle of informed consent is predicated upon the notions of respect for persons as individuals and as autonomous agents.[19] This is at variance with more relational definitions of the person found in other societies, especially in Africa, which stress the embeddedness of the individual within society and define a person by his or her relations to others.[20]

From this variation in the definition of a person arise important practical implications. Where the notion of persons as individuals is not dominant, the consent process may shift from the individual to the family or to the community.[21] It may be necessary to secure the consent of a subject's family or social group instead of or in addition to the consent of the subject himself.

Culturally-defined views of personhood may also find expression in determinations of who is deemed able to give informed consent for others. This is acknowledged in the CIOMS guidelines:

> Where individual members of a community do not have the necessary awareness of the implications of participation in an experiment to give adequately informed consent directly to the investigators, it is desirable that the decision whether or not to participate should be elicited through the intermediary of a trusted community leader.[22]

There will be considerable variation by culture as to who is acknowledged to be a "community leader" and whether such an individual will meet the investigator's expectation regarding who can appropriately give proxy consent.

The principle of community leader consent may be the only alternative—however unsatisfactory by Western standards—to individual consent in many cases where beneficial research is essential. This alternative may not necessarily be ethically incorrect for the society of which the research subject is a member. Indeed, the desire of research subjects to cooperate with respected local authorities can be instrumental in the success of research in many settings.[23] His or her obedience to a local authority should not be abused, however, by a Western researcher to the detriment of a Third World subject of research. A researcher must respect an individual's manifest refusal to participate, even if consent has been elicited from some other person or group.

Western investigators should also appreciate that what appears to them to be coercion may, from the perspective of local inhabitants, represent cooperation and identification with the group to which the individual belongs. This does not relieve Western investigators of the responsibility to avoid coercion arising from their *own* actions. They must be aware that it is difficult to avoid coercing subjects in most settings where clinical investigation in the developing world is conducted. African subjects with relatively little understanding of medical aspects of research participation, indisposed toward resisting the suggestions of Western doctors, perhaps operating under the mistaken notion that they are being treated, and possibly receiving some ancillary benefits from participation in the research, are very susceptible to coercion. Their vulnerability warrants greater care in procuring consent and necessitates greater sensitivity to protect this class of research subjects.

It is clear that the type of consent practiced in the West, with the signing of an informed consent document containing medical terms, is inappropriate for illiterate or semi-literate peoples. Indeed, signing or even thumbprinting a consent form may be deemed highly suspect in certain societies, as may a physician's "excessive" explanation of the purpose of the research (which may be taken as indicative of some hidden, detrimental purpose). In some cultural settings it may be extremely difficult to convey an accurate understanding of the idea of randomization or other essential scientific concepts.[24] Moreover, there may be cultural variations in the understanding of disease, at odds with Western scientific notions, that make truly *informed* consent impossible.[25] In the context of an AIDS vaccine trial in Africa, the foregoing concerns will allow for significant variability in the information conveyed in obtaining the subject's consent. Nevertheless, investigators must seek to explain the purpose of the research in culturally relevant terms.

The principle of respect for persons is also ordinarily taken to imply a respect for individual privacy and confidentiality. In some societies, as we have seen, it may be necessary that this individual claim yield to a somewhat larger group, as with, for example, informing a husband of his wife's participation in a research endeavor. Yet, insofar as feasible, confidentiality should be respected. One example of unnecessary violation of this principle that has led to irritation on the part of some African officials is the practice of publishing photographs of African AIDS patients in the Western press.[26]

A relational concept of personhood may also result in ethical decisions that, by Western standards, unduly favor the interests of society at large over those of the individual. Western ethical standards generally accord considerable import to the welfare of the individual in the conduct of research. The Declaration of Helsinki, for example, states that "concern for the interests of the subject must always prevail over the interests of science and society. . . ."[27] The Belmont Report, an ethical standard developed within the U.S., more explicitly acknowledges the difficulties in balancing the rights of the individual versus those of society and states that ethical codes "have required that risks to subjects be outweighed by the sum of both the anticipated benefit to the subject, if any, and the anticipated benefit to society. . . ." It notes, however, that "in balancing these different elements, the risks and benefits affecting the immediate research subject will normally carry special weight."[28]

The calculus of such balancing will be different in different sociocultural settings. In some situations, cultural expectations may be that the anticipated benefit to society will justifiably outweigh the anticipated risk to the individual. Societal values may be such that the interests of the subject do not take precedence over the interests of society. Thus, furthering the interest of society at large may not necessarily compromise the rights and interests of the individual research participant within the particular value system the individual espouses. Even more fundamentally, an African may perceive that it is "difficult to see how the interests of the subject conflict with the interests of the society except, of course, if the society is not his own."[29] That is, the interest of the subject and of society are necessarily congruent. Problems arise only if the values and expectations of a society of which the individual is not a member are imposed upon him. In this light, imposing Western ethical values upon African research subjects is inappropriate.

Considerations of beneficent treatment of research subjects are also modified by cultural and social concerns. In developing countries, resources are often so scarce as to force particularly difficult decisions regarding allocation.[30] Moreover, assessment of the acceptability of a particular medical intervention will differ in developed as compared with developing countries as a result of different patterns of illness and different medical and practical constraints acting upon the population. Risk/benefit assessments may yield different outcomes, and hence different acceptabilities, depending on the society.[31] AIDS may be so widespread and deadly a disease in Africa that a higher degree of research risk must perforce be tolerated to deal with the problem, and this may well be socially sanctioned.

But while greater risk may be tolerated in Africa, this does not mean that Westerners should indiscriminately benefit from research conducted in Africa if Africans are systematically subjected to excess research risks with the prospect of deriving but little benefit. This would violate the principle of justice. This principle involves a sense of "fairness in distribution" or "what is deserved," and as applied to human subjects research is usually taken to address the question of who should receive the benefits of the research and who should bear the burdens.

Under the principle of justice, research subjects should be chosen "for reasons directly related to the problem being studied," and not "because of their easy availability, their compromised position, or their manipulability."[32] Thus, the practical concerns that make an AIDS vaccine trial easier to conduct in Africa do not alone constitute sufficient justification to use Africans as subjects. Only the scientific concerns related directly to the problem of establishing the ability of a vaccine to prevent HIV infection are relevant.

The principle of justice also requires that those who stand to benefit from the research should, in fact, be those to bear the burden. Much of the world stands to gain from the development of an effective AIDS vaccine and the burden of research risks should therefore be fairly distributed, as should the benefits. In Central and Western Africa much of the population at large stands to gain by introduction of an effective vaccine. Yet economic constraints may well prevent even moderately extensive distribution of a beneficial vaccine in Africa, should one become available. The benefits to Africans are thus only hypothetical unless there is a financial commitment by the developed world to provide the vaccine. In this light, it would be frankly unethical to subject Africans to a disproportionate share of the research risks. A contingency of any trial of an AIDS vaccine in Africa by Western scientists should thus be to provide access to the technology once it is developed—possibly in the form of free or subsidized vaccine.

RESEARCH ETHICS IN THE FACE OF A PANDEMIC

Conduct of research throughout the world on a pandemic disease—which perforce occurs in disparate sociocultural settings—forces reevaluation of a uniform, international view of research ethics. The straightforward application of the ethical standards across cultural barriers is problematic.[33]

Confronting AIDS will require a rethinking of a narrow, parochial formulation of ethics.

This is not to assert that standards for research ethics should be culturally relative, but rather that they should be culturally *relevant.* Some ethical standards can and should be met worldwide. An important challenge to Western scientists conducting AIDS vaccine trials is to conform to certain minimum ethical standards regardless of the setting: (1) The trial should be of suitable design and scientific merit; (2) it should involve the free, and where possible, informed consent of the participants; (3) all participants should benefit from proper counseling regarding avoidance of risky behaviors; (4) due consideration should be given to the risks of research participation, using the highest standard of risk/benefit analysis possible; and (5) the countries participating in the study should be allowed fair access to any vaccine arising from the research.

An equally important—and possibly more difficult—challenge to investigators conducting AIDS vaccine trials throughout the world is to be culturally sensitive. Proper conduct of an AIDS vaccine trial must be informed not only by the epidemiology and biology of HIV infection in different settings, but also by the ethical norms and cultural constraints prevailing in such settings. Beyond certain minimum standards, there should be tolerance of variability. Variability, as we have seen, is especially apt to arise in the informational content of consent, in the acceptability of proxy consent, and in the tolerance of an increased risk/benefit ratio.

What is essential is not that the research meet the same ethical standard worldwide. What is essential is that the research manifest a culturally sensitive and ethically sophisticated concern for the well-being of subjects throughout the world.

ACKNOWLEDGMENTS

I am grateful to Robert J. Levine, M.D., Larry Gostin, J.D., Richard Cash, M.D., Erika Zuckerman, and especially to Allan M. Brandt, Ph.D., for their helpful criticism of earlier drafts of this manuscript. This work was partially supported by a grant from the Harvard School of Public Health Alumni Association.

NOTES

1. Daniel Zagury *et al.,* "Immunization Against AIDS in Humans," *Nature* 326 (1987), 249–50. See also, "First Human AIDS Vaccine Trial Goes Ahead Without Official OK," *Nature* 325 (1987), 290.
2. Alfred J. Fortin, "The Politics of AIDS in Kenya," *Third World Quarterly* 9:3 (1987), 906–19; "Special SIDA: Des Millions D'Africains Condamnès á Mort?" *Jeune Afrique Magazine* (February 1987), 81–93 (at 87). See also, "Who Will Volunteer for an AIDS Vaccine?" *The New York Times,* April 15, 1986, C1: "AIDS: Racist Myths, Hard Facts." *Afric-Asia* (May 1987), 50–55.
3. "Zaire, Ending Secrecy, Attacks AIDS Openly," *The New York Times,* February 8, 1987, A1.
4. Council for International World Organizations of Medical Sciences and the World Health Organization, *Proposed International Guidelines for Biomedical Research Involving Human Subjects* (Geneva: CIOMS, 1982), 32.
5. CIOMS, *Proposed International Guidelines,* 23.
6. Wendy K. Mariner and Robert C. Gallo, "Getting to Market: The Scientific and Legal Climate for Developing an AIDS Vaccine," *Law, Medicine & Health Care* 15:1–2 (1987), 17–25.
7. Donald P. Francis and John C. Petricciani, "The Prospects for and Pathways Toward a Vaccine for AIDS," *New England Journal of Medicine* 313:25 (1985), 1586–90.
8. "Zaire, Ending Secrecy, Attacks AIDS Openly."
9. For the accuracy of HIV tests, see: Michael J. Barry, Paul D. Cleary, and Harvey V. Fineberg, "Screening for HIV Infection: Risks, Benefits, and the Burden of Proof," *Law, Medicine & Health Care* 14:5–6 (1986) 259–67.
10. Thomas C. Quinn *et al.,* "AIDS in Africa: An Epidemiologic Paradigm," *Science* 234 (1986), 955–63; Gerald H. Friedland and Robert S. Klein, "Transmission of the Human Immunodeficiency Virus," *New England Journal of Medicine* 317:18 (1987), 1125–35. Regarding heterosexual transmission in Africa, see Peter Piot, *et al.,* "Acquired Immunodeficiency Syndrome in Heterosexual Population in Zaire," *The Lancet* ii (1984), 65–69; N.

Clumeck *et al.*, "Heterosexual Promiscuity Among African Patients with AIDS," *New England Journal of Medicine* 313:3 (1985), 182; Jonathan M. Mann *et al.*, "Prevalence of HTLV-III/LAV in Household Contacts of Patients with Confirmed AIDS and Controls in Kinshasa, Zaire," *Journal of the American Medical Association* 256:6 (1986), 721–24.

11. Phyllis J. Kanki et al, "Human T-Lymphotropic Virus Type 4 and the Human Immunodeficiency Virus in West Africa," *Science* 236 (1987) 827–31: Joan K. Kreiss *et al.*, "AIDS Virus Infection in Nairobi Prostitutes," *New England Journal of Medicine* 314:7 (1986), 414–18; Jonathan Mann *et al.*, "Condom Use and HIV Infection Among Prostitutes in Zaire," *New England Journal of Medicine* 316:6 (1987), 345; and Phylllis J. Kanki *et al.*, "Absence of Antibodies to HIV2/HTLV4 in Six Central African Nations," *AIDS Research and Human Retroviruses,* Phyllis J. Kanki, ed., in press.
12. Alvin Novick, Nancy Neveloff Dubler, and Sheldon H. Landesman, "Do Research Subjects Have the Right Not to Know Their HIV Antibody Test Results?" *IRB: A Review of Human Subjects Re-search* 8:5 (September/October 1986), 6–9.
13. Beverly Merz, "HIV Vaccine Approved for Clinical Trials," *Journal of the American Medical Association* 258:11 (1987), 1433–34.
14. National Commission for the Protection of Human Subjects of Biomedical and Behavioral Research, *The Belmont Report: Ethical Principles and Guidelines for the Protection of Human Subjects of Research* (Washington, DC: Department of Health, Education and Welfare, 1979), 4.
15. Don C. Des Jarlais and Samuel R. Friedman, "AIDS Prevention Among IV Drug Users: Potential Conflicts Between Research Design and Ethics," *IRB: A Review of Human Subjects Research* 9:1 (January/February 1987), 6–8.
16. Des Jarlais and Friedman, "AIDS Prevention Among IV Drug Users."
17. "Zaire, Ending Secrecy, Attacks AIDS Openly."
18. See, for example, Allan M. Brandt, "Racism and Research: The Case of the Tuskegee Syphilis Study,"*Hastings Center Report* 8:6 (December 1978), 21–29.
19. Belmont Report, 4.
20. Willy De Craemer, "A Cross-Cultural Perspective on Personhood," *Millbank Memorial Fund Quarterly* 61:1 (1983), 19–34; Renee C. Fox and David P. Willis, "Personhood, Medicine, and American Society," *Millbank Memorial Fund Quarterly* 61:1 (1983), 127–47; J.M. Janzen, *The Quest for Therapy in Lower Zaire* (Berkeley: The University of California Press, 1978), 169, 189.
21. See, for example, H. Tristram Engelhardt, "Bioethics in the People's Republic of China," *Hastings Center Report* 10:2 (April 1980), 7–10.
22. CIOMS, *Proposed International Guidelines,* 26–27; see also p. 24.
23. See Robert J. Levine, "Validity of Consent Procedures in Technologically Developing Countries" in *Human Experimentation and Medical Ethics,* Z. Bankowski and N. Howard-Jones, eds. (Geneva: CIOMS, 1982), 16–30. There is potential for abuse of authority if a community leader acts to the detriment of his or her constituency; see, for example, Francis Moore Lappe, Joseph Collins, and David Kinley, *Aid as Obstacle* (San Francisco: Food First, 1981), at questions 7, 11.
24. M. Beiser, "Ethics in Cross Cultural Perspective," in E.F. Foulks *et al., Current Perspectives in Cultural Psychiatry* (New York: Spectrum Publications, 1977), 125–37.
25. Ebun O. Ekunwe and Ross Kessel, "Informed Consent in the Developing World," *Hastings Center Report* 14:3 (June, 1984), 23–24.
26. "Racist Bigotry on AIDS," *African Concord,* June 4, 1987, 25. See also Margaret Mead, "Research with Human Beings: A Model Derived from Anthropological Field Practice," *Daedalus* 98 (1969), 361–86.
27. World Medical Assembly, "Declaration of Helsinki," revised 1975, in CIOMS, *Proposed International Guidelines,* Appendix 5: principle I.5.
28. *Belmont Report,* 7.
29. O.O. Ajayi, "Taboos and Clinical Research in West Africa," *Journal of Medical Ethics* 6:1 (1980) 61–63.
30. John F. Kilner, "Who Shall Be Saved? An African Answer," *Hastings Center Report* 14:3 (June 1984), 19–22.
31. See, for example, Carol Levine, "Depo-Provera and Contraceptive Risk: A Case Study of Values in Conflict," *Hastings Center Report* 9:4 (August 1979), 8–11.
32. *Belmont Report,* 5.
33. Regarding international variation in ethical decision-making, see, for example, Arthur I. Eidelman, K.N. Siva Subramanian, and Rihito Kimura, "Caring for Newborns: Three World Views," *Hastings Center Report* 16:4 (August 1986), 18–23; "Biomedical Ethics: A Multinational View," *Hastings Center Report* 17:3 (June 1987), Special Supplement.

THE AIDS EPIDEMIC — SUPPLEMENTARY READINGS

ALMOND, BRENDA. and CAROLE ULANOWSKY "HIV and Pregnancy." *Hastings Center Report,* March–April 1990.

ARRAS, JOHN D. "Noncompliance in AIDS Research." *Hastings Center Report,* September–October 1990.

BELL, NORA KISER. "Women and AIDS: Too Little, Too Late?" *Hypatia,* vol. 4 (3), Fall 1989.

CHAMBERS, DONALD. "AIDS Testing: An Insurers Viewpoint," in *AIDS: Ethics and Public Policy,* Pierce and VanDeVeer, editors, Belmont, CA: Wadsworth, 1988.

CRISP, ROGER. "Autonomy, Welfare and the Treatment of AIDS." *Journal of Medical Ethics,* vol. 15, June 1989.

DANIELS, NORMAN. "Duty to Treat or Right to Refuse." *The Hastings Center Report,* vol. 21, March–April 1991.

MAYO, DAVID, "AIDS, Quarantines and Noncompliant Positives," in *AIDS: Ethics and Public Policy,* Pierce and VanDeVeer, editors, Belmont, CA: Wadsworth, 1988.

RIDSDALE, LEONE. "When Keeping Secrets May Cause Harm." *Journal of Medical Ethics,* vol. 16, June 1990.

SPOHN, WILLIAM C. "The Moral Dimensions of AIDS." *Theological Studies,* vol. 49, March 1988.

TAPPIN, D.M., and F. COCKBURN. "Ethics and Ethics Committees: HIV Serosurveillance in Scotland." *Journal of Medicine and Philosophy,* vol. 18, March 1992.

WALTERS, LEROY. "Ethical Issues in the Prevention and Treatment of AIDS." *Science,* vol. 239, February 5, 1988.

WAYMACK, MARK. "AIDS, Ethics and Health Insurance." *Business & Professional Ethics Journal,* vol. 10, Spring 1991.

VIII

Abortion

In their remarkable joint decision, Justices Sandra Day O'Connor, Anthony M. Kennedy and David H. Souter directly addressed the American people, clearly seeking their support for a compromise legal position . . . the three conservative justices turned middle-of-the-roaders . . . noted that a few times each generation the "Court's interpretation of the Consitutution calls the contending sides of a national controversy to end their national division by accepting a common mandate rooted in the Constitution."

—St. Louis Post Dispatch[1]

Abortion has been one of the most controversial issues in the United States over the last 25 years. While many people have an exclusively emotional reaction to this issue, there are many important philosophical questions that need to be addressed. In this section, our essays survey the three main positions that have been taken in the debate and provide philosophical defense for these positions. In addition, we turn to other cultures and find that there has been substantial consensus rather than hostility on this issue.

The liberal position on abortion was well articulated in the U.S. Supreme Court's 1973 ruling in *Roe* v. *Wade*. An overwhelming majority ruled that abortion constituted a "fundamental right" of women. Until the fetus is viable (able to live outside the womb), the court ruled that the woman's right to decide what to do with her own body was paramount. After the fetus attained viability (during the third trimester of gestation), then restrictions could be placed on abortion rights, because only at that point was there a competing (human) right. Abortion was seen as one of many rights to privacy, along with the right to obtain and use birth control devices. These rights were considered to be akin to the rights against unreasonable search and seizure and to speech and peaceable assembly.

The conservative position generally regards all abortions as morally unjustifiable. The fetus is regarded as a full-fledged human person from the moment of conception. And since the fetus is regarded by conservatives as a paradigmatic innocent human being, its rights are thought to outweigh the woman's right to control her body. Many who hold the conservative position also hold that any attempt to interfere with the natural process of gestation and birth, even many forms of birth control, is morally unjustifiable. The paramount concern is for the fetus's right to life, a right so important that it overrides all other considerations. Conservatives argue that if a child is unwanted, adoption rather than abortion is the only morally acceptable solution.

Various difficulties plague both sides of the abortion dispute in the United States. Many conservatives have long been bothered by cases of pregnancy due to rape or incest, as well as pregnancies that threaten the life of the pregnant woman. Liberals have been bothered by the issue of whether, on their own principles, they are committed to justifying some forms of infanticide, such as the killing of greatly deformed newborn babies. A consideration of such problem cases has caused some people to adopt one of many moderate, compromise positions on abortion, accepting some types of abortion while also prohibiting some others.

The recent U.S. Supreme Court decision in *Casey* v. *Planned Parenthood,* referred to above, recognizes a compromise position. Abortion is not regarded as a fundamental right, one which would override most others; but neither is the fetus considered to have an absolute right to life. Instead, abortion is considered to be a relatively important right, but one which can be restricted, as long as the restrictions do not place an "undue burden" on the woman in question. This compromise position is far from being a consensus position in America today, but perhaps it will become so. Yet even if this compromise is accepted by the vast majority, this does not resolve the question of the *moral* justifiability of abortion.

Mary Anne Warren is quite clear in arguing that only human persons have strong rights, and that the notion of personhood needs to be philosophically examined before a decision is reached about whether the fetus is a human person whose rights can override the pregnant woman's rights. Warren argues that there are five features that are central to the concept of human personhood: consciousness, reasoning, self-motivated activity, capacity to communicate, and selfawareness. These are the features that make a being a member of a human community. Fetuses do not generally have enough of these features to be considered human persons even though they may resemble human persons in other respects. Fetuses are merely potential persons and as such have merely potential rights, not the sort of rights that could override a woman's right to control her own body.

Don Marquis takes the opposing, conservative position, that what is important about a life is its future possibilities, and that what is so tragic about killing is that it deprives someone of this future. Marquis contends that if this is understood as the main criterion of a valuable life, then animals and fetuses share this feature in common with adult human beings. And what makes it wrong to kill adult human beings is also what makes it wrong to kill animals or fetuses. Marquis thus concludes that most abortions are morally unjustified, and this is true no matter what the current consensus is about abortion.

Mary Mahowald represents one of the many compromise positions that can be taken in the abortion debate. She contends that while the rights of the fetus need to be taken into account, so do the rights of the pregnant woman, since after all, there cannot be fetuses without women. Mahowald focuses on the difficult case of fetal tissue transplantation. As with the case of population control, addressed below, fetal tissue cases point up the fact that abortions can sometimes have extremely beneficial results for the society at large. In this case, many otherwise incurable diseases can be treated with the tissues of aborted fetuses, once again raising questions of whether an extreme conservative position on abortion can be justified.

Christine Overall also provides a challenge to the extreme conservative position by presenting the case of multiple fetuses growing in the same womb where it is highly unlikely that any can be carried to term unless at least one is aborted. If all fetuses have an absolute right to life, how are we to resolve this puzzling case? Overall argues that in this case an antiabortion stance is actually contrary to the conservative prescription to support pregnancy to term. The women who seek abortions in these multiple fetus cases generally do so with a hope of continuing, not ending, their pregnancy. A consideration of such cases certainly makes it harder to hold an unbending conservative position.

In addition, Ren-Zong Qiu, Chun-Zhi Wang and Yuan Gu raise the question of population control in certain societies as a possible basis for justifying even some late-term abortions. In many parts of the world, hunger and starvation are intimately linked with birth control measures, and abortion is one of the many forms of birth control. It is positions like these that profoundly worry conservatives on the abortion issue. They are afraid that late-term abortion will become an accepted form of birth control. However, Qiu, Wang and Gu suggest that in many cultures women are so stigmatized if they become pregnant that they will find it difficult to admit their condition until it is too late to have anything but a late-term abortion. And adoption may not always be an alternative, especially if control of population growth is considered a vital social goal.

William LaFleur points us toward a society that has largely reached a consensus about abortion. In contemporary Japan, a strong emphasis on conservative family values has had an effect opposite to that which has occurred in America. Abortion is regarded as a necessary feature in assuring that families will have only those members who are wanted. Interestingly, the consensus reached in Japan is one that is tempered by the feeling that abortion is a tragic necessity. No matter where a consensus compromise is reached on abortion, there will probably always be this tragic dimension to our choices on the abortion issue.

NOTE

1. *St. Louis Post Dispatch,* July 1, 1992, p. 12A, concerning *Casey* v. *Planned Parenthood.*

On the Moral and Legal Status of Abortion

Mary Anne Warren

Mary Anne Warren is a professor of philosophy at San Francisco State University. She is the author of The Nature of Woman *(1980) and* Gendercide: The Implications of Sex Selection *(1985).*

Warren provides the classic "liberal" defense of abortion rights. She maintains that once one concedes that the fetus is a person, then one must accept limitations on the right to abortion. But, she argues, the fetus is not a person. Her argument proceeds by examining the various criteria that have been employed to establish personhood. Eventually, Warren constructs what she regards as the most plausible definition of a human person, and then shows that a fetus does not conform to the definition. Neither the resemblance of the fetus to a person, nor the fact that it may become a human person, are sufficient reasons for regarding the fetus as a human person whose rights could override a pregnant woman's right to decide whether or not to have an abortion.

We will be concerned with both the moral status of abortion, which for our purposes we may define as the act which a woman performs in voluntarily terminating, or allowing another person to terminate, her pregnancy, and the legal status which is appropriate for this act. I will argue that, while it is not possible to produce a satisfactory defense of a woman's right to obtain an abortion without showing that a fetus is not a human being, in the morally relevant sense of that term, we ought not to conclude that the difficulties involved in determining whether or not a fetus is human make it impossible to produce any satisfactory solution to the problem of the moral status of abortion. For it is possible to show that, on the basis of intuitions which we may expect even the opponents of abortion to share, a fetus is not a person, and hence not the sort of entity to which it is proper to ascribe full moral rights.

Of course, while some philosophers would deny the possibility of any such proof,[1] others will deny that there is any need for it, since the moral permissibility of abortion appears to them to be too obvious to require proof. But the inadequacy of this attitude should be evident from the fact that both the friends and the foes of abortion consider their position to be morally self-evident. Because proabortionists have never adequately come to grips with the conceptual issues surrounding abortion, most if not all, of the arguments which they advance in opposition to laws restricting access to abortion fail to refute or even weak-

Reprinted from *The Monist,* 1973. [Edited]

en the traditional antiabortion argument, i.e., that a fetus is a human being, and therefore abortion is murder.

These arguments are typically of one of two sorts. Either they point to the terrible side effects of the restrictive laws, e.g., the deaths due to illegal abortions, and the fact that it is poor women who suffer the most as a result of these laws, or else they state that to deny a woman access to abortion is to deprive her of her right to control her own body. Unfortunately, however, the fact that restricting access to abortion has tragic side effects does not, in itself, show that the restrictions are unjustified, since murder is wrong regardless of the consequences of prohibiting it; and the appeal to the right to control one's body, which is generally construed as a property right, is at best a rather feeble argument for the permissibility of abortion. Mere ownership does not give me the right to kill innocent people whom I find on my property, and indeed I am apt to be held responsible if such people injure themselves while on my property. It is equally unclear that I have any moral right to expel an innocent person from my property when I know that doing so will result in his death.

Furthermore, it is probably inappropriate to describe a woman's body as her property, since it seems natural to hold that a person is something distinct from her property, but not from her body. Even those who would object to the identification of a person with his body, or with the conjunction of his body and his mind, must admit that it would be very odd to describe, say, breaking a leg, as damaging one's property, and much more appropriate to describe it as injuring *oneself*. Thus it is probably a mistake to argue that the right to obtain an abortion is in any way derived from the right to own and regulate property.

But however we wish to construe the right to abortion, we cannot hope to convince those who consider abortion a form of murder of the existence of any such right unless we are able to produce a clear and convincing refutation of the traditional antiabortion argument, and this has not, to my knowledge, been done. With respect to the two most vital issues which that argument involves, i.e., the humanity of the fetus and its implication for the moral status of abortion, confusion has prevailed on both sides of the dispute.

Thus, both proabortionists and antiabortionists have tended to abstract the question of whether abortion is wrong to that of whether it is wrong to destroy a fetus, just as though the rights of another person were not necessarily involved. This mistaken abstraction has led to the almost universal assumption that if a fetus is a human being, with a right to life, then it follows immediately that abortion is wrong (except perhaps when necessary to save the woman's life), and that it ought to be prohibited. It has also been generally assumed that unless the question about the status of the fetus is answered, the moral status of abortion cannot possibly be determined. . . .

The question which we must answer in order to produce a satisfactory solution to the problem of the moral status of abortion is this: How are we to define the moral community, the set of beings with full and equal moral rights, such that we can decide whether a human fetus is a member of this community or not? What sort of entity, exactly, has the inalienable rights to life, liberty, and the pursuit of happiness? Jefferson attributed these right to all *men*, and it may or may not be fair to suggest that he intended to attribute them *only* to men. Perhaps he ought to have attributed them to all human beings. If so, then we arrive, first, at the problem of defining what makes a being human, and, second, at the equally vital question . . . namely, What reason is there for identifying the moral community with the set of all human beings, in whatever way we have chosen to define that term?

On the Definition of "Human"

One reason why this vital second question is so frequently overlooked in the debate over the moral status of abortion is that the term "human" has two distinct, but not often distinguished, senses. This fact results in a slide of meaning, which serves to conceal the fallaciousness of the traditional argument that since (1) it is wrong to kill innocent human beings, and (2) fetuses are innocent human beings, then (3) it is wrong to kill fetuses. For if "human" is used in the same sense in both (1) and (2) then, whichever of the two senses is meant, one of these premises is question-begging. And if it is used in two different senses then of course the conclusion doesn't follow.

Thus, (1) is a self-evident moral truth,[2] and avoids begging the question about abortion, only if "human being" is used to mean something like "a full-fledged member of the moral community." (It may or may not also be meant to refer exclusively to members of the species *Homo sapiens*.) We may call this the *moral* sense of "human." It is not to be confused with what we will call the *genetic* sense, i.e., the sense in which *any* member of the species is a human being, and no member of any other species could be. If (1) is acceptable only if the moral sense is intended, (2) is non-question-begging only if what is intended is the genetic sense.

In "Deciding Who is Human," Noonan argues for the classification of fetuses with human beings by pointing to the presence of the full genetic code, and the potential capacity for rational thought.[3] It is clear that what he needs to show, for his version of the traditional argument to be valid, is that fetuses are human in the moral sense, the sense in which it is analytically true that all human beings have full moral rights. But, in the absence of any argument showing that whatever is genetically human is also morally human, and he gives none, nothing more than genetic humanity can be demonstrated by the presence of the human genetic code. And, as we will see, the *potential* capacity for rational thought can at most show that an entity has the potential for *becoming* human in the moral sense.

Defining the Moral Community

Can it be established that genetic humanity is sufficient for moral humanity? I think that there are very good reasons for not defining the moral community in this way. I would like to suggest an alternative way of defining the moral community, which I will argue for only to the extent of explaining why it is, or should be, self-evident. The suggestion is simply that the moral community consists of all and only *people,* rather than all and only human beings;[4] and probably the best way of demonstrating its self-evidence is by considering the concept of personhood, to see what sorts of entity are and are not persons, and what the decision that a being is or is not a person implies about its moral rights.

What characteristics entitle an entity to be considered a person? This is obviously not the place to attempt a complete analysis of the concept of personhood, but we do not need such a fully adequate analysis just to determine whether and why a fetus is or isn't a person. All we need is a rough and approximate list of the most basic criteria of personhood, and some idea of which, or how many, of these an entity must satisfy in order to properly be considered a person.

In searching for such criteria, it is useful to look beyond the set of people with whom we are acquainted, and ask how we would decide whether a totally alien being was a person or not. (For we have no right to assume that genetic humanity is necessary for personhood.) Imagine a space traveler who lands on an unknown planet and encounters a race of beings utterly unlike any he has ever seen or heard of. If he wants to be sure of behaving morally toward these beings, he has to somehow decide whether they are people, and hence have full moral rights, or whether they are the sort of thing which he need not feel guilty about treating as, for example, a source of food.

How should he go about making this decision? If he has some anthropological background, he might look for such things as religion, art, and the manufacturing of tools, weapons, or shelters, since these factors have been used to distinguish our human from our prehuman ancestors, in what seems to be closer to the moral than the genetic sense of "human." And no doubt he would be right to consider the presence of such factors as good evidence that the alien beings were people, and morally human. It would, however, be overly anthropocentric of him to take the absence of these things as adequate evidence that they were not, since we can imagine people who have progressed beyond, or evolved without ever developing, these cultural characteristics.

I suggest that the traits which are most central to the concept of personhood, or humanity in the moral sense, are, very roughly, the following:

(1) consciousness (of objects and events external and/or internal to the being), and in particular the capacity to feel pain;
(2) reasoning (the *developed* capacity to solve new and relatively complex problems);
(3) self-motivated activity (activity which is relatively independent of either genetic or direct external control);
(4) the capacity to communicate, by whatever means, messages of an indefinite variety of types, that is, not just with an indefinite number of possible contents, but on indefinitely many possible topics;
(5) the presence of self-concepts, and self-awareness, either individual or racial, or both.

Admittedly, there are apt to be a great many problems involved in formulating precise definitions of these criteria, let alone in developing universally valid behavioral criteria for deciding when they apply. But I will assume that both we and our explorer know approximately what (1)–(5) mean, and that he is also able to determine whether or not they apply. How, then, should he use his findings to decide whether or not the alien beings are people? We needn't suppose that an entity must have *all* of these attributes to be properly considered a person; (1) and (2) alone may well be sufficient for personhood, and quite probably (1)–(3) are sufficient. Neither do we need to insist that any one of these criteria is *necessary* for personhood, although once again (1) and (2) look like fairly good candidates for necessary conditions, as does (3), if "activity" is construed so as to include the activity of reasoning.

All we need to claim, to demonstrate that a fetus is not a person, is that any being which satisfies *none* of (1)–(5) is certainly not a person. I consider this claim to be so obvious that I think anyone who denied it, and claimed that a being which satisfied none of (1)–(5) was a person all the same, would thereby demonstrate that he had no notion at all of what a person is—perhaps because he had confused the concept of a person with that of genetic humanity. If the opponents of abortion were to deny the appropriateness of these five criteria, I do not know what further arguments would convince them. We would probably have to admit that our conceptual schemes were indeed irreconcilably different, and that our dispute could not be settled objectively.

I do not expect this to happen, however, since I think that the concept of a person is one which is very nearly universal (to people), and that it is common to both proabortionists and antiabortionists, even though neither group has fully realized the relevance of this concept to the resolution of their dispute. Furthermore, I think that on reflection even the antiabortionists ought to agree not only that (1)–(5) are central to the concept of personhood, but also that it is a part of this concept that all and only people have full moral rights. The concept of a person is in part a moral concept; once we have admitted that *x* is a person we have recognized, even if we have not agreed to respect, *x*'s right to be treated as a member of the moral community. It is true that the claim that *x* is a *human being* is more commonly voiced as part of an appeal to treat *x* decently than is the claim that *x* is a person, but this is either because "human being" is here used in the sense which implies personhood, or because the genetic and moral senses of "human" have been confused.

Now if (1)–(5) are indeed the primary criteria of personhood, then it is clear that genetic humanity is neither necessary nor sufficient for establishing that an entity is a person. Some human beings are not people, and there may well be people who are not human beings. A man or woman whose consciousness has been permanently obliterated but who remains alive is a human being which is no longer a person; defective human beings, with no appreciable mental capacity, are not and presumably never will be people; and a fetus is a human being which is not yet a person, and which therefore cannot coherently be said to have full moral rights. Citizens of the next century should be prepared to recognize highly advanced, self-aware robots or computers, should such be developed, and intelligent inhabitants of other worlds, should such be found, as people in the fullest sense, and to respect their moral rights. But to ascribe full moral rights to an entity which is not a person is as absurd as to ascribe moral obligations and responsibilities to such an entity.

Fetal Development and the Right to Life

Two problems arise in the application of these suggestions for the definition of the moral community to the determination of the precise moral status of a human fetus. Given that the paradigm example of a person is a normal adult human being, then (1) How like this paradigm, in particular how far advanced since conception, does a human being need to be before it begins to have a right to life by virtue, not of being fully a person as of yet, but of being *like* a person? and (2) To what extent, if any, does the fact that a fetus has the *potential* for becoming a person endow it with some of the same rights? Each of these questions requires some comment.

In answering the first question, we need not attempt a detailed consideration of the moral rights of organisms which are not developed enough, aware enough, intelligent enough, etc., to be considered people, but which resemble people in some respects. It does seem reasonable to suggest that the more like a person, in the relevant respects, a being is, the stronger is the case for regarding it as having a right to life, and indeed the stronger its right to life is. Thus we ought to take seriously the suggestion that, insofar as "the human individual develops biologically in a continuous fashion . . . the rights of a human person might develop in the same way."[5] But we must keep in mind that the attributes which are relevant in determining whether or not an entity is enough like a person to be regarded as having some of the same moral rights are no different from those which are relevant to determining whether or not it is fully a person—i.e., are no different from (1)–(5)—and that being genetically human, or having recognizably human facial and other physical features, or detectable brain activity, or the capacity to survive outside the uterus, are simply not among these relevant attributes.

Thus it is clear that even though a seven- or eight-month fetus has features which make it apt to arouse in us almost the same powerful protective instinct as is commonly aroused by a small infant, nevertheless it is not significantly more personlike than is a very small embryo. It is *somewhat* more personlike; it can apparently feel and respond to pain, and it may even have a rudimentary form of consciousness, insofar as its brain is quite active. Nevertheless, it seems safe to say that it is not fully conscious, in the way that an infant of a few months is, and that it cannot reason, or communicate messages of indefinitely many sorts, does not engage in self-motivated activity, and has no self-awareness. Thus, in the *relevant* respects, a fetus, even a fully developed one, is considerably less personlike than is the average mature mammal, indeed the average fish. And I think that a rational person must conclude that if the right to life of a fetus is to be based upon its resemblance to a person, then it cannot be said to have any more right to life than, let us say, a newborn guppy (which also seems to be capable of feeling pain), and that a right of that magnitude could never override a woman's right to obtain an abortion, at any stage of her pregnancy.

There may, of course, be other arguments in favor of placing legal limits upon the stage of pregnancy in which an abortion may be performed. Given the relative safety of the new techniques of artificially inducing labor during the third trimester, the danger to the woman's life or health is no longer such an argument. Neither is the fact that people tend to respond to the thought of abortion in the later stages of pregnancy with emotional repulsion, since mere emotional responses cannot take the place of moral reasoning in determining what ought to be permitted. Nor, finally, is the frequently heard argument that legalizing abortion, especially late in the pregnancy, may erode the level of respect for human life, leading, perhaps, to an increase in unjustified euthanasia and other crimes. For this threat, if it is a threat, can be better met by educating people to the kinds of moral distinctions which we are making here than by limiting access to abortion (which limitation may, in its disregard for the rights of women, be just as damaging to the level of respect for human rights).

Thus, since the fact that even a fully developed fetus is not personlike enough to have any significant right to life on the basis of its personlikeness shows that no legal restrictions upon the stage of pregnancy in which an abortion may be performed can be justified on the grounds that we should protect the rights of the older fetus; and since there is no other apparent justification for such restrictions, we may conclude that they are entirely unjustified. Whether or not it would be *indecent* (whatever that means) for a woman in her seventh month to obtain an abortion just to avoid having to postpone a trip to Europe, it would not, in itself, be *immoral,* and therefore it ought to be permitted.

Potential Personhood and the Right to Life

We have seen that a fetus does not resemble a person in any way which can support the claim that it has even some of the same rights. But what about its *potential,* the fact that if nurtured and allowed to develop naturally it will very probably become a person? Doesn't that alone give it at least some right to life? It is hard to deny that the fact that an entity is a potential person is a strong prima facie reason for not destroying it; but we need not conclude from this that a potential person has a right to life, by virtue of that potential. It may be that our feeling that it is better, other things being equal, not to destroy a potential person is better explained by the fact that potential people are still (felt to be) an invaluable resource, not to be lightly squandered. Surely, if every speck of dust were a potential person, we would be much less apt to conclude that every potential person has a right to become actual.

Still, we do not need to insist that a potential person has no right to life whatever. There may be something immoral, and not just imprudent, about wantonly destroying potential people, when doing so isn't necessary to protect anyone's rights. But even if a potential person does have some prima facie right to life, such a right could not possibly outweigh the right of a woman to obtain an abortion, since the rights of any actual person invariably outweigh those of any potential person, whenever the two conflict. Since this may not be immediately obvious in the case of a human fetus, let us look at another case.

Suppose that our space explorer falls into the hands of an alien culture, whose scientists decide to create a few hundred thousand or more human beings, by breaking his body into its component cells, and using these to create fully developed human beings, with, of course, his genetic code. We may imagine that each of these newly created men will have all of the original man's abilities, skills, knowledge, and so on, and also have an individual self-concept, in short that each of them will be a bona fide (though hardly unique) person. Imagine that the whole project will take only seconds, and that its chances of success are extremely high, and that our explorer knows all of this, and also knows that these people will be treated fairly. I maintain that in such a situation he would have every right to escape if he could, and thus to deprive all of these potential people of their potential lives; for his right to life outweighs all of theirs together, in spite of the fact that they are all genetically human, all innocent, and all have a very high probability of becoming people very soon, if only he refrains from acting.

Indeed, I think he would have a right to escape even if it were not his life which the alien scientists planned to take, but only a year of his freedom, or, indeed, only a day. Nor would he be obligated to stay if he had gotten captured (thus bringing all these people-potentials into existence) because of his own carelessness, or even if he had done so deliberately, knowing the consequences. Regardless of how he got captured, he is not morally obligated to remain in captivity for *any* period of time for the sake of permitting any number of potential people to come into actuality, so great is the margin by which one actual person's right to liberty outweighs whatever right to life even a hundred thousand potential people have. And it seems reasonable to conclude that the rights of a woman will outweigh by a similar margin whatever right to life a fetus may have by virtue of its potential personhood.

Thus, neither a fetus's resemblance to a person, nor its potential for becoming a person provides any basis whatever for the claim that it has any significant right to life. Consequently, a woman's right to protect her health, happiness, freedom, and even her life,[6] by terminating an unwanted pregnancy, will always override whatever right to life it may be appropriate to ascribe to a fetus, even a fully developed one. And thus, in the absence of any overwhelming social need for every possible child, the laws which restrict the right to obtain an abortion, or limit the period of pregnancy during which an abortion may be performed, are a wholly unjustified violation of a woman's most basic moral and constitutional rights.

ACKNOWLEDGMENT

My thanks to the following people, who were kind enough to read and criticize an earlier version of this paper: Herbert Gold, Gene Glass, Anne Lauterbach, Judith Thomson, Mary Mothersill, and Timothy Binkley.

NOTES

1. For example, Roger Wertheimer, who in "Understanding the Abortion Argument" (*Philosophy and Public Affairs,* 1, No. 1 [Fall, 1971], 67–95), argues that the problem of the moral status of abortion is insoluble, in that the dispute over the status of the fetus is not a question of fact at all, but only a question of how one responds to the facts.
2. Of course, the principle that it is (always) wrong to kill innocent human beings is in need of many other modifications, e.g., that it may be permissible to do so to save a greater number of other innocent human beings, but we may safely ignore these complications here.
3. John Noonan, "Deciding Who Is Human," *Natural Law Forum,* vol. 13 (1968), p. 135.
4. From here on, we will use "human" to mean genetically human, since the moral sense seems closely connected to, and perhaps derived from, the assumption that genetic humanity is sufficient for membership in the moral community.
5. Thomas L. Hayes, "A Biological View," *Commonweal,* 85 (March 17, 1967), 677–78; quoted by Daniel Callahan, in *Abortion, Law, Choice, and Morality* (London: Macmillan & Co., 1970).
6. That is, insofar as the death rate, for the woman, is higher for childbirth than for early abortion.

Why Abortion Is Immoral

Don Marquis

Don Marquis is a professor of philosophy at the University of Kansas.

Marquis provides a sustained defense of one variation of the "conservative" position that abortion is morally unjustified. He begins by explaining why both sides of the debate engage in serious conceptual mistakes in the way they regard the fetus. Then he argues that "it is wrong to kill us" because such killing deprives us of all the value of our futures. Contrary to Warren, Marquis argues that fetuses are sufficiently like us to permit the assertion that it is just as wrong to kill them as it is to kill us, or wantonly to kill innocent animals. In all three cases, it is wrong to kill because of the deprivation of a valuable future. Marquis allows, at the end, that this argument does not make all abortion wrong since there may be overriding considerations in some cases.

The view that abortion is, with rare exceptions, seriously immoral has received little support in the recent philosophical literature. No doubt most philosophers affiliated with secular institutions of higher education believe that the anti-abortion position is either a symptom of irrational religious dogma or a conclusion generated by seriously confused philosophical argument. The purpose of this essay is to undermine this general belief. This essay sets out an argument that purports to show, as well as any argument in ethics can show, that abortion is, except possibly in rare cases, seriously immoral, that it is in the same moral category as killing an innocent adult human being.

The argument is based on a major assumption. Many of the most insightful and careful writers on the ethics of abortion—such as Joel Feinberg, Michael Tooley, Mary Anne Warren, H. Tristram Engelhardt, Jr., L. W. Sumner, John T. Noonan, Jr., and Philip Devine[1]—believe that whether or not abortion is morally permissible stands or falls on whether or not a fetus is the sort of being whose life it is seriously wrong to end. The argument of this essay will assume, but not argue, that they are correct.

Also, this essay will neglect issues of great importance to a complete ethics of abortion. Some anti-abortionists will allow that certain abortions, such as abortion before implantation or abortion when the life of a woman is threatened by a pregnancy or abortion after rape, may be morally permissible. This essay will not explore the casuistry of these hard cases. The purpose of this essay is to develop a general argument for the claim that the overwhelming majority of deliberate abortions are seriously immoral.

A sketch of standard anti-abortion and pro-choice arguments exhibits how those

Reprinted with permission of *The Journal of Philosophy* and Donald Marquis, from *The Journal of Philosophy,* April 1989. [Edited]

arguments possess certain symmetries that explain why partisans of those positions are so convinced of the correctness of their own positions, why they are not successful in convincing their opponents, and why, to others, this issue seems to be unresolvable. An analysis of the nature of this standoff suggests a strategy for surmounting it.

Consider the way a typical anti-abortionist argues. She will argue or assert that life is present from the moment of conception or that fetuses look like babies or that fetuses possess a characteristic such as a genetic code that is both necessary and sufficient for being human. Anti-abortionists seem to believe that (1) the truth of all of these claims is quite obvious, and (2) establishing any of these claims is sufficient to show that abortion is morally akin to murder.

A standard pro-choice strategy exhibits similarities. The pro-choicer will argue or assert that fetuses are not persons or that fetuses are not rational agents or that fetuses are not social beings. Pro-choicers seem to believe that (1) the truth of any of these claims is quite obvious, and (2) establishing any of these claims is sufficient to show that an abortion is not a wrongful killing.

In fact, both the pro-choice and the anti-abortion claims do seem to be true, although the "it looks like a baby" claim is more difficult to establish the earlier the pregnancy. We seem to have a standoff. How can it be resolved?

As everyone who has taken a bit of logic knows, if any of these arguments concerning abortion is a good argument, it requires not only some claim characterizing fetuses, but also some general moral principle that ties a characteristic of fetuses to having or not having the right to life or to some other moral characteristic that will generate the obligation or the lack of obligation not to end the life of a fetus. Accordingly, the arguments of the anti-abortionist and the pro-choicer need a bit of filling in to be regarded as adequate.

Note what each partisan will say. The anti-abortionist will claim that her position is supported by such generally accepted moral principles as "It is always prima facie seriously wrong to take a human life" or "It is always prima facie seriously wrong to end the life of a baby." Since these are generally accepted moral principles, her position is certainly not obviously wrong. The pro-choicer will claim that her position is supported by such plausible moral principles as "Being a person is what gives an individual intrinsic moral worth" or "It is only seriously prima facie wrong to take the life of a member of the human community." Since these are generally accepted moral principles, the pro-choice position is certainly not obviously wrong. Unfortunately, we have again arrived at a standoff.

Now, how might one deal with this standoff? The standard approach is to try to show how the moral principles of one's opponent lose their plausibility under analysis. It is easy to see how this is possible. On the one hand, the anti-abortionist will defend a moral principle concerning the wrongness of killing which tends to be broad in scope in order that even fetuses at an early stage of pregnancy will fall under it. The problem with broad principles is that they often embrace too much. In this particular instance, the principle "It is always prima facie wrong to take a human life" seems to entail that it is wrong to end the existence of a living human cancer-cell culture, on the grounds that the culture is both living and human. Therefore, it seems that the anti-abortionist's favored principle is too broad.

On the other hand, the pro-choicer wants to find a moral principle concerning the wrongness of killing which tends to be narrow in scope in order that fetuses will *not* fall under it. The problem with narrow principles is that they often do not embrace enough. Hence, the needed principles such as "It is prima facie seriously wrong to kill only persons" or "It is prima facie wrong to kill only rational agents" do not explain why it is wrong to kill infants or young children or the severely retarded or even perhaps the severely mentally ill. Therefore, we seem again to have a standoff. The anti-abortionist charges, not unreasonably, that pro-choice principles concerning killing are too narrow to be acceptable; the pro-choicer charges, not unreasonably, that anti-abortionist principles concerning killing are too broad to be acceptable.

Attempts by both sides to patch up the difficulties in their positions run into further difficulties. The anti-abortionist will try to remove the problem in her position by reformulating her principle concerning killing in terms of human beings. Now we end up with: "It is always prima facie seriously wrong to end the life of a human being." This principle has the advantage of avoiding the problem of the human cancer-cell culture counterexample. But this advantage is purchased at a high price. For although it is clear that a fetus is both human and alive, it is not at all clear that a fetus is a human *being*. There is at least something to be said for the view that something becomes a human being only after a process of development, and that therefore first trimester fetuses and perhaps all fetuses are not yet human beings. Hence, the anti-abortionist, by this move, has merely exchanged one problem for another.[2]

The pro-choicer fares no better. She may attempt to find reasons why killing infants, young children, and the severely retarded is wrong which are independent of her major principle that is supposed to explain the wrongness of taking human life, but which will not also make abortion immoral. This is no easy task. Appeals to social utility will seem satisfactory only to those who resolve not to think of the enormous difficulties with a utilitarian account of the wrongness of killing and the significant social costs of preserving the lives of the unproductive.[3] A pro-choice strategy that extends the definition of "person" to infants or even to young children seems just as arbitrary as an anti-abortion strategy that extends the definition of "human being" to fetuses. Again, we find symmetries in the two positions and we arrive at a standoff.

. . . We can start from the following unproblematic assumption concerning our own case: it is wrong to kill *us*. Why is it wrong? Some answers can be easily eliminated. It might be said that what makes killing us wrong is that a killing brutalizes the one who kills. But the brutalization consists of being inured to the performance of an act that is hideously immoral; hence, the brutalization does not explain the immorality. It might be said that what makes killing us wrong is the great loss others would experience due to our absence. Although such hubris is understandable, such an explanation does not account for the wrongness of killing hermits, or those whose lives are relatively independent and whose friends find it easy to make new friends.

A more obvious answer is better. What primarily makes killing wrong is neither its effect on the murderer nor its effect on the victim's friends and relatives, but its effect on the victim. The loss of one's life is one of the greatest losses one can suffer. The loss of one's life deprives one of all the experiences, activities, projects, and enjoyments that would otherwise have constituted one's future. Therefore, killing someone is wrong, primarily because the killing inflicts (one of) the greatest possible losses on the victim. To describe this as the loss of life can be misleading, however. The change in my biological state does not by itself make killing me wrong. The effect of the loss of my biological life is the loss to me of all those activities, projects, experiences, and enjoyments which would otherwise have constituted my future personal life. These activities, projects, experiences, and enjoyments are either valuable for their own sakes or are means to something else that is valuable for its own sake. Some parts of my future are not valued by me now, but will come to be valued by me as I grow older and as my values and capacities change. When I am killed, I am deprived both of what I now value which would have been part of my future personal life, but also what I would come to value. Therefore, when I die, I am deprived of all of the value of my future. Inflicting this loss on me is ultimately what makes killing me wrong. This being the case, it would seem that what makes killing *any* adult human being prima facie seriously wrong is the loss of his or her future.[4]

How should this rudimentary theory of the wrongness of killing be evaluated? It cannot be faulted for deriving an "ought" from an "is," for it does not. The analysis assumes that killing me (or you, reader) is prima facie seriously wrong. The point of the analysis is to establish which natural property ultimately explains the wrongness of the killing, given that it is wrong. A natural property will ultimately explain the wrongness of killing, only if (1) the explanation fits with our intuitions about the matter and (2) there is no other natural property that provides the basis for a better explanation of the wrongness of killing. This analysis rests on the intuition that what makes killing a particular human or animal wrong is what it does to that particular human or animal. What makes killing wrong is some natural effect or other of the killing. Some would deny this. For instance, a divine-command theorist in ethics would deny it. Surely this denial is, however, one of those features of divine-command theory which renders it so implausible.

The claim that what makes killing wrong is the loss of the victim's future is directly supported by two considerations. In the first place, this theory explains why we regard killing as one of the worst of crimes. Killing is especially wrong, because it deprives the victim of more than perhaps any other crime. In the second place, people with AIDS or cancer who know they are dying believe, of course, that dying is a very bad thing for them. They believe that the loss of a future to them that they would otherwise have experienced is what makes their premature death a very bad thing for them. A better theory of the wrongness of killing would require a different natural property associated with killing which better fits with the attitudes of the dying. What could it be?

The view that what makes killing wrong is the loss to the victim of the value of the victim's future gains additional support when some of its implications are examined. In the first place, it is incompatible with the view that it is wrong to kill only beings who are biologically human. It is possible that there exists a different species from another planet whose members have a future like ours. Since having a future like that is what makes killing someone wrong, this theory entails that it would be wrong to kill members of such a species. Hence, this theory is opposed to the claim that only life that is biologically human has great moral worth, a claim which many anti-abortionists have seemed to adopt. This opposition, which this theory has in common with personhood theories, seems to be a merit of the theory.

In the second place, the claim that the loss of one's future is the wrong-making feature of one's being killed entails the possibility that the futures of some actual nonhuman mammals on our own planet are sufficiently like ours that it is seriously wrong to kill them also. Whether some animals do have the same right to life as human beings depends on adding to the account of the wrongness of killing some additional account of just what it is about my future or the futures of other adult human beings which makes it wrong to kill us. No such additional account will be offered in this essay. Undoubtedly, the provision of such an account would be a very difficult matter. Undoubtedly, any such account would be quite controversial. Hence, it surely should not reflect badly on this sketch of an elementary theory of the wrongness of killing that it is indeterminate with respect to some very difficult issues regarding animal rights.

In the third place, the claim that the loss of one's future is the wrong-making feature of one's being killed does not entail, as sanctity of human life theories do, that active euthanasia is wrong. Persons who are severely and incurably ill, who face a future of pain and despair, and who wish to die will not have suffered a loss if they are killed. It is, strictly speaking, the value of a human's future which makes killing wrong in this theory. This being so, killing does not necessarily wrong some persons who are sick and dying. Of course, there may be other reasons for a prohibition of active euthanasia, but that is another matter. Sanctity-of-human-life theories seem to hold that active euthanasia is seriously wrong even in an individual case where there seems to be good reason for it independently of public policy considerations. This consequence is most implausible, and it is a plus for the claim that the loss of a future of value is what makes killing wrong that it does not share this consequence.

In the fourth place, the account of the wrongness of killing defended in this essay does straightforwardly entail that it is prima facie seriously wrong to kill children and infants, for we do presume that they have futures of value. Since we do believe that it is wrong to kill defenseless little babies, it is important that a theory of the wrongness of killing easily account for this. Personhood theories of the wrongness of killing, on the other hand, cannot straightforwardly account for the wrongness of killing infants and young children.[5] Hence, such theories must add special ad hoc accounts of the wrongness of killing the young. The plausibility of such ad hoc theories seems to be a function of how desperately one wants such theories to work. The claim that the primary wrong-making feature of a killing is the loss to the victim of the value of its future accounts for the wrongness of killing young children and infants directly; it makes the wrongness of such acts as obvious as we actually think it is. This is a further merit of this theory. Accordingly, it seems that this value of a future-like-ours theory of the wrongness of killing shares strengths of both sanctity-of-life and personhood accounts while avoiding weaknesses of both. In addition, it meshes with a central intuition concerning what makes killing wrong.

The claim that the primary wrong-making feature of a killing is the loss to the victim of the value of its future has obvious consequences for the ethics of abortion. The future of a standard fetus includes a set of experiences, projects, activities, and such which are identical with the futures of adult human beings and are identical with the futures of young children. Since the reason that is sufficient to explain why it is wrong to kill human beings after the time of birth is a reason that also applies to fetuses, it follows that abortion is prima facie seriously morally wrong.

This argument does not rely on the invalid inference that, since it is wrong to kill persons, it is wrong to kill potential persons also. The category that is morally central to this analysis is the category of having a valuable future like ours; it is not the category of personhood. The argument to the conclusion that abortion is prima facie seriously morally wrong proceeded independently of the notion of person or potential person or any equivalent. Someone may wish to start with this analysis in terms of the value of a human future, conclude that abortion is, except perhaps in rare circumstances, seriously morally wrong, infer that fetuses have the right to life, and then call fetuses "persons" as a result of their having the right to life. Clearly, in this case, the category of person is being used to state the *conclusion* of the analysis rather than to generate the *argument* of the analysis.

The structure of this anti-abortion argument can be both illuminated and defended by comparing it to what appears to be the best argument for the wrongness of the wanton infliction of pain on animals. This latter argument is based on the assumption that it is prima facie wrong to inflict pain on me (or you, reader). What is the natural property associated with the infliction of pain which makes such infliction wrong? The obvious answer seems to be that the infliction of pain causes suffering and that suffering is a misfortune. The suffering caused by the infliction of pain is what makes the wanton infliction of pain on me wrong. The wanton infliction of pain on other adult humans causes suffering. The wanton infliction of pain on animals causes suffering. Since causing suffering is what makes the wanton infliction of pain wrong and since the wanton infliction of pain on animals causes suffering, it follows that the wanton infliction of pain on animals is wrong.

This argument for the wrongness of the wanton infliction of pain on animals shares a number of structural features with the argument for the serious prima facie wrongness of abortion. Both arguments start with an obvious assumption concerning what it is wrong to do to me (or you, reader). Both then look for the characteristic or the consequence of the wrong action which makes the action wrong. Both recognize that the wrong-making feature of these immoral actions is a property of actions sometimes directed at individuals other than postnatal human beings. If the structure of the argument for the wrongness of the wanton infliction of pain on animals is sound, then the structure of the argument for the prima facie serious wrongness of abortion is also sound, for the structure of the two arguments is the same. The structure common to both is the key to the explanation of how the wrongness of abortion can be demonstrated without recourse to the category of person. In neither argument is that category crucial.

This defense of an argument for the wrongness of abortion in terms of a structurally similar argument for the wrongness of the wanton infliction of pain on animals succeeds only if the account regarding animals is the correct account. Is it? In the first place, it seems plausible. In the second place, its major competition is Kant's account. Kant believed that we do not have direct duties to animals at all, because they are not persons. Hence, Kant had to explain and justify the wrongness of inflicting pain on animals on the grounds that "he who is hard in his dealings with animals becomes hard also in his dealing with men."[6] The problem with Kant's account is that there seems to be no reason for accepting this latter claim unless Kant's account is rejected. If the alternative to Kant's account is accepted, then it is easy to understand why someone who is indifferent to inflicting pain on animals is also indifferent to inflicting pain on humans, for one is indifferent to what makes inflicting pain wrong in both cases. But, if Kant's account is accepted, there is no intelligible reason why one who is hard in his dealings with animals (or crabgrass or stones) should also be hard in his dealings with men. After all, men are persons: animals are no more persons than crabgrass or stones. Persons are Kant's crucial moral category. Why, in short, should a Kantian accept the basic claim in Kant's argument?

Hence, Kant's argument for the wrongness of inflicting pain on animals rests on a claim that, in a world of Kantian moral agents, is demonstrably false. Therefore, the alternative analysis, being more plausible anyway, should be accepted. Since this alternative analysis has the same structure as the anti-abortion argument being defended here, we have further support for the argument for the immorality of abortion being defended in this essay.

Of course, this value of a future-like-ours argument, if sound, shows only that abortion is prima facie wrong, not that it is wrong in any and all circumstances. Since the loss of the future to a standard fetus, if killed, is, however, at least as great a loss as the loss of the future to a standard adult human being who is killed, abortion, like ordinary killing, could be justified only by the most compelling reasons. The loss of one's life is almost the greatest misfortune that can happen to one. Presumably abortion could be justified in some circumstances, only if the loss consequent on failing to abort would be at least as great. Accordingly, morally permissible abortions will be rare indeed unless, perhaps, they occur so early in pregnancy that a fetus is not yet definitely an individual. Hence, this argument should be taken as showing that abortion is presumptively very seriously wrong, where the presumption is very strong—as strong as the presumption that killing another adult human being is wrong. . . .

The purpose of this essay has been to set out an argument for the serious presumptive wrongness of abortion subject to the assumption that the moral permissibility of abortion stands or falls on the moral status of the fetus. Since a fetus possesses a property, the possession of which in adult human beings is sufficient to make killing an adult human being wrong, abortion is wrong. This way of dealing with the problem of abortion seems superior to other approaches to the ethics of abortion, because it rests on an ethics of killing which is close to self-evident, because the crucial morally relevant property clearly applies to fetuses, and because the argument avoids the usual equivocations on "human life," "human being," or "person." The argument rests neither on religious claims nor on Papal dogma. It is not subject to the objection of "speciesism." Its soundness is compatible with the moral permissibility of euthanasia and contraception. It deals with our intuitions concerning young children.

Finally, this analysis can be viewed as resolving a standard problem—indeed, *the* standard problem—concerning the ethics of abortion. Clearly, it is wrong to kill adult human beings. Clearly, it is not wrong to end the life of some arbitrarily chosen single human cell. Fetuses seem to be like arbitrarily chosen human cells in some respects and like adult humans in other respects. The problem of the ethics of abortion is the problem of determining the fetal property that settles this moral controversy. The thesis of this essay is that the problem of the ethics of abortion, so understood, is solvable.

NOTES

1. Feinberg, "Abortion," in *Matters of Life and Death: New Introductory Essays in Moral Philosophy,* Tom Regan, ed. (New York: Random House, 1986), pp. 256–293; Tooley, "Abortion and Infanticide," *Philosophy and Public Affairs,* II, 1 (1972):37–65, Tooley, *Abortion and Infanticide* (New York: Oxford, 1984); Warren, "On the Moral and Legal Status of Abortion," *The Monist,* I. VII, 1 (1973): 43–61; Engelhardt, "The Ontology of Abortion,"

Ethics, I.XXXIV, 3 (1974):217–234; Sumner, *Abortion and Moral Theory* (Princeton: University Press, 1981); Noonan, "An Almost Absolute Value in History," in *The Morality of Abortion: Legal and Historical Perspectives,* Noonan, ed. (Cambridge: Harvard, 1970); and Devine, *The Ethics of Homicide* (Ithaca: Cornell, 1978).

2. For interesting discussions of this issue, see Warren Quinn, "Abortion: Identity and Loss," *Philosophy and Public Affairs,* XIII, 1 (1984): 24–54; and Lawrence C. Becker, "Human Being: The Boundaries of the Concept," *Philosophy and Public Affairs,* IV, 4 (1975): 334–359.
3. For example, see my "Ethics and The Elderly: Some Problems," in Stuart Spicker, Kathleen Woodward, and David Van Tassel, eds., *Aging and the Elderly: Humanistic Perspectives in Gerontology* (Atlantic Highlands, NJ: Humanities, 1978), pp. 341–355.
4. I have been most influenced on this matter by Jonathan Glover, *Causing Death and Saving Lives* (New York: Penguin, 1977), ch. 3; and Robert Young. "What Is So Wrong with Killing People?" *Philosophy,* 1. IV, 210 (1979):515–528.
5. Feinberg, Tooley, Warren, and Engelhardt have all dealt with this problem.
6. "Duties to Animals and Spirits," in *Lectures on Ethics,* Louis Infeld, trans. (New York: Harper, 1963), p. 239.

As If There Were Fetuses without Women: A Remedial Essay

Mary B. Mahowald

Mary Mahowald is a professor of medical ethics at the University of Chicago. She is the author of An Idealistic Pragmatism *(1972) and* Women and Children in Health Care *(1992). She is the editor of* Philosophy of Woman *(1978 and 1983).*

Mahowald enters the debate by pointing out that one needs to realize that the fetus is not an independent entity in its own right. Focusing on the case of fetal tissue transplantation, Mahowald provides a moderate view of the abortion controversy. She argues that abortion involves a "tragic choice" which is made worse when it is realized that aborted fetuses can provide valuable tissues to cure otherwise incurable diseases that afflict millions of adults. Mahowald is sympathetic to the use of fetal tissue for these purposes but worries that women may be exploited concerning their tragic choices. She argues that we need to proceed cautiously so as not to induce women to abort who would otherwise choose not to.

INTRODUCTION

As with abortion, most of the moral controversy regarding fetal tissue transplantation focuses on fetuses rather than pregnant women. In both of these related issues, that focus needs to be corrected so as to avoid the fallacy of abstraction, that is, consideration of an object as if it exists without a context. For example, "pro-life" arguments are generally based on the claim that the fetus is a person, and "pro-choice" arguments are generally based on the claim that the fetus is not a person.[1] Assuming the validity of arguments on both sides, the truth status of their conclusions depends on whether the criteria for personhood have been met by the fetus. Despite the fact that fetuses do not exist apart from women, who are inevitably affected by decisions about fetuses, women are ignored by either side so long as fetuses are the pivotal focus of the argument.

With regard to fetal tissue transplantation, women are ignored to the extent that arguments supporting and opposing it are linked with abortion as the means through which the tissue is made available. Women are also ignored where the focus is solely on commercialization of fetal tissue, the experimental status of the technique, or the needs of potential recipients. Interestingly, the important parallels between this issue and others

Mary B. Mahowald, "As If There Were Fetuses Without Women," in *Reproduction, Ethics, and the Law,* edited by Joan Callahan (Bloomington, IN: Indiana University Press, 1993). Reprinted with permission of Indiana University Press and the author. [Edited]

that principally and undeniably affect women (such as contract motherhood, egg provision, and prostitution) is that women have been neglected, and in some cases, flatly ignored.

In this paper, I want to redress the omission that prevails by reviewing the issue of fetal tissue transplantation with a focus that explicitly includes women as necessary participants in the process. In doing so, I will compare and contrast this with other issues that particularly affect women, and examine different frameworks for ethical assessment of fetal tissue transplantation. First, however, I want to say why it is wrong to focus on fetuses apart from their relationship to women.

FETUSES AS SUCH

The term "fetus" is defined in dictionaries and medical texts as "the unborn young of an animal while still in the uterus."[2] Fortunately or unfortunately, medical technology has not yet produced an artificial uterus, and it may be biologically impossible to do so. To speak of the uterus without acknowledgment that it is within a woman is thus another example of prescinding from necessary context. According to *Stedman's Medical Dictionary,* the human fetus "represents the product of conception from the end of the eighth week to the moment of birth."[3] Human birth is understood to mean the emergence of a fetus from a woman's body. *Stedman's* defines the human embryo as "the developing organism from conception until approximately the end of the second month."[4] Since the advent of *in vitro* fertilization techniques, development of a conceptus can be initiated and sustained for several days apart from a woman's body. By definition, nonviable fetuses cannot be so sustained. No matter how early the gestation, a viable fetus removed from a woman's body is no longer a fetus but a newborn. If a nonviable fetus is removed from a woman's body, it is an abortus. In other words, no fetus as such exists apart from a woman's body.

Two major (overlapping) feminist criticisms of traditional ethics are exemplified in our insistence that fetuses not be considered as if they were not present in women. First is the objection that traditional ethics calls for a deductive process through which universal principles are applied to cases.[5] Starting from different principles, whether these are *a priori* or *a posteriori* in their derivation, the process (if conducted correctly) leads inexorably to answers about what should be done in specific situations. Feminists argue that this type of deductive analysis cannot adequately attend to the complexity and uniqueness of real cases and issues. To rectify the inadequacy, attention to context is essential.[6]

Second is the objection that much of traditional ethics emphasizes the rights of individuals, neglecting the realm of relationships.[7] In fact, through its assumption that impartiality is a requirement of ethically justifiable judgments, traditional ethics eschews considerations based on particular relationships such as occur between pregnant women and their fetuses. Many of the arguments in which abortion is supported or opposed solely on grounds of the moral status of the fetus exemplify this. In contrast, feminists insist on the moral relevance of relationships, whether these are based on choice, chance, genetics, or affection.[8] The ethics of care elaborated by Carol Gilligan and Nel Noddings provide frameworks for understanding the essential role that relationships play in moral decision making.[9]

When it is consistently recognized that fetuses exist only in relationship to women who are inevitably affected by decisions regarding them, the above concerns are addressed. Inattention to this ongoing relationship is unscientific because it neglects an element of analysis that affects the validity of scientific interpretation. It is unethical because it ignores the interest and preferences of pregnant women, which may be at odds with the interests of the fetus.

USE OF FETAL TISSUE IN TRANSPLANTATION

An accurate understanding of reality can only be attained through analysis of the complexity of context. With regard to fetal tissue transplantation, the analysis involves at least the following variables: (1) the empirical status of fetuses or abortuses used for grafts, (2) different purposes and sites of tissue retrieval or implantation, (3) therapeutic potential for the recipient, (4) the means through which fetuses are made available for transplantation, and (5) possible motives, "donors," and recipients of fetal tissue.[10]

Regarding (1), human fetuses or abortuses used for tissue grafts may be living or dead. Living fetuses or abortuses may be viable, nonviable or possibly viable, and they may be sentient, nonsentient or possibly sentient, depending in part on the duration of gestation.[11] Viability is particularly relevant because it implies that others in addition to the pregnant woman can maintain the fetus *ex utero* if it is to be delivered or aborted. Sentience is relevant because the *prima facie* obligation to avoid inflicting pain on others applies to fetuses regardless of whether they are persons. While that obligation does not imply that killing is always wrong, it does imply that pain relief should be attempted for all sentient, or even possibly sentient, individuals.

Regarding (2), the procedure may be undertaken solely for research purposes, as experimental treatment, or (if and when the procedure becomes standard therapy) solely as therapy for recipients. Ordinarily, therapeutic reasons are more compelling than research reasons for medical procedures. Thus governmental and institutional regulations are more strict for research protocols than for therapeutic protocols.[12] Tissue may be retrieved from the brain or from other parts of a fetus, and implanted directly into a recipient's brain or into other regions of a recipient's body. Brain grafts are generally more problematic than nonbrain grafts because the brain is usually seen as, and may in fact be, the source of a person's identity as well as cognitive function. Nonetheless, the small amount and immaturity of tissue used in transplants serve to minimize this concern.

Regarding (3), non-neural fetal tissue has been transplanted for many years to treat diseases such as DeGeorge's syndrome and diabetes mellitus, without creating public controversy.[13] The prospects that have evoked public debate involve use of neural tissue for treatment of severe and previously incurable neurological disorders. Among the neurological conditions that are potentially treatable are Alzheimer's disease, Parkinson's disease, amyotrophic lateral sclerosis (Lou Gehrig's disease), Huntington's disease, multiple sclerosis, spinal cord injury, epilepsy, and stroke.[14] The research is most advanced in treatment of Parkinson's disease, but only a few Parkinson's patients in the United States have thus far been treated. One case of apparent success in treatment of Hurler's syndrome (through fetus to fetus transplant) has also been reported.[15] While preliminary results are promising, there are far too little data as yet to generalize about the treatment's effectiveness.

Regarding (4), abortion is the means through which human fetal tissue becomes available for transplantation. Abortions may be spontaneous or induced, and induced abortions may be performed for medical or non-medical reasons. Medical reasons for induced abortion include those based on the pregnant woman's health, those based on fetal anomaly, or both. While use of tissue obtained from spontaneous abortions may be less morally controversial than use of tissue obtained from induced abortions, the tissue from spontaneously aborted fetuses is unlikely to be normal or suitable for transplantation.[16] Because of that probability, it may be argued that use of tissue from spontaneously aborted fetuses constitutes undue risk to the recipient. Nonetheless, the first reported human use of fetal neural tissue for treatment of Parkinson's patients involved tissue retrieved from a spontaneously aborted fetus. This report has evoked criticism from researchers involved in neurografting.[17]

Regarding (5), fetal tissue may be "donated" for altruistic reasons, self-interested reasons, or both. Ordinarily, the recipient is unrelated and unknown to the pregnant woman. Anonymity has been proposed by at least two panels reviewing the issue as a requirement for donor status.[18] However, an ethic that emphasizes relationships supports a decision to donate the tissue on the part of someone such as a friend or spouse who is both known and related to the recipient. A care ethic may also support a decision to become pregnant in order to provide the tissue to someone with whom one has a special relationship.

Further, a pregnant woman might herself be the recipient, and could deliberately become pregnant in order to provide the fetal tissue that might lead to her own cure. There is one published report of a woman with severe aplastic anemia who was transplanted with the liver of her own fetus after an elective abortion.[19] Although the details of the case are sketchy, there are two reasons why the pregnancy was probably not initiated with the intention of providing the fetal tissue. First, pregnancy is a serious risk to women with this disease, and second, the fetus would not necessarily be an appropriate tissue match for the woman. Nonetheless, a woman's right to self-preservation supports such an attempt to provide the tissue for her own treatment.

From a feminist perspective, all of the above variables are morally relevant to determination of whether fetal tissue transplantation is justified in specific cases. Particularly important is the means through which fetal tissue is obtained, namely, abortion. In order to insure respect for women's autonomy, decisions to terminate pregnancies must be separable from decisions to provide fetal tissue for transplantation. (Note that I have used the word "separable" rather than "separate.") As we will see in the next section, however, the possibility of separating the two has been disputed.

FETAL TISSUE TRANSPLANTATION AND ABORTION

Although the connection between grafts of human fetal tissue and abortion might have triggered public controversy decades ago, this did not occur until reports circulated early in 1987 about the prospect of using the tissue for treatment of neurological disorders.[20] Apparent reasons for the shift include the fact that abortion was not the volatile issue that it is today when fetal tissue was first used for research or therapeutic purposes. Another reason is that the type of diseases that the tissue may now be used to treat afflict literally millions of people who are severely debilitated with otherwise incurable diseases. There seems to be little doubt that political interests have been at work in establishing the moratorium on government funding for research projects involving use of fetal tissue obtained from abortions. Legislative efforts to overturn the moratorium have thus far failed.[21]

The problematic connection between fetal tissue transplantation and abortion was first noted by a group who reviewed the issue in Cleveland in 1986. In collaboration with neuroscientist Jerry Silver, I had organized the meeting in order to facilitate informed public debate. In March 1987, a consensus statement of our group appeared in *Science*.[22] We maintained that the procedure held "the promise of great benefit to victims of serious neurological disorders." Despite the legality of abortion, fetal tissue transplantation "was acknowledged to be ethically controversial because of its association with abortion." In light of that controversy, we proposed "separation between decisions related to the acquisition of tissue and decisions regarding the transplantation of tissue into a recipient." Two years later a panel of experts convened by the National Institutes of Health (NIH), several of whom had signed the earlier consensus statement, offered a similar recommendation.[23]

Feminist support for distinguishing between decisions about abortion and decisions about fetal tissue transplantation is mainly based on concerns about possibilities for exploiting women or pressuring them to undergo abortions, or to delay or modify abortion procedures in order to provide fetal tissue to prospective recipients. As yet, it has not been necessary to delay or modify abortion procedures for treatment by means of fetal tissue grafts. While feminists generally support the right of women to terminate pregnancies, most see abortion as a "forced" and tragic option.[24] It is regrettable that a woman must choose between continuation and termination of her pregnancy because both alternatives involve burdens or harms. Accordingly, we would not like to see the option of providing fetal tissue for transplantation precipitate an increase in abortions. Ironically, this concern coincides with one of the concerns mentioned in minority reports of the NIH Human Fetal Tissue Transplantation Research panel (hereafter, NIH panel). Several members of the panel argued against government support for the procedure on grounds that it would constitute an inducement to abortion, at least for pregnant women who had not yet decided whether to terminate their pregnancies.[25] There are no data supporting this claim.

A further concern of a minority of the NIH panel was that participation in fetal tissue transplantation constitutes complicity in, and legitimation of, abortion. According to James Bopp and James Burtchaell,

> Whatever the researcher's intentions may be, by entering into an institutionalized partnership with the abortion industry as a supplier of preference, he or she becomes complicit, though after the fact, with the abortions that have expropriated the tissue for his or her purposes.[26]

They thus maintain that those who use fetal tissue from elective abortions ally themselves with the "evil" that abortion represents.

Bopp and Burtchaell further claim that legitimation occurs when pregnant women considering abortion construe the possibility of benefiting someone by donating fetal tissue a positive endorsement of abortion. The abortion is then seen as a less tragic choice than it would otherwise be, and in some circumstances it might even be seen as virtuous. Legitimation would occur on a social level if the good of successful treatment through fetal tissue transplantation became so compelling that the means of achieving the success were never critically assessed. The end would then have justified the means, at least as perceived by those who pursue the end without scrutinizing the end in its own right.

The legitimation argument illustrates more general concerns about slippery slope reasoning. Questions such as the following are then raised: if we now approve use of fetal tissue for transplants under restrictive conditions, are we not likely in time to relax the conditions if the therapy proves highly successful or if the restrictive conditions limit its usefulness? Most people agree that some restrictions are necessary to avoid abuses that could accompany use of the technology; they disagree about where to place wedges along the slippery slope.[27]

Some have proposed less restrictive guidelines than those recommended by the NIH panel, particularly with regard to commercialization. For example, Lori Andrews argues that a woman should be allowed to sell the tissue of a fetus she has agreed to abort. Feminists, she maintains, are inconsistent with their commitment to promote women's right to control their own bodies if they oppose commercial surrogacy.[28] Most feminists, however, oppose both contract motherhood and commerce in fetal tissue because of the possibility they present for exploiting women. Unlike Andrews, we thus place greater emphasis on social equality than on individual liberty. Social equality is seen as a necessary condition for authentic choice. Until and unless gender equality prevails, the liberty of individual women is inevitably curtailed.

Different views regarding abortion also give rise to different views regarding the consent necessary for fetal tissue transplantation. Those who are morally opposed to elective abortion generally deny that women who choose abortion have a right to donate fetal tissue.[29] Such women, they allege, have forfeited that right even as parents may forfeit their right to consent for their child if they abuse or abandon the child. On the other side of the issue are those who stress the importance of the pregnant woman's consent to use of fetal tissue because she has the right to abortion and because the tissue belongs to her.[30] Among those who consider abortion a separable issue from fetal tissue transplantation, some insist that the pregnant woman's consent is necessary because the timing and procedure for abortion may be altered in order to maximize the chance for a successful graft.[31] In other words, if the pregnant woman may herself be affected, her consent to use fetal tissue is morally indispensable.

On therapeutic grounds alone, a comparison of the potential advantages of using fetal tissue from electively aborted fetuses with the potential and actual disadvantages of treatment through other means provides a strong case for use of fetal tissue from induced abortions. Many of the diseases that are potentially curable with fetal tissue grafts are curable by no other known means. However, therapeutic efficacy alone doesn't constitute moral justification. This returns us, then, to the question of whether the question of induced abortion is morally separable from the question of fetal tissue transplantation. The issue calls for reexamination of the traditional moral dilemma involving the relationship between means and ends. Does the end justify the means in transplantation of fetal tissue for cure of otherwise incurable disorders?

A simplistic version of utilitarianism supports an affirmative answer to the question. In other words, the tremendous good that might be accomplished through the new technique outweighs the harm that might be done through induced abortion. However, if endorsement of the procedure led to widespread increase in induced abortions and to exploitation of women, such undesirable consequences might outweigh the potential benefit of the technique. So, even if ends can justify means, it is not clear that the end justifies the means in this case. Whether or not the overall consequences of treating debilitating disorders through fetal tissue transplantation will generally constitute a preponderance of harms over benefits is an empirical issue for which more data is needed to support a credible utilitarian position.

From a deontological point of view, a good end does not justify means that are otherwise morally unacceptable, but this does not imply that fetal tissue transplantation is morally unjustified. The individual who knowingly and freely pursues a specific end also knowingly and freely chooses the means to its fulfillment. Intention is thus crucial to the moral relevance of the relationship. If a woman were to deliberately become pregnant, choose abortion or persuade another to do so solely for the sake of fetal tissue transplantation, she would then be responsible for both means and end because she would be intending both. As we already noted, the motive of the decision may be altruistic, self-interested, or both. Although worthy motives are morally relevant, they do not alter the fact that the intention in such cases applies to both ends and means.

In other situations involving fetal tissue transplantation, the individual who intends to use the tissue need not even be aware of the abortion through which the tissue becomes available. Presumably, she does intend the retrieval procedure. However, just as a transplant surgeon may retrieve essential organs from the brain-dead victim of a drunk-driving accident without any implication that she endorses the behavior that led to the availability of the organs, so may a neurosurgeon who is totally opposed to abortion transplant neural tissue from an electively aborted fetus into a severely impaired patient, without thereby compromising her moral convictions. In fact, one may argue that a truly pro-life position favors the saving or prolonging of life that the transplantation intends, while acknowledging the negation of life that abortion implies. When the abortion decision has already been made by others, a decision not to transplant seems less in keeping with a position that is genuinely pro-life than its opposite. One opponent of abortion found support for fetal tissue transplants in the biblical account of creation:

> God formed one human being from the tissue of another. Not only does God approve of this [transplantation], he himself performed the first one.[32]

Even on religious grounds, then, fetal tissue grafts may be interpreted as affirmation of another's life. . . .

CONCLUSION

Like abortion, and probably because of its association with abortion, the issue of fetal tissue transplantation has become a political quagmire. Ironically, both feminists and those opposed to elective abortion are concerned about its association with abortion because for the former it represents possible pressures on women to initiate or terminate pregnancies, and for the latter it expresses complicity in, and legitimation of, abortion. From a feminist standpoint, there is strong support for keeping the two issues separable, but not necessarily separate. "Separable" allows for the possibility that individual women may choose to connect their abortions with the provision of fetal tissue. If the issues are "separate," that connection is precluded.

Because fetuses do not exist apart from women, fetal tissue transplantation raises concerns that may be seen in other troublesome issues that centrally affect women: contract motherhood, egg provision, and prostitution. Examination of the similarities and dissimilarities among these issues facilitates a better grasp of problematic aspects of the involvement of women in fetal tissue transplantation. If abortion decisions are separable from decisions about use of fetal tissue, the problematic aspects are reduced.

Of the frameworks that have been proposed for moral assessment of fetal tissue transplantation, the use of fetal remains from abortions is more like the use of discarded tissue than use of tissue from research subjects or from cadaver donors. Whether the abortion through which fetal tissue becomes available is spontaneous or induced, the tissue used for grafts is discarded from the body of the pregnant woman. However, even the analogy with use of discarded tissue misses the uniqueness and complexity of the relationship between pregnant women and fetuses. The uniqueness and complexity of that relationship call for explicit attention to the fact that human fetuses do not exist without women. Good science and good ethics can do no less.

NOTES

1. My use of the terms "pro-life" and "pro-choice" accords with popular usage. In another article I have noted that this usage is not fully affirmative of life and choice, respectively. See my "Abortion and Equality," in Sidney Callahan and Daniel Callahan, *Abortion* (New York: Plenum Press, 1984), 179–180. One notable exception to the tendency to base "pro-choice" arguments on the status of the fetus is Judith Jarvis Thomson's "A Defense of Abortion," in *Philosophy and Public Affairs* 1, 1 (1971), 47–66. Thomson defends a woman's right to abortion *even* if the fetus is a person.
2. E.g., see *Webster's New World Dictionary,* 2nd College ed. (New York: Simon & Schuster, 1982), 517; also, see *Butterworth's Medical Dictionary,* 2nd ed. (Boston: Butterworth Publishers, Inc., 1978), 654.
3. *Stedman's Medical Dictionary,* 23rd ed. (Baltimore: Williams and Wilkins, 1976), 516. This calculation of the duration of gestation is based on the first day of the last menstrual period rather than fertilization. If duration of gestation is calculated from fertilization, the fetal stage of development commences at six weeks. See James Knight and Joan Callahan, *Preventing Birth* (Salt Lake City: University of Utah Press, 1989), 205.
4. *Stedman's,* 453. However, Knight and Callahan note that the term "embryo" refers to the developing human organism between weeks 2 and 6 of gestation (205). Implantation in the uterus occurs about two weeks after fertilization. Between fertilization and implantation, the conceptus may be referred to as a "pre-implantation embryo." The term "pre-embryo" is sometimes used by in vitro fertilization specialists to refer to the conceptus before implantation. In popular usage, however, the term "embryo" is often used to characterize the conceptus from fertilization until fetal stage.
5. Susan Sherwin develops this criticism on the part of medical ethics as well as feminist ethics. See her "Feminist and Medical Ethics: Two Different Approaches to Contextual Ethics," *Hypatia* 4, 2 (Summer 1989): 57–72.
6. Marilyn Friedman, "Care and Context in Moral Reasoning," *Women and Moral Theory,* ed. by Eva F. Kittay and Diana T. Meyers (Totowa, New Jersey: Rowman and Littlefield, 1987), 190–204.
7. See Friedman; also see Christine Sommers, "Filial Morality," in Kittay and Meyers, 69–84.
8. Some feminists argue that the genetic tie is hardly relevant in defining parental relationships. See, e.g., Barbara Katz Rothman, *Recreating Motherhood* (New York: W.W. Norton and Company, 1989), 37–40. In some cases, however, the law insists on the significance of the genetic tie. For example, known (genetic) fathers are legally responsible for support of their children. It is well known that statutes requiring such support are only occasionally enforced.
9. Carol Gilligan, *In a Different Voice* (Cambridge: Harvard University Press, 1982), and Nel Noddings, *Caring* (Berkeley: University of California Press, 1984).
10. I have discussed these variables at greater length in "Neural Fetal Tissue Transplantation—Should We Do What We Can Do?" *Neurologic Clinics* 7, 4 (November 1989): 745–753.
11. Technically, a viable or even a nonviable (living) "abortus" is a newborn. What is relevant here, however, is not that technical difference but the moral significance of viability and sentience for any developing organism.
12. Although research with human subjects, including fetuses, must be reviewed by an institutional review board, no such review is necessary for established therapies.
13. Dorothy E. Vawter, Warren Kearney, and Karen G. Gervais *et al., The Use of Human Fetal Tissue: Scientific, Ethical and Policy Concerns* (Minneapolis: University of Minnesota, January 1990), 45–67, 2128–2129.
14. Cf. U.S. Congress, Office of Technology Assessment, *Neural Grafting: Repairing the Brain and Spinal Cord,* OTA-BA-462 (Washington, D.C.: U.S. Government Printing Office, September 1990), 93–107.
15. Barbara J. Culliton, "Needed: Fetal Tissue Research," *Nature* 355 (January 23, 1992): 295.
16. Vawter *et al.,* 136–138.
17. Vawter *et al.,* 109, 138.

18. These were the *Forum on Transplantation of Neural Tissue from Fetuses,* convened by the Case Western Reserve University School of Medicine, Cleveland, December 4–5, 1986, and the National Institutes of Health *Human Fetal Tissue Transplantation Research Panel,* which met in Washington, D.C. late in 1988.
19. Cited in Vawter *et al.*, 42 from E. Kelemen, "Recovery from Chronic Idiopathic Bone Marrow Aplasia of a Young Mother after Intravenous Injection of Unprocessed Cells from the Liver (and Yolk Sac) of Her 22 m. CR-length Embryo. A Preliminary Report," *Scandinavian Journal of Haemotology* 10 (1973): 304–308.
20. The first of these was a letter in *Science* signed by Mary B. Mahowald, Judith Areen, Barry J. Hoffer, Albert R. Jonsen, Patricia King, Jerry Silver, John R. Sladek, Jr., and LeRoy Walters, "Transplantation of Neural Tissue from Fetuses," *Science* 235 (Mar. 13, 1987): 1307–1308.
21. Culliton, 295. As a result, researchers in the United States have only been able to pursue this line of research through use of private funds, in states (such as Colorado and Connecticut) where laws permit use of tissue from electively aborted fetuses.
22. Mahowald *et al.*, Science, 1308–1309.
23. Consultants to the Advisory Committee to the Director, National Institutes of Health, *Report of the Human Fetal Tissue Transplantation Research Panel* (hereafter NIH Report), Vol. II (December 1988), A2.
24. It is "forced" in the sense that William James delineates as one of the marks of a genuine option. In other words, choice is unavoidable. See "The Will to Believe," in William James, *Essays on Faith and Morals* (Cleveland: Meridian Books, 1962), 34.
25. In addition to three chairs, the NIH panel consisted of 18 members, three of whom disagreed with the majority view.
26. *Report of the Human Fetal Tissue Transplantation Research Panel* (NIH Report), Vol. I, (December 1988), 70.
27. Cf. my "Placing Wedges along the Slippery Slope," *Clinical Research* 36, 3 (1988): 220–222.
28. Cf. NIH Report I, 56, and Lori B. Andrews, "Feminism Revisited: Fallacies and Policies in the Surrogacy Debate," *Logos* 9: 81–96.
29. Cf. NIH Report I, 47–50.
30. Cf. Lori Andrews, "My Body, My Property," *Hastings Center Report* 16, 5 (October 1986): 28–38, and John Robertson, "Rights, Symbolism, and Public Policy in Fetal Tissue Transplants," *Hastings Center Report* 18, 6 (December 1988): 9–10. A key point here is whether externalization of the fetus through birth or abortion terminates or reduces the woman's claims to ownership of the tissue. Mary Ann Warren distinguishes the rights of fetuses and infants, arguing that even late term fetuses cannot have "the full and equal rights" to which newborns may be entitled. See her "The Moral Significance of Birth," *Hypatia* 4, 3 (Fall 1989), 63.
31. Cf. Mary B. Mahowald, Jerry Silver, and Robert A. Ratcheson, "The Ethical Options in Fetal Transplants," *Hastings Center Report* 17, 1 (February 1987): 13.
32. Culliton, 295. This statement was attributed to the Baptist father of a baby who had prenatally received grafted cells from an aborted fetus for treatment of Hurler's syndrome. Two older children had already died of the disease. Both parents were strongly opposed to abortion and remain so.

Selective Termination of Pregnancy and Women's Reproductive Autonomy

Christine Overall

Christine Overall is a professor of philosophy at Queen's University in Canada. She is the author of Ethics and Human Reproduction: A Feminist Analysis *(1987), and the editor of* Feminist Perspectives *(1988) and* The Future of Human Reproduction *(1989).*

Overall tackles the difficult question of abortion where a woman is carrying two or more fetuses. The case is difficult, because unlike standard abortion cases, the decision to abort is not a decision to end pregnancy but rather often a decision to enhance the likelihood of continuing a pregnancy full term. Overall also points out that the decision to abort one of the fetuses occurs as a result of a technological intervention which has made it much more likely than otherwise that multiple fetuses will form in the first place. The so-called "demand" for abortion in these cases is actually seen as a necessary effect of the artificially produced hyperfertility of certain women. Overall concludes that fetuses cannot all have a right to be carried to term by a woman.

The development of techniques for selective termination of pregnancy has added further questions to debates about women's reproductive self-determination. The procedure is performed during the first or second trimester in some instances of multiple pregnancy, either to eliminate a fetus found through prenatal diagnosis to be handicapped or at risk of a disability, or simply to reduce the number of fetuses in the uterus. More than two hundred cases of selective termination are known to have been performed around the world.[1]

Physicians and ethicists have expressed reservations about selective termination, both with respect to its moral justification and to the formation of social policy governing access to and resource allocation for this procedure. Selective termination has been viewed as invoking a right to kill a fetus rather than to control one's body, as with abortion,[2] and some commentators have recommended restricting the procedure to pregnancies of three or more[3] and even stipulated a need for national guidelines for the procedure.[4]

Many discussions appear to assume that selective termination is primarily a matter of acting against some fetus(es) on behalf of others. For example, Diana Brahams describes the issue as follows:

> Is it ethical and legally appropriate to carry out a selective reduction of pregnancy—

Reprinted with permission of *The Hastings Center Report,* May/June 1990.

> that is, to destroy one or more fetuses in order to give the remaining fetus or fetuses a better chance?[5]

However, this construction of the problem is radically incomplete, since it omits attention to the women—their bodies and their lives—who should be at the center of any discussion of selective termination. When Margaret Somerville, for example, expresses concern about "the right to kill a fetus who is competing with another for space," she neglects to mention that the "space" in question is the pregnant woman's uterus. In fact, selective termination vividly instantiates many of the central ethical and policy concerns that must be raised about the technological manipulation of women's reproductive capacities.

Evans and colleagues state that "the ethical issues [of selective termination] are the same in multiple pregnancies whether the cause is spontaneous conception or infertility treatment" (293). Such a claim is typical of many discussions in contemporary bioethics, which abstract specific moral and social problems from the cultural context that produced them. But the issue of selective termination of pregnancy demonstrates the necessity of examining the social and political environment in which issues in biomedical ethics arise.

Selective termination itself must be understood and evaluated with reference to its own particular context. The apparent need or demand for selective termination in fact is created and elaborated in response to prior technological interventions in women's reproductive processes, themselves the result of prevailing cultural interpretations of infertility.

Hence, it is essential to explore the significance of selective termination for women's reproductive autonomy. The issue acquires added urgency at this point in both Canada and the United States when access to and allocation of funding for abortion are the focus of renewed controversy. Although not precisely the same as abortion, selective termination is similar insofar as in both cases one or more fetuses are destroyed. They differ in that in abortion the pregnancy ends whereas in selective termination, ideally, the pregnancy continues with one or more fetuses still present. I will argue that, provided a permissive abortion policy is justified (that is, a policy that allows abortion until the end of the second trimester), a concern for women's reproductive autonomy precludes any general policy restricting access to selective termination of pregnancy, as well as clinical practices that discriminate on nonmedical grounds as to which women will be permitted to choose the procedure or how many fetuses they must retain.

A TECHNOLOGICAL FIX

In recent discussions of selective termination, women with multiple pregnancies are often represented as demanding the procedure—sometimes by threatening to abort the entire pregnancy if they are not allowed selective termination.[6]

The assumption that individual women "demand" selective termination of pregnancy places all moral responsibility for the procedure on the women themselves. However, neither the multiple pregnancies nor the "demands" for selective termination originated *ex nihilo*. An examination of their sources suggests both that moral responsibility for selective termination cannot rest solely on individual women and that the "demand" for selective termination is not just a straightforward exercise of reproductive freedom.

Deliberate societal and medical responses to the perceived problem of female infertility generate much of the demand for selective termination, which is but one result of a complex system of values and beliefs concerning fertility and infertility, maternity and children. Infertility is not merely a physical condition; it is both interpreted and evaluated within cultural contexts that help to specify the appropriate beliefs about and responses to the condition of being unable to reproduce. According to the prevailing ideology of pronatalism, women must reproduce, men must acquire offspring, and both parents should be biologically related to their offspring. A climate of acquisition and commodification encourages and reinforces the notion of child as possession. Infertility is seen as a problem for which the solution must be acquiring a child of one's own, biologically related to oneself, at almost any emotional, physical, or economic costs.[7]

The recent increase in numbers of multiple pregnancies comes largely from two steps taken in the treatment of infertility. The use of fertility drugs to prod women's bodies into ovulating and producing more than one ovum at a time results in an incidence of multiple gestation ranging from 16 to 39 percent.[8] Gamete intrafallopian transfer (GIFT) using several eggs, and in vitro fertilization (IVF) with subsequent implantation of several embryos in the woman's uterus to increase the likelihood that she will become pregnant may also result in multiple gestation. As Brahams notes, "Pregnancy rate increments are about 8 percent for each pre-embryo replaced in IVF, giving expected pregnancy rates of 8, 16, 24, and 32 percent for 1, 2, 3, and 4 pre-embryos, respectively" (1409). A "try anything" mentality is fostered by the fact that prospective IVF patients are often not adequately informed about the very low clinical success rates ("failure rates" would be a more appropriate term) of the procedure.[9] A case reported by Evans and colleagues dramatically illustrates the potential effects of these treatments: One woman's reproductive history included three cesarean sections, a tubal ligation, a tuboplasty (after which she remained infertile), in vitro fertilization with subsequent implantation of four embryos, selective termination of two of the fetuses, revelation via ultrasound that one of the remaining twins had "severe oligohydramnios and no evidence of a bladder or kidneys," spontaneous miscarriage of the abnormal twin, and intrauterine death of the remaining fetus (291).

In a commentary critical of selective termination, Angela Holder quotes Oscar Wilde's dictum: "In this world, there are only two tragedies. One is not getting what one wants, and the other is getting it" (22). But this begs the question of what is meant by saying that women "want" multiple pregnancy, or "want" selective termination of pregnancy.[10] What factors led these women to take infertility drugs and/or participate in an IVF program? How do they evaluate fertility, pregnancy, motherhood, children? How do they perceive themselves as women, as potential mothers, as infertile, and where do children fit into these visions? To what degree were they adequately informed of the likelihood that they would gestate more than one fetus? Were they provided with adequate support to enable them to clarify their own reasons and goals for seeking reproductive interventions, and to provide assistance throughout the emotionally and physically demanding aspects of the treatment? Barbara Katz Rothman's appraisal of women who abort fetuses with genetic defects has more general applicability:

> They are the victims of a social system that fails to take collective responsibility for the needs of its members, and leaves individual women to make impossible choices. We are spared collective responsibility, because we individualize the problem. We make it the woman's own. She "chooses," and so we owe her nothing.[11]

Uncritical use of the claim that certain women "demand" selective termination implies that they are just selfish, unable to extend their caring to more than one or two infants, particularly if one has a disability. But this interpretation appears unjustified. In general, participants in IVF programs are extremely eager for a child. They are encouraged to be self-sacrificing, to be acquiescent in the manipulations the medical system requires their bodies to undergo. As John C. Hobbins notes, these women "have often already volunteered for innovative treatments and may be desperate to try another." The little evidence so far available suggests that if anything these women are, by comparison to their male partners, somewhat passive in regard to the making of reproductive decisions.[12] There is no evidence to suggest that most are not willing to assume the challenges of multiple pregnancy.

An additional cause of multiple pregnancy is the conflicting attitudes toward the embryo and fetus manifested in infertility research and clinical practice. One report suggests that multiple pregnancies resulting from IVF are generated not only because clinicians are driven by the motive to succeed—and implantation of large numbers of embryos appears to offer that prospect—but also because of "intimidation of medical practitioners by critics and authorities who insist that all fertilized eggs or pre-embryos be immediately returned to the patient."[13] Such "intimidation" does not, of course, excuse clinicians who may sacrifice their patients' well-being. Nevertheless, conservative beliefs in the necessity and inevitability of procreation and the sacredness and "personhood" of the embryo may contribute to the production of multiple pregnancies.

Thus, the technological "solutions" to some forms of female infertility create an additional problem of female hyperfertility—to which a further technological "solution" of selective termination is then offered. Women's so-called "demand" for selective termination of pregnancy is not a primordial expression of individual need, but a socially constructed response to prior medical interventions.

The debate over access to selective pregnancy termination exemplifies a classic no-win situation for women, in which medical technology generates a solution to a problem itself generated by medical technology—yet women are regarded as immoral for seeking that solution. While women have been, in part, victimized through the use of reproductive interventions that fail to respect and facilitate their reproductive autonomy, they are nevertheless unjustifiably held responsible for their attempts to cope with the outcomes of these interventions in the forms made available to them. From this perspective, selective termination is not so much an extension of women's reproductive choice as it is the extension of control over women's reproductive capacity—through the use of fertility drugs, GIFT, and IVF as "solutions" to infertility that often result, when successful, in multiple gestations; through the provision of a technology, selective termination, to respond to multiple gestation that may create much of the same ambivalence for women as is generated by abortion; and finally through the imposition of limitations on women's access to the procedure.

In decisions about selective termination, women are not simply feckless, selfish, and irresponsible. Nor are they mere victims of their social conditioning and the machinations of the medical and scientific establishments. But they must make their choices in the face of extensive socialization for maternity, a limited range of options, and sometimes inadequate information about outcomes. When women "demand" selective termination of pregnancy they are attempting to take action in response to a situation not of their own making, in the only way that seems available to them. Hence my argument is not that women are merely helpless victims and therefore must be permitted access to selective termination, but rather that it would be both socially irresponsible and unjust for a health care system that contributes to the generation of problematic multiple pregnancies to withhold access to a potential, if flawed, response to the situation.

SELECTIVE TERMINATION AND ABORTION

There is reason to believe that women's attitudes toward selective termination may be similar to their attitudes toward abortion. Although abortion is a solution to the problem of unwanted pregnancy, and the general availability of abortion accords women significant and essential reproductive freedom, it is often an occasion for ambivalence, and remains, as Caroline Whitbeck has pointed out, a "grim option" for most women.[14] Women who abort are, after all, undergoing a surgical invasion of their bodies, and some may also experience emotional distress. Moreover, for some women the death of the fetus is a source of grief, particularly when the pregnancy is wanted and the abortion is sought because of severe fetal disabilities.[15]

Comparable factors may contribute to women's reservations about selective termination of pregnancy. Those who resort to this procedure surely do not desire the invasion of their uterus, nor do they make it their aim to kill fetuses. In fact, unlike women who request abortions because their pregnancy is unwanted, most of those who seek selective termination are originally pregnant by choice. And as Evans and colleagues note, such pregnancies are "not only wanted but achieved at great psychological and economic cost after a lengthy struggle with infertility" (292).

For such women a procedure that risks the loss of all fetuses as selective termination does, may be especially troubling. The procedure is still experimental, and its short- and long-term outcomes are largely unknown. Richard C. Berkowitz and colleagues suggest that "[a]lthough the risks associated with selective reduction are known, the dearth of experience with the procedure to date makes it impossible to assess their likelihood" (1046). Further, in their report on four cases of selective termination, Evans and coworkers state that:

> [A]ny attempt to reduce the number of fetuses [is] experimental and [can] result in miscarriage, and . . . infection, bleeding, and other unknown risks [are] possible. If successful, the attempt could theoretically damage the remaining fetuses (290).

Note that "success" in the latter case would be seriously limited, assuming that the pregnant woman's goal is to gestate and subsequently deliver one or more healthy infants. In fact, success in this more plausible sense is fairly low.[16] As a consequence, in their study of first trimester selective termination, Berkowitz *et al.* mention the "psychological difficulty of making the decision [to undergo selective termination]," a difficulty partly resulting from "emotional bonding" with the fetuses after repeated ultrasound examinations (1046).

Thus, women undergoing selective termination, like those undergoing abortion, are choosing a grim option; they are ending the existence of one or more fetuses because the alternatives—aborting all the fetuses (and taking the risk that they will never again succeed in becoming pregnant), or attempting to maintain all the fetuses through pregnancy, delivery, and childbearing—are unacceptable, morally, medically, or practically.

THE CHALLENGES OF MULTIPLE GESTATION

Why don't women who seek selective termination simply continue their pregnancies? No matter how much it is taken for granted, the accomplishment of gestating and birthing even one child is an extraordinary event; perhaps even more praise should be given to the woman who births twins or triplets or quadruplets. Rather than setting policy limits on women who are not able or willing to gestate more than one or two fetuses, we should recognize and understand the extraordinary challenges posed by multiple pregnancies.

There are good consequentialist reasons why a woman might choose to reduce the number of fetuses she carries. For the pregnant woman, continuation of a multiple pregnancy means, Evans notes, "almost certain preterm delivery, prefaced by early and lengthy hospitalization, higher risks of pregnancy-induced hypertension, polyhydramnios, severe anemia, preeclampsia, and postpartum blood transfusions" (292).[17]

The so-called "minor discomforts" of pregnancy are increased in a multiple pregnancy, and women may suffer severe nausea and vomiting or become depressed or anxious. There is also an increased likelihood of cesarean delivery, entailing more pain and a longer recovery time after the birth.[18]

Infants born of multiple pregnancy risk "premature delivery, low infant birthweight, birth defects, and problems of infant immaturity, including physical and mental retardation."[19] Moreover, as Evans and colleagues note, there is a high likelihood that these infants "may . . . suffer a lengthy, costly process of dying in neonatal intensive care" (295). Thus a woman carrying more than one fetus also faces the possibility of becoming a mother to infants who will be seriously physically impaired or will die.

It is also important to count the social costs of bearing several children simultaneously, where the responsibilities, burdens, and lost opportunities occasioned by childrearing fall primarily if not exclusively upon the woman rather than upon her male partner (if any) or more equitably upon the society as a whole—particularly when the infants are disabled. A recent article on Canada's first set of "test-tube quintuplets" reported that the babies' mother, Mae Collier, changes diapers fifty times a day, and goes through twelve liters of milk a day and 150 jars of baby food a week. Her husband works full time outside of the home and "spends much of his spare time building the family's new house."[20]

Moreover, while North American culture is strongly pronatalist, it is simultaneously anti-child. One of the most prevalent myths of the West is that North Americans love and spoil their children. A sensitive examination—perhaps from the perspective of a child or a loving parent—of the conditions in which many children grow up puts the lie to this myth.[21] Children are among the most vulnerable victims of poverty and malnutrition. Subjected to physical and sexual abuse, educated in schools that more often aim for custody and confinement than growth and learning, exploited as opportunities for the mass marketing of useless and sometimes dangerous foods and toys, children, the weakest members of our society, are often the least protected. Children are virtually the last social group in North America for whom discrimination and segregation are routinely countenanced. In many residential areas, businesses, restaurants, hotels, and other "public" places, children are not welcome, and except in preschools and nurseries, there is usually little or no accommodation to their physical needs and capacities.

A society that is simultaneously pronatalist but anti-child and only minimally supportive of mothering is unlikely to welcome quintuplets and other multiples—except for their novelty—any more than it welcomes single children. The issue, then, is not just how many fetuses a woman can be required to gestate, but also how many children she can be required to raise, and under what sort of societal conditions.

To this argument it is no adequate rejoinder to say that such women should continue their pregnancies and then surrender some but not all of the infants for adoption by eager childless and infertile couples. It is one thing for a woman to have the choice of making this decision after careful thought and with full support throughout the pregnancy and afterward when the infants have been given up. Such a choice may be hard enough. It would be another matter, however, to advocate a policy that would restrict selective termination in such a way that gestating all the fetuses and surrendering some becomes a woman's only option.

First, the presence of each additional fetus places further demands on the woman's physical and emotional resources; gestating triplets or quadruplets is not just the same as gestating twins. Second, to compel a woman to continue to gestate fetuses she does not want for the sake of others who do is to treat the woman as a mere breeder, a biological machine for the production of new human beings. Finally, it would be callous indeed to ignore the emotional turmoil and pain of the woman who must gestate and deliver a baby only to surrender it to others. In the case of a multiple gestation an added distress would arise because of the necessity of somehow choosing which infant(s) to keep and which to give up.

REPRODUCTIVE RIGHTS

Within the existing social context, therefore, access to selective termination must be understood as an essential component of women's reproductive rights. But it is important to distinguish between the right to reproduce and the right not to reproduce. Entitlement to access to selective termination, like entitlement to access to abortion, falls within the right not to reproduce.[22]

Entitlement to choose how many fetuses to gestate, and of what sort, is in this context a limited and negative one. If women are entitled to choose to end their pregnancies altogether, then they are also entitled to choose how many fetuses and of what sort they will carry. If it is unjustified to deny a woman access to an abortion of all fetuses in her uterus, then it is also unjustified to deny her access to the termination of some of those fetuses. Furthermore, if abortion is legally permitted in cases where the fetus is seriously handicapped, it is inconsistent to refuse to permit the termination of one handicapped fetus in a multiple pregnancy.

One way of understanding abortion as an exercise of the right not to reproduce is to see it as the premature emptying of the uterus, or the deliberate termination of the fetus's occupancy of the womb. If a woman has an entitlement to an abortion, that is to the emptying of her uterus of all its occupants, then there is no ground to compel her to maintain all the occupants of her uterus if she chooses to retain only some of them. While the risks of multiple pregnancy for both the fetuses and the pregnant woman increase with the number of fetuses involved, it does not follow that restrictions on selective termination for pregnancies with smaller numbers of fetuses would be justified. Legal or medical policy cannot consistently say, "you may choose whether to be pregnant, that is, whether your uterus shall be occupied, but you may not choose how many shall occupy your uterus."

More generally, if abortion of a healthy singleton pregnancy is permitted for any reason, as a matter of the woman's choice, within the first five months or so of pregnancy, it is inconsistent to refuse to permit the termination of one or more healthy fetuses in a multiple pregnancy. To say otherwise is unjustifiably to accord the fetuses a right to occupancy of the woman's uterus. It is to say that two or more human entities, at an extremely immature stage in their development, have the right to use a human person's body. But no embryo or fetus has a right to the use of a pregnant woman's body—any more than any other human being, at whatever stage of development, has a right to use another's body.[23] The absence of that right is recognized through state-sanctioned access to abortion. Fetuses do not acquire a right, either collectively or individually, to use a woman's uterus simply because there are several of them present simultaneously. Even if a woman is willingly and happily pregnant she does not surrender her entitlement to bodily self-determination, and she does not, specifically, surrender her entitlement to determine how many human entities may occupy her uterus.

Although I defend a social policy that does not set limits on access to selective termination of pregnancy, there can be no denying that the procedure may raise serious moral problems. As some persons with disabilities have pointed out, there is a special moral significance to the termination of a fetus with a disability such as Down syndrome.[24] The use of prenatal diagnosis followed by abortion or selective termination may have eugenic overtones, when the presupposition is that we can ensure only high quality babies will be born, and that "defective" fetuses can be eliminated before birth.[25] The fetus is treated as a product for which "quality control" measures are appropriate. Moreover, as amniocentesis and chorionic villus sampling reveal the sex of offspring, there is also a possibility that selective termination of pregnancy could be used, as abortion already is, to eliminate fetuses of the "wrong" sex—in most cases, that is, those that are female.[26]

These possibilities are distressing and potentially dangerous to disabled persons and to women generally. The way to deal with these and other moral reservations about selective termination is not to prohibit the procedure or to limit access to it on such grounds as fetal disability or fetal sex choice. Instead, part of the answer is to change the conditions that promote large numbers of embryos and fetuses. For example, since as Evans and colleagues astutely note, "[m]any of the currently known instances of grand multiple pregnancies should have never happened" (296), the administration of fertility drugs to induce ovulation can be carefully monitored, and for IVF and GIFT procedures, more use can be made of the natural ovulatory cycle and of cryopreservation of embryos.[27] The number of eggs implanted through GIFT and the number of embryos implanted after IVF can be limited—not by unilateral decision of the physician, but after careful consultation with the woman about the chances of multiple pregnancy and her attitudes toward it.[28] To that end, there is a need for further research on predicting the likelihood of multiple pregnancy.[29] And, given the experimental nature of selective termination, genuinely informed choice should be mandatory for prospective patients, who need to know both the short- and long-term risks and outcomes of the procedure. Acquiring this information will necessitate the "long-term follow-up of parents and children . . . to assess the psychological and physical effects of fetal reduction."[30] By these means the numbers of selective terminations can be reduced, and the women who seek selective termination can be both protected and empowered.

More generally, however, we should carefully reevaluate both the pronatalist ideology and the system of treatments of infertility that constitute the context in which selective termination of pregnancy comes to seem essential. There is also a need to improve social support for parenting, and to transform the conditions that make it difficult or impossible to be the mother of triplets, quadruplets, etc. or of a baby with a severe disability. Only through the provision of committed care for children and support for women's self-determination will genuine reproductive freedom and responsibility be attained.

ACKNOWLEDGMENT

I would like to acknowledge the assistance of Monica Webster, Queen's University Health Sciences Library, in locating resource material for this paper.

NOTES

1. Marie T. Mulcahy, Brian Roberman, and S.E. Reid, "Chorion Biopsy, Cytogenetic Diagnosis, and Selective Termination in a Twin Pregnancy at Risk of Haemophilia" (letter), *The Lancet*, 13 October 1984, 866; "Selective Fetal Reduction" (review article), *The Lancet*, 1 October 1988, 773; Dorothy Lipovenko, "Infertility Technology Forces People to Make Life and Death Choices," *The Globe and Mail*, 21 January 1989, A4.
2. "Multiple Pregnancies Create Moral Dilemma," *Kingston Whig Standard*, 21 January 1989, 3.
3. Mark I. Evans *et al.*, "Selective First-Trimester Termination in Octuplet and Quadruplet Pregnancies: Clinical and Ethical Issues," *Obstetrics and Gynecology* 71:3, pt. 1 (1988), 289–296, at 293; Richard L. Berkowitz, *et al.*, "Selective Reduction of Multifetal Pregnancies in the First Trimester," *New England Journal of Medicine* 118:16 (1988), 1043. Berkowitz and colleagues regard even triplet pregnancies as constituting a "gray area" for physician and patient. However, it is not clear whether this hesitation is based on moral scruples in addition to the medical risks.
4. Lipovenko, "Infertility Technology."
5. Diana Brahams, "Assisted Reproduction and Selective Reduction of Pregnancy," *The Lancet*, 12 December 1987, 1409; cf. John C. Hobbins, "Selective Reduction—A Perinatal Necessity?," *New England Journal of Medicine* 318:16 (1988), 1063; Evans *et al.*, "Selective First-Trimester Termination," 295.
6. One television interviewer who talked to me about this issue described women as "forcing" doctors to provide the procedure! See also "Multiple Pregnancies Create Moral Dilemma"; Angela R. Holder and Mary Sue Henifin, "Selective Termination of Pregnancy," *Hastings Center Report* 18:1 (1988), 21–22.
7. Christine Overall, *Ethics and Human Reproduction: A Feminist Analysis* (Boston: Allen & Unwin, 1987), 139–56.
8. Hobbins, "Selective Reduction," 1062.
9. Gena Corea and Susan Ince, "Report of a Survey of IVF Clinics in the U.S.," in *Made to Order: The Myth of Reproductive and Genetic Progress*, Patricia Spallone and Deborah Lynn Steinberg, eds. (Oxford: Pergamon Press, 1987), 133–45.
10. Compare the ambiguity of the claim "women want it" in connection with in vitro fertilization. See Christine Crowe, "Women Want It: In Vitro Fertilization and Women's Motivations for Participation" in Spallone and Steinberg, *Made to Order*, 84–93.
11. Barbara Katz Rothman, *The Tentative Pregnancy: Prenatal Diagnosis and the Future of Motherhood* (New York: Viking, 1986), 189.
12. Judith Lorber, "In Vitro Fertilization and Gender Politics," in *Embryos, Ethics, and Women's Rights*, Elaine Hoffman Baruch, Amadeo F. D'Adamo, Jr., and Joni Seager, eds. (New York: Haworth Press, 1988), 123–26.
13. "Selective Fetal Reduction," 774.
14. Caroline Whitbeck, "The Moral Implications of Regarding Women as People: New Perspectives on Pregnancy and Personhood," in *Abortion and the Status of the Fetus*, William B. Bondeson *et al.*, eds. (Boston: Reidel, 1984), 251–52.
15. Rothman, *The Tentative Pregnancy*, 177–216. She describes abortion in the case of fetal defect as "the chosen tragedy" (180).
16. Evans *et al.* give a success rate of 50% (p. 289), while Berkowitz *et al.* give 66-2/3% (1043). Angela Holder quotes a success rate of 55% (21).
17. Cf. Berkowitz *et al.*, "Selective Reduction," 1045; and Alastair H. MacLennan, "Multiple Gestation: Clinical Characteristics and Management," in *Maternal-Fetal Medicine: Principles and Practice*, Robert K. Creasy and Robert Resnick, eds. (Philadelphia: W.B. Saunders, 2nd ed., 1989), 581–84.
18. Jose C. Scerbo, Powan Rattan, and Joan E. Drukker, "Twins and Other Multiple Gestations," in *High-Risk Pregnancy: A Team Approach*, Robert A. Knuppel and Joan E. Drukker, eds. (Philadelphia: W.B. Saunders, 1986) 347–48, 358; Martin L. Pernoll, Gerda I. Benda, and S. Gorham Babson, *Diagnosis and Management of the Fetus and Neonate at Risk: A Guide for Team Care* (St. Louis: C.V. Mosby, 5th ed., 1986), 192–93.

19. "Selective Fetal Reduction," 773.
20. Victoria Stevens, "Test-Tube Quints Celebrate First Birthday," *The Toronto Star,* 6 February 1989, A7.
21. See Letty Cottin Pogrebin, *Family Politics: Love and Power on an Intimate Frontier* (New York: McGraw-Hill, 1983), 42.
22. Overall, *Ethics and Human Reproduction,* 166–68.
23. Overall, *Ethics and Human Reproduction, 76–79.*
24. Adrienne Asch, "Reproductive Technology and Disability," in *Reproductive Laws for the 1990s,* Sherrill Cohen and Nadine Taub, eds. (Clifton, NJ: Humana Press, 1989), 69–117; Marsha Saxton, "Prenatal Screening and Discriminatory Attitudes About Disability," in *Embryos, Ethics, and Women's Rights,* 217–24.
25. Ruth Hubbard, "Eugenics: New Tools, Old Ideas," in *Embryos, Ethics, and Women's Rights,* 225–35.
26. Cf. Robyn Rowland, "Motherhood, Patriarchal Power, Alienation and the Issue of 'Choice' in Sex Preselection," in *Man-Made Women,* 74–87.
27. Hobbins, "Selective Reduction," 1063; "Selective Fetal Reduction," 773, 774.
28. Brahams, "Assisted Reproduction," 1409.
29. Ian Craft *et al.,* "Multiple Pregnancy, Selective Reduction, and Flexible Treatment" (letter), *The Lancet,* 5 November 1988, 1087.
30. "Selective Fetal Reduction," 775.

Can Late Abortion Be Ethically Justified?

Ren-Zong Qiu, Chun-Zhi Wang and Yuan Gu

Ren-Zong Qiu is the director of the Medical Ethics program, Institute of Philosophy, Academy of Social Sciences of China, Beijing, People's Republic of China.

Chun-Zhi Wang is the chief of the Unit for Medical Ethics at Capital Medical College, Beijing, People's Republic of China.

Yuan Gu is chief of the Unit for Philosophy of Science at Capital Medical College, Beijing, People's Republic of China.

Qui, Wang and Gu defend the current policy in the People's Republic of China favoring late-term abortions for those who are unmarried or who already have a child. Concerning unmarried women, the authors point out that in China there is no possibility of supporting a child on the wages one person can earn. This consideration makes even late-term abortion potentially justifiable. For women who already have one child, control of the world's largest population is in conflict with considerations of fetal survival and the woman's health. In general, these authors argue for a consequentialist approach to abortion that could, in some circumstances, justify late-term abortion.

THORNY CASES

Miss A is a 25-year-old unmarried woman working in a factory. She lived with her boyfriend and became pregnant. She was not aware of her condition in the early stage of her pregnancy, because she lacked education in reproduction. After she realized that she was pregnant, she was afraid to undergo an abortion. She used a cloth to bind her waist to hide her illegitimate pregnancy from others, and she was burdened with anxieties every day. Her pregnancy was revealed when the fetus was eight months old. Responsible men in her factory escorted her to the hospital and asked the physician to perform an abortion. The physician agreed, because the young woman did not want the child, and because she had no birth quota as an unmarried woman.[1] The physician performed the abortion using an intraamniotic injection of Huangyan Flower,[2] and a 2800 g. dead baby was expelled the next day.

Mrs. B is another story. She is a 30-year-old accountant, the wife of an army officer. She has been pregnant two times, but only gave birth once, to a girl, and was given a "One Child" certificate.[3] When she became aware of being pregnant the third time, she felt a physical difference, and she inferred that the fetus might possibly be a boy. Her husband was performing his duty outside Beijing at that time. She made every effort to

Reprinted by permission of *The Journal of Medicine and Philosophy*, 1989.

hide the truth for seven months. During this period she economized on food and clothing, and she worked very hard to save money for the penalty fine;[4] both courses of action jeopardized her health. When her husband came home to visit, he persuaded her to give up the fetus in the interests of their family and country. Mrs. B. agreed, and was escorted by her husband to the hospital to undergo an abortion. After examination, the physician found her malnourished, dropsical, Hgb 4g., heart rate 120/min., fetal heartbeat quite weak. She was given supportive treatment first, and then an intraamniotic injection of Rivanol several days later. A 1800 g. dead baby was born the next day.

The experience of Mrs. C. is somewhat different. She is a 40-year-old worker in a state-owned factory, with two daughters and one son from five pregnancies. She wanted more children. When she conceived the sixth time, she succeeded in covering the truth until seven months later, when the cadres of her factory discovered her condition. The cadres asked her to give up the fetus, but she refused, because she believed the Chinese maxim "More children, more happiness." She said she did not care if she were fined. One month later she was persuaded to undergo an abortion, but the physician refused to perform the operation. The cadres of her factory complained that if she gave birth to a fourth child, the rewards of all of the workers would be diminished, because they had broken the birth quota assigned to the factory.[5] Finally the physician was convinced, and he performed the abortion with an intraamniotic injection of Huangyan Flower. The next day a 3000 g. live baby was born, and later adopted by an infertile couple.

REASONS FOR LATE ABORTIONS

From the cases described above we know that there are two groups of pregnant women who undergo late abortion: the unmarried woman, and those who want more than one child but who are convinced at a late date to forgo the fetus.

The rate of pregnancy in unmarried women has increased in recent decades. With the wide application and free distribution of contraceptives, and the opening of the door to foreign cultures, China is undergoing its own form of the "sexual revolution." But sex education is still unavailable to young men, including knowledge on how to use contraceptives. According to one study in nine villages of Jiangbei County in the Sichuan Province, the average rate of illegitimate pregnancies was 50–82%. In one village it was as high as 90%; and in another village the rates in 1979, 1980, and 1981 were 44%, 53%, and 71% respectively (Hua, 1984). We think that the figures may not be representative, but only indicative. In a region of Shanghai city, among the pregnant women who underwent abortion, the rate of unmarried women was 8.4%; but in recent years it has been as high as 40% in some hospitals in Beijing and other cities.

In the early stages of pregnancy, these unmarried women made every effort to hide the truth from others. However, it is hardly possible for them to raise a child by themselves, for moral and economic reasons. The average income of a young woman is below 100 yuan ($27) per month. And changes in the moral environment lag behind the change in the sexual behavior of youth. In Chinese public opinion, premarital sexual relations are still considered unethical, an illegitimate pregnancy even more so. In some cities, abortion in hospitals was allowed only for married women, in an attempt to decrease or put an end to illegitimate pregnancies. As a result, however, there was an increase in the rate of late and illegal abortions which usually led to the death of both mother and fetus.

In our opinion, appropriate sex and reproductive education should be provided to young people, and there should be a change of attitude toward premarital sexual relations and illegitimate pregnancies. We believe that the attitude should be more lenient, in order to make it easier for pregnant girls to tell the truth and to have an abortion earlier and more safely, if they do not want to carry the pregnancy to term.

The case of pregnancy in a woman who already has a child is much more complicated. It is the Confucian cultural tradition which encourages the Chinese to have more children. Confucius said "Among the three vices that violate the principle of filial piety, the biggest is to be without offspring." The Chinese turned this negative warning into a positive maxim: "More children, more virtues." In the case of Mrs. B, she wanted a male child. Chinese tradition values male children more highly than females, because genealogy is continued through the male. But the desire to have more children, or a male child, often conflicts with the state policy of "one couple, one child." In Mrs. B's case, it also conflicted with the interests of her colleagues in the factory where she worked. However, Mrs. B and Mrs. C were finally persuaded to agree to undergo an abortion in the interest of their country and their colleagues. Can this be ethically justified?

CONFLICTS OF VALUES

There are conflicts of values around the ethical issue of late abortion which cannot be solved exclusively by deontological theory. The Chinese Ministry of Health has promulgated a regulation to prohibit late abortions after 28 weeks, with the purpose of protecting the health and life of the mother as well as of the fetus. But at the same time, since the beginning of the 1980s, the Chinese government has promulgated a regulation of birth control which permits a couple to have only one child. These two regulations are in conflict, but the latter is the more powerful. It is argued that this regulation ("one couple, one child") is in the maximum interest of the maximum number of people. Rewards in a factory are connected not only with one's work performance, but also with one's reproductive behavior.

If you give birth to a second child, you will be fined *and* the rewards of all of your colleagues will be deducted. This practice forces a fertile married woman to consider the consequences of her reproductive behavior for others before making a decision. Some married women, most of whom are professionals and intellectuals, do not want more than one child. A few of them do not even want to get married. Some want more than one child, but they are reluctant to be in a position to be fined, or they think they should put the interest of their country first by carrying out the birth control policy. But there are still a few women who insist on having another child. The outcome is usually that they are finally persuaded to undergo an abortion, or they give birth to the child in spite of the financial or psychological pressures from their colleagues or their employers.

In our opinion, it is difficult to say which conduct is moral or immoral. For a woman not to have any more children, for whatever reason, may be labeled praiseworthy conduct; but if a woman wants more than one child, it is not a vicious desire. "Moral" or "immoral" may be too strong a label to apply in such cases.

But value conflicts exist. In preceding years, when the technology for late abortion was underdeveloped and no third party intruded, the balance would usually incline towards rejecting late abortion in the interest of protecting the mother and the viable fetus. Now the scale is more evenly stacked. On the one side is the presumed interest of the viable fetus; on the other are the interests of a big third party: the country, the factory and colleagues, and the family. If the mother stands on the latter side, she tips the balance against the fetus. If she insists on giving birth, or if the late abortion would jeopardize the mother's life, the scale could be a match, or the interests of the fetus could even prevail.

PHYSICIAN'S DILEMMAS

In two of the three cases described above, the physician did not hesitate to perform a late abortion. In the third case the physician was persuaded to perform the abortion by cadres of the factory where the pregnant woman worked.

There is a schism between physicians, ethicists, and the public over late abortions.

The first to explicitly defend prohibiting abortions after seven months was an obstetrician, Dr. J.K. Liu, at the 2nd National Conference on Medical Ethics (*Liu*, 1983, pp. 213–218). We have asked our obstetrician friends their opinions on this issue. They always say, "I don't know what I should do." Some of them prefer not to perform late abortions except for women with particularly troubled pregnancies. Others take their responsibility to society into account first, and perform late abortions with less hesitation. The overwhelming majority of Chinese physicians are employed by state-owned hospitals; they are labeled "state cadres" and have the responsibility of carrying out state policy. But all of them are perplexed; either way they harm one side, either the mother and fetus or society. Especially thorny is the case in which the aborted fetus is alive. Although the fertility rate is increasing now in China, and infertile couples are willing to adopt such a baby, should the physician tell the truth to the mother who had expressed a desire to give up the fetus? In some cases physicians do not do so, because they are afraid that the mother might change her mind and keep the baby.

The author of *An Outline of Medical Moral Theory* claims that in some cases, because a woman was coerced into an abortion in order to keep the birth rate low, the physician was coerced to perform late abortions, thereby violating both policy and medical morality (p. 80). But the author of *Essential Medical Ethics* claims that, "when the perinatal care came into conflict with birth control and eugenics, it must be subordinated to the needs of the latter, because these are in the interest of the whole nation and the whole of mankind, as well as in accord with the greatest morality" (pp. 191–192).

A questionnaire showed that 16% of the respondents assented to performing late abortions on women with second pregnancies, in order to conform with the state policy, 7% supported respect for the woman's free will without any interference, and 77% believed the late abortion should not be performed, but that a fine should be imposed. As for the question of who should make the decision on late abortion, 32% supported the pregnant woman and her family as the primary decision makers, 32% the physician, 9% the responsible men of the unit (factory, school, institute, etc.) where the woman was working; and 27% an ethical committee (unpublished report).

When making the decision to undergo or perform a late abortion, should the responsible parties take into account the interests of the third party, or only the interest of the woman, or only the interest of the fetus?

SOCIAL GOOD

Even as a member of an individualist society, one should be concerned about the social good, although more attention might be paid to individual rights or interests. If you are a carrier of the AIDS virus, do you have the right to have sex freely and spread the disease to others? No. A socialist country operating under the guiding ideology of Marxism favors a holistic social philosophy which asserts that a society is not merely the sum of its members but a non-additive whole which is more than the sum. Every member should put the interest of society as a whole in the first position and subordinate his or her interest to that of society. The problem is, Who is the representative of society and its interests, and how is the interest of a society as a whole known? Usually, someone claims that he is the representative, and it later turns out that this is not the case. However, in China the "one couple, one child" policy has been accepted by the majority of the Chinese people as in the best interest of the society as a whole. Of course, birth control is not the only factor, but it is one of the most important factors in modernizing underdeveloped countries in Asia, Africa, and Latin America. In a sense, the success or failure of development depends on the use of birth control. Everyone, including the married couple and the physician, should take this into account.

But we should practice birth control in a more human way. We should make every effort to avoid late abortions, i.e., to use effectively the contraceptives and to perform the abortions earlier. In the case of a late abortion, voluntary consent of the mother is indispensable. The physician should determine whether the late abortion would cause any harm to the mother's health or endanger her life, and he should refuse to perform it if there is a high risk.

In preceding years the second pregnancy was treated with more leniency and flexibility than at present. If a couple in a rural area had a child who was disabled, or if they live in a rural area that has a birth rate lower than the quota, they were permitted to give birth to a second child. But this flexibility in policy has raised the birth level, and an upsurge of second births amongst China's rural families is jeopardizing the attempt to limit the population to 1.2 billion by the year 2000. The State Statistics Bureau reports that 40% of rural women have given birth to three or more children over the past several years. Compared with 1985, the number of second births last year climbed by 1.37 million people to 6.92 million, and the number of third or more births topped 2.88 million, 240.000 more than the previous year (*China's Daily*, 1987).

CONCLUSION

Our conclusion is that the late abortion can be justified ethically in China: (1) if the "one couple, one child" policy is justifiable; (2) if the couple and the physician take the social good into account; (3) if the mother expresses her voluntary consent, no matter whether the decision is made on the basis of her own original desire or after persuasion by others that is not coercive; and (4) if the late abortion will entail only a low risk to the mother's health or life.

NOTES

1. Every married woman gets a birth quota before pregnancy; also see note 5.
2. The extraction from an herb used as an effective drug to induce abortion.
3. Whoever has such a certificate enjoys favored treatment, such as additional rewards at the factory, enrollment in a kindergarten for their child, etc.
4. If you give birth to a second child, you will be fined about 1000 yuan ($270), which can be about one year's wages.
5. Every factory, school, or institute has a birth quota set by the authorities. Female workers are allowed to give birth to only a certain number per year, and the quotas are assigned to the married women on the basis of consultation with them each year.

REFERENCES

China's Daily: 1987 (July 1).

Hua, Jinma: 1984, "Sex Education Is an Urgent Need," *Popular Medicine* 12.

Liu, J.K.: 1983, in the *Proceedings of the 2nd National Conference on Medical Ethics. An Outline of Medical Moral Theory:* 1983, The Health Press, Beijing.

Essentials of Medical Ethics: 1985, Jiangxi People's Press, Beijing.

Contestation and Consensus: The Morality of Abortion in Japan

William R. LaFleur

William R. LaFleur is a professor in the Department of Japanese Studies at the University of Pennsylvania. He is the author of The Karma of Words: Buddhism and Literary Arts in Medieval Japan *(1983), and* Liquid Life: Abortion and Buddhism in Japan *(1992). He is the editor of* Dogen Studies *(1985).*

LaFleur examines the traditional Buddhist doctrine that abortion is morally justifiable. Even though abortion is considered justifiable, it is nonetheless regarded as a necessary evil and also as a necessary sorrow. Abortion is considered to be an important component in the preservation of family values in Japan as well as in keeping the population in check. Because of these two considerations, there is a consensus in Japan that abortion is morally justifiable. He contends that the controversy in Japan concerns the question of whether retribution or guilt is appropriate for those who have abortions.

. . . The scholarly community, especially in the West, has habitually by-passed or denigrated vast amounts of materials that are important to understand the history of ethical thinking in Japan. It has also led to a systematic pattern of ignoring and downplaying those times and ways in which there was real conflict and contestation in Japanese ethical and religious life. In keeping with the fact that some recent works in Japanese have paid increasing attention to the reality and energy of intellectual contestation in Japanese history,[1] I am here suggesting that we, at least for heuristic purposes, reject as flawed the common assumption that there usually was a neat division of intellectual labor in Japan. To assume that Buddhists merely plugged Confucianism into their teachings as a kind of caretaker for "the world," ethics, and the family is an assumption that tends to flatten the real shape of ethical discourse in Japan. It also reads as complementary and "harmonized" certain points that were, in fact, often fraught with conflict over both principles and practice.

ABORTION IN JAPAN: THE CONTESTATION

I believe this to be eminently true in the case of Japanese thinking about abortion. I have elsewhere narrated what I take to be the history of Japanese Buddhist thinking about abortion as a moral and religious problem.[2] Within that history I have located a phase in the early half of the nineteenth century when what I call a distinct difference between Buddhists on the one hand and

Reprinted by permission of the University of Hawaii Press, from its journal *Philosophy East and West, Vol. 40/4,* October, 1990. [Edited]

Confucians and Shinto-based Kokugaku scholars on the other took shape. I detail why it is clear that the Buddhists for the most part took the position that abortion was what we call a "necessary evil"—although their term was a "necessary sorrow." Their opponents rejected all abortion as morally and religiously wrong. A common Buddhist position, in this sense comparatively "soft" on abortion, is expressed in the tradition of memorial rituals (*kuyō*) provided in cases of abortion; it can also be known from the materials in which Buddhists were attacked on this point by their opponents.

This is not to say that Buddhists had no qualms about abortion or did not recognize a tension between its practice and the precept against taking life. It is merely to note that they were more flexible on this point than were the Confucians and proponents of late Kokugaku. The latter, especially, mixed religion and politics unabashedly; beginning in the nineteenth century a family's reproductivity was read as an index to patriotism. This became intense in the Meiji (1868–1912) period—an eloquent demonstration of Bellah's observation that in Japan "the family does not stand over against the polity but is integrated into it and to an extent penetrated by it."[3]

Therefore, the Buddhist stance at that time was charged with being a threat to national well-being and as a flagrant offense to the gods—gods that protect the nation and are happiest when people's "seeds" germinate into whole persons in great numbers. Of course, the fact that there was a political aspect to the entire discourse also helps explain why the Buddhists dared to express their "soft" stand only indirectly. In fact, the Buddhist "position" on this was articulated not so much through treatises as through ritual, surely a "safer" medium in their situation. I would, however, point out that this indirect, mixed, or muted discourse on specific moral questions had by this point already become "traditional" for Japanese Buddhists. Here was an instance where a traditional mode of expression also happened to be the only politically viable one; that it came in a muted form, however, does not mean it was not a distinct and *discernible* position. Its opponents knew it was at odds with their view and we, too, can reconstruct why that was so—and, therefore, its structure as an ethical stance on abortion.

During the later half of the nineteenth century much changed within Japan. What the government perceived as a "population stagnation" conflicted with imperial designs. Japan's growing need for human manpower, a need that was to grow with rapid industrialization and a military buildup for foreign wars, fit hand-in-glove with the antiabortion arguments advanced early in the nineteenth century by Kokugaku advocates and Confucians. This meant that a process was in place that led to the criminalization of abortion soon after the Meiji Restoration in 1868. During the latter half of the nineteenth century and the first half of the twentieth, therefore, the case against abortion, identifiable with this Shinto revival and with Confucian points of view, held sway in Japan. What I call "fecundism" became the order of the day and was associated in the public mind with "family" values.

Given the fact that in 1945 with its total defeat in World War II Japan underwent as thorough and total a crisis as can be imagined, the ban on abortion, too, began to be rethought. Whereas during the decades of rapid industrialization, militarization, colonial expansion, and war, abortion had been proscribed, after the Pacific War things were completely different. To some degree what had been the Kokugaku/Confucian opposition to abortion had been totally discredited by the events of history, most especially

Japan's own defeat in 1945. Beginning at that time—especially given the tightness of basic resources—there was a deep concern about an explosion of the population. Thus once again a more "Buddhist" view, traditionally amenable to seeing abortion as a "necessary suffering," was the view that for all practical purposes was adopted when, in 1948, the process was begun to legalize abortion once again. Although what we here call "the Buddhist view" was not articulated in terms of explicit arguments, it was implicit in Buddhism's readiness to provide "rituals of memorial" for aborted fetuses (*mizuko*), a view widely perceived as tolerating abortion. It is probably not an exaggeration to say that, at least since 1948, on this ethical question it has been the Buddhist view which, consciously or not, has been what underlies actual practice.

The point that I want to emphasize here is not the one that ethical positions merely traipse along in the wake of political needs but, in fact, a quite different one—namely, that ethical discourse in Japan has in fact been much more diverse and conflict-ridden than most commentators assume. It also interests me that, once we begin to derive our readings of ethical positions from materials that are "mixed" and do not necessarily come in a genre recognizable as "*the* ethical treatise," we can more readily reconstruct what clearly seems historically to have been a distinctly Buddhist approach to abortion in Japan, a position in actuality quite different from the total opposition—at least from the early nineteenth to the mid-twentieth centuries—to it by persons self-consciously representing Confucianism and the Neo-Shinto phase of Kokugaku. This is not to say that certain schools of Buddhists, especially those in the Pure Land tradition, have not objected both to abortion and to the *mizuko* rites. It is merely to note a trajectory of comparative tolerance of the practice.

ABORTION IN JAPAN: CONSENSUS

What are we to make of the fact that, whereas what I call Japan's conflict over abortion was most aggravated in the middle of the nineteenth century, there is relatively little debate today—when in Europe and America the debate has become strong and often acrimonious?

One might expect that, given the high rate of abortion in Japan as well as the diversity of religious positions represented there, Japan would have been the locus of protracted and spirited debates about the ethics of abortion in recent years. Such, however, has not been the case. What is impressive, at least to the Western scholar looking for such, is the fact that comparatively little has been written on this topic during the past few decades—and that what has appeared has for the most part dealt with the politics of abortion, the legalization of the contraceptive pill, and criticisms of certain entrepreneurial temples for capitalizing on the *mizuko* boom. Voices advocating the repeal of legalized abortion have, by contrast, been almost nonexistent. I think it significant that what a century ago had been strongly expressed Confucian and neo-Shintō objections to legalized abortion have today in Japan largely dissipated and disappeared.

There are groups—such as Seichō no Ie (The House of Life), a "new religion"—that vocally oppose abortion. Such groups during the early 1980s evoked strong opposition from the Women's Movement in Japan, but as far as the general public is concerned these rather small groups opposed to abortion are little more than a blip on the screen of public consciousness. Some Buddhist and Christian groups express alarm at the *number* of abortions performed, yet in Japan today there could hardly be anything that could rightly be called a real or wide public debate on this issue. Books on abortion as a public policy problem can scarcely be found. Many assume that the legalization of the pill will in time cut back the abortion rate. In fact, it is the *absence* of such a debate at the present time which, in my opinion at least, is the salient datum that deserves exploration and interpretation.

I would contend that this absence of public debate also needs to be interpreted as a sign of something *present*—namely, a fairly wide consensus on this matter. There is a consensus that abortion constitutes a painful social necessity and as such must remain legal and available, although religio-psychological mechanisms for relieving bad feelings about abortion—the *mizuko* rites, for instance—in most cases probably play a positive, therapeutic role. And, of course, this is to say that it is now what I have termed a Buddhist position on abortion which has, for all practical purposes, won the day.

A "position" is expressed not only by what is said but also by what goes unsaid. Therefore, in my view, it is significant that within the Japanese Buddhist community the discussion of abortion is now limited largely to criticisms of those temples and temple-like organizations which employ the notion of "fetal retribution" to coerce the "parents" of an aborted fetus into performing rituals that memorialize the fetus, remove its "grudges," and facilitate its rebirth or its Buddhahood. Many Buddhists find repugnant such types of manipulation of parental guilt—especially when expressed in the notion that a fetus in limbo will wreak vengeance (*tatari*) on parents who neglect to memorialize it.

But, of course, the focus here is on the morality of using this concept of retribution; the question of the morality of abortion per se is, by comparison, something that goes almost without discussion. In other words, it seems now widely accepted that the Buddhist praxis developed over centuries on this issue is itself basically a moral and viable way of handing this complex and vexing problem.

Although I cannot here recapitulate things discussed in more detail elsewhere, a very rudimentary statement of the matter is that most Japanese Buddhists have accepted abortion as a necessary sorrow but at the same time have contextualized the termination of pregnancy—and also infanticide in an earlier epoch—through Buddhist ritual. One result of my analysis has been to demonstrate that historically the belief in transmigration and rebirth effectively attenuated any sense of "finality" in abortion—thus giving the "parents" of an aborted fetus the expectation that the fetus' entry into the world had been merely postponed.

Thus parental prayers and ritual memorializations were expected to palliate guilt, create what is taken to be a continuing relationship between parents in this world and a fetus in a Buddhist "limbo," and render close to moot many of the West's protracted debates about life's inception, fetal rights, and ownership of the bodies of women. Although those Japanese Buddhists who take this position face various conceptual and ethical problems in its wake, these are rather different—and in terms of upheaval in the larger society certainly less severe—than the problems we have faced in trying to deal with abortion in the West in general and the United States in particular.[4]

This is not to say that women's rights advocates feel no need for vigilance vis-à-vis Buddhist institutions on this matter. It is merely to call attention to the fact that, even though their acknowledged concerns are political and focus on the danger of being, as women, manipulated, those feminists who have written about Buddhism and abortion have tended to focus their criticisms on those who employ the concept of "fetal retribution," and that is something which, as noted above, many Buddhists themselves are quick to condemn.[5] My sense is that many feminists in Japan find, at least in the present context, a kind of odd, unanticipated ally in the Buddhists. Those feminists who are also ideologically Marxists are troubled by this convergence, but most feminists show reluctance to refuse the Buddhist hand that seems to render indirect help to this part of their cause. Obviously the Marxist critique of religion is itself "softened" in this.

My own personal conversations with representatives of various religious constituencies in Japan leads me to conclude that, especially if the legalization of "the pill" and a wider use of contraceptive devices can effectively reduce the *number* of abortions, there will be no deep objection to the continued legalization of abortion and the tendency to keep in place those Buddhist rituals that ritually memorialize fetuses and may serve as a conscience-solace for parents. The status quo, especially if numbers can be reduced, is acceptable to a surprisingly wide spectrum of persons engaged in discussions of religious and ethical questions. To that degree at least—and in contrast to American society—there is in Japan a fairly wide public consensus on this matter.

MORAL HIGH GROUND

Sometimes on moral questions a consensus forms because the participants in a protracted debate are exhausted or the issue no longer seems so important. On other occasions, however, consensus comes into being because something tagged as a "higher" value is recognized and respected by those who had earlier been partisans of differing positions; in such instances the "higher" can begin to override the former concern to sharpen differences. If a sense of exhaustion happens to coincide with a sense of moving towards a value deemed "higher" by both sides, the potential for consensus becomes eminently realizable.

My view is that in Japan's consensus on abortion today we can observe an instance where these two motives have, in fact, coincided quite remarkably. Interest in opening the old wounds is minimal—especially given the high social cost of the years of abortion-proscription. In addition, there is a widely generalized perception that abortion, however much regretted as a source of suffering, is not only demographically necessary but even a means for protecting what are felt to be "family" values. In most basic terms it is necessary to prevent the hemorrhaging of population in a land where the density is already unusually high. More importantly, however, abortion is perceived as a mechanism whereby families can maximize the opportunities for their children by a "rational" investment of resources in the education and upbringing of a limited number of children, usually two. It would not be too much to say that in Japan the high emphasis placed upon family life is itself a factor in the current consensus in favor of keeping abortion legal and available.

Religious institutions—perhaps Buddhist ones in particular—articulate and reinforce these family values in Japan. This means that in most instances such institutions cannot be expected to move in any significant way to curtail a practice they perceive as a regrettable but necessary component in ensuring the persistence of good family life and national life. The consensus among religious groups to leave abortion legal and available will, I suspect, remain as long as it seems clear to the majority that, however unpleasant and painful abortion may be, family life in the aggregate is far better served by having it available than by criminalizing it once again. In my own conversations with Buddhist clergy in Japan on this problem I detect two concerns, but they are not, it should be noted, of sufficient weight to prompt any strong movement for a change in the rather liberalized law.

The first concern is that people not become inured to abortion and trivialize it. Many Buddhists are worried that, especially if there is no real grief and ritual, a kind of personal degradation becomes the pattern: from repeated abortions to a flippant acceptance of the practice and from there to a deterioration in a person's (read: woman's) capacity for generalized sensitivity. This consists in a "hardening," something serious because in the psychoethical vocabulary of the Japanese this is a matter of the *kokoro* or "heart." If too many people within society become persons who take abortion as simply a matter of course, then the tenor of society itself will change for the worse.

The legal and social admission of abortion as a practice is different from being psychologically and spiritually inured to it. Japanese Buddhists worry more about the latter than the former and focus their energies accordingly. Japanese Buddhists will often go on to argue that the meaningful performance of remembrance rites can, in fact, offset what is to be most feared. That is, the ritual of *mizuko kuyō*, a kind of "requiem mass" for the fetus, can, it is claimed, do much to prevent this "hardening" of the *kokoro* and dehumanization.

The second concern is for a possible nexus between the accessibility of abortion and an appreciable growth in the numbers of persons who adopt what is now called the "single" (*shingaru*) style of the larger urban centers. Within Buddhist periodicals, for instance, there can be found more and more discussions of the single life-style as a threat to family life. A decline is detected and projected: from the extended family to the nuclear family and from there to the single life-style and the one-parent "family." It is important to note that virtually every Buddhist institution is committed to the superior values of the traditional family and is itself dependent upon such a family's readiness to support temples for the performance of ancestral rites. Partially no doubt because of this, the single life-style is pinpointed as a threat to societal values in general. It is also seen as an index to the growth of a dangerous form of (Western-style) individualism, and fundamentally contrary to traditional values that are at the same time understood to be "national" values.

On the basis of things I have heard and read, it probably can be predicted that, if the single life-style were to become really widespread, the ready accessibility of abortion could eventually come under attack. To date, however, this does not seem likely. The anxiety about a nexus between "liberated sex" and a changing structure of the family has for now focused on the danger of making "the pill" readily available. If that anxiety tends to deepen, it will more likely jeopardize the legalization of the contraceptive pill rather than the availability of abortion.

In fact, "conservative" views in Japan can at times take strikingly unexpected turns—at least when judged by what would be expected if they are thought to be the equivalent of "conservative" views in American public life. For instance, one privately will often be told in Japan that the availability of abortion is in fact *protective of family values* to the degree that it makes unnecessary the birthing of unwanted children. Then, because it is assumed, first, that unwanted children are both pitiable and more prone to become problematic for society itself and, second, that family strength and well-being are maximized when it can be assumed that all persons within it are *wanted* and valued, logic seems to compel the conclusion that abortion is needed as a necessary "safety valve" to ensure familial, societal, and national strength. Buddhists go on from this to argue that, especially if the "hearts" of persons who have had abortions can be "softened" via the rituals that keep alive a sensitivity to the departed fetus as still alive in the Buddhist limbo (*sai no kawara*), the cumulative danger to society is reduced.

In Japan, surprisingly then, it seems to be the case that the most politically effective argument for legalized abortion, even though it comes down in muted forms, is based on fairly "conservative" concerns for the quality of family life. To many persons with fairly traditional religious and social views in Japan it is difficult to imagine why "conservative" Americans can be found favoring a public policy—the criminalization of abortion—that will in effect result not only in giving birth to obviously unwanted children but, beyond that, also to the psychic pain, both individual and social, that is bound to follow such a policy. In addition it is assumed in Japan that there must be some close correlations in any society among the degree to which children are wanted, such children's perceptions of being wanted and loved, the quality of the care they receive, and whether or not their subsequent behavior becomes deviant or criminal.

To criminalize abortion, thus, looks irrational and socially foolhardy. To Japanese ready to express candid views on these things, this scarcely seems to be the direction in which American public life should sensibly be moving today. Given the existing problem of large numbers of unwanted children as well as the exorbitant crime rate in America, those who push for abortion's recriminalization appear to be courting what to some Japanese looks like a kind of social suicide. To some Japanese it is even somewhat baffling why certain Americans, viewing themselves to be "conservative" in their views of the family, do not recognize that forcing others to have children they do not really want is itself a morally questionable stance.

Clearly that location called the "moral high ground" can be approached from different directions. What is interesting—and potentially instructive—in the Japanese case is that interpretations of the relationship between religion and abortion have not been forced down the either/or chutes of "rights of the unborn" or "rights of the woman." In part that is undoubtedly because the Japanese traditional concern for social order (*chitsujo*) still seems almost automatically to take immediate precedence over any public scenario of "rights" and "liberation."

ABORTION AND THE POLIS

I believe the chief value in the study of Japanese thinking about abortion may be heuristic. That is, in this way we can see a society permitting abortion while avoiding interminable debate over conflicting rights. In a sense we can see a society that, through trial and error, has learned to opt for access to abortion as a way of enhancing the quality of social life itself. Neither the rights of the individual fetus nor those of the individual woman are highlighted; instead these claims—often taken in the West as "opposite"—are both seen as driven by the ideology of individualism. There are other reasons to legitimate abortion, reasons which, it is felt, have to do with the quality of common life of the society itself. The health of the larger society is at issue.

Robert Nisbet grasped this point. As an advocate of the contemporary relevance of the position on these things held by ancient Greeks and Romans rather than by medieval Christians, Nisbet found in the Japanese case a ready instance of exactly what he had in mind. In the entry on "abortion" in his *Prejudices: A Philosophical Dictionary*, he wrote:

> In the contemporary world it would be hard to find a family system more honored and more important in its authority than that of Japan. But abortion there has for long been easily available.[6]

My own analysis has suggested that, although Nisbet did not realize how historically complicated things really had been in Japan and how painful had been the process to legalize abortion there,[7] he was entirely accurate in his grasp of the nexus between tolerance of abortion in Japan and the high valorization of family life there *today.* That is, he grasped that there is an argument for abortion based upon familial and societal values, an argument furthermore that is not bound to prioritize individuals and individual rights.

Alasdair MacIntyre, in his *Whose Justice? Which Rationality?* refers to "the unborn" in a way that suggests how he reads the history of Europe very differently from Nisbet. In depicting what he calls the emergence of the "Augustinian alternative" to Aristotelianism, MacIntyre locates the moral payoff of that alternative as making itself evident in the following way:

> The law of the *civitas Dei* requires a kind of justice to the unborn which Aristotle's proposed measures for controlling the size of the population of a *polis* deny to them.[8]

It would be difficult to find a more pithy statement of what many in the West have often held to be how Christianity gained its own moral high ground, a position assumed to be superior even to that of Aristotle.

The problem, of course, is that the trajectory right into individualism seems to have been prepared at the same time. Augustine, says MacIntyre, had found a way to require "a kind of justice to the unborn" but he neglects to point out that in Augustine the importance of the *polis* was at the same time being drastically reduced. In his *De nuptiis et concupiscentia,* the Bishop Hippo, having declared that childbearing is "the end and aim of marriage," goes on to judge that, unless they have the intent of being fecund, a man and woman, however legally married, are really only having sinful sex. Without the aim of propagation a woman is just her "husband's harlot" and the man is his own "wife's adulterer."[9] Ultimately marriage is something for the Church to define, not the state.

Once such views were injected into the consciousness of the West—and later defined in such a way that something uniquely "Western" and morally "higher" was implied in their observance—it became extremely difficult to go back and recapture Aristotle's important and still valid point about eugenics and the quality of life in the polis. That point had been compromised, of course, because Aristotle had viewed it, unnecessarily I think, as something the polis must force upon its citizens. But the Christians went beyond merely objecting to the coercion. With their polemic against paganism, Christians tended toward the obscuring of the view that the *polis* might have eugenic concerns that are legitimate and, in fact, ethically worthy. In this way, what was important in Aristotle was effectively obliterated by the "Augustinian alternative," and with the articulation of that alternative the course of the West was set.

If eugenics became a matter of consensus rather than coercion, however, the picture changes significantly. Then it appears possible to avoid, on one side, the forced compliance that Aristotle mandated and, on the other, the prizing of individual rights—either to "life" in the fetus' case or to "choice" in the pregnant woman's—at the expense of what is good for the larger social entity.[10] While I do not imply that the Japanese have arrived at a perfect solution to these problems, their present practice with respect to abortion and the family avoids, I wish to suggest, some of the most serious pitfalls of our own practices. In addition, an understanding of how their practice has been put together as an instance of moral "reasoning" is—however initially odd by our usual criteria—itself a reason for studying it with care.

NOTES

1. For example, Imai Jun and Ozawa Tomio, eds., *Nihon shisô ronsôshi* (Tokyo: Perikansha, 1979).
2. William R. LaFleur, *Liquid Life: Buddhism, Abortion, and the family in Japan,* Princeton: Princeton University Press, 1992. Published studies on *mizuko* in English to date include: Anne Page Brooks, "*Mizuko kuyō* and Japanese Buddhism," *Japanese Journal of Religious Studies* 8, nos. 3–4 (September–December 1981): 119–147; Emiko Ohnuki-Tierney, *Illness and Culture in Contemporary Japan: An Anthropological View* (Cambridge: Cambridge University Press, 1984), pp. 78–81; Hoshino Eiki and Takeda Dōshō, "Indebtedness and Comfort: The Undercurrents of *Mizuko Kuyō* in Contemporary Japan," *Japanese Journal of Religious Studies* 14, no. 4 (December 1987): 305–320; and Bardwell Smith, "Buddhism and Abortion in Contemporary Japan: *Mizuko kuyō* and the Confrontation with Death," *Japanese Journal of Religious Studies* 15, no. 1 (March 1988): 3–24. There is, of course, an extensive bibliography in Japanese.
3. Robert N. Bellah, *Tokugawa Religion: The Values of Pre-Industrial Japan* (Glencoe, Illinois: The Free Press, 1957), p. 19.
4. For the incredulous, somewhat appalled response of a Japanese woman legal expert present at European debates trying to pinpoint the exact time of a soul's entry into the body, see Nakatani Kinko, "Chūzetsu, Dataizai no Toraekata," in Nihon Kazoku Keikaku Renmei, ed., *Onna no jinken to sei* (Tokyo: Kōmichi Shobō, 1984), p. 29.
5. See, for example, Anzai Atsuko, "'Mizuko kuyō' shōbai no ikagawashisa,: in Nihon Kazoku Keigaku Renmei, ed., *Kanashimi o sabakemasu ka* (Tokyo: Ningen no Kagakusha, 1983), pp. 137–148. The critique of *tatari* from within Buddhism, however, is also strong. There is widespread censure of it, for instance, in a special issue devoted to this problem in the interdenominational Buddhist journal *Daihōrin,* vol. 54 (July 1987). For details see my *Liquid Life,* pp. 160–176.
6. Robert Nisbet, *Prejudices: A Philosophical Dictionary* (Cambridge, Massachusetts: Harvard University Press, 1982), p. 1.
7. See my *Liquid Life,* pp. 69–139.
8. Alasdair MacIntyre, *Whose Justice? Which Rationality?* (Notre Dame: University of Notre Dame Press, 1988), p. 163.
9. Augustine, "Of Marriage and Concupiscence," in Marcus Dods, ed., *The works of Aurelius Augustine, Bishop of Hippo,* trans. Peter Holmes (Edinburgh: T & T Clark, 1985), vol. 12, p. 116.
10. For a discussion of how, in fact, history shows there is nothing absolute about "respect for life" in the West's religions, see John A. Miles, Jr., "Jain and Judaeo-Christian Respect for Life,"*Journal of the American Academy of Religion* 44, no. 3 (1976): 453–457.

ABORTION—SUPPLEMENTARY READINGS

ARMSTRONG, ROBERT L. "The Right to Life." *Journal of Social Philosophy,* vol. 8(1), January 1977.

BAYLES, MICHAEL D. "Genetic Choice." in *Ethical Issues in the New Reproductive Technologies,* David Hull, editor. Belmont, CA: Wadsworth, 1990.

BOLTON, MARTHA BRANDT. "Responsible Women and Abortion Decisions." in *Having Children,* O'Neill and Ruddick, editors. New York: Oxford University Press, 1979.

KOERNER, UWE, AND HANNELORE KOERNER. "Ethics in Reproductive Medicine in the German Democratic Republic." *The Journal of Medicine and Philosophy,* vol. 14(3), June 1989.

MARKOWITZ, SALLY. "Abortion and Feminism." *Social Theory and Practice,* Spring 1990.

MENKITI, IFEANYI A. "Person and Community in African Traditional Thought," in *African Philosophy: An Introduction,* third edition, Richard Wright, editor. Lanham, MD: University Press of America, 1984.

MURRAY, THOMAS H. "Moral Obligations to the Not-Yet Born: The Fetus as Patient," in *Ethical Issues in the New Reproductive Technologies,* David Hull, editor. Belmont, CA: Wadsworth, 1990.

NOONAN, JOHN. "Responding to Persons: Methods of Moral Argument in the Debate Over Abortion." *Theology Digest,* 1973.

PAPP, ZOLTAN. "Genetic Counseling and Termination of Pregnancy in Hungary." The *Journal of Medicine and Philosophy,* vol. 14(3), June 1989.

SISTARE, CHRISTINE. "Reproductive Freedom and Women's Freedom: Surrogacy and Autonomy." *Philosophical Forum,* vol. 19(4), 1987.

SUMNER, L. WAYNE. "The Morality of Abortion." *Abortion and Moral Theory,* Princeton, NJ: Princeton University Press, 1981.

THOMSON, JUDITH JARVIS. "A Defense of Abortion." *Philosophy and Public Affairs,* vol. 1(1), Fall 1971.

IX

Euthanasia and Sustaining Life

> Should his demand to die be respected? . . . Another question occurred to me as I watched this blind, maimed, and totally helpless man defy and baffle everyone: could his adamant stand be the only way available for him to regain his independence after such a prolonged period of helplessness and total dependence? Consequently I decided to assist him . . .
>
> —Robert B. White, M.D.[1]

There is a right to life but is there also a right to die? This is the first question we take up in this section. The second question is this: given that there is a right to life, what do we do when rights to life conflict, as in situations where not everyone's life can be sustained due to a scarcity of medical resources? These questions push our discussion of human rights into the domain of very difficult cases. Those who demand the right to die are often opposed by those who think that the right to life is too precious to be compromised. Discussions about the allocation of scarce medical resources also involve the right to life, since, when not all can be saved, someone's right to life will seemingly be regarded as not being paramount.

The right to life is often thought to be connected to the right to decide how to live one's life. If one can be killed against one's will, this calls into question the right to decide how to live one's life. Similarly, if one can be forced to stay alive against one's will, then autonomy doesn't amount to much. And yet it seems odd to say that there is a right to die that is on the same level as the right to live. Isn't the right to die in some sense unnatural? Should people be allowed to decide to end their lives whenever they wish? Should the rest of us have to assist them in their decision to die with the same vigor as if the person's right to life were at stake? These are many of the questions that make our final topic such a difficult one.

"Euthanasia" literally means "good or happy death." The term is often equated with mercy killing. There are two types of euthanasia: active and passive. Active euthanasia refers to the practice of directly bringing about a person's death, according to or against that person's wishes. A person who wishes to die may request that a lethal injection be administered, and such an injection would constitute active euthanasia. Passive euthanasia is the practice of doing nothing to prevent death from occurring. If someone is suffering greatly and wants to die, a decision may be made not to treat the person's current pneumonia, for example, thereby allowing the person to die naturally. There are difficult cases that will not easily fit into this scheme, such as the decision to remove someone from life support systems. Some argue that this is a way of directly causing a person's death, while others argue that it is a way of merely allowing a person to die naturally.

In many, but not all societies, active euthanasia is condemned. We will examine the practices and their justification in a number of societies in hopes of understanding the complexities of the morality of euthanasia. We will also examine how decisions are made about whom to save when not all can be saved. In both of these topics we will be forced to confront the possible limits of the right to life, as well as the justification of certain medical practices, such as physician-assisted suicide, that are currently some of the most controversial in Western society and in many other societies.

We begin with a very influential essay written by James Rachels. Rachels argues that the distinction between active and passive euthanasia is not a morally relevant one. He points out that one can directly bring about a person's death with the best of intentions, and one can let someone die with the worst of intentions. The intentions make a moral difference, but whether the death is actively or passively brought about is not relevant. Similarly, from a consequentialist perspective, one can produce very good results by actively bringing about someone's death, and one can produce very bad results by letting someone die. The consequences make a moral difference but the type of euthanasia does not. Rachels contends that those who argue for or against an instance of euthanasia, merely because it is either active or passive, have made a conceptual mistake.

Margaret Battin argues in favor of a form of active euthanasia called physician-assisted suicide. She points out that in the Netherlands various forms of euthanasia have been practiced without major difficulties. Physician-assisted suicide has the advantage of keeping things under a physician's scrutiny, but it also gives the patient a greater range of autonomy, especially for those who are suffering greatly. Battin also talks about the successes in Germany, where assisted suicide but not active euthanasia is allowed. Cultural differences as well as cultural similarities are addressed in urging that the United States allow more forms of euthanasia than it currently does.

Henk ten Have and Jos Welie present the other side of the picture in the Netherlands. They argue that euthanasia is largely unregulated, and that as a result the number of cases of abuse is larger than people realize. Contrary to what Battin suggests, ten Have and Welie contend that a large part of the problem concerns the role of physicians in the process. Physicians report that often they engage in active euthanasia because they have made the decision that the patient's case is hopeless, rather than because they think that this is what the patient wants. Ten Have and Welie conclude that allowing any form of active euthanasia opens the door to substantial abuse, especially when the physicians are faced with the futility of continuing to treat a dying patient.

Carl Becker enters the debate from a Buddhist perspective. Unlike contemporary Westerners, Buddhists do not regard death as an evil or even as something to be avoided. Indeed, the Buddha is said to have praised certain persons who committed suicide. For Buddhists, what is most important is that a person be mentally and physically prepared to die. Once this has occurred, then the only morally relevant question concerns how this person can best die with dignity. To keep someone alive who is prepared to die and wants to die is generally considered inhumane in Japan, where Buddhism is very strong.

Issues about what is humane and about what rights we have are also of central importance to discussions of scarce medical resource allocation. Indeed, one of the questions raised in the literature on this subject is whether a physician acts wrongly by refusing to save the life of one patient when such a refusal will allow another patient's life to be saved. The refusal to save the one life is, in many respects, similar to euthanasia. But in this case it is not consistent with the wishes of the patient whose life is not sustained. Hence, the issues of explicit coercion arise in the scarce medical resource literature in ways that they do not generally arise in the euthanasia literature.

John Harris presents us with a highly controversial example of scarce resource allocation. He asks what would be wrong if one person were killed so that his organs could be used to save two other people who would otherwise die. This essay presents a similar problem to that presented by John Arthur in the section on hunger and poverty, but Harris takes quite a different tack on this issue. He argues that it may be justified to kill this person, and that the system that would be the most morally unobjectionable for selecting those to be killed is some form of lottery. But, as he admits, it would be a nearly insoluble problem to decide who should be in the lottery, that is, who would be in the class of possible donors.

John Kilner provides an interesting challenge to the standard consequentialist way of deciding who should be saved. From an African perspective an older patient's life is valued over that of a younger patient, in situations where both cannot be saved. Usefulness to society, the category often used in the West to decide hard cases in favor of those who are young, is not valued as much in Africa as is how much one needs help. Equality is also very highly valued, and this is true to such an extent that some form of lottery, such as first-come-first-served, is often a preferred strategy for selection in cases where two people cannot both be saved. If one values need or equality ahead of usefulness, then consequentialist analyses that favor the young are not necessarily those that are viewed as preferable.

Susan Sherwin discusses the way in which gender, race and class differences contribute to the way that scarce medical resources are allocated. She contends that if one is female or nonwhite or poor, one is much less likely to have access to scarce resources than if one is male, white, and wealthy. And if one is both female and poor, or both female and nonwhite, one is at the bottom of the pool of those who obtain scarce medical resources. Indeed, those at the bottom don't even have studies done about them to determine which resources they most need. Sherwin argues that this situation should be changed by empowering all health consumers so that they can effectively fight for their medical rights.

NOTE

1. Robert B. White, MD, "A Demand To Die," *Hastings Center Report,* June 1975.

Active and Passive Euthanasia

James Rachels

James Rachels is professor of philosophy at the University of Alabama at Birmingham. He is the author of The Elements of Moral Philosophy *(1986),* The End of Life: Euthanasia and Morality *(1986), and* Created from Animals: The Moral Implications of Darwinism *(1990). He is the editor of* The Right Thing To Do *(1989).*

In this essay, Rachels treats the distinction between active and passive euthanasia as an example of the distinction between killing and letting die. Rachels argues that there is no morally relevant difference between actively killing someone and passively letting a person die. He argues that if this is true, then policies of the American Medical Association and other institutions that rely on the distinction need to be changed. What is important morally are the motivations or consequences of actively or passively killing, and only after these factors have been evaluated in each case can it be said that euthanasia is morally justifiable.

The distinction between active and passive euthanasia is thought to be crucial for medical ethics. The idea is that it is permissible, at least in some cases, to withhold treatment and allow a patient to die, but it is never permissible to take any direct action designed to kill the patient. This doctrine seems to be accepted by most doctors, and it is endorsed in a statement adopted by the House of Delegates of the American Medical Association on 4 December 1973:

> The intentional termination of the life of one human being by another—mercy killing—is contrary to that for which the medical profession stands and is contrary to the policy of the American Medical Association.
>
> The cessation of the employment of extraordinary means to prolong the life of the body when there is irrefutable evidence that biological death is imminent is the decision of the patient and/or his immediate family. The advice and judgment of the physician should be freely available to the patient and/or his immediate family.

However, a strong case can be made against this doctine. In what follows I will set out some of the relevant arguments, and urge doctors to reconsider their views on this matter.

To begin with a familiar type of situation, a patient who is dying of incurable cancer of the throat is in terrible pain, which can no longer be satisfactorily alleviated. He is certain to die within a few days, even if present treatment is continued, but he does not want to go on living for those days since the pain is unbearable. So he asks the doctor for

James Rachels, "Active and Passive Euthanasia," in *The New England Journal of Medicine,* Vol. 292, © 1975, pp. 78–80. Reprinted by permission of *The New England Journal of Medicine.*

an end to it, and his family joins in the request.

Suppose the doctor agrees to withhold treatment, as the conventional doctrine says he may. The justification for his doing so is that the patient is in terrible agony, and since he is going to die anyway, it would be wrong to prolong his suffering needlessly. But now notice this. If one simply withholds treatment, it may take the patient longer to die, and so he may suffer more than he would if more direct action were taken and a lethal injection given. This fact provides strong reason for thinking that, once the initial decision not to prolong his agony has been made, active euthanasia is actually preferable to passive euthanasia, rather than the reverse. To say otherwise is to endorse the option that leads to more suffering rather than less, and is contrary to the humanitarian impulse that prompts the decision not to prolong his life in the first place.

Part of my point is that the process of being "allowed to die" can be relatively slow and painful, whereas being given a lethal injection is relatively quick and painless. Let me give a different sort of example. In the United States about one in 600 babies is born with Down's syndrome. Most of these babies are otherwise healthy—that is, with only the usual pediatric care, they will proceed to an otherwise normal infancy. Some, however, are born with congenital defects such as intestinal obstructions that require operations if they are to live. Sometimes, the parents and the doctor will decide not to operate, and let the infant die. Anthony Shaw describes what happens then:

> When surgery is denied [the doctor] must try to keep the infant from suffering while natural forces sap the baby's life away. As a surgeon whose natural inclination is to use the scalpel to fight off death, standing by and watching a salvageable baby die is the most emotionally exhausting experience I know. It is easy at a conference, in a theoretical discussion to decide that such infants should be allowed to die. It is altogether different to stand by in the nursery and watch as dehydration and infection wither a tiny being over hours and days. This is a terrible ordeal for me and the hospital staff—much more so than for the parents who never set foot in the nursery.[1]

I can understand why some people are opposed to all euthanasia, and insist that such infants must be allowed to live. I think I can also understand why other people favor destroying these babies quickly and painlessly. But why should anyone favor letting "dehydration and infection wither a tiny being over hours and days"? The doctrine that says a baby may be allowed to dehydrate and wither, but may not be given an injection that would end its life without suffering, seems so patently cruel as to require no further refutation. The strong language is not intended to offend, but only to put the point in the clearest possible way.

My second argument is that the conventional doctrine leads to decisions concerning life and death made on irrelevant grounds.

Consider again the case of the infants with Down's syndrome who need operations for congenital defects unrelated to the syndrome to live. Sometimes, there is no operation, and the baby dies, but when there is no such defect, the baby lives on. Now an operation such as that to remove an intestinal obstruction is not prohibitively difficult. The reason why such operations are not performed in these cases is, clearly, that the child has Down's syndrome and the parents and the doctor judge that because of that fact it is better for the child to die.

But notice that this situation is absurd, no matter what view one takes of the lives and potentials of such babies. If the life of such an infant is worth preserving what does it matter if it needs a simple operation? Or, if one thinks it better that such a baby should not live on, what difference does it make that it happens to have an unobstructed intestinal tract? In either case, the matter of life and death is being decided on irrelevant grounds. It is the Down's syndrome, and not the intestines, that is the issue. The matter should be decided, if at all, on that basis, and not be allowed to depend on the essentially irrelevant question of whether the intestinal tract is blocked.

What makes this situation possible, of course, is the idea that when there is an intestinal blockage, one can "let the baby die," but when there is no such defect there is nothing that can be done, for one must not "kill" it. The fact that this idea leads to such results as deciding life or death on irrelevant grounds is another good reason why the doctrine would be rejected.

One reason why so many people think that there is an important moral difference between active and passive euthanasia is that they think killing someone is morally worse than letting someone die. But is it? Is killing, in itself, worse than letting die? To investigate this issue, two cases may be considered that are exactly alike except that one involves killing whereas the other involves letting someone die. Then, it can be asked whether this difference makes any difference to the moral assessments. It is important that the cases be exactly alike, except for this one difference, since otherwise one cannot be confident that it is this difference and not some other that accounts for any variation in the assessments of the two cases. So, let us consider this pair of cases:

In the first, Smith stands to gain a large inheritance if anything should happen to his six-year-old cousin. One evening while the child is taking his bath, Smith sneaks into the bathroom and drowns the child, and then arranges things so that it will look like an accident.

In the second, Jones also stands to gain if anything should happen to his six-year-old cousin. Like Smith, Jones sneaks in planning to drown the child in his bath. However, just as he enters the bathroom Jones see the child slip and hit his head, and fall face down in the water. Jones is delighted; he stands by, ready to push the child's head back under if it is necessary, but it is not necessary. With only a little thrashing about, the child drowns all by himself, "accidentally," as Jones watches and does nothing.

Now Smith killed the child, whereas Jones "merely" let the child die. That is the only difference between them. Did either man behave better, from a moral point of view? If the difference between killing and letting die were in itself a morally important matter, one should say that Jones's behavior was less reprehensible than Smith's. But does one really want to say that? I think not. In the first place, both men acted from the same motive, personal gain, and both had exactly the same end in view when they acted. It may be inferred from Smith's conduct that he is a bad man, although that judgment may be withdrawn or modified if certain further facts are learned about him—for example, that he is mentally deranged. But would not the very same thing be inferred about Jones from his conduct? And would not the same further considerations also be relevant to any modification of this judgment? Moreover, suppose Jones pleaded, in his own defense, "After all, I didn't do anything except just stand there and watch the child drown. I didn't kill him; I only let him die." Again, if letting die were in itself less bad than killing, this defense should have at least some weight. But it does not. Such a "defense" can only be regarded as a grotesque perversion of moral reasoning. Morally speaking, it is no defense at all.

Now, it may be pointed out, quite properly, that the cases of euthanasia with which doctors are concerned are not like this at all. They do not involve personal gain or the destruction of normal healthy children. Doctors are concerned only with cases in which the patient's life is of no further use to him, or in which the patient's life has become or will soon become a terrible burden. However, the point is the same in these cases: the bare difference between killing and letting die does not, in itself, make a moral difference. If a doctor lets a patient die, for humane reasons, he is in the same moral position as if he had given the patient a lethal injection for humane reasons. If his decision was wrong—if, for example, the patient's illness was in fact curable—the decision would be equally regrettable no matter which method was used to carry it out. And if the doctor's decision was the right one, the method used is not in itself important.

The AMA policy statement isolates the crucial issue very well; the crucial issue is "the intentional termination of the life of one human being by another." But after identifying this issue, and forbidding "mercy killing," the statement goes on to deny that the cessation of treatment is the intentional termination of a life. This is where the mistake comes in, for what is the cessation of treatment, in these circumstances, if it is not "the intentional termination of the life of one human being by another"? Of course it is exactly that, and if it were not, there would be no point to it.

Many people will find this judgment hard to accept. One reason, I think, is that it is very easy to conflate the question of whether killing is, in itself, worse than letting die, with the very different question of whether most actual cases of killing are more reprehensible than most actual cases of letting die. Most actual cases of killing are clearly terrible (think, for example, of all the murders reported in the newspapers), and one hears of such cases every day. On the other hand, one hardly ever hears of a case of letting die, except for the actions of doctors who are motivated by humanitarian reasons. So one learns to think of killing in a much worse light than of letting die. But this does not mean that there is something about killing that makes it in itself worse than letting die, for it is not the bare difference between killing and letting die that makes the difference in these cases. Rather, the other factors—the murderer's motive of personal gain, for example, contrasted with the doctor's humanitarian motivation—account for different reactions to the different cases.

I have argued that killing is not in itself worse than letting die; if my contention is right, it follows that active euthanasia is not any worse than passive euthanasia. What arguments can be given on the other side? The most common, I believe, is the following:

> The important difference between active and passive euthanasia is that, in passive euthanasia, the doctor does not do anything to bring about the patient's death. The doctor does nothing, and the patient dies of whatever ills already afflict him. In active euthanasia, however, the doctor does something to bring about the patient's death: he kills him. The doctor who gives the patient with cancer a lethal injection has himself caused his patient's death; whereas if he merely ceases treatment, the cancer is the cause of death.

A number of points need to be made here. The first is that it is not exactly correct to say that in passive euthanasia the doctor does nothing, for he does do one thing that is very important: he lets the patient die. "Letting someone die" is certainly different, in some respects, from other types of action—mainly in that it is a kind of action that one may perform by way of not performing certain other actions. For example, one may let a patient die by way of not giving medication, just as one may insult someone by way of not shaking his hand. But for any purpose of moral assessment, it is a type of action none the less. The decision to let a patient die is subject to moral appraisal in the same way that a decision to kill him would be subject to moral appraisal: it may be assessed as wise or unwise, compassionate or sadistic, right or wrong. If a doctor deliberately let a patient die who was suffering from a routinely curable illness, the doctor would certainly be to blame for what he had done, just as he would be to blame if he had needlessly killed the patient. Charges against him would then be appropriate. If so, it would be no defense at all for him to insist that he didn't "do anything." He would have done something very serious indeed, for he let his patient die.

Fixing the cause of death may be very important from a legal point of view, for it may determine whether criminal charges are brought against the doctor. But I do not think that this notion can be used to show a moral difference between active and passive euthanasia. The reason why it is considered bad to be the cause of someone's death is that death is regarded as a great evil—and so it is. However, if it has been decided that euthanasia—even passive euthanasia—is desirable in a given case, it has also been decided that in this instance death is no greater an evil than the patient's continued existence. And if this is true, the usual reason for not wanting to be the cause of someone's death simply does not apply.

Finally, doctors may think that all of this is only of academic interest—the sort of thing that philosophers may worry about but that has no practical bearing on their own work. After all, doctors must be concerned about the legal consequences of what they do, and active euthanasia is clearly forbidden by the law. But even so, doctors should also be concerned with the fact that the law is forcing upon them a moral doctrine that may be indefensible, and has a considerable effect on their practices. Of course, most doctors are not now in the position of being coerced in this matter, for they do not regard themselves as merely going along with what the law requires. Rather, in statements such as the AMA policy statement that I have quoted, they are endorsing this doctrine as a central point of medical ethics. In that statement, active euthanasia is condemned not merely as illegal but as "contrary to that for which the medical profession stands," whereas passive euthanasia is approved. However, the preceding considerations suggest that there is really no difference between the two, considered in themselves (there may be important moral differences in some cases in their *consequences,* but as I pointed out, these differences may make active euthanasia, and not passive euthanasia, the morally preferable option). So, whereas doctors may have to discriminate between active and passive euthanasia to satisfy the law, they should not do any more than that. In particular, they should not give the distinction any added authority and weight by writing it into official statements of medical ethics.

NOTE

1. Shaw, Anthony, "Doctor, Do We Have a Choice?" *The New York Times Magazine,* 30 Jan. 1972, p. 54.

Euthanasia: The Way We Do It, the Way They Do It

Margaret Battin

Margaret Battin is a professor of philosophy at the University of Utah. She is the author of Ethical Issues in Suicide *(1982),* Ethics in the Sanctuary *(1990), and* The Least Worst Death *(1990). She is coeditor of* Ethical Issues in the Professions *(1989).*

Battin examines euthanasia practices in three societies: the Netherlands, where active euthanasia is allowed; Germany where active euthanasia is disallowed but assisted suicide is allowed; and the United States, where neither active euthanasia nor assisted suicide is allowed, but where passive euthanasia in the form of withdrawal or withholding of treatment is common. Battin argues that the United States does not supply an adequate range of options to patients who are near death. After considering arguments from many sides of the issue, Battin concludes that the United States should allow "physician-assisted suicide."

INTRODUCTION

Because we tend to be rather myopic in our discussions of death and dying, especially about the issues of active euthanasia and assisted suicide, it is valuable to place the question of how we go about dying in an international context. We do not always see that our own cultural norms may be quite different from those of other nations, and that our background assumptions, and actual practices, differ dramatically. Thus, I would like to examine the perspectives on end-of-life dilemmas in three countries, the Netherlands, Germany, and the USA.

The Netherlands, Germany, and the United States are all advanced industrial democracies. They all have sophisticated medical establishments and life expectancies over 70 years of age; their populations are all characterized by an increasing proportion of older persons. They are all in what has been called the fourth stage of the epidemiologic transition[1]—that stage of societal development in which it is no longer the case that most people die of acute parasitic or infectious diseases. In this stage, most people do not die of diseases with rapid, unpredictable onsets and sharp fatality curves; rather, the majority of the population—as much as perhaps 70%–80%—dies of degenerative diseases, especially delayed degenerative diseases, that are characterized by late, slow onset and extended decline. Most people in highly industrialized countries die from cancer, atherosclerosis, heart disease (by no means always suddenly fatal), chronic obstructive pulmonary disease, liver, kidney or other organ disease, or degenerative neurological disorders. Thus, all three of these countries are alike in facing a common problem: how to deal with the characteristic new ways in which we die.

DEALING WITH DYING IN THE UNITED STATES

In the United States, we have come to recognize that the maximal extension of life-prolonging treatment in these late-life degenerative conditions is often inappropriate. Although we could keep the machines and tubes—the respirators, intravenous lines, feeding tubes—hooked up for extended periods, we recognize that this is inhumane, pointless, and financially impossible. Instead, as a society we have developed a number of mechanisms for dealing with these hopeless situations, all of which involve withholding or withdrawing various forms of treatment.

Some mechanisms for withholding or withdrawing treatment are exercised by the patient who is confronted by such a situation or who anticipates it; these include refusal of treatment, the patient-executed DNR order, the Living Will, and the Durable Power of Attorney. Others are mechanisms for decision by second parties about a patient who is no longer competent or never was competent. The latter are reflected in a long series of court cases, including *Quinlan, Saikewicz, Spring, Eichner, Barber, Bartling, Conroy, Brophy,* the trio *Farrell, Peter* and *Jobes,* and *Cruzan*. These are cases that attempt to delineate the precise circumstances under which it is appropriate to withhold or withdraw various forms of therapy, including respiratory support, chemotherapy, antibiotics in intercurrent infections, and artificial nutrition and hydration. Thus, during the past 15 years or so, roughly since *Quinlan* (1976), we have developed an impressive body of case law and state statute that protects, permits, and facilitates our characteristic American strategy of dealing with end-of-life situations. These cases provide a framework for withholding or withdrawing treatment when we believe there is no medical or moral point in going on. This is sometimes termed *passive euthanasia;* more often, it is simply called *allowing to die,* and is ubiquitous in the United States.

For example, a recent study by Miles and Gomez indicates that some 85% of deaths in the United States occur in health-care institutions, including hospitals, nursing homes, and other facilities, and of these, about 70% involve electively withholding some form of life-sustaining treatment.[2] A 1989 study cited in the *Journal of the American Medical Association* claims that 85%–90% of critical care professionals state that they are withholding and withdrawing life-sustaining treatments from patients who are "deemed to have irreversible disease and are terminally ill."[3] Still another study identified some 115 patients in two intensive-care units from whom care was withheld or withdrawn; 110 were already incompetent by the time the decision to limit care was made. The 89 who died while still in the intensive care unit accounted for 45% of all deaths there.[4] It is estimated that 1.3 million American deaths a year follow decisions to withhold life support;[5] this is a majority of the just over 2 million American deaths per year. Withholding and withdrawing treatment is the way we in the USA go about dealing with dying, and indeed "allowing to die" is the only legally protected alternative to maximal treatment recognized in the United States. We do not legally permit ourselves to actively cause death.

DEALING WITH DYING IN THE NETHERLANDS

In the Netherlands, voluntary active euthanasia is also an available response to end-of-life situations. Although active euthanasia remains prohibited by statutory law, it is protected by a series of lower and supreme court decisions and is widely regarded as legal, or, more precisely, *gedoeken,* legally "tolerated." These court decisions have the effect of protecting the physician who performs euthanasia from prosecution, provided the physician meets a rigorous set of guidelines.

These guidelines, variously stated, contain five central provisions:

1. that the patient's request be voluntary;
2. that the patient be undergoing intolerable suffering;
3. that all alternatives acceptable to the patient for relieving the suffering have been tried;
4. that the patient have full information;
5. that the physician consult with a second physician whose judgment can be expected to be independent.

Of these criteria, it is the first which is central: euthanasia may be performed only at the voluntary request of the patient. This criterion is also understood to require that the patient's request be a stable, enduring, reflective one—not the product of a transitory impulse. Every attempt is to be made to rule out depression, psychopathology, pressures from family members, unrealistic fears, and other factors compromising voluntariness.

Putting an end to years of inflammatory discussion in which speculation about the frequency of euthanasia had ranged from 2,000 (close to correct) to 20,000 cases a year, a comprehensive study requested by the Dutch government was published in late 1991; an English version appeared in *The Lancet.*[6] Popularly known as the Remmelink Commission report, this study provided the first objective data about the incidence of euthanasia as well as a wider range of medical practices at the end of life: the withholding or withdrawal of treatment, the use of life-shortening doses of opioids for the control of pain, and direct termination, including active euthanasia, physician-assisted suicide, and life-ending procedures not termed euthanasia. This study was supplemented by a second empirical examination, focusing particularly carefully on the characteristics of patients and the nature of their euthanasia requests.[7]

About 130,000 people die in the Netherlands every year, and of these deaths, about 30% are acute and unexpected; 70% are predictable and foreseen, usually the result of degenerative illnesses comparatively late in life. Of the total deaths in the Netherlands, the Remmelink Commission's study found, about 17.5% involved decisions to withhold or withdraw treatment although continuing treatment would probably have prolonged life; another 17.5% involved the use of opioids to relieve pain but in dosages probably sufficient to shorten life. A total of 2.9% of all deaths involved euthanasia and related practices.

About 2,300 people, 1.8% of the total deaths in the Netherlands, died by euthanasia, understood as the termination of the life of the patient at the patient's explicit and persistent request. Another 400 people, 0.03% of the total, chose physician-assisted suicide. About 1,000 additional patients died as the result of "life-terminating procedures," not technically called euthanasia, in virtually all of which euthanasia had either been previously discussed with the patient or the patient had expressed in a previous phase of the disease a wish for euthanasia if his or her suffering became unbearable, or the patient was near death and clearly suffering grievously, yet verbal contact had become impossible.

Although euthanasia is thus not frequent—a small fraction of the total annual mortality—it is nevertheless a conspicuous option in terminal illness, well known to both physicians and the general public. There has been *very* widespread public discussion of the issues in euthanasia during the last several years, especially as the pros and cons of full legalization have been debated, and surveys of public opinion show that the public support for a liberal euthanasia policy has been growing: from 40% in 1966 to 81% in 1988.[8] Doctors too support this practice, and although there is a vocal opposition group, the opposition is in the clear minority. Some 54% of Dutch physicians said that they performed euthanasia or provided assistance in suicide, including 62% of *huisarts* or general practitioners, and an additional 34% said that although they had not actually done so, they could conceive of situations in which they would be prepared to do so. Thus, although many who had practiced euthanasia mentioned that they would be most reluctant to do so again and that "only in the face of unbearable suffering and with no alternatives would they be prepared to take such action,"[9] some 88% of Dutch physicians appear to accept the practice in some cases. As the Remmelink Commission commented, ". . . a large majority of physicians in the Netherlands see euthanasia as an accepted element if medical practice under certain circumstances."[10]

In general, pain alone is not the basis for euthanasia, since pain can, in most cases, be effectively treated. Rather, "intolerable suffering," among the criteria for euthanasia, is understood to mean suffering that is intolerable in the patient's (rather than the physician's) view, and can include a fear of or unwillingness to endure *entluisterung,* that gradual effacement and loss of personal identity that characterizes the end stages of many terminal illnesses. In a year, about 25,000 patients seek reassurance from their physicians that they will be granted euthanasia if their suffering becomes severe; there are about 9,000 explicit requests, and more than two-thirds of these are turned down, usually on the grounds that there is some other way of treating the patient's suffering, and in just 14% on the grounds of psychiatric illness.

In Holland, many hospitals now have protocols for the performance of euthanasia; these serve to ensure that the court-established guidelines have been met. However, euthanasia is often practiced in the patient's home, typically by the *huisarts* or general practitioner who is the patient's long-term family physician. Euthanasia is usually performed after aggressive hospital treatment has failed to arrest the patient's terminal illness; the patient has come home to die, and the family physician is prepared to ease this passing. Whether practiced at home or in the hospital, it is believed that euthanasia usually takes place in the presence of the family members, perhaps the visiting nurse, and often the patient's pastor or priest. Many doctors say that performing euthanasia is never easy, but that it is something they believe a doctor ought to do for his or her patient, when nothing else can help.

Thus, in Holland a patient facing the end of life has an option not openly practiced in the United States: to ask the physician to bring his or her life to an end. Although not everyone does so—indeed, about 97% of people who die in a given year do not—it is a choice widely understood as available.

FACING DEATH IN GERMANY

In part because of its very painful history of Nazism, Germany appears to believe that doctors should have no role in causing death. Although societal generalizations are always risky, it is fair, I think, to say that there is vigorous and nearly universal opposition in Germany to the notion of active euthanasia. Euthanasia is viewed as always wrong, and the Germans view the Dutch as stepping out on a dangerously slippery slope.

However, it is an artifact of German law that, whereas killing on request (including voluntary euthanasia) is prohibited, assisting suicide is not a violation of the law, provided the person is *tatherrschaftsfähig,* capable of exercising control over his or her actions, and also acting out of *freiverantwortliche Wille,* freely responsible choice. Responding to this situation, there has developed a private organization, the *Deutsche Gesellschaft für Humanes Sterben* (DGHS), or German Society for Humane Dying, which provides support to its very extensive membership (over 50,000 persons) in choosing suicide as an alternative to terminal illness.

After a person has been a member of the DGHS for at least a year, and provided that he or she has not received medical or psychotherapeutic treatment for depression or other psychiatric illness during the last two years, he or she may request a copy of DGHS's booklet *Menschenwürdiges und selbstverantworliches Sterben,* or "Dignified and Responsible Death." This booklet provides a list of about ten drugs available by prescription in Germany, together with the specific dosages necessary for producing a certain, painless death. (The DGHS no longer officially recommends cyanide, though its president, Hans Henning Atrott, was recently charged with selling it.) DGHS recommends that the members approach a physician for a prescription for the drug desired, asking, for example, for a barbiturate to help with sleep, or chloroquine for protection against malaria on a trip to India. If necessary, the DGHS may also arrange for someone to obtain drugs from neighboring countries, including France, Italy, Spain, Portugal, and Greece, where they may be available without prescription. In unusual cases, the DGHS will also provide what it calls *Sterbebegleitung* or "accompaniment in dying," providing a companion to remain with the person during the often extended period that is required for the lethal drug to take full effect. However, the *Sterbebegleiter* is typically a layperson, not someone medically trained, and physicians play no role in assisting in these cases of suicide. To preclude suspicion by providing evidence of the person's intentions, the DGHS also provides a form—printed on a single sheet of distinctive pink paper—to be signed once when joining the organization, expressing the intention to determine the time of one's own death, and to be signed again at the time of the suicide and left beside the body.

Because assisting suicide is not illegal in Germany, provided the person is competent and in control of his or her own will, there is no legal risk for family members, *Sterbebegleiter,* or others in reporting information about the methods and effectiveness of suicide attempts, and the DGHS encourages its network of regional bureaus (five, in major cities throughout the country) to facilitate feedback. On this basis, it regularly updates and revises the drug information it provides. It claims some 2,000–3,000 suicides per year among its members.

To be sure, assisted suicide is not the only option open to the terminally ill patient in Germany, nor is there clear evidence concerning its frequency either within the DGHS or in nonreported cases outside it. There is increasing emphasis on help in dying that does not involve direct termination, and organizations like Ormega, offering hospice-style care and an extensive program of companionship, are attracting increasing attention. Furthermore, there has been recent scandal directed towards the founder and president of the DGHS, Hans Henning Atrott, accused in late 1991 of selling cyanide to an attorney hospitalized for mental illness; in May 1992 police raided his office, finding capsules of cyanide, barbiturates, and a large amount of cash. What the outcome of this event will be remains at this writing to be seen, though it is clear that the scandal focuses on Atrott's alleged profiteering and assisting a mentally ill person, rather than with the DGHS's regular practice of assisting competent terminally ill individuals in suicide. Furthermore, the DGHS is a conspicuous, widely known organization, and many Germans appear to be aware that assisted suicide is available even if they do not use the services of the DGHS.

OBJECTIONS TO THE THREE MODELS OF DYING

In response to the dilemmas raised by the new circumstances of death, in which the majority of the population in each of the advanced industrial nations dies of degenerative diseases after an extended period of terminal deterioration, different countries develop different practices. The United States legally permits only withholding and withdrawal of treatment, though of course active euthanasia and assisted suicide do occur. Holland also permits voluntary active euthanasia, and although Germany rejects euthanasia, it tolerates assisted suicide. But there are serious moral objections to be made to each of these practices, objections to be considered before resolving the issue of which practice our own culture ought to adopt.

Objections to the German Practice

German law does not prohibit assisting suicide, but postwar German culture discourages physicians from taking any active role in death. This gives rise to distinctive moral problems. For one thing, it appears that there is little professional help or review provided for patients' choices about suicide; because the patient makes this choice essentially outside the medical establishment, medical professionals are not in a position to detect or treat impaired judgment on the part of the patient, especially judgment impaired by depression. Similarly, if the patient must commit suicide assisted only by persons outside the medical profession, there are risks that the patient's diagnosis and prognosis are inadequately confirmed, that the means chosen for suicide will be unreliable or inappropriately used, that the means used for suicide will fall into the hands of other persons, and that the patient will fail to recognize or be able to resist intrafamilial pressures and manipulation. The DGHS policy for providing assistance requires that the patient be terminally ill and have been a member of the DGHS for at least one year in order to make use of its services, the latter requirement is intended to provide evidence of the stability of such a choice. However, these minimal requirements are hardly sufficient to answer the charge that suicide decisions, which are made for medical reasons but must be made without medical help, may be rendered under less than ideally informed and voluntary conditions.

Objections to the Dutch Practice

The Dutch practice of physician-performed active voluntary euthanasia also raises a number of ethical issues, many of which have been discussed vigorously both in the Dutch press and in commentary on the Dutch practices from abroad. For one thing, it is sometimes said that the availability of physician-performed euthanasia creates a disincentive for providing good terminal care. I have seen no evidence that this is the case; on the contrary, Peter Admiraal, the anesthesiologist who is perhaps Holland's most vocal proponent of voluntary active euthanasia, insists that pain should rarely or never be the occasion for euthanasia, as pain (in contrast to suffering) is comparatively easily treated.[11] Instead, it is a refusal to endure the final stages of deterioration, both mental and physical, that motivates requests.

It is also sometimes said that active euthanasia violates the Hippocratic Oath.

Indeed, it is true that the original Greek version of the Oath prohibits the physician from giving a deadly drug, even when asked for it; but the original version also prohibits performing surgery and taking fees for teaching medicine, neither of which prohibitions has survived into contemporary medical practice. Dutch physicians often say that they see performing euthanasia—where it is genuinely requested by the patient and nothing else can be done to relieve the patient's condition—as part of their duty to the patient, not as a violation of it.

The Dutch are also often said to be at risk of starting down the slippery slope, that is, that the practice of voluntary active euthanasia for patients who meet the criteria will erode into practicing less-than-voluntary euthanasia on patients whose problems are not irremediable, and perhaps by gradual degrees develop into terminating the lives of people who are elderly, chronically ill, handicapped, mentally retarded, or otherwise regarded as undesirable. This risk is often expressed in vivid claims of widespread fear and wholesale slaughter, claims that are repeated in the right-to-life press in both the Netherlands, and the USA, though there is no evidence for these claims. However, the Dutch are now beginning to agonize over the problems of the incompetent patient, the mentally ill patient, the newborn with serious deficits, and other patients who cannot make voluntary choices, though these are largely understood as issues about withholding or withdrawing treatment, not about direct termination.[12]

What is not often understood is that this new and acutely painful area of reflection for the Dutch—withholding and withdrawing treatment from incompetent patients—has already led in the United States to the development of a vast, highly developed body of law: namely that series of cases just cited, beginning with *Quinlan* and culminating in *Cruzan*. Americans have been discussing these issues for a long time, and have developed a broad set of practices that are regarded as routine in withholding and withdrawing treatment. The Dutch see Americans as much further out on the slippery slope than they are, because Americans have already become accustomed to second-party choices about other people. Issues involving second-party choices are painful to the Dutch in a way they are not to us precisely because *voluntariness* is so central in the Dutch understanding of choices about dying. Concomitantly, the Dutch see the Americans' squeamishness about first-party choices—voluntary euthanasia, assisted suicide—as evidence that we are not genuinely committed to recognizing *voluntary* choice after all. For this reason, many Dutch commentators believe that the Americans are at a much greater risk of sliding down the slippery slope into involuntary killing than they are. I fear, I must add, that they are right about this.

Objections to the American Practice

There may be moral problems raised by the German and the Dutch practices, but there are also moral problems raised by the American practice of relying on withholding and withdrawal of treatment in end-of-life situations. The German, Dutch, and American practices all occur within similar conditions—in industrialized nations with highly developed medical systems, where a majority of the population dies of illnesses exhibiting characteristically extended downhill courses—but the issues raised by our own response to this situation may be even more disturbing than those of the Dutch or the Germans. We often assume that our approach is "safer" because it involves only letting someone die, not killing him or her; but it too raises very troubling questions.

The first of these issues is a function of the fact that withdrawing and especially withholding treatment are typically less conspicuous, less pronounced, less evident kinds of actions than direct killing, even though they can equally well lead to death. Decisions about nontreatment have an invisibility that decisions about directly causing death do not have, even though they may have the same result, and hence there is a much wider range of occasions in which such decisions can be made. One can decline to treat a patient in many different ways, at many different times—by not providing oxygen, by not instituting dialysis, by not correcting electrolyte imbalances, and so on—all of which will cause the patient's death; open medical killing also brings about death, but is a much more overt, conspicuous procedure. Consequently, letting die also invites many fewer protections. In contrast to the standard slippery slope argument which sees killing as riskier than letting die, the more realistic slippery slope argument warns that because our culture relies primarily on decisions about nontreatment, grave decisions about living or dying are not as open to scrutiny as they are under more direct life-terminating practices, and hence, are more open to abuse.

Second, and closely related, reliance on withholding and withdrawing treatment invites rationing in an extremely strong way, in part because of the comparative invisibility of these decisions. When a health care provider does not offer a specific sort of care, it is not always possible to discern the motivation; the line between believing that it would not provide benefit to the patient and that it would not provide benefit worth the investment of resources in the patient can be very thin. This is a particular problem where health care financing is highly decentralized, as in the United States, and where rationing decisions without benefit of principle are not always available for easy review.

Third, relying on withholding and withdrawal of treatment can often be cruel. It requires that the patient who is dying from one of the diseases that exhibits a characteristic extended, downhill course (as the majority of patients in the Netherlands, Germany and the U.S. do) must in effect wait to die until the absence of a certain treatment will cause death. For instance, the cancer patient who foregoes chemotherapy or surgery does not simply die from this choice; he or she continues to endure the downhill course of cancer until the tumor finally destroys some crucial bodily function or organ. The patient with amyotrophic lateral sclerosis who decides in advance to decline respiratory support does not die at the time the choice is made, but continues to endure increasing paralysis until breathing is impaired and suffocation occurs. We often try to ameliorate these situations by administering pain medication or symptom control at the same time we are withholding treatment, but these are all ways of disguising the fact that we are letting the disease kill the patient rather than directly bringing about death. But the ways diseases kill people are far more cruel than the ways physicians kill patients when performing euthanasia or assisting in suicide.

THE PROBLEM: A CHOICE OF CULTURES

Thus we see three similar cultures and countries and three similar sets of circumstances, but three different basic practices in approaching death. All three of these practices generate moral problems; none of them, nor any others we might devise, is free of moral difficulty. But the question that faces us is this: which of these practices is best?

It is not possible to answer this question in a less-than-ideal world without some attention to the specific characteristics and deficiencies of the society in question. In asking which of these practices is best, we must ask which is best *for us.* That we currently employ one set of these practices rather than others does not prove that it is best for us; the question is, would practices developed in other cultures or those not yet widespread in any be better for our own culture than that which has developed here? Thus, it is necessary to consider the differences between our society and these European cultures that have real bearing on which model of approach to dying we ought to adopt.

First, notice that different cultures exhibit different degrees of closeness between physicians and patients—different patterns of contact and involvement. The German physician is sometimes said to be more distant and more authoritarian than the American physician; on the other hand, the Dutch physician is sometimes said to be closer to his or her patients than either the American or the German is. In the Netherlands, basic primary care is provided by the *huisarts,* the general practitioner or family physician, who typically lives in the neighborhood, makes house calls frequently, and maintains an office in his or her own home. The *huisarts* is usually the physician for other members of the patient's family, and will remain the family's physician throughout his or her practice. Thus, the patient for whom euthanasia becomes an issue—say, the terminal cancer patient who has been hospitalized in the past but who has returned home to die—will be cared for by the trusted family physician on a regular basis. Indeed, for a patient in severe distress, the physician, supported by the visiting nurse, may make house calls as often as once a day, twice a day, or more (after all, it is right in the neighborhood), and is in continuous contact with the family. In contrast, the traditional American institution of the family doctor who makes house calls is rapidly becoming a thing of the past, and although some patients who die at home have access to hospice services and house calls from their long-term physician, many have no such long-term care and receive most of it from staff at a clinic or housestaff rotating through the services of a hospital. The degree of continuing contact the patient can have with a familiar, trusted physician clearly influences the nature of his or her dying, and also plays a role in whether physician-performed active euthanasia, assisted suicide, and/or withholding and withdrawing treatment is appropriate.

Second, the United States has a much more volatile legal climate than either the Netherlands or Germany; our medical system is increasingly litigious, much more so than that of any other country in the world. Fears of malpractice action or criminal prosecution color much of what physicians do in managing the dying of their patients. We also tend to evolve public policy through court decisions, and to assume that the existence of a policy puts an end to any moral issue. A delicate legal and moral balance over the issue of euthanasia, as is the case in the Netherlands, would not be possible here.

Third, we in the United States have a very different financial climate in which to do our dying. Both the Netherlands and Germany, as well as every other industrialized nation except South Africa, have systems of national health insurance or national health care. Thus the patient is not directly responsible for the costs of treatment, and consequently the patient's choices about terminal care and/or euthanasia need not take personal financial considerations into account. Even for the patient who does have health insurance in the United States, many kinds of services are not covered, whereas the national health care or health insurance programs of many other countries variously provide many sorts of relevant services, including at-home physician care, home nursing care, home respite care, care in a nursing-home or other long-term facility, dietitian care, rehabilitation care, physical therapy, psychological counseling, and so on. The patient in the United States needs to attend to the financial aspects of dying in a way patients in many other countries do not, and in this country both the patient's choices and the recommendations of the physician are very often shaped by financial considerations.

There are many other differences between the USA on the one hand and the Netherlands and Germany, with their different models of dying, on the other. There are differences in degrees of paternalism in the medical establishment and in racism, sexism, and ageism in the general cultures, as well as awareness of a problematic historical past, especially Nazism. All of these and the previous factors influence the appropriateness or inappropriateness of practices such as active euthanasia and assisted suicide. For instance, the Netherlands' tradition of close physician/patient contact, its absence of malpractice-motivated medicine, and its provision of comprehensive health insurance, together with its comparative lack of racism and ageism and its experience in resistance to Nazism, suggest that this culture is able to permit the practice of voluntary active euthanasia, performed by physicians, without risking abuse. On the other hand, it is sometimes said that Germany still does not trust its physicians, remembering the example of Nazi experimentation, and given a comparatively authoritarian medical climate in which contact between physician and patient is quite distanced, the population could not be comfortable with the practice of active euthanasia. There, only a wholly patient-controlled response to terminal situations, as in nonphysician-assisted suicide, is a reasonable and prudent practice.

But what about the United States? This is a country where (1) sustained contact with the personal physician is decreasing, (2) the risk of malpractice action is increasing, (3) much medical care is not insured, (4) many medical decisions are financial decisions as well, (5) racism is on the rise, and (6) the public is naive about direct contact with Nazism or similar totalitarian movements. Thus, the United States is in many respects an untrustworthy candidate for practicing active euthanasia. Given the pressures on individuals in an often atomized society, encouraging solo suicide, assisted if at all only by nonprofessionals, might well be open to considerable abuse too.

However, there are several additional differences between the United States and both Holland and Germany that seem relevant here.

So far, the differences cited between the U.S. and both the Netherlands and Germany are negative ones, ones in which the U.S. falls far short. But there are positive differences as well, differences in which distinctive aspects of American culture are more favorable than those of Holland or Germany to the practice of euthanasia and assisted suicide. For example:

First, although the U.S. is indeed afflicted by a great deal of racism and sexism, it is also developing an increasingly strong tradition of independence in women. In many other countries, especially the Far East and the Islamic countries, the role of women still involves much greater disempowerment and expectations of subservience; in contrast, the U.S. is particularly advanced—though, of course, it has a long way to go. The U.S. may even be ahead of the Netherlands and perhaps Germany in this respect. Whatever the case, this issue is of particular importance with respect to euthanasia, especially among elderly persons, because it is women whose life expectancies are longer than those of men and hence are more likely to be confronted with late-life degenerative terminal conditions.

Second, American culture is more confrontational than many others, including Dutch culture. While the Netherlands prides itself rightly on a long tradition of rational discussion of public issues and on toleration of others' views and practices, the U.S. (and to some degree, also Germany) tends to develop highly partisan, moralizing oppositional groups. In general, this is a disadvantage; but in the case of euthanasia it may serve to alert a public to issues and possibilities it might not otherwise consider, and especially to the risks of abuse.

Third, though this may at first seem to be a trivial difference, it is Americans who are particularly given to personal self-analysis. This tendency is evident not only in America's high rate of utilization of counseling services, including religious counseling, psychological counseling, and psychiatry, but is even more clearly evident in its popular culture: its diet of soap operas, situation comedies, and pop psychology books. It is here that the ordinary American absorbs models for analyzing his or her own personal relationships and individual psychological characteristics. While of course things are changing and our cultural tastes are widely exported, the fact remains that the ordinary American's cultural diet contains more in the way of both professional and do-it-yourself amateur psychology and self-analysis than anyone else's. This long tradition of self-analysis may put us in a better position for certain kinds of end-of-life practices than many other cultures—despite whatever other deficiencies we have, just because we live in a culture that encourages us to inspect our own motives, anticipate the impact of our actions on others and scrutinize our own relationships with others, including our physicians. This disposition is of importance in euthanasia contexts because euthanasia is the kind of fundamental choice about which one may have somewhat mixed motives, be subject to various interpersonal and situational pressures, and so on. If the voluntary character of these choices is to be protected, it may be a good thing to inhabit a culture in which self-inspection of one's own mental habits and motives is encouraged.

Finally, the U.S. is also characterized by a kind of "do-it-yourself" ethic, an ethic that does not rely on others to direct you or provide for you, but encourages individual initiative and responsibility. (To be sure this feature has been somewhat eclipsed in recent years, and is little in evidence in the series of court cases cited earlier, but it is still part, I think, of the American character.) This is coupled with a sort of resistance to authority that is sometimes also said to be basic to the American temperament. If these things are the case, it would seem to suggest that Americans would seek a style of end-of-life practices which would emphasize these characteristics rather than others.

These, of course, are all mere conjectures about features of American culture which would have a positive effect on the practice of euthanasia, or assisted suicide. These are the features that one would want to reinforce, should these practices become general, in part to minimize the effects of the negative features. But, of course, these positive features will differ from one country and culture to another, just as negative features do. In each country, a different architecture of antecedent assumptions and cultural features develops around the issues of the end of life, and in each country the practice of euthanasia, if it is to be free from abuse at all, must be adapted to the culture in which it takes place.

What, then, is appropriate for our own cultural situation? Physician-performed euthanasia, though not in itself morally wrong, is morally jeopardized where the legal, time, and especially financial pressures on both patients and physicians are severe;

thus, it is morally problematic in our culture in a way that it is not in the Netherlands. Solo suicide outside the institution of medicine (as in Germany) may be problematic in a culture (like the United States) that is increasingly alienated, offers deteriorating and uneven social services, is increasingly racist, and in other ways imposes unusual pressures on individuals despite opportunities for self-analysis. Reliance only on withholding and withdrawing treatment (as in the United States) can be, as we've seen, cruel, and its comparative invisibility invites erosion under cost containment and other pressures. These are the three principal alternatives we've considered; but none of them seems wholly suited to our actual situation for dealing with the new fact that most of us die of extended-decline, deteriorative diseases. However, permitting physicians to supply patients with the means for ending their own lives grants physicians some control over the circumstances in which this can happen—only, for example, when the prognosis is genuinely grim and the alternatives for symptom control are poor—but leaves the fundamental decision about whether to use these means to the patient alone. It is up to the patient then—the independent, confrontational self-analyzing, do-it-yourself, authority-resisting patient—and his or her advisors, including family, clergy, physician, other health-care providers, and a raft of pop-psychology books, to be clear about whether he or she really wants to use these means or not. Thus, the physician is involved, but not directly; and it is the patient's choice, but the patient is not alone in making it. We live in a quite imperfect world, but, of the alternatives for facing death—which we all eventually must—I think the practice of permitting physician-assisted suicide is the one most nearly suited to the current state of our own somewhat flawed society. This is a model not yet central in any of the three countries examined here—the Netherlands, Germany, or the United States—but it is the one I think suits us best.

NOTES

1. Olshansky SJ. Ault AB. The fourth stage of the epidemiological transition: the age of delayed degenerative diseases. *Milbank Memorial Fund Quarterly/Health and Society* 1986;64:355–391.
2. Miles S. Gomez C. *Protocols for elective use of life-sustaining treatment*. New York: Springer-Verlag. 1988.
3. Sprung CL. Changing attitudes and practices in foregoing life-sustaining treatments. *JAMA* 1990; 263:2213.
4. Smedira NG et al. Withholding and withdrawal of life support from the critically ill. *N Engl J Med* 1990; 322:309–315.
5. *New York Times*, July 23, 1990, p. A13.
6. Paul J. van der Maas, Johannes J.M. vanDelden, Loes Pijnenborg, and Casper W.N. Looman, "Euthanasia and Other Medical Decisions Concerning the End Of Life," *The Lancet* 338 (Sept. 14, 1991): 669–674.
7. G. van der Wal, J. Th. M. van Eijk, H.J.J. Leenen, and C. Spreeuwenberg, "Euthanasie en hulp bij selfdoding door artsen in de thuissituatie. I. Diagnosen, leeftijd en geslacht van de patienten," *Nederlands Tijdschrift voor Geneesekunde* 135 (1991: 1593–1598: and II. "Lijden van de patienten," 1500–1603.
8. Else Borst-Eilers, paper delivered at the conference "Controversies in the Care of Dying Patients," University of Florida, Orlando, Feb. 14–16, 1991.
9. Van der Maas, p. 673.
10. Van der Maas, p. 671.
11. Admiraal P. *Euthanasia in a general hospital*. Address to the Eighth World Congress of the International Federation of Right-To-Die Societies, Maastricht. Holland. June 8, 1990.
12. Ten Have, H. "Coma: controversy and consensus." *Newsletter of the European Society for Philosophy of Medicine and Health Care* (May 1990) 8:19–20.

Euthanasia: Normal Medical Practice?

Henk A. M. J. ten Have and Jos V. M. Welie

Henk A. M. J. ten Have is a professor of medical ethics and chair of the Department of Ethics, Philosophy and History of Medicine, Catholic University of Nijmegen, The Netherlands.

Jos V. M. Welie is executive director of the International Program in Bioethics Education and Research, Catholic University of Nijmegen, The Netherlands.

Ten Have and Welie raise serious questions about the Dutch practice of allowing active euthanasia. The authors begin by pointing out that active euthanasia in the Netherlands is widely tolerated and more common than various recent studies have indicated. They provide many reasons for worrying about the increasing practices of active euthanasia. Most troubling of all is the fact that physicians are often not especially concerned about the express wishes of the patient. Perhaps as disturbing is their claim that most active euthanasia is not performed to put the patient out of his or her suffering but because of such factors as low quality of life, futility of treatment, and the belief on the physician's part that death should not be postponed. They conclude that the Dutch practice simply gives too much power to physicians and thereby curtails patient autonomy.

Since the 1973 Leeuwarden trial of a doctor who killed a patient requesting euthanasia, public debate on euthanasia in the Netherlands has become more intense. Despite the fact that, legally, active euthanasia is a criminal offense, physicians are quite open about practicing it. For example, in 1983 several general practitioners published case reports in influential Dutch medical journals.[1] However, the overall incidence of active euthanasia in medical practice was unknown; estimates varied between 2,000 and 20,000 cases a year.

In the 1970s and 1980s a pattern of jurisprudence developed that reflected a considerable judicial lenience toward physicians practicing euthanasia under strict conditions.[2] At least three conditions have been repeatedly referred to in court decisions and bills: (1) the patient's voluntary and persistent request; (2) the hopeless situation of the patient; (3) consultation of a colleague.

Early in 1989 two legislative proposals were submitted to Parliament pertaining to the practice of euthanasia but could not be discussed, as shortly afterwards the Cabinet resigned. In November 1989 the government (a coalition of the Christian Democratic Party and the Socialist Party) announced its intention to suspend political debate on legislation in order to obtain an empirical under-

Reprinted with permission of *The Hastings Center Report*, March/April 1992.

standing of the frequency and nature of euthanasia in medical practice. In January 1990 a new committee consisting of three lawyers and three physicians was established by the Ministers of Justice and Public Health to investigate medical practices regarding decisions at the end of life. In September 1991 the committee published its report, followed by new legislative proposals issued by the government on 8 November 1991 and scheduled to be discussed in Parliament about May 1992.

These developments suggest that the current debate in the Netherlands has shifted from the level of medical-ethical arguments, justifying or opposing euthanasia within the doctor-patient relationship, to the socioethical and political problem of whether and how to regulate or legalize the actual practice of euthanasia, given newly accumulated empirical data. Medical-ethical viewpoints regarding euthanasia in clinical practice have been moved to the background.

In this contribution, we will discuss the present state of the debate, first through an analysis of research into the practice of euthanasia and then through a moral evaluation of its political and legal implications.

RESEARCH INTO THE PRACTICE OF EUTHANASIA

In the fall of 1991 the results of two empirical studies on euthanasia were published. Van der Wal and his associates reported on the results of an exploratory, descriptive, retrospective study of morbidity, age, and sex of patients whose family doctors helped them to die; the study also tried to assess the level of suffering these patients experienced.[3] More influential was the report of the Committee on the Study of Medical Practice concerning Euthanasia (also called the Remmelink Committee after its president, attorney general of the Supreme Court J. Remmelink). The task of this committee was not to advise the government about legalizing euthanasia, but to investigate the current practice in the Netherlands.[4]

Some 130,000 people die in the Netherlands each year. In some 49,000 of these instances physicians have to decide whether to continue life support, withhold treatment, increase the dose of morphine to provide adequate pain relief even at a potentially lethal level, assist in suicide, or actually kill the patient. Although the committee was asked to investigate only the medical practice of terminating life, it decided to look into the whole field, that is "all situations in which physicians make decisions that aim (also) at ending suffering by hastening the end of the patient's life or in which the probability of a hastening of the end of life must be taken into account."[5]

To obtain data concerning such medical practices, the Institute of Public Health and Social Medicine of the Erasmus University of Rotterdam was requested to undertake an empirical research project. The research group decided (1) to initiate a retrospective study by interviewing a random population of some 400 physicians; (2) to verify the true cause of death of a random sample of some 8,500 recent deaths; (3) to undertake a prospective study in which the 400 interviewed physicians were asked to provide information anonymously about the true cause of death of each of their patients dying in the next six months; and (4) to interview a number of physicians with different specialties to eliminate the possibility, left open by the three previous studies, that particular specialties attract a much higher incidence of euthanasia.

It was found that assisted suicide was relatively uncommon, occurring only some 400 times a year, Euthanasia, defined as "any action that intentionally ends the life of someone else, on the request of that person," is practiced some 2,300 times, or in 5 percent of those 49,000 cases. Since every year some 9,000 patients request euthanasia, asking that it be performed within a few weeks—primarily patients suffering severely from cancer but virtually all mentally competent—physicians grant such wishes in less than half of the number of cases. Euthanasia has the highest incidence among family physicians/general practitioner, whereas physicians in nursing homes commit euthanasia relatively seldom.

The results of the study by Van der Wal and colleagues provide some insight into the context of euthanasia decisions, although in their publications no distinction is made between euthanasia (defined as the Remmelink Committee defines it) and assisted suicide. Data were gathered through an anonymous questionnaire in a random sample of family practitioners as well as through an analysis of police reports involving family doctors practicing euthanasia in the province of North Holland (in 1986–89). In 85 percent of these cases the patients suffered from malignant neoplasm; a high percentage of patients had AIDS or multiple sclerosis. In approximately 20 percent, a secondary, usually chronic disease had been diagnosed. Among patients under the age of thirty and over eighty-five euthanasia or assisted suicide were relatively rare.

Van der Wal also examined the nature and extent of the physical and emotional suffering of patients culminating in a request for euthanasia or assisted suicide. Questionnaires were sent to a random sample of family practitioners asking them to rate twenty-four aspects of suffering as well as to assess the life expectancy of the patient they most recently euthanized. According to the respondents, 90 percent of these patients showed severe physical suffering and 71 percent severe emotional suffering. "General weakness or tiredness," "dependence or being in need of help," "loss of dignity," and "pain" were the most frequently identified aspects of suffering. In 63 percent of the cases life expectancy at the moment of execution of the request was estimated as less than two weeks; in 10 percent it was more than three months.

INTERPRETATION OF THE DATA

In the media, one of the early conclusions drawn from the research reports was that euthanasia apparently was not as frequent as had been assumed by both protagonists and antagonists. This conclusion is not necessarily false, but upon careful consideration of the data presented in the Remmelink Report itself, it turns out to be rather meaningless. Medical decisions aimed at ending human life are more nuanced and heterogeneous than reflected in the definition. Many physicians do not interpret or classify their actions as euthanasia, even when those actions fall strictly under the range of the definition employed in the report (and common in the Netherlands). Consequently, the figure of 2,300 is not at all a specific or representative indicator of medical decisions leading to patients' death. The report clearly shows that other forms of intentional hastening of death are common practice in the Netherlands, yet fully escape professional, judicial, and social scrutiny.

The empirical data reveal that in 6 percent of the total number of 22,500 cases in which pain medication with a possible lethal effect was administered, hastening death was the very purpose of the administration, and in as many as 30 percent it was at least one of the purposes. Including these figures would increase the incidence of euthanasia to some 8,100 cases.

There also seem to be about 1,000 patients whose death was caused or hastened by physicians without any such request at all. These are patients who no longer were competent to make decisions, yet apparently suffered severely. Notice that these cases do not involve withholding or withdrawing medically futile treatments, since such treatments always have to be withdrawn. Nonetheless, the committee felt that these 1,000 cases are not morally troublesome; moreover, they should be considered "providing assistance to the dying." Nonvoluntary euthanasia was justified because the suffering of those patients had become "unbearable" and life must be considered "given-up" according to medical standards. Death would have occurred quickly (usually within a week), if the physician had not acted. Elsewhere, the committee adds that actively ending life when "the vital functions have started failing" is "indisputably normal medical practice."[6]

In some 28 percent of these 1,000 cases, patients had previously expressed the wish to be killed if, for example, the pain ever became unbearable or their situation inhuman. These cases, therefore, can be classified as euthanasia in the strict sense. Yet physicians mentioned "previously uttered request of the patient" as the reason to kill in a mere 17 percent of the cases. The researchers explained this discrepancy by arguing that physicians more often are guided by their own impressions of the patient's unspoken but probable wishes than by explicit oral or written requests. One may wonder whether such "impressions" are always correct. At any rate, a paradox emerges between this kind of reasoning and the very opposite reasoning of a number of courts and legislators to the effect that suffering is a purely subjective phenomenon and that, consequently, only the patient can decide whether his or her suffering has become unbearable. It seems that advocates of euthanasia use the subjective argument when defending the right of the competent patient to opt for euthanasia autonomously, and the impressionist argument when defending the practice of euthanasia on the mentally incompetent patient.

A similar ambiguity is reflected in the research methodology of Van der Wal and colleagues. Diagnoses can best be made by physicians, so there is nothing controversial about classifying diseases of euthanized patients by means of questionnaires mailed to family doctors. However, the assessment of patient's suffering is another matter; it is problematic to ask a physician to assess the depth as well as the nature of his patient's suffering—all the more so in retrospect when the physician has already performed euthanasia on his patient. Quite predictably these physicians claim the condition of 90 percent of the patients was characterized by severe physical suffering. Furthermore, dividing suffering into twenty-four "aspects" is highly problematic, since the relationship between suffering and "pain," "dependence," "nausea," "thirst," "constipation," "itch" is variable and subjective. The researchers seem to assume that the individual nature of suffering can be objectified by collecting a multitude of subjective opinions. But even then the data only provide an idea of what *doctors* think about the nature of suffering in their patients. The conclusion that the majority of euthanized patients experience severe physical and emotional suffering is not warranted. It can merely be concluded that the doctors in retrospect think this about their patients, but it is hardly an unexpected finding that euthanizing physicians justify their actions in precisely such terms.

The Remmelink Committee furthermore found that in 45 percent of the 1,000 nonvoluntary euthanasia cases, treatment of pain was no longer adequate to relieve the patient's suffering. However, the impossibility of treating the pain adequately was the reason for killing the patient in only 30 percent of the cases. The remaining 70 percent were killed for different reasons, such as: (1) low quality of life; (2) no prospect of improvement; (3) all forms of medical treatment had become futile; (4) all treatment was withdrawn but the patient did not die; or (5) one should not postpone death. In one-third of the cases, the fact that family and friends no longer could bear the situation played a role in the decisionmaking and indeed one respondent even indicated that economic considerations such as shortage of beds played a role. One may wonder how the committee's judgment that from a medical standpoint these patients were correctly "given up" should be understood. Certainly, such actions are not "indisputably" normal medical practice.

Finally the Remmelink Report mentions one more category that merits attention: the 20,000 cases in which physicians withhold or withdraw treatment neither because the patient so requests, nor because the treatment is futile, but because only limited benefit is to be expected and there are other reasons to withdraw or withhold. Looking at these "other reasons," we find that in 16 percent of the nonvoluntary withholdings or withdrawings, hastening death was the point of the decision and in another 19 percent hastening death was one of the reasons. Again, given the definitions of the committee itself, in which intention is the keyword, the cases, at least those where death is the primary point, must be considered nonvoluntary euthanasia which would imply an increase from 1,000 to 4,200 or even 8,000 such cases.

DISCUSSION OF THE COMMITTEE'S CONCLUSIONS

Although the Remmelink Committee was not asked to advise on the political consequences of the empirical data, it apparently could not resist the temptation. As we have tried to show, the committee's particular interpretation of the data itself reveals political bias. The committee clearly tried to remove any societal anxieties about the practice of euthanasia. Similar practices are brought under dissimilar headings to keep the numbers low. And at crucial places, particularly with the 1,000 nonvoluntary euthanasia cases, the committee uses fallacious rhetoric to emphasize that there is nothing to worry about. The committee's ideas on the legal status of euthanasia—for example, its views on the nonpunishment of a physician who carries out euthanasia in accordance with the cautionary standards and on the adequacy of the existing procedure for disclosing euthanasia—seem to imply that the committee favors legalization of euthanasia. The committee identifies certain constraints, but under those constraints it does not consider euthanasia an illegal practice.

Legalization, obviously, assumes the context of a particular legal system. A detailed review of the Dutch criminal law cannot be provided within the framework of this article, but a few remarks may clarify the context.[7] Since euthanasia is still illegal and, according to the letter of the law, can be penalized with up to twelve years' imprisonment, past jurisprudence has always looked for a "punishment exception." The legislators of the Dutch criminal law in 1886 realized that the letter of the law in certain exceptional circumstances might be unfair, and they therefore added a few articles listing possible grounds for nonpunishment. Without further explanation the Remmelink Committee claims that when a physician commits euthanasia in accordance with certain safeguards, there must always be a strong presumption that the physician's obligation to the patient justified trespassing the criminal law. Since such a conflict of duties constitutes one of those punishment exceptions, the physician should not be punished.

The committee simply contends that its interpretation of euthanasia by physicians is in accord with past Dutch jurisprudence. It maintains that the patient's situation is "inhumanly dishonorable," due to "unacceptably severe suffering," the physician is placed in a situation of *force majeure* that in turn justifies euthanasia.

As a matter of fact, Dutch jurisprudence, including Supreme Court verdicts, is not very clear or consistent at all about the applicability of that particular punishment exclusion. Since by law euthanasia is not a genuine medical intervention but an illegal action, and since the criminal law applies to every Dutch citizen equally—that is, no occupation or profession can claim special exemptions—the fact that the person who commits euthanasia is a physician may not be taken into consideration. Consequently, the euthanizing physician has to justify breaking the criminal law on nonmedical grounds that a layman could use just as well. The Supreme Court has underwritten this philosophy by explicitly rejecting the "medical exception." Yet on the other hand, society—the courts included—seems to take it for granted that if anybody should be allowed to practice euthanasia it should be physicians only.

This paradox is not merely a legalistic problem. A legal solution can be provided by simply adding a paragraph to the section on murder, manslaughter, and suicide, stating that physicians are allowed to commit such acts. The paradox is rather an ethical problem, for it is still not clear what circumstances can provide a justification. Traditionally, it is argued that an autonomous patient has the right to determine the course of his or her own life as well as the moment of its ending. Empirical research, however, indicates that the lives of many patients are deliberately shortened without any patient request whatsoever. The Remmelink Committee is not at all anxious about the extent of nonvoluntary euthanasia, yet fails to explain what it considers to be the justification of the practice. Indeed, the question about justification is not even asked. It is simply taken for granted that physicians are allowed, perhaps even obligated, intentionally to shorten life on a regular basis. After all, on medical criteria such life must be regarded as "given up."

THE RESPONSE OF THE CABINET

In its response to the Remmelink Report, the current government issued a statement containing a proposal to change the law on the Disposal of the Dead.[8] In writing a proposal, the government's leading consideration has been that the practice of euthanasia must remain open to legal audit. Consequently, the criminal law (particularly Article 293) will not be changed and the practice of euthanasia remains illegal. How, then, is this proposal supposed to resolve the tension of maintaining the criminal prohibition against euthanasia while still assuring that the practice of euthanasia is open to proper legal scrutiny? Some resolution must be offered since the Socialists advocate a more liberal stance toward euthanasia than the Christian Democrats.

The proposal is in many regards very similar to the one presented by the former coalition government of Christian Democrats and Liberals. In the former proposal, as in the current one, the criminal law remained unchanged. But in the Medical Practices Act a paragraph was to be added, listing various procedural safeguards to be followed when a physician decides to perform euthanasia. The Liberals explained that this proposal clearly reflected a liberalization of euthanasia, for judges now could take into account an explicit, legally binding list of criteria when judging a case of euthanasia. The only thing a physician would need to do was to abide by those criteria. The Christian Democrats, however, took the very same proposal as a clear message that euthanasia was still illegal. The criteria in the Medical Practices Act were merely practical suggestions; in and of themselves, they could not provide a justification for breaking the criminal law. In short, it was a fine example of a political compromise that suited both parties, but left the public confused and the future open.

A similar political compromise seems to have been struck in the latest proposal of the Christian Democrats and the Socialists. The criminal law remains unchanged, but this time the law on the Disposal of the Dead is amended. This law contains instructions for the attending physician, who is to write up a medical report on the cause of the patient's death. Currently, only two possible causes can be listed: natural or unnatural death. When the latter category is checked, as in cases of manslaughter, suicide, or any other unusual death, a legal mechanism is set into motion, involving the coroner, police, and the prosecution council. Euthanasia, obviously, is not a natural death, yet most physicians were accustomed to check that category upon committing euthanasia. Consequently, no coroner, police, or prosecution council would become involved (unless it happened that a family member or nurse, knowing about but disagreeing with the event, informed the authorities), and no legal audit could be performed. Both the Christian Democrats and the Socialists agreed that this situation of an undercover euthanasia practice is the worst possible situation. For that reason, as early as November 1990 a new regulation was issued pertaining to the disclosure of euthanasia. The regulation stated that attending physicians no longer should check "natural death" but should check neither alternative. The attending physician should simply hand the case to the coroner, who would inform the prosecution council. The prosecutor then would decide whether to prosecute. This new regulation and the very lenient policy of the prosecution council, however, could not prevent a large majority of physicians from refusing to disclose their act of euthanasia. Unwilling to change the criminal law, making euthanasia legal but unverifiable, the government now has proposed to change the law on the Disposal of the Dead, making the 1990 regulation positive law. Furthermore, the government proposed to expand the regulation to encompass nonvoluntary termination of life as well.

Both propositions—the legal formalizing of the regulation and its expansion—could be justified in purely pragmatic terms. Undercover euthanasia is an undesirable situation; undercover nonvoluntary termination of patient lives is even worse; therefore, a formal law pertaining to the disclosure of such practices is necessary even though it is rather unusual and paradoxical to draft a law requiring a transgressor to disclose his or her illegal deed. Indeed, the proposal explicitly states that these changes do not imply a pseudo-legalization of euthanasia. On the contrary, it is declared that current Dutch jurisprudence does not support the conclusion of the Remmelink Committee that nonvoluntary termination of life when vital functions have started failing is normal medical practice.

On the other hand, those taking a more liberal stance toward euthanasia could argue that the criteria in the law on the Disposal of the Dead constitute an incentive for the prosecution council to be even more lenient with physicians who have committed euthanasia. In other words, the proposal is open to diametrically opposed interpretations.

But it is problematic in other regards as well. For unlike the 1990 regulation, the proposal extends to nonvoluntary termination of life as well, a practice the Remmelink Committee found to occur in some 1,000 cases per year, but that as we suggested above, we believe occurs in even more instances. The government explains that it is undesirable to allow this practice to escape legal audit. Therefore, it is necessary to mandate that physicians disclose their actions in the same way as they are supposed to do in cases of ordinary euthanasia. Again, this part of the proposal is quite paradoxical in nature, for it requires a physician to assist in his or her own arrest, that is, to disclose actions that legally constitute the crime of murder; it furthermore prescribes how to commit such a crime, and it provides physicians with official documents to be used when disclosing this crime.

From a purely pragmatic point of view, this solution may be justifiable. But it goes so far against the system of the law that a quite different interpretation of this proposal presents itself, in spite of explicit remarks by the government to the contrary. The literal text of the proposal may not do so, but the intention clearly reflects a positive attitude toward euthanasia, including nonvoluntary euthanasia. Indeed, the government takes the committee's interpretation of the empirical data for granted, along with the conclusion that physicians almost always exercise the greatest possible caution prior to deciding in favor of euthanasia. A small but relevant detail may further clarify this point. The proposal requires physicians to disclose only euthanasia, physician-assisted suicide, and active medical interventions aimed at hastening the patient's death without the patient's request. In other words, withholding or withdrawing treatment, which traditionally is considered a passive action, does not fall within the range of this proposal, even if it is aimed at hastening the patient's death. The proposal sanctions the 7,000 such decisions that are made annually.

FINAL COMMENTS

Although the outcome of the current debate is still unclear, the results of the empirical studies raise fundamental questions concerning euthanasia and medical practice. In the 1970s the "euthanasia movement" in the Netherlands began as a protest against the power of contemporary medicine to alienate individuals from their own dying. Instead of counterbalancing that power and enhancing the individual's autonomy and control over his or her own life, it seems that social acceptance of euthanasia is resulting in physicians' acquiring even more power over the life and death of their patients. As the Remmelink Report shows, in most cases of ending human life, it is the physician who decides that it is appropriate to hasten death. Furthermore, it is quite remarkable how easily the morally most important cautionary standard established by jurisprudence—the patient's voluntary and persistent request—is brushed aside in the report. The motion adopted by the General Assembly of the Dutch Society of Health Law, published in the *Hastings Center Report* in late 1988, as well as various letters to the editor, repudiate the statement that doctors who terminate the life of patients without request remain unpunished. The latest empirical data prove exactly the opposite.

NOTES

1. See E.G.H. Kenter, "Euthanasie in een huisartsenpraktijk" [Euthanasia in a family practice], *Medisch Contact* 38 (1983): 1179–83; B. Meyboom-De Jong, "Actieve euthanasie" [Active euthanasia], *Nederlands Tijdschrift voor Geneeskunde* 127 (1983): 946–50; B.P. Ponsioen, "Hoe leert de huisarts leven met euthansie?" [How is the general practitioner learning to cope with euthanasia?],

Nederlands Tijdschrift voor Geneeskunde 127 (1983): 961–64.

2. See, for instance, J.K.M. Gevers, "Legal Developments Concerning Active Euthanasia on Request in the Netherlands," *Bioethics* 1, no. 2 (1987): 156–62; H.J.J. Leenen, "Euthanasia in the Netherlands," in *Medicine, Medical Ethics and the Value of Life,* ed. P. Byrne (Chichester: Wiley, 1990), pp. 1–14; M.A.M. de Wachter, "Active Euthanasia in the Netherlands," *JAMA* 262, no. 23 (1989): 3216–319; Henk ten Have, "Euthanasia in the Netherlands: The Legal Context and the Cases," *HEC Forum* 1, no. 1 (1989): 41–45.
3. G. van der Wal, J.T.M. van Eijk, H.J.J. Leenen, and C. Spreeuwenberg, "Euthanasie en hulp bij zelfdoding door artsen in de thuissituatie. I. Diagnosen, leeftijd en geslacht van de patienten," and II. Lijden van de patienten" [Euthansia and medically assisted suicide in the home situation. I Diagnoses, age, and sex of the patients, and II. Suffering of the patients]. *Nederlands Tijdschrift voor Geneeskunde* 135 (1991): 1593–1603.
4. Commissie Onderzock Medische Praktijk inzake euthansie, *Medische Beslissingen rond het Levenseinde* [Medical decisions concerning the end of life] (The Hague: SDU Uitgeverji, 1991); P.J. van der Maas J.J.M. van Delden, L. Pijnenborg, and C.W.N. Looman, "Euthanasia and Other Medical Decisions Concerning the End of Life," *Lancet* 338 (1991): 669–74.
5. Commissie Onderzock Medische Praktijk inzake euthanasie, *Medische Beslissingen,* p. 11.
6. Commissie Onderzock Medische Praktijk inzake euthanasie, *Medische Beslissingen,* p. 32.
7. For more information on the Dutch criminal law and jurisprudence pertaining to euthanasia, and a detailed discussion of legal-ethical complexities surrounding legalization of euthanasia, see J. Welie, "The Medical Exception: Physician, Euthanasia and the Dutch Criminal Law," *Journal of Medicine and Philosophy,* Spring 1992 (forthcoming).
8. Tweede Kamer, "Stanpunt van het Kabinet inzake medische beslissingen rond het levenseinde: Concept voorstel wijziging van de Wet op de Lijkbezorging" [Government statement on medical decisions concerning the end of life: proposal to amend the Law on the Disposal of the Dead], *Handelingen van de Tweede Kamer* 20, no. 14 (1991–1992): 383.

Buddhist Views of Suicide and Euthansia

Carl B. Becker

Carl B. Becker is a professor of Asian studies at the University of Hawaii. He has been a visiting professor of philosophy at University of Tsukuba, Japan. He is the author of Japan: My Teacher, My Love.

Becker explores Buddhist views of death and suicide and attempts to apply these ideas to recent debates about euthanasia. Traditionally, Buddhism does not view death as a bad thing or even as an ending. Rather, death is a transition from one stage of life to another. Because of this, suicide was not condemned, as long as the person had placed himself or herself in the right state of mind. A key to this is that a person accepts responsibility for his or her own life choices. When suicide or euthanasia is prohibited, it means that a person is deprived of the final act of taking responsibility for his or her own life. Hence, Becker argues, disallowing suicide and euthanasia is inhumane.

BIOETHICS AND BRAIN DEATH: THE RECENT DISCUSSION IN JAPAN

Japanese scholars of ethics and religions have been slow to come to grips with issues of bioethics, suicide, and death with dignity. Although the practical problems are frequently addressed in the popular press, and scattered citizen groups are beginning to draw attention to the issues, few people outside of the medical community have seriously addressed these issues.[1] As one recent representative example of this situation, consider the 39th annual meeting of the Japan Ethics Association (the academic association of ethicists from the entire country) held at Waseda University in October of 1988. The title of the annual meeting, in deference to the late Emperor's ailing condition and growing urgency of bioethical issues, was "Life and Ethics." Ostensibly, this was a chance to further the discussion among medical, religious, and philosophical ethicists on topics such as euthanasia and death with dignity. In fact, more than half of the presentations discussed classical views of life, such as those of Hippocrates, Confucius, Vico, Kant, Nietzsche, and so forth. The periods planned for open discussion were entirely usurped by the panelists' overtime reading of such papers. To their credit, however, there were a few Japanese scholars who boldly attempted to establish some more-Japanese views on the topics in bioethics, particularly euthanasia and death with dignity. While not without their problems, these presentations displayed less a Buddhist than a popular Japanese approach to the issue. The majority

Reprinted by permission of the University of Hawaii Press, from its journal *Philosophy East and West, Vol. 40/4,* October 1990.

agreed with Anzai Kazuhiro's early presentation that brain death should not be equated with human death.[2] Anzai's reasoning runs as follows: If brain death implies human death, then, by contraposition, human life must imply conscious (brain) life. Now there are clearly segments of our lives in which we are alive but not always conscious. Therefore it is wrong to conclude that a human is dead because he or she lacks consciousness. Of course, this argument can be faulted for collapsing conscious life and brain life, and for failing to distinguish periods of unconsciousness with the expectation of future revival (like deep sleep) from periods of unconsciousness with no expectation of future revival (like irreversible coma). But it is representative of a widely seen Japanese rejection of brain-death criteria.

This rejection comes partly from the Japanese association of brain-death criteria with organ transplantation. Many Japanese continue to manifest a distaste for organ transplantation, a distaste which dates back to Confucian teachings that the body, a gift from heaven and from one's parents, must be buried whole, and never cut. For this reason, dissections and autopsies were late in coming to Japan, not widely permitted until the nineteenth century. The modern Japanese practices of universal cremation, of surgical operations, and of flying to other countries to have organ transplants all have superseded the old Confucian prejudice against body-cutting. However, there remains a fear that if brain-death criteria were widely accepted, less conservative elements of society might abuse it for the sake of the "distasteful" practice of organ transplantation.

In his keynote address about Buddhist ethics, Tsukuba Professor Shinjō Kawasaki implied that this rejection of brain-death criteria may also be grounded in a Buddhist view of life and death.[3] He cited the *Visuddhimagga,* which indicates that life energy *(ayus)* is supported by body warmth and conscious faculties (broadly interpretable to include reflexes).[4] If either body heat or reflexes remain, then a person cannot be considered dead. Now Buddhism admits situations (such as meditative trances or hypothermia) in which neither body warmth nor reflexes are externally detectable, but the subject is not yet dead. So lack of warmth and reflexes is a necessary but not sufficient indicator of death; if either persists, it can be said that the body is not yet dead. In other words, Buddhism does not equate life with warmth and reflexes, but holds that body heat and reflexes are the "supports" of life, and therefore life cannot be empirically measurable except through such variables. Kawasaki also reaffirms the widespread Japanese Buddhist view that death is not the end of life, but merely a brief transition to another state, commonly thought to last for forty-nine days, intermediate between life in this body and life in the next. The reluctance to dismiss a body as "dead" prior to its loss of warmth and reflexes is not based on a fear of personal extinction or annihilation, but rather on a Buddhist view of the basic components of the life system.[5]

Chiba's Iida Tsunesuke expands this view by arguing that "persons are not merely the meaningless "subjects of rights," but personalities, "faces," embodying the possibilities of fulfilling the dreams of their parents or loved ones . . . recipients of love, and therefore worthy of honoring."[6] This argument begs the question of "possibilities," since in the case of brain-dead victims, it is precisely such possibilities which are missing. Logically speaking, the "possibilities" argument has long ago been laid to rest by philosophers like Mary Anne Warren, who have demonstrated that we need not treat potential presidents as presidents, potential criminals as criminals, or potential humans as humans.[7] (Japanese society might differ in this respect; until recently, suspicion of crime or likelihood of committing crime were sufficient grounds for arrest, children of nobles [potential lords] were often honored or killed as real lords.)[8]

However, Iida's argument is important less for its logical persuasion than for its revelation of the Japanese attitude: that persons are not subjects with rights and individual free wills, but rather objects of the attention of others. (Japanese treatment of infants and children reinforces this view that Japanese children are not seen as persons but as possessions of their parents; this was the legal as well as philosophical status of women and servants as well as children prior to the twentieth century.)

This position is further developed by Ohara Nobuo, who argues that "although a body may be treated as a "thing" or a corpse by physicians, it remains a body of value and meaning, and in that sense, a *person,* to members of its family. . . . In this sense, even vegetative humans and brain-dead corpses can give joy to other people."[9] Of course this point of view is pregnant with problems which Ohara himself seems loath to acknowledge. Only in the most metaphorical of senses can a corpse "give" anything to anyone; rather, it is the family who may *derive* some sense of joy by beholding the face of one dear to them, even though that person is incapable of ever being conscious in that body again.

This attitude is akin to the Japanese reverence for pictures, sculptures, and myths; it provides no useful guidelines whatsoever to the medical faculty as to when to continue or desist from what kinds of treatment for the patient. To the question "When does a body stop being a person?" the Oharan answer, "It never stops being a person to those who love it," may be psychologically correct for some people, but is a dead end in medical ethics, for it fails to answer the question, "When should a body be treated not as a living person but as a dead body?"

Moreover, even if it were thought to have some utility in the case where relatives or "significant others" remain alive and concerned with the fate of the deceased, it values the person (or corpse) entirely in terms of his value *to others*. In cases where old people die alone and uncared for, the absence of concerned others leaves the medical practitioner utterly without guidelines. (This is consistent with the frequently noted proposition that Japanese without social contexts seem morally at a loss.)[10]

This position also presumes a wishful naïveté on the part of the parent or family, a failure to distinguish between a living human with a potential for interaction and a dead body with only the resemblance of a loved one. This may not bother many Japanese parents, for whom children are indeed "objects." In fact, there are "rehabilitation hospitals" in Japan in which anencephalic infants are cared for and raised for as many years as their parents' finances and interest dictate; they are propped up and made to "greet" their parents whenever their parents desire to visit.[11]

Such unwillingness to admit the finality of death or the fundamental suffering of the human condition runs counter to the basic tenets of Buddhism. We are reminded of the famous story of the woman who asked the Buddha to revive her baby. In response, the Buddha instructed her to ask for food from any house in which no one had died. In the process of asking around the entire village, the woman came to realize that all humans must die and deal with death. In this way she gained enlightenment, stopped grieving for her dead child, and became a follower of the Buddha. The relatives who refuse to pronounce dead a relative as long as he has a "face," or the parents who insist on artificially prolonging the appearance of life in an anencephalic infant, cannot claim to understand Buddhism.

A much larger misunderstanding lurks behind the whole discussion between "brain-death advocates" and "brain-dead opposers" in Japan. The real issue is not whether or not every body should immediately be scavenged for spare parts as soon as the brain is isoelectric, as some opponents would purport. Rather, the question is whether it is ever acceptable to desist from treatment after brain death (turning the hospital's valuable and limited resources to other waiting patients). In the absence of brain-death criteria, many otherwise hopeless bodies remain on artificial support systems almost indefinitely. Even if the brain-death criteria were accepted, nothing would prevent families from finding hospitals which would preserve the bodies of their beloved on artificial support systems indefinitely, nor would anything require organ donation if the patient and family did not desire it. Thus the issue, like that of suicide and euthanasia, is not, "Should everyone be forced to follow these criteria?" but rather, "May people who desire it be allowed to follow these criteria?" Groundless fears of widespread organ sales or piracy have made this issue into a much greater hobgoblin than it ever needed to become.

This is not merely to criticize the recently voiced opinions of Japanese ethicists. Rather, I introduce this body of evidence to demonstrate the slow growth of Japanese thought in bioethics, and particularly their concerns with *bodies of value to others* rather than with *subjects of value to themselves*. This concern finds no support either in Japanese Buddhism nor in samurai teaching, but in the level of popular belief, it may have serious ramifications for Japanese bioethics for many generations to come.

The World Federation of the Right To Die Society held an International Conference in Nice (France) in 1984. Although many Japanese attended this conference, apparently none of them contributed to the West's understanding of Buddhist views of euthanasia. When the President of the Society published a book on world attitudes on euthanasia the following year, only 2 percent (2.5 out of 150 pages) was about Buddhist attitudes, and those ideas were gained from California Buddhists, not from the Japanese Buddhists at Nice.[12]

Buddhists have a big contribution to make to the humanization and naturalization of medicine and bioethics. I may not speak for all of Japanese Buddhism, but I shall be happy if this article inspires further dialogue and contributions from the Japanese Buddhist side.

EARLY BUDDHIST VIEWS OF DEATH, SUICIDE, AND EUTHANASIA

Japan has long been more aware of and sensitive to the dying process than modern Western cultures. Moreover, Japan already has its own good philosophical and experiential background to deal effectively with "new" issues of bioethics, such as euthanasia. Japanese Buddhists have long recognized what Westerners are only recently rediscovering: that the manner of dying at the moment of death is very important. This fundamental premise probably predates Buddhism itself, but is made very explicit in the teachings of the Buddha.[13] In his meditations, the Buddha noticed that even people with good karma were sometimes born into bad situations, and even those with bad karma sometimes found inordinately pleasant rebirths. Buddha declared that the crucial variable governing rebirth was the nature of the consciousness at the moment of death. Thereafter, Buddhists placed high importance on holding the proper thoughts at the moment of death. Many examples of this idea can be found in two works of the

Theravāda canon. The *Petavatthu* and the *Vimānavatthu* ("Stories of the Departed"). Indeed, in many sutras, monks visit laymen on their deathbeds to ensure that their dying thoughts are wholesome,[14] and the Buddha recommends that lay followers similarly encourage each other on such occasions.[15]

Buddhism sees death as not the end of life, but simply a transition; suicide is therefore no escape from anything. Thus, in the early *sangha* (community of followers of the Buddha), suicide was in principle condemned as an inappropriate action.[16] But the early Buddhist texts include many cases of suicide which the Buddha himself accepted or condoned. For example, the suicides of Vakkali[17] and of Channa[18] were committed in the face of painful and irreversible sickness. It is significant, however, that the Buddha's praise of the suicides is *not* based on the fact that they were in terminal states, but rather that their minds were selfless, desireless, and enlightened at the moments of their passing.

This theme is more dramatically visible in the example of Godhika. This disciple repeatedly achieved an advanced level of *samādhi,* bordering on *parinirvāna,* and then slipped out of the state of enlightenment into normal consciousness again. After this happened six times, Godhika at last vowed to pass on to the next realm while enlightened, and quietly committed suicide during his next period of enlightenment. While cautioning his other disciples against suicide, the Buddha nonetheless blessed and praised Godhika's steadiness of mind and purpose, and declared that he had passed on to *nirvāna*. In short, the acceptability of suicide, even in the early Buddhist community, depended not on terminal illness alone, but upon the state of selfless equanimity with which one was able to pass away. It is interesting in passing that all these suicides were committed by the subject knifing himself, a technique which came to be standardized in later Japanese ritual suicide.

When asked about the morality of committing suicide to move on to the next world, the Buddha did not criticize it.[19] He emphasized that only the uncraving mind would be able to move on towards *nirvāna,* and that, conversely, minds desiring to get free or flee something by their death might achieve nothing. Similarly, there are stories in the Jatāka tales of the Buddha giving his own body (in former lives) to save other beings, both animals and humans. Thus death out of compassion for others is also lauded in the scriptures.[20] It is also well known that in the Jain tradition, saints were expected to fast until their deaths,[21] and thereafter there have been those both in China and Japan who have followed this tradition.[22]

In China, it is believed that a disciple of Zendō's jumped out of a tree in order to kill himself and reach the Pure Land. Zendō's response was not that the action of suicide was right or wrong in and of itself, but that the disciple who wanted so strongly to see the Pure Land was doubtless ready to reach it.[23] Other more recent examples may be found in the Buddhist suicides of the Vietnamese monks protesting against the Vietnam government.[24] Whether or not these stories are all historical fact is not at issue here. The point is that they demonstrate the consistent Buddhist position toward suicide: there is nothing intrinsically wrong with taking one's own life, if it is not done in hate, anger, or fear. Equanimity or preparedness of mind is the main issue.

In summary, Buddhism realizes that death is not the end of anything, but a transition. Buddhism has long recognized persons' rights to determine when they should move on from this existence to the next. The important consideration here is not whether the body lives or dies, but whether the mind can remain at peace and in harmony with itself.

The Jōdo, (Pure Land) tradition tends to stress the continuity of life, while the Zen tradition tends to stress the importance of the time and manner of dying. Both of these ideas are deeply rooted in the Japanese consciousness.

RELIGIOUS SUICIDE AND DEATH WITH DIGNITY IN JAPAN

Japanese Buddhists demonstrated an unconcern with death even more than their neighbors. Japanese valued peace of mind and honor of life over length of life. While the samurai often committed suicide on the battlefield or in court to preserve their dignity in death, countless commoners chose to commit suicide in order to obtain a better future life in the Pure Land. On some occasions, whole masses of people committed suicide at the same time. In others, as in the situation depicted in Kurosawa's famous film "Red Beard," a poverty-stricken family would commit suicide in order to escape unbearable suffering in this life and find a better life in the world to come. Often parents would kill their children first, and then kill themselves; this kind of *shinjū* can still be seen in Japan today. The issue for us today is: how does Buddhism appraise such suicide in order to gain heavenly rebirth?

On a popular level, the desire to "leave this dirty world and approach the Pure Land" (*Enri edo, gongu jōdo*) was fostered by wandering itinerant monks such as Kūya in the Heian period, and Ippen in the Kamakura period. The tradition of committing suicide by entering a river or west-facing seashore apparently began in the Kumano area, but rapidly spread throughout the nation along with the Pure Land faith upon which it was based. The common tradition was to enter the water with a rope tied around one's waist, held by one's retainers or horse.[25] If one's nerve and single-minded resolution failed, then one would not achieve rebirth in the Pure Land as desired. In such an instance, either the suicide himself, or his retainers (judging from his countenance), might pull him out of the water and save him from dying with inappropriate thoughts. However, if the suicide retained a peaceful and unperturbed mind and countenance throughout the drowning, the retainers were to let him die in peace, and simply retain the body for funeral purposes. Such situations clearly demonstrate that what is at stake here is not the individual's right to die, but rather his ability to die with peace of mind. If a death with a calm mind is possible, then it is not condemned.

A paradigmatic example of this situation can be found in the records of Saint Ippen.[26] Ajisaka Nyūdō, a Pure Land aspirant possibly of noble descent, gave up his home and family to follow the teachings of Saint Ippen. For unclear reasons, Ippen refused admission to his band of itinerant mendicants, but advised him that the only way to enter the Pure Land was to die holding the Nembutsu (name and figure of Amida) in mind. Nyūdō then committed suicide by drowning himself in the Fuji River.

The scene is vividly depicted in the scroll paintings.[27] Here, Ajisaka is seen with a rope around his waist. His attendants on the shore hold one end of the rope. As he bobs above the current, he is seen perfectly preserving the *gasshō* position, at peace and in prayer. Music is heard from the purple clouds above him, a common sign of Ōjō, or rebirth in the Pure Land.

When Ippen heard of this suicide, he praised Ajisaka's faith, interpreting the purple clouds and Ajisaka's unruffled demeanor as proof of his attainment of rebirth in the Pure Land. At the same time, he warned his other disciples, repeating Ajisaka's last words (*nagori o oshimuna*), not to grieve over their master's passing.[28]

When Ippen himself died, six of his disciples also committed suicide in sympathy, hoping to accompany their master to the Pure Land. This occasioned some other debate about the propriety of "sympathy suicide." Shinkyō, Ippen's disciple and second patriarch of the Ji School, declared that the disciples had failed to obtain rebirth in the Pure Land, for their action was seen as "self-willed," and Pure Land faith relies entirely on the power and will of Amida Buddha. Assertion of self-will is seen as running counter to the reliance on other power demanded by the Amida faith.[29]

Several important points can be learned from these examples. First, suicide is never condemned per se. Rather it is the state of mind which determines the rightness or wrongness of the suicide situation. The dividing line between choosing one's own time and place of death with perfectly assured peace of mind, and self-willing one's own death at the time of one's master's death is perhaps a thin grey one, but this should not obscure the criteria involved: death with desire leads not to rebirth in the Pure Land, but death with calm assurance does. Even the method of water suicide, using a rope as a preventative backup, stresses the importance of the state of mind in this action.

Secondly, Ajisaka's famous phrase, "Nagori o oshimuna," means that Buddhists are not to kill themselves in "sympathy" when others die. A literal translation would be that we are not to cling to what remains of the name or person, but to let the deceased go freely on to the next world. In other words, when someone dies with an assured state of mind, it is not for those who remain either to criticize or to wish that he had not died in this situation. Those who are left behind are to respect and not resent, reject, or grieve for a death which might seem to them untimely.

It is not coincidental that the word for euthanasia in Japanese is *anrakushi,* a term with Buddhist meanings. In Buddhist terminology, *anrakukoku* is another name for the Pure Land, the next world of Amida Bodhisattva, to which each Japanese expects to go after death. German-educated doctor and historical novelist Mori Ōgai's famous book *Takasebune* specifically deals with *anrakushi;* it is the story of Yoshisuke killing his sickly young brother who wants to die but lacks the strength to kill himself.[30] Many famous twentieth-century Japanese authors wrote of suicide, and some, such as Akutagawa, Dazai, Kawabata, and Mishima, actually committed suicide. Following the deaths of each emperor (Meiji, Taishō, and, last year, Shōwa), faithful retainers have also committed suicide in sympathy with their departed leaders. While some of these suicides are not Buddhistic (they show anger, pessimism, nihilism, and so forth), they are still reminders that the Japanese Buddhist world view does not condemn suicide.

Japanese law does not criminalize suicide, and European law is slowly beginning to follow the Japanese model in this regard. However, Japanese law does hold it to be a crime to assist or encourage a suicide. In normal situations, this is only wise and prudent, for healthy people should be encouraged to live and make the most of their lives. But in the situations where *songenshi* (death with dignity) is requested, it is precisely because the person is facing imminent death that it is morally acceptable to assist his suicide, particularly if the motive is mercy.

SAMURAI, *SEPPUKU,* AND EUTHANASIA

Among the warrior elite, who usually followed Zen Buddhism, suicide was considered an honorable alternative to being killed by others or continuing a life in shame or misery. Beginning with the famous *seppuku* of Minamoto no Tametomo and Minamoto no Yorimasi in 1170, *seppuku* became known as the way that a vanquished but proud Buddhist warrior would end his life.[31] Soon thereafter, headed by Taira Noritsune and Tomomori, hundreds of Taira warriors and their families committed suicide in the battle of Dannoura of 1185. Famous suicides included that of Kusunoki Masashige in 1336, in the battle between Nitta and Hosokawa, and that of Hideyori Toyotomi, under siege by Tokugawa Ieyasu in 1615. In the Tokugawa period, love suicides were dramatized in a dozen plays by Chikamatsu Monzaemon including *Sonezaki shinjū, Shinjū ten no Amijima, and Shinjū mannensō.*[32] The forty-seven Akō *rōnin,* who committed suicide after avenging their master's death, was another famous true story, dramatized in the *Chūshingura* plays and films.[33] The samurai's creed, to be willing to die at any moment, was dramatically spelled out by the *Hag-akure*.[34] According to the *Hagakure,* the important concern was not whether one lived or died, but (1) being pure, simple, single-minded, (2) taking full responsibility for doing one's duty, and (3) unconditionally serving one's master, without concern for oneself.

Although *seppuku* may seem like a violent death to the observer, it was designed to enable the samurai to die with the greatest dignity and peace.

It is particularly noteworthy that the samurai's code of suicide included a provision for euthanasia: the *kaishakunin* (attendant). Cutting of the *hara* alone was very painful, and would not lead to a swift death. After cutting their *hara,* few samurai had enough strength to cut their own necks or spines. Yet without cutting their necks, the pain of the opened *hara* would continue for minutes or even hours prior to death. Therefore, the samurai would make arrangements with one or more *kaishakunin* to assist his suicide. While the samurai steadied his mind and prepared to die in peace, the *kaishakunin* would wait by his side. If the samurai spoke to the *kaishakunin* before or during the *seppuku* ceremony, the standard response was *"go anshin"* (set your mind at peace). All of the interactions and conversations surrounding an officially ordered *seppuku* were also fixed by tradition, so that the suicide might die with the least tension and greatest peace of mind. After the samurai had finished cutting to the prearranged point, or gave some other signal, it was the duty of the *kaishakunin* to cut the neck of the samurai to terminate his pain by administering the coup de grâce.[35]

Many samurai suicides were in fact the moral equivalent of euthanasia. The reasons for a samurai's suicide were either (1) to avoid an inevitable death at the hands of others, or (2) to escape a longer period of unbearable pain or psychological misery, without being an active, fruitful member of society. These are exactly the sorts of situations when euthanasia is desired today: (1) to avoid an inevitable death at the hands of others (including disease, cancer, or bacteria), (2) to escape a longer period of pain or misery without being a fruitful, active member of society.

In regard to (1), most Japanese are now cut down in their seventies by the enemies of cancer and other diseases, rather than in their youth on a battlefield. Regardless of whether the person is hopelessly surrounded by enemies on a battlefield, or hopelessly defeated by enemy organisms within his body, the morality of the situation is the same. In regard to (2), it might be argued that there is a difference between the pain or misery of the permanent incapacitation of a samurai, and the pain or misery of the permanent incapacitation of a hospital patient.

But if anything, the hospital patient is in even less of a position to contribute to society or feel valued than is the samurai, so he has even more reason to be granted the option of leaving this arena (world) when he chooses. The samurai tradition shows that the important issue is not the level of physical pain, but the prospect for meaningful and productive interaction with other members of society. If there are no prospects for such interactions, the samurai society claimed no right to prevent the person from seeking more meaningful experiences in another world.

Now in both cases, there may be relatives or retainers in the area who do not wish to see their friend die. The issue in these cases is not whether or not the besieged person will die; it is only a question of how soon, and in what manner. From ancient times, Japanese have respected the right of the individual to choose the moment and manner of dying. The Buddhist principle ought to apply equally well to the modern medical battles against the enemies of the body. The argument that if a body still has a face, it is still a person to those around him, is a basically un-Buddhist failure to understand (a) the difference between body and life, (b) the importance of each person's determination of his own mental states, and (c) the importance of placing mercy over desire in Buddhism.

Of course there need to be safeguards in such situations, and those safeguards have already been spelled out by the decision of the Nagoya High Court. In case of euthanasia, the Nagoya High Court (22 December 1962) defined certain conditions under which euthanasia could be considered acceptable:

1. The disease is considered terminal and incurable by present medicine.
2. The pain is unbearable—both for the patient and those around him.
3. The death is for the purpose of his peaceful passing.
4. The person himself has requested the death, while conscious and sane.
5. The killing is done by a doctor.
6. The method of killing is humane.

If these safeguards are followed, it seems there is no moral reason that Buddhists should oppose euthanasia.

CONCLUSIONS

There are Japanese who hold that the Japanese lack the independent decision-making abilities of Western people, and that therefore doctors should make the decisions for their patients. This logic is backwards. The reason patients cannot make good independent judgments is because the doctors refuse them the information and freedom to do so, not because they lack the mental abilities or personal characteristics to make judgments.[36] Buddhism has always recognized the importance of individual choice, despite social pressures; examples range from the Buddha himself, through Kūkai, Hōnen, Shinran, and Nagamatsu Nissen. The ability of Japanese to take personal responsibility for important decisions in times of stress, danger, or anguish has been repeatedly shown in the historical examples of these bold Buddhist reformers.

In order for the patient to make an intelligent decision about when and how he wants to die, he needs to know the facts about the nature of his disease, not only its real name, but the realistic prospects and alternative outcomes of all available forms of treatment. This means renouncing the paternalistic model held by present Japanese medicine, and granting substantial freedom to the patient in deciding his own case. Some Japanese doctors have argued that (1) patients do not really want to know the bad news about themselves, that (2) knowing the truth may harm their conditions, and that (3) the physicians can judge more intelligently than the patient. However, studies in the West show that none of these claims is true. As Bok points out, "The attitude that what [the patient] doesn't know won't hurt him is proving unrealistic—it is rather what patients do not know but vaguely suspect that causes them corrosive (destructive) worry."[37] People recover faster from surgery and tolerate pain with less medication when they understand their own medical problems and what can and cannot be done about them.[38] In any case, doctors' withholding of information from patients is based not on statistical proof or ethical principles, but on the physician's desires to retain control over patients.[39] This is a situation that clear-thinking Buddhists naturally oppose. There is no reason to believe that these findings, long known and supported in Western medicine, should prove any different for the Japanese.

One important question for Buddhists today remains: what, if any, are the differences between suicide and euthanasia? Obviously one important difference is in the case where the person receiving euthanasia is unconscious. In this case, we have no way of knowing whether the patient genuinely desires euthanasia, unless he or she has previously made a declaration of wishes in a living will. On the other hand, once the consciousness has permanently disassociated itself from the body, there is no reason in Buddhism to continue to nourish or stimulate the body, for the body deprived of its *skandhas* is not a person. The Japan Songenshi Kyōkai (Association for Death with Dignity) has done much to improve the ability of the individual Japanese to choose his time and manner of death.

Another issue is the relation of pain-killing to prolonging life and hastening death itself. The Japan Songenshi Kyōkai proposes the administering of painkilling drugs even if they hasten the death of the patient. Buddhists would agree that relief of pain is desirable, and whether the death is hastened or not is not the primary issue. However, consider a case where the pain is extreme and only very strong drugs will stop the pain. Here there may be a choice between: (a) no treatment at all, (b) pain-killing which only blurs or confuses the mind of the patient, and (c) treatment which hastens the end while keeping the mind clear. In such a situation, the Buddhist would first prefer the most natural way of (a) no treatment at all. But if his mind were unable to focus or be at peace because of the great pain, the Buddhist would choose (c) over (b), because clarity of consciousness at the moment of death is so important in Buddhism.

Doctors who do not like the idea of shortening a person's life would prefer to prolong the material life-processes, regardless of the mental quality of that life. This is where Buddhists disagree with materialistic Western medicine. But there need be no conflict between Buddhism and medicine. There is no reason to assign the doctor the "responsibility" for the death of the patient. Following the guidelines of the Nagoya court, patients potentially eligible for euthanasia are going to die soon anyway, so that is not the fault of the doctor. And the patient has the right to determine his own death. The fact that he is too weak to hold a sword or to cut short his own life is not morally significant. If his mind is clear, calm, and ready for death, then the one who understands and compassionately assists that person is also following Buddhist morality. In summary, the important issue for Buddhists here is whether or not the person will be allowed responsibility for his own life and fate. The entire Buddhist tradition, and particularly that of suicide within Japan, argues that personal choice in time and manner of death is of extreme importance, and anything done by others to dim the mind or deprive the dying person of such choice is a violation of Buddhist principles. Japanese Buddhists may respect this decision more than Western cultures, and lead humanitarian bioethics in a different perspective towards dignified death.

NOTES

1. Morioka Masahiro, "Nōshi to wa nan de atta ka" (What was brain death?), in *Nihon Rinri Gakkai kenkyū happyō yoshi* (Japanese Ethics Association outline of presentations) (Japan Ethics Association 39th Annual Conference, Waseda University, October 14–15, 1988), p. 7.
2. Anzai Kazuhiro, "Nō to sono ishiki" (Brain and its consciousness), in *Nihon Rinri Gakkai,* p. 6.
3. Kawasaki Shinjō, "Tōyō kodai no seimei juyō" (The accepted understanding of life in the ancient Orient), in *Nihon Rinri Gakkai,* p. 26.
4. *Visuddhimagga,* pp. 229ff.
5. Kawasaki, "Tōyō kodai no seimei juyō." p. 27.
6. Iida Tsunesuke, "Bioethics wa nani o nasu no ka" (What does bioethics accomplish?), in *Nihon Rinri Gakkai,* pp. 40ff.
7. Mary Anne Warren, "Do Potential People Have Moral Rights?" *Canadian Journal of Philosophy* 7 no. 2 (1978): 275–289.
8. Carl Becker, "Old and New: Japan's Mechanisms for Crime Control and Social Justice," *Howard Journal of Criminal Justice,* 27 no. 4 (November 1988): 284–285.
9. Ohara Nobuo, "Sei to shi no rinrigaku" (The ethics of life and death), in *Nihon Rinri Gakkai,* pp. 54–55.
10. Carl Becker, "Religion and Politics in Japan," chap. 13 of *Movements and Issues in World Religions,* ed. C. W-H. Fu and G. S. Spiegler (New York: Greenwood Press, 1987), p. 278.
11. Among the author's students are nurses at such hospitals.
12. Gerald A. Larue, *Euthanasia and Religion: A Survey of the Attitudes of World Religions to the Right-To-Die* (Los Angeles: The Hemlock Society, 1985).
13. Cf. *Hastings Encyclopedia of Religion,* Vol. 4, p. 448.
14. *Majhima Nikāya* II, 91; III, 258.
15. *Samyutta Nikāya* V, 408.
16. Tamaki Koshirō, "Shino oboegaki" (Memoranda on death), in *Bukkyo shisō,* vol. 10, ed. Bukkyō Shiso Kenkyukai, Tokyo (September 1988), pp. 465–475.
17. *Sūtta Vibhanga, Vinaya* III, 74; cf. *Samyutta Nikaya* III, 119–124.
18. *Majhima Nikāya* III, 263–266 (*Channovada-sūtta); Samyutta Nikāya* IV, 55–60 (*Channavaga).*
19. *Samyutta Nikāya* I, 121.
20. *Jatakā Suvarna Prabhāsa* 206ff.
21. *Acāranga Sūtra* I, 7, 6.
22. A mummified body of one such monk is preserved at the Myorenji temple, close to Tsukuba University.
23. Ogasawara Senshū, *Chūgoku Jōdokyō no kenkyū* (Researches in Chinese Pure Land Buddhism) (Kyoto: Heirakuji, 1951), pp. 60ff.
24. Thich Nhat Hanh, *The Lotus in the Sea of Fire* (London, 1967).
25. Kurita Isamu, *Ippen Shōnin, tabi no shisakuska* (Saint Ippen, the meditative wayfarer) (Tokyo: Shinchosha, 1977), pp. 165–169.
26. Ōhashi Shunnō, *Ippen* (Tokyo: Yoshikawa Kobunkan, 1983), pp. 105ff.
27. *Ippen goroku,* scroll 6, stage 2 (*maki 6, dan 2).*
28. Kurita, *Ippen Shōnin.*
29. Ōhashi, *Ippen,* pp. 107ff.
30. Mori Ōgai, *Takasebune* (Tokyo: Iwanami Bunko, 1978).
31. Jack Seward, *Hara-Kiri: Japanese Ritual Suicide* (Tokyo: Charles E. Tuttle, 1968), Seward describes these and many other significant suicides in detail.
32. Donald Keene, trans., *Major Plays of Chikamatsu* (New York: Columbia University Press, 1961).
33. Fujino Yoshiō, ed., *Kanatehon Chushingura: Kaishaku to kenkyū* (Chushingura) (Tokyo: Ofūsha, 1975).
34. Watsuji Tetsurō, ed., *Hagakure* (Tokyo: Iwanami Bunko, 1970).
35. All condensed from Seward, *Hara-Kiri.*
36. *Kimura Ribito,* "In Japan, Parents Participate but Doctors Decide," *Hastings Center* Report 16, no. 4 (1986): 22–23.
37. Sisela Bok, "Lies to the Sick and Dying," in *Lying: Moral Choice in Public and Private Life* (New York: Pantheon Books, 1978).
38. Lawrence Egbert, George Batitt, et al., "Reduction of Post-operative Pain by Encouragement and Instruction of Patients," *New England Journal of Medicine* 270 (1964): 825–827; and Howard Waitzskin and John Stoeckle, "The Communication of Information About Illness," *Advances in Pyschosomatic Medicine* 8 (1972): 185–215.
39. Cf. Bernard Gert and Charles Culver, "Paternalistic Behavior," *Philosophy and Public Affairs* 6 (Summer 1976); and Allen Buchanan, "Medical Paternalism," ibid., vol. 7 (Summer 1978).

The Survival Lottery

John Harris

John Harris is a reader in philosophy at the faculty of education of the University of Manchester, England. He is the author of Violence and Responsibility *(1980),* The Value of Life: An Introduction to Medical Ethics *(1985), and* Wonderwoman and Superman: The Ethics of Human Biotechnology *(1992).*

In this provocative essay, Harris argues that a lottery to determine who should live and who should die, given that organs are scarce, can be justified. Such a justification calls into question many of our deepest intuitions, especially concerning the moral importance of not directly killing a person, even if that person's death will save the lives of others who would die naturally otherwise. Among other things, Harris argues that the person who loses the lottery, and must give up his or her life so that others may be saved, is no more innocent than those who would otherwise die without his or her organs. So, Harris contends, the most obvious objection to such a practice is not defensible.

Let us suppose that organ transplant procedures have been perfected; in such circumstances if two dying patients could be saved by organ transplants then, if surgeons have the requisite organs in stock and no other needy patients, but nevertheless allow their patients to die, we would be inclined to say, and be justified in saying, that the patients died because the doctors refused to save them. But if there are no spare organs in stock and none otherwise available, the doctors have no choice, they cannot save their patients and so must let them die. In this case we would be disinclined to say that the doctors are in any sense the cause of their patients' deaths. But let us further suppose that the two dying patients, Y and Z, are not happy about being left to die. They might argue that it is not strictly true that there are no organs which could be used to save them. Y needs a new heart and Z new lungs. They point out that if just one healthy person were to be killed his organs could be removed and both of them be saved. We and the doctors would probably be alike in thinking that such a step, while technically possible, would be out of the question. We would not say that the doctors were killing their patients if they refused to prey upon the healthy to save the sick. And because this sort of surgical Robin Hoodery is out of the question we can tell Y and Z that they cannot be saved, and that when they die they will have died of natural causes and not of the neglect of their doctors. Y and Z do not agree, however, they insist that if the doctors fail to kill a healthy man and use his organs to save them, then the doctors will be responsible for their deaths.

Reprinted with permission of John Harris and Cambridge University Press from *Philosophy*, The Journal of the Royal Institute of Philosophy, Vol. 50, 1975.

Many philosophers have for various reasons believed that we must not kill even if by doing so we could save life. They believe that there is a moral difference between killing and letting die. On this view, to kill A so that Y and Z might live is ruled out because we have a strict obligation not to kill but a duty of some lesser kind to save life. A. H. Clough's dictum "Thou shalt not kill but need'st not strive officiously to keep alive" expresses bluntly this point of view. The dying Y and Z may be excused for not being much impressed by Clough's dictum. They agree that it is wrong to kill the innocent and are prepared to agree to an absolute prohibition against so doing. They do not agree, however, that A is more innocent than they are. Y and Z might go on to point out that the currently acknowledged right of the innocent not to be killed, even where their deaths might give life to others, is just a decision to prefer the lives of the fortunate to those of the unfortunate. A is innocent in the sense that he has done nothing to deserve death, but Y and Z are also innocent in this sense. Why should they be the ones to die simply because they are so unlucky as to have diseased organs? Why, they might argue, should their living or dying be left to chance when in so many other areas of human life we believe that we have an obligation to ensure the survival of the maximum number of lives possible?

Y and Z argue that if a doctor refuses to treat a patient, with the result that the patient dies, he has killed that patient as sure as shooting, and that, in exactly the same way, if the doctors refuse Y and Z the transplants that they need, then their refusal will kill Y and Z, again as sure as shooting. The doctors, and indeed the society which supports their inaction, cannot defend themselves by arguing that they are neither expected, nor required by law or convention, to kill so that lives may be saved (indeed, quite the reverse) since this is just an appeal to custom or authority. A man who does his own moral thinking must decide whether, in these circumstances, he ought to save two lives at the cost of one, or one life at the cost of two. The fact that so-called "third parties" have never before been brought into such calculations, have never before been thought of as being involved, is not an argument against their now becoming so. There are, of course, good arguments against allowing doctors simply to haul passers-by off the streets whenever they have a couple of patients in need of new organs. And the harmful side-effects of such a practice in terms of terror and distress to the victims, the witnesses and society generally, would give us further reasons for dismissing the idea. Y and Z realize this and have a proposal, which they will shortly produce, which would largely meet objections to placing such power in the hands of doctors and eliminate at least some of the harmful side-effects.

In the unlikely event of their feeling obliged to reply to the reproaches of Y and Z, the doctors might offer the following argument: they might maintain that a man is only responsible for the death of someone whose life he might have saved, if, in all the circumstances of the case, he ought to have saved the man by the means available. This is why a doctor might be a murderer if he simply refused or neglected to treat a patient who would die without treatment, but not if he could only save the patient by doing something he ought in no circumstances to do—kill the innocent. Y and Z readily agree that a man ought not to do what he ought not to do, but they point out that if the doctors, and for that matter society at large, ought on balance to kill one man if two can thereby be saved, then failure to do so will involve responsibility for the consequent deaths. The fact that Y's and Z's proposal involves killing the innocent cannot be a reason for refusing to consider their proposal, for this would just be a refusal to face the question at issue and so avoid having to make a decision as to what ought to be done in circumstances like these. It is Y's and Z's claim that failure to adopt their plan will also involve killing the innocent, rather more of the innocent than the proposed alternative.

To back up this last point, to remove the arbitrariness of permitting doctors to select their donors from among the chance passers-by outside hospitals, and the tremendous power this would place in doctors' hands, to mitigate worries about side-effects and lastly to appease those who wonder why poor old A should be singled out for sacrifice, Y and Z put forward the following scheme: they propose that everyone be given a sort of lottery number. Whenever doctors have two or more dying patients who could be saved by transplants, and no suitable organs have come to hand through "natural" deaths, they can ask a central computer to supply a suitable donor. The computer will then pick the number of a suitable donor at random and he will be killed so that the lives of two or more others may be saved. No doubt if the scheme were ever to be implemented a suitable euphemism for "killed" would be employed. Perhaps we would begin to talk about citizens being called upon to "give life" to others. With the refinement of transplant procedures such a scheme could offer the chance of saving large numbers of lives that are now lost. Indeed, even taking into account the loss of the lives of donors, the numbers of untimely deaths each year might be dramatically reduced, so much so that everyone's chance of living to a ripe old age might be increased. If this were to be the consequence of the adoption of such a scheme, and it might well be, it could not be dismissed lightly. It might of course be objected that it is likely that more old people will need transplants to prolong their lives than will the young, and so the scheme would inevitably lead to a society dominated by the old. But if such a society is thought objectionable, there is no reason to suppose that a program could not be designed for the computer that would ensure the maintenance of whatever is considered to be an optimum age distribution throughout the population.

Suppose that inter-planetary travel revealed a world of people like ourselves, but who organized their society according to this scheme. No one was considered to have an absolute right to life or freedom from interference, but everything was always done to ensure that as many people as possible would enjoy long and happy lives. In such a world a man who attempted to escape when his number was up or who resisted on the grounds that no one had a right to take his life, might well be regarded as a murderer. We might or might not prefer to live in such a world, but the morality of its inhabitants would surely be one that we could respect. It would not be obviously more barbaric or cruel or immoral than our own.

Y and Z are willing to concede one exception to the universal application of their scheme. They realize that it would be unfair to allow people who have brought their misfortune on themselves to benefit from the lottery. There would clearly be something unjust about killing the abstemious B so that W (whose heavy smoking has given him lung cancer) and X (whose drinking has destroyed his liver) should be preserved to over-indulge again.

What objections could be made to the lottery scheme? A first straw to clutch at would be the desire for security. Under such a scheme we would never know when we would hear *them* knocking at the door.

Every post might bring a sentence of death, every sound in the night might be the sound of boots on the stairs. But, as we have seen, the chances of actually being called upon to make the ultimate sacrifice might be slimmer than is the present risk of being killed on the roads, and most of us do not lie trembling a-bed, appalled at the prospect of being dispatched on the morrow. The truth is that lives might well be more secure under such a scheme.

If we respect individuality and see every human being as unique in his own way, we might want to reject a society in which it appeared that individuals were seen merely as interchangeable units in a structure, the value of which lies in its having as many healthy units as possible. But of course Y and Z would want to know why A's individuality was more worthy of respect than theirs.

Another plausible objection is the natural reluctance to play God with men's lives, the feeling that it is wrong to make any attempt to re-allot the life opportunities that fate has determined, that the deaths of Y and Z would be "natural," whereas the death of anyone killed to save them would have been perpetrated by men. But if we are able to change things, then to elect not to do so is also to determine what will happen in the world.

Neither does the alleged moral difference between killing and letting die afford a respectable way of rejecting the claims of Y and Z. For if we really want to counter proponents of the lottery, if we really want to answer Y and Z and not just put them off, we cannot do so by saying that the lottery involves killing and object to it for that reason, because to do so would, as we have seen, just beg the question as to whether the failure to save as many people as possible might not also amount to killing.

To opt for the society which Y and Z propose would be then to adopt a society in which saintliness would be mandatory. Each of us would have to recognize a binding obligation to give up his own life for others when called upon to do so. In such a society anyone who reneged upon this duty would be a murderer. The most promising objection to such a society, and indeed to any principle which required us to kill A in order to save Y and Z, is, I suspect, that we are committed to the right of self-defense. If I can kill A to save Y and Z then he can kill me to save P and Q, and it is only if I am prepared to agree to this that I will opt for the lottery or be prepared to agree to a man's being killed if doing so would save the lives of more than one other man. Of course, there is something paradoxical about basing objections to the lottery scheme on the right of self-defense since, *ex hypothesi*, each person would have a better chance of living to a ripe old age if the lottery scheme were to be implemented. None the less, the feeling that no man should be required to lay down his life for others makes many people shy away from such a scheme, even though it might be rational to accept it on prudential grounds, and perhaps even mandatory on utilitarian grounds. Again, Y and Z would reply that the right of self-defense must extend to them as much as to anyone else, and while it is true that they can only live if another man is killed, they would claim that it is also true that if they are left to die, then someone who lives on does so over their dead bodies.

It might be argued that the institution of the survival lottery has not gone far to mitigate the harmful side-effects in terms of terror and distress to victims, witnesses, and society generally, that would be occasioned by doctors simply snatching passers-by off the streets and disorganizing them for the benefit of the unfortunate. Donors would after all still have to be procured, and this process, however it was carried out, would still be likely to prove distressing to all concerned. The lottery scheme would eliminate the arbitrariness of leaving the life and death decisions to the doctors, and remove the possibility of such terrible power falling into the hands of any individuals, but the terror and distress would remain. The effect of having to apprehend presumably unwilling victims would give us pause. Perhaps only a long period of education or propaganda could remove our abhorrence. What this abhorrence reveals about the rights and wrongs of the situation is, however, more difficult to assess. We might be inclined to say that only monsters could ignore the promptings of conscience so far as to operate the lottery scheme. But the promptings of conscience are not necessarily the most reliable guide. In the present case Y and Z would argue that such promptings are mere squeamishness, an over-nice self-indulgence that costs lives. Death, Y and Z would remind us, is a distressing experience whenever and to whomever it occurs, so the less it occurs the better. Fewer victims and witnesses will be distressed as part of the side-effects of the lottery scheme than would suffer as part of the side-effects of not instituting it.

Lastly, a more limited objection might be made, not to the idea of killing to save lives, but to the involvement of "third parties." Why, so the objection goes, should we not give X's heart to Y or Y's lungs to X, the same number of lives being thereby preserved and no one else's life set at risk? Y's and Z's reply to this objection differs from their previous line of argument. To amend their plan so that the involvement of so called "third parties" is ruled out would, Y and Z claim, violate their right to equal concern and respect with the rest of society. They argue that such a proposal would amount to treating the unfortunate who need new organs as a class within society whose lives are considered to be of less value than those of its more fortunate members. What possible justification could there be for singling out one group of people whom we would be justified in using as donors but not another? The idea in the mind of those who would propose such a step must be something like the following: since Y and Z cannot survive, since they are going to die in any event, there is no harm in putting their names into the lottery, for the chances of their dying cannot thereby be increased and will in fact almost certainly be reduced. But this is just to ignore everything that Y and Z have been saying. For if their lottery scheme is adopted they are not going to die anyway—their chances of dying are no greater and no less than those of any other participant in the lottery whose number may come up. This ground for confining selection of donors to the unfortunate therefore disappears. Any other ground must discriminate against Y and Z as members of a class whose lives are less worthy of respect than those of the rest of society.

It might more plausibly be argued that the dying who cannot themselves be saved by transplants, or by any other means at all, should be the priority selection group for the computer program. But how far off must death be for a man to be classified as "dying"? Those so classified might argue that their last few days or weeks of life are as valuable to them (if not more valuable) than the possibly longer span remaining to others. The problem of narrowing down the class of possible donors without discriminating unfairly against some sub-class of society is, I suspect, insoluble.

Such is the case for the survival lottery. Utilitarians ought to be in favor of it, and absolutists cannot object to it on the ground that it involves killing the innocent, for it is Y's and Z's case that any alternative must also involve killing the innocent. If the absolutist wishes to maintain his objection he must point to some morally relevant difference between positive and negative killing. This challenge opens the door to a large topic with a whole library of literature, but Y and Z are dying and do not have time to explore it exhaustively. In their own case the most likely candidate for some feature which might make this moral difference is the malevolent intent of Y and Z themselves. An absolutist might well argue that while no one intends the deaths of Y and Z, no one necessarily wishes them dead, or aims at their demise for any reason, they do mean to kill A (or have him killed). But Y and Z can reply that the death of A is no part of their plan, they merely wish to use a couple of his organs, and if he cannot live without them. . .*tant pis*! None would be more delighted than Y and Z if artificial organs would do as well, and so render the lottery scheme otiose.

One form of absolutist argument perhaps remains. This involves taking an Orwellian stand on some principle of common decency. The argument would then be that even to enter into the sort of "macabre" calculations that Y and Z propose displays a blunted sensibility, a corrupted and vitiated mind. Forms of this argument have recently been advanced by Noam Chomsky (*American Power and the New Mandarins*) and Stuart Hampshire (*Morality and Pessimism*). The indefatigable Y and Z would of course deny that their calculations are in any sense "macabre," and would present them as the most humane course available in the circumstances. Moreover they would claim that the Orwellian stand on decency is the product of a closed mind, and not susceptible to rational argument. Any reasoned defense of such a principle must appeal to notions like respect for human life, as Hampshire's argument in fact does, and these Y and Z could make conformable to their own position.

Can Y and Z be answered? Perhaps only by relying on moral intuition, on the insistence that we do feel there is something wrong with the survival lottery and our confidence that this feeling is prompted by some morally relevant difference between our bringing about the death of A and our bringing about the deaths of Y and Z. Whether we could retain this confidence in our intuitions if we were to be confronted by a society in which the survival lottery operated, was accepted by all, and was seen to save many lives that would otherwise have been lost, it would be interesting to know.

There would of course be great practical difficulties in the way of implementing the lottery. In so many cases it would be agonizingly difficult to decide whether or not a person had brought his misfortune on himself. There are numerous ways in which a person may contribute to his predicament, and the task of deciding how far, or how decisively, a person is himself responsible for his fate would be formidable. And in those cases where we can be confident that a person is innocent of responsibility for his predicament, can we acquire this confidence in time to save him? The lottery scheme would be a powerful weapon in the hands of someone willing and able to misuse it. Could we ever feel certain that the lottery was safe from unscrupulous computer programmers? Perhaps we should be thankful that such practical difficulties make the survival lottery an unlikely consequence of the perfection of transplants. Or perhaps we should be appalled.

It may be that we would want to tell Y and Z that the difficulties and dangers of their scheme would be too great a price to pay for its benefits. It is as well to be clear, however, that there is also a high, perhaps an even higher, price to be paid for the rejection of the scheme. That price is the lives of Y and Z and many like them, and we delude ourselves if we suppose that the reason why we reject their plan is that we accept the sixth commandment.

ACKNOWLEDGMENT

Thanks are due to Ronald Dworkin, Jonathan Glover, M. J. Inwood, and Anne Seller for helpful comments.

Who Shall Be Saved? An African Answer

John F. Kilner

John F. Kilner is currently at the Parkridge Center for the Study of Health, Faith and Ethics in Chicago. He has taught medical ethics and social ethics at the University of Kentucky. He is the author of Who Lives? Who Dies? Ethical Criteria in Patient Selection *(1990).*

Kilner bases his essay on interviews he conducted in Africa among witch doctors and other traditional healers. The focus of his study is the question: If there are two people who need help and you can only help one, how do you choose? Kilner claims that it is quite common for a health practitioner in Africa to prefer an older to a younger patient. In addition, equality of treatment is extremely important for a number of practitioners. This was true to such an extent that a significant number of healers would not choose one patient over another. In such cases they would not treat either patient, thereby letting them both die.

Daniel Ngwala and I drive our dusty, dented four-wheel drive Subaru into a little market area where cars are not often seen. Getting out, Ngwala wanders over to where several older men are talking while younger faces eye me cautiously. Ngwala asks if there are any traditional healers in the area. With a casual gesture, someone tells him: a witch-doctor named Kavili Nduma lives "out that way," but why does he want to know? After due assurances that we are not government agents come to cause trouble, Ngwala returns to the car and we head "that way."

A mile or so down the rutted dirt road we stop to greet a woman with fifty pounds of firewood on her back, and we ask the whereabouts of Nduma. She says we have gone too far and must return to the second path on (she points) "that" side of the road. We do so, taking the car as far down the path as we can before thornbushes and rocks force us to stop.

We leave the car at a mud and grass hut nearby, but only after we have secured a pledge from an adult to keep the fascinated children from pulling the car apart. Now setting out on foot, we travel twenty minutes through meandering maize fields and up a rocky hill, finally reaching Nduma's home—and she is home, thank God! Ngwala explains the reason we have come, and Nduma calls others to bring us chairs. Though the chairs are rickety and lack upright backs, I quickly forget how uncomfortable they are during the two-and-a-half hour interview that follows.

Questioned about how best to cope with the frequent scarcity of medical resources, which may allow her to save only one of two dying people, Nduma says to save an old man rather than a young, a man without

Reprinted with permission of *The Hastings Center Report,* June 1984.

children rather than a father supporting five. She affirms these priorities even when it is revealed that in both cases those preferred arrived second rather than first for treatment. When she adds that it really would be better to try to save none rather than one, little doubt remains that I have encountered a perspective on scarce resource allocation very different from those generally found in the United States.

In fact, this was precisely the reason for the long journey to Africa. The trip was inspired by my conviction that an ethical analysis of alternative approaches to the microallocation of scarce lifesaving medical resources would be greatly enhanced by discussing the problem with people operating out of a different cultural framework. (Microallocation focuses on determining who gets how much of a particular lifesaving medical resource, once budgetary and other limitations have determined the total amount of the resource available.) With support and guidance both in the United States and Kenya, I decided to investigate in particular the views of the Akamba people of Machakos district, Kenya, by means of personal interviews. Special assistance was provided by Ngwala, one of the Akamba himself, life-long resident of Machakos, and part-time farmer with a variety of skills.

The Akamba are traditionally subsistence farmers and herders. But their young men are increasingly seeking jobs in the district's towns or the nation's capital, Nairobi, as the rapidly growing population of 1.2 million fills the district's 14,183 square kilometers (5,475 sq. mi.). The land is largely semi-arid—a major exception being some very hilly areas—so life here is not easy. Moreover, droughts are not unusual; roads and infrastructure are not yet well developed, and government services are limited.

Health care in Machakos reflects the general scarcity of resources. While much development is taking place, the efforts of government and religion (mainly Christian) have so far produced only a few modest hospitals, health centers, and health subcenters (four or five each). Most public health care is provided at the more than fifty small dispensaries scattered throughout the district. But even the most basic critical drugs such as penicillin are frequently out of stock, especially in the dispensaries. Accordingly, many, if not a majority, of the people still depend upon traditional healing even though for the most part it has been forbidden by the government, which is promoting a more "modern" (Western) approach to health care.

Having decided to focus upon the Akamba people, I next had to identify those in the Akamba culture who are most knowledgeable about the ethical as well as medical issues involved in allocating scarce medical resources. I learned that those I was seeking are the "healers" of the culture, for Akamba healers have consistently been concerned with both physical and religious/moral health. Akamba healers are of two types: traditional healers (witchdoctors, herbalists, and midwives) and health workers (those who work in government or mission health care facilities). I randomly selected a sample population of 132 persons, with equal representation of both groups.[1]

Since the Akamba think in terms of stories,[2] it seemed appropriate to pose my questions as a series of stories (see "Two Dying Patients, One Dose of Herbs," on p. 542). The stories focused mainly on a healer named Mutua and two patients. Mbiti and Kioko. Resources are so scarce that only one of the two can be saved. In each situation, Mbiti arrives earlier, which, according to the Akamba, is a presumptive reason for treating him before Kioko. But different facts about the two people are also stated in successive questions—for example, Kioko is helping many people in his area whereas Mbiti is not—in order to see if the Akamba ever view such considerations as more important than order of arrival.

People were generally willing to talk at great length about these matters, with a few notable exceptions. One witchdoctor suddenly stopped in the middle of an answer, and said that she could tell me no more. When asked why, she replied that not she but a spirit had been speaking up to that point and the spirit refused to continue today. Plead as we might, she insisted she had nothing more to say but we could return the next day for more. We did, and she finished the interview. Was she merely eccentric? Another witchdoctor told us she could not be a Christian because whenever she started going to church an evil spirit killed a member of her family after telling her the day the murder would happen. She had lost her husband and two children this way, a fact that others confirmed. If I had not accepted the reality of spiritual beings before going to Kenya I might well have left a believer. Such spiritual involvement added a striking dimension to the tremendous friendliness, hospitality, and thoughtfulness of the Akamba people.

THE AKAMBA VIEW OF LIFE

The answers to our questions proved well worth waiting for, especially where they reflected outlooks different from those commonly encountered in the United States. For instance, where only one person can be saved, many Akamba favor saving an old man before a young, even where the young man is first in line. Whereas in the United States we tend to value the young more highly than the old because they are more productive economically, these Akamba espouse a more relational view of life. Life, they insist, is more than atomistic sums of individual economic contributions; it is a social fabric of interpersonal relation. The older a person becomes, the more intricately interwoven that person becomes in the lives of others, and the greater the damage done if that person is removed. At the same time, the older person has wisdom—a perspective on life that comes only with age—which is considered to be a particularly important social resource.

Another Akamba priority documented by the study is: where only one person can be saved, save a man without children rather than one with five. Whereas in the United States many would favor the opposite choice for the children's sake, many Akamba counter that the man without children faces annihilation and must be allowed to live so he can "raise up a name" for himself by having children. The self, for the Akamba, is not solely an individual, mortal life in the present; it is also a vital link in a chain that reaches through time, To drop a link before subsequent links have been fashioned is to destroy all future links (persons) as well as the perpetual life of the link in question,

A third surprising (by U.S. standards) priority acknowledged by numerous Akamba is the insistence that it is better to give a half-treatment to each of two dying patients—even where experience dictates that a half-treatment is insufficient to save either—than to provide one patient with a full treatment which would almost certainly be lifesaving. Under these circumstances many in the United States would abandon substantive equality (or equal treatment, which would here probably mean equal death) in favor of procedural equality (or equal access, which would here probably entail saving one person according to a first-come, first-served principle).

But many Akamba argue that the whole point of equality is what a person receives. They live according to the proverb, "no matter how many Akamba are gathered the mbilivili will be shared." (A mbilivili is the smallest bird known to Akamba and one that provides very little food.) Their outlook is sustained by the conviction that God is prone to heal not only where medical personnel have faithfully applied all available scientific knowledge but also where they have been faithful to the moral law as they are capable of knowing it. As long as healers remain faithful (that is, moral), they maintain, the responsibility for patients' lives remains God's.

These views bring into question some Western assumptions that dictate allocation decisions in the United States and elsewhere. Moreover, they remind us of the error in too quickly concluding, from the fact that people of different cultures support conflicting policies or actions, that morality is relative and that people's basic moral sensibilities may differ significantly. Often, as here, the difference is one of knowledge or beliefs (about what contributions benefit society most, or the nature of eternal life, or God's role in healing) rather than of moral judgment.

Cultural differences affect more allocation decisions, however. They help shape the way that medical personnel view and treat patients. For instance, because the Akamba traditionally see God as active in healing and people as both spiritual and material beings, they are more likely than their Western counterparts to perceive a need for treatment that addresses health problems on a spiritual as well as physical level. While Akamba healers do not generally distinguish a psychological component of illness, their emphasis on relationships (regarding their valuing of the elderly) disposes them, together with the entire community, to provide the care and support required to meet this dimension of illness.

The different approaches of Akamba health workers and Akamba traditional healers reflect similar considerations. Health workers, shaped as they are by Western education and medical training, are much more apt to see an illness in purely physical terms and to be skeptical about spiritual diagnoses, not to mention spiritual treatment. To be sure, of the three types of traditional healer, only the witchdoctors make use of spiritual powers (to help those who have been spiritually victimized by "witches" or "wizards"). Yet, even the more physically oriented herbalists and midwives display a level of caring and personal availability to patients that sets them apart from many of the more Western health workers.

Health workers concentrate more on efficient treatment, and are more apt to devote time to research. They are more likely to employ varied (and scientifically better) treatments, even if their quality of caring does not always equal that of traditional healers. Health workers also use Western developed medicines rather than the traditional herbs, though the administering and even effectiveness of the two do at times appear to be similar.

SCORING VALUES

Though I was eager to understand the full range of Akamba perspectives on the allocation of scarce lifesaving medical resources, I was especially interested to learn what significance, if any, they attach to four basic values frequently invoked in the U.S. allocation debate. Informal preliminary research revealed that the Akamba appeal to these values in the following particular form:

- *Equality:* All people are fundamentally equal where life itself is at stake, so the first to arrive should be treated when only one life can be saved.
- *Usefulness:* The most important goal in deciding whom to treat is to achieve the greatest social benefit possible.
- *Need:* Whoever is in the greatest danger of dying right away should be saved.

- *Life:* The most important goal in deciding who to treat is to save as many lives as possible.

To determine the significance that the Akamba attach to these values, we asked our participants twenty-four questions and assigned value-significance points to their answers according to the values they expressed. Participants could earn a point for equality on twenty-three of the questions. Six questions pertained to usefulness; three to need; three to life; and others to a variety of values such as choice. For example, if a healer maintained that Mbiti, who arrives first, is to be treated rather than the patient Kioko, who is involved in projects to benefit the community, then the healer received an equality point. However, to receive this point the healer had to justify her or his choice with some sort of reference to the notion that people equally warrant treatment where life-threatening health problems are concerned. The implicit idea expressed here is that treatment should do nothing but proceed according to the natural lottery; first-come, first-served. (As noted previously, a significant number of healers were so strongly egalitarian that they never chose one patient over another. These healers automatically received a high number of equality points.)

Average Value-Significance Scores by Education

Type of Healer	Level of Education	*Average Scores* Equality	Usefulness	Need	Life
Health Workers	None–Standard 7	15.5	1.6	2.3	2.1
	Standard 8–Form 2	14.1	2.1	2.4	2.7
	Form 3–Form 4	9.8	3.8	2.4	2.9
Traditional	None–Standard 8	15.2	1.8	2.4	2.2

Where Kioko rather than Mbiti was chosen because of his greater social usefulness, then the healer received a usefulness point rather than an equality point. Other questions presented the possibility of receiving, say, a need or life point as against an equality point. In nearly all of the questions it was possible to accumulate either an equality point or a point of some other type—the three categories mentioned here being the major ones. That virtually every question involved a possible equality point does not mean that equality is in some sense more "important" than the other values but merely reflects the manner in which the moral choice typically arises for the Akamba healers. They must choose between their adopted norm of first-come, first-served and some competing moral claim arising from the particulars of the case before them.

Once assigned in this manner, points of each type were summed for each person. The resulting equality scores ranged from 3 to 23 (average 14.3), usefulness scores from 0 to 6 (average 2.1), need scores from 0 to 3 (average 2.4), and life scores from 0 to 3 (average 2.3). (In each case the highest score reflects the number of questions pertaining to that category.)

As the averages suggest, most of those interviewed placed a high value on need and life. Perhaps this is to be expected since the Akamba working in health care settings are dedicated to the health of their people. Another finding was somewhat less predictable. While one-third of those questioned viewed usefulness as completely irrelevant in the context under consideration, the remaining two-thirds saw it as a legitimate consideration, at least sometimes, when deciding whose life to save. This latter outlook had a definite impact upon the significance accorded to equality. Nearly two-thirds of the Akamba scored less than 17 on the equality scale—17 being the score of one who would allow the claims of equality to be set aside only where need, life, or choice (not usefulness) is at stake.[3]

What accounts for a healer's particular set of value-significance scores? Whether a person is a health worker or traditional healer appears to matter, for equality, usefulness, and life scores. But what, more precisely, accounts for the difference between the two groups? In order to attempt a partial answer to this question, personal information was gathered at the start of each participant's interview. Specifically, we ascertained each person's sex, age, marital status, length of marriage, number of children, level of education, length of (medical) training, job responsibility, years worked, and religion. Doing so was not always easy. Age was particularly troublesome since many people did not know their age. Sometimes only through the ingenuity of Ngwala—who quizzed them about their knowledge of certain natural disasters and their estimated age at the time of those they could remember—was it possible to obtain this information. We examined potentially significant relationships between the ten personal factors and the value-significance scores.

With regard to nine of the ten items no consistent correlation emerged between the factors and the value-significance scores. (Perhaps surprisingly, religion was one of the nine. Probably this is because the only two religions our respondents acknowledged were the traditional Akamba religion and Christianity. Both, as the Akamba understand them, promote a fairly egalitarian outlook and place similar degrees of emphasis upon the three other basic values examined in this study.) Only education appeared to make a difference. In the table above, the health workers were divided as evenly as possible into three groups according to the highest level of education completed. (Kenyans completed the "standard" grades and then the "forms" before becoming eligible to enter a college or university.) Because none of the traditional healers interviewed had more than a primary education, they were treated here as a separate group and served as a check upon the other results, as will be explained shortly.

Statistical analysis of the scores suggests that the importance health workers attach to equality, usefulness, and life (not need) is significantly influenced by their education. (In fact, all three correlations are statistically significant at well above a 99 percent confidence level.) The more education one has received, the lower her or his equality score. This drop corresponds to a rise in both usefulness and life scores. However, when the weight ascribed to equality is changing most rapidly—beyond the primary educational level—the rise in usefulness scores is the primary change associated with the drop in equality scores.

Two other findings would appear to substantiate these conclusions. First, since the educational level of the traditional healers as a whole is only a little above that of the least-educated group of health workers, one would expect their mean value-significance scores to fall between the mean scores of the two least-educated health worker groups, though closer to those of the least-educated group. The table confirms that such is the case for all four values.

Second, in order to obtain a fourth educational level and thereby ascertain whether or not the observed trends continue through university education, the only three Akamba "doctors" (in the Western, university-educated sense) of Machakos district were interviewed. None had previously been selected through the sampling procedure employed. All of the observed trends do in fact persist at this fourth level. To the average equality scores (see the table) of 15.5, 14.1, and 9.8 the doctors add a 7.0; to the average usefulness scores of 1.6, 2.1, and 3.8 they add a 5.3; and to the average life scores of 2.1, 2.7, and 2.9 they add a 3.0.

My language regarding correlations between education and value-significance scores has been purposely tentative. Any quantitative measurement of the significance that people attach to particular values can only be approximate. Furthermore, while the data lead me to think that a decreasing equality-oriented and increasingly usefulness-oriented outlook is traceable directly to the Kenyan educational system, I am aware that this contention has not been conclusively proven. For instance, those who go on for more education may—at least theoretically—be those who already have a more usefulness-oriented outlook.

However, two considerations cast doubt on this alternate explanation. First, this explanation gives no account of what does prompt the values to change. Since the nine other items apparently do not account for the differences in values according to this study, the best explanation seems to be education is affecting values rather than vice-versa. Second, it seems highly unlikely that the reason many people stay in school through secondary school and beyond is their preference for one particular moral value over another. However, this question could be studied empirically.

If in fact basic values are being altered by the educational process in Kenya, then the institution of education, even when "purged" of religious instruction, is not as "value-free" as some contend. The real issue may be *which* values education is going to instill—those that it teaches implicitly, or "better" (if different) values, which are explicitly taught and otherwise encouraged.

A SHARED EXPERIENCE

As we brought the interviewing to a close I did not know exactly what the results of the study would be, but I knew it would be long before I forgot the process by which the results were obtained. One of the greatest challenges came near the very end. We completed the interviews a week ahead of schedule, but the heavy rains came ten days early. Those last three days were quite muddy. I never did get the hang of walking down a steep mud-path in the rain—without the dubious pleasure of sitting down in it at least once. But what a privilege to be able to see the task of healing through very different eyes.

In exchange for sharing their perspective, the Akamba health workers and traditional healers were eager to learn my views of medical resource allocation as well as the views of other Akamba. The problem of allocating scarce lifesaving medical resources, particularly the resource of their own time, is tragically real and urgent. One worker described to me a more than weekly occurrence at the district hospital. In a typical scenario, she is providing "intensive care" for a child who will not survive the night without her when another child who also requires her undivided attention in order to live through the night is unexpectedly brought into the hospital. She herself is the scarce resource, and the allocation decision is hers.

In response to the interest expressed by many of those I interviewed, I decided to write up a final report for the participants. The report was translated into Kikamba and hand-delivered even to the most remotely located participants by persons who could read the reports out loud to those who were not able to read for themselves. The participants were grateful, even as they had been gracious in sharing their outlooks. They also remain eager to learn what others think of their views.

The dusty journey across the plains and hills of central Kenya was more than a strenuous physical trek. It was a moral excursion of the most challenging kind. Confronted by strange, new perspectives on an old and familiar problem, I found that my capacity to wrestle with these perspectives depended upon my willingness to question and struggle anew with my own views and my fixed notions of the range of viable alternatives. While the study is done, the journey continues.

ACKNOWLEDGEMENTS

In addition to those who were interviewed, many others have made important contributions to this study. I am deeply grateful to Daniel Ngwala, my ever-present Akamba research assistant, as well as to others in Kenya who provided governmental, academic, and personal support and counsel. Francis Massakhalia, James Kagia, Dan Kaseje, Dennis Willms, and Joyce Scott stand out among many others. In the United States, the Danforth Foundation and Harvard University (Sheldon Fellowship) provided major funding for the study, while key planning assistance and critical evaluation were provided by Margot Gill, Ralph Potter, Preston Williams, and Sissela Bok. A special word of thanks belongs to Arthur Dyck who helped guide this project from start to finish.

NOTES

1. For a detailed explanation of the methodology, including a description of the sampling technique and questionnaire pre-testing as well as a copy of the basic questionnaire, see John F. Kilner, "Who Shall Be Saved?: An Ethical Analysis of Major Approaches to the Allocation of Scarce Lifesaving Medical Resources" (Cambridge, MA: Ph.D. dissertation, Harvard University, 1983).
2. Cf. John S. Mbiti, *Akamba Stories* (Oxford: Oxford University Press, 1966).
3. The issue of choice arises once in the questionnaire, when the respondents are asked whether or not patients should be allowed to forego treatment voluntarily (e.g., when they discover that all of the waiting patients cannot be treated). For a normative defense of a United States allocation policy which would more or less allow equality (as expressed in random selection) to be over-ridden only where need, life, or choice is at stake, see John F. Kilner, "A Moral Allocation of Scarce Lifesaving Medical Resources," *Journal of Religious Ethics* 9 (Fall 1981), 245–85.

TWO DYING PATIENTS, ONE DOSE OF HERBS

Mutua was an herbalist in Ukambani, who treated people for many different illnesses. Some patients such as those with kiathi (a severe bacterial infection), received a rare herb called kitawa. But sometimes Mutua's supply of kitawa would run out. Mutua had seen people die because there was no kitawa. One morning a person dying of kiathi was waiting when Mutua finished treating his first patient. The person's name was Mbiti. But before Mutua called Mbiti in to examine and treat him, another person came in and asked to speak to Mutua. He told Mutua that a man named Kioko was dying from kiathi and had just arrived. The person urged Mutua to see Kioko right away. Mutua knew that there was only enough kitawa left to cure one person.

Suppose that Kioko was involved in a number of projects of great benefit to the people in Mutua's area. Moreover, if he died the projects would probably soon fail. Should Mutua save the life of Kioko or that of Mbiti, who had arrived earlier? Why?

Suppose that Kioko was the father of five children, whereas Mbiti had no children. Should Mutua save the life of Kioko or that of Mbiti, who had arrived earlier? Why?

Suppose that Mbiti was over sixty years old, whereas Kioko was twenty-five. Should Mutua save the life of Kioko or that of Mbiti, who had arrived earlier? Why?

—Example of scenario with some follow-up questions.

Gender, Race, and Class in the Delivery of Health Care

Susan Sherwin

Susan Sherwin is a professor of philosophy and women's studies at Dalhousie University in Canada. She is the author of No Longer Patient: Feminist Ethics and Health Care *(1992). She is a coeditor of* Moral Problems in Medicine, second edition *(1983).*

Sherwin begins by noting that women are the primary users of health care, but they often receive care that is inadequate given their needs. She argues that when a woman is also an ethnic minority member, or if she is poor, this can further compound the problem of discrimination in the delivery of health care. She contends that women as a group are more vulnerable to be harmed by poor health care than are men. The health-care needs of minority women, especially in the Third World, are simply not being adequately addressed. Sherwin ends by considering various feminist proposals for redressing the problems that women find in seeking adequate health care.

OPPRESSION AND ILLNESS

It is widely recognized throughout the field of biomedical ethics that people's health care needs usually vary inversely with their power and privilege within society. Most bioethical discussions explain these differences solely in economic terms, observing that health and access to health resources are largely dependent on income levels. Poverty is an important determining factor in a person's prospects for health: being poor often means living without access to adequate nutrition, housing, heat, clean water, clothing, and sanitation, and each of these factors may have a negative impact on health (Lewis 1990). Further, the poor are more likely than others to work in industries that pose serious health risks (Stellman 1988) and to do without adequate health insurance (Tallon and Block 1988). And the poor suffer higher rates of mental illness and addiction (Paltiel 1988) than do other segments of the population. Financial barriers also often force the poor to let diseases reach an advanced state before they seek professional help; by the time these individuals do receive care, recovery may be compromised.

It is not sufficient, however, just to notice the effects of poverty on health; it is also necessary to consider who is at risk of becoming the victim of poverty. In a hierarchical society such as the one we live in, members of groups that are oppressed on the basis of gender, race, sexuality, and so forth are the people who are most likely to be poor. Moreover, not only does being oppressed lead to poverty and poverty to poor health but being oppressed is itself also

From *No Longer Patient: Feminist Ethics and Health Care* by Susan Sherwin (Philadelphia: Temple University Press, 1992). Reprinted by permission. [Edited]

a significant determining factor in the areas of health and health care. Those who are most oppressed in society at large are likely to experience the most severe and frequent health problems and have the least access to adequate medical treatment.[1] One reason for this vulnerability is that oppressed individuals are usually exposed to high levels of stress by virtue of their oppressed status, and excessive stress is responsible for many serious illnesses and is a complicating factor in most diseases. Another important factor to consider, as we shall see, is that the same prejudices that undermine the status of the oppressed members of society may affect the treatment they receive at the hands of health care workers.

North American society is characteristically sexist, racist, classist, homophobic, and frightened of physical or mental imperfections; we can anticipate, then, that those who are oppressed by virtue of their gender, race, class, sexual orientation, or disabilities—and especially, those who are oppressed in a number of different ways—will experience a disproportional share of illness and will often suffer reduced access to resources. Moreover, the connection between illness and oppression can run in both directions; because serious or chronic illness is often met with fear and hostility, it may also precipitate an individual's or family's slide into poverty and can therefore lead to oppression based on class.

The damaging connections between oppression and illness are profoundly unfair. Because this situation is ethically objectionable, bioethicists have a responsibility to consider ways in which existing medical institutions can be modified to challenge and undermine these connections, rather than contribute to them. Ethical analyses of the distribution of health and health care must take into consideration the role that oppression plays in a person's prospects for health and well-being.

PATIENTS AS MEMBERS OF OPPRESSED GROUPS

Throughout this book I have argued that women constitute an oppressed group, which is at a clear disadvantage in the health care system. Women are the primary consumers of health care, but the care they receive does not always serve their overall health interests. In a report presented to the American Medical Association, Richard McMurray (1990) reviewed recent studies on gender disparities in clinical decision-making; he found that although women are likely to undergo more medical procedures than do men when they present the same symptoms and condition, they have significantly less access than men do to some of the major diagnostic and therapeutic interventions that are considered medically appropriate for their conditions. In some cases the discrepancies were quite remarkable: for example, despite comparable physical needs, women were 30 percent less likely than men to receive kidney transplants, 50 percent as likely to be referred for diagnostic testing for lung cancer, and only 10 percent as likely to be referred for cardiac catheterization. The studies were unable to identify any biological difference that would justify these discrepancies. In addition, even though biological differences are sometimes significant in the course of various diseases and therapies, McMurray found that medical researchers have largely ignored the study of diseases and medications in women; for instance, cardiovascular disease is the leading cause of death in women in the United States, but research in this area has been almost exclusively conducted on men.

Therefore, as a group, it appears that women are particularly vulnerable to poor health care. Although they receive a great deal of medical treatment, the relevant research data are frequently missing, and specific treatment decisions seem to be biased against them. When women are medically treated, they are often overtreated, that is, subjected to excessive testing, surgery, and prescription drugs (Weaver and Garrett 1983). Sometimes they are simply not offered the treatment that physicians have judged to be preferable; for example, most professionals who work in the area of fertility control encourage women seeking birth control to go on the pill, despite its known risks. Interestingly, the majority of practitioners choose barrier methods for themselves and their spouses (Todd 1989); they do not seem to trust ordinary women to be conscientious in the use of the safer, less medically intrusive methods.

Physicians are trained in the stereotypical views of women as people who are excessively anxious, devious, and unintelligent; they are taught not to take all women's complaints seriously (Ehrenreich and English 1979; Corea 1985a; Todd 1989). Researchers have found that physicians are often condescending toward their women patients, and many deliberately withhold medical information from them out of concern for their inability to interpret it correctly (Corea 1985a; Todd 1989). Having medicalized the very condition of being female, many doctors have seized opportunities to intervene and modify those bodies in ways they are unwilling to apply to men—for example, psychosurgery, an exceedingly controversial therapy, is performed twice as often on women as on men, and ultrasound was widely practiced on women before being introduced as a therapy for men (Corea 1985a).

Nevertheless, not all women experience the health care system in the same ways. There are many important differences among women that result in different sorts of experiences within the health care system; in particular, differences that are associated with race, economic class, and ethnicity compound the difficulties most women experience in their various encounters with health care workers. Alexandra Todd observed that "the darker a woman's skin and/or the lower her place on the economic scale, the poorer the care and efforts at explanation she received" (Todd 1989, 77). Other factors that contribute to the sort of health care a woman is likely to receive include age, sexuality, body size, intelligence, disabilities, and a history of mental illness. It is a matter of serious moral concern that social factors play a significant role in determining the quality of health care a woman receives.

If we expand our scope to that of a global perspective, then it is obvious that women in other parts of the world face distinct health problems, such as those created by malnutrition, often to the point of starvation, and by the absence of a safe source of drinking water; many women must cope with the ravages of war or the hazards of living under brutally repressive political regimes. Third World women must frequently rely on unsafe drugs, which have failed to meet minimum safety standards and therefore are dumped in developing countries by manufacturers determined to make a profit from them (McDonnell 1986). Some prominent concerns of bioethicists, such as the need to obtain informed consent for treatment and research, are deemed to be the products of Western ideals and are likely to go unrecognized in nations where all personal liberties are severely curtailed; elsewhere, the ethical "niceties" are often ignored in the face of the pressing demands posed by crippling poverty and illiteracy.

The injustice represented by the differing health options and standards of care based on different levels of power and privilege is not restricted to the Third World. Inadequate prenatal care and birth services are common to poor women everywhere, and the lack of safe, effective birth control and abortion services is more a matter of politics than of economics. In North America women of color are at a higher risk than white women for many life-threatening conditions; for example, black American women are four times more likely to die in childbirth and three times more likely to have their newborns die than are white women (Gordon-Bradshaw 1988, 256). Black women in the United States are twice as likely to die of hypertensive cardiovascular disease as are white women; they have three times the rate of high blood pressure and of lupus as do white women; they are more likely than white women to die from breast cancer (despite having lower rates of incidence); they are twelve times more likely than white women to contract the AIDS virus; and they are four times more likely than white women to die of homicide (Davis 1990).

In the United States the poor usually have (at best) access only to inadequate health services. Many people who find themselves employed full time but receiving annual incomes well below established poverty lines fail to qualify for Medicaid support (Tallon and Block 1988). Those who do receive subsidized health care must confront the fact that many physicians and hospitals refuse to accept Medicaid patients. In 1985, for example, four out of ten physicians who provided obstetrical service refused to take Medicaid patients (McBarnette 1988).

Canadians have so far avoided the two-tiered system of private and public health care. In Canada poor women are not turned away from hospitals or doctors' offices,[2] but they may not be able to afford travel to these facilities. Rural women are often restricted from access to needed health care by lack of transportation. Many Canadian communities lack suitably qualified health care specialists, and some provinces simply refuse to provide needed services, especially abortion, thus making it unavailable to women who cannot travel to a private clinic in another jurisdiction. Despite its guaranteed payment for health care, then, the Canadian health care system still reflects the existence of differential patterns of health and illness, associated with both race and income level (York 1987; Paltiel 1988).

In both countries the services available to women through the health care system are predominantly those that meet the needs of the most privileged and articulate women, namely, those who are white, middle-class, educated, and urban. The health needs of other women are likely to be invisible or to slip through the cracks of the structures and funding of the system. In most cities, for example, prenatal programs, exercise counseling, mammography facilities, and hormone replacement therapy for menopausal women are available, but other urgent services, such as programs for alcohol- or drug-dependent women, are less easily found. Although some private programs exist for affluent women with substance-abuse problems, poor women have virtually no place to which they can turn. Further, if they should manage to find a program that is not too alienating to their experience to be of value, then they may face the problem of finding child care for the duration of the program, and if they are poor, then they are liable to lose custody of their children to the state when they admit to having a problem with addiction.

Although most urban centers offer nutritional guidance to affluent women trying to lose weight (even if their main goal is to fit the cultural ideals and medically mandated norms of slimness), few programs help women on welfare learn how to stretch their inadequate welfare checks to provide nutritious meals or to locate the resources for a healthy diet. Battered women who arrive at emergency rooms are patched up by the specialists on duty and perhaps referred to local, short-term shelters—if space can be found.[3] Preventive health care, which would help the abuser find nonviolent ways of behaving, is usually not available. As a result, many women get trapped in the cycle of returning home to their violent partner, returning to hospital with increasingly severe injuries (where they encounter frustrated staff members, who frequently blame them for repeat episodes), and recuperating in a temporary shelter. In the meantime, their children become intimately acquainted with violence as a means of addressing personal tensions and become primed to continue the pattern in the next generation.

In bioethics literature the issue of justice is often raised, but most discussions focus on whether or not everyone has a right to health care and, if so, what services this right might entail. Accessibility is viewed as the principal moral concern, but even where there is universal health insurance (for example, in Canada); the system is not designed to respond to the particular health needs of many groups of women. Being subject to violence, at risk of developing addictions to alcohol or other mood-altering drugs, and lacking adequate resources to obtain a nutritious food supply are all factors that affect peoples' prospects for health and their ability to promote their own well-being. Such threats to health are a result of the social system, which promotes oppression of some groups by others. Health care alone will not correct all these social effects, but as long as the damage of oppression continues, it is necessary to help its victims recover from some of the harms to their health that occur as a result of their oppressed status.

Bioethicists share with health care professionals and the rest of the community an ethical responsibility to determine how the health needs generated by oppressive structures can best be met. Medical care per se will not always be the most effective means of restoring or preserving the health of oppressed persons. Investigation of how best to respond to these socially generated needs is a topic that must be added to the traditional agenda of health care ethics.

THE ORGANIZATION OF HEALTH CARE

Much of the explanation for the different ways in which health care providers respond to the needs of different social groups can be found in the very structures of the health care delivery system. The dominance structures that are pervasive throughout society are reproduced in the medical context; both within and without the health care delivery system, sex, race, economic class, and able-bodied status are important predictors in determining someone's place in the hierarchy. The organization of the health care system does not, however, merely mirror the power and privilege structures of the larger society; it also perpetuates them.

Within existing health care structures, women do most of the work associated with health care, but they are, for the most part, excluded from making the policy decisions that shape the system. They are the principal providers of home health care, tending the ill members of their own families, but because this work is unpaid, it is unrecorded labor, not even appearing in statistical studies of health care delivery systems; it carries no social authority, and the knowledge women acquire in caring for the ill is often dismissed by those who have power in the system. Furthermore, support is not made available to provide some relief to women carrying out this vital but demanding work.

In the formal institutions of health care delivery, women constitute over 80 percent of paid health care workers, but men hold almost all the positions of authority.[4] Health policy is set by physicians, directors, and legislators, and these positions are filled overwhelmingly by men. Despite recent dramatic increases in female enrollment in medical schools, most physicians are men (78.8 percent in Canada and 84.8 percent in the United States as of 1986);[5] further, female physicians tend to cluster in less influential specialties, such as family practice and pediatrics, and they are seldom in positions of authority within their fields. Most medical textbooks are written by men, most clinical instructors are men, and most hospital directors are men.[6] The professional fields that women do largely occupy in the health care system are ones associated with traditionally female skills, such as nursing, nutrition, occupational and physical therapy, and public health. Women who work in health administration tend to be situated in middle-management positions, where their mediating skills may be desirable but their influence on policy is limited.

Research, too, is largely concentrated in male hands. Few women have their own labs or the budgets to pursue projects of their own choosing. The standards by which research is evaluated are those that have been developed by privileged men to meet their needs. They do not incorporate considerations that some female scientists and most feminist philosophers of science find important, such as including space in the design of a project for a measure of participant control, reducing the separation between subject and object, and resisting restrictive, medicalized analysis.

When we focus directly on issues of race and economic class, the isolation of health care provider from consumer becomes even more pronounced. Although many members of minority races and plenty of poor people are involved in the delivery of health care, very few hold positions of authority. Working-class and minority employees are concentrated in the nonprofessional ranks of cleaners, nurses' aides, orderlies, kitchen staff, and so forth. Women from these groups generally have the lowest income and status in the whole health care system. They have no opportunity to shape health care policy or voice their concerns about their own health needs or those of persons for whom they are responsible. One result of this unbalanced representation is that there has been virtually no research into the distinct needs of minority women (White 1990). Both those empowered to do medical research and those expected to respond to identified health needs come almost entirely from the socially defined groups and classes most removed from the experiences of women of color and poor and disabled women.

The gender and racial imbalances in the health care system are not accidental; they are a result of specific barriers designed to restrict access to women and minorities to the ranks of physicians. Regina Morantz-Sanchez (1985) documents how the medical profession organized itself over the last century to exclude and harass women who sought to become doctors, and Margaret Campbell (1973) shows that many of these mechanisms are still with us. Blacks, too, have been subject to systematic barriers, which keep them out of the ranks of physicians. For example, it is necessary to serve as an intern to become licensed to practice medicine, but until the 1960s, few American hospitals would grant internship positions to black physicians; those blacks who did manage to become qualified to practice medicine often encountered hospitals that refused to grant them the opportunity to admit patients (Blount 1990). Because black women must overcome both gender and race barriers, they face nearly insurmountable obstacles to pursuing careers as physicians (Weaver and Garrett 1983; Gamble 1990). Therefore, although blacks make up 12 percent of the population of the United States, they account for only 3 percent of the population of practicing doctors, and black women constitute only 1 percent of the nation's physicians; further, blacks represent only 2 percent of the faculty at medical schools (Gamble 1990).

Racism and sexism in health care have been exacerbated by the fact that different oppressed groups have long been encouraged to perceive their interests as in conflict, so that race often divides women who might otherwise be expected to unite. Darlene Clark Hine (1989) has shown that racial struggles have plagued the nursing profession since 1890. For much of that period, white nurses acted on their own racist views and fought to exclude black women from their ranks. Although their racism is not excusable, it is perhaps understandable: Hine explains that white nurses felt compelled to fight for professional status and autonomy. Acting within a predominantly racist culture, they feared that their claims for recognition would be undermined if they were to welcome black nurses into the profession on an equal footing. In other words, because the combined forces of racism and sexism made it especially difficult for black nurses to obtain respect as professionals, white nurses chose to accept the implicit judgments behind such attitudes and to distance themselves from their black colleagues, rather than joining them in the struggle to counter racial prejudice.

Moreover, the racial struggles of nurses are just one symptom of a larger problem. The hierarchical structures that operate throughout the health care system motivate each social group to pursue the pragmatic strategy of establishing its relative superiority over yet more disadvantaged groups, rather than working collectively to challenge the structures themselves. Although white nurses did seek to dissociate themselves from black nurses and claimed greater commonality with the higher-ranked (white) male physicians, black nurses were themselves driven to seek distance from other black women who were employed in the system as domestic staff or nurses' aides, by claiming an unreciprocated identity with white nurses. Within hierarchical structures, all participants have reason to foster connections with those ranked higher and to seek distance from those ranked lower. This motive breeds an attitude that encourages submission to those above and hostility and a sense of superiority toward those below; in this way, all but the most oppressed groups become complicit in maintaining the hierarchical structure of the health care system. Thus the organization of the health care system itself helps reinforce the oppressive structures and attitudes of society at large. . . .

The power and authority that society has entrusted to doctors give them the opportunity to destroy many of the patriarchal assumptions about women collectively and the racist, classist, homophobic, and other beliefs about various groups of women that are key to their oppression. Few physicians, however, have chosen to exercise their social power in this way. Many doctors have accepted uncritically the biases of an oppressive society, and some have offered evidence in confirmation of such values. As a group, physicians have held onto their own power and privilege by defending the primacy of the authoritarian medical model as a necessary feature of health care. Most have failed to listen honestly to the alternative perspectives of oppressed people who are very differently situated in society.

The medical model organizes our current attempts at defining and responding to health needs. It has been conceived as a structure that requires a hierarchically organized health care system, in which medical expertise is privileged over other sorts of knowledge. It grants license to an elite class of experts to formulate all matters of health and to determine the means of responding to them. As we have seen, however, there are several serious moral problems with this model. First, it responds differently to the health needs of different groups, offering less and lower-quality care to members of oppressed groups. Second, its structures and presuppositions support the patterns of oppression that shape our society. Finally, it rationalizes the principle of hierarchy in human interactions, rather than one of equality, by insisting that its authoritarian structures are essential to the accomplishment of its specific ends, and it tolerates an uneven distribution of positions within its hierarchy.

We need, then, different models to guide our thinking about ways to organize the delivery of health care. In addition to the many limits to the medical model that have been named in the bioethics literature, the traditional model reflects and perpetuates oppression in society. I conclude by summarizing some feminist suggestions that I believe should be incorporated into alternative models, if they are to be ethically acceptable.

A model that reflects the insights of feminist ethics would expand its conceptions of health and health expertise. It would recognize social as well as physiological dimensions of health. In particular, it would reflect an understanding of both the moral and the health costs of oppression. Thus it would make clear that those who are committed to improving the health status of all members of the population should assume responsibility for avoiding and dismantling the dominance structures that contribute to oppression.

Such a model would require a change in traditional understandings of who has the relevant knowledge to make decisions about health and health policy. Once we recognize the need to include oppression as a factor in health, we can no longer maintain the authoritarian medical model, in which physicians are the experts on all matters of health and are authorized to respond to all such threats. We need also to recognize that experiential knowledge is essential to understanding how oppression affects health and how the damage of oppression can be reduced. Both political and moral understandings may be necessary to address these dimensions of health and health care. Physiological knowledge is still important, but it is not always decisive.

Therefore, a feminist model would resist hierarchical structures and proclaim a commitment to egalitarian alternatives. Not only would these alternatives be more democratic in themselves and hence more morally legitimate, they would also help to produce greater social equality by empowering those who have been traditionally disempowered. They would limit the scope for domination that is available to those now accustomed to power and control. More egalitarian structures would foster better health care and higher standards of health for those who are now oppressed in society; such structures would recognize voices that are now largely unheard and would be in a position to respond to the needs they express.

The current health care system is organized around the central ideal of pursuing a "cure" in the face of illness, wherein "cure" is interpreted with most of the requisite agency belonging to the health care providers. A feminist alternative would recommend that the health care system be principally concerned with empowering consumers in their own health by providing them with the relevant information and the means necessary to bring about the changes that would contribute to their health. The existing health care system, modeled as it is on the dominance structures of an oppressive society, is closed to many innovative health strategies that would increase the power of patients; a feminist model would be user-controlled and responsive to patient concerns.

Such a change in health care organization would require us to direct our attention to providing the necessities of healthy living, rather than trying only to correct the serious consequences that occur when the opportunities for personal care have been denied. Moreover, as an added benefit, a shift to a more democratized notion of health needs may help to evolve a less expensive, more effective health care delivery system; most patients seem to be less committed than are their professional health care providers to a costly high-tech, crisis-intervention focus in health care (York 1987).

A health care system that reflects feminist ideals would avoid or at least lessen the contribution that the system of health care makes in the maintenance of oppression. It would be significantly more egalitarian in both organization and effect than anything that we are now accustomed to. This system not only would be fairer in its provision of health services but would also help to undermine the ideological assumptions on which many of our oppressive practices rest. Such an alternative is required as a matter of both ethics and health.

To spell out that model in greater detail and with an appropriate understanding, it is necessary to democratize the discipline of bioethics itself—hence, bioethics, as an area of intellectual pursuit, must also recognize the value of incorporating diverse voices in its discussions and analyses. Like medicine or any other discipline, bioethics is largely defined by the perspective of its participants. If we hope to ensure a morally adequate analysis of the ethics of health care, then we should ensure the participation of many different voices in defining the central questions and exploring the promising paths to answers in the field.

NOTES

1. Writers who are concerned about oppression are likely to make the connection prominent; for example, Beverly Smith states: "The reason that Black women don't have good health in this country is because we are so oppressed. It's just that simple" (quoted in Lewis 1990, 174).
2. Nevertheless many provinces would like to reinstitute a "small" user fee. Quebec has recently announced plans to proceed with a five-dollar charge for each visit to a hospital emergency room.
3. Women who gain entry to shelters learn that there are limits to the amount of time any woman can stay; most also find that low-cost housing is not available for them to move into once their prescribed time is exhausted, especially if they have children in tow and welfare is their only means of support.
4. Canada census data statistics for 1986 list 104,315 men and 418,855 women employed in the areas of medicine and health. Brown (1983) reports that over 85 percent of all health-service and hospital workers in the United States are women.
5. The Canadian figure is from Statistics Canada census figures; the American figure is taken from Todd (1989).
6. To correct the apparently systematic gender bias in the provision of health care McMurray (1990) recommends that efforts be made to increase "the number of female physicians in leadership roles and other positions of authority in teaching, research and the practice of medicine" (10).

REFERENCES

BLOUNT, MELISSA. 1990. "Surpassing Obstacles: Pioneering Black Women Physicians." *In Black Women's Health Book*. See White.

CAMPBELL, MARGARET. 1973. *Why Would a Woman Go Into Medicine? Medical Education in the United States: A Guide for Women*. Old Westbury, NY: Feminist Press.

COREA, GENA. 1985. *The Hidden Malpractice: How American Medicine Mistreats Women*. rev. ed. New York: Harper Colophon Books.

DAVIS, ANGELA Y. 1990. "Sick and Tired of Being Sick and Tired: The Politics of Black Women's Health." In *Black Women's Health Book*. See White.

EHRENREICH, BARBARA, and DEIDRE ENGLISH. 1979. FOR HER OWN GOOD: 150 YEARS OF THE EXPERTS' ADVICE TO WOMEN. Garden City, NY: Anchor Books.

GAMBLE, VANESSA NORTHINGTON. 1990. "On Becoming a Physician: A Dream Not Deferred." In *Black Women's Health Book.* See White

GORDON-BRADSHAW, RUTH H. 1988. "A Social Essay on Special Issues Facing Poor Women of Color." In *Too Little, Too Late.* See Stellman.

HINE, DARLENE CLARK. 1989. *Black Women in White: Racial Conflict and Cooperation in the Nursing Profession,* 1890–1950. Bloomington: Indiana University Press.

LEWIS, ANDREA. 1990. "Looking at the Total Picture: A Conversation with Health Activist Beverly Smith." In *Black Women's Health Book.* See White.

MCBARNETTE, LORNA. 1988. "Women and Poverty: The Effects on Reproductive Status." In *Too Little, Too Late.* See Stellman.

MCDONNELL, KATHLEEN. 1984. *Not an Easy Choice: A Feminist Re-examines Abortion.* Toronto: Women's Press.

MCMURRAY, RICHARD J. 1990. "Gender Disparities in Clinical Decision-Making." Report to the American Medical Association Council on Ethical and Judicial Affairs.

MORANTZ-SANCHEZ, REGINA MARKELL. 1985. *Sympathy and Science: Women Physicians in American Medicine.* New York: Oxford University Press.

PALTIEL, FREDA L. 1988. "Is Being Poor a Mental Health Hazard?" In *Too Little, Too Late.* See Stellman, 1988.

STELLMAN, JEAN MAGER. 1988. "The Working Environment of the Working Poor: An Analysis based on Worker's Compensation Claims, Census Data and Known Risk Factors." In *Too Little, Too Late: Dealing with the Health Needs of Women in Poverty,* ed. Cesar Perales and Lauren Young. New York: Harrington Park Press.

TALLON, JAMES R. JR., and RACHEL BLOCK. 1988. "Changing Patterns of Health Insurance Coverage: Special Concerns for Women." In *Too Little, Too Late.* See Stellman, 1988.

TODD, ALEXANDRA DUNDAS. 1989. *Intimate Adversaries: Cultural Conflict Between Doctors and Women Patients.* Philadelphia: University of Pennsylvania Press.

WEAVER, JERRY L., and SHARON D. GARRETT. 1983. "Sexism and Racism in the American Health Care Industry: A Comparative Analysis." In *Women and Health: The Politics of Sex in Medicine,* ed. Elizabeth Fee. Farmingdale, NY: Baywood.

WHITE, EVELYN C., ed. 1990. *Black Women's Health Book: Speaking for Ourselves.* Seattle: Seal Press.

YORK, GEOFFREY. 1987. *The High Price of Health: A Patient's Guide to the Hazards of Medical Politics.* Toronto: James Lorimer and Company.

EUTHANASIA AND SUSTAINING LIFE—SUPPLEMENTARY READINGS

BATTIN, MARGARET P. "Assisted Suicide: Can We Learn from Germany?" *Hastings Center Report*, March–April 1992.

BAYLES, MICHAEL D. "Allocation of Scarce Medical Resources." *Public Affairs Quarterly*, vol. 4(1), January 1990.

BELL, NORA K. "What Setting Limits Might Mean: A Feminist Critique." *Hypatia*, Summer 1989.

BROCK, DAN W. "Voluntary Active Euthanasia." *Hastings Center Report*, March–April 1992.

BUCHANAN, ALLEN. "The Right to a Decent Minimum of Health Care." *Philosophy and Public Affairs*, Winter 1984.

FENIGSEN, RICHARD. "A Case Against Dutch Euthanasia." *Hastings Center Report*, January–February 1989.

HEVI, JACOB. "In Ghana, Conflict and Complementarity." *Hastings Center Report*, July–August 1989.

KIMURA, RIHITO. "Anencephalic Organ Donation: A Japanese Case." *The Journal of Medicine and Philosophy*, vol. 14(1), February 1989.

KUHSE, HELGA, and PETER SINGER. "Age and the Allocation of Medical Resources." *The Journal of Medicine and Philosophy*, vol. 13(1), February 1988.

MALM, M.H. "Killing, Letting Die, and Simple Conflicts." *Philosophy and Public Affairs*, vol. 18(3), Summer 1989.

RESCHER, NICHOLAS. "The Allocation of Exotic Lifesaving Therapy." *Ethics*, April 1969.

SIVA SUBRAMANIAN, K.N. "In India, Nepal and Sri Lanka, Quality of Life Weighs Heavily." *Hastings Center Report*, August 1986.